Field Guide to American Antique Furniture

Field Guide to American Antique Furniture

by
JOSEPH T. BUTLER

in collaboration with
Kathleen Eagen Johnson

illustrations by
RAY SKIBINSKI

A Roundtable Press Book

An Owl Book
Henry Holt and Company • New York

A Roundtable Press Book

Editorial: Susan E. Meyer and Marsha Melnick

Design: Betty Binns Graphics

Layout: Jeffrey Fitschen

Text copyright © 1985 by Joseph T. Butler and Roundtable Press, Inc.
Illustrations copyright © 1985 by Ray Skibinski and Roundtable Press, Inc.
Acknowledgements for the sources of the furniture illustrated appear on pages 364 and 365.
All rights reserved, including the right to reproduce this book or portions thereof in any form.
Published by Henry Holt and Company, Inc.,
115 West 18th Street, New York, New York 10011.
Published in Canada by Fitzhenry & Whiteside Limited.
195 Allstate Parkway, Markham, Ontario L3R 4T8.

Library of Congress Cataloging-in-Publication Data
Butler, Joseph T.
Field guide to American antique furniture.
"An Owl Book."
Reprint. Originally published: Illustrated guide to American antique furniture. New York, N.Y.: Facts on File, 1985.
Includes index.
1. Furniture—United States—History. I. Johnson, Kathleen Eagen, II. Skibinski, Ray. III. Title.
NK2405.B87 1986 749.213 86-12099
ISBN 0-8050-0124-7 (pbk.)

Henry Holt books are available at special discounts for bulk purchases for sales promotions, premiums, fund-raising, or educational use. Special editions or book excerpts can also be created to specification.

For details contact:

Special Sales Director
Henry Holt and Company, Inc.
115 West 18th Street
New York, New York 10011

First published in hardcover by Facts on File, Inc., in 1985.

First Owl Book Edition—1986

Printed in the United States of America
10 9 8 7 6 5 4 3

Preface

By using a systematic visual approach, this book chronologically traces the evolution of style in American antique furniture from the 17th century through the early 20th century. The 1700 illustrations are arranged in sequence by type of furniture: chairs; tables; beds; daybeds, sofas, and settees; lift-top chests; chests with movable drawers; desks and bookcases; and miscellaneous. The forms are further divided by style, then by geographic origin from the north to south along the eastern seaboard. In the section on the 19th century, other major furniture centers are treated.

Carefully-created line drawings offer the reader a clear means of comparing and identifying furniture styles. As the reader studies the illustrations and the text, the salient characteristics of each style will emerge and comparisons among styles can also be made. Although cabinetmakers sometimes combined elements from several styles in the design of one piece of furniture, for instructive purposes examples shown here are designed to illustrate style in its purest form.

The framework for presenting historical American furniture styles has been based on the finest examples of the period. Individual pieces have been identified as specifically as possible, including maker, working dates, place of origin, and date, when known. Because certain furniture forms have been made over a number of centuries, they are difficult to date by means of stylistic attributes. These long-lived vernacular forms of furniture are treated, therefore, in the time period when they first developed.

While the guide is designed to provide the information needed to identify any major style of antique furniture popular in America before World War I, it does not, and cannot, treat the subject of authenticity. That sort of knowledge can only be acquired through frequent and thorough examination of the actual furniture. For a more in-depth look at fine examples of furniture, the reader is strongly advised to visit the major collections listed on page 366. This book can help educate the eye to distinguish differences in styles, but there is no substitute for seeing the furniture first hand.

Contents

PART TWO

Field Guide to American Antique Furniture

Anatomy of Furniture

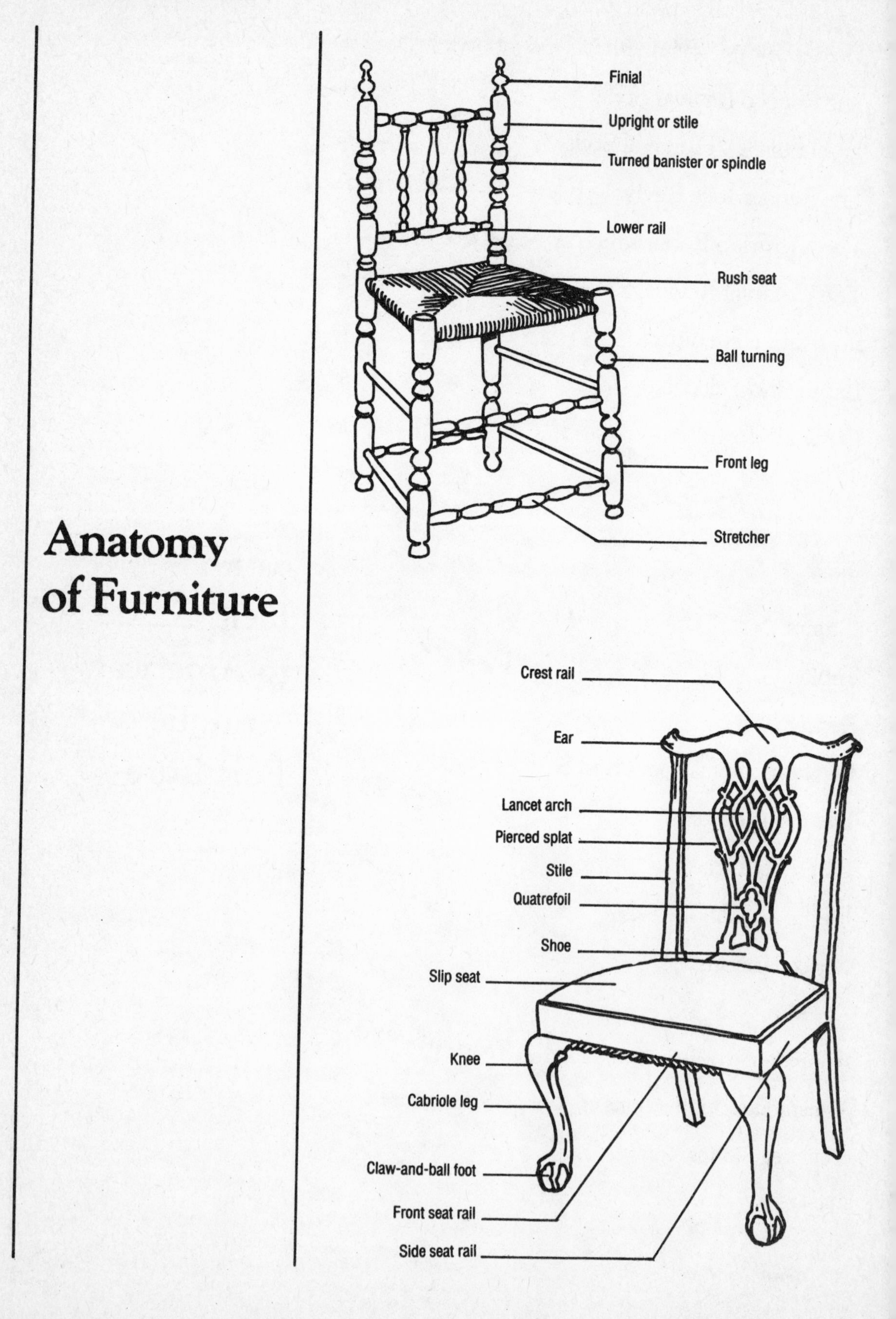

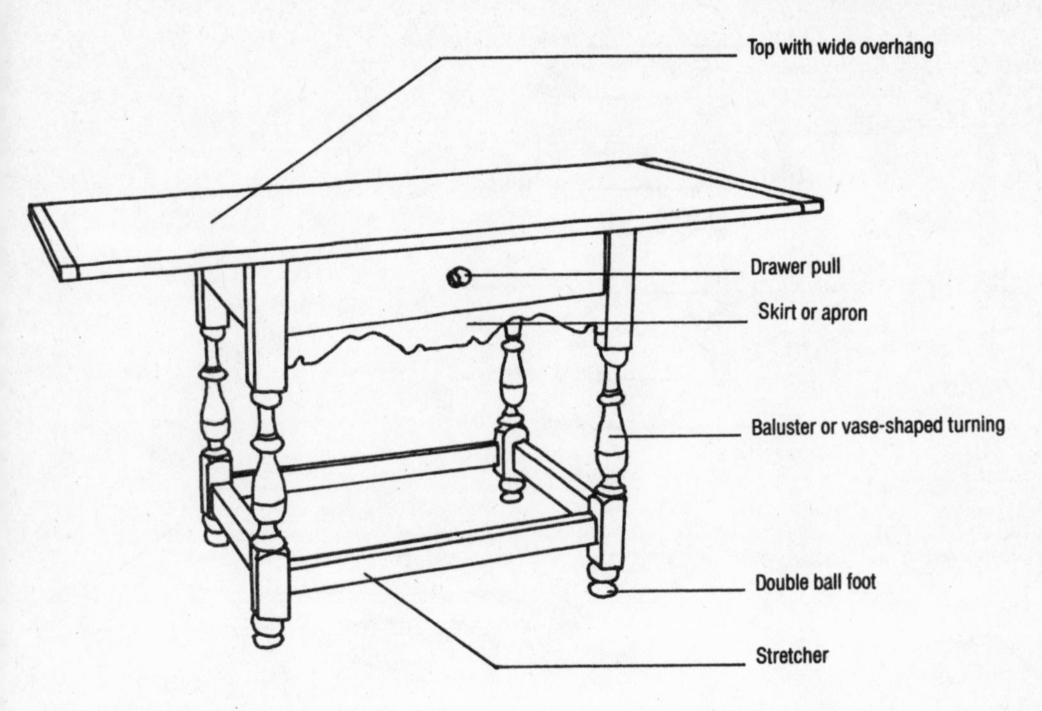
Top with wide overhang
Drawer pull
Skirt or apron
Baluster or vase-shaped turning
Double ball foot
Stretcher

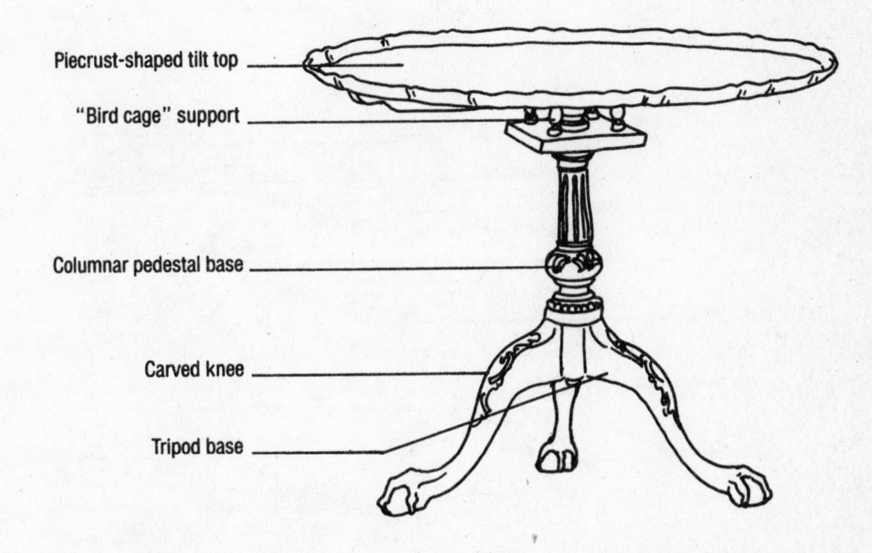
Piecrust-shaped tilt top
"Bird cage" support
Columnar pedestal base
Carved knee
Tripod base

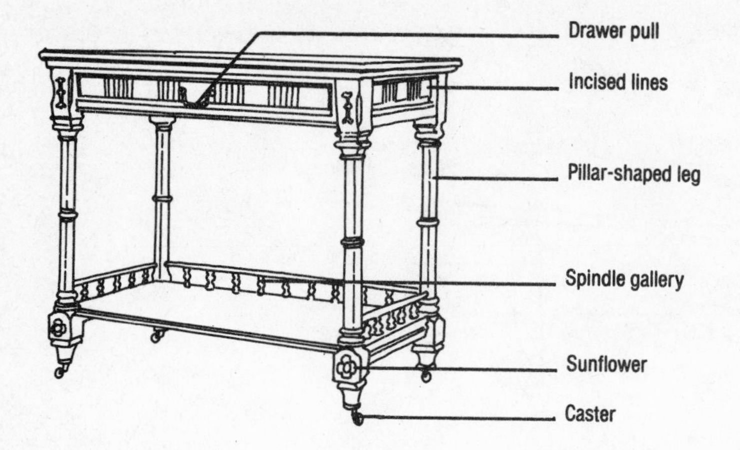
Drawer pull
Incised lines
Pillar-shaped leg
Spindle gallery
Sunflower
Caster

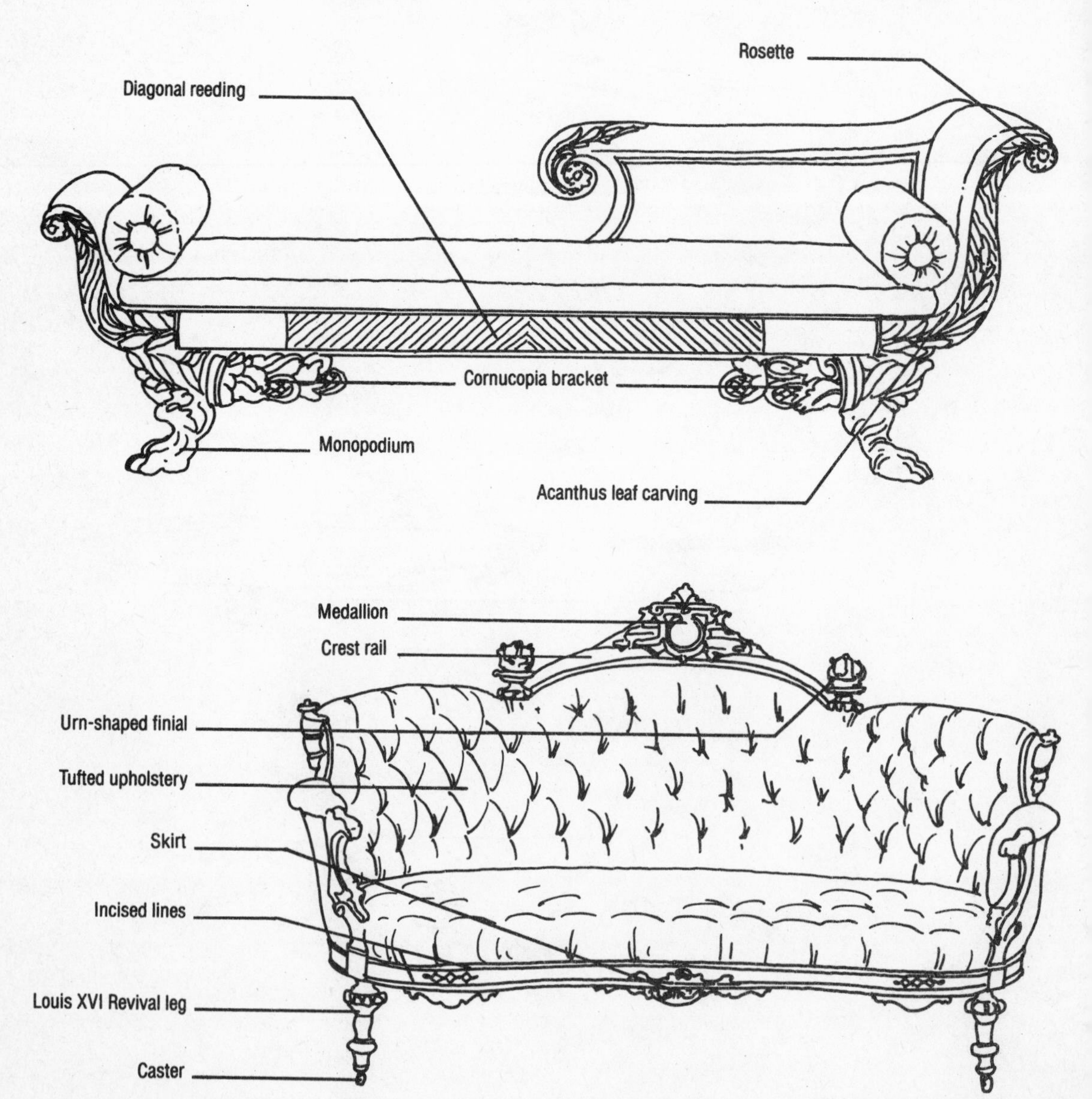
Rosette
Diagonal reeding
Cornucopia bracket
Monopodium
Acanthus leaf carving
Medallion
Crest rail
Urn-shaped finial
Tufted upholstery
Skirt
Incised lines
Louis XVI Revival leg
Caster

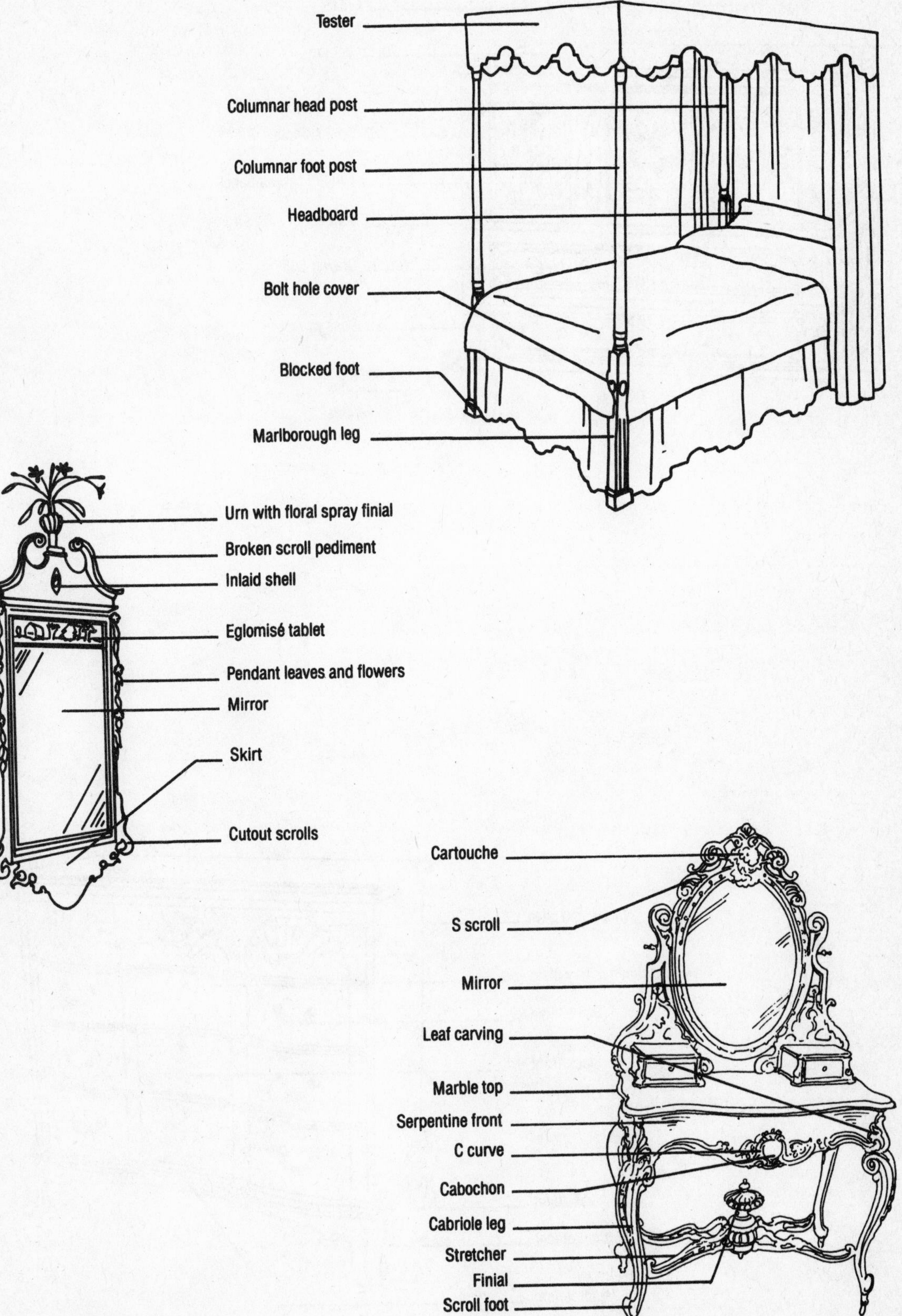
Tester
Columnar head post
Columnar foot post
Headboard
Bolt hole cover
Blocked foot
Marlborough leg
Urn with floral spray finial
Broken scroll pediment
Inlaid shell
Eglomisé tablet
Pendant leaves and flowers
Mirror
Skirt
Cutout scrolls
Cartouche
S scroll
Mirror
Leaf carving
Marble top
Serpentine front
C curve
Cabochon
Cabriole leg
Stretcher
Finial
Scroll foot
Caster

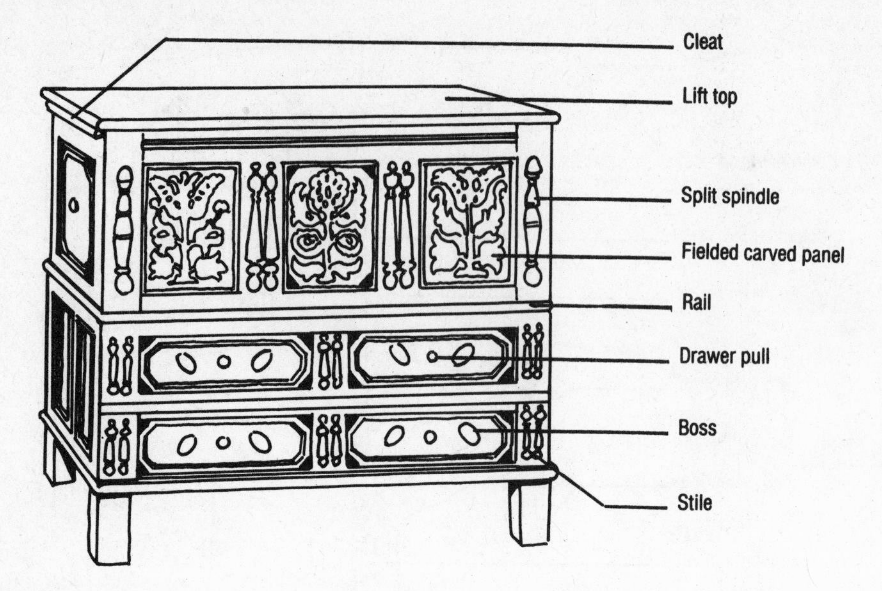
Cleat
Lift top
Split spindle
Fielded carved panel
Rail
Drawer pull
Boss
Stile

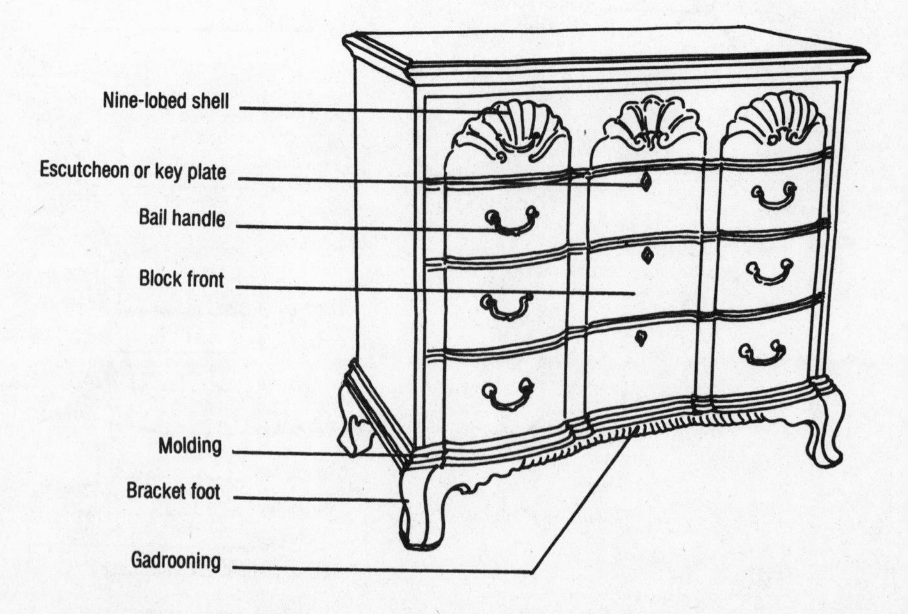
Nine-lobed shell
Escutcheon or key plate
Bail handle
Block front
Molding
Bracket foot
Gadrooning

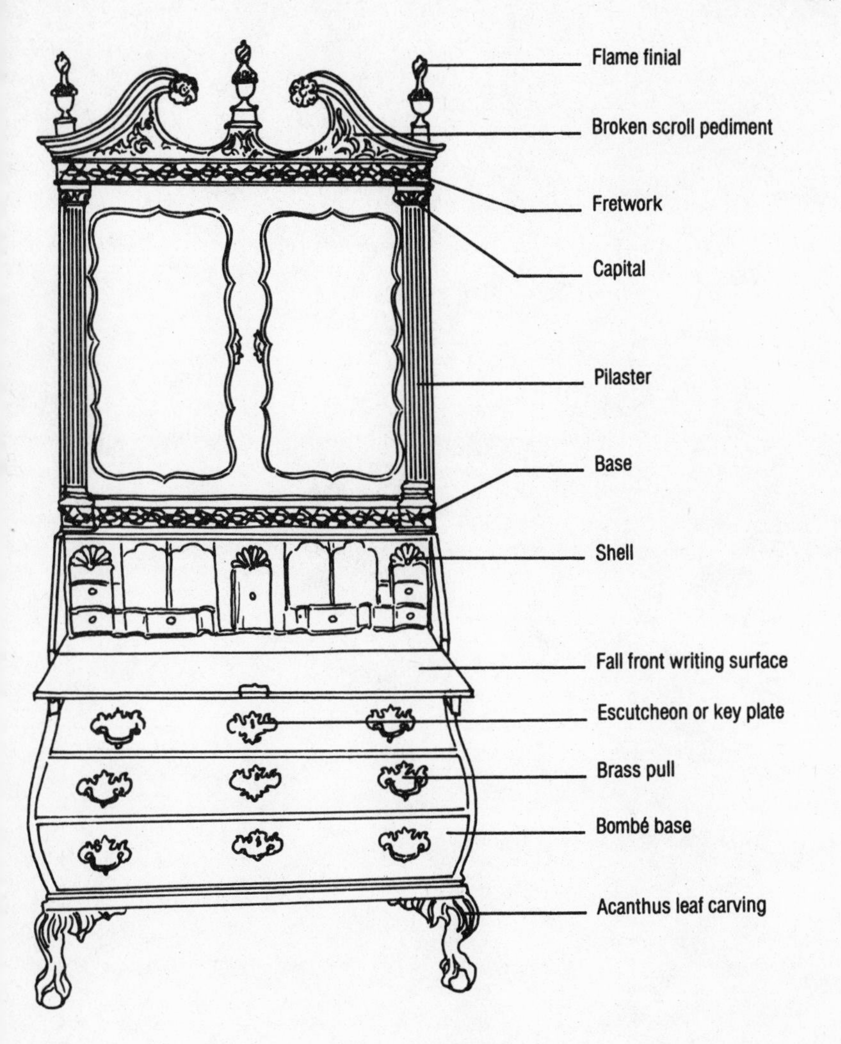
Flame finial
Broken scroll pediment
Fretwork
Capital
Pilaster
Base
Shell
Fall front writing surface
Escutcheon or key plate
Brass pull
Bombé base
Acanthus leaf carving

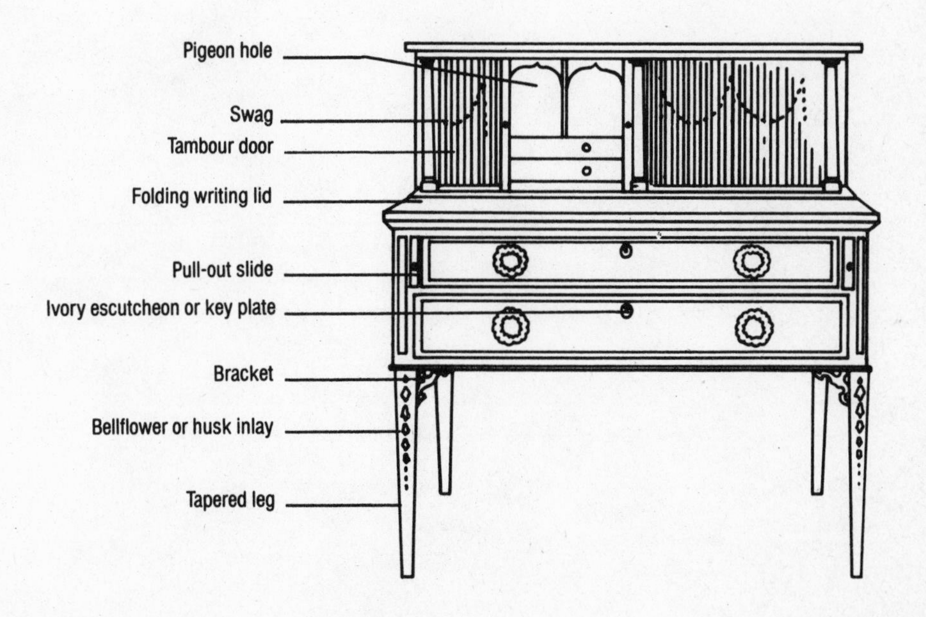
Pigeon hole
Swag
Tambour door
Folding writing lid
Pull-out slide
Ivory escutcheon or key plate
Bracket
Bellflower or husk inlay
Tapered leg

History of American Furniture

Origins of American Furniture

WHEN the colonists settled along the Eastern seaboard of North America during the 17th century, they brought their European traditions with them. Because their domestic customs—how they lived and worked—reflected this Old World heritage, it is small wonder that the style and construction of their furniture also was derived from European sources. Settlers arriving from different countries brought with them the training and the styles of their native lands, so, for example, 17th-century New England furniture displays a strong English flavor, while that made in New York reveals the tastes of the Dutch.

Of course, the European influence on American furniture was not unique to the 17th century. Until the end of the 19th century, American furniture styles continued to evolve principally from European sources, a phenomenon that has made American furniture making a fascinating but occasionally perplexing subject of study.

First, some definitions are in order. *Furniture making* is a comprehensive term that can be divided into two categories: cabinetry and joinery. Cabinetmaking was the regulated trade that produced fine furniture. A cabinetmaker generally served an apprenticeship through which he learned to construct and, in particular, to carve furniture. A fine piece of furniture produced in a good European cabinet shop commonly followed the style established by the reigning monarch; this style eventually reached the colonies.

Joined and turned furniture tended to be less style-conscious. The joiner was not as well trained as a cabinetmaker. He used a draw knife and constructed mortise-and-tenon joints to pin furniture together. Another type of craftsman, a turner, was skilled in making parts of furniture on a lathe. While often derivative of high-style furniture, such pieces are sometimes termed *country* or *primitive*. But since

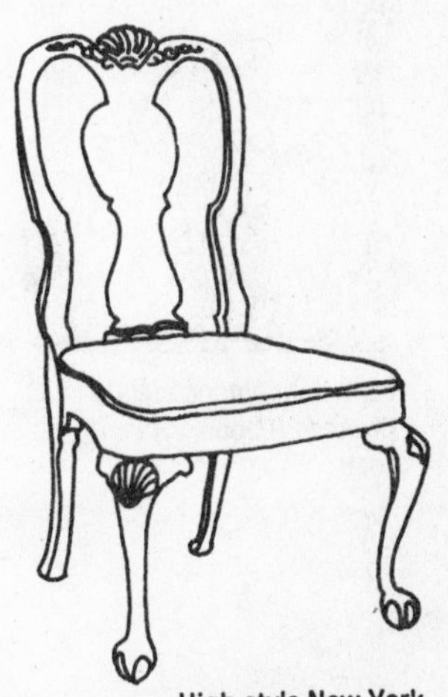

High style New York Queen Anne chair made by a cabinetmaker.

Fiddle-back chair made by a turner.

joiners operated in urban as well as rural areas, *vernacular* is a more accurate term for describing joined, or less sophisticated, furniture.

Finally, the term *hand-made* is used to mean exactly that: furniture created with simple tools. After the first quarter of the 19th century, the machine was applied to furniture making and the factory method of production began.

The Transmission of European Styles

European furniture styles crossed the Atlantic in several ways. The original colonists constructed native furniture according to their recent training and the ideas they brought with them to the New World; 17th-century furniture makers used their skills to construct pieces in the medieval and Renaissance forms they remembered. In the 17th and 18th centuries, some European furniture was actually imported by wealthy settlers. These pieces served as models for colonial furniture makers.

Plate from Chippendale's *Director*. Ribbon-back chair.

European furniture styles were also transmitted through published pattern and design books. Fine cabinet shops in Europe owned pattern books that pictured the popular styles of the time. Engravings in these books showed furniture that the shop might produce for a patron. In turn, the patron might also refer to these patterns in order to show the cabinetmaker details he or she wished incorporated into a commissioned piece. There is little documented evidence to substantiate the use of such publications in America before the mid-18th century. However, the close similarity of actual pieces of 18th-century American furniture to illustrations in the pattern books shows that American craftsmen were at least familiar with these books.

Regardless of how European styles reached the New World, a certain time lag naturally occurred between the two continents. What was fashionable in Europe might not appear in America until twenty or more years later. This phenomenon has created some confusion in the naming of American styles. For example, the William and Mary style did not develop in America until after the actual reign of those monarchs in England. (The William and Mary period in England is 1689–1702, while in America, the style predominated in 1700–1725.) Periods in American furniture are further confused because they shift from the names of English monarchs to the name of a designer (Chippendale) or to an overall design movement (Classicism).

One factor that strongly affected the appearance of American furniture is a phenomenon called the regional characteristic. The European stylistic ideas that arrived on the Eastern seaboard were adapted in a slightly different form in each individual region. Regions of America were somewhat isolated from one another because communication and travel among the colonies was slow. Furthermore, groups of craftsmen in each region came from different places and brought with them the stylistic interpretations of the centers from which they emigrated. Thus, the differences among the colonial craftsmen, as well as the varying influences they found when they settled in the New World, created strong regional distinctions in the style and construction of American furniture. By the middle of the 18th century, these characteristics had become so highly evolved that it is possible to distinguish the work of several East Coast furniture centers through the stylistic treatment and/or construction of individual pieces. Furthermore, the styles that were fashionable in the urban areas eventually filtered down to influence country furniture, so it is sometimes possible to identify localized rural adaptations.

In considering the evolution of American furniture, therefore, it is vital to bear in mind these factors:

1. Style was transmitted to America by craftsmen, actual objects, and pattern books.

2. The names of the stylistic periods do not necessarily correspond to the historical events to which they seem to refer, and sometimes forms related to a particular historical period were actually made well into another.

3. American furniture-making centers developed individual interpretations of European styles in accordance with regional characteristics.

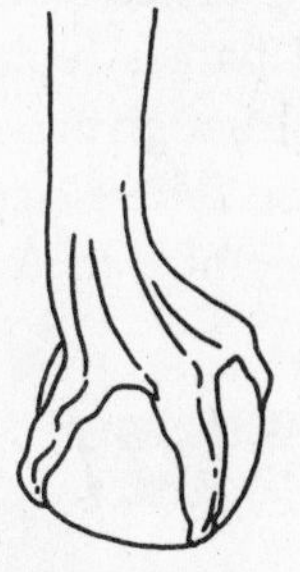
Massachusetts claw-and-ball foot.

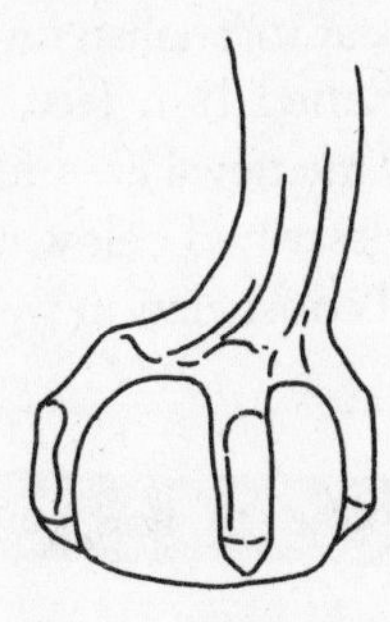
Connecticut claw-and-ball foot.

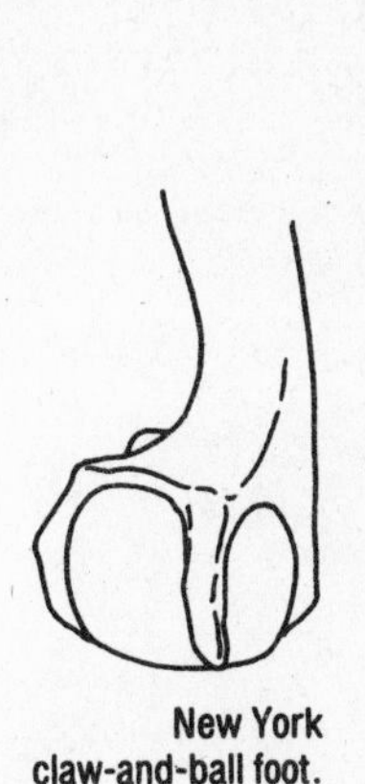
New York claw-and-ball foot.

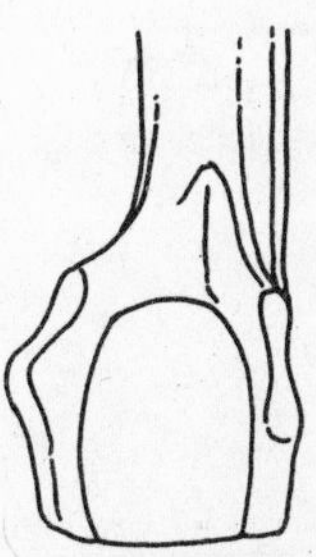
Philadelphia claw-and-ball foot.

The 17th Century

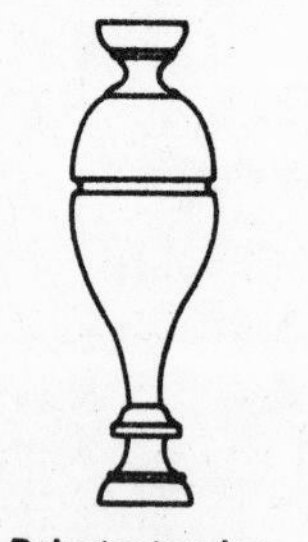
Baluster turning.

WHEN the two earliest American colonies were founded—Jamestown (1607) and Plymouth (1620)—James I (1603–1625) was the reigning monarch in England. For this reason, the term *Jacobean* is sometimes used to describe the earliest American furniture. However, because this earliest type of colonial furniture is derived from a combination of several earlier design sources, the term *17th century* is used here to denote this period.

The Renaissance Influence

Bun foot.

At the end of the 16th century, northern Europe was just emerging from the Middle Ages. The importation of Flemish pattern books and the immigration of Flemish-Huguenot craftsmen began to bring the influence of Italian Renaissance design to England. As this new style was introduced into a somewhat backward country, basic Renaissance elements began to appear in English furniture. Heavy, turned baluster supports, flattened bun feet, and arcaded panels replaced the traditional medieval linenfold patterns, although paneled construction described below remained in use. These elements of design and construction were then transplanted to America.

General Features of 17th-Century Furniture

Because it is heavy, durable, and well suited to the massive, rectilinear character of such furniture—and because it was widely available in great quantities—oak was the chief wood used in both England and America during the 17th century. Ash and maple were also used because both woods are easily turned and whittled, making them suitable for the varieties of rounded forms found in this period. Although little evidence survives today, much 17th-century furniture was originally painted.

Rounded shapes turned on the lathe provided an important decorative element in 17th-century furniture forms. Turned balusters, spindles, and bun feet, formed in a variety of shapes, appeared frequently on case furniture. Split spindles were created by gluing two blocks together with a thin strip of wood between the blocks. After the blocks were turned, the strip of wood was knocked out, leaving two half (or "split") spindles which could be applied to case furniture.

Shallow carved geometric panels were also used as decorative elements. In fact, paneled construction was widely used in 17th-century America. A medieval development, these inset panels were fitted into slots within an overall frame so that they could expand and contract with changes in humidity and temperature.

The technique of creating joints with mortise and tenon was widely used in 17th-century furniture. With this technique, a hole, usually square or rectangular, was chiseled into one member and a tongue shaped to fit this hole was chiseled into the other. A peg was then placed through both pieces to secure them together, forming the joint.

Several types of iron hinges and lock plates were held in place by wrought iron nails in much 17th-century case furniture. And movable drawers, developed in Renaissance Italy, also appeared in 17th-century American furniture.

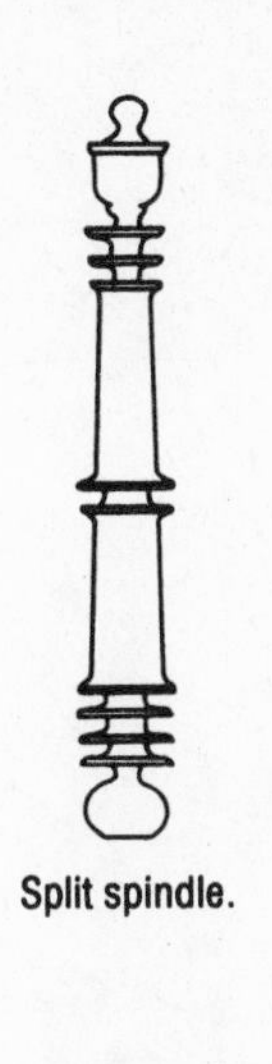

Split spindle.

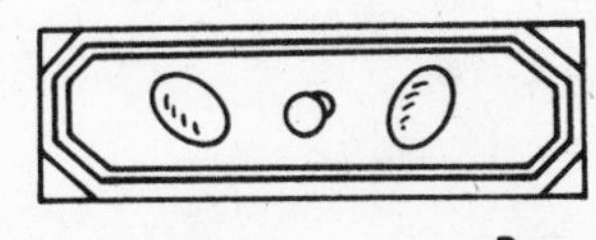

Boss.

17th-Century Furniture Forms

Not many pieces of American furniture have survived from the 17th century, and much that presently exists was heavily restored in the early 20th century, when this style was very popular. Of the surviving pieces, most come from Massachusetts, but examples are also known from New Hampshire, Connecticut, New York, and Virginia.

Carved panel.

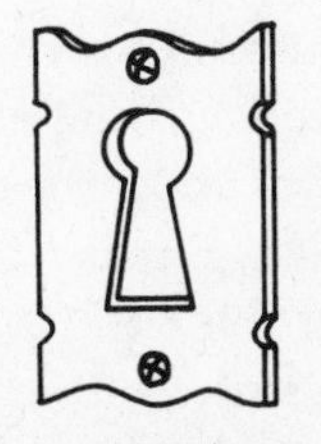

Lock plate (escutcheon).

Hinge and whole nail.

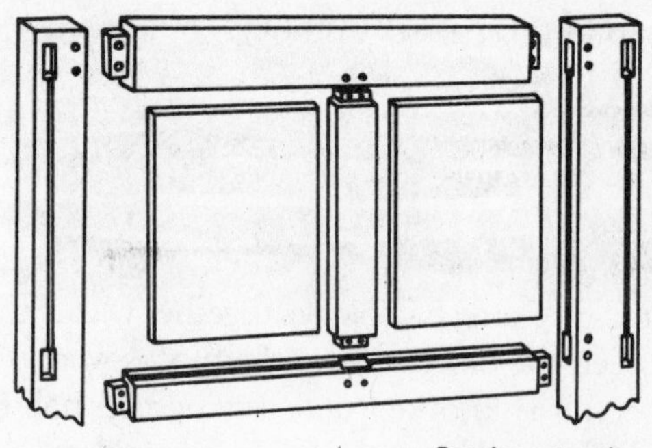
Panel construction.

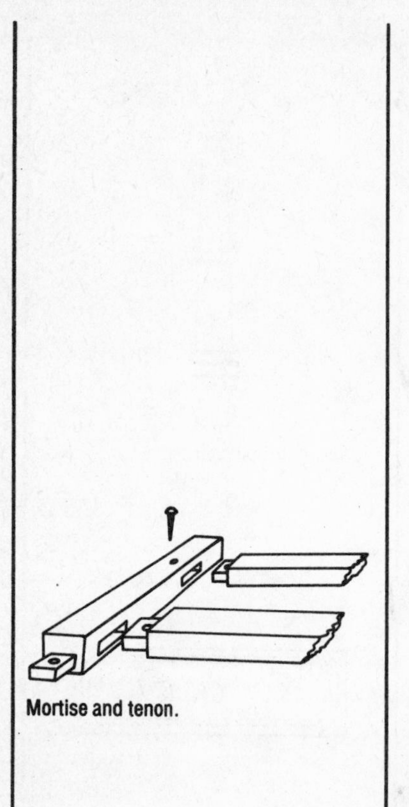
Mortise and tenon.

Side view of movable drawer.

Seventeenth-century chairs came in a number of varieties. Massive turned armchairs represented symbols of authority in the household. Slat-back chairs—with plank, splint, or rush seats—were introduced in the 17th century, and variants are still made today. The wainscot chair, with a plank seat, contained a paneled back that was often carved with dates, initials, and geometric, floral, and strapwork details. Derivative of the English Cromwellian or farthingale chair, leather-covered chairs were also made at this time; the rectangular upholstered back and seat were separated by an open space. This form, upholstered with leather or turkeywork that was held in place with brass-headed nails, was expanded to create a couch that could seat two people.

Also related to the chair, the joint stool was used both as a seat and as a table. Ruggedly constructed, the stool had a rectangular top supported by four turned legs connected by stretchers. The "form," an expanded version of the joint stool, was used as a bench at long tables.

Seventeenth-century beds, extremely rare today, contained turned elements similar to those of the turned chair. Beds for babies—wicker cradles, in fact—were also in use at the time.

Trestle tables derived from medieval forms and were often of monumental proportions. Two or three stanchions, connected by a stretcher, supported the top, which was often detachable, so that the table could be easily disassembled. X-shaped supports, placed at either end, were used in a variant of this table. The draw-top table, rarely seen today, contained flat leaves that could be drawn at either end from under the tabletop so that the table's size could double. Also popular was the multiple purpose chair-table, with a convertible top.

Derivative of the Renaissance Italian *cassone*, or dower chest, the lift-top chest—quite common in the 17th century—

was often of paneled construction. In some instances, the panels were flat-carved; in others, plain. Other chests contained movable drawers below the lift-top section. A group of these chests, featuring sunflower and tulip carving on the inset panels, has been identified with the Hartford-Wethersfield area of Connecticut. Chests from the region around Hadley, Massachusetts, farther up the Connecticut River, are related to the Hartford-Wethersfield chests, but they display less carved detail. True chests of drawers, as we know them today, began to be made near the end of the century and often rested on bun feet.

The cupboard was the most important type of 17th-century storage furniture, however. Containing shelves for folded fabric and clothing, this form was marked by strong architectural lines. A surprisingly sophisticated piece for the 17th century was the chamber table, supported on turned legs and containing a lift top and drawers. The most imposing pieces with drawers, though, were the court and press cupboards. Used for storage and for display of important possessions, the court cupboard contained a cabinet with doors above and an open shelf below. The press cupboard contained cabinets above and below. To simulate the rich effect of ebony, which was popular in Europe at the time, the ornamentation was often painted black (ebonized). Split spindles were also frequently ebonized, as were bosses or jewels (small, oval pieces of wood).

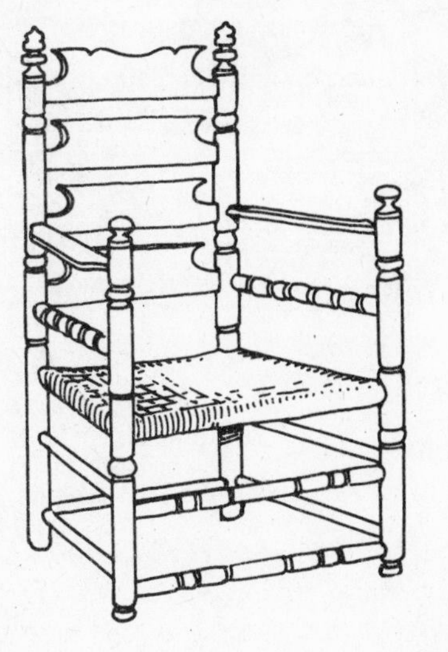

Slat-back chair.

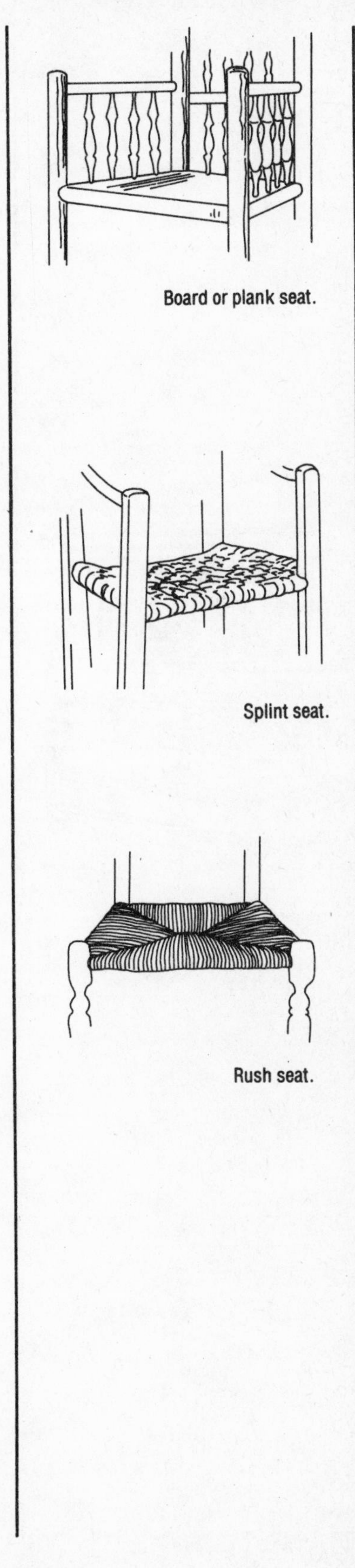

Board or plank seat.

Splint seat.

Rush seat.

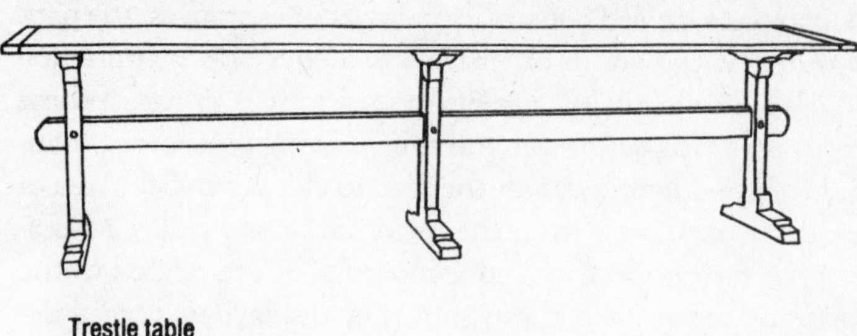

Trestle table
with stanchions
connected by stretcher.

Court cupboard
containing doors
above and an
open shelf below.

Identifying 17th-Century Furniture

Because documentary evidence is scant, dating furniture from this period is especially difficult. The few pieces that survive provide little more than the broadest outline of regional differences and techniques of special joiners. Little is known about the actual makers of this early furniture. Thomas Dennis (active 1663–1706) and William Searle (active 1634–1667), both of Ipswich, Massachusetts, are two of the earliest known American furniture makers. Peter Blin of Wethersfield, Connecticut, is associated with the sunflower chest, and John Allis and Samuel Belding, followed by their sons, are associated with the Hadley chest.

Wethersfield chest
featuring sunflower
and tulip carving
on inset panels.

The William and Mary Style (1700–1725)

WHEN the Dutch stadholder William III of Orange and his wife, Mary II, became joint monarchs of England in 1689, that country became linked directly to the Continent and ceased to be a provincial island. William reigned until his death in 1702 (Mary died in 1694). His rule was marked not only by the adoption of many Dutch traditions, but by the importations of Dutch craftsmen to England.

This Anglo-Dutch taste had its roots in the French court style of Louis XIV, which in turn had been influenced by Italian Baroque design. Elaborate turnings, carvings in high relief, severe curves, large unified shapes, and contrasts of color were typical elements of this style. Also, trade with China prompted the vogue for Oriental objects at this time, and furniture incorporated japanning (a simulation of Oriental lacquer) and woven cane panels. An original English contribution was a form of case furniture with simple, flat surfaces and architectural trim that would be the chief influence on American furniture for more than a century.

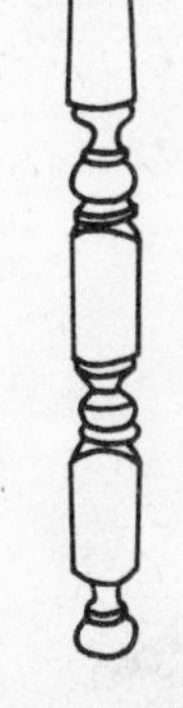

Split spindle turning.

American Adaptations of the William and Mary Style

By the 18th century, a simplified version of Baroque William and Mary style began to appear in the interiors of American buildings. At this time, the first formal interior architectural paneling was introduced, and rooms were enriched with imported luxuries from Europe and the Orient. Turnings and cutouts whose shapes resembled Oriental vases began to be used. A tapering scroll foot—often called a *paintbrush* or *Spanish foot*—became an important design element. (The form actually seems to have originated in Portugal, not Spain.) The carved elements in the cresting piece of chairs often reflected

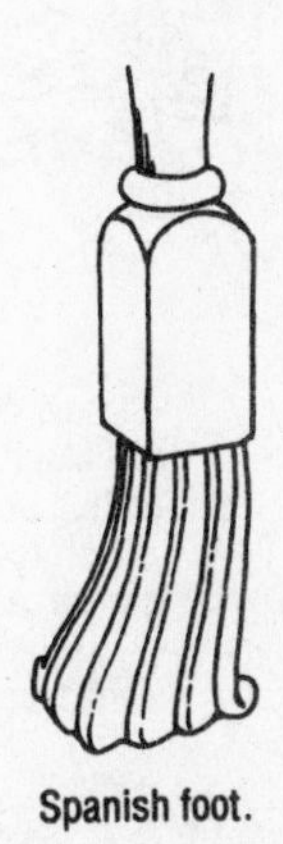

Spanish foot.

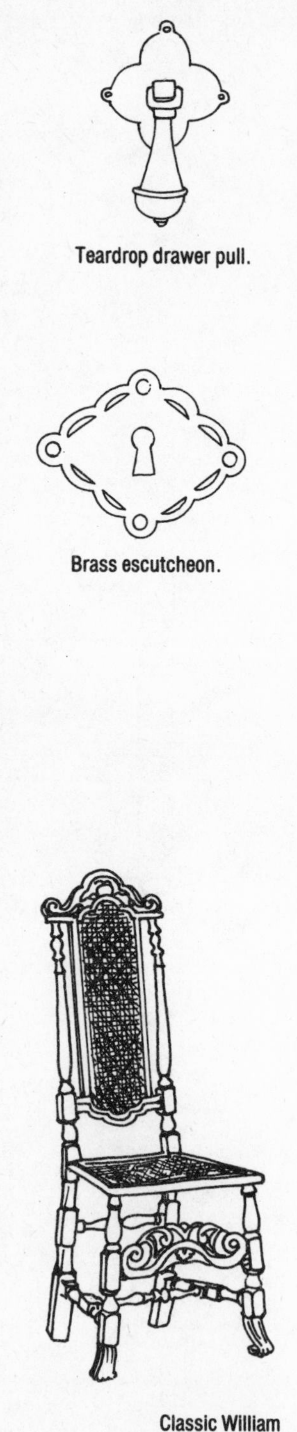

Teardrop drawer pull.

Brass escutcheon.

Classic William and Mary chair, incorporating Spanish feet, rounded carved cresting pieces, and caned surfaces.

the designs of the Huguenot craftsman Daniel Marot, who was employed by William and Mary in England.

Since sculptural carving was a chief component of the William and Mary style, it might be said that the era of the cabinetmaker had arrived. Walnut was a favored wood because it was readily available and lent itself to carving, and veneers cut from walnut burl added decorative interest to William and Mary furniture. Maple was also used, and ebonized finishes remained popular. By now, hardware was being imported to America, with engraved brass key plates and teardrop drawer pulls particularly favored.

Although vigorous in its execution, native furniture was now beginning to reveal the simplicity of detail and the flat plain surfaces that clearly distinguished American designs from their European prototypes. While cabinetmaking centers extended from New England to the Carolinas, only scant material survives about the makers of American William and Mary furniture.

The Baroque influence was reflected in the elaborately carved scrolls and arched cresting pieces and use of Spanish feet seen in William and Mary chairs. While retaining 17th-century outlines, for example, the William and Mary banister-back chairs incorporated rounded carved cresting pieces. As cane began to be imported from the Orient, it was frequently used in chair-back panels and in seats, providing additional comfort. Large armchairs, with leather backs and seats attached with brass-headed nails, looked almost thronelike. A simpler form of leather chair contained a center backsplat that was upholstered, as was the seat. Made in great quantities until after the mid-18th century, this so-called *Boston chair* was shipped to many ports along the Eastern seaboard.

The easy chair, called a wing chair today, was an innovation of this period and offered a great degree of seating comfort. This high-back armchair, with padding and upholstery on its back, sides, arms, and seat, was most often used in the bedchamber as an invalid's chair.

William and Mary settees or benches carried on 17th-century traditions. Paneled construction dominated the surface of these pieces; some had leather seats for extra comfort.

An important innovation of the period was the daybed or couch, a long, cotlike form with a back (like a chair back) that could be adjusted.

Gateleg tables, with turned supports and drop leaves, were made in a variety of sizes during this period. The length of the leaves determined the number of "gates" needed to support them securely. The so-called butterfly table used wing-shaped supports for the drop leaves. A variety of small tables, derivative of the joint stool, also continued to be made.

Preserving 17th-century traditions, divided boxlike chests were also made in the William and Mary period. A type of chest made in the Guilford, Connecticut, area included a drawer, rather like the Wethersfield and Hadley chests; chests with drawers were sometimes placed in turned frames. An important innovation of this period was a high chest of drawers (highboy), in which a top section with drawers was placed on a stand, also containing drawers. The stand of the highboy had Baroque twist or trumpet-shaped legs, and sometimes burled veneers were used on the fronts of drawers. The dressing table, or lowboy, could be made en suite with such a piece.

In Dutch-influenced areas, such as New York and New Jersey, the *kast*, or large wardrobe, was popular. This piece had a heavy cornice door on the front with shelves inside and a drawer below. It rested on removable feet. Based on the Dutch *kast*, which was often elaborately inlaid, the American variant was generally plain, although a few more ornate and painted American examples do exist. This unique form was made into the second quarter of the 19th century, by which time bracket feet had replaced bun feet.

Another important development of the William and Mary period was the desk, which evolved from the bureau-cabinet, a form that had drawers above and a fall front over the drawers that provided a writing surface.

Boston chair with leather back and seat.

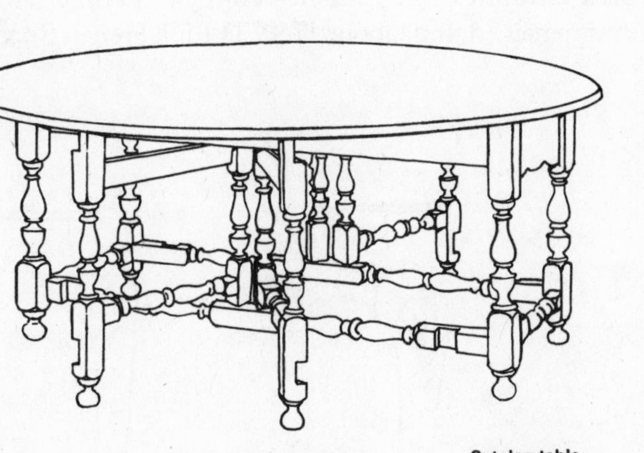

Gateleg table with turned supports and drop leaves.

Easy chair, now called wing chair.

The Queen Anne Style (1725–1755)

Curved crest rail.

Scroll.

BY 1720, certain stylistic changes in American furniture were taking place. Transitional forms between the William and Mary and Queen Anne styles appeared at that time, and the new style was firmly established by about 1725.

The introduction of the fluid, curving line represented the fundamental stylistic change during the Queen Anne period. These curves were based on a scroll-like element first seen in French decorative art in about 1700 and was now expressed in the rounded cabriole leg, curved cresting piece, vase-shaped splat, and shell carving. Some of these innovations of the Queen Anne style carried over into the Chippendale period.

The Queen Anne Style in England

The cabriole leg was introduced as a Baroque element in English furniture during the reign of Queen Anne (1702–1714) and remained until about 1760. The full French Rococo style

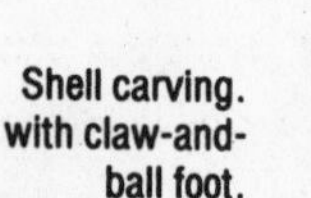

Shell carving. with claw-and-ball foot.

Cabriole leg terminating in pad foot.

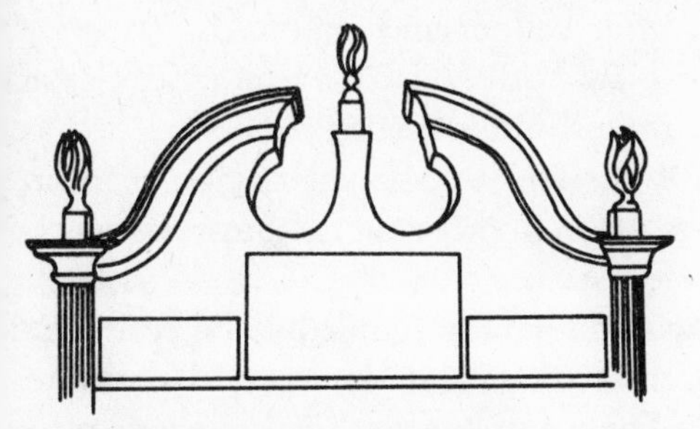

Architectural or broken arch pediment.

was marked in England by 1750 by a more delicate cabriole leg. This later evolution was named the Chippendale period. In case furniture, strong architectural forms using balanced proportions, moldings, and pediments, which had begun to develop under William and Mary, were characteristic of the Queen Anne style.

English Queen Anne chairs generally assumed two forms. One was the English interpretation of the Chinese chair, with an almost flat cresting, rounded at each end, and straight stiles. The other used curving cabriole-shaped stiles with an ornament carved in the center of a hoop-shaped cresting. Both types had vase-shaped splats and pad and hoof feet, although claw-and-ball feet became popular during the first quarter of the 18th century.

Americans adopted the English Queen Anne style and simplified it in several ways, drawing from three English periods: Queen Anne, George I (1714–1727), and George II (1727–1760). In ornamentation, carving was more important than inlay, which was restricted primarily to star and sunburst patterns and bands of striping on drawer fronts. Finials, carved as urns or flames, were used on pediments. Veneering was applied to drawer fronts and to chair splats. Cabriole legs terminated in pad feet. Japanning continued to be popular, primarily in Boston, but also in New York and, in a limited way, in Connecticut.

Regional Characteristics in America

The introduction of the Queen Anne style in the colonies occurred at a time when strong regional characteristics were developing. Although walnut was the wood most generally used, other types of wood began to be associated with certain areas. In New England, for example, walnut, cherry, and maple were

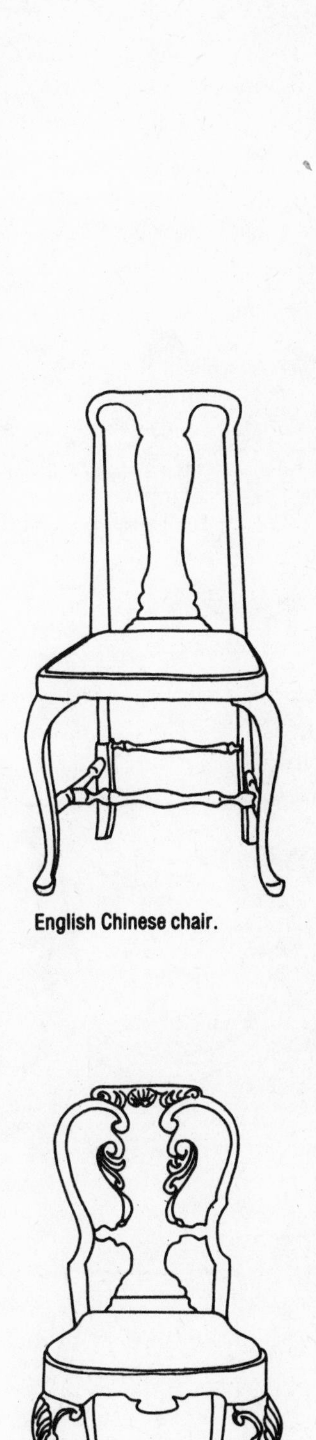

English Chinese chair.

English hoop-shaped chair.

Inlaid star.

Flame finial.

Pad foot.

Seat frame with corner blocks.

the preferred woods, while walnut and imported mahogany were more popular in New York and Philadelphia. Regional characteristics in craftsmanship became more pronounced as well, and it is frequently possible to distinguish a piece made in one locale from that made in another on the basis of stylistic and construction details.

Because New England furniture tended to be conservative, characteristics of the William and Mary period tended to disappear more slowly. For example, stretchers connecting the legs of chairs persisted, even though the triangular corner of glue blocks used inside the seat construction to strengthen the corners made them unnecessary. Massachusetts furniture is generally delicate and spare, with a strong verticality that is unique among colonial pieces. Delicate tea and card tables, placed on slender cabriole legs, display the Massachusetts interpretation of the Queen Anne style to good advantage. Highboys tended to be slender and vertical, rising on delicate cabriole legs. In chairs, the vase-shaped splat was notably simple, and a pinched back was typical of Massachusetts side chairs.

The introduction of blocking in New England is an important contribution of the Queen Anne period. Requiring virtuoso skill, blocking involves cutting a single piece of solid wood to form raised and depressed areas on the front of a case piece. A technique derived from Continental craftsmanship, blocking represents a high point in New England cabinetmaking.

Newport, Rhode Island, emerged as a highly original center of American cabinetmaking during the Queen Anne pe-

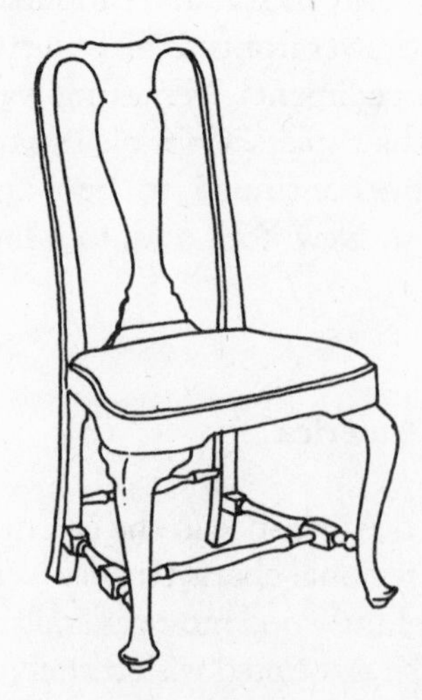

Boston side chair with slip seat.

Massachusetts tea table.

riod and flourished by mid-century. Here, Santo Domingo mahogany was used almost exclusively, having become fashionable as a result of widening international trade. The claw-and-ball foot was adapted quite early and was characterized by its oval, rather than round, shape, with slender and outstretched talons that were sometimes undercut just above the ball. Reminiscent of English work, this feature is especially associated with the cabinetmaker John Goddard. Splats on Newport chairs were generally narrow and often scrolled; the shell carved on the cresting was silhouetted (a characteristic also found on New York chairs). On some Newport chairs, there was also a flat serpentine stretcher. Newport is chiefly remembered for its case furniture, particularly the blockfront, which reached its height in the Chippendale style, and is associated with the Goddard and Townsend families of cabinetmakers.

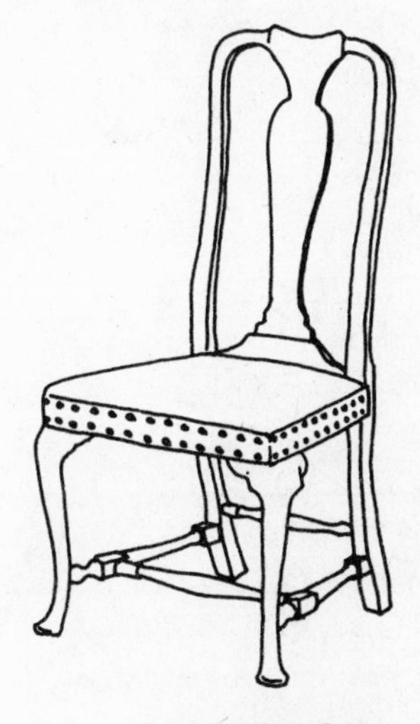

Side chair from Boston with upholstered seat.

Massachusetts card table.

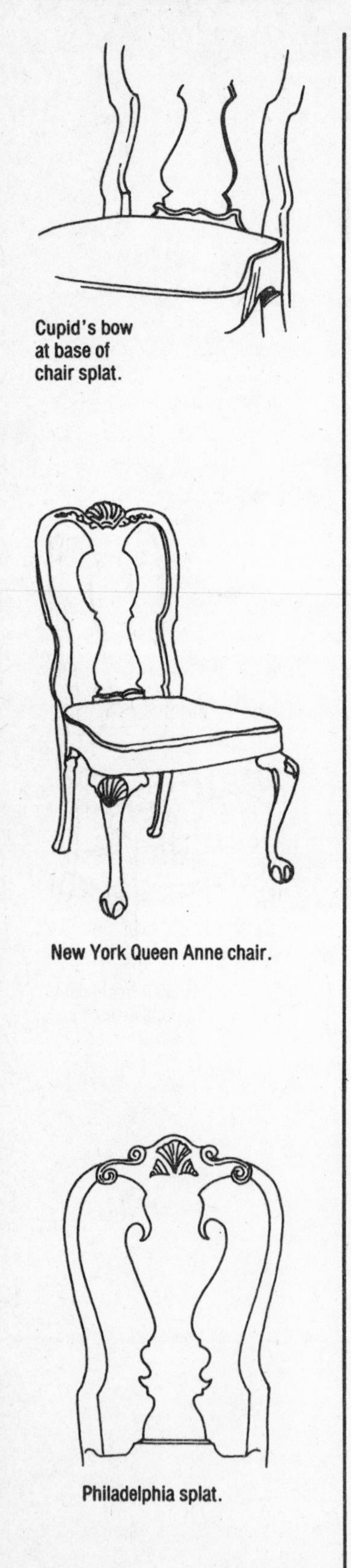

Cupid's bow at base of chair splat.

New York Queen Anne chair.

Philadelphia splat.

Silhouetted shell.

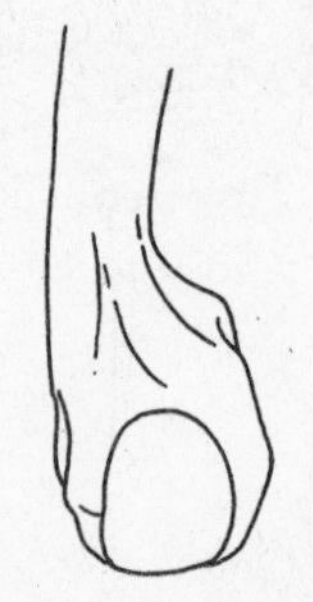

Newport claw-and-ball.

Although the Dutch controlled the New York area relatively briefly, certain characteristics of Dutch Baroque design persisted there and were integrated with English Queen Anne and early Georgian design. New York furniture tended to contain square, squat, and heavy elements. The chair was often nearly square, and the cabriole legs had a sturdiness not found elsewhere. The claw-and-ball foot also displayed a squarish quality, and the rear leg, which was tapered and rounded, terminated in a small, square foot. A scroll called a cupid's bow was often found at the base of the splat in New York chairs.

Highly decorative Queen Anne chairs were produced in Philadelphia. Here, cresting was fashioned like a hoop, carved with S-shaped spirals; if a shell was included at all, it tended to be contained within the design, not silhouetted or set off by itself. The splat had curved volutes and scrolls, and the seat was horseshoe-shaped. The trifid foot, characteristic of Philadelphia-area chairs, was often paneled. Similar paneling is also seen with the club-and-slipper foot, a feature that seems to have originated in Ireland. The rear leg in Philadelphia chairs is often of the stump type—severely plain and round, although sometimes chamfered.

Furniture made in New Jersey and Maryland bore a strong resemblance to that of the Philadelphia school. The trifid foot appeared on some New Jersey chairs, and Maryland furniture maintained the same general shape as that of Philadelphia, but lacked the carved detail.

Much of the documented Southern furniture does not display the height or architectural proportions associated with Northern centers. Rather, it tends to demonstrate a close link with English country prototypes. Walnut and some fruitwoods were the principal materials, with Southern yellow pine used as a secondary wood. Tables from the South reveal straight, rounded legs ending in slanting pad feet, while case pieces had simple bracketed feet.

New Furniture Forms

The Queen Anne style did not introduce quite as many new furniture forms as the William and Mary period did. Although the William and Mary side and armchairs and the easy chair now incorporated Queen Anne characteristics, a slipper chair with upholstered back and seat and a comfortable open armchair were actual innovations of the Queen Anne style. True sofas with curved cresting and cabriole legs were also introduced.

The daybed continued to be made with stylistic modifications. Tester beds (with a framework for holding curtains) became popular, now having short front cabriole legs with pad feet. Easily disassembled field beds, probably named because they were associated with military campaigns, were also developed during this period.

Drop-leaf tables also continued to be made, now with cabriole legs to support the leaves. Side tables, mixing tables, and tea and card tables were specialized types associated with the Queen Anne style.

High chests and dressing tables continued to be made as well. Some of the latter forms were conceived with blocked

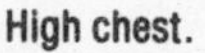

High chest.

Philadelphia cresting piece.

Trifid foot.

Maryland side chair.

fronts. Desks with bookcases followed the same form as in the William and Mary period but now tended to include broken pediments with finials as ornaments.

Looking-glass frames were also architectural, containing broken pediments and scrolls. They were made exclusively of wood or of wood with gilded plaster.

Cabinetmakers

More information is available about cabinetmakers working in the Queen Anne style than those active in earlier periods because more craftsmen labeled and/or signed their pieces. The most important New England cabinetmakers included Thomas Johnston (also spelled Johnson), an engraver and artist who produced japanned surfaces on furniture in Boston between 1732 and 1766, and the Goddard and Townsend families of Newport, Rhode Island. Job Townsend and his son-in-law John Goddard founded this line of cabinetmakers, who would become especially important during the Chippendale era.

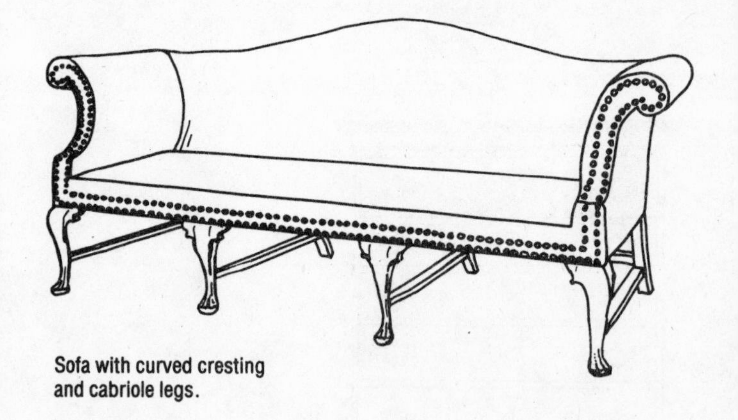

Sofa with curved cresting and cabriole legs.

The Chippendale Style (1755–1780)

IN about 1755, the Chippendale style was introduced to colonial America from England. It flourished in the 1760s and 1770s. With the Chippendale style, Baroque and Queen Anne forms took on a new delicacy and a playful character. Mahogany, which was available through trade, became the most widely used wood in cabinetmaking, and rich ornamental carving was favored over veneer and inlay. The claw-and-ball foot became extremely popular.

Origins of the Chippendale Style

Originating in England during the late 1730s and 1740s, the Chippendale style combined three ingredients: French Rococo; Chinese ornamentation, known from imported objects; and the Gothic style. These elements were often added to fur-

English Rococo chair.

English Chinese chair.

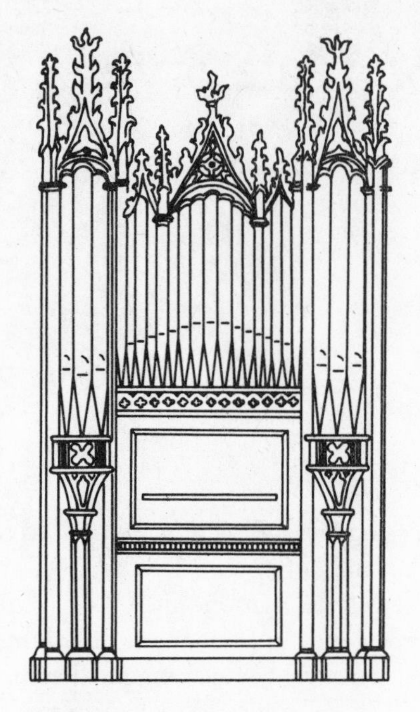

English Gothic organ.

niture that reflected the Baroque architectural influences that had been so popular during the William and Mary and Queen Anne periods. Thus, the broken pediment, pilaster, and classical entablature remained essential parts of furniture design, though the Chippendale style introduced new elements as well.

The Rococo style, widely accepted in England during the 1740s, originated in France about two decades earlier when lighter forms and more playful curvilinear lines were introduced. The name derived from the French words *rocaille*, referring to rockwork or rock forms, and *coquille*, or shell patterns. The fanciful and fantastic combinations of these two motifs in asymmetrical patterns formed the Rococo elements of the Chippendale style.

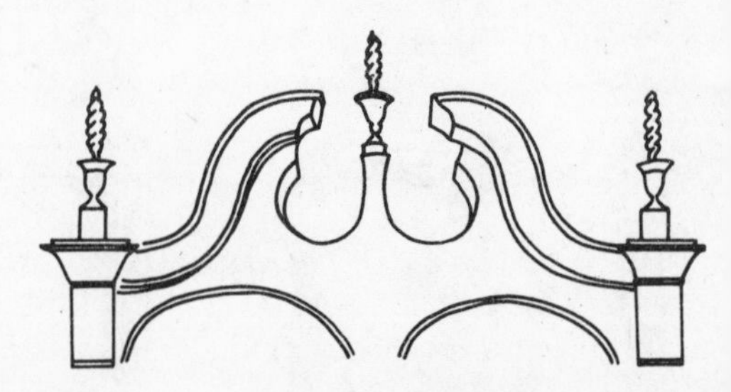

Architectural or broken arch pediment.

The Chinese influence on the Chippendale style had two chief components: the adaptation of actual Far Eastern furniture from pieces that were being widely imported from the Orient; and the imaginative Western interpretations of Chinese designs, called *chinoiserie*.

As an architectural influence, Gothic detail has never altogether disappeared from the English design vocabulary. However, the Gothic influence had had little or no impact on actual medieval English furniture, and Gothic elements were often so blended with Rococo and Chinese forms that it is difficult to distinguish them.

It was Thomas Chippendale (1718(?)–1779) who codified this style, which was later named after him in both England and America. Although he, his father, and his sons were all furniture makers, Chippendale is remembered primarily for his pattern book called the *Gentleman and Cabinet-Makers Director*, which was first published in 1754. This book, and the two editions that followed, illustrated furniture that combined Rococo, Chinese, and Gothic elements. The *Director* was circulated among the nobility as well as among the cabinetmakers and other craftsmen both in England and America, but its exact influence on American cabinet shops has not been determined. Chippendale's name probably did not become identified with the style until the 19th century.

Rocaille.

Chinoiserie.

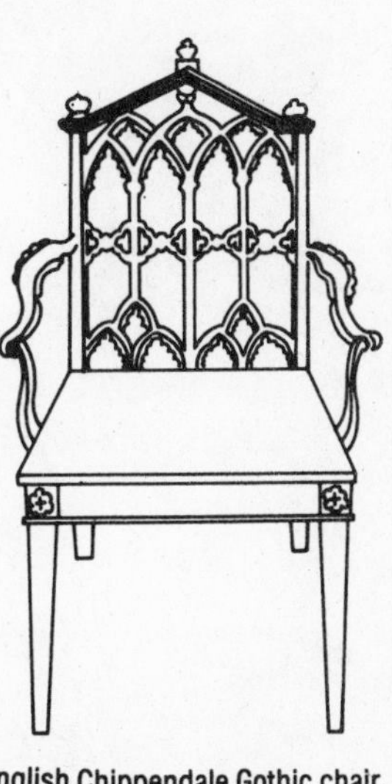

English Chippendale Gothic chair.

Coquille.

Regional Characteristics in American Chippendale Furniture

Massachusetts claw-and-ball.

Corkscrew finial, popular in Massachusetts.

Regional characteristics were highly pronounced during the Chippendale period. In Massachusetts, furniture remained conservative, still slower to change there than in other areas. The slender and highly refined cabriole leg was typical of this area, and a block-and-spindle stretcher was often used, a hold-over from the Queen Anne period. The Massachusetts claw-and-ball foot was crisply carved, with the side talon turned back sharply, forming a triangle with the center claw when seen from the side.

The same feeling of delicacy in Massachusetts furniture is displayed in the tall, slender cabriole legs of tables. The turreted or buttress-top tea table is particularly identified with Massachusetts: circular projections, resembling turrets, extended from the top to hold teacups. Chests-on-chests and secretary-bookcases often had flattened pilasters to frame the upper section. Corkscrew finials were popular, and carved human figures occasionally were used as well.

Blocked fronts were also characteristic of Massachusetts furniture, although the blocking was somewhat flatter than that found on Newport pieces. The master of the blockfront in the Boston area was the cabinetmaker Benjamin Frothingham (1734–1809).

Of all the innovations characteristic of the Massachusetts school, the most ambitious was the kettle or *bombé* form on case furniture. Derived from Continental Baroque and Rococo designs, these great bulging forms had sides that were

Carved finial from Connecticut.

Massachusetts chair.

fashioned from a single piece of wood, as in blocking. The Boston cabinetmaker John Cogswell (known to be active in 1769, died in 1818) is most closely identified with this technique.

In Newport, three generations, including twenty-three members, of the Goddard and Townsend families made furniture that ranged stylistically from the Queen Anne to the Empire style, and their handling of the blockfront and shell represents a unique contribution to American cabinetmaking. Using primarily highly patterned Santo Domingo mahogany, the Goddards and Townsends created skillful blockfront surfaces. Shells, which were sometimes applied, were carved in high relief and contained fine carved detail. The pieces were often adorned with a flattened finial, which has been termed a "cupcake," with a corkscrew extending from it. The ogee-bracketed foot contained a small scroll, and a palmette was sometimes carved on the knees. The claw-and-ball foot was oval, and the talons were sometimes undercut.

Connecticut produced an original, though somewhat less sophisticated, type of Chippendale furniture. The favored wood there was cherry, which was plentiful. Elements of Queen Anne design, including the pad foot, persisted for a long time in this area. Although Connecticut furniture reveals the influence of Massachusetts, Newport, and Philadelphia, a simpler treatment of the blockfront, a shallow version of the shell, and carved sunbursts or pinwheel patterns are generally characteristic. More sophisticated design elements included cut latticework pediments and scallops on the skirts of case pieces.

The Chapin family was prominent among Connecticut cabinetmakers. Bringing the Philadelphia style with him when he moved to East Windsor, Connecticut, in 1771, Eliphalet Chapin (1741–1807) used elaborate latticework and scrolled

Undercut claw-and-ball from Newport.

Newport cupcake finial.

Newport blockfront with bracket feet.

Lattice-cut pediment from Connecticut.

Connecticut blockfront.

New York tassel and ruffle.

pediments and a distinct type of finial, characterized by a pierced four-sided cartouche. His second cousin, Aaron Chapin (1753–1773), of Hartford, worked in virtually the same manner. Benjamin Burnham of Colchester, Connecticut (active 1769–1773) was another leading cabinetmaker of the Connecticut school.

New York furniture was also conservative stylistically, and Rococo ornamentation made only slow headway there. In New York, Dutch Baroque design still tended to combine with the English style. Prior to the American Revolution, the strong reliance on architectural form, reminiscent of the design vocabulary of George III's reign, dominated the furniture made in New York City; the tassel and ruffle and strapwork enclosing a diamond in chair backs reflected that earlier style.

The influence of Chippendale can be seen, though, in the use of Gothic motifs and the serpentine form common in New York card tables. These tables, as well as the New York chairs,

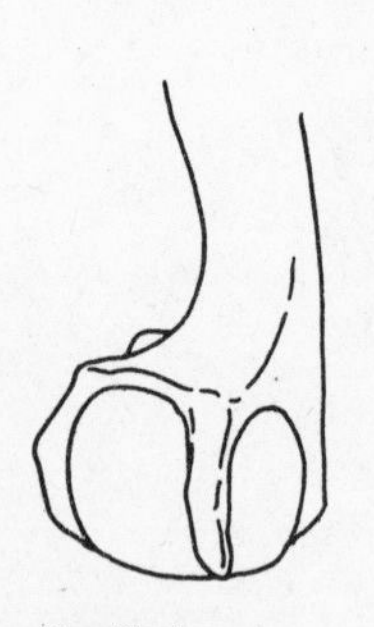

New York claw-and-ball.

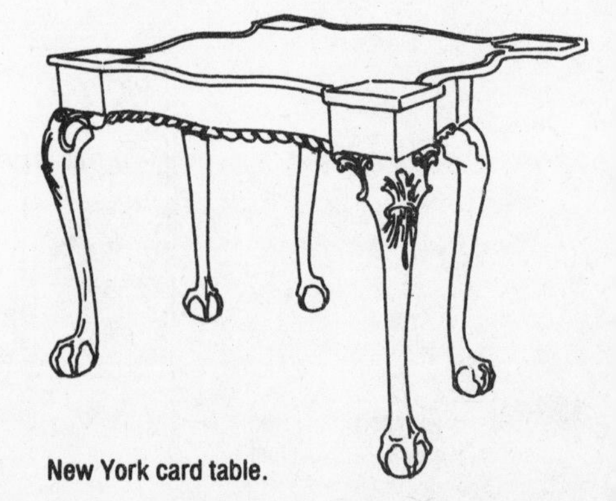

New York card table.

often had skirts carved with gadrooning, endowing them with elegance and demonstrating the persistence of the Continental Baroque tradition. Acanthus-leaf carving here tended to be stringy. On the whole, New York furniture was generally square and heavy, and had a somewhat squat quality. The distinctive New York claw-and-ball foot had talons closely grasping a squarish ball, while rear legs tapered to a squared foot in the English manner. Although New York Chippendale furniture is known chiefly for its tables and seat furniture, several pedimented secretaries have also survived. Gilbert Ash (1717–1785) was a prominent New York cabinetmaker, as was Thomas Burling, who worked in the city from 1772–1775.

By the third quarter of the 18th century, Philadelphia was the second-largest English-speaking city in the world, so, not surprisingly, very sophisticated furniture was made there. By the late 1780s, more than 100 Philadelphia joiners and cabinetmakers and their journeymen marched in the parade celebrating the ratification of the Constitution. Cabinetmakers trained in the British Isles, primarily in London and Dublin, immigrated to Philadelphia, bringing with them the influence of their own tradition.

Philadelphia furniture, generally more elaborate than that of other American centers, often contained details taken directly from Chippendale's *Director*. For example, the French scrolled toe often depicted in this publication was frequently

Scrolled toe popular in Philadelphia.

Philadelphia cartouche and cabochon.

Philadelphia cabriole leg.

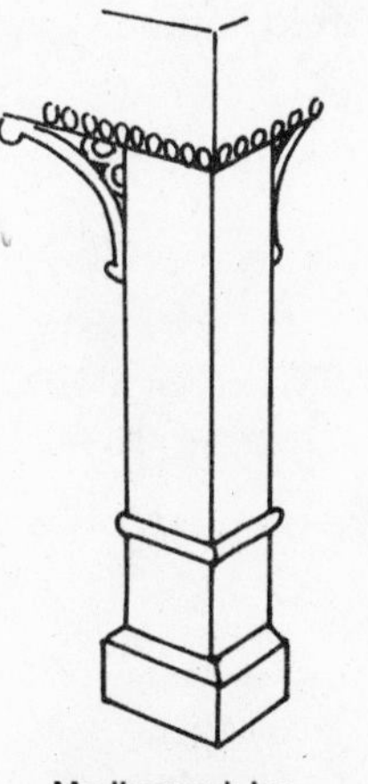

Marlborough leg from Philadelphia

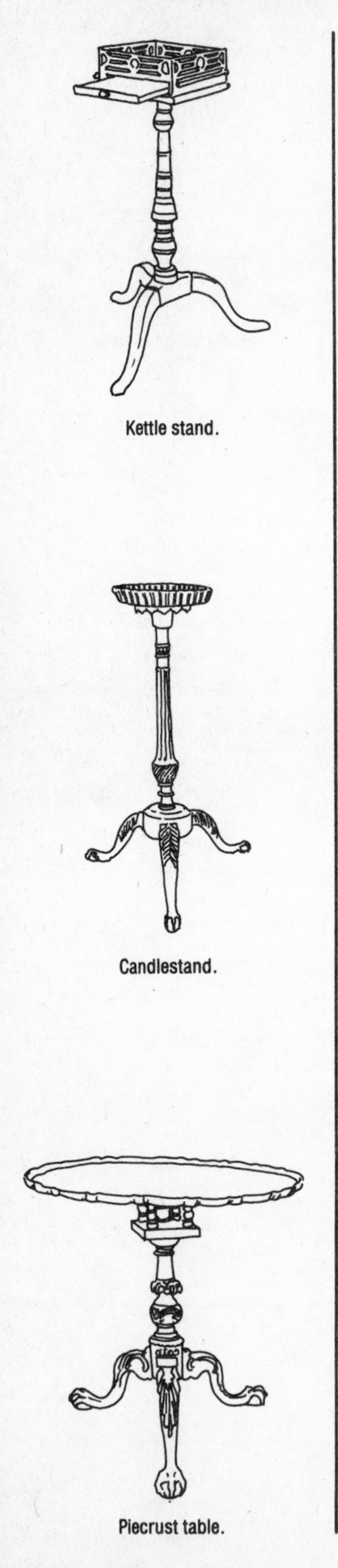

Kettle stand.

Candlestand.

Piecrust table.

used here. Surface carving, sometimes illustrating Aesop's fables, embraced delicate Rococo details. The cartouche was highly developed, frequently containing a central asymmetrical element called a *cabochon*. In Philadelphia, the claw-and-ball foot achieved a sculptural quality, with the talons finely articulated. The cabriole leg was often carved with an acanthus leaf in relief and, in a few rare instances, terminated in a hairy paw foot. Furniture with straight square Marlborough legs, generally terminating in a block or plinth, was also a favorite form of the Philadelphia school.

One of the leading Philadelphia exponents of the Chinese Chippendale style was Thomas Affleck (1740–1795). Other noteworthy cabinetmakers in this city included William Savery (1721–1788), a Quaker craftsman; Benjamin Randolph (active c. 1760–1790); James Gillingham (1736–1781); Daniel Trotter (1747–1800) and his son-in-law Ephraim Haines (1775–1811); John Folwell (active 1762, died 1780) and Adam Hains (born 1768, active c. 1815).

Furniture made south of Philadelphia was sometimes produced by itinerant craftsmen, so it is more difficult to identify individual cabinetmakers there than in the North. Furniture made in Maryland during the Chippendale period shows the strong influence of Philadelphia taste; Baltimore did not become an important port until after the Revolution.

The many varieties of walnut that grow in the South were generally preferred for furniture, though Charleston, South Carolina, makers tended to use mahogany, sometimes adding walnut as a secondary wood. In Charleston, a thriving school of cabinetmaking developed. It produced sophisticated furniture closely related to English prototypes. Until recently, almost all Charleston furniture was attributed to Thomas Elfe (active 1747–1775), who was English by birth and training. But more recent research suggests that other cabinetmakers crafted some of these pieces.

Pembroke table.

Innovative Forms

Few new forms developed during the Chippendale period. Chairs and sofas continued to be made in the same shapes as those of the Queen Anne style. Tester beds were made with claw-and-ball feet, rather than pad feet, and the daybed virtually disappeared.

The new and widespread fashion for tea drinking resulted in new furniture forms: the kettle stand, containing a small, easily movable slide to hold a teacup; the fret-top "China table," used to hold the tea service; and the elaborately carved "piecrust" top designed for the three-legged tilt-top tea table.

The Chippendale period also introduced the Pembroke table, a breakfast table with short leaves. Candlestands, designed to hold candlesticks, were also developed during this time. Because case furniture remained highly architectural, blocking and *bombé* were both important during the Chippendale period. The secretary-bookcase came to be supplemented, particularly in England, by the breakfront, a highly architectural piece conceived in several sections, with bookcases, a desk, and closed cupboards. This form is rare in America. Looking-glasses, also architectural in form, often displayed elements borrowed from the *Director.*

Chippendale looking-glass.

Elfe desk and bookcase.

Windsor Furniture

English Windsor.

DURING the Chippendale era, Windsor furniture carried on the turner's tradition. Its name seems to be derived from Windsor, an important English market town, where such furniture was sold. Produced in quantity in England beginning in the 17th century, Windsor chairs are characterized by stick legs and spindles driven into a plank seat. Hickory and ash—tough, springy, and easily shaped—were ideal woods for Windsor construction, which required no screws or nails.

Because Windsor chairs were being made in large numbers in Philadelphia by the mid-18th century, they were occasionally called "Philadelphia" chairs. The first Windsors made in Philadelphia had low backs; they were followed by fan backs, sack backs, and bow backs. A New England version was fashioned with a continuous hoop and arm. During the second half of the 18th century, Windsors were being made in quantity in most major American cities, and Connecticut became

Fan-back.

an important Windsor-manufacturing center. One of the most important Connecticut craftsmen working in this style was Ebenezer Tracy (1744–1803).

Because these chairs and settees were constructed with a number of types of wood, they were painted in such colors as red, black, blue, yellow, rose, or gray. Some pieces had floral decorations to conceal the differences in the materials.

Other Windsor forms included cradles, high chairs, stools, and writing armchairs.

Bow-back.

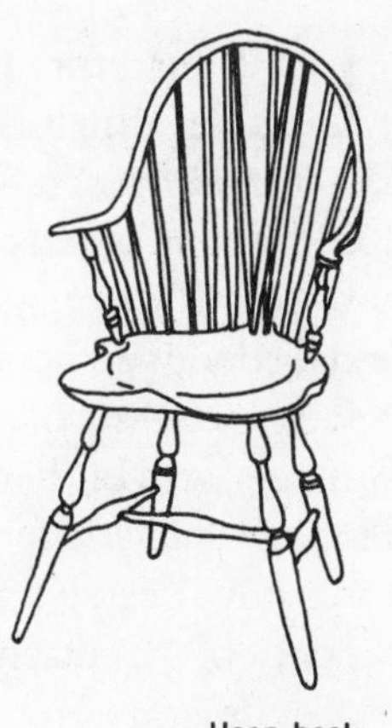

Hoop-back (continuous arm).

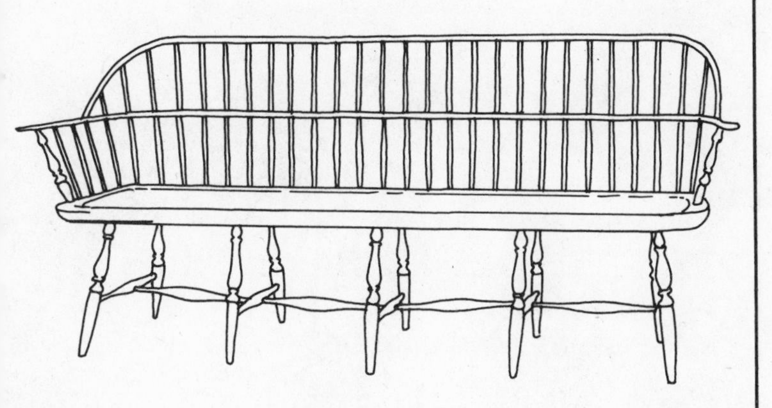

Settee.

Germanic Furniture

Birds on trees motif.

Unicorn motif.

Flower in panel motif.

THE furniture discussed so far was generally conceived under English influence, with Continental—notably Dutch and French—traditions playing a part as well. But by 1683, settlers began to arrive from the Rhineland in Germany and from Switzerland, bringing with them a peasant culture and distinctive traditions. Generally belonging to dissident religious sects—such as the Mennonites, Amish, Moravians, Dunkers, and Lutherans—these groups settled in southeastern Pennsylvania and farther west. Those who settled in Pennsylvania have been popularly called "Pennsylvania Dutch" (a corruption of "Deutsch"), but *Pennsylvania German* is a more proper designation.

The Germanic cabinetmakers produced furniture that represented very old traditions; many of their decorative motifs had originated in medieval illuminations. These decora-

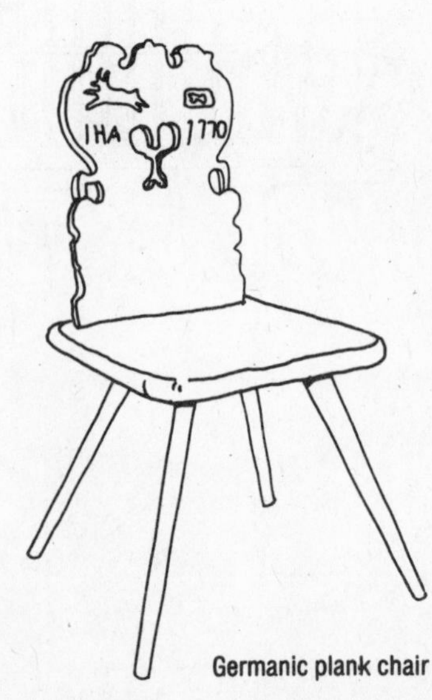

Germanic plank chair

Schrank.

tions were brightly painted on furniture, often with accompanying names and dates. Typical forms known from the second half of the 18th century include dower chests; chairs with scrolled solid backs, solid seats and stick legs; dressers; cupboards; and wardrobes. The chief woods used were walnut, oak, yellow pine, and tulipwood.

The most prominent of the true Pennsylvania German cabinetmakers was Christian Seltzer (1749–1831). Chippendale influence, which is unusual in Pennsylvania German furniture, can be seen in the work of Lancaster cabinetmakers of the Bachman family, who worked in the 1770s.

Germanic lift-top chest

New Influences on Furniture Design

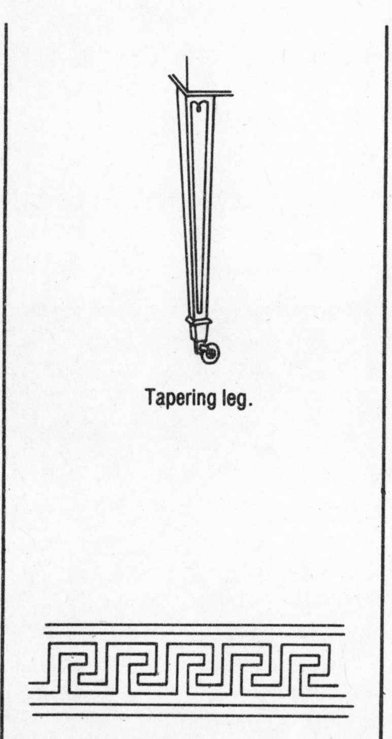

Tapering leg.

Greek key (running fret).

FOLLOWING the American Revolution, furniture styles fell under a general design influence that extended throughout the entire 19th century: revivalism, or the borrowing of decorative detail, or even the entire design vocabulary, of a style that had been popular at an earlier time. Revivalism first appeared at the end of the 18th century in the form of Neoclassicism (employing discreet Greco-Roman ornamentation), which evolved into other classical styles by the early 19th century. Classicism was not the only revival style to develop during this era, however. The 19th century also saw the introduction of Gothic, Rococo, Louis XVI, and Renaissance Revival styles, and this fascination with the past continued for about 125 years.

European Classicism

Just as American furniture styles had derived from European sources during the 17th and 18th centuries, American taste continued to be shaped by European fashions throughout the 19th century as well. The classical styles were no exception.

Since the beginning of the 18th century, European intellectuals and travelers had shown a keen interest in the relics and monuments of classical antiquity. Archeological discoveries at Herculaneum, in Italy, aroused a deep romantic interest

Egg and dart pattern.

in the past, and many books were published describing these findings. The discovery of Pompei later in the 18th century and its exploration in the early 19th added impetus to the classical influence. As early as 1730, the English architect William Kent (1684–1748) had begun to apply classical motifs to his Baroque furniture forms—such devices, for example, as Greek keys and egg-and-dart moldings. Kent's innovation, of course, was merely the application of classical motifs to the *surface* of the existing piece, rather than the creation of classical forms of furniture, and his example continued to be followed in England and France well into the 1750s and 1760s.

Prince of Wales feathers.

European Neoclassicism

A further development was the alteration of the furniture form itself—most particularly by incorporating a straight tapered or turned leg, in direct contrast to the earlier curvilinear lines of the Rococo style. This change in the furniture form signaled the first significant development in what is called *Neoclassicism*. Although the Scottish architect Robert Adam (1728–1792) is often credited with this innovation, the straight leg may have been already in use in France at about time as well. Nevertheless, Adam's ideas were codified and circulated widely—primarily through their translation into furniture designs by George Hepplewhite in his *Cabinetmaker and Upholsterer's Guide* (1788) and by Thomas Sheraton in *The Cabinet-Maker and Upholsterer's Drawing-Book* (1791–1794). These books were largely responsible for disseminating Neoclassicism throughout Europe, and later throughout America.

Wheat shuck.

In general, the Neoclassical forms shown in these books are delicate and balanced. Satinwoods and other exotic woods

Armchair by Robert Adam.

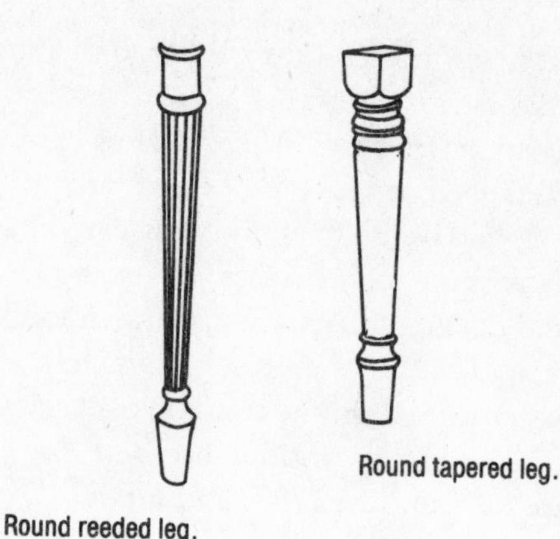

Round reeded leg.

Round tapered leg.

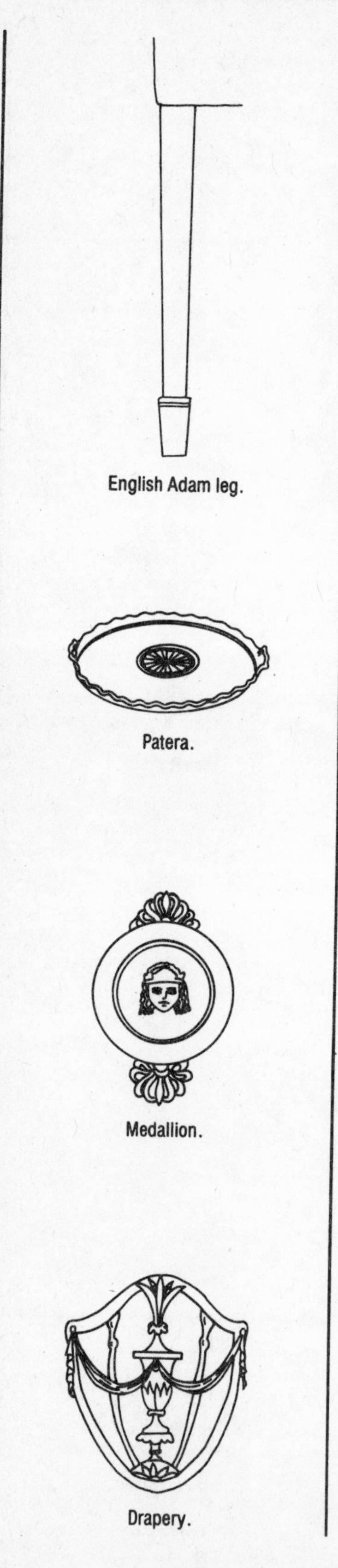

English Adam leg.

Patera.

Medallion.

Drapery.

were used primarily for inlay. Hepplewhite's and Sheraton's illustrations tended to be quite similar, but there were some general distinctions between the two. Hepplewhite, for example, preferred the square tapering leg, which sometimes terminated in a spade foot. He also favored inlay and decorative motifs—particularly Prince of Wales feathers, medallions, drapery, and sheaves of wheat. His chair backs tended to be either shield- or heart-shaped. A limited number of his designs continued the Rococo tradition through the use of curved lines; Hepplewhite called this the *French style*. Sheraton, on the other hand, favored the round, turned, and reeded leg, which tended to be more faithful to the spirit of the late Louis XVI style in France. Sheraton's favorite chair backs were composed of bars that created a trellis effect.

Empire Style

A subsequent phase of Classicism evolved when the intense interest in contemporary archeological discoveries prompted the copying of actual Greco-Roman furniture forms. This phase is known as *Archeological Classicism* or the *Empire style*. Two forms in particular characterize the Empire style: a chair form called the *klismos* and a bench and chair form called the *curule*. The *klismos* had flaring saber legs placed in opposition to one another, while the *curule* had a familiar X-shaped support.

Archeological forms were adapted in France by two French architect-designers, Charles Percier and Pierre F. L. Fontaine, who published—first in 1801, then again in 1812—a collection of illustrations called *Recueil de Décorations Intérieures*. When Napoleon established his Empire in 1804, he appointed Percier and Fontaine his official court architects and

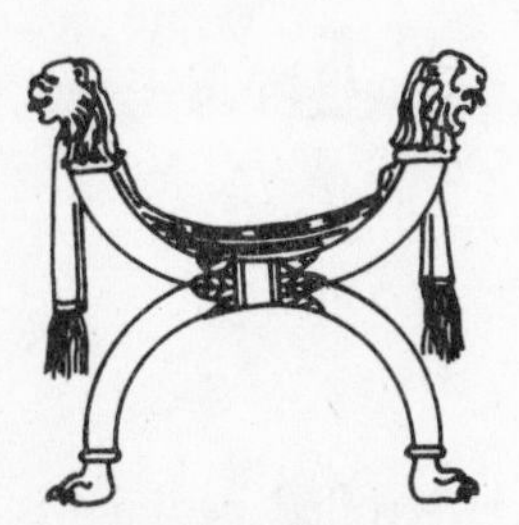
English curule bench.

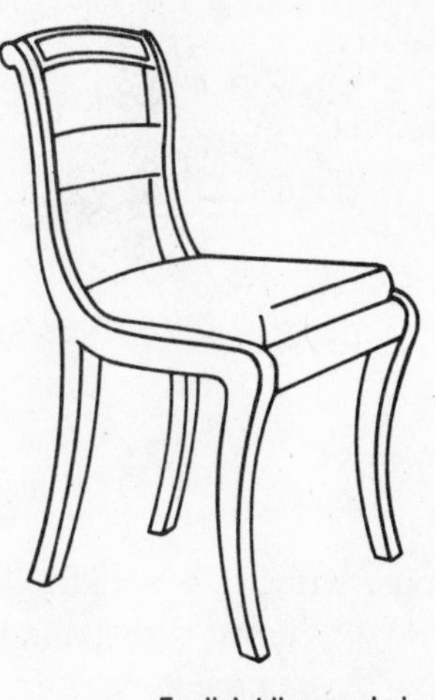
English klismos chair.

Acanthus leaf.

decorators, and the publication of their book played a large role in the creation of the Empire style.

Some of the Greco-Roman motifs identified with the Empire style include acanthus leaves, cornucopias, swans, eagles, dolphins, and monopodia (single elements combining animal heads and legs). Napoleon's Egyptian campaign popularized still another source of ancient decorative motifs and elements—the ancient Egyptian forms, such as the lotus, sphinx, hawk, and hieroglyphics. Made of mahogany and rosewood and elaborately decorated with ormolu mounts, Empire furniture was massive and cubical.

Cornucopia.

The English version of the Empire style became popular chiefly through the work of Thomas Hope, a friend of Charles Percier, who wrote *Household Furniture and Interior Decoration* (1807). This book helped to create what is generally referred to in England as the *Regency* style, after the Prince Regent (later King George IV), an active patron of art and architecture.

Lotus motif.

Late Classicism

The designs of Hope, Percier, and Fontaine were intended for the wealthy. But almost simultaneously with the appearance of Hope's *Household Furniture* in England, other design publications were issued there for more widespread consumption; George Smith's *A Collection of Designs for Household Furniture and Interior Decoration* (1808), a monthly English periodical, Rudolph Ackermann's *Repository* (published 1809–1829), and Loudon's *Encyclopedia of Cottage, Farm and Villa Architecture and Furniture* (first edition, 1833). These illustrated a popular variant of the Empire style that was massive, heavy, and bul-

Swan motif.

Hieroglyphics.

Hawk motif.

Dolphin motif.

Monopodium motif.

Eagle motif.

Sphinx motif.

bous, with such details as architectural scrolled pediments, heavy columns with capitals, and winged lion's-paw feet. This new development signaled the third and final stage of Classicism, which might be called *Late Classicism*. Meanwhile, in France a simplified version of classical furniture was created during the reign of Charles X (1824–1830), a period and style referred to as the *Restauration*. With Restauration furniture, ormolu mounts disappeared and light fruitwoods were favored over mahogany.

In considering classical furniture, then, we can see three phases: Neoclassicism—in which Greco-Roman motifs were applied to contemporary furniture forms; the Archeological Empire style, in which furniture was based on pieces from ancient Greece, Rome, and Egypt; and Late Classicism, which has both English and French influences. The evolution of these classical styles was paralleled in the United States.

French Restauration chair.

Late Classical English chair.

American Neoclassicism—The Federal Style (1780–1820)

CLASSICISM was introduced to America only gradually. The Chippendale style persisted into the 1790s, though it began to be often seen in combination with classical decorative motifs as well. The architectural term *Federal* is often used—and will be used here—to denote this period in American furniture, since the classical styles were introduced during America's Federal age.

After the Revolution, a new wave of cabinetmakers began to arrive in the infant United States from England, Ireland, Scotland, and—in the early 19th century—France. Bringing with them ideas from the popular European furniture pattern books, these craftsmen catered, in the East, to a rising new class of wealthy merchants who were anxious to keep abreast of fashionable trends in Europe.

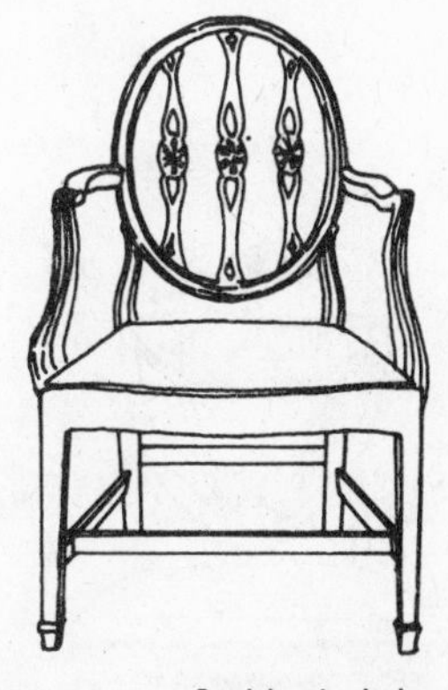
Oval-back chair.

New Furniture Forms

With the introduction of the Federal style of furniture, the dressing table and high chest disappeared. Continuing in limited popularity, the chest-on-chest now became embellished with elaborate carving. The most important new form to develop in this period was the sideboard, a logical development from the earlier side or mixing table. One kind of sideboard had square legs and a recessed center section; another had a kidney-shaped top and rounded ends. In the South, the huntboard developed as a regional variation of the sideboard.

Designed specifically with the needleworker in mind, the work table also appeared at this time. It was fitted with a set of drawers containing compartments or divisions. A cloth (or, rarely, wooden) "bag" to hold sewing was placed below the surface of the table. Card tables remained popular, and they either

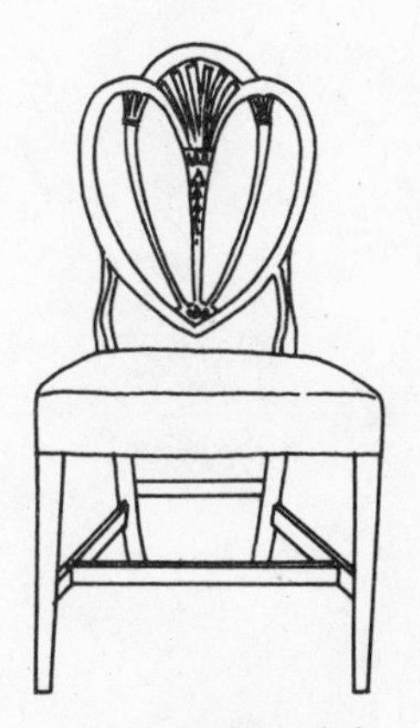
Heart-back chair.

continued to retain the swing leg of their Chippendale predecessors or incorporated a folding top that swiveled. The sectional dining table became a well-known Federal form, as did the dressing table with an attached looking-glass.

During the Federal period, the fall front chest of drawers, with a column at either end, developed as a variation of the Chippendale chest. The fall front desk generally was replaced by the tambour desk. Chairs reflected the delicacy and symmetry of the Neoclassical style: shield- and heart-shaped chair backs became standard, as did rectangular and oval backs.

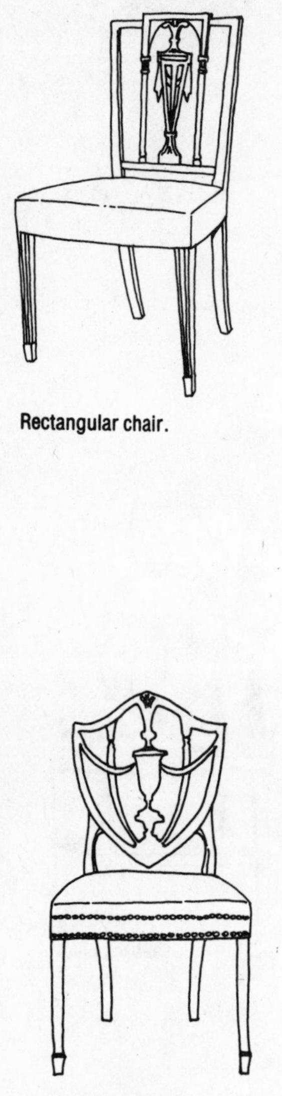

Rectangular chair.

Shield-back chair.

Regional Characteristics

Regional characteristics became less pronounced during the Federal period, although some lingered, making it possible to determine certain areas of manufacture.

Designed with great delicacy, New England furniture still remained the most conservative; only here, for example, did stretchers continue to connect chair legs. Heart- and shield-shaped backs were popular here for chairs. Salem chairs often featured a large urn as a splat, with festoons radiating from it, and rear legs that had an inward curve near the bottom. The bow front chest, with contrasting light and dark veneers, was a typical New England form, as was the dressing table (with attached looking-glass), and the breakfront.

In the Boston-Salem area, several cabinetmakers excelled. The Seymour family produced several master craftsmen, for example. John Seymour (1738–1818) immigrated from England to Boston. His son Thomas (1771–1848) worked with him from the beginning of the 19th century, although John is given credit for most of the superb design and execution.

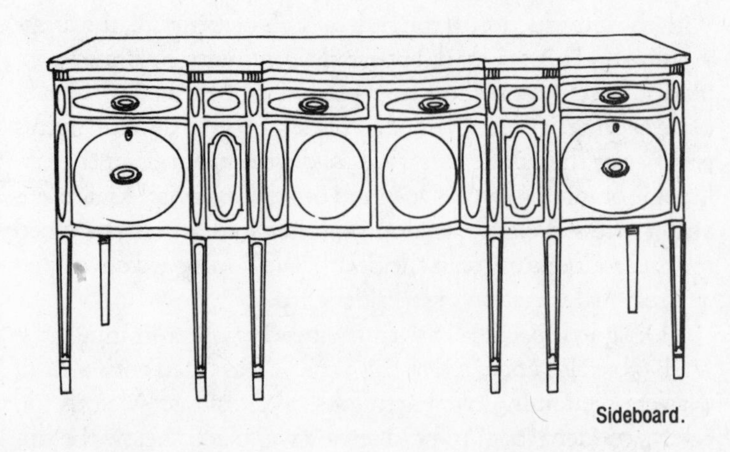

Sideboard.

Samuel McIntire (1757–1811) is remembered not only as a furniture carver but as an architect and a carver of architectural trim as well. Coming from a family of carvers, McIntire became prominent in 1782 as the architect and builder of the Pierce-Nicholas house in Salem. Of the surviving pieces of McIntire's furniture, sofas and chairs seem to predominate. McIntire decorated these with motifs that resembled those he used on his houses: baskets of fruit and flowers; sheaves of wheat; alternating fluting and rosettes; eagles; husks; cornucopias; bunches of grapes; urns with festoons and flowers; and laurel wreaths. While most of the pieces attributed to McIntire were constructed in mahogany, he also used bird's-eye maple and satinwood. McIntire's sofas and chairs were made with both rectangular and rounded backs; the carved ornamentation was sometimes set against a background created with a woodworking tool called a snowflake punch.

Other Salem cabinetmakers included Nehemiah Adams (1769–1840), whose work was once confused with McIntire's; Nathaniel Appleton, Sr. (active 1803); Edmund Johnson (active 1793–1811); William Hook (1777–1867); Elijah Sanderson (1752–1825) and his brother Jacob (1758–1810); John Doggett (d. 1857); and Joseph Short (1771–1819).

In Rhode Island, cabinetmakers developed a characteristic type of chair back, a shield shape centered by a flattened Greek urn or dish called a *kylix*. The Rhode Island card table was quite distinctive also, often having tapering geometric inlay on the legs, which is surmounted by a small "book" inlay.

Newport was no longer regarded as an especially important center of cabinetmaking during the Federal period. John Goddard's sons, Stephen and Thomas, made some pieces in the classical style, as did Holmes Weaver (1767–1848) and Adam S. Coe (1782–1862), but the city had lost its leadership in furniture fashion.

Although mahogany generally remained the principal wood in the Federal period, Connecticut furniture continued to be made of cherry. Connecticut Federal furniture is characterized by elaborate inlays: a pattern of wavy lines resembling a pinwheel was particularly favored, along with bellflowers with "dot" outlines, "carrot" inlays, and eagles with shields. The Chapin family, who worked in Hartford and East Windsor, continued to make furniture, and other well-known cabinetmakers in the state included Lemuel Adams (active c. 1792) and Silas Cheney (1776–1821).

In New York, Federal furniture is generally associated with the quarter-fan inlay, although this detail appears in furniture made in New Jersey as well. New York chair backs of this pe-

Seymour chair.

McIntire snowflake punch.

Kylix.

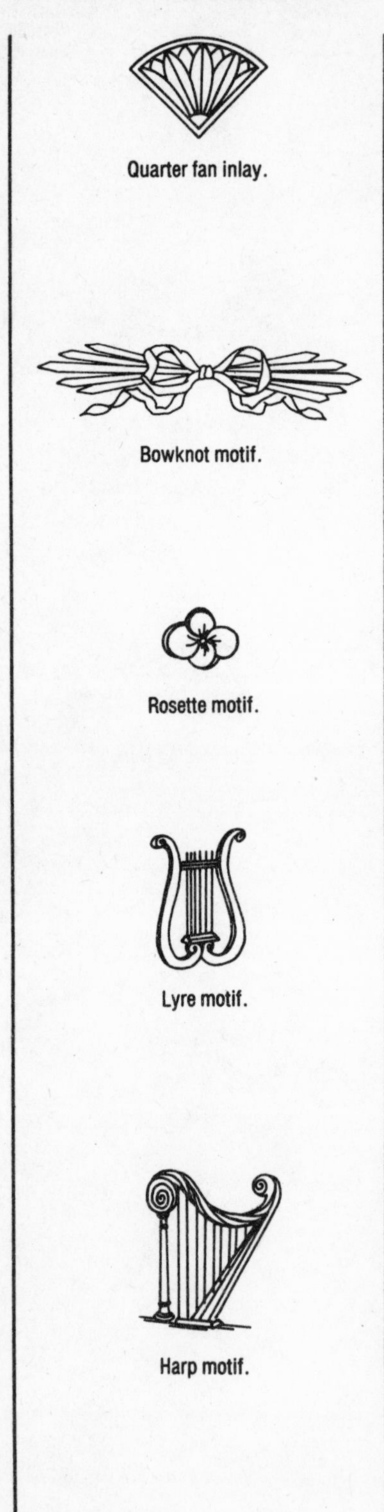

Quarter fan inlay.

Bowknot motif.

Rosette motif.

Lyre motif.

Harp motif.

riod tend to be square, with elongated urns as splats and carved Prince of Wales feathers.

New York City became extremely important after the Revolution as an arbiter of American taste. Several cabinetmakers who had emigrated from Europe settled in New York and had a considerable impact. Most prominent of all was Duncan Phyfe (1768–1854), one of the most famous names in American cabinetmaking. Born in Scotland, Phyfe came to New York City in about 1794 and established a cabinet shop. His firm continued under the name Duncan Phyfe & Sons until 1847, when Phyfe retired, having accumulated a sizable fortune.

Phyfe's work at the turn of the 19th century reflected the designs of Sheraton, although slightly after 1800, he came under the influence of French Directoire design (named after the Directory, the group of five leaders who ruled France in 1795–1799). He preferred the rich mahogany from Cuba and Santo Domingo and combined these with carefully cut veneered panels for dramatic effects. After 1830, though, Phyfe tended to favor the more fashionable rosewood.

Phyfe was one of the first American cabinetmakers to successfully incorporate the factory method into the cabinet workshop. He employed master craftsmen, journeymen, and apprentices, as well as carvers, turners, and upholsterers; each craftsman performed the operation for which he was best trained. Because of this division of labor, it is more correct to refer to the "school" or "workshop" of Duncan Phyfe, rather than to attribute the furniture directly to him.

Phyfe's early work comprised virtually every category of furniture, combining delicate Greco-Roman motifs in an entirely original manner. In the Federal furniture produced in his workshop, favorite decorative motifs include the lyre, acanthus leaf, plume, cornucopia, drapery, laurel, sheaf of wheat,

Early Phyfe chair.

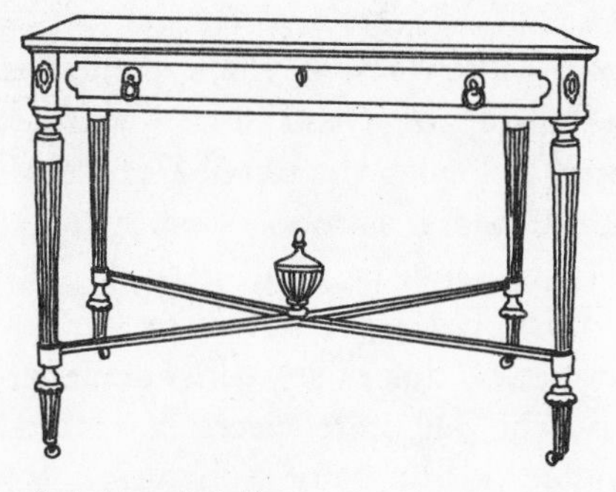
Early Lannuier table.

thunderbolt, bow knot, trumpet, harp, and rosette. Reeding was a universal ingredient of this furniture, and brass and ormolu pulls and feet were frequently used.

Other cabinetmakers working in New York at the time were also producing very high-quality furniture. In the 1790s, Charles-Honoré Lannuier (1779–1819) arrived in New York from France with his two brothers and established his own shop and employed another Frenchman, John Gruez, as a foreman. Lannuier's early work is in the Directoire style, but, like Phyfe, he eventually embraced Archeological Classicism.

Just as Lannuier's furniture can be misattributed to Phyfe, so can that of Michael Allison (active in New York 1800–1845). Along with these three cabinetmakers, several others were working in New York at this time as well: John Budd (active 1817–1840); Mills & Demming; Slover & Taylor (active 1802–1804); William Wilmerding (active 1785–1794); and looking-glass makers Charles, Joseph, and John Del Vecchio (active 1801–1844).

Furniture created during the early 19th century in northern New Jersey demonstrated that, in some areas, several styles were being produced simultaneously. The shop of Matthew Egerton, Sr., in New Brunswick, for example, was producing furniture in the fashionable Federal style while it was still making the much earlier Baroque *kast* for more conservative patrons.

In Philadelphia, the rectangular-back chair was popular, characterized by urn-and-drapery decoration or by urns in the back intersected with vertical balusters. Elegant painted chairs, as well as sideboards with rounded ends, were specialties of Philadelphia cabinetmakers. The chief Philadelphia cabinetmakers during this period were Ephraim Haines (1755–1837) and Henry Connelly (1770–1826). Both employed an oak-leaf type of carving and created delicate furni-

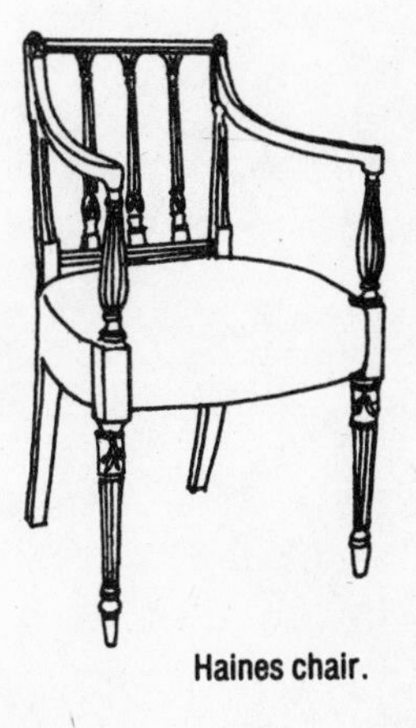
Haines chair.

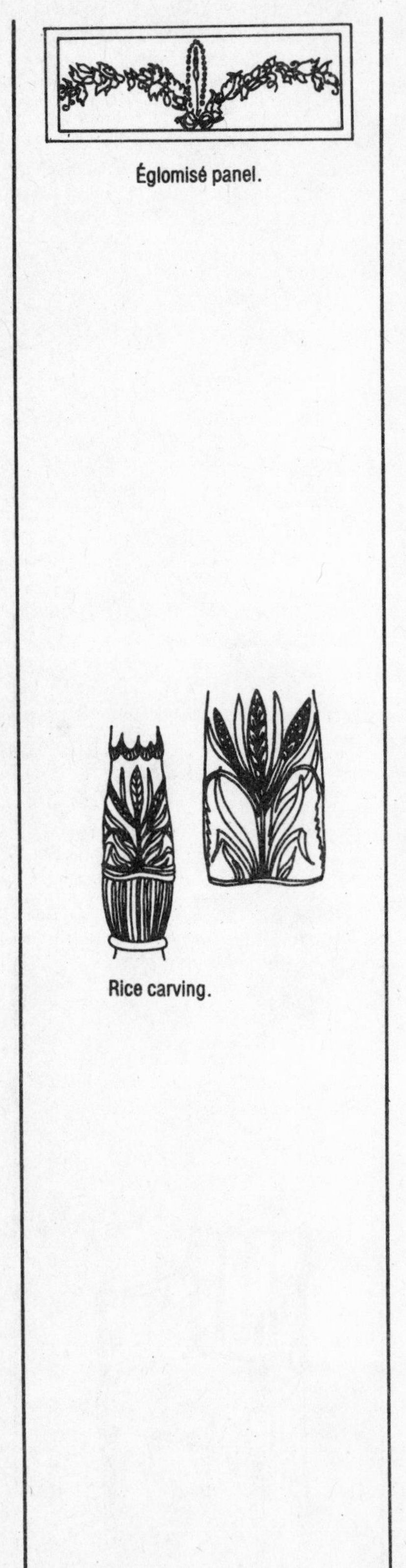

Églomisé panel.

Rice carving.

ture with balloon-shaped feet and square and vertical turned balusters in chair backs. John Aitken (active 1755) was another craftsman associated with Philadelphia Neoclassical furniture.

In the years immediately following the Revolution, Baltimore became an important port, and a school of cabinetmaking flourished there during the Federal period. The sophistication and grace of the Baltimore school of cabinetmaking can hardly be matched by that of any other area, particularly as exemplified by the elaborate pieces of painted furniture created here. In addition to painted furniture, the Baltimore school is known for its use of *églomisé*, glass panels with allegorical figures. Large ovals inlaid in mitered panels are also characteristic, as is the inlay or carving of the bellflower, in which each petal is carefully delineated from the others.

Since Baltimore was a thriving metropolis, a number of outstanding cabinetmakers settled there, but scholars have only recently discovered their names. Like Baltimore, Annapolis also became an important Maryland cabinetmaking center; the most prominent craftsman from this city was John Shaw (1745–1829).

In Federal furniture from Charleston, South Carolina, a distinct type of "rice carving" is seen, resembling the ripe grain of the rice plant that is grown in that region. Other Southern characteristics are more difficult to detect because furniture continued to be shipped to the South from England and from other parts of the United States, which explains the strong stylistic affinity between Charleston's and New York's classical furniture.

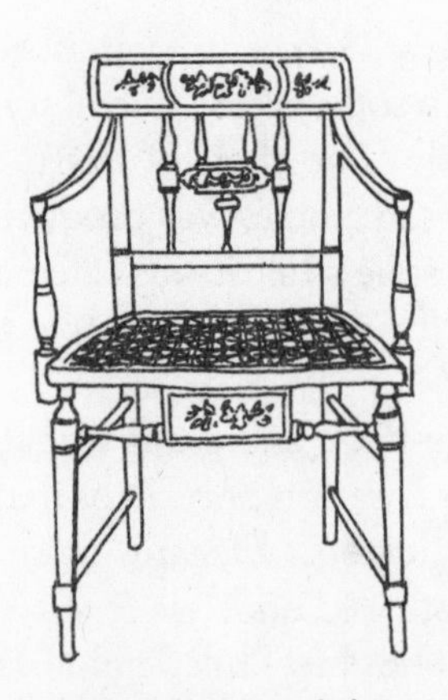

Painted Baltimore chair.

The Empire Style (1820–1840)

IN the United States, as in Europe, the second phase of Classicism is called the *Empire style* or *Archeological Classicism*, a period which reflected a fascination with recent discoveries of actual Greek and Roman furniture and stimulated a taste for living and dressing as the ancients had. Modern versions of classical furniture thus became fashionable.

While other American cities continued to produce furniture in the Federal style, New York cabinetmakers began to create pieces in the Empire style. Duncan Phyfe was the most important individual to introduce the Empire style in this city. He must have been familiar with the Regency designs of Sheraton's *Cabinet Dictionary*, for he was using saber legs on *klismos* chairs as early as 1807. Other forms popularized by Phyfe included the *curule*, or Roman base, on chairs and settees; chairs with a lyre or eagle splat; the Grecian couch or *recamier* with scrolled ends; and cabinet pieces with Egyptian-style animal legs and feet. The last of Phyfe's pieces—his "Voltaire" chairs, for example—revealed the first signs that curved lines were reappearing.

Klismos by Phyfe.

Voltaire by Phyfe.

Curule by Phyfe.

American Sheraton fancy chair.

Since Charles-Honoré Lannuier had trained as a cabinetmaker in Paris before immigrating to New York, his work showed the influence of both the Directoire and Empire styles. Lannuier's furniture was often more ornate than Phyfe's. Until his early death in 1819, Lannuier produced pieces in the most severe and correct French Empire manner, and his work was marked by a generous use of imported ormolu mounts.

After 1820, stenciled decoration became increasingly popular, a fashion that was allied with the production of "fancy" chairs. These chairs followed Sheraton-style designs. They were of light construction, generally with rushed or caned seats and painted decoration. On some, the cresting piece was painted with romantic views; on others, the full back was shaped into an eagle, shield, or other patriotic emblem.

Fancy armchair from New York.

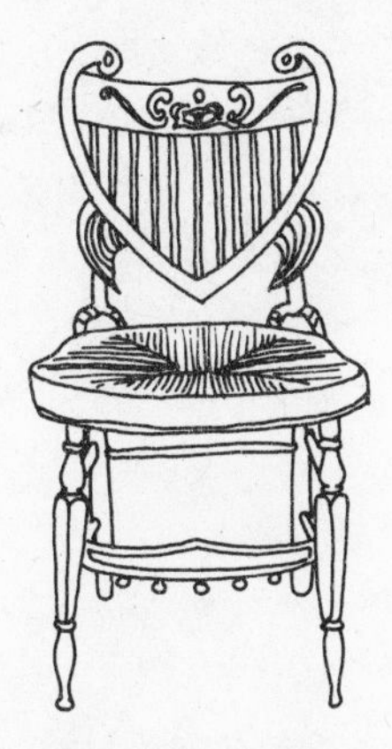

Eagle-back chair.

Probably the best-known type of "fancy" chair produced in America at the time was made in the 1830s by Lambert Hitchcock at his factory at Hitchcockville (now Riverton), Connecticut. Popular across America, Hitchcock chairs were mass-produced in several variations with similar characteristics. Frames were generally made of birch or maple, with a broad curved cresting piece, a wide curved slat, and a crosspiece below. The stiles were continuations of the legs; the front legs and lower stretchers were turned. Seats of rush, and later plank, were wider at the front than the back. Sold for $1.50 retail, the chairs were marked on the back of the seat with a stencil with this approximate wording: "L. HITCHCOCK, HITCHCOCKVILLE, CONNECTICUT, WARRANTED."

Hitchcock chair.

Late Classicism and the Restauration Style (1835–1850)

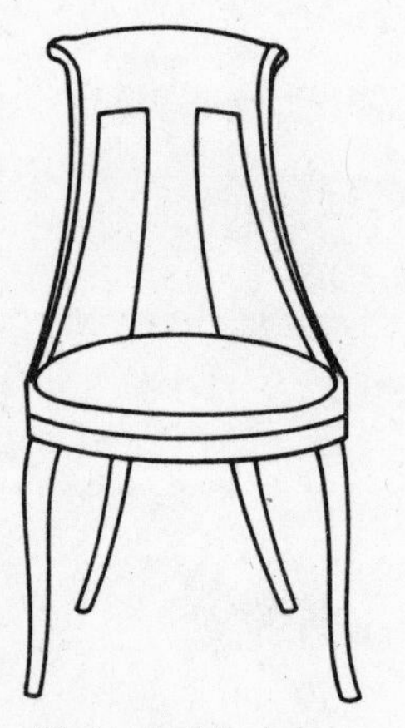
Meeks gondola chair.

DURING the 1830s, an even greater massiveness came to dominate furniture design, and plain, undecorated surfaces and scroll supports appeared—features distinctly influenced by the style of the French Restauration period. Again New York took the lead. One of the most important cabinetmaking firms to disseminate this last phase of Classicism in America was Joseph Meeks & Sons (active 1797–1868) of New York. A lithograph printed in 1833 for the firm by Endicott & Semett shows forty-one pieces of furniture and two sets of draperies; this is the first known American print to illustrate complete furniture designs. Popular furniture in this style tended to contain projecting columns in the French manner and an extraordinary use of S- and C-scrolls. Indeed, it might be said that the scroll represents the key to the style of the

Pillar-and-scroll table.

Late Classical French type or sleigh bed.

1830s. By then, the massive architectural lines of this furniture were virtually all that remained of the classical influence.

The style, sometimes called *pillar and scroll*, was widely popularized through a Baltimore publication of 1840, John Hall's *The Cabinet Maker's Assistant*, which contained 198 plates showing furniture forms whose design was completely dominated by single and double scrolls. Hall believed that the elliptical curve was the most beautiful single ingredient of design, and he combined S- and C-scrolls in every conceivable way. Because his designs were intended for inexpensive furniture, the individual parts could be cut simply with a bandsaw, and the base wood was generally pine or tulip poplar whose surface was veneered with mahogany.

Meeks table.

Shaker Furniture

Classic Shaker chair.

THE furniture created by the Shakers, a religious sect, made a significant contribution to American design. The founders of this group came to America from England in 1774 and by the early 19th century had established settlements in various parts of New England, New York, Kentucky, and Ohio. Within these communities, the Shakers created a distinct type of furniture—functional, devoid of all ornamentation, and revealing graceful and delicately constructed lines and proportions. Although Shaker design is often considered unique, analysis reveals the influence of Neoclassical lines, proportions, and overall delicacy. Shaker furniture continued to be made into the 20th century, and later pieces were affected by other 19th-century revival styles.

Shaker dining table.

The Gothic and Elizabethan Revival Styles (1825–1865)

AS we have seen, revivalism first appeared in furniture of Greek and Roman influence. But almost simultaneous with their taste for the classical, designers were turning to other historical sources for inspiration as well. Whether borrowed from the designs of the Middle Ages, the Bourbon courts, or the Ottoman Empire, styles of the past were being widely reinterpreted by 19th-century designers.

By the end of the first quarter of the 19th century, America was feeling the powerful effects of the Industrial Revolution. While some furniture manufacturers, such as Phyfe and Allison, had already begun to use machinery and the assembly-line technique, by 1825 it was possible to make nearly the entire frame for a piece of furniture by machine. As a result, the time-honored pride in craftsmanship began to decline in favor of mass production. The increasing demand for comfort influenced the design of furniture and stimulated

Davis chair.

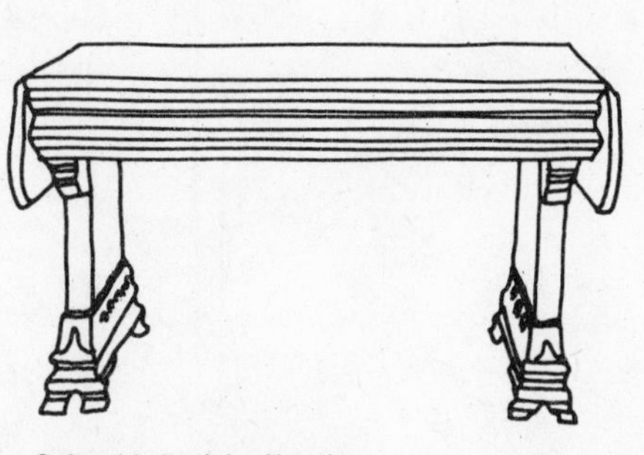

Sofa table by John Needles.

more elaborate tufted upholstery. Although many designers and furniture manufacturers of the 19th century were convinced they were actually making replicas of antique furniture by carefully following the lines of earlier models, a close look will generally distinguish the 19th-century piece from the earlier prototype.

The Gothic Revival style was rooted in England, where medieval elements had never altogether disappeared from the architectural vocabulary. In the 17th century, William Kent applied Gothic as well as classical motifs to Baroque furniture forms, and a number of designs in Thomas Chippendale's *Director* showed Gothic influence. The style again appeared in Smith's *Household Furniture* (1808), along with numerous pieces designed in the classical taste. The pieces in Smith's publication applied Gothic architectural ornamentation to contemporary furniture forms; they did not actually imitate Gothic furniture, about which very little was then known.

In America, the Gothic style never achieved the same degree of popularity that it had in England. The Gothic style was associated with the church, and it was principally used in great

Gothic Revival bedstead incorporating lancet arches and crockets.

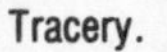
Tracery.

Trefoil rosette.

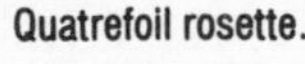
Quatrefoil rosette.

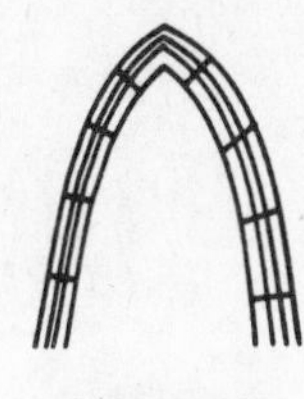

Lancet arch.

houses designed by important architects. One of the chief exponents of American Gothic style, for example, was the prominent architect Alexander Jackson Davis (1803–1892). Of the American furniture surviving in the style, much was designed by architects for specific buildings, and these pieces tend to reiterate the similar architectural details: pointed and lancet arches, trefoil and quatrefoil rosettes, heraldic devices, crockets, finials, and tracery. The earliest of the Gothic-influenced furniture delicately incorporated this architectural vocabulary into classical forms. The first American design book to illustrate Gothic furniture in America was the *Cabinet Maker's Assistant* (1842) by Robert Conner, an English-born cabinetmaker and designer. Craftsmen working in this style included Richard Byrne (1805–1883), Ambrose Wright (c. 1794–post 1866), Alexander and Frederick Roux (in partnership 1837–1881), John Needles (1786–1878), and John Jelliff (active 1835–1890).

Heraldic devices.

Finial.

Crockets.

Twist-turned chair.

Elizabethan chair.

Cottage chair.

The Elizabethan Revival style was closely related to the Gothic, for both relied largely on openwork surfaces and the play of light through their openings. In fact, the term *Elizabethan* is a misnomer for this style—although it was so-called in the 19th century—because it was actually inspired by the design vocabulary of the eras of Charles I (1626–1649) and Charles II (1660–1685), rather than that of Elizabeth I (1558–1603). Chief ingredients of the Elizabethan style included Baroque turnings with the characteristic spiral and ball—details derived from the designs of French architectural designer Daniel Marot (1660?–1712). Hall chairs and *prie dieux* were often conceived in this style.

In the United States, the Elizabethan style was applied chiefly to simple mass-produced cottage furniture, highly advocated for country residences by tastemakers because it was practical, attractive, and inexpensive. In these pieces, the spiral twist was reduced to a simple ball- or spool-turned straight member. Generally made of cheap softwood, mass-produced Elizabethan-style furniture was painted and decorated in various colors and could be fitted with marble tops if desired. Its floral and scroll decoration announced the coming of another popular revival style: the Rococo.

Cottage chest of drawers.

The Rococo Revival Style (1845–1900)

THE Rococo Revival or "French Antique" style was popular in Paris and London as early as 1840; numerous design books illustrating it appeared in both cities and were circulated in America. From the 1840s through the end of the century, Rococo was the most popular furniture style in the United States. (Indeed, Rococo furniture has never ceased being made, and some factories still produce versions of it today.) Its inspiration was the style of the court of Louis XV, and its chief features included the cabriole leg, shell and other fanciful carvings, curved surfaces, and a profuse use of delicate S- and C-scrolls. Since the curved line had never totally disappeared from the design repertory, Rococo was, in a sense, not so much a revival as an exaggeration of previous styles. Nevertheless, it is not difficult to distinguish this 19th-century revival style from its 18th-century antecedent: lines tend to become heavier, the cabriole leg is less delicate (sometimes terminating in an S-scroll toe); and the rear leg is chamfered at its base to give a sense of solidity. Heaviness is also evident in the elaborate scrolls that display the naturalistic carving of birds, fruit, flowers, and so on.

The cost of Rococo Revival furniture depended on the amount of carving on the piece; the least expensive was the simple "finger-rolled" carving. Walnut was a popular wood for inexpensive pieces of Rococo furniture, while rosewood was reserved for the more costly. The Industrial Revolution made it possible to produce furniture of this type, including even the carving, completely by machine, and the most popular forms were the parlor sets, which included a sofa and arm and side chairs.

John Henry Belter

The most famous cabinetmaker associated with the American Rococo Revival style was John Henry Belter (1804–1863).

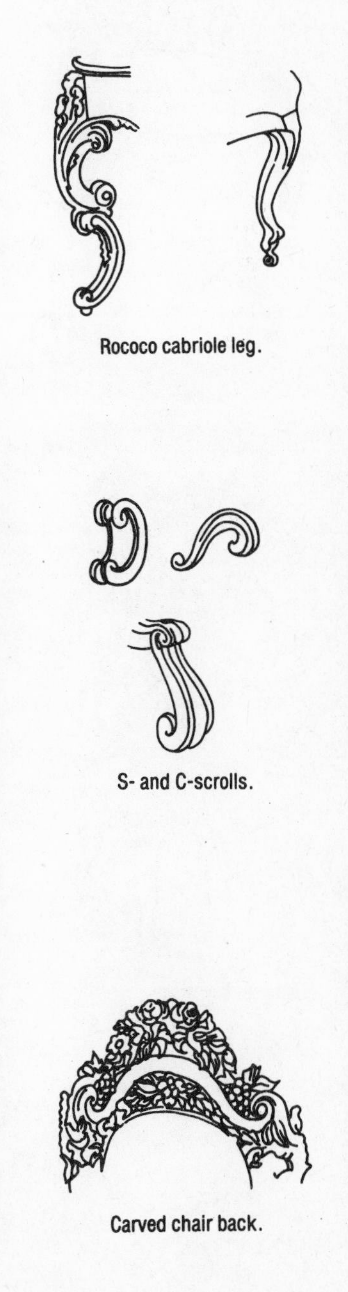

Rococo cabriole leg.

S- and C-scrolls.

Carved chair back.

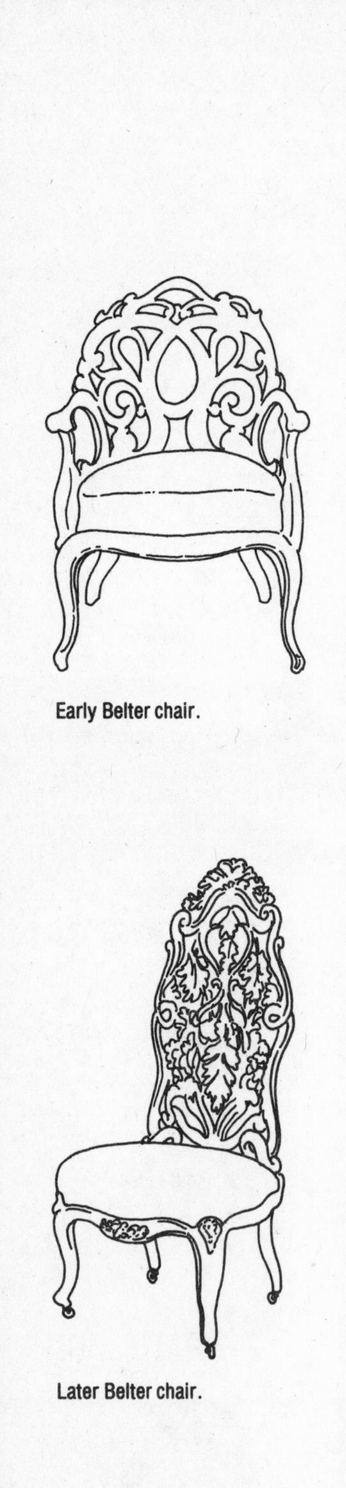

Early Belter chair.

Later Belter chair.

Belter table.

Trained in Württemberg, Germany, Belter immigrated to New York, where he replaced Duncan Phyfe as that city's most fashionable cabinetmaker.

Belter used laminated wood panels to produce this furniture. First he glued together 1/16″ layers of rosewood, oak, or ebonized hardwood so that the grain of each layer ran perpendicular to the grains of the layer next to it. There were typically six to eight layers, although there could be as few as three or as many as sixteen. Belter's lamination process was unusual in that he steamed the laminated panels under great pressure in molds, or "cawls," to achieve great undulating curves, which he would then carve. Another feature distinguishing Belter's work was his production of extra ornamentation by applying pieces of solid wood to the frame.

During the course of Belter's career, the style of his work changed considerably. In the late 1840s and early 1850s, his fur-

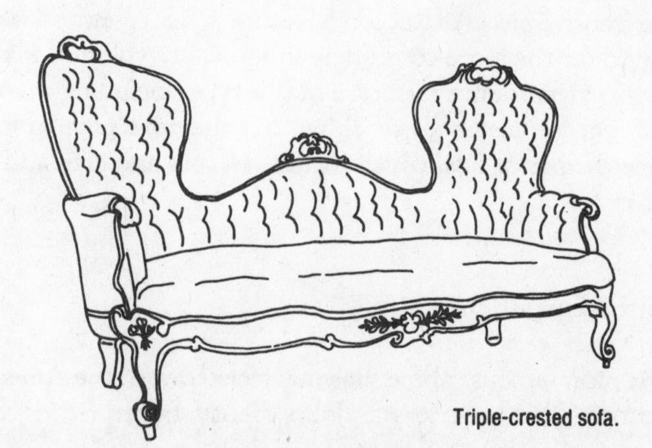

Triple-crested sofa.

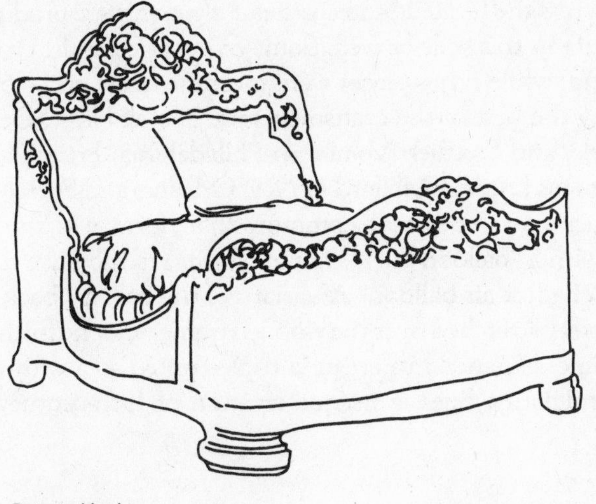

Patented bed.

niture was rather loose in form, although it was conceived in the Rococo Revival style. He achieved a tighter form after the mid-1850s, when the popularity of the Louis XIV, Louis XVI, and Renaissance Revival styles were reflected in his work. Some early Belter pieces had backs constructed entirely of scrolls, which enclosed an area dominated by naturalistic carving. Some of Belter's greatest work is seen in the high backs of his slipper and hall chairs. In his earlier work, scrolls were combined with naturalistic details—such as flower, fruit, and vine motifs; later, the scrolls disappeared, and the backs were formed completely of naturalistic detail. With the growing popularity of the Renaissance and Louis XVI styles, Belter's furniture assumed a more balanced form. At this time Belter applied for several patents for his laminating and steaming process, as well as for a specially designed bed.

For many years, all elaborate laminated rosewood furniture was identified as "Belter." However, an important manuscript notebook by another New York cabinetmaker, Ernest Hagen, came to light in the 1950s, indicating that Charles H. Baudouine (active 1845–1900) had infringed on Belter's patents and created similar furniture, although he used more than one panel.

Belter wardrobe.

Other Cabinetmakers

Although he was the most famous, Belter was certainly not the only New York cabinetmaker working in the Rococo Revival style. Others included August Jansen, the Meeks brothers, Alexander Roux, Leon Marcotte, and Gustave Herter.

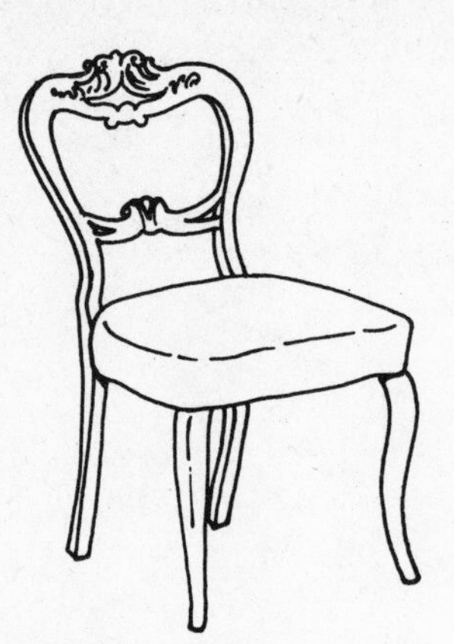

Balloon-back chair.

Across the United States, other craftsmen were producing furniture in this style as well. Some of it was carefully created by hand, while other pieces were machine-made and clumsy. Among the best of the craftsmen were Daniel Pabst, George Henkels, and Gottlieb Volmer in Philadelphia; François Signouret and Prudent Mallard in New Orleans; and S. S. Johns in Cincinnati. The most common chair form was the side chair with a "balloon back," named for its resemblance to the shape of a hot-air balloon. A variant of the balloon back had upholstery stretched over the wooden frame, and the form was sometimes expanded to create a triple-crested sofa with deep and undulating lines, a unique creation of 19th-century design.

The Louis XIV Revival Style

A style related to the Rococo was the Louis XIV Revival style, but it was not as popular, possibly because it was generally massive and busy. Reintroducing symmetrical form, Louis XIV Revival furniture was generally reserved for case pieces with such motifs as heroic figures, broken pediments, geometric detail, and naturalistic garlands. Louis XIV sideboards seemed to drip flowers, fruit, and trophies of game.

The Louis XVI Revival Style (1860–1890)

THE beginnings of the Louis XVI Revival style date to the 1850s, when Empress Eugénie of France began to restore the private apartments of the palaces of the Tuileries and St. Cloud. The style reintroduced a formal classicism with oval backs, straight stiles, arm supports, and legs. Delicate classical motifs were inlaid and porcelain plaques and ormolu medallions became a part of the vocabulary. Ebonized frames became popular, and Aubusson or other French fabrics were used for upholstery.

By the 1860s, the style was popular in the eastern United States. Jelliff in Newark, New Jersey, and Henkels in Philadelphia began to produce pieces in the Louis XVI Revival style. New York, however, became the chief center for the style, and cabinetmakers such as Christian and Gustave Herter, Alexander Roux, Leon Marcotte, Szypher firm, and Thomas Brooks excelled in its production. The style was popular into the 1880s and 1890s.

Chair with finger-rolled carving.

Library table by Marcotte.

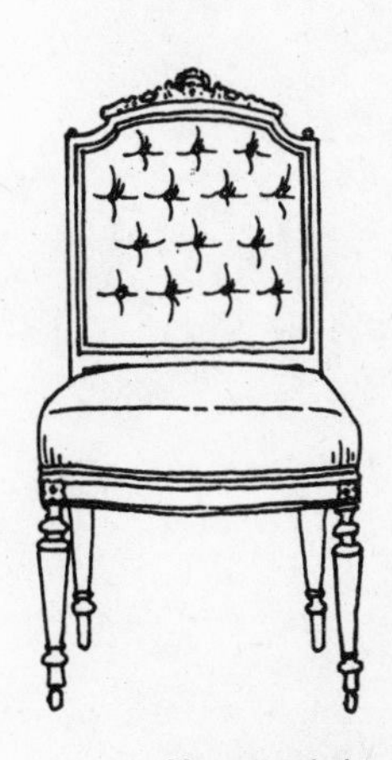

Marcotte chair.

The Renaissance Revival Style (1860–1885)

THE last half of the 19th century saw an even further expansion of revivalism to incorporate other historical periods as well. By then, virtually every period had been tapped for inspiration, and occasionally designs from different sources were even incorporated into a single piece. Novelty was the watchword as designers vied to produce even more elaborate and showy pieces.

Pabst sideboard.

Emerging in popularity at around the time of the Civil War (1861–1865), the Renaissance Revival style had been referred to by writers earlier than 1850; it was mentioned by architect Alexander Jackson Downing in that year as well. Inspired by Renaissance architecture, this style was characterized by massive, square, architectural forms, broken pediments, applied medallions, acorn trim, and tapering baluster-turned legs.

Belter used the Renaissance Revival style in his later pieces, and George Hunzinger of New York also produced some sensitive furniture in this style. German by birth, Hunzinger was working in New York by the 1860s (he had patented a chair in 1866), and his work shows a remarkable mastery of the Renaissance design vocabulary. Other important makers were John Jelliff in Newark, Daniel Pabst in Philadelphia, and Thomas Brooks in Brooklyn. Mass-produced in Grand Rapids, Michigan, furniture in the Renaissance Revival style found popular favor and was made in quantity and shipped to every part of America by such companies as Berkey & Gay.

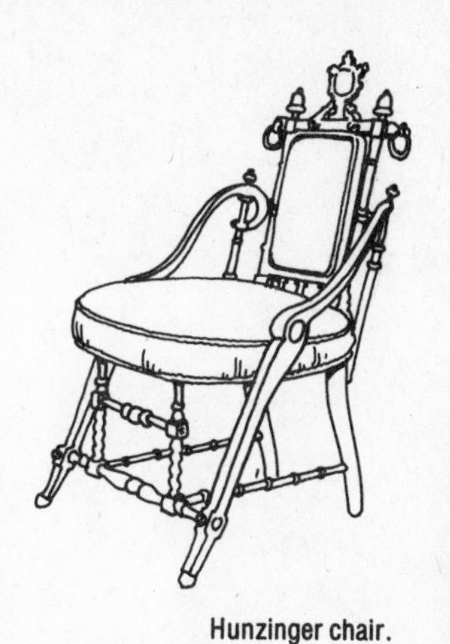

Hunzinger chair.

Berkey & Gay bedstead.

The Victorian Renaissance or Neo-Grec Style (1860–1880)

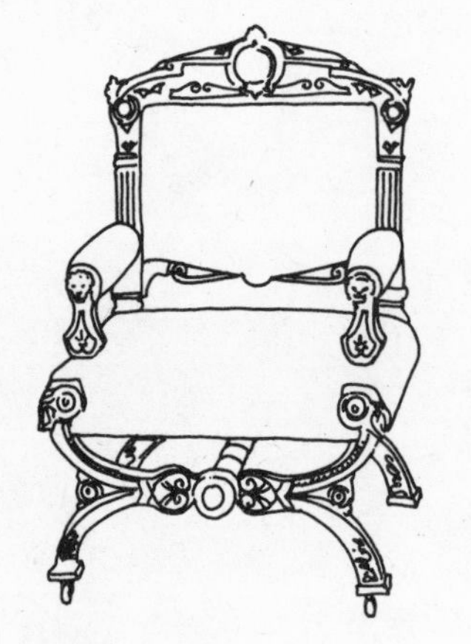

Neo-Grec chair.

LOUIS XVI design, reintroduced during the 1860s, eventually merged with the Renaissance Revival style to create still another revival style which was introduced by the Paris- and New York-based firm of Ringuet, Le Prince, & Marcotte. Their pieces followed late 18th-century stylistic precedents and led to a fashion that the French called the *Neo-Grec* style. This style is often called *Victorian Renaissance* to distinguish it from the more ponderous true Renaissance style. In this style, classical ornaments were introduced in ormolu and other metalwork, porcelain terra cotta, and mother-of-pearl plaques.

Chest of drawers with looking-glass in the Neo-Grec style by Marcotte.

The Colonial Revival Style (1875–1910)

IT became fashionable to collect antiques during the 1870s. Not only the wealthy but also the middle class adopted this pursuit when they were advised that old Japanese screens and Spanish chairs could do much to improve their interiors. Simultaneously, a revival of interest in the furniture of America's colonial past developed. At the Philadelphia Centennial Exhibition of 1876, for example, interest focused on the past, and one particularly popular display featured a colonial kitchen and a set of furniture made from one of the oldest trees in Philadelphia. This exhibition stimulated a zeal for collecting old pieces of American furniture and also sparked the creation of antique reproduction pieces.

In hindsight, it is easy to see that 17th- and 18th-century furniture, as well as Federal and Empire pieces, were all indiscriminately regarded as "colonial." Many reproductions of such furniture were made in the latter years of the 19th century. Some of this reproduction furniture was so well made, in fact, that today it is often difficult to distinguish these pieces from the originals.

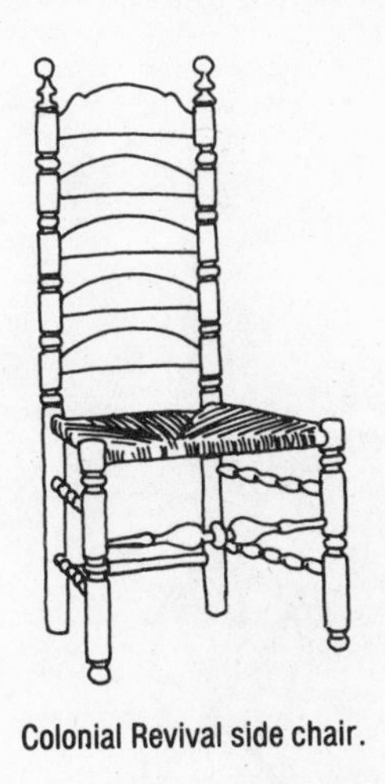

Colonial Revival side chair.

Rocker.

Innovative Furniture (1800–1900)

THE advent of the machine and the fervent experimentation with new materials during the 19th century led to the development of some highly innovative furniture. In some instances, technical advances were used in the construction of furniture; in other cases, a mechanical contrivance was actually incorporated into the furniture form.

Laminated Furniture

Thonet chair.

Lamination was one of the most important innovations in 19th-century furniture construction, a technique characteristic of Belter and his imitators, as we have seen. A European designer whose technique was related was Michael Thonet (1796–1871), who began to experiment with lamination and shaping by steam in Germany and Austria between 1836 and 1840. By 1850, Thonet had perfected a method of bending birch wood into highly fanciful shapes. Known as *bentwood*, Thonet's furniture displays sinuous curves reminiscent of the Rococo Revival style. Because bentwood furniture could be broken down into a number of component parts, it could be shipped unassembled and screwed together later. During the 19th century, large quantities were imported into the United States, and American furniture factories created imitations, which generally lack the quality of the original. Thonet furniture is still made today.

Papier-Mâché

The invention of efficient pressing and molding machines made it possible to produce furniture from *papier-mâché*, a durable substance created by binding together ground paper pulp or strips of paper and glue under pressure. Parts were assembled, and the piece was treated with numerous coats of heavy lacquer (often black) before being decorated with gild and inlaid mother-of-pearl. Many large and elaborate *papier-mâché* pieces were shown at the London Crystal Palace Exhibition in 1851. *Papier-mâché* furniture was imported to America in large quantities during the second half of the century. The major producer of *papier-mâché* furniture in England was the firm of Jennens & Bettridge; this furniture was also made in France. In the United States, it was made in limited quantities at Litchfield, Connecticut.

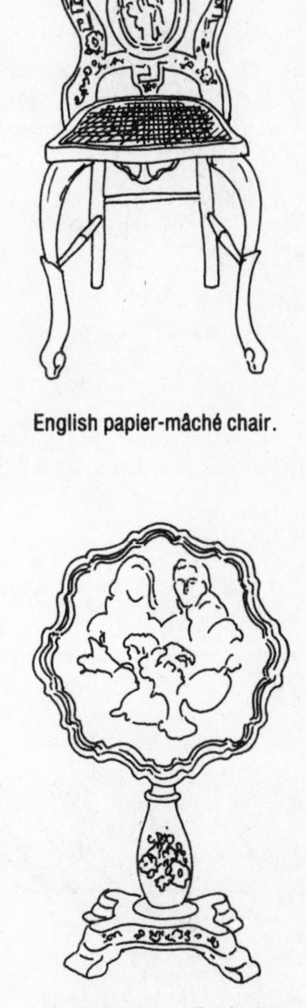

English papier-mâché chair.

English papier-mâché table.

Metal in Furniture

Metal was another material from which innovative furniture was constructed during the 19th century. Iron and steel had been used in a limited manner during the 18th century for furniture construction and bracing, but by the mid-19th century, the iron industry was greatly expanded and iron objects were being mass-produced in molds. During the 1840s, French factories produced chairs with hollow tubular frames that were often reinforced with a glue or plaster core to lend durability. One of the most popular of all tubular chairs was a rocker made during the late 1840s and 1850s, in which two bent pieces of metal tubing formed the entire substructure of the piece. An American version of this chair, said to have been made by manufacturer Peter Cooper (1791–1883), used flattened metal members rather than tubes.

The most highly popular metal furniture, however, was constructed of cast iron. Designed for both interior and exterior use and often highly ornamental, with details drawn from the popular revival styles, a single piece of cast iron furniture

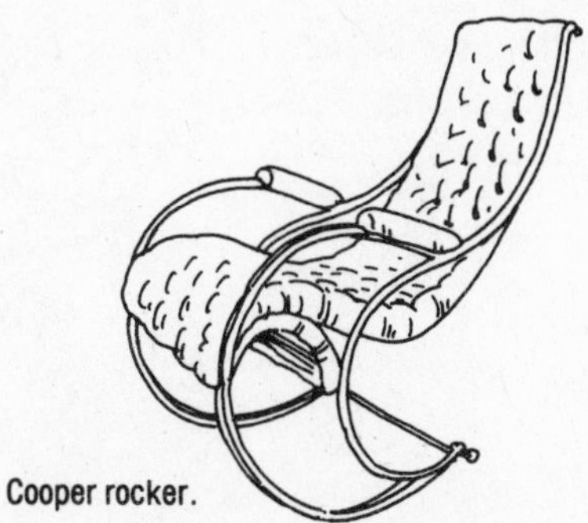

Cooper rocker.

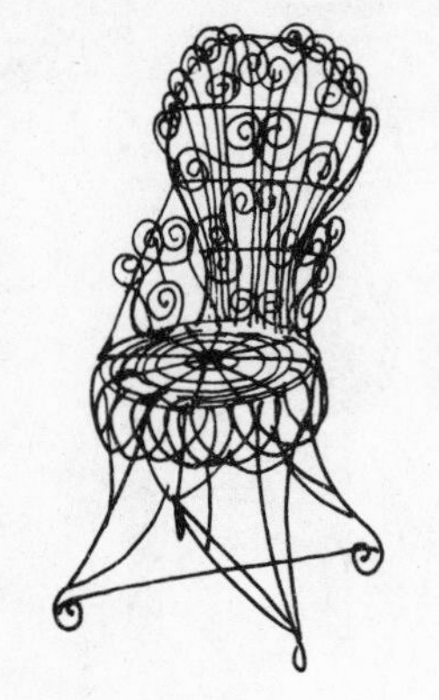

Wire chair.

was made by screwing together parts that had been cast in individual molds. The form that survives in large quantities today is the garden bench, sometimes combining a wooden seat and back with an iron frame. Many firms that produced iron furniture also made furniture of wire, using new wire-making machines that mass-produced the material. It is possible to twist this adaptable material into elaborate and fanciful shapes reminiscent of the Rococo Revival style.

Mechanical Devices

Other innovative furniture actually incorporated some clever mechanical device within the form itself. Movable and collapsible furniture has fascinated people since ancient times, and beginning in the 1850s, an enthusiastic interest in furniture that reclined, converted, and folded stimulated patents for varieties of such pieces.

The introduction of the metal coil spring represented one of the greatest mechanical innovations in furniture design. Although no precise date is known for its invention, the coil spring was in use by mid-century, when the upholsterer's trade was flourishing. Tufting, buttons, and fringes became important adjuncts to upholstery, which influenced forms such as the circular ottoman and easy chair. The use of springs generated a type of furniture that concealed the structure of the piece with upholstery. Incorporating what is known as *Turkish-frame construction*, the entire form was made from wire spring bundles and then completely upholstered. The overall chair shape was created with an iron frame that was screwed onto a wooden frame at the base, supported by wooden legs.

Turkish frame chair.

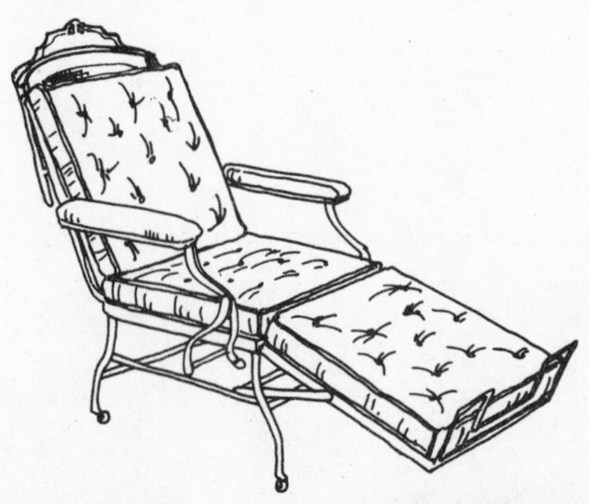

Convertible chair.

Rustic table.

Natural Materials

In total contrast to this "mechanical" furniture, other furniture was being made by hand from natural materials. These pieces were generally intended for country houses and outdoor settings, where picturesque effects were desired. For example, rustic furniture made from tree branches and roots to form a natural chair or table became popular during the second half of the 19th century.

Cane (wicker or rattan) furniture was also made in great quantities at this time. Originating from the durable stem and tendril of a climbing palm growing in the East Indies, the cane was woven around furniture frames made from white oak or hickory. A closely related type of furniture was made from bamboo fashioned in an Oriental shape, with cane panels used as well.

One exotic type of furniture was made from animal horns. The vogue for antlers and horns had existed for a long time, and furniture was built of these materials in Europe by the late 18th century. In the United States, where exploration of the West made steer and buffalo horns available, they were used to fashion fantastic pieces of furniture.

Horn chair.

Bamboo chair.

Exotic and Eclectic (1885–1910)

Turkish-style chair.

A fascinating revival of the late 1880s and 1890s resulted from the renewed interest in Orientalism and exoticism. In fact, during most of the century, there existed an affection for Islamic (Moorish or Saracenic) designs, but this was combined, by the end of the century, with a taste for varied influences to create highly exotic furniture best described by the term *eclectic*.

Electicism and confusion of design source typified revival furniture at the end of the 19th century. By this time, much American furniture was mechanically produced, and even so-called "custom-built" pieces were created by machine, enabling these eclectic pieces to be circulated widely. At the same time, great architectural firms dominated New York fashion with their preference for European design. Furniture shown at the Chicago Columbian Exhibition in 1893 revealed the state of American furniture: in the catalogue, endless revival styles were represented, from a hopelessly debased version of the classical revival to the most eclectic trends. In some instances, in fact, the styles were so completely mixed within a single piece that it is virtually impossible to distinguish the original design inspiration.

Turkish-style easy chair.

Design Reform (1850–1930)

BY the mid-19th century, the poor design, bad taste, misuse of historical ornamentation, and dominance of the machine came under heavy attack by certain critics. When the displays at the London Crystal Palace exhibition in 1851 included pieces with motifs borrowed indiscriminately from various historical styles inappropriately mixed together, Henry Cole (1808–1882), one of the organizers of the exhibition, and designer Owen Jones (1809–1874) both published works reacting to the overblown taste of the time.

Design Reformers

Early reformers decried the overuse of ornamentation and urged the honest use of materials and a return, in some measure, to handcrafting in furniture making. A leader in this reform was the English art critic John Ruskin (1819–1900), whose books won a wide audience both at home and in America. Ruskin was interested in the forms and organizations found in nature and their application to design and architecture.

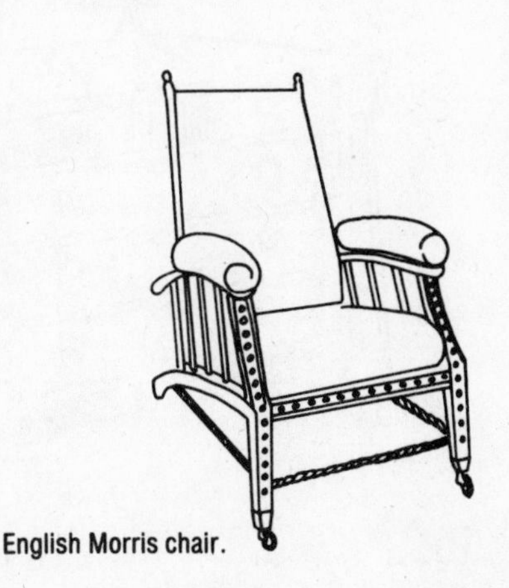

English Morris chair.

In England, a strong protest against the machine came from William Morris (1834–1898) and the group of artists with whom he was associated. Trained as an architect, Morris turned to furniture design in 1861, when he founded a company that would offer only furniture of good taste. Morris and his colleagues turned to the English Gothic style of the 13th century for inspiration. Rather than imitate the grammar of Gothic ornamentation in literal terms, however, they looked to the basic structure, line, and proportions of medieval design. All furniture made by the Morris firm was built and decorated by hand, so it was too costly for popular consumption—a fact that tended to defeat his basic intention of improving popular taste.

Eastlake Influence

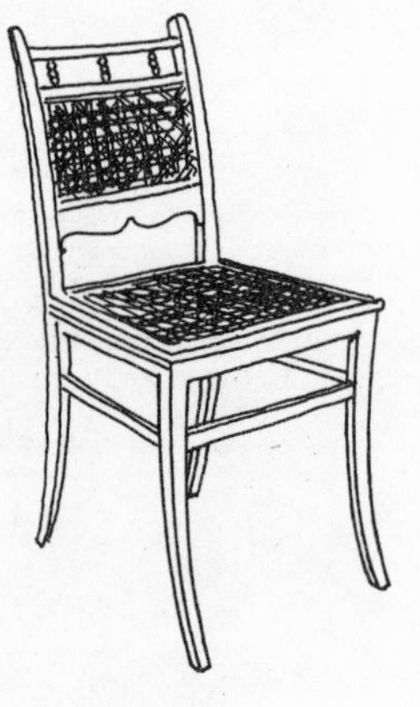

Caned chair in Eastlake tradition.

Charles Locke Eastlake (1836–1906) was another popular English exponent of good taste in the Morris manner. His work *Hints on Household Taste* (1868), first published in the United States in 1872, was reprinted and circulated until the end of the century. Eastlake was opposed to the then-popular revival styles and advocated furniture that was simple, straightforward, and early English in style. The illustrations in his publication displayed furniture made of oak with simple incised decoration. Although some American furniture at this time did reveal the influence of Eastlake, it did not precisely interpret the examples in his book.

Dresser by Eastlake.

Art and Japanese–Inspired Furniture (1870–1890)

Art Furniture began to appear in England and America during the 1870s; its name signified useful furniture to which artistic decoration was added. It was light in construction and often showed the influence of Japanese design. In New York, the firms of Christian Herter and Kimbel & Cabus were particularly well-known for their production of Art Furniture.

Art furniture in Anglo-Japanese taste made by Herter Brothers.

Art Nouveau

Art Nouveau, a movement that developed in Europe in about 1900, also represented a revolt against revivalism. Relying on a whiplash curve and organic ornamentation as its chief ingredients, Art Nouveau had a strong influence on glass and ceramic design in the United States but only rarely affected American furniture design.

Whiplash curve.

The Arts and Crafts Movement (1850–1900)

The philosophy of Ruskin and the work of Morris created what is called the *Arts and Crafts movement*. From the 1880s until about 1910, this movement stressed humble, hand-made products and brought about a revival of cottage crafts. Crafts guilds developed in England to encourage the creation of objects that emphasized proper material and craftsmanship.

Art Nouveau chair.

Art Nouveau cabinet.

Stickley mark.

Roycroft mark.

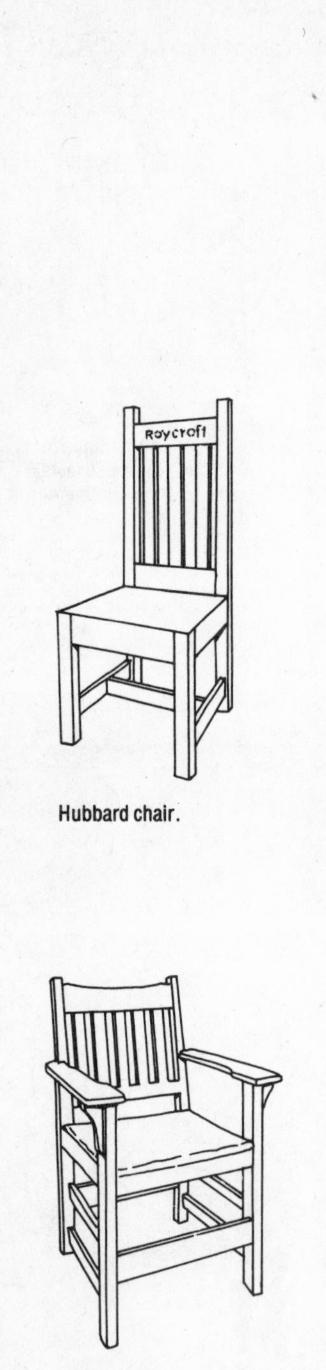

Hubbard chair.

Stickley chair.

In the United States the Arts and Crafts movement was not as thoroughly organized as in England, but craftsmen did band together at various centers at the end of the 19th century. One of the most famous of such groups was the Roycrofters, founded by Elbert G. Hubbard (1856–1915) in East Aurora, New York. The Roycrofters produced a variety of decorative objects, including furniture. Their pieces were rectilinear and simple, often made of oak, and identified with a Roycroft mark.

By 1900, Gustav Stickley (1858–1942) of Eastwood, New York, had formulated his ideas about Craftsman furniture. Stickley's furniture, also made of oak, had square lines and visible mortise-and-tenon joints. Upholstery and tabletops were made of brown leather or green canvas. Such furniture created what came to be known as the *Mission style*, a name that came from the functional "mission" for which the furniture was intended.

The Art Workers Guild of Providence, Rhode Island, was an Arts and Crafts group whose composition resembled that of Morris's association. Here, designers, cabinetmakers, and painters pooled their talents to produce furniture. Important members of this group included Charles W. Stetson, painter; Sydney Burleigh, cabinetmaker and carver; and John G. Aldrich, architect.

Henry Hobson Richardson (1838–1886) was a Boston-based architect who designed furniture of ususual vitality. His oak furniture was integrated in both scale and style with the architectural setting for which it was intended. Because it was handcrafted, Richardson's work can be linked to the Arts and Crafts movement.

Also continuing the tradition of design reform in America were a smaller number of architect-designers in Chicago and on the Pacific Coast. For example, the Midwestern architect Frank Lloyd Wright (1869–1959) greatly influenced Chicago's furniture manufacturers (most notably the Tabey Furniture Company) to produce basic, straightforward designs decorated with a small amount of natural organic ornamentation that usually anticipated the square Craftsman-style furniture. Brothers Charles and Henry Greene (active 1893–1912) of Pasadena, California, were two other important architects of the time, creating simple Craftsman furniture, influenced by Japanese design, to adorn their houses.

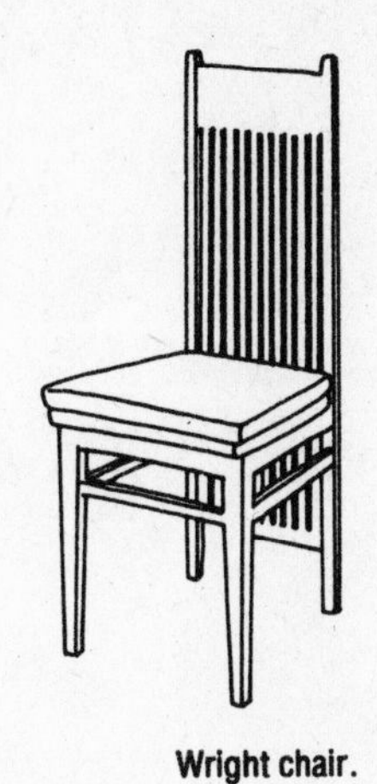

Wright chair.

The Bauhaus (1919–1933)

The European *Bauhaus* movement—named for the school of design that flourished in Germany in 1919–1933 where many of its leaders taught—also had a great influence on American furniture. Ludwig Mies van der Rohe (1886–1969), Walter Gropius (1883–1969), and Marcel Breuer (1902–1981) all designed furniture sympathetic to the streamlined architecture they advocated. The technology reflected in this furniture is still very popular today.

During each of its stylistic periods, American furniture shows originality which sets it apart from European models. The succeeding styles and revivals carefully mirror American taste in each of its periods.

American furniture has unquestionably come into its own and collectors are continually stimulated by it.

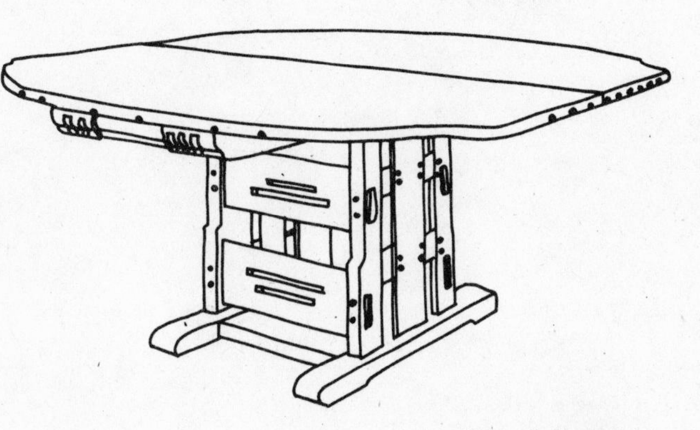

Greene & Greene table.

Chairs

1. Wainscot armchair. Connecticut. Example of joiner's mortise-and-tenon (panel) construction. 1640–1660.

2. Wainscot armchair. Ipswich, Massachusetts. Delicately carved chair of complex design. (Attributed to William Searle, 1634–1667.) 1663–1667.

3. Wainscot armchair. Essex County, Massachusetts. Many joiners carved, rather than turned, elements such as legs and arm supports. 1670–1700.

4. Turned armchair. Probably England. Belonged to Governor John Carver of Plymouth Colony. Chairs like this one are called "Carver-type." 1600–1620.

5. Turned armchair. Plymouth Colony, Massachusetts. Belonged to William Brewster. Chairs of similar design are called "Brewster type." Missing some spindles. 1620–1630.

6. Turned armchair. Probably New York. Reminiscent of medieval chairs. 1640–1670.

7. Carver-type chair. Guilford, Connecticut. Thick, baluster-shaped turnings on back uprights and thin spindles of similar shape were regional characteristics. 1680–1710.

8. Turned armchair. Suffolk, Virginia. Many thin spindles were a 17th-century Southern characteristic. 1680–1700.

9. Slat-back armchair. New York. Flaring slats were a Dutch characteristic. 1680–1720.

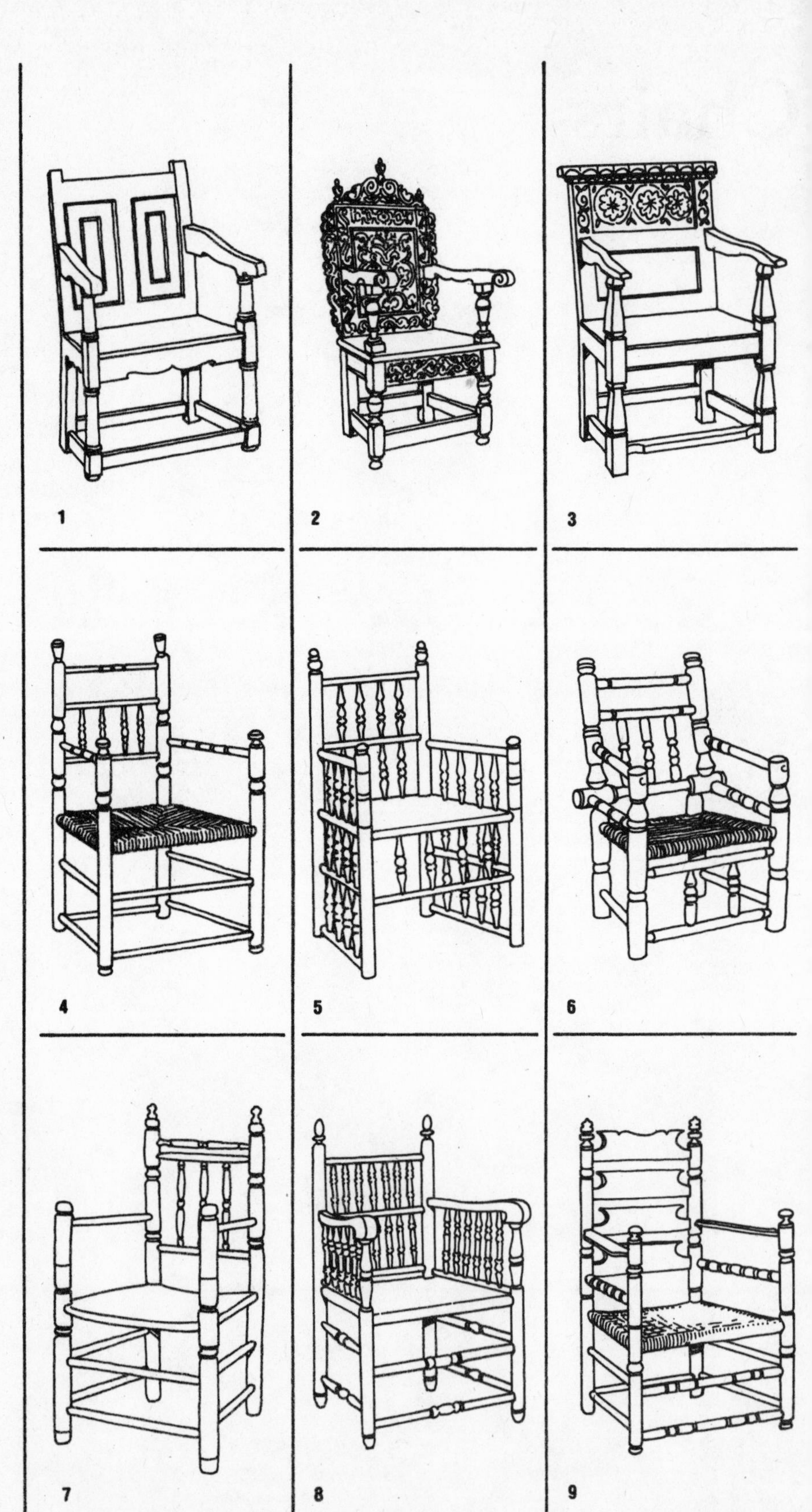

CHAIRS

1

2

3

4

5

6

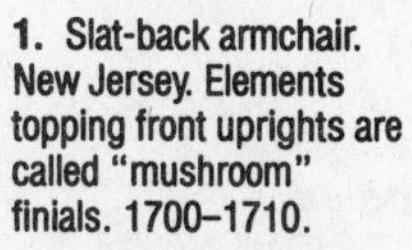

1. Slat-back armchair. New Jersey. Elements topping front uprights are called "mushroom" finials. 1700–1710.

2. Chair. New York and New Jersey. Almost identical to Netherlandish prototypes, but made of American wood. 1680–1710.

3. Twist-turned chair. Philadelphia. Twists are hand-carved, not turned on a lathe. 1680–1710.

4. Leather armchair. Boston. Note 17th-century style tack configuration and use of large, fluffy pillow. 1660–1670.

5. Leather chair. Boston. Type sometimes called "Cromwellian" or "farthingale" chair. 1675–1695.

6. Turned high chair. Probably New England. Note massive turned members typical of many 17th-century chairs. 1680–1710.

1. Caned chair. South Shore, Massachusetts. Scroll feet and carving on back panel were somewhat unusual. Double-ball or Spanish feet and molding on the back panel were more common. 1690–1735.

2. Caned chair. Probably Boston. Its strongly vertical design, carved crest rail, front stretcher, turned members, and Spanish feet were typical. 1690–1730.

3. Caned armchair. Pennsylvania. Stylistically similar to English examples, but made of American black walnut. 1690–1735.

4. Leather chair. Boston. Classic early example. Because of widespread exportation, also called "Boston" chair. 1700–1725.

5. Leather armchair. Boston. Molded crest rail suggests slightly later date than others shown here. 1710–1740.

6. Leather chair. Probably Boston. Double rows of tacks were an original upholstery technique. 1700–1730.

7. Leather armchair. New York City. The pattern of reel, egg-shaped, and columnar turnings on back uprights suggests Continental influence. 1700–1730.

8. Banister-back chair. Eastern Massachusetts. More economical version of caned or leather chair. 1690-1720.

9. Banister-back chair. Connecticut. Note that turned split spindles match uprights in outline. 1710–1750.

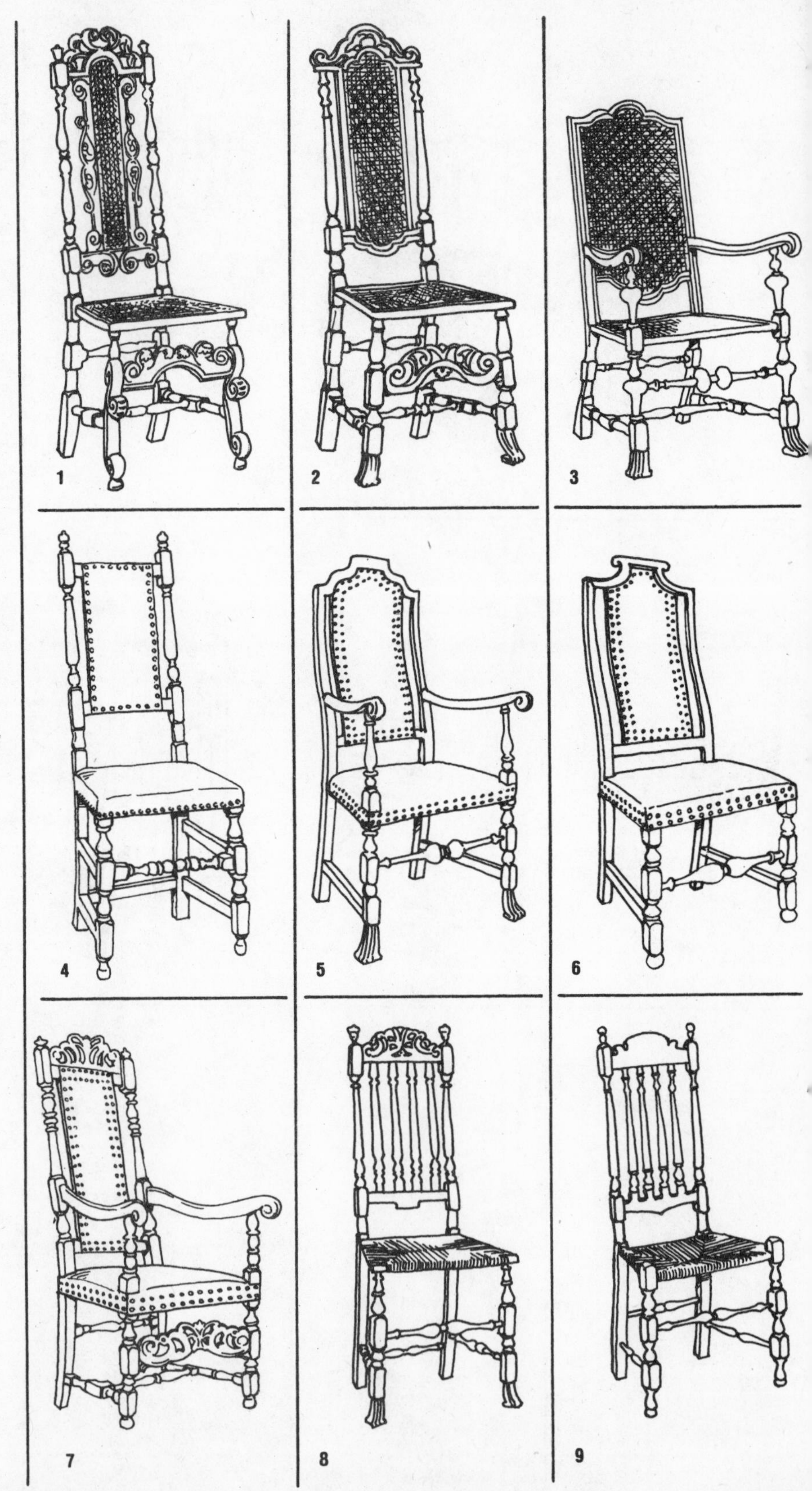

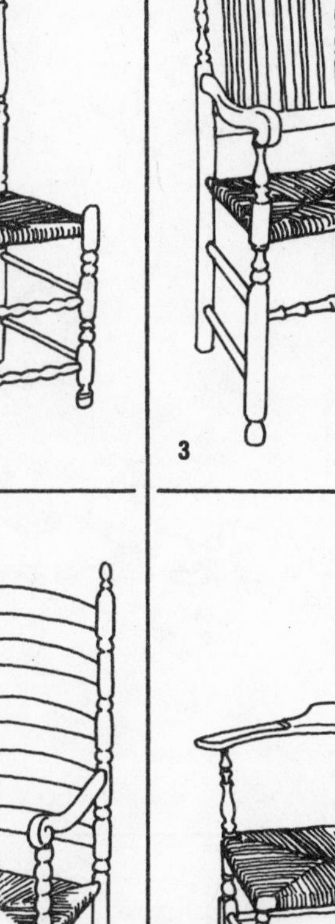

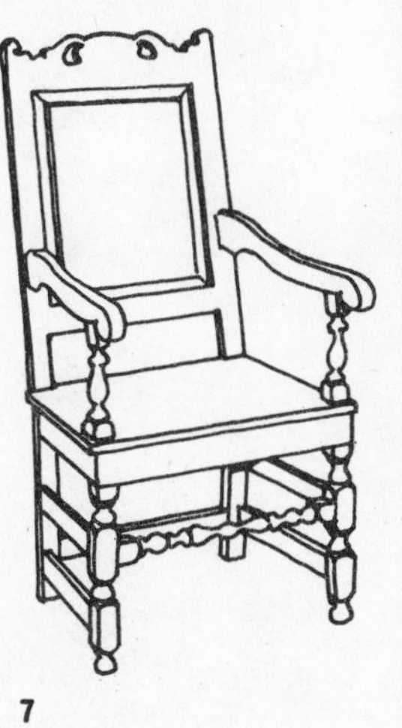

1 2 3 4 5 6 7

1. Banister-back armchair. Stratford, Connecticut. Called "hearts and crowns" type because of its carved crest rail. Popular along Connecticut coast. (Attributed to shop of Thomas Salmon, 1693–1749.) 1735–1745.

2. Banister-back chair. Connecticut. Double-ball turnings on front legs and "sausage" turnings on front stretchers suggest Dutch, probably New York, influence. 1710–1760.

3. Banister-back armchair. Delaware Valley, Pennsylvania. Molded banisters and gently arching crest rail relate to provincial English prototypes. 1720–1750.

4. Slat-back chair. New England. Note William and Mary period's emphasis on verticality of overall design when compared to 17th-century examples. 1700–1725.

5. Slat-back armchair. New York or New Jersey. Fairly common type of chair with broad proportions. 1710–1750.

6. Corner chair. New England. Also called "roundabout"; both period terms. Preferred armchair for use at a desk. 1700–1730.

7. Wainscot armchair. Chester County, Pennsylvania. Closely related to rural English prototypes. 1700–1750.

CHAIRS

1. Easy chair. New England. Form introduced to America during William and Mary period. Note boldly curving crest and arms. 1710–1725.

2. Easy chair. Massachusetts. During 18th century, form was often reserved for the elderly or infirm. 1715–1730.

3. "Spanish," "Portuguese," or "paintbrush" foot; "clawfoot" was period term. Found in all regions. 1690–1720.

4. Scroll leg. Seen relatively frequently on American chairs. 1690–1735.

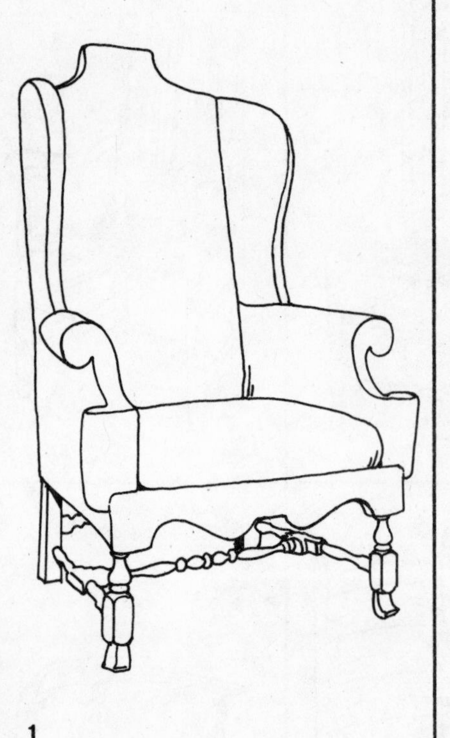

1

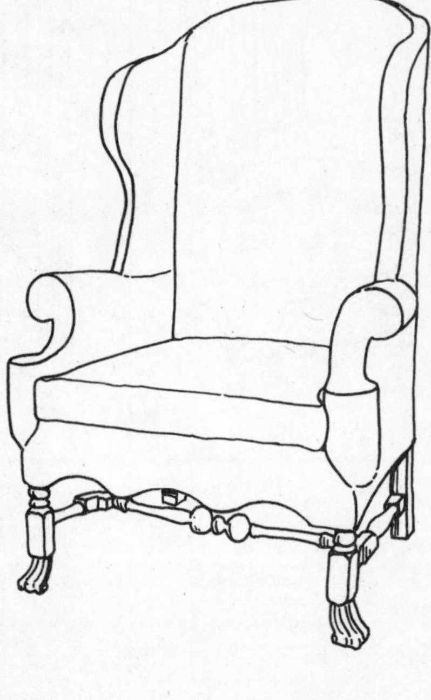

2

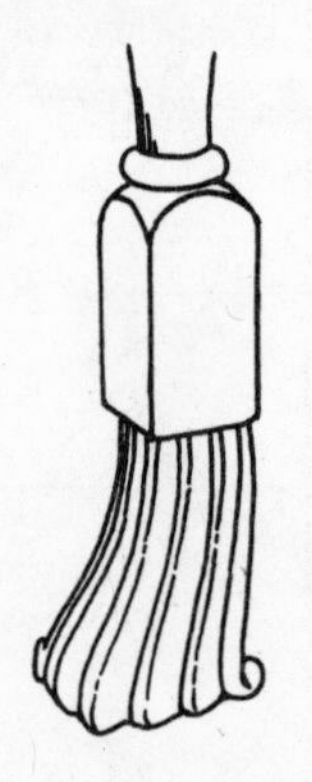

3

4

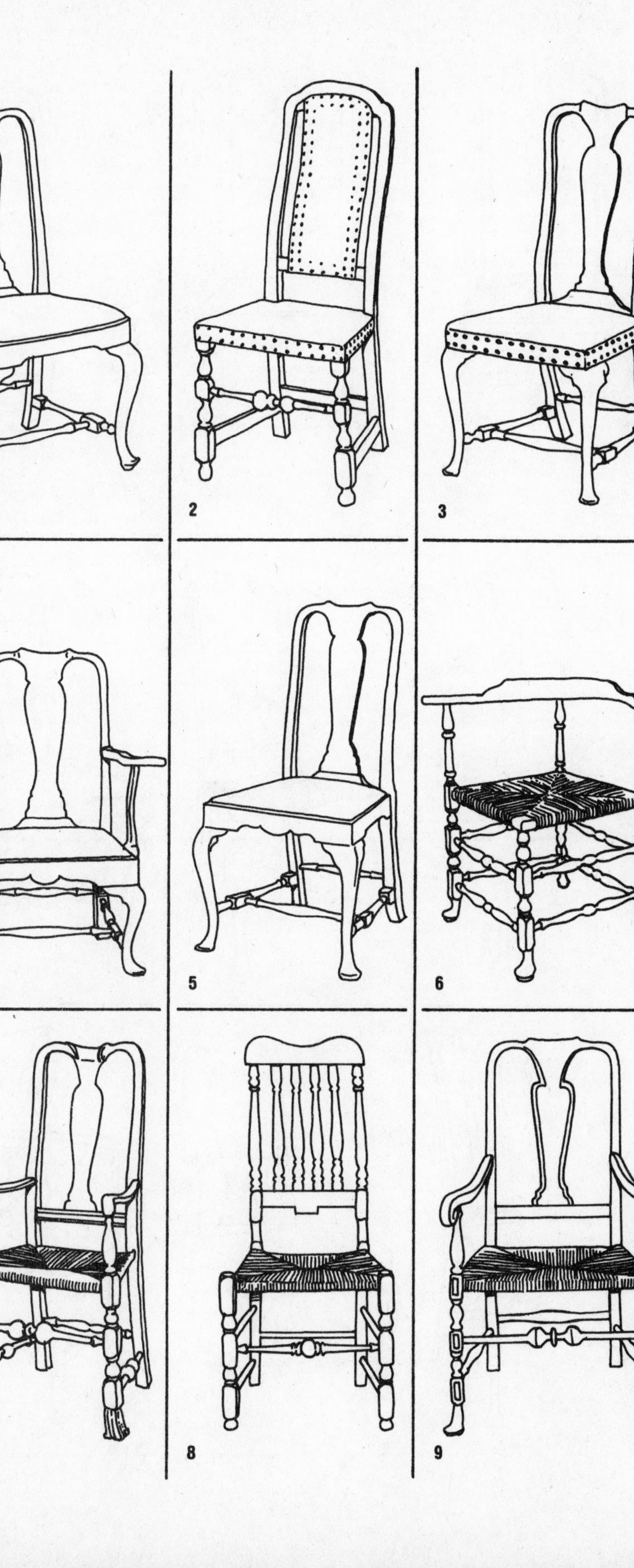

1. Chair. Boston area. Typical Massachusetts example with thin splat, stretchers, compass seat, and rather "clubby" pad feet. 1730–1760.

2. Leather chair. Boston. Rounded crest suggests influence of Queen Anne style. 1720–1740.

3. Chair. Boston. Such tall, thin proportions and upholstery over the rail were fairly unusual features. 1730–1750.

4. Low armchair. Massachusetts. Low, broad proportions relate it to "slipper" and easy chairs. 1730–1760.

5. Chair. New England. Has trapezoidal seat with squared-off corners, rather than compass seat with rounded corners. 1730–1760.

6. Roundabout chair. New England. Its pad feet were stylistically newer features than its block and vase turnings. 1725–1740.

7. Armchair. New England. Molded stiles, yoke-shaped crest rail, and splat all Queen Anne-style characteristics, combined with William and Mary-style turnings and Spanish feet. 1730–1750.

8. Banister-back chair. New England. Essentially William and Mary in style, though yoke-shaped crest rail is associated with Queen Anne style. 1750–1775.

9. Armchair. Massachusetts. A turner's adaptation of Queen Anne style, which generally featured carved rather than turned ornamentation. 1750–1800.

1. Chair. Portsmouth, New Hampshire. Carved and pierced crest rail unusual for period in overall design and openness of piercing. Its turned legs are William and Mary in style. (Attributed to John Gaines, 1704–1743.) 1730–1743.

2. Chair. Connecticut. Extremely thin splat and cyma-curved seat rail were typical Connecticut characteristics. 1730–1760.

3. Chair. Connecticut. Country example, rather rigid in overall design. 1740–1760.

4. Chair. Wethersfield, Connecticut. Of slender proportions. Compass seat was a common alternative to trapezoidal seat. 1730–1760.

5. Chair. Connecticut. Cabriole legs were joined to seat rail by means of turned members. 1730–1760.

6. Chair. Newport, Rhode Island. Classic Rhode Island attributes include sharply beaked parrots' heads in voids of back, thickly carved shells, and fairly broad overall proportions. 1750–1770.

7. Chair. Newport, Rhode Island. Straight splat suggests Chinese influence. C-curves on knees appear on other Rhode Island chairs of period. 1725–1760.

8. Chair. Newport, Rhode Island. Flat, curved stretchers associated with Rhode Island or Pennsylvania. 1730–1760.

9. Roundabout chair. Newport, Rhode Island. X-shaped stretchers seen on some Rhode Island chairs. 1735–1750.

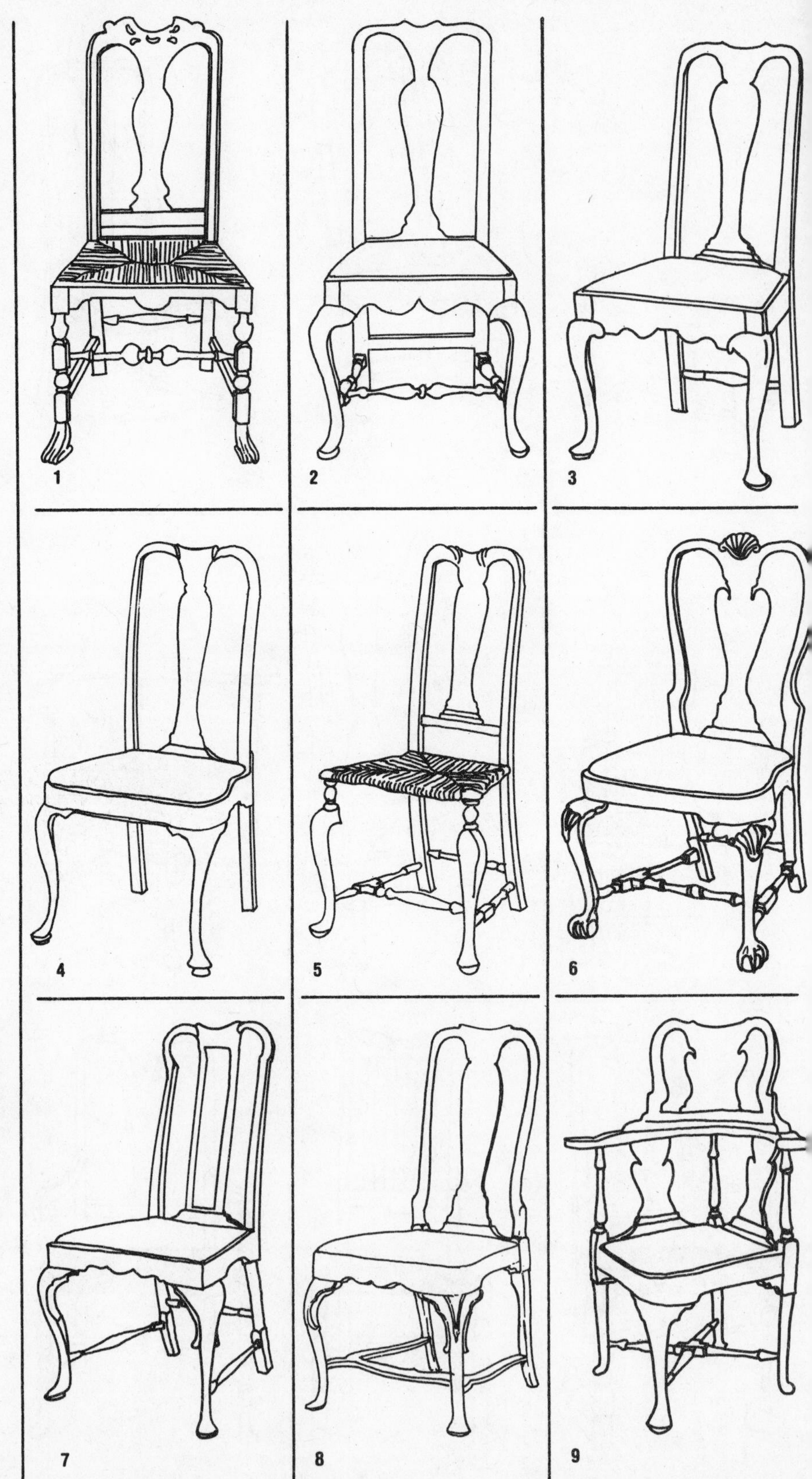

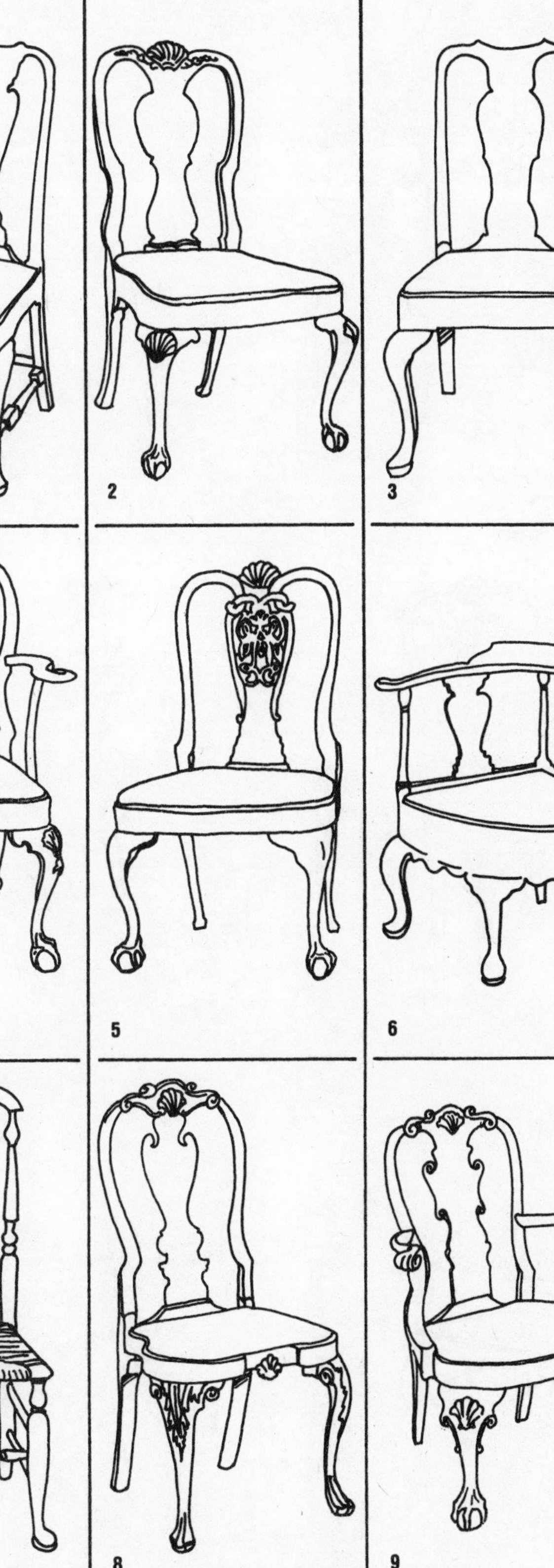

1. Chair. Newport, Rhode Island. Deep-cut seat rail seen on other Newport examples. 1730–1760.

2. Chair. New York City. Broad proportions, "hoof" rear legs, and Cupid's bow carving at base of splat were New York characteristics. c. 1750.

3. Chair. New York. Rounded stiles and pointed pad feet seen here are more often associated with English work. 1730–1760.

4. Armchair. New York. Typical New York example. Shell with pendant carving on knee also seen on Rhode Island chairs. 1740–1795.

5. Chair. New York. Letters R, M, and L worked into the splat of this broadly proportioned chair stand for Robert and Margaret Beekman Livingston, members of two important New York families who were married in 1742. 1742–1770.

6. Roundabout chair. New York City. Deep skirt hides toilet apparatus. 1755–1790.

7. Fiddle-back chair. New York City. A turner's version of a Queen Anne chair. Note that carved cabriole legs have been substituted by turned conical legs. A number of such chairs stamped "Jacob" and "Smith" on seat blocks survive. (By Jacob Smith, active 1760–1812.) 1760–1812.

8. Chair. Philadelphia. Its Philadelphia attributes include bold carving, horseshoe-shaped seat, shell carving on seat rail, trifid front feet, and stump rear legs. 1745–1760.

9. Armchair. Philadelphia. Note strong carving of crest rail, splat, arms, and legs, as well as chair's bold stance. 1745–1760.

1. Armchair. Philadelphia. Elegant example, lacking heavy ornamentation. 1730–1750.

2. Armchair. Philadelphia. Note saddled (or scooped) crest rail and distinctive C-shaped arm supports, both Philadelphia attributes. 1745–1760.

3. Chair. Delaware River Valley. Considerably simpler than some Philadelphia chairs, this example nonetheless has trifid front feet. 1740–1760.

4. Chair. Philadelphia. Highly carved chair shows Rococo influence, particularly in splat. 1740–1760.

5. Roundabout chair. Philadelphia. Note double-winged splats and spade feet. 1740–1750.

6. "Slipper" chair. Pennsylvania. So-called because one theory suggests that such chairs were low to the ground for ease in putting on shoes. 1730–1750.

7. Chair. Philadelphia. Example of quieter taste often associated with Quaker communities. (Possibly by William Savery, 1721–1788.) 1740–1790.

8. Armchair. Probably Maryland. Stylistically similar to Philadelphia chairs. 1740–1760.

9. Armchair. Edenton, North Carolina. Its rear cabriole leg was an unusual feature in an American chair. 1750–1770.

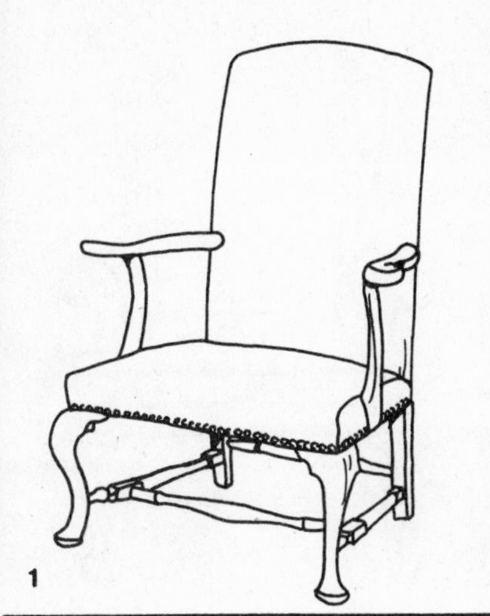

1

2

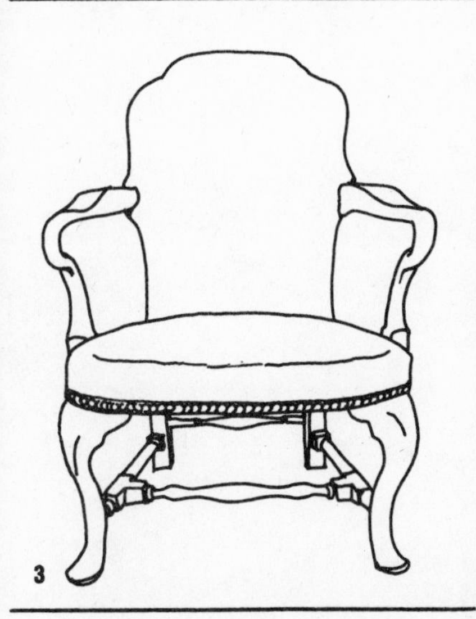

3

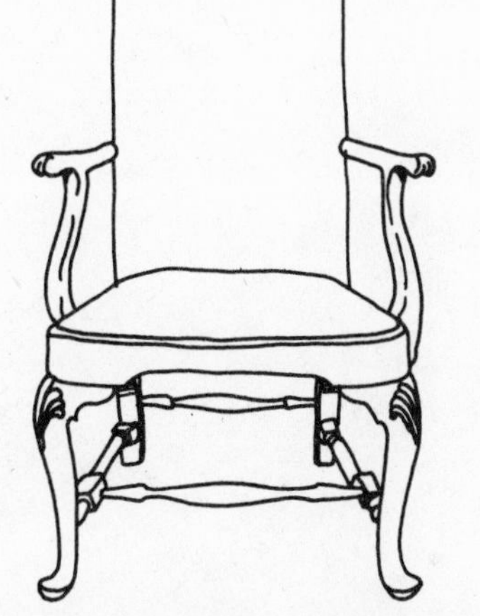

4

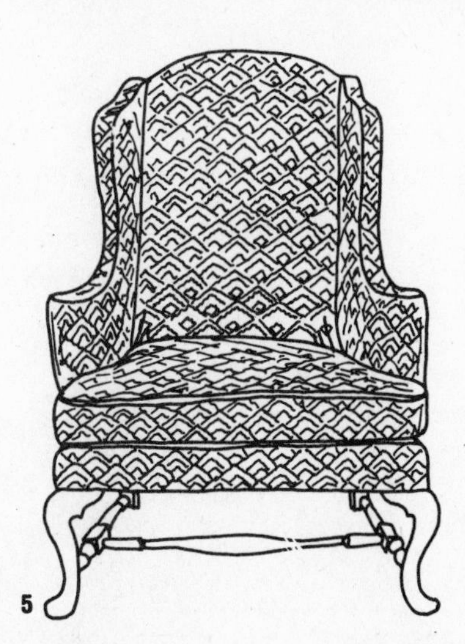

5

6

1. Upholstered armchair. Massachusetts. Horizontally scrolled arms replaced easy chair's wings. 1730–1760.

2. Easy chair. Boston. Still has vertical roll of arms associated with earlier examples. 1740–1760.

3. Upholstered chair. Newport, Rhode Island. Reverse scroll arms intensify chair's curvaceous design. 1730–1750.

4. Upholstered armchair. Newport, Rhode Island. Note knuckled arm ends on continuous arms, and shell with pendant carving on knees. 1740–1750.

5. Easy chair. Newport, Rhode Island. American easy chairs upholstered in canvaswork (needlepoint) were rare. Chair bears inscription "Gardiner Junr [Junior] New Port 1758." Such inscriptions add to an object's monetary and historical value. Dated 1758.

6. Upholstered armchair. New York. Extreme flaring of back was very rare in American chairs. 1735–1750.

1. Easy chair. Philadelphia. Note front feet and stump rear legs. 1735–1750.

2. Easy chair. Philadelphia. Example with trifid feet and flat stretcher base. 1740–1750.

1

2

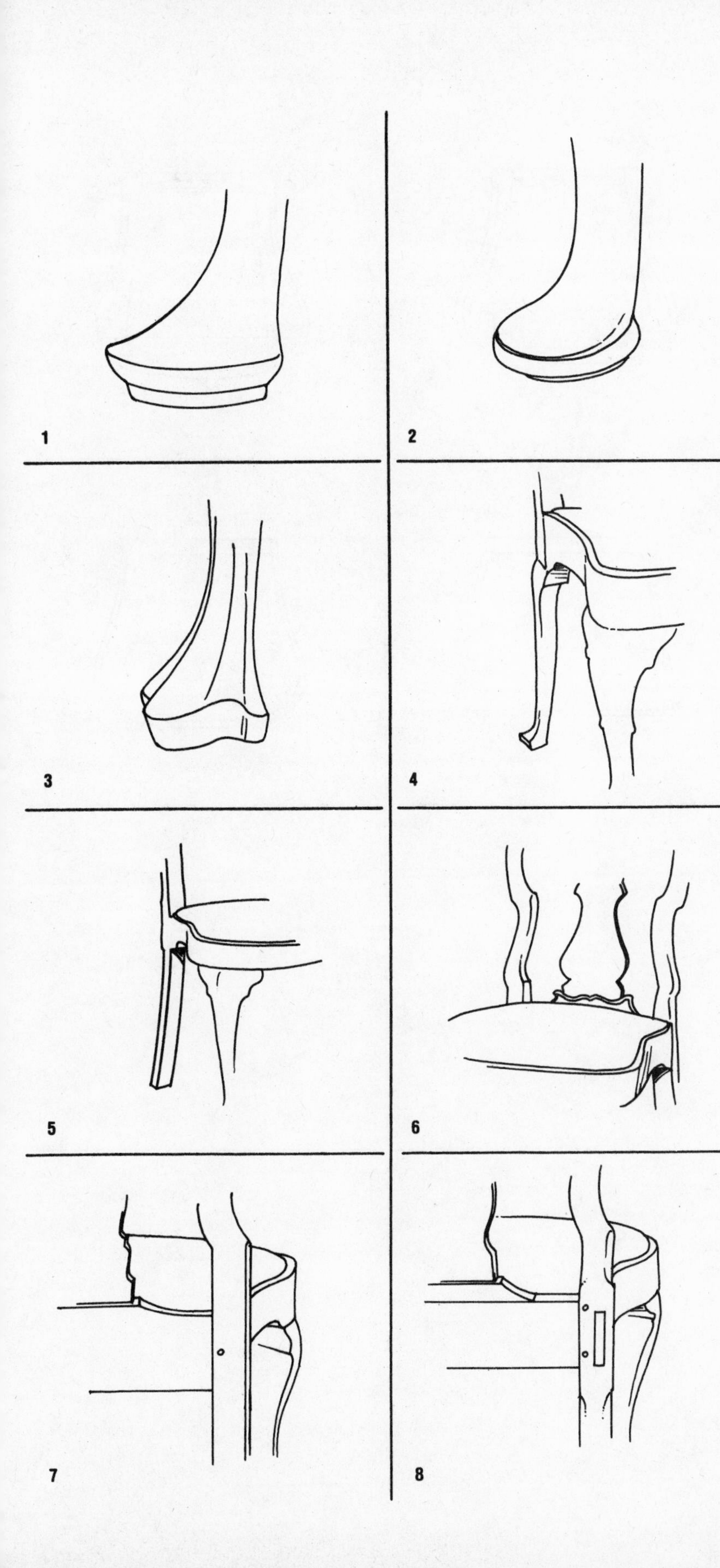

1. New England pad foot. Somewhat flat and "clubby." 1730–1750.

2. Pad foot. Philadelphia. Note softly rounded shape and disk beneath. 1730–1750.

3. Trifid foot. Philadelphia. This example has shaped center rib. 1740–1760.

4. Hoofed rear leg from New York chair. English holdover. 1730–1750.

5. Stump rear leg. Philadelphia feature. 1740–1760.

6. "Cupid's bow" or cyma curve at base of splat, seen on New York chairs. 1730–1760.

7. Rear stile of New England chair. One pin supported seat. 1740–1760.

8. Through-tenon and double-pinning seen on Philadelphia and a few Connecticut chairs. 1740–1760.

1. New England seat frame construction with seat supports. Corner blocks reinforce legs. 1740–1760.

2. Philadelphia seat framing has wide supports. Legs are doweled into front seat support. 1740–1760.

3. Slip seat from Connecticut chair with trapezoidal outline. Many Connecticut chairs had squared-off seats. 1740–1770.

4. Bird's-eye view of horseshoe-shaped seat from New York chair. 1740–1770.

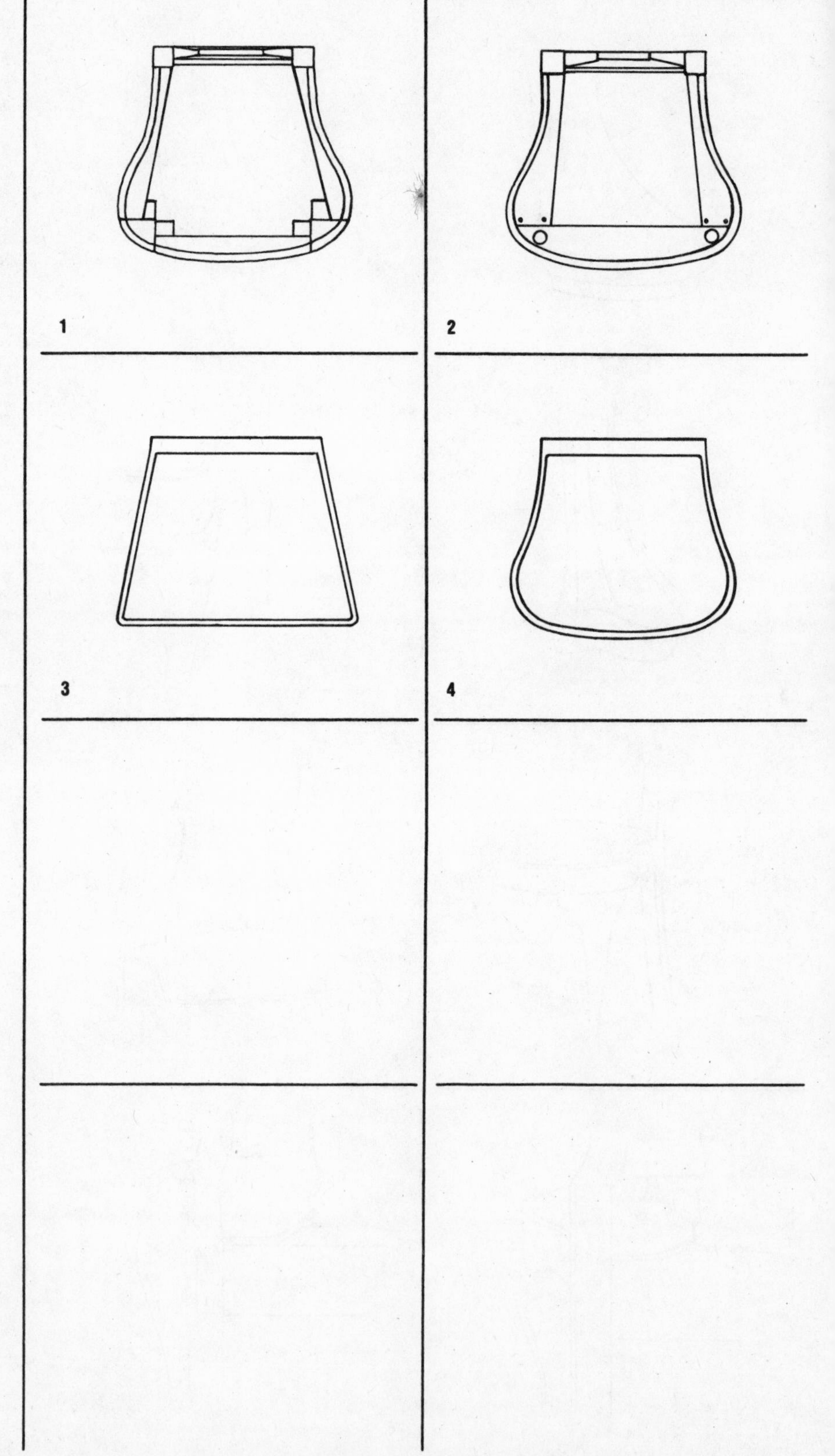

1 2 3 4 5 6

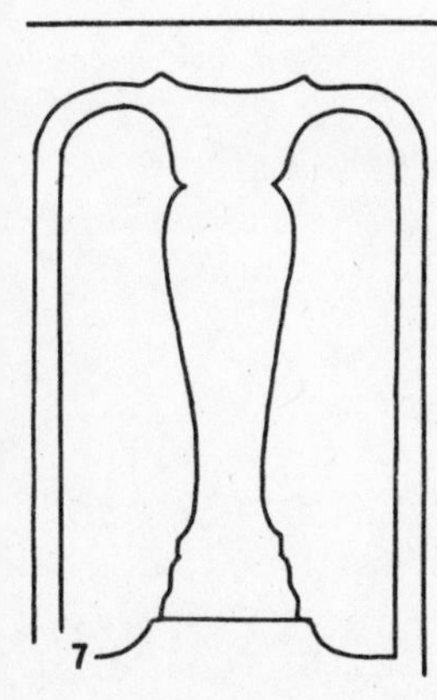

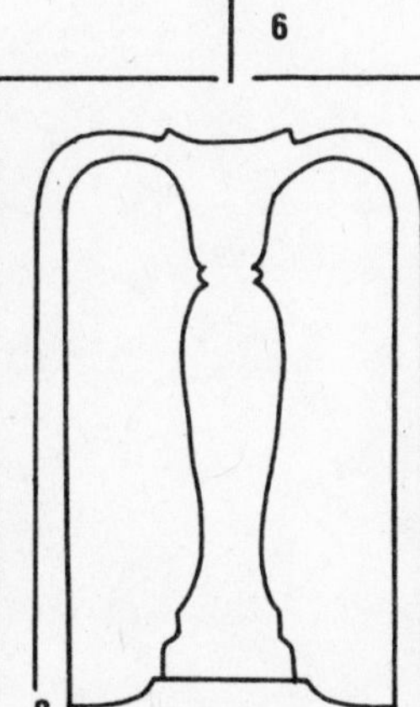

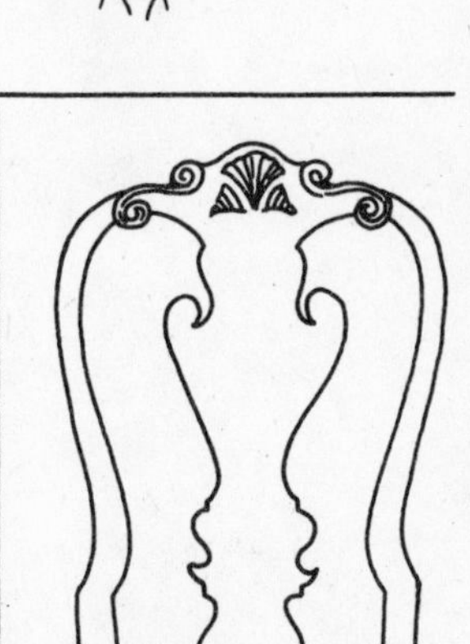

1. Crest rail from Boston side chair, slightly scooped. 1730–1760.

2. Connecticut crest rail, similar in style to Boston examples. 1730–1760.

3. Crest rail from Newport side chair, with deeply carved shell above a volute. 1740–1770.

4. New York crest rail, with shell and flat leafy carving, both associated with that city. 1740–1790.

5. Philadelphia crest rail with carved scroll volutes flanking a scallop shell. 1745–1760.

6. Crest rail from North Carolina chair is nearly covered by flat, leafy carving. c. 1760.

7. Thin, long splat from Massachusetts. 1730–1760.

8. Thin splat without shoulders from Wethersfield, Connecticut. 1730–1780.

9. Elaborate trophy-shaped Philadelphia splat with deep cuts. 1740–1770.

1. Plain knee from Massachusetts side chair. 1730–1760.

2. Pointed knee carving with C-curves from Newport chair. 1740–1770.

3. Shell with pendant carving from New York. Also used on Newport chairs. 1740–1760.

4. Flat, stringy acanthus leaf carving on New York side chair knee. 1740–1790.

5. Naturalistic shell on Philadelphia knee. 1740–1790.

6. Boldly carved acanthus leaf carving on knee of Philadelphia chair. 1745–1760.

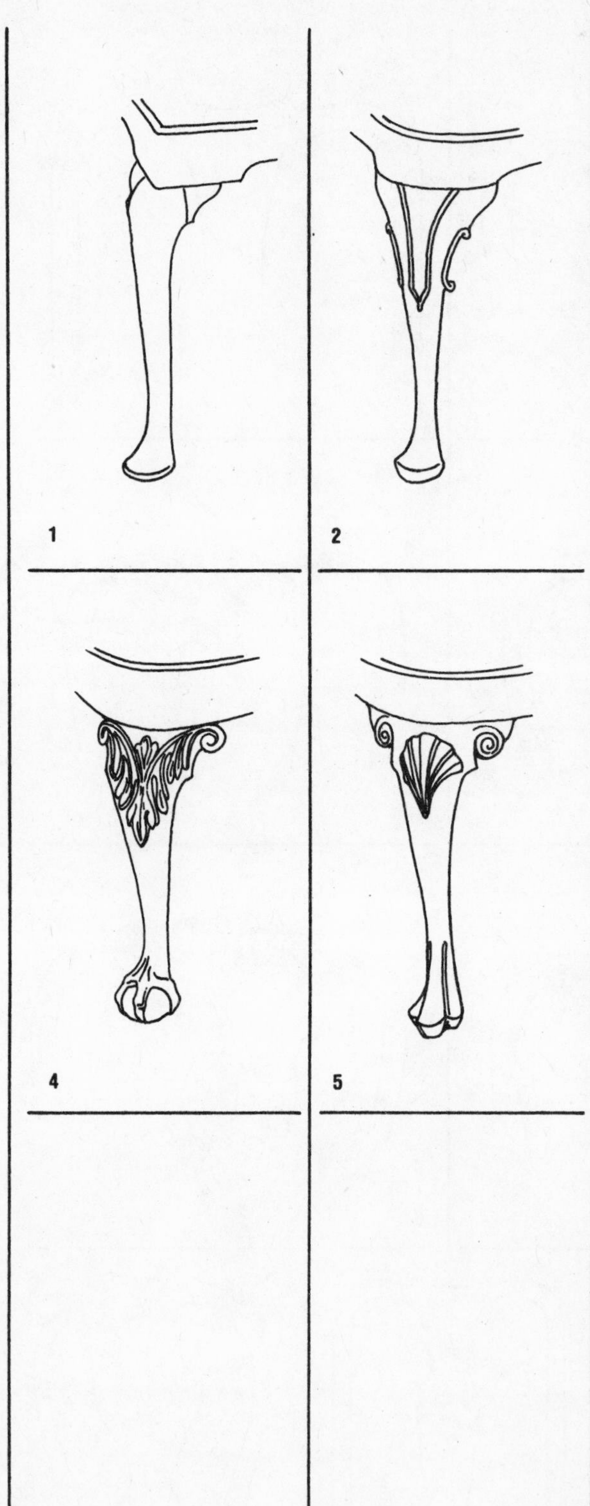

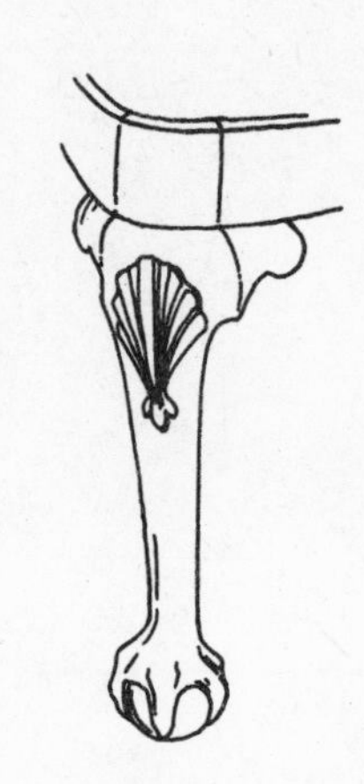

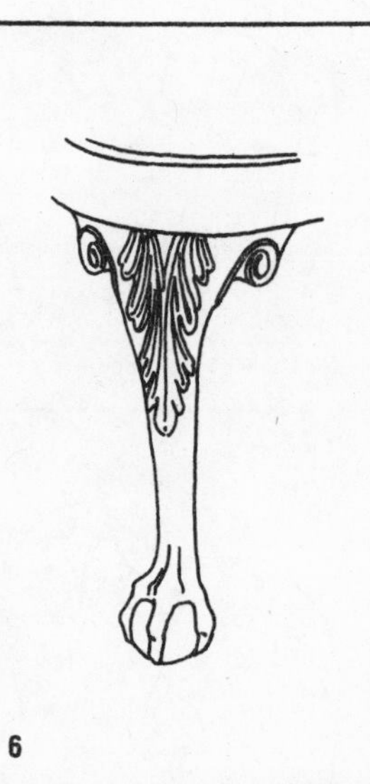

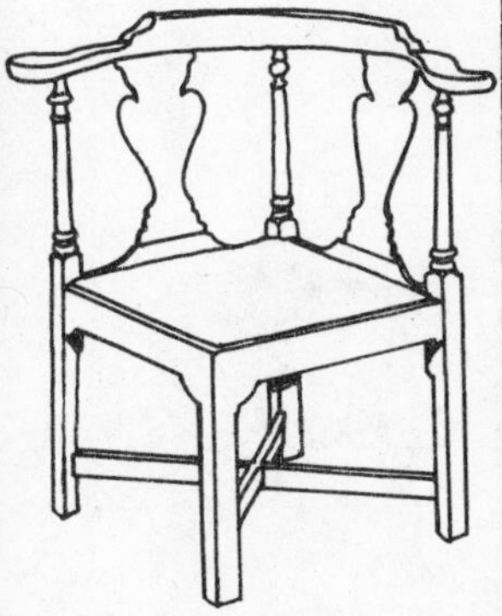

1

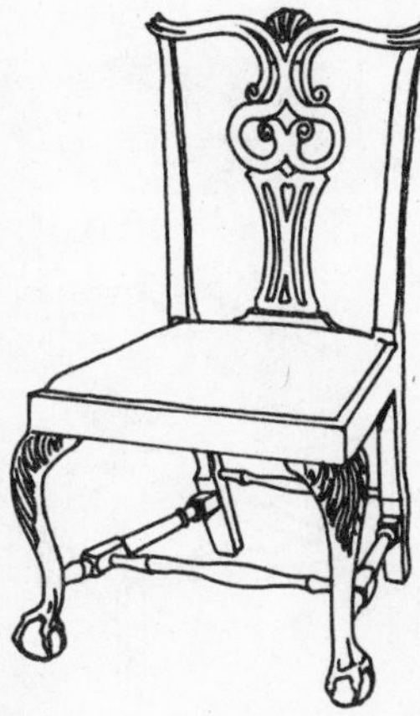

2

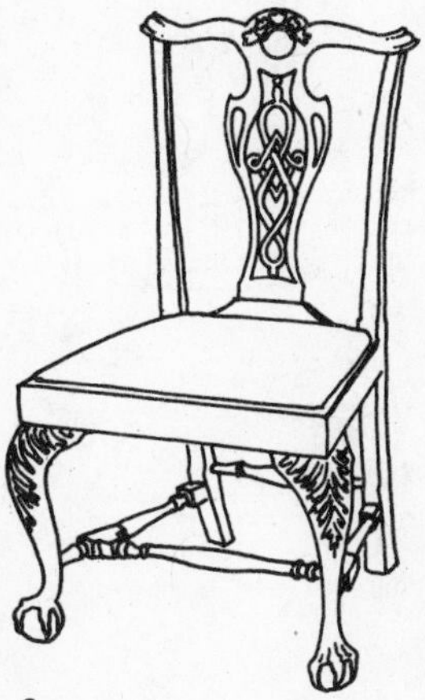

3

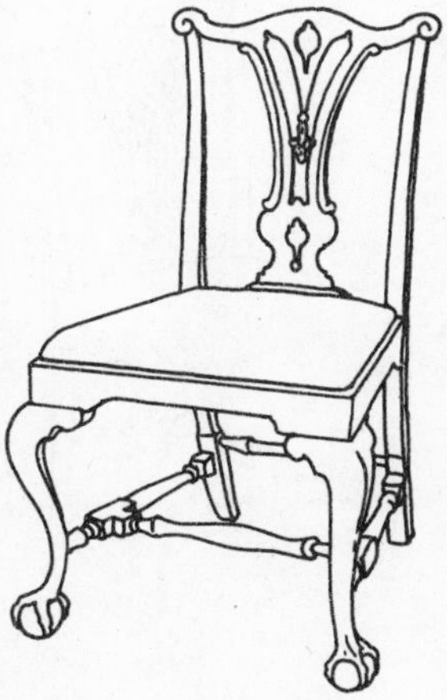

4

5

6

7

8

9

1. Roundabout chair. Massachusetts. Use of straight, or "Marlborough," leg associated with Chippendale style. 1740–1760.

2. Chair. Massachusetts. Typical Massachusetts scroll-back chair. Note continued use of stretchers. 1755–1795.

3. Chair. Massachusetts. Diamond-and-figure-eight-interlaced splat also seen on Philadelphia chairs. 1755–1795.

4. Chair. Massachusetts. Closely related to design in Plate 16 of Chippendale's *Gentleman and Cabinet-Maker's Director* (1762). 1755–1795.

5. Chair. Massachusetts. Inspired by English prototypes. Note two-part Gothic-style splat. 1755–1795.

6. Chair. Massachusetts. Similarly molded stiles, curved crest rail, and carved splat appear on English chairs. 1755–1795.

7. Armchair. Possibly Newburyport, Massachusetts. Gothic splat derived from English models. 1760–1795.

8. Armchair. Probably Boston. One of the most elaborate splats used on a Massachusetts chair. 1765–1785.

9. Chair. Salem or Boston, Massachusetts. Based on Plate 9 in Robert Manwaring's *The Cabinet and Chair-Maker's Real Friend and Companion* (1765). 1765–1790.

1. Armchair. Boston. Gothic splat also seen on English and Philadelphia chairs. 1765–1780.

2. Chair. Newburyport, Massachusetts. Chairs with pierced slats called "riddle-backs." 1785–1800.

3. Chair. New England. Lathe-turned version of Chippendale-style chair. 1776–1800.

4. Chair. Possibly Portsmouth, New Hampshire. Pad foot cheaper alternative to claw-and-ball foot. 1785–1800.

5. Chair. Goffstown or Bedford, New Hampshire. Highly individualized interpretation of Chippendale style. (By Major John Dunlap, 1746–1792, member of an important New Hampshire family of cabinetmakers.) 1770–1790.

6. Chair. Norwich area, Connecticut. Scrolled splat reveals Gothic influence. Note simple knee brackets. 1760–1795.

7. Armchair. East Windsor, Connecticut. Diamond design in splat most often seen in New York, but also in Connecticut and Massachusetts work. (Possibly by Eliphalet Chapin, 1741–1807.) 1771–1795.

8. Chair. East Windsor, Connecticut. Very similar to Philadelphia examples in overall design and construction. Maker trained in Philadelphia. (By Eliphalet Chapin.) 1781.

9. Chair. Connecticut. Example of a simpler Chippendale style. 1775–1800.

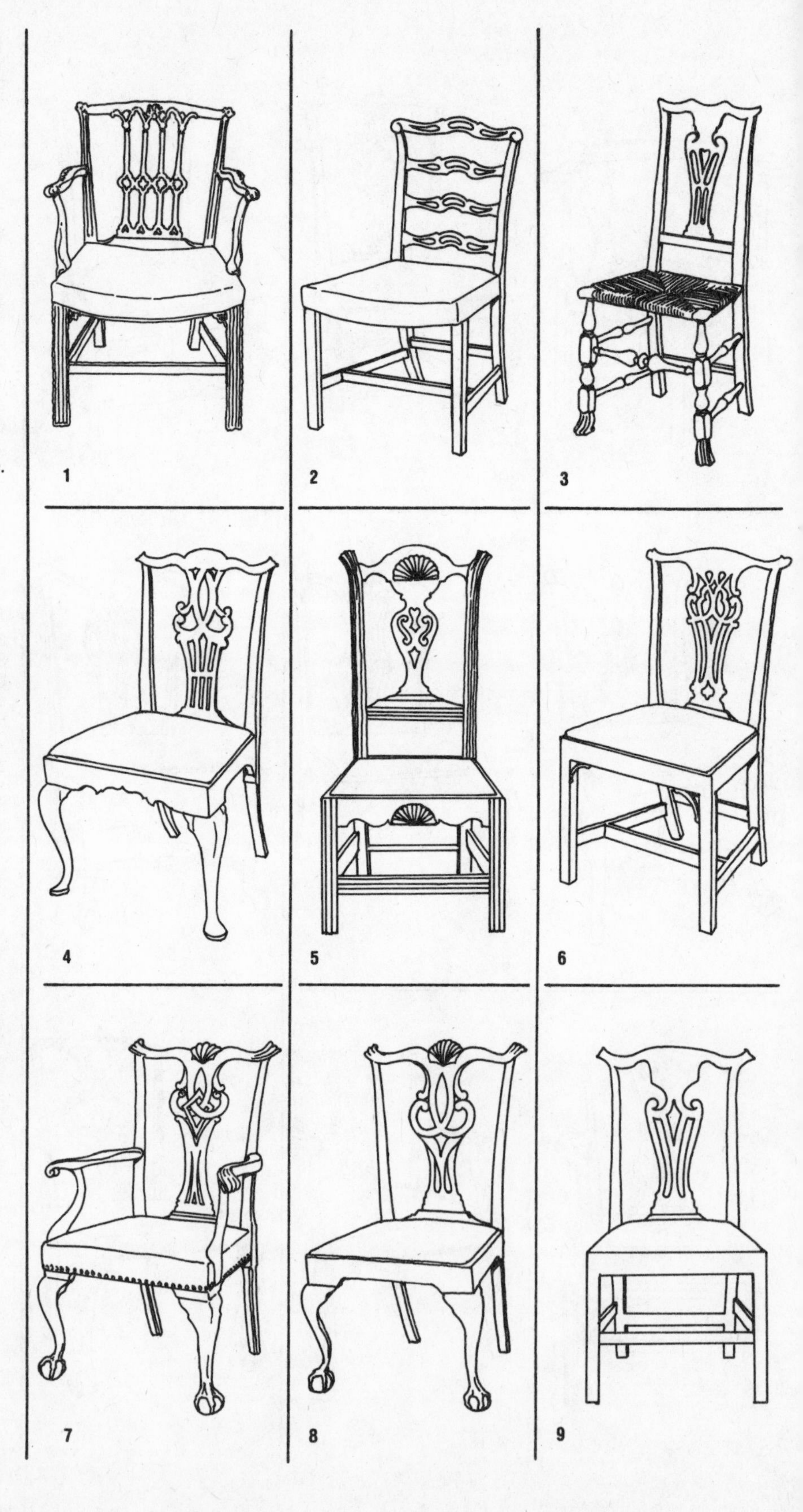

1. Chair. Connecticut. Shows influence of Chinese furniture design. 1750–1780.

2. Chair. Newport, Rhode Island. Newport version of scrolled splat. 1755–1795.

3. Low or "slipper" chair. Rhode Island. This splat seen on simple Rhode Island chairs, on English prototypes, and on a few Massachusetts chairs. 1755–1795.

4. Roundabout chair. Newport, Rhode Island. Splats canting outward added to chair's comfort. (Possibly by John Goddard I, 1723–1785.) 1755–1780.

5. Low or "slipper" chair. Rhode Island. Note how Chippendale ears were combined with Queen Anne-style rounded back. 1760–1780.

6. Chair. Rhode Island. Distinctive ears associated with Rhode Island. Uncommon use of Gothic-style splat in Rhode Island work. 1760–1795.

7. Chair. Newport, Rhode Island. Made by Newport's most famous cabinetmakers, the Townsend-Goddard school. 1780–1790.

8. Chair. New York. Scroll-and-diamond splat often associated with New York. (Inscribed in pencil by maker Gilbert Ash, 1717–1785.) 1755–1785.

9. Chair. New York. Shell carving with pendant on knees seen on Newport chairs. Unusual use of "club" foot in place of claw-and-ball foot. 1745–1795.

1. Chair. New York. Tassel-and-ruffle splat most often associated with New York. New York chairs usually had broad proportions. 1755–1795.

2. Chair. New York. Identical splat seen on Massachusetts chair no. 6, page 105. Rare in New York. 1755–1795.

3. Chair. New York. Very broad knees with C-curve accents. Splat also seen in Rhode Island. 1755–1795.

4. Chair. New York. Compass seat common in New York chairs. Splat had English prototype. 1755–1795.

5. Chair. New York. Overall design similar to Plate 9 in Manwaring's pattern book. 1755–1795.

6. Chair. New York. Note relatively simple Gothic splat and gadrooned edge of seat rail. Gothic taste rarely seen in New York. 1755–1795.

7. Toilet chair. New York. Stringy leaf carving on knees was New York characteristic. 1760–1790.

8. Chair. New York. Earliest possible date based on chair's design source, Chippendale's *Director,* Plate 12. 1762–1780.

9. Upholstered chair. New York. Note rectilinearity of back and delicately pierced knee brackets. 1760–1780.

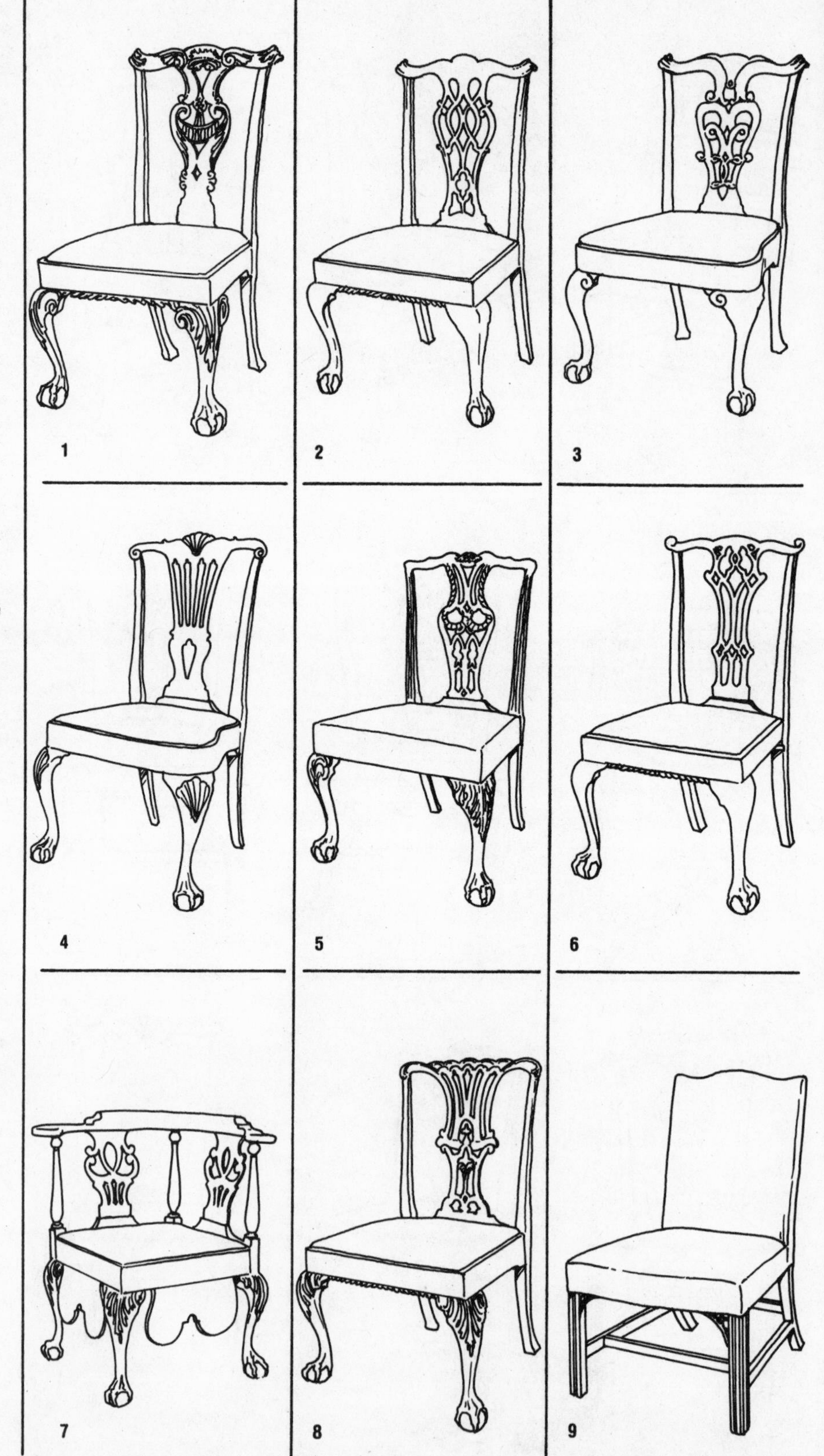

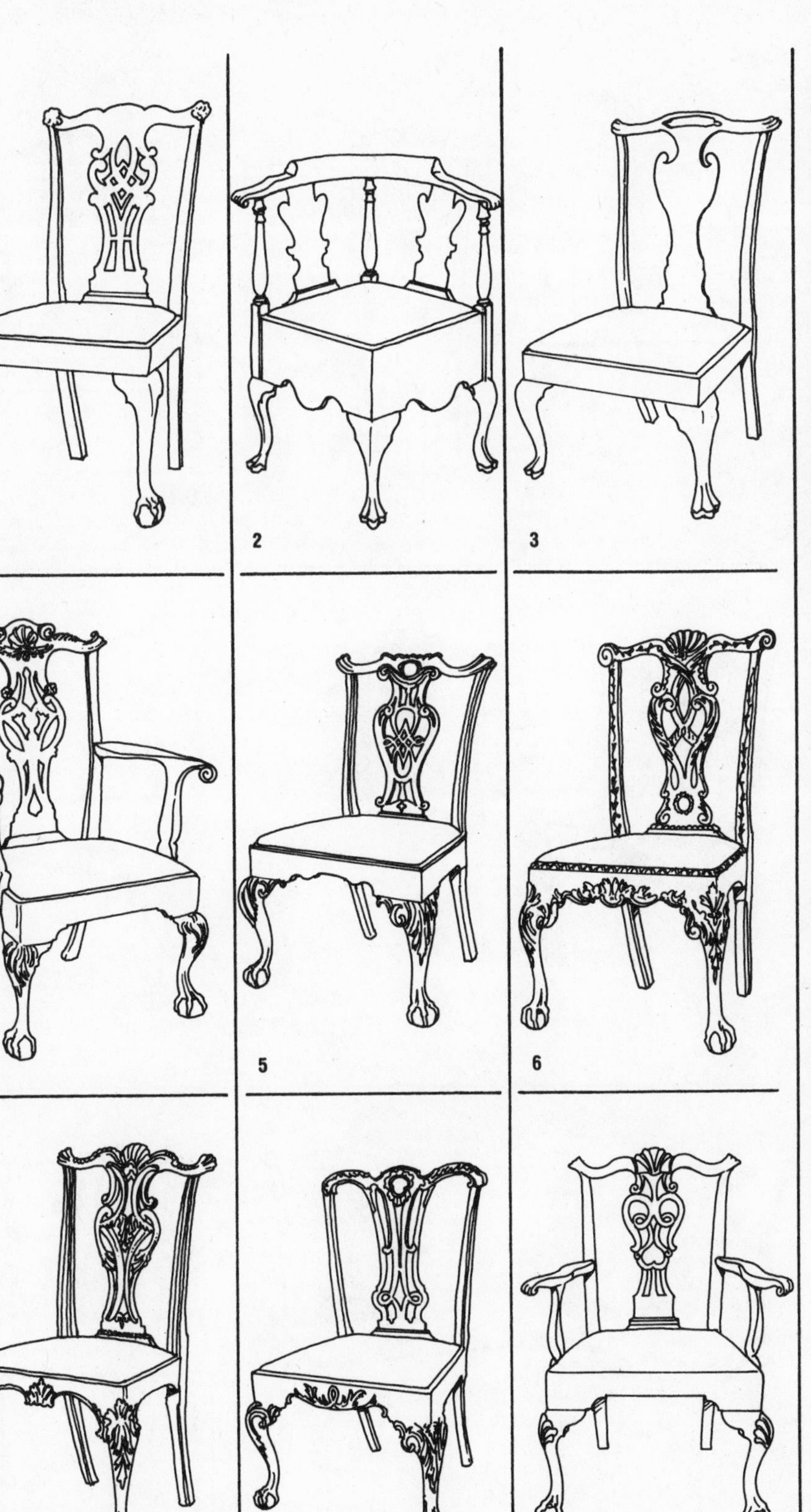

1. Chair. New Jersey. Diamond-and-scroll splat suggests New York influence, while feet resemble Philadelphia examples. 1770–1780.

2. Toilet chair. Philadelphia. Trifid feet and "wings" on splats were Philadelphia characteristics. 1740–1760.

3. Low or "slipper" chair. Philadelphia. Note stump rear legs, wide splat, and hand-hold carved in crest for ease in moving. (Possibly by William Savery, 1721–1788.) 1745–1795.

4. Armchair. Philadelphia. Monumental in size. Deeply carved and exaggerated ears on crest rail and knuckles on arms seen on other Philadelphia chairs. 1755–1795.

5. Chair. Philadelphia. Diamond-and-figure-eight splat also seen on Massachusetts chairs. Note sweep of crest rail. 1755–1795.

6. Chair. Philadelphia. Note heavy, naturalistic foliage carving on splat and on knees. 1755–1795.

7. Chair. Delicate carving covers much of chair's surface. 1775–1795.

8. Armchair. Philadelphia. Based on Chippendale's *Director,* Plates 13 and 14. 1760–1780.

9. Armchair. Philadelphia. Similarly scrolled splat appears on English chairs. 1755–1795.

1. Armchair. Philadelphia. (Labeled by Quaker cabinetmaker William Savery, known for chairs of conservative design and sturdy construction.) 1755–1788.

2. Chair. Philadelphia. Splat similar to those seen on some Southern chairs. Note naturalistically carved scallop shell, Philadelphia hallmark. 1755–1795.

3. Armchair. Philadelphia. Openwork splat. Fine foliate carving covers much of chair. 1755–1795.

4. Chair. Philadelphia. Elegant and airy in design. (Labeled by Thomas Tuft, c. 1738–1788.) 1760–1780.

5. Chair. Philadelphia. Note ribbon-back splat, type seen in Chippendale's designs. 1760–1780.

6. Chair. Philadelphia. Splat taken from Plate 12 of Chippendale's *Director* (1754). 1760–1780.

7. Chair. Philadelphia. Relatively rare example of Chinese-inspired design in America. 1760–1780.

8. Chair. Philadelphia. Splat copied directly from Chippendale's *Director*. Extremely masterful chair. (Attributed to Thomas Affleck, 1740–1795, one of the most talented of the newly-arrived British cabinetmakers.) 1763–1795.

9. Armchair. Philadelphia. Gothic style extremely popular in Philadelphia. 1765–1785.

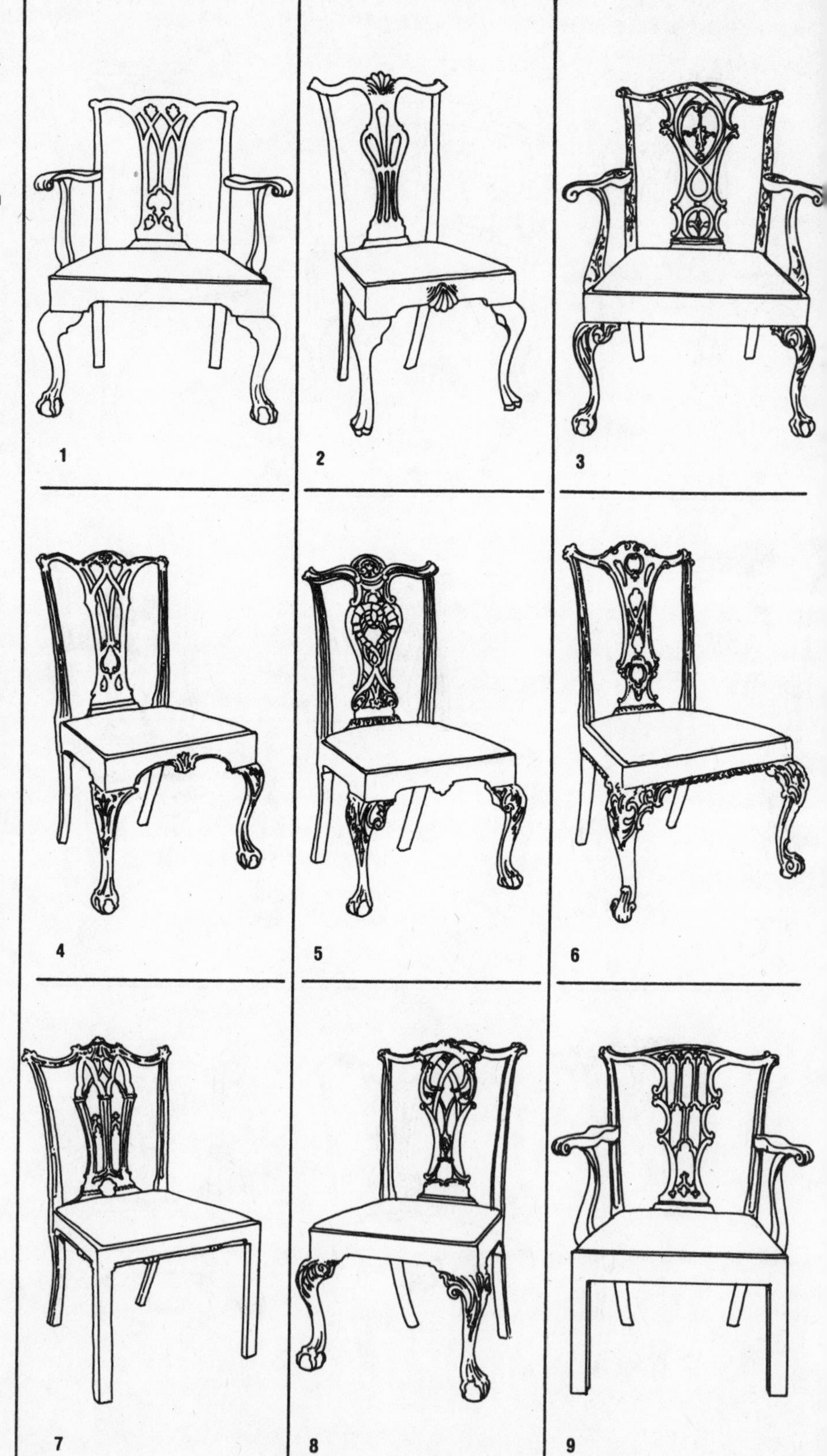

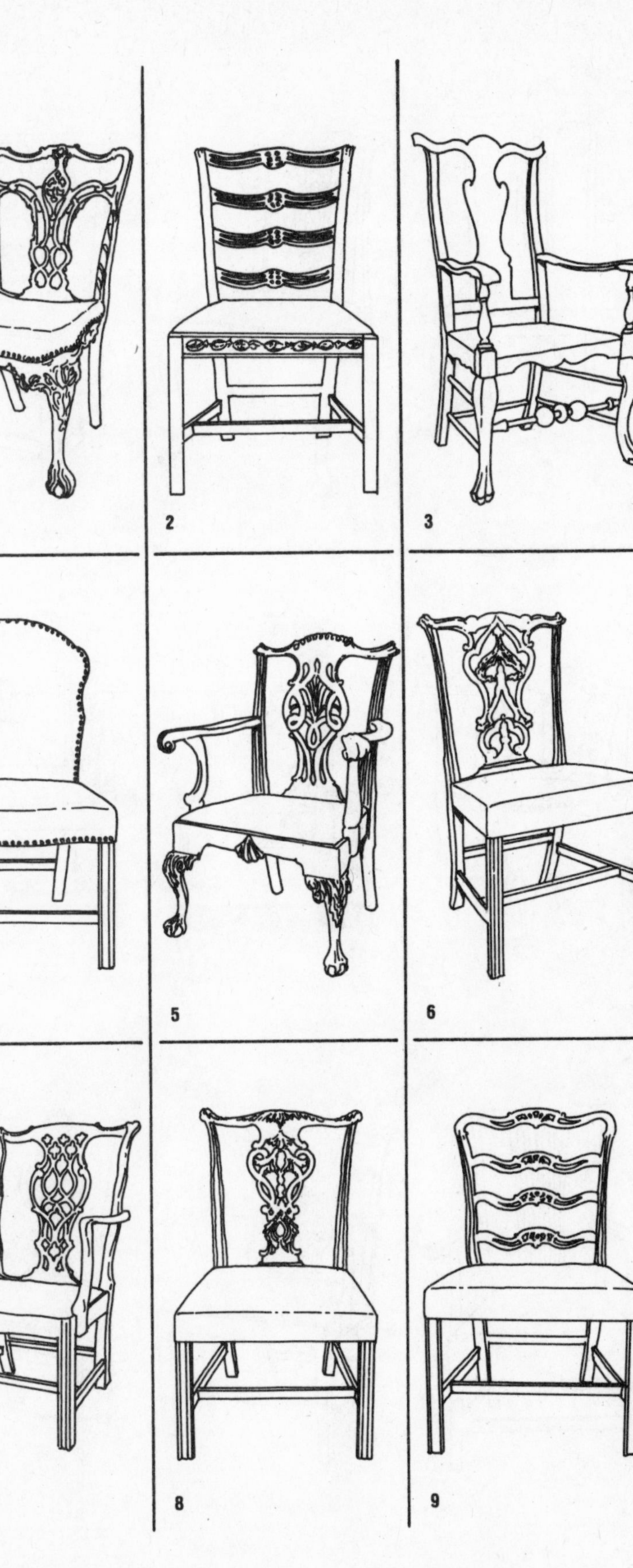

1. Chair. Philadelphia. Once thought to be English because of extreme high style. Note saddle seat, partial over-the-rail upholstery, and flowing splat. (By Benjamin Randolph, 1721–1791.) 1770–1772.

2. Chair. Philadelphia. Riddle-back of very elegant design. (Attributed to Daniel Trotter, 1747–1800.) 1780–1790.

3. Armchair. Philadelphia. Double-undercut arms and distinctive bold turnings on front stretchers seen in Philadelphia work. 1750–1790.

4. Upholstered chair. Philadelphia. Unusual example with serpentine back. 1760–1775.

5. Armchair. Probably Baltimore. Shares some Philadelphia characteristics, such as broad proportions, swept-back crest rail, and trifid feet. Style of splat and presence of cedar corner blocks suggests Maryland origin. 1755–1765.

6. Chair. Baltimore. Wide, interlacing splat and Marlborough legs strongly suggest Maryland provenance. 1765–1785.

7. Armchair. Baltimore. Wavy stiles borrowed from Chippendale's designs. 1765–1780.

8. Chair. Baltimore. One of set originally owned by Charles Carroll the Barrister. Illustrates Marylanders' taste for complicated, pierced splats. 1760–1780.

9. Riddle-back chair. Maryland. Delicately pierced, undulating slats. Fanciest form of slat-back produced in America. 1770–1780.

1. Chair. Probably Virginia. Elegant chair with typically Southern "ribbed" splat. 1755–1795.

2. Chair. Virginia. Claw-and-ball foot was rare on Southern furniture. 1755–1800.

3. Chair. Probably Virginia. Directly related to English prototypes. 1760–1810.

4. Toilet chair. Fredericksburg area, Virginia. Note awkwardness of base. 1760–1770.

5. Masonic master's armchair. Williamsburg, Virginia. Masonic symbols incorporated into back of highly unusual chair. (Bears stamped signature of Benjamin Bucktrout, owner of Anthony Hay's shop.) 1767–1770.

6. Armchair. Northeastern North Carolina. Resembles roundabout chair in crest rail and use of three splats. 1755–1800.

7. Toilet chair. Probably Edenton area, North Carolina. Illustrates typical Southern characteristics of flaring, straight-sided back, four-rib splat, and Marlborough legs. 1755–1810.

8. Armchair. Probably Edenton area, North Carolina. Note figure-eights incorporated into four-rib splat. 1760–1800.

9. Chair. Charleston, South Carolina. Softly molded ears seen on many Southern chairs. Use of looped-figure splat in South often associated with Thomas Elfe. 1755–1795.

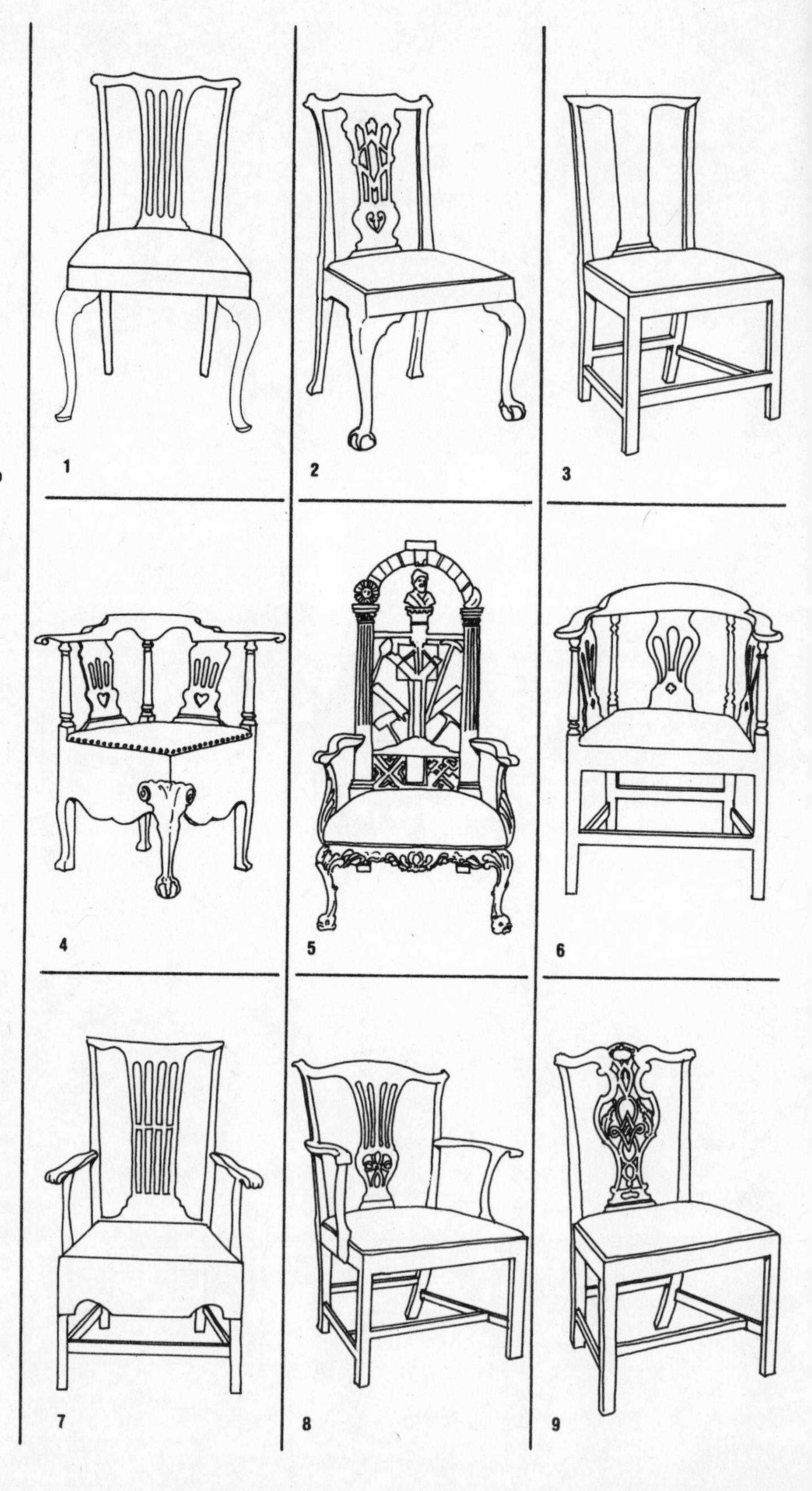

1

2

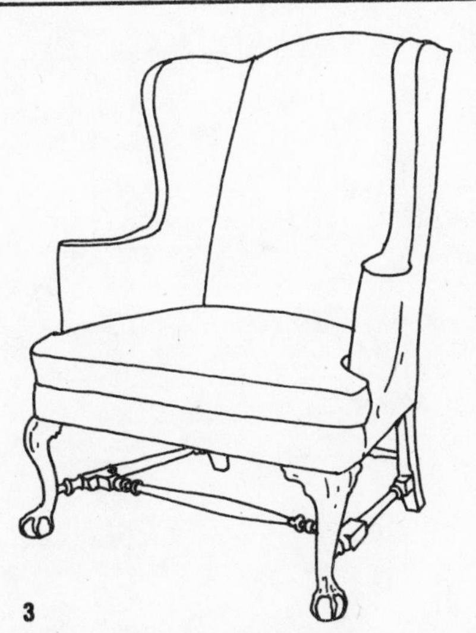

3

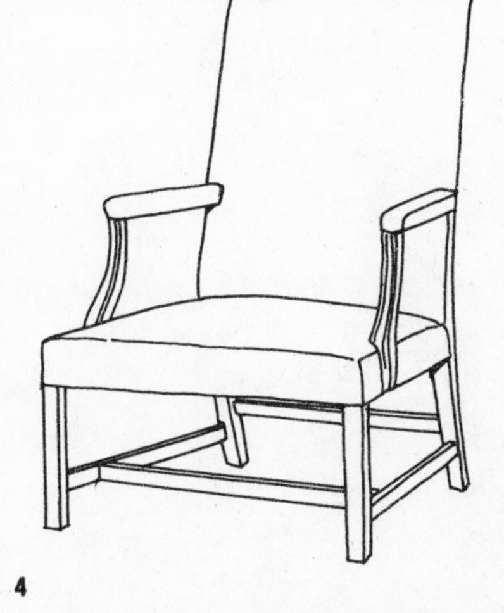

4

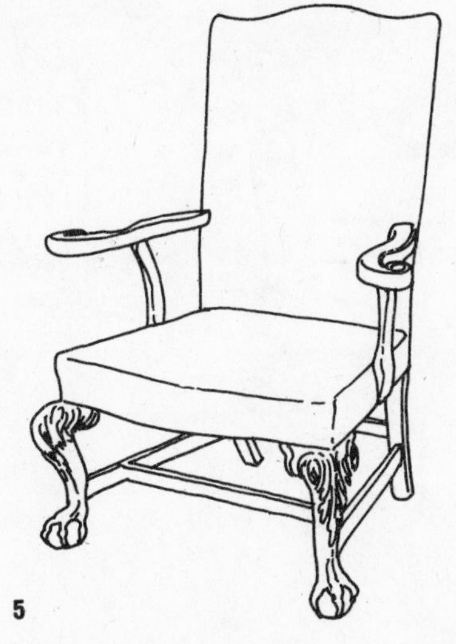

5

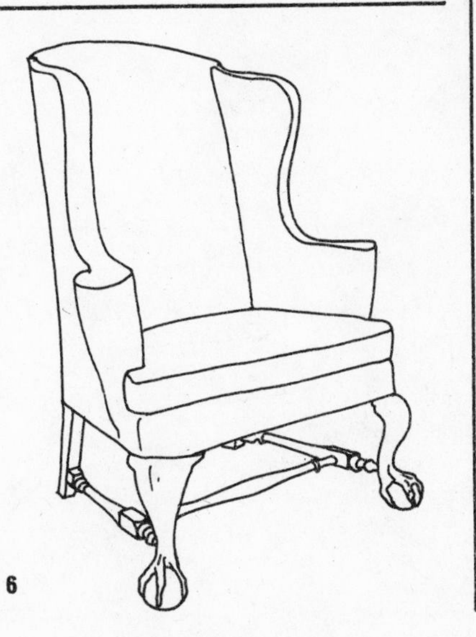

6

1. Chair. Charleston, South Carolina. Maker was very familiar with high-style English work. Made for Drayton Hall, an important Charleston country house. 1760–1780.

2. Chair. Probably South Carolina. Crest rail and splat borrowed from Philadelphia. 1760–1800.

3. Easy chair. Massachusetts. Chair has claw-and-ball feet and vertically rolled arms, generally associated with stylistically earlier period. 1765–1780.

4. Upholstered armchair. Massachusetts. Antecedent of Federal period's lolling chair. 1760–1785.

5. Upholstered armchair. Salem, Massachusetts. Extremely unusual example, with horizontally scrolled arms and highly carved cabriole legs ending in claw-and-ball feet. 1770–1790.

6. Easy chair. Newport, Rhode Island. Turned stretchers continued to appear on New England easy chairs. 1765–1780.

1. Easy chair. New York. Boldly swept wings and overall broad proportions. Note carved knees. 1760–1775.

2. Upholstered armchair. Philadelphia. Distinctive C-scrolled arm supports seen on other Philadelphia armchairs. 1740–1760.

3. Upholstered armchair. Philadelphia. Note blocked foot on Marlborough leg and bracket ornament. Chippendale called this type "French" chair. 1760–1780.

4. Easy chair. Philadelphia. Local attributes include C-scrolled arms, cartouches carved on knees, and stump rear legs. 1755–1795.

5. Easy chair. Philadelphia. Unique American example. Note exposed and carved arms and seat rail. (Attributed to Benjamin Randolph, 1721–1791, and carver Hercules Courtenay, 1744?–1784.) 1770–1772.

6. Easy chair. Probably Virginia. Note wide knees and thick hoofed rear feet. 1745–1755.

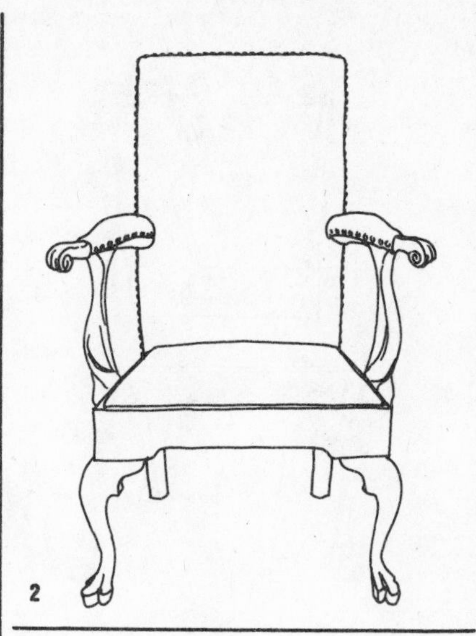

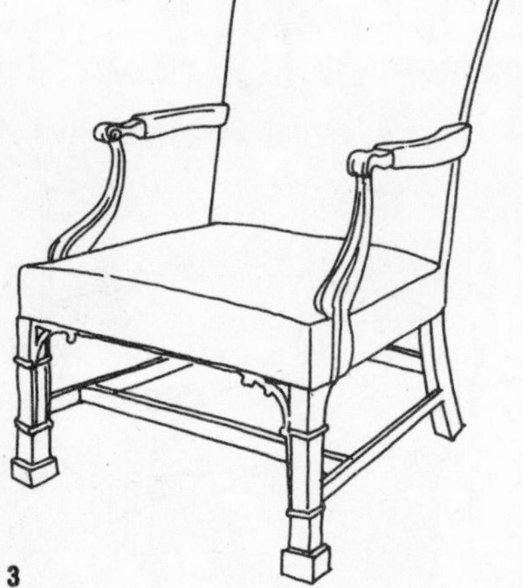

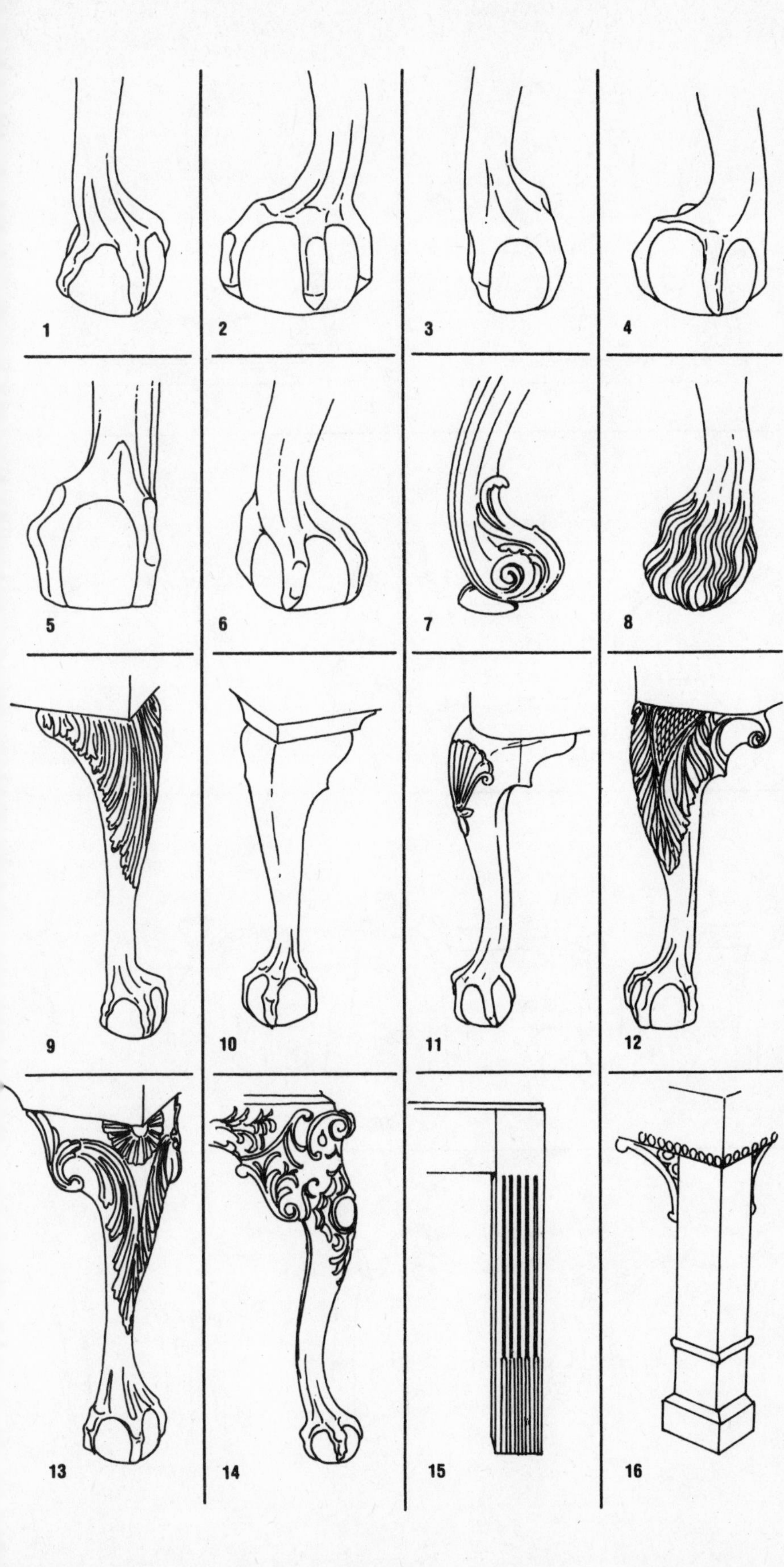

1. Eastern Massachusetts. Sharply curved, elongated talons and swept-back side talons. 1750–1790.

2. Connecticut. Broader talons, roughly carved. 1750–1790.

3. Newport, Rhode Island. Some examples have webbing between talons. 1750–1790.

4. New York. This version boxy in shape. 1750–1790.

5. Philadelphia. Talons well-carved. 1750–1790.

6. Virginia. Talons softly modeled. 1750–1790.

7. Philadelphia scroll foot. Rarely used. 1760–1780.

8. Philadelphia hairy-paw foot. Sometimes used in Massachusetts. 1760–1790.

9. Leafy carving in Massachusetts. Rather flat and stiff in character. 1750–1790.

10. Squared-off cabriole leg apparently never decorated in Connecticut. 1750–1790.

11. Rhode Island. Shell with volutes and pendant. 1750–1790.

12. New York. Flat carving and cross-hatched center of knee. 1750–1790.

13. Philadelphia. Fluid and deeply carved two-part foliage on leg. 1750–1790.

14. Intricately carved South Carolina leg similar to English work. 1760–1780.

15. Rhode Island Marlborough leg with stop fluting. 1760–1790.

16. Philadelphia Marlborough leg, blocked foot, and knee bracket. 1760–1780.

1. Squared seat. Massachusetts. Contains triangular corner blocks. 1750–1790.

2. Squared seat frame. Philadelphia. Has rounded corner blocks. 1750–1790.

3. Note blunt-ended ears on Massachusetts crest rail. 1750–1790.

4. Connecticut crest rail with flaring, rolled back ears and Philadelphia-style shell. 1770–1790.

5. Newport crest rails show variety in treatment. This one relatively plain. 1750–1790.

6. Serpentine crest rail with long knuckles on ears and bold shells and foliage carving seen in some other New York chairs. 1750–1790.

7. Philadelphia crest rail with scrolled, deeply carved ears and elaborate cartouche. 1750–1790.

8. Southern chairs often had simple crest rails ending in gently rounded ears. 1760–1810.

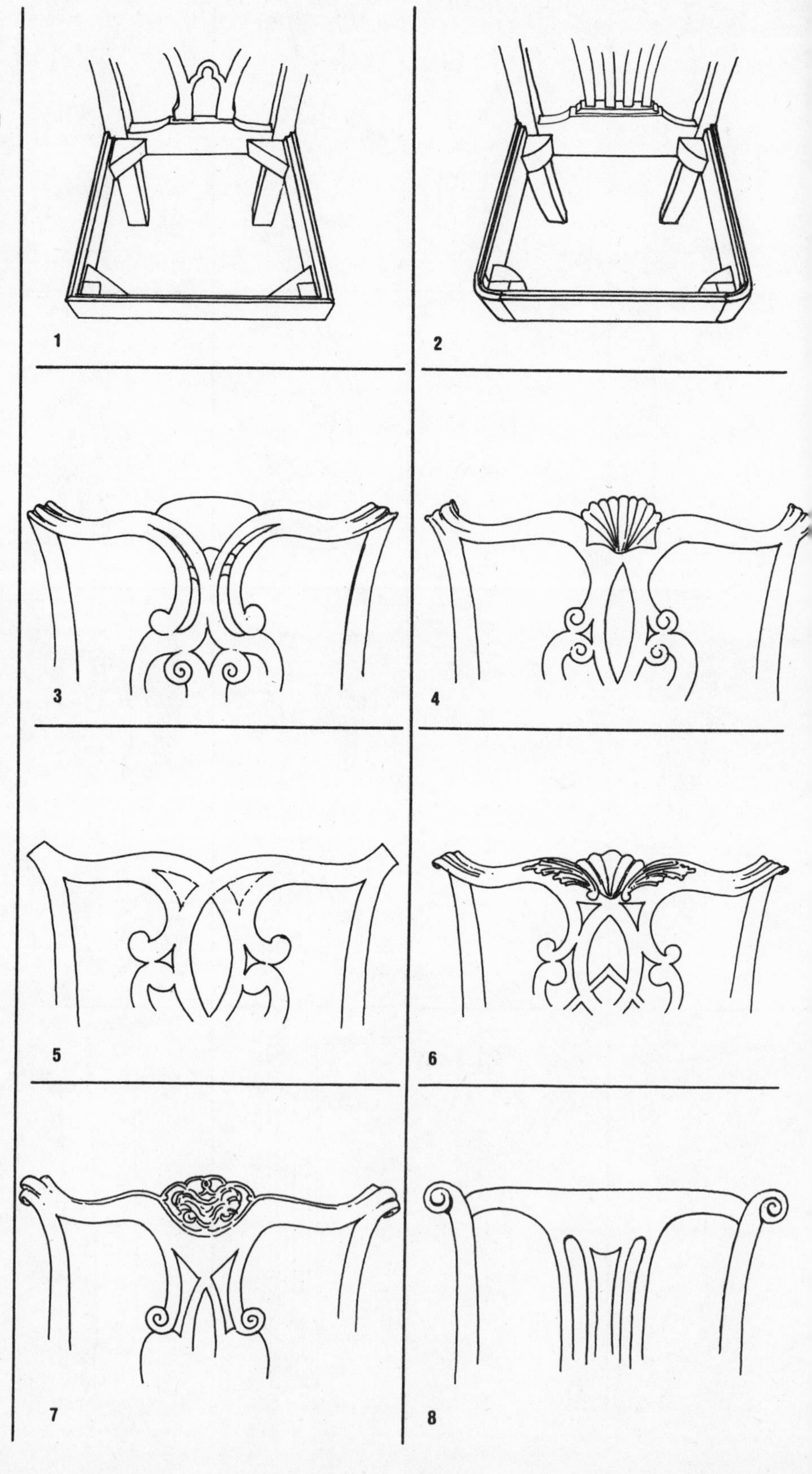

1. Sack-back armchair with comb attachment. Massachusetts. Unusual form also called "triple-back." 1770–1790.

2. Sack-back armchair rocker. Boston. Rockers original, not added at later date as is most often the case. (Branded "Seaver." By William Seaver, a relatively obscure chair maker.) 1790–1800.

3. Child's sack-back armchair. New York. Children's Windsors not common. Bold "milk bottle" turnings on legs were New York feature. 1795–1800.

4. Sack-back armchair. Philadelphia. Type made in large numbers for Philadelphia export trade. Branded "I Henzy." (By Joseph Henzy, b. 1743–?.) 1765–1780.

5. Sack-back armchair. Lancaster County, Pennsylvania. Back originally covered with removable cloth sack for draft protection, not unlike wing chair. 1780–1800.

6. High-backed armchair. Probably Connecticut. Cross-stretchers and swollen legs, also seen on English Windsors. 1760–1800.

7. High-backed writing armchair. Lisbon, Connecticut. Writing surface and drawers for storage incorporated into broadly comfortable chair. (By Ebenezer Tracy, 1744–1803, a well-known Windsor maker.) 1765–1785.

8. High-backed armchair. Philadelphia. Turnings very similar in style to those on Philadelphia William and Mary furniture. Possibly earliest extant American Windsor. 1730–1740.

9. High-backed high chair. Philadelphia. Distinctive turnings on medial stretcher indicate early date. 1730–1750.

1. Low-backed armchair. Rhode Island. Cross-stretchers associated with Rhode Island. 1750–1770.

2. Low-backed armchair. East Hampton, New York. Semioval seat with straight front and slight swell typical of New York. (Inscribed "Nat Dominy/ makg 10/November 11, 1794/ W. R." By Nathaniel Dominy V, 1770–1852, member of a well-documented family of furniture and clock makers.) Dated 1794.

3. Child's low-backed armchair. Probably New Jersey. Late, decorated version. 1840–1850.

4. Low-backed armchair. Philadelphia. Well-defined turnings and "blunt-arrow" feet were Philadelphia characteristics. 1765–1780.

5. Low-backed writing armchair. Philadelphia. Unusual form, especially in Philadelphia. (Branded "A. Steele" by maker Anthony Steele.) 1780–1790.

6. Fan-back armchair. Massachusetts. Distinctive ears on crest rail and serpentine arms ending in deeply carved knuckles were New England characteristics. Note use of bracing spindles to support back. 1780–1800.

7. Fan-back chair. Connecticut. Boldly turned with unusual scalloped crest rail. 1775–1795.

8. Fan-back chair. Probaby Norwich area, Connecticut. Later features include flattened-rod crest rail and bamboo turnings. 1790–1800.

9. Fan-back chair. Connecticut. Note wide splay of legs and braces. 1795–1810.

1. Fan-back chair. Rhode Island. Disked ears on crest rail and pronounced ring turning on leg were Rhode Island characteristics. 1780–1800.

2. Bow-back, continuous armchair. Lisbon, Connecticut. Handsomely turned. Swollen back spindles associated with Connecticut. (Branded by Ebenezer Tracy.) 1785–1795.

3. Bow-back high chair. Probably Connecticut. High peak on front of seat and vertically scrolled arms seen on other New England chairs. 1780–1810.

4. Bow-back chair. New England, probably Connecticut. Bamboo turnings on legs introduced in 1780s. 1790–1810.

5. Bow-back armchair. Rhode Island. Delicately turned back spindles in this design were unusual, but also occasionally seen on Connecticut, New York, and other Rhode Island chairs. 1790–1805.

6. Bow-back, continuous armchair. New York. Illustrates typical Windsor feature of turnings on arm supports echoing those on legs. (Branded by the fairly prolific Walter MacBride, active 1785–1810.) 1785–1810.

7. Bow-back armchair. Philadelphia. Seat originally upholstered. (Branded by little-known maker W. Cox, active 1767–1796.) 1785–1796.

8. Bow-back armchair. Philadelphia. Usual spindle back substituted by pierced slats. 1785–1800.

9. Bow-back armchair. Philadelphia. Note Gothic arches in back. (By John B. Ackerly.) c. 1800.

1. Rod-back chair. Salem, Massachusetts. Unusual arched crest rail greatly adds to overall design. (By James Chapman Tuttle.) 1800–1810.

2. Rod-back chair. Possibly Connecticut. Typical features include double crest rail and squarish, flat seat. 1815–1830.

3. Rod-back armchair. Lancaster, Pennsylvania. Medallions suggest Federal fancy-chair design. (Made by Frederick and Jacob Fetter and decorated by James Williams.) c. 1811.

4. Arrow-back chair. New England. Flaring, curved back and flattened spindles give chair vertical thrust. Common form. 1800–1840.

5. "Stepdown" chair. Farmington, Maine. "Stepdown" refers to shaped crest rail. (By Daniel Stewart.) c. 1820.

6. Arrow-back writing armchair. New England. Shows influence of Empire style in crest rail. 1815–1840.

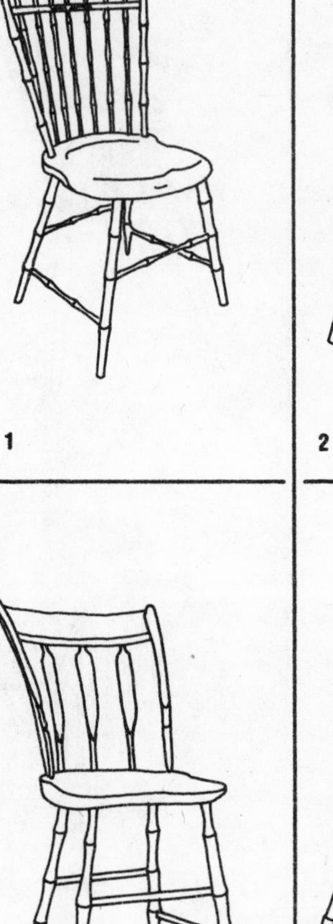

2

3

5

6

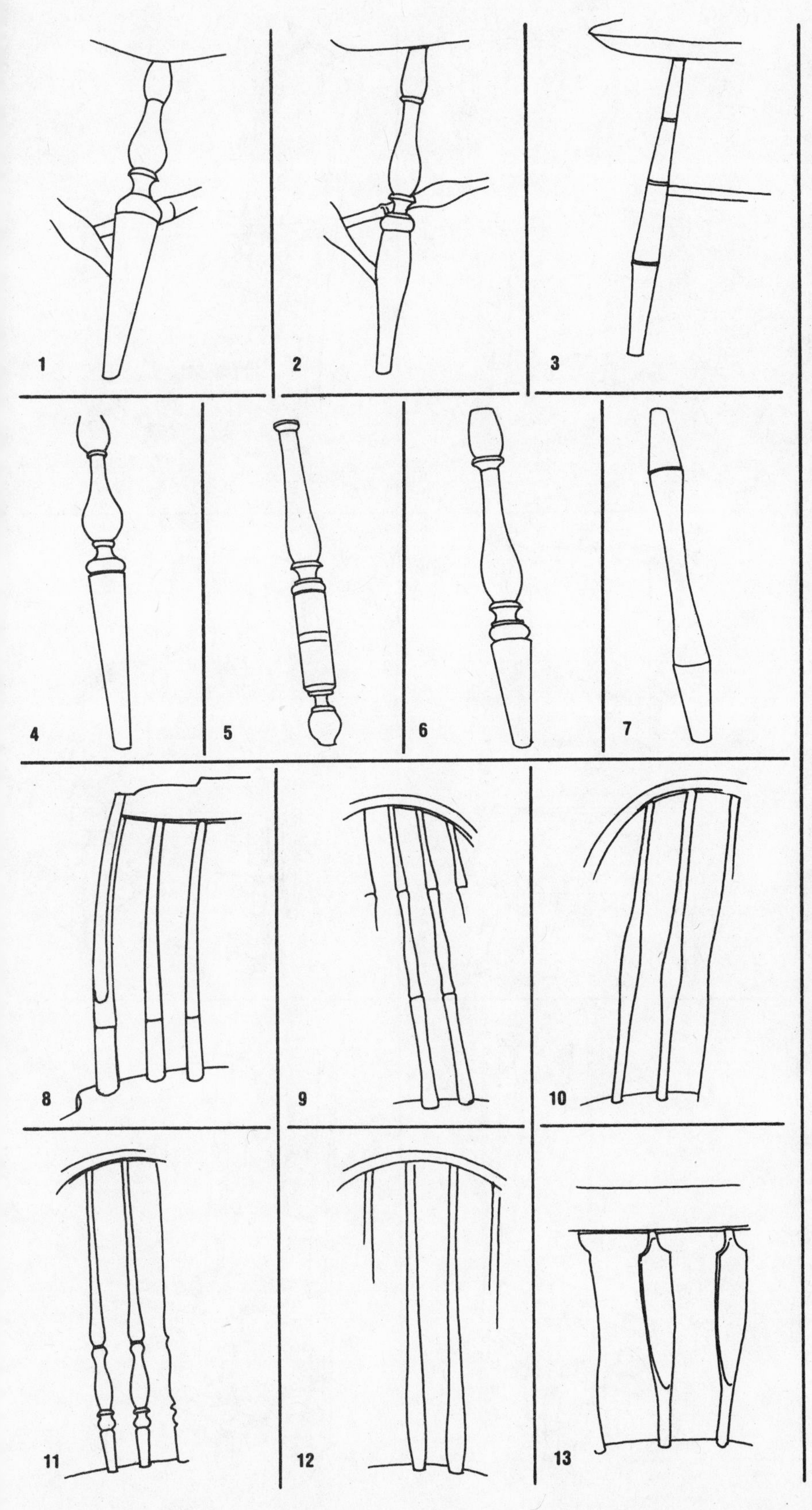

1. Connecticut baluster and ring-turned leg. 1770–1800.

2. Rhode Island baluster and ring-turned leg. Note stop-turning at top baluster and shape of tapered section. Rhode Island baluster turnings tend to be longer than those made by Connecticut craftsmen. 1780–1800.

3. Bamboo turning from New England chair. 1800–1820.

4. Rounded plump baluster with ring turning on New York Windsor leg. 1770–1800.

5. Philadelphia Windsor leg with tall baluster ring and cylindrical turnings ending in blunt arrow foot. 1740–1790.

6. Philadelphia turned leg ending in taper. 1765–1790.

7. Bamboo-turned leg with two swells introduced before one leg with three swells. Philadelphia. 1780–1800.

8. Bent spindle from Maine stepdown Windsor. c. 1820.

9. Bamboo-turned spindle from Massachusetts armchair. 1800–1820.

10. Connecticut spindles tended to swell in the middle. 1770–1800.

11. This distinctively turned spindle is seen on some Rhode Island chairs. 1775–1800.

12. Some spindles on New York chairs thick at bottom. 1770–1800.

13. Arrow from back of Pennsylvania chair. 1820–1840.

1. Armchair. Pennsylvania. Leather-covered chair with modified "wings." Found in Bethlehem. 1730–1750.

2. Armchair. Pennsylvania. Also upholstered in leather, including tops of arms. 1760–1780.

3. Leather armchair. Pennsylvania. Boldly designed armchair, from crest with vine-and-shell carving to hoof-shaped feet. 1760–1790.

4. Armchair. Possibly Lancaster County, Pennsylvania. Joined and turned version of Queen Anne-style chair. 1740–1760.

5. Chair. Pennsylvania. Cruder example of Queen Anne-style chair. 1730–1760.

6. Side chair. Wachovia (now Salem), North Carolina. Made at Moravian settlement. Gently rounded ears on crest rail were Southern features. 1750–1780.

1

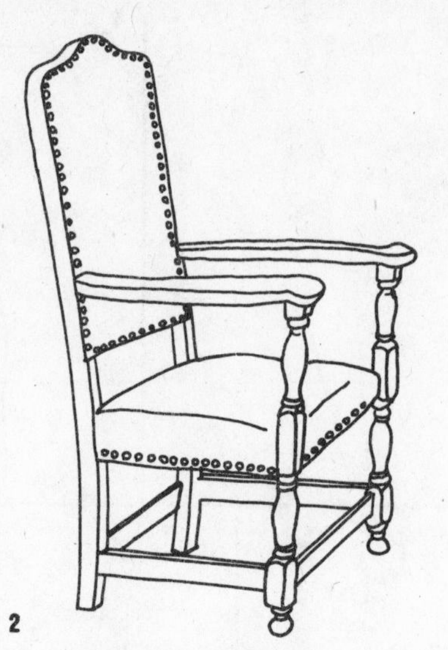

2

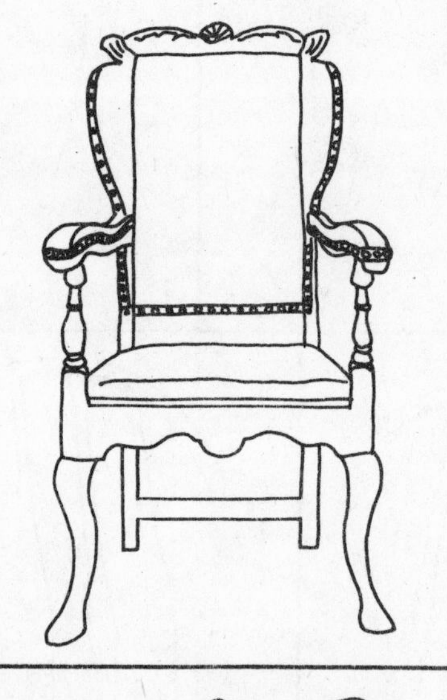

3

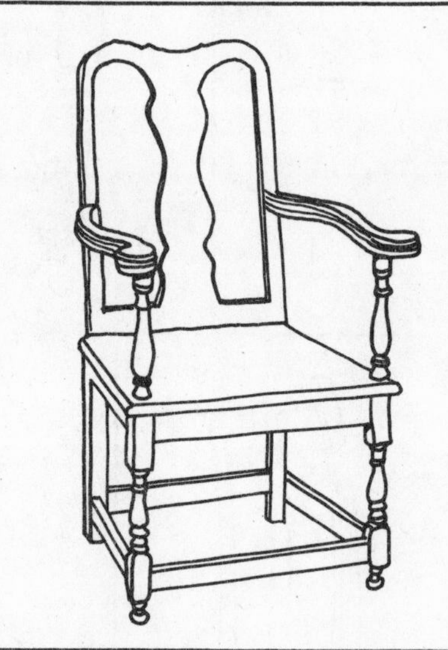

4

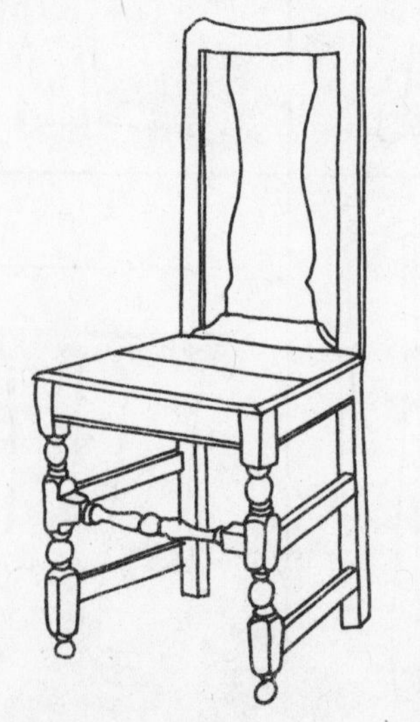

5

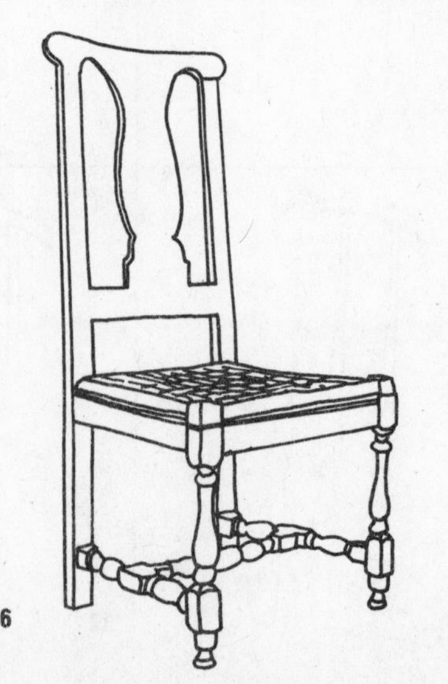

6

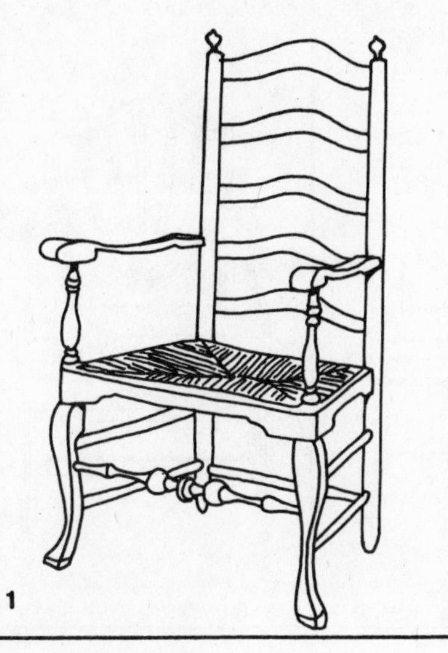

1

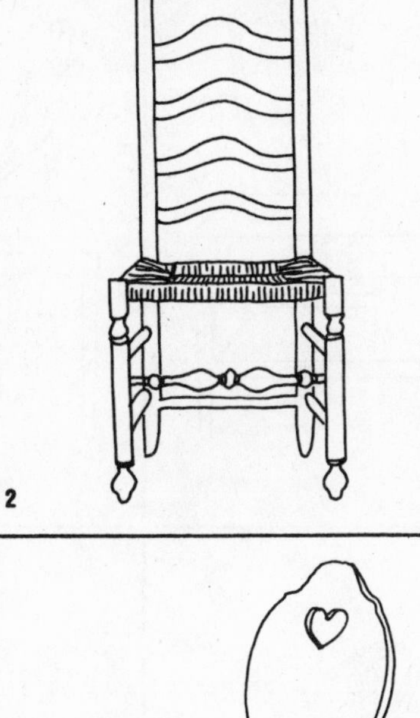

2

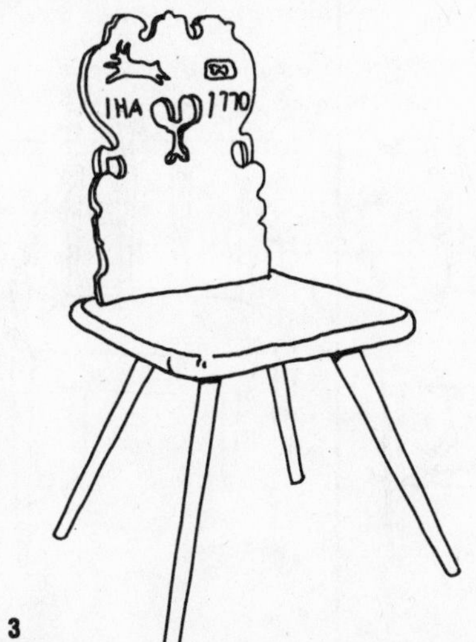

3

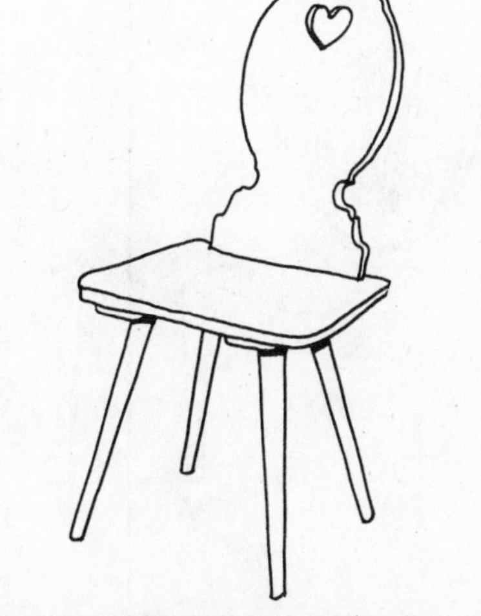

4

1. Armchair. Delaware River Valley. Bulbous finials, serpentine slats, undercut arms, cut seat rail, boldly turned front stretcher, and sharply squared-off cabriole legs all distinctive features. 1730–1800.

2. Chair. Delaware River Valley. Extremely long-lived regional form. 1750–1850.

3. Plank chair. Pennsylvania. Once-common seating form, inspired by northern European prototypes. Dated 1770.

4. Plank chair, or *brettstuhl.* Zoar, Ohio. Made by the communal group the Society of Separatists. Later version of plank chair. 1850–1875.

1. Shield-back chair. Probably Salem, Massachusetts. Very similar to English examples. 1790–1810.

2. Shield-back chair. Salem, Massachusetts. Samuel McIntire may have carved this chair, made for Elias Hasket Derby, the richest merchant in Salem. 1790–1810.

3. Shield-back armchair. Northeastern Massachusetts. Shield-back design seen in both George Hepplewhite's *The Cabinetmaker and Upholster's Guide* and Thomas Sheraton's *Cabinet-Maker and Upholster's Drawing-Book.* 1790–1810.

4. Shield-back chair. Dorchester Lower Mills, Massachusetts. Of heavier proportions than most Federal chairs. Four-ribbed splat seen on other Massachusetts chairs. (Stamped "S. Badlam" for maker Stephen Badlam.) c. 1795.

5. Shield-back chair. Charlestown, Massachusetts. Sharply cornered shield with tasseled splats seen on other Massachusetts chairs. (Labeled by maker Jacob Forster, active 1786–1838.) c. 1795.

6. Square-back armchair. Salem, Massachusetts. Copied from Sheraton's *Drawing-Book,* Plate 33. Possibly carved by Samuel McIntire. 1792–1810.

7. Square-back chair. Salem, Massachusetts. Gothic back with intersecting splats borrowed from plate in Hepplewhite's *Guide.* c. 1800.

8. Square-back armchair. Boston. Chair is painted and has carved seat. (Possibly by John Seymour, c. 1738–1815, and/or Thomas Seymour, 1771–1848.) c. 1800.

9. Shield-back chair. New England. Vernacular version with rush seat. 1790–1810.

1

2

3

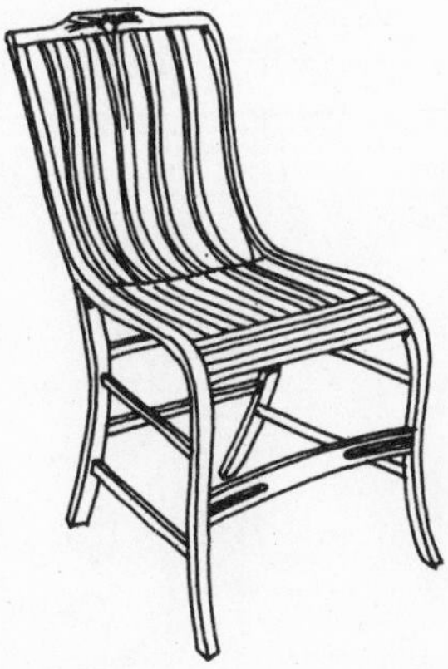

4

5

6

7

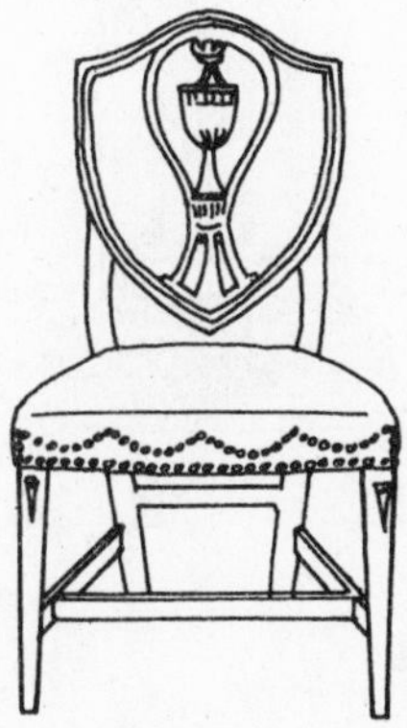

8

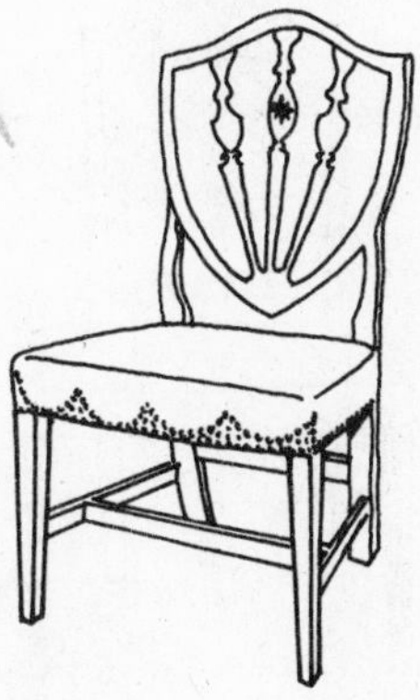

9

1. Square-back chair. Boston. Mahogany chair highlighted by figured birch veneer. (Attributed to John and/or Thomas Seymour.) 1805–1815.

2. Oval-back chair. Salem, Massachusetts. Feather-and-ribbon back also seen on English chairs. 1790–1810.

3. Oval-back chair. Eastern Massachusetts. Chair with painted decoration made for Elias Hasket Derby. 1790–1800.

4. Chair. Boston. Samuel Gragg (active 1800–1830) patented this "elastic" chair of steam-bent wood in 1808.

5. Chair. Eastern Massachusetts. Such Sheraton-painted fancy chairs were very popular. This one made for George Crowninshield's *Cleopatra's Barge*, an early American pleasure yacht. 1815–1830.

6. Chair. Probably New England. Shape of back similar to those on some Chippendale chairs. c. 1795.

7. Heart-back chair. Connecticut. Inspired by shield-back. Chair more curvaceous than most shield-backs. c. 1795.

8. Shield-back chair. Hartford, Connecticut. Copied from Plate 5 of Hepplewhite's *Guide* (1788). c. 1800.

9. Shield-back chair. Connecticut. Note inlaid decoration and tacks arranged in swag pattern. c. 1800.

1. Chair. Hartford, Connecticut. Shares many attributes with Chippendale-style chairs. This type of chair with this specific splat associated with Connecticut and Rhode Island. (Attributed to Samuel Kneeland and Lemuel Adams, in partnership 1792–1796.) c. 1795.

2. Chair. Connecticut. Although it contains the same distinctive splat, the taller back makes the overall proportions of this chair more awkward. c. 1795.

3. Toilet chair. Probably Connecticut. Yet another version, this less sophisticated example has Chippendale-style ears and a carved, ribbed shell on the front. 1795–1815.

4. Chair. Connecticut or Rhode Island. Top of back follows serpentine line of shield-back. c. 1795.

5. Chair. Rhode Island. In this chair, splat bearing drapery and kylix substitutes for splat with urn. c. 1795.

6. Square-back chair. New York. Design derived from Sheraton's *Drawing-Book*, Plate 36, Number 1. Often copied by New York chair makers. 1795–1815.

7. Square-back chair. New York. Based on Plate 36, Number 2, of Sheraton's *Drawing-Book*. Note reeded spade legs favored in New York. c. 1800.

8. Square-back chair. New York or Albany. Painted white with gilt and red decoration. 1800–1810.

9. Square-back chair. New York. Design associated with chair makers Abraham Slover and Jacob Taylor (in partnership 1802–1805), but also made in other New York shops. 1800–1810.

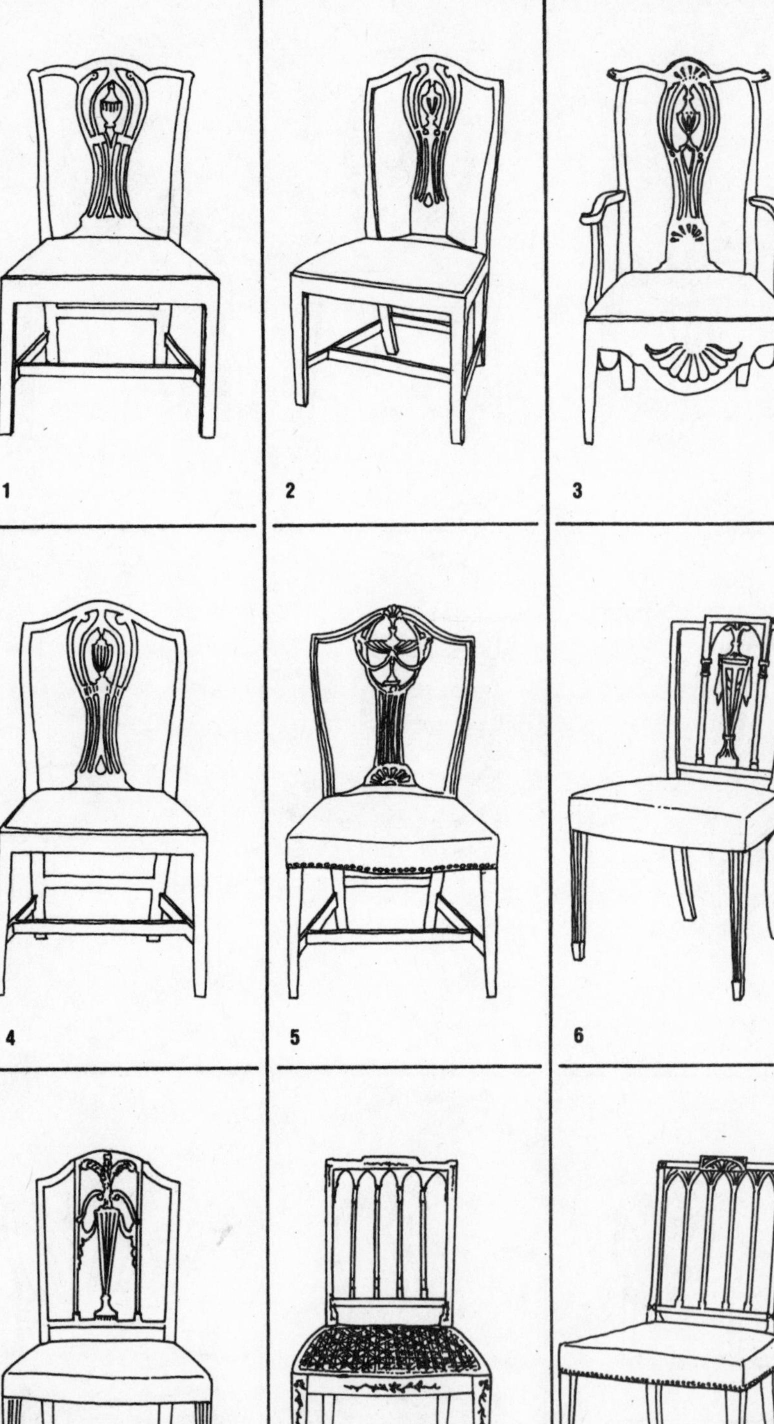

1 2 3 4 5

6

7 8

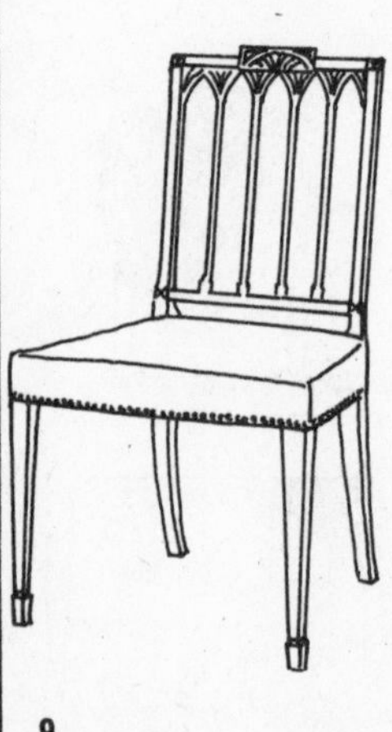

9

1. Square-back armchair. New York. Has drapery rather than sunburst in tablet at top. 1800–1810.

2. Shield-back armchair. New York. Flaring front legs associated with New York when seen on an American chair. Concave arm supports and serpentine arms seen on other New York chairs. 1790–1800.

3. Shield-back chair. New York. Shape of back based on Hepplewhite's *Guide*, Plate 2. 1790–1800.

4. Shield-back chair. New York. Unusual combination of carving and inlay. Design of splat more common on Philadelphia and Baltimore chairs. 1790–1800.

5. Shield-back chair. New York. Drapery and feather splats seen on other New York chairs. Stretchers rare. 1795–1800.

6. Scroll-back armchair. New York. Part of a set of ten side chairs and another armchair. (Produced by the workshop of Duncan Phyfe; documented by a bill.) 1807.

7. Scroll-back chair. New York. Single-cross-backed chairs cheaper than double-cross ones. Turned and reeded leg interchangeable with saber leg. (Attributed to the workshop of Duncan Phyfe.) c. 1807.

8. Chair. New York. Fancy chair with landscape painted on back. This particular chair belonged to the Van Rensselaer family. 1815–1825.

9. Square-back chair. New York City. Similar chairs found in Connecticut and on Long Island. Of seemingly modern design. 1780–1810.

1. Chair. Connecticut, Rhode Island, or New York. Overall form, including pierced splat, similar to that of other New England chairs. 1785–1810.

2. Shield-back chair. Philadelphia. Loosely based on Hepplewhite's *Guide*, Plate 7. Note serpentine seat rail seen on other Philadelphia Federal chairs. 1790–1800.

3. Shield-back chair. Philadelphia or the South. Inspired by Hepplewhite's *Guide*, Plate 4. Broad back with round bottom. 1790–1800.

4. Shield-back chair. Philadelphia or the South. Design of the urn and ribbed splat not often seen. 1790–1800.

5. Shield-back chair. Pennsylvania. Chairs with five splats and tassel carvings in the back made in many states and in England. 1790–1810.

6. Square-back armchair. Philadelphia. Part of a specialty order of furniture made of ebony. (By the workshop of Ephraim Haines, 1755–1837.) 1807.

7. Square-back chair. Philadelphia. Design of back based on Plate 28 in Sheraton's *Drawing-Book* (1802). Also seen in New York furniture. c. 1800.

8. Square-back chair. Philadelphia. Here, chair maker has combined two plates from Sheraton's *Drawing-Book*, rather than simply copying one. c. 1800.

9. Square-back chair. Philadelphia. Several such Philadelphia "urn-back" chairs survive. c. 1800.

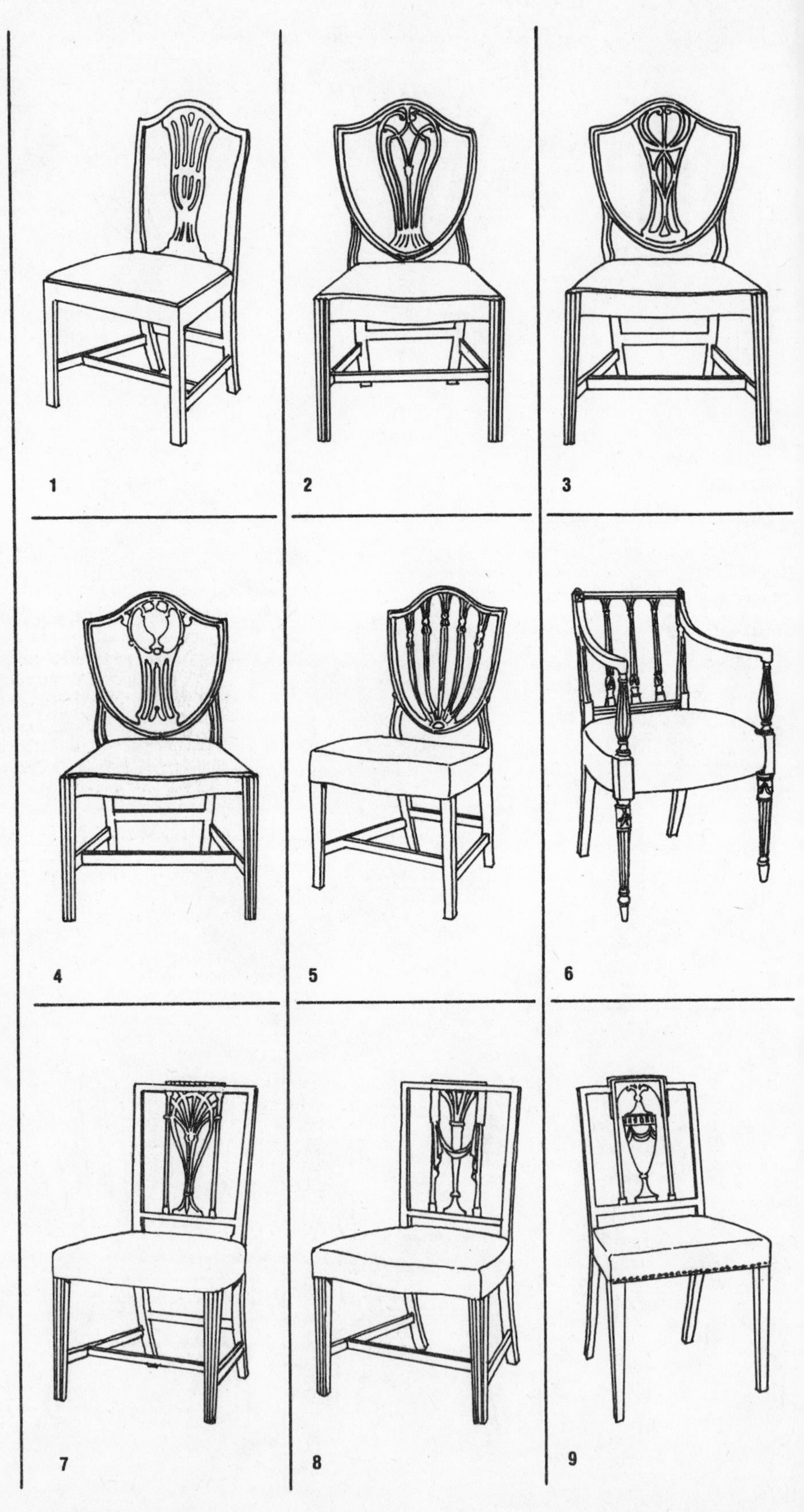

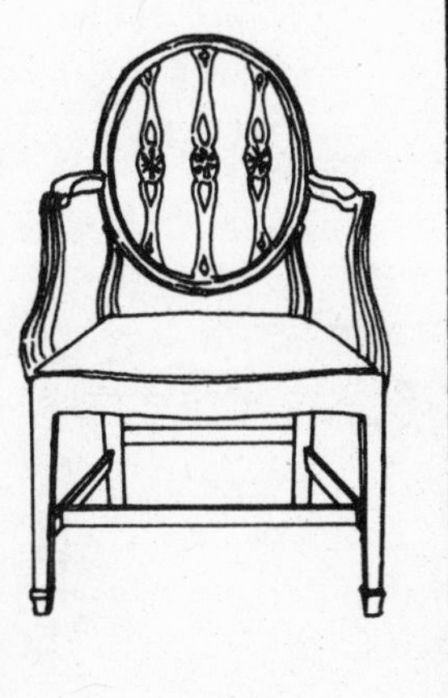
1

2

3

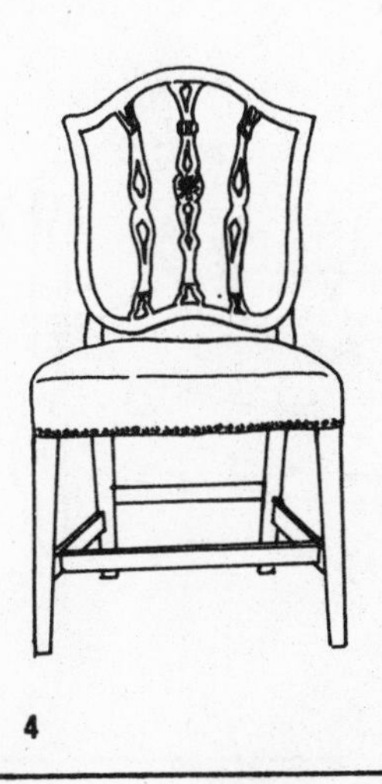
4

5

6

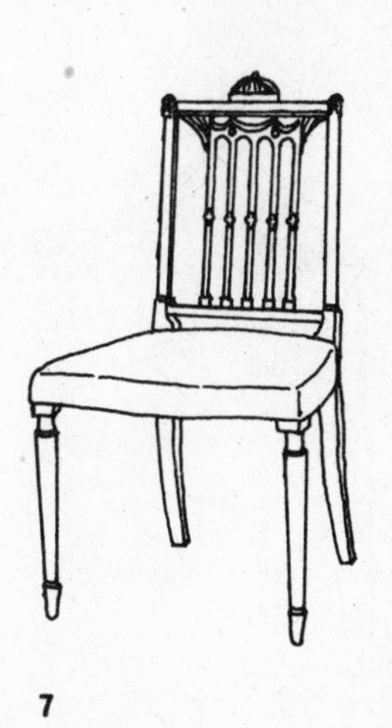
7

8

9

1. Oval-back armchair. Philadelphia or Maryland. Apparently, chairs of this design were more popular in Britain than in America. 1785–1795.

2. Shield-back chair. Maryland. Four-ribbed splat had been popular during the Chippendale period in the South. 1785–1810.

3. Shield-back chair. Annapolis, Maryland. With double eagle's heads in splat, highly patriotic chair. (Labeled by noted furniture maker John Shaw, 1745–1829.) c. 1795.

4. Chair. Maryland. Pierced splats similar to those seen on riddle-back chairs. c. 1800.

5. Shield-back chair. Baltimore or Annapolis, Maryland. Back combines a corn-husk motif from Hepplewhite's *Guide* with overall design from Sheraton's *Drawing-Book*. Other Maryland chairs had partial upholstery over the seat rail. c. 1800.

6. Heart-back chair. Baltimore, Maryland. Heart-backs were made all along the East Coast. Note inlaid detail on back. 1790–1800.

7. Square-back chair. Maryland. Crown-topped square-back copied from Hepplewhite's *Guide*, Plate 9. 1790–1810.

8. Chair. Baltimore, Maryland. Baltimore was noted for fine painted furniture during this period. 1800–1810.

9. Chair. Baltimore, Maryland. Some painted furniture was extremely high style during Federal period. (Matching sofa signed by Thomas S. Renshaw and John Barnhart, the decorator.) c. 1815.

1. Shield-back chair. Charleston, South Carolina. Drapery carving within shield most often seen on Massachusetts and New York chairs. 1795–1800.

2. Lolling chair. Massachusetts. One form of easy chair popular during the Federal period. c. 1795.

3. Lolling chair. Massachusetts or Rhode Island. Note unusual serpentine line of sides and top. 1800–1810.

4. Upholstered tub-shaped armchair. Boston. One of a set of thirty made for Boston's State House by George Bright (1727–1805). 1797.

5. Lolling chair. Boston. Well-proportioned chair with flaring back. (Labeled by maker Lemuel Churchill, active 1805–c. 1828.) c. 1805.

6. Lolling chair. Salem, Massachusetts. Inspired by Plate 35 in Sheraton's *Drawing-Book*. One of a set of chairs made *en suite* with a sofa. c. 1805.

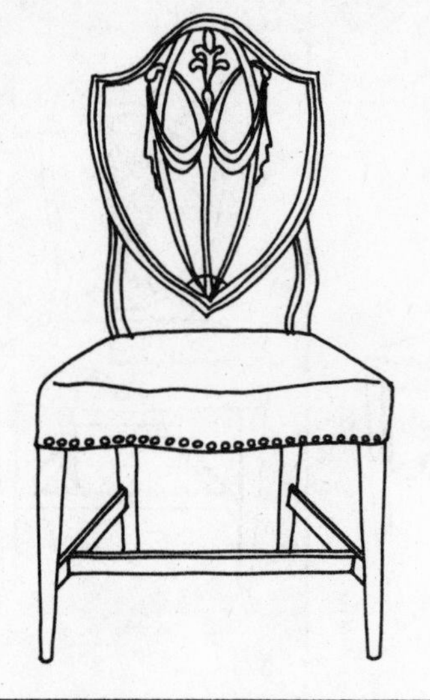

1

2

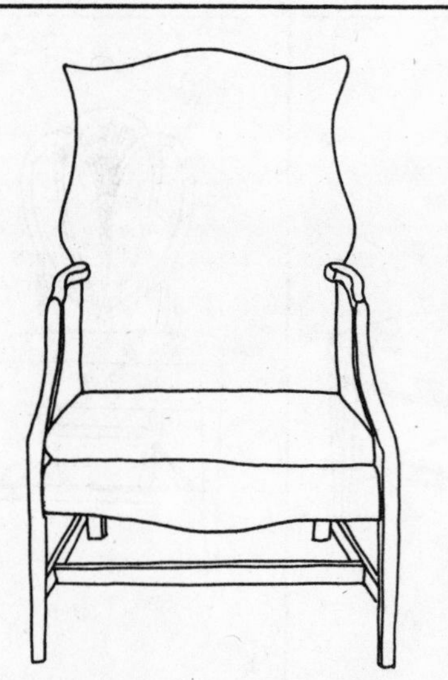

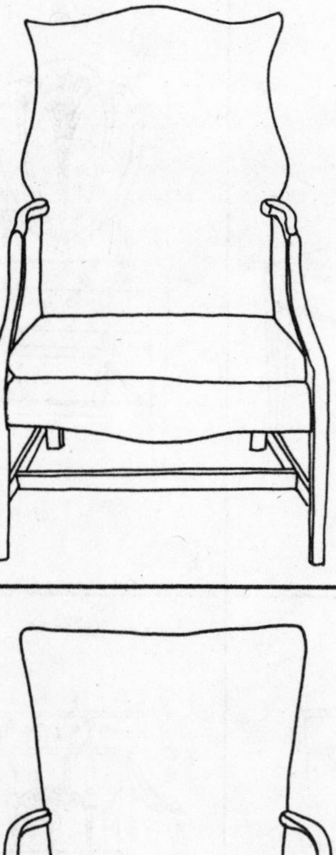

3

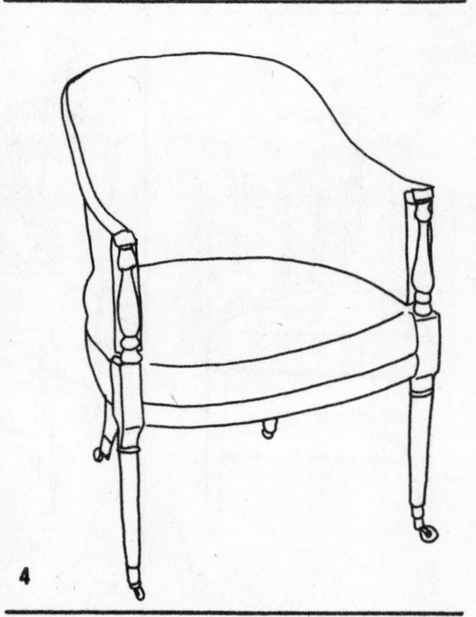

4

5

6

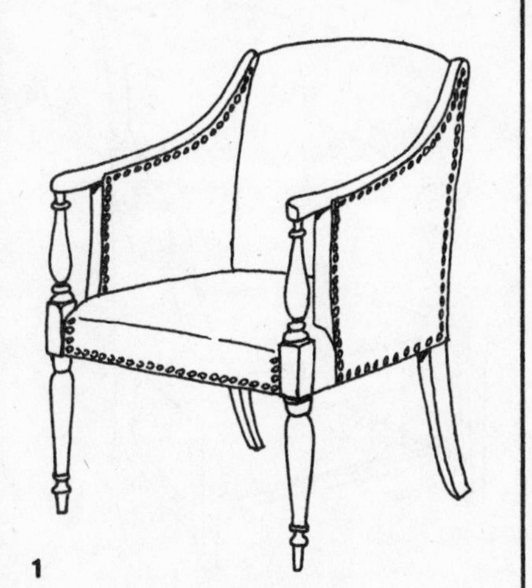

1

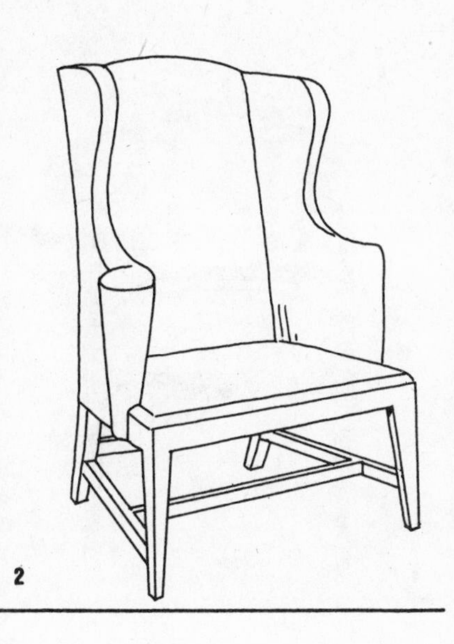

2

3

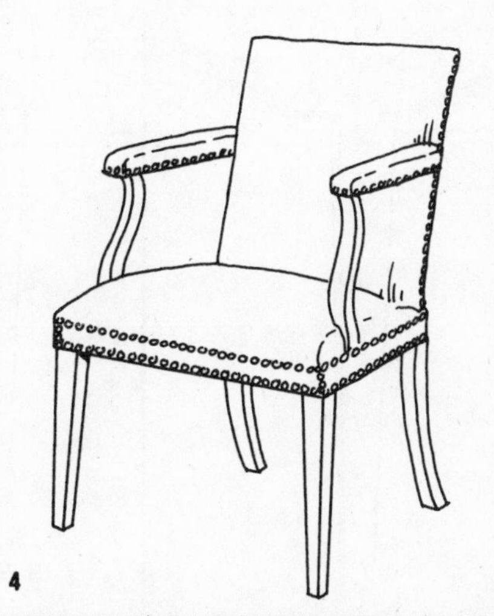

4

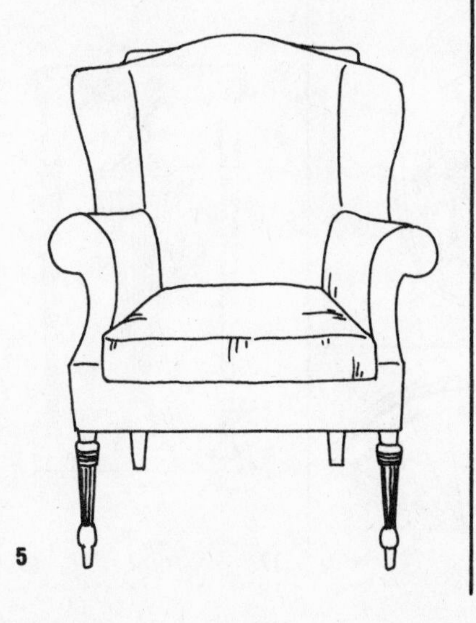

5

6

1. Upholstered armchair. Boston. Note delicate carving of arm supports and legs. 1800–1810.

2. Easy chair. New England, possibly Connecticut. Combination toilet–easy chair has exposed seat rail and sharply tapering front legs. 1790–1810.

3. Easy chair. New York. Later features include cylindrical legs, softly C-scrolled arms, and serpentine back. 1800–1810.

4. Upholstered armchair. Philadelphia. One of many chairs made by Thomas Affleck for the Senate and House of Representatives when Congress met in Philadelphia. 1791–1793.

5. Easy chair. Philadelphia. Reeded legs and bulb feet associated with Philadelphia. Federal easy chairs tend to have deeper wings than their Chippendale counterparts. 1800–1810.

6. Circular easy chair. Philadelphia. Form popular among chair makers of this city. 1805–1815.

1. "Cabriole" armchair. Philadelphia. Painted white and gold after the French fashion. Such chairs called "cabriole" chairs by Heppelwhite and "drawing-room" chairs by Sheraton. c. 1800.

2. Easy chair. Baltimore, Maryland. Downward slanting arms were Baltimore characteristic. 1790–1800.

3. Tapered leg seen in all regions during Federal period. 1790–1810.

4. Spade leg differs from the tapered leg in that it has a block at the bottom of the leg. 1790–1810.

5. Reeded leg popular through much of first half of 19th century.

6. Sunburst inlay from back of Connecticut shield-back, c.1800.

7. Patera inlay from Boston side chair dated c. 1800.

8. Eagle inlay common motif on Federal furniture. When placed on heart-shaped chair back, often considered a Baltimore characteristic.

9. Fan inlay used at base of shield-back chairs. This example from Charlestown, Massachusetts. c. 1795.

10. Commonly found splat on New York square-back chairs enlivened by inlay. 1790–1800.

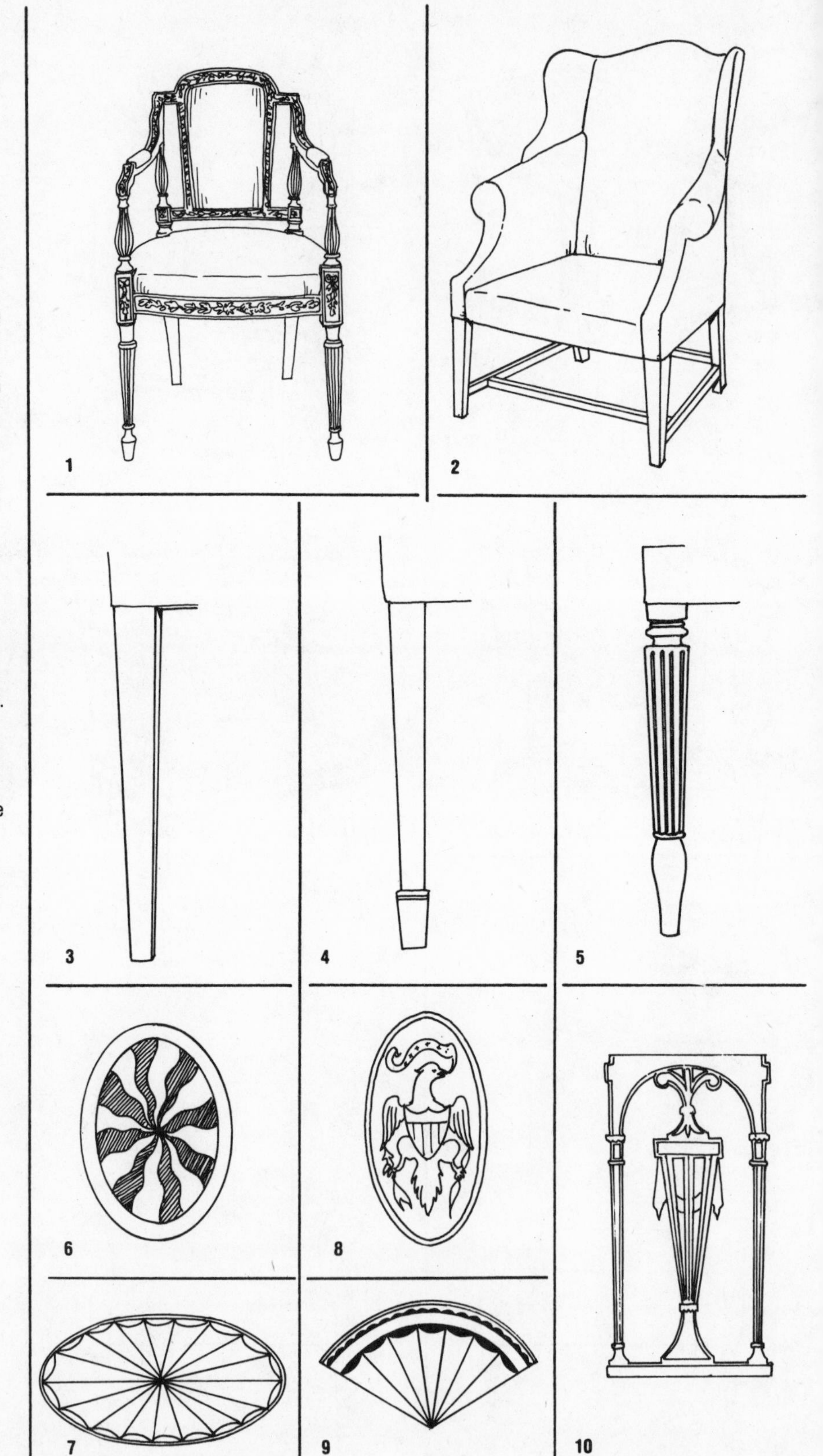

1

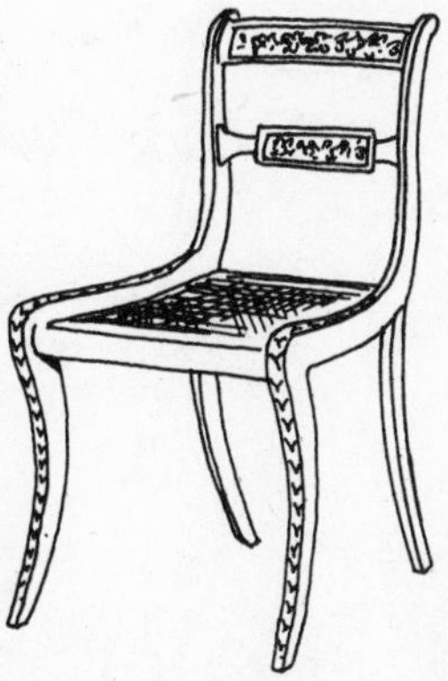

2

3

4

5

6

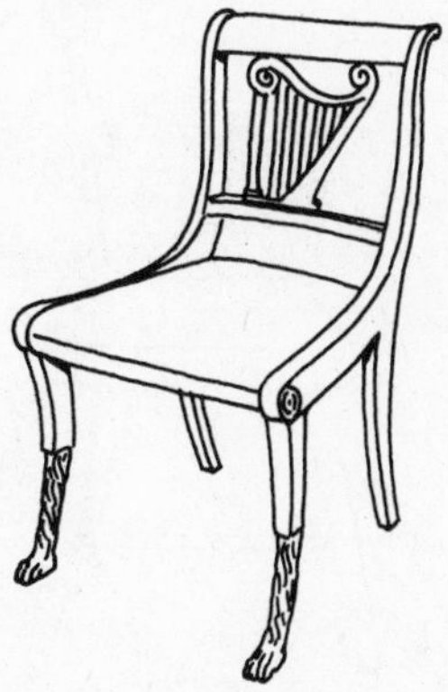

7

8

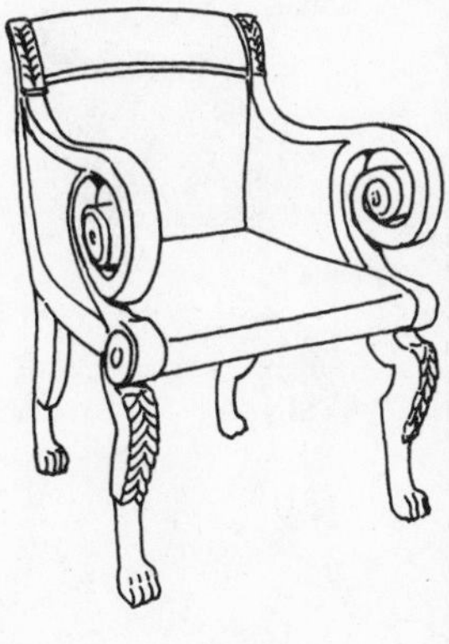

9

1. Armchair. Boston. Klismos chair inspired by ancient Greek prototype. 1815–1830.

2. Chair. Boston. Typical klismos side chair with wide top rail and curved stiles that "flow" into saber legs. This example had brass inlay. 1818–1830

3. Armchair. Massachusetts. Classical motifs include dolphins in crest rail and as arm supports, animal paw feet, and detailing around seat rail. c. 1825.

4. Chair. Possibly Connecticut. Turned and painted version of eagle-back klismos chair. 1820–1840.

5. Chair. Hitchcocksville, Connecticut. The Hitchcock factory produced this chair featuring freehand and stenciled decoration; other factories made similar pieces. (Stenciled on the back of seat rail "Hitchcock Alfred Co. Hitchcocksville, Conn. Warranted.") 1829–1843.

6. Chair. New York. Lyre-back chairs once fairly common. 1810–1820.

7. Chair. New York. Back incorporates Classical harp motif. Such chairs were made by many New York chairmakers. 1810–1820.

8. Chair. New York. Patriotic eagle symbol was variant splat used on scroll-back chairs. 1810–1820.

9. Armchair. New York or Philadelphia. Note strong scroll of arms and seat rail and animal feet. 1815–1825.

1. Chair. New York. Decoration includes gilded ornamentation, anthemia, acanthus leaves, and gadrooning along the seat rail; this last element also seen on New York Chippendale chairs. 1815–1825.

2. Chair. New York. This klismos (or scroll-back) chair has a cornucopia back and animal paw front legs. 1815–1825.

3. Chair. New York. Much simpler oval splat used on this klismos chair. 1810–1820.

4. Chair. New York. "Curule" or "Grecian cross-legged" chair apparently made only in New York during this period and then rarely. 1810–1815.

5. Armchair. New York. Fancy armchair ornamented by gilt decoration and metal mounts of Classical design. 1815–1825.

6. Chair. Albany, New York. Originally had carved eagle head attached to top of crest rail. (Attributed to William Buttre on the basis of a newspaper advertise-ment.) c. 1815.

7. Chair. Philadelphia. Very similar to ancient Greek forms. Lavish painted decoration incorporates motifs from several ancient civilizations. 1820–1830.

8. Chair. Probably Philadelphia. Made for Nicholas Biddle's house Andalusia. Scrolled crest rail not often seen on klismos side chairs. c. 1830.

9. Chair. Possibly Pennsylvania. Wide crest rail seen on Classical chairs incorporated into turned, less sophisticated ones. 1830–1850.

1

2

3

4

5

6

1. Chair. Baltimore, Maryland. Painted klismos chair with caned seat. 1820–1830.

2. Chair. Baltimore, Maryland. Designs for such a chair appeared in J. C. Loudon's *Encyclopaedia of Cottage, Farm, and Villa Architecture and Furniture* (1833). 1830–1840.

3. Sling-seated, Campeachy, or Spanish armchair. New York. Another version of the Roman curule chair. 1810–1820.

4. Circular easy chair. Philadelphia. Bold example with typical Philadelphia legs. 1805–1815.

5. Easy chair. Possibly Annapolis, Maryland. Note heavy turnings on legs. 1810–1820.

6. Armchair. America. Arm supports resemble swans' necks. Called "Voltaire" chair. 1815–1830.

1. Armchair. New England. Simplified Grecian forms continued to be popular through much of the 19th century. Wide splat and crest rail indicative of relatively late date. 1830–1845.

2. "Boston" rocking armchair. New England. Extremely popular furniture form, not necessarily invented in Boston. This relatively early example dates from 1825–1840.

3. Chair. Massachusetts. Similar to chairs designed by Joseph Meeks and John Hall. 1830–1850.

4. Chair. New York. Egyptian Revival influence seen in splat and seat rail. c. 1830.

5. Chair. New York. Part of a set of furniture made for New York lawyer Samuel Foot. (By Duncan Phyfe.) 1837.

6. Chair. New York. Note feminine outline of chair back and simple saber legs. c. 1840.

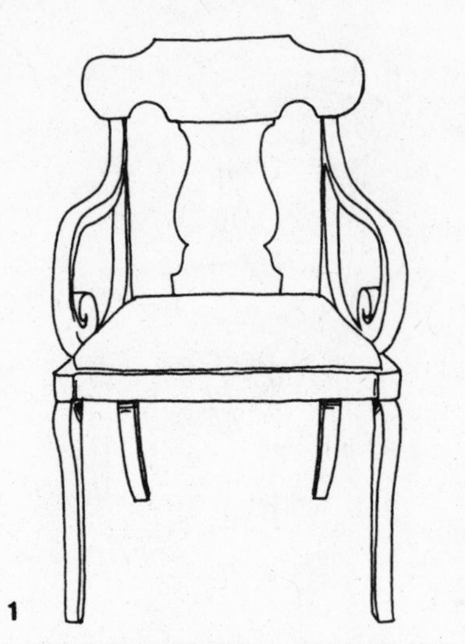
1

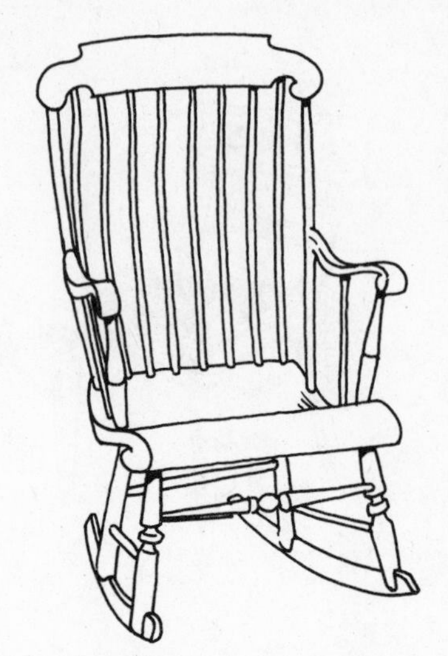
2

3

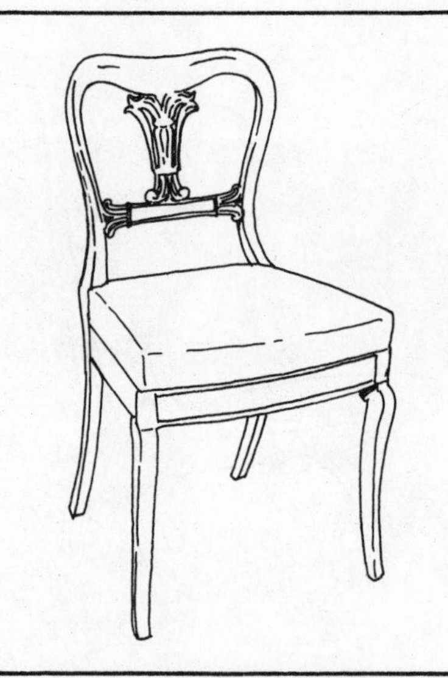
4

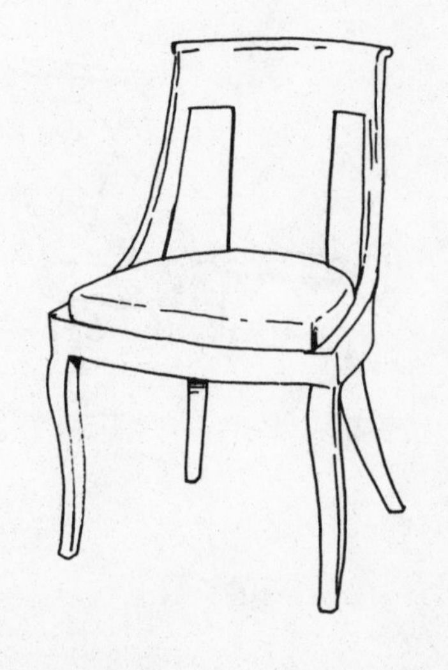
5

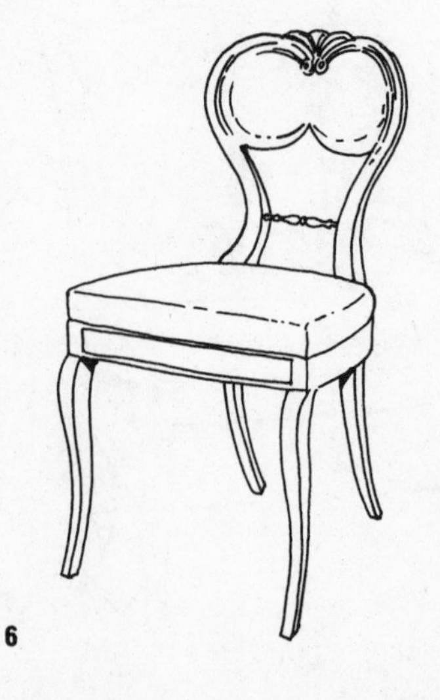
6

1

2

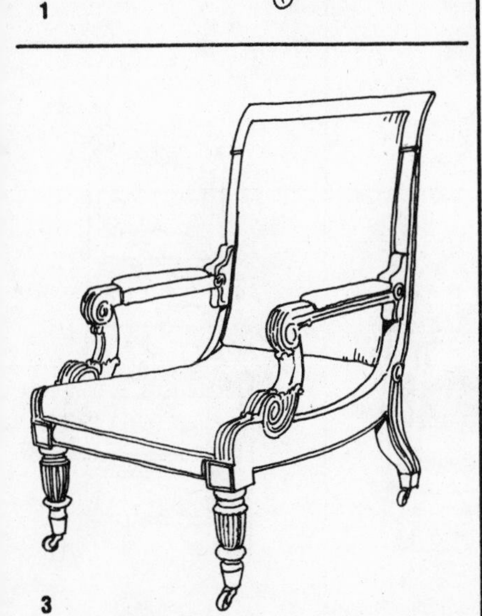

3

4

5

6

1. Chair. America. Has simplified lyre-back and broad curves. 1835–1840.

2. Armchair. Boston or Salem, Massachusetts. Based on English prototypes. 1830–1840.

3. Upholstered armchair. Boston. Has reclining back and footrest which pulls out. (Labeled by maker William Hancock, active 1820–1849.) 1829–1831.

4. Upholstered armchair. New York. Type of easy chair referred to as "Voltaire" chair; period term. 1815–1840.

5. Upholstered armchair. New York. Based on French Restauration style. 1830–1840.

6. Upholstered armchair. America. Type known as "bergère," with rounded, relatively low back. 1820–1840.

1. Rocking chair. Canterbury, New Hampshire. Relatively early version. 1820–1860.

2. Chair. Enfield, New Hampshire. Characteristics associated with Enfield include "candle-flame" finials, relatively thin stiles, and caned seat. 1840–1870.

3. Dining chair. Hancock, Massachusetts. Dining chairs had low backs so that they could be stored underneath tables. 1840–1850.

4. Rocking chair. Hancock, Massachusetts. Has distinctive rounded finials on back stiles and flattened "mushroom" finials on arms. Unlike Mount Lebanon examples of same date, not marked. c. 1890.

5. Rocking chair. Mount Lebanon, New York. Early and rather crude Shaker rocker. c. 1810.

6. Chair. Mount Lebanon, New York. Typical rush-bottomed Shaker chair. 1830–1850.

7. Chair. Mount Lebanon, New York. Note tilters on back legs to aid in leaning back. The Shakers invented such tilters. 1840–1870.

8. Rocking chair. Mount Lebanon, New York. Extremely narrow chair made to order for a sister in New England. c. 1850.

9. Revolving swivel chair. Mount Lebanon, New York. Form invented by Shakers for use in workplaces in mid-19th century. 1850–1875.

1

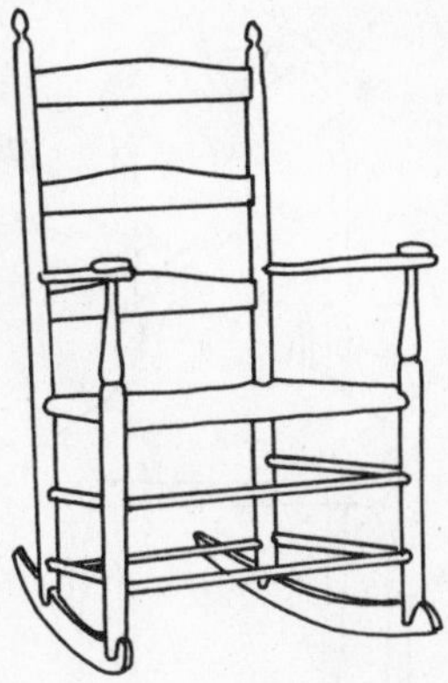

2

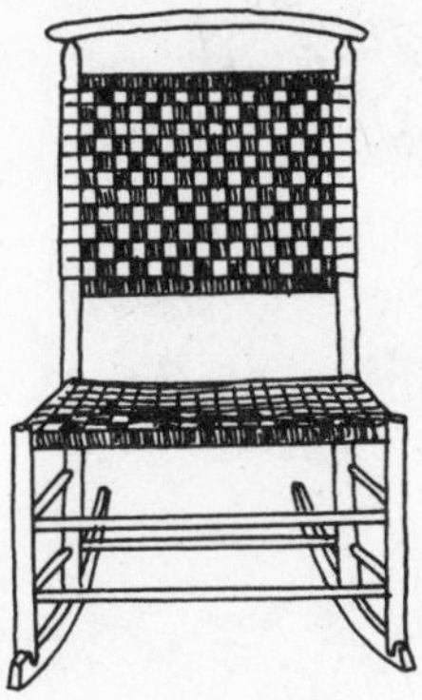

3

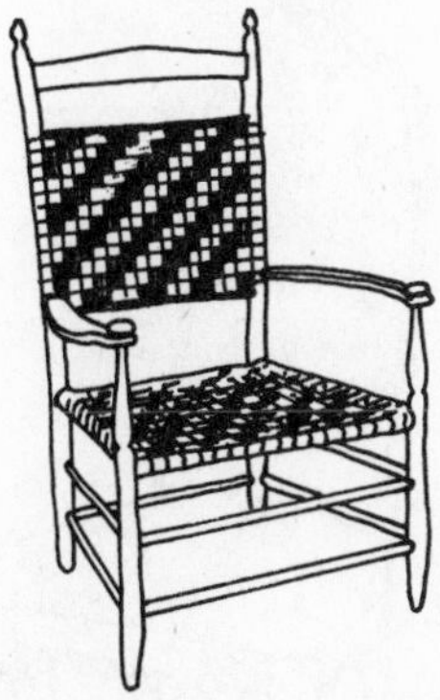

4

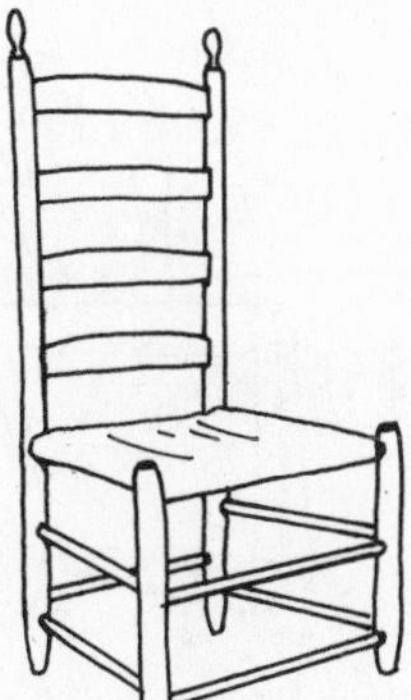

5

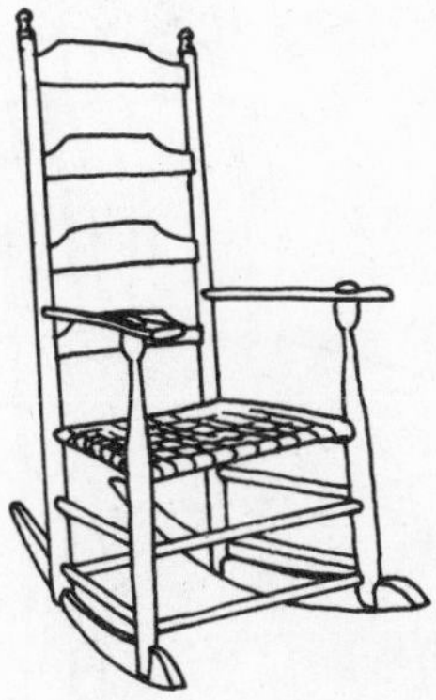

6

1. Rocking chair. Mount Lebanon, New York. Design influenced by Thonet bentwood furniture and patented by Shakers in 1874. (Made by the South family.) 1874–1900.

2. Rocking chair. Mount Lebanon, New York. Representative of commercial line introduced for public consumption in 1875. (Labeled "Shaker's/N° 3/Trade Mark/Mt. Lebanon, NY.") 1875–1900.

3. Rocking chair. Mount Lebanon, New York. Shaker chairs noted for woven tape seats and backs. Bar at top used to hang cushions. 1875–1910.

4. Armchair. Mount Lebanon, New York. No. 7 was largest chair size sold. Chairs from this community usually have pointed, yet rounded finials and dome-shaped "mushroom" finials on arms. 1875–1910.

5. Chair. North Union, Ohio. Four-slat side chairs are often associated with the Western Shaker communities. 1840–1875.

6. Rocking chair. Union Valley, Ohio. Slats with notched corners seen on other chairs from Western communities. c. 1850.

1. Chair. Boston or New York. Note twist turnings on legs and uprights. Gothic Revival style not as popular in United States as it was in Britain. 1840–1850.

2. Chair. New York. Note prevalence of organic forms from rustic, "hoofed" feet to foliated crockets. (Designed by architect Alexander Jackson Davis, 1803–1892.) 1830–1840.

3. Chair. New York. Chair made for Hudson River Valley villa Lyndhurst, designed in the Gothic style by A. J. Davis. Davis also designed this wheel-shaped-back chair. (Made by Richard Byrne, 1805–1883, or Ambrose Wright, c. 1794–after 1866.) c. 1842.

4. Chair. New York. Lancet arches and trefoils worked into back. (Stenciled by makers Alexander and Frederick Roux, in partnership 1837–1881.) 1842.

5. Upholstered armchair. Probably New York. American easy chairs with Gothic ornamentation were rare. c. 1850.

6. Chair. Newark, New Jersey. During 19th century, Gothic style was thought most suitable for library furniture. (By John Jelliff, active 1835–1890.) c. 1855.

7. Chair. New York. Twist turning characteristic of Elizabethan Revival, as the style was called during the 19th century. 1845–1855.

8. Chair. New York. Elizabethan Revival style hall chair made for Astor family. (Labeled by Alexander Roux, active 1837–1881.) 1850–1857.

9. Armchair. "Spool-turned" objects generally termed Elizabethan Revival in style. 1865–1885.

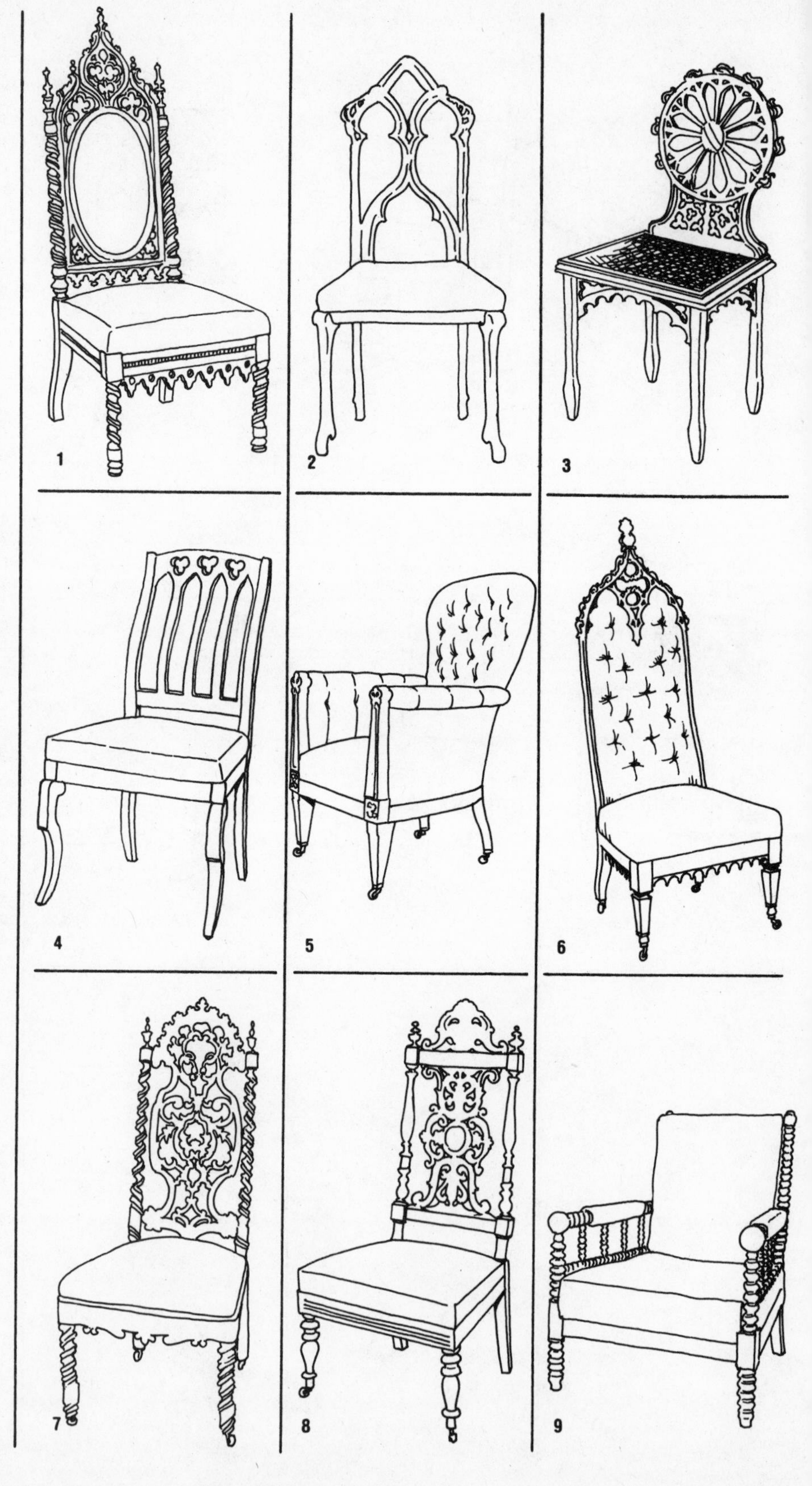

1. Armchair. New York. Back composed entirely of scrolls. John Henry Belter (1804–1863), noted cabinetmaker who worked in the Rococo Revival style, used such backs during his early years. c. 1850.

2. Chair. New York. Foliate carving restricted to top of this scroll-back chair. (Attributed to John Henry Belter.) 1850–1860.

3. Chair. New York. Wide, looping scrolls and lush fruit and foliage carving associated with John Henry Belter. Process of steaming permitted such curved and delicately carved backs. 1850–1860.

4. Armchair. New York. Similar motifs used on chair with upholstered back. (Attributed to Belter.) 1850–1860.

5. Chair. New York. Cannot be assigned to a specific maker. Many cabinetmakers worked in this style, particularly in New York. 1850–1860.

6. Upholstered armchair. New York. This chair is attributed to the firm of J. & J. W. Meeks (in partnership 1836–1860) on the basis of a similar set of furniture given to the latter's daughter as a wedding present in 1859. Design of floral carving on crest rail associated with this firm. c. 1860.

7. Chair. New York. Type of chair known as "balloon-back." Painted white with gilt decoration in the Rococo manner. 1850-1860.

8. Easy chair. New York. Made *en suite* with the previous balloon-back chair. 1850–1860.

9. Armchair. New York. Has subdued gilt ornament on ebonized frame. (By Auguste Pottier and William Pierre Stymus, in partnership 1859–after 1883.) c. 1860.

1. Easy chair. New England. Has exposed wooden crest rail and arms and tufted back. c. 1850.

2. Chair. New England. Has "finger-rolled" molding and fine floral carving. c. 1860.

3. Armchair. Philadelphia. Part of a suite of furniture ordered by President James Buchanan. (By Gottlieb Volmer.) 1859.

4. Chair. America. Balloon-back chairs extremely common during mid-19th century. c. 1860.

5. Upholstered chair. America. Has thin strip of exposed wood along curve of arms and back. c. 1860.

6. Chair. America. Rococo Revival furniture continued to be popular through the end of the 19th century. 1865–1875.

Louis XVI Revival

1. Slipper chair. New York. Note "finger-rolled" molding around edges of chair. Has Louis XVI-style ornamentation on legs. (Made by Alexander Roux.) c. 1860.

2. Chair. New York. Ebonized with gilt details. (Attributed to Leon Marcotte.) c. 1860.

3. Chair. New York. Form inspired by Louis XVI-style chairs. Has mother-of-pearl and brass inlay. 1865–1870.

1. Upholstered chair. Brooklyn, New York. The trumpet-turned leg is a characteristic of the Renaissance Revival style. (By Thomas Brooks, 1811–1887.) 1856–1876.

2. Chair. New York. Hall chair with caned bottom. Made for a New Jersey country house designed by James Renwick (1818–1895). Chair may also have been designed by him. c. 1865.

3. Chair. New York. Made by Leon Marcotte & Co. according to Roosevelt family tradition for the parents of Theodore Roosevelt. c. 1870.

4. Chair. New York. Has acorn finials and ring pendants; the latter hang from the chair's shoulders. Stamped on rear seat rail by maker George Hunzinger (1835–1889). 1870–1880.

5. Chair. New York. George Hunzinger developed a number of innovative chair designs including this one, patented in 1869. 1870–1880.

6. Armchair. New York. Based closely on true Renaissance chair design. By Herter Brothers (in partnership after 1865–c. 1900). 1882.

7. Chair. Grand Rapids, Michigan. Like the Rococo Revival style, the Renaissance Revival style was popular for a long time among a variety of consumer levels. Trumpet-turned legs and pendant drops from shoulders seen on other Renaissance Revival chairs. c. 1880.

8. Armchair. Grand Rapids, Michigan. Here, Renaissance Revival–style incised designs are grafted onto a turned chair. c. 1880.

9. Armchair. Grand Rapids, Michigan. This turned chair has some Renaissance Revival detailing in the crest rail. c. 1880.

1. Upholstered armchair. Probably Boston. The ornamentation on Renaissance Revival chairs tends to be geometric and architectural. c. 1875.

2. Upholstered armchair. Probably New York. Pendants hang from corners of back, a feature seen on other Renaissance Revival chairs, and a mother-of-pearl medallion is set into the cresting piece. c. 1870.

3. Upholstered armchair. Carved seat rail and stretchers reminiscent of Renaissance design. Displayed at the Centennial Exposition in Philadelphia of 1876. (By Pottier & Stymus.) c. 1875.

4. Upholstered armchair. New York. (Designed by architect John Quincy Adams Ward, 1830–1910.) Note fanciful use of crocodiles on arms. 1886.

5. Upholstered armchair. Newark, New Jersey. Has caryatid arm supports and carved tassel pendants. (By John Jelliff.) 1865–1870.

6. Upholstered armchair. Grand Rapids, Michigan. By this time, Grand Rapids was perhaps the leading furniture manufacturing center in the United States. 1870–1880.

1

2

3

4

5

6

1

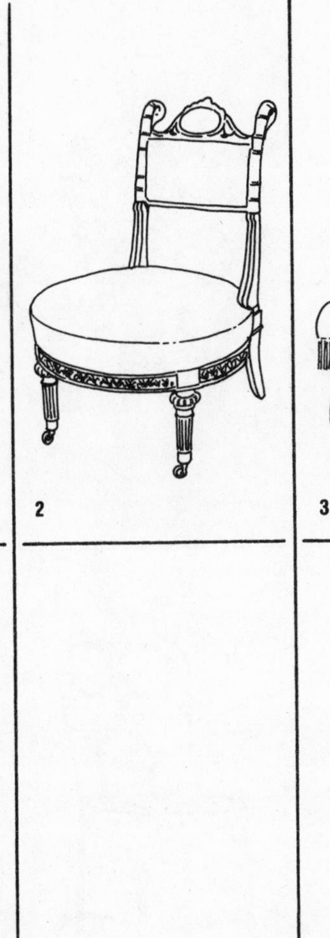

2

3

1. Upholstered armchair. New York. This example suggests the characteristics of the Neo-Grec style: Classical and, at times, Renaissance forms and details, often highlighted by incised and gilded decoration. 1860–1870.

2. Chair. New York. The Neo-Grec style was disseminated from France. This chair, attributed to the Herter Brothers, resembles chairs made during France's Second Empire. 1860–1870.

3. Chair. America. Lounging chair had X-shaped base with incised and gilded ornamentation as well as bosses. 1870–1880.

1

2

3

Colonial Revival

1. Chair. Framingham, Massachusetts. Uprights and front legs heavier than on 18th-century examples. (By famous antiquarian Wallace Nutting, 1861–1941, who also made furniture.) 1917–1936.

2. Armchair. Gardner, Massachusetts. Skirt below seat not seen on period Windsors (By the little-known company of Bent & Brothers.) c. 1900.

3. Rocking armchair. America. Shield-back rockers did not exist during Federal period. In Colonial Revival style, earlier styles and forms were often adapted. c. 1900.

1. Chair. America. Rustic cast iron chair. 1860–1890.

2. Chair. America. Cast iron chair of organic design and therefore appropriate for garden settings. 1860–1890.

3. Garden chair. America. Balloon-back chair of wire and iron. c. 1870.

4. Garden chair. New York. Patented in 1866 by French designer François A. Carré, but made widely. Made of steel strips and rods. (By Lalance and Grosjean, active 1852–after 1900.) c. 1900.

5. Chair. Chicago. Wire chairs popular in cafés earlier in 20th century. (By Royal Metal Manufacturing Co., 1900–1962.) Patented in 1909.

6. Spring armchair. Troy, New York. This upholstered armchair, which bounces on springs, was designed by Thomas W. Warren (active 1849–1852) and made by the American Chair Co. (1828–1858). Patented 1849.

7. Rocking chair. Trenton, New Jersey. Iron painted in imitation of blonde tortoiseshell. (Experimental rarity by Peter Cooper, 1791–1883.) 1850–1860.

8. Reclining armchair. New York. Iron-frame folding armchair designed by Cevedra B. Sheldon (active 1873–1877) and made by Marks Adjustable Folding Chair Co. (1877–1897). Patented 1876.

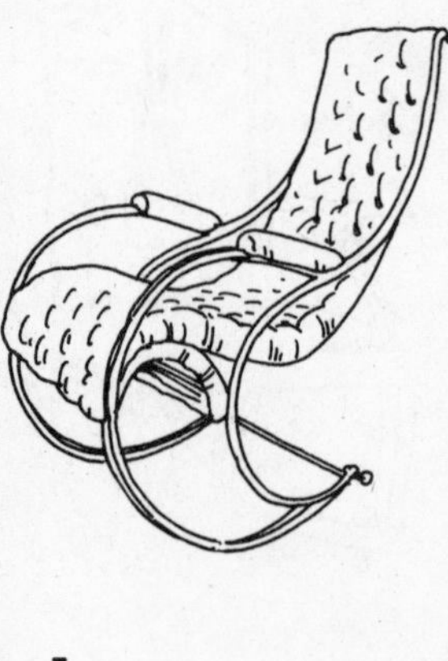

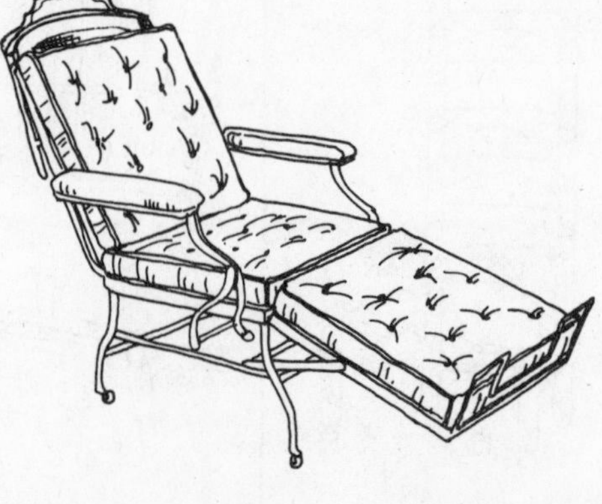

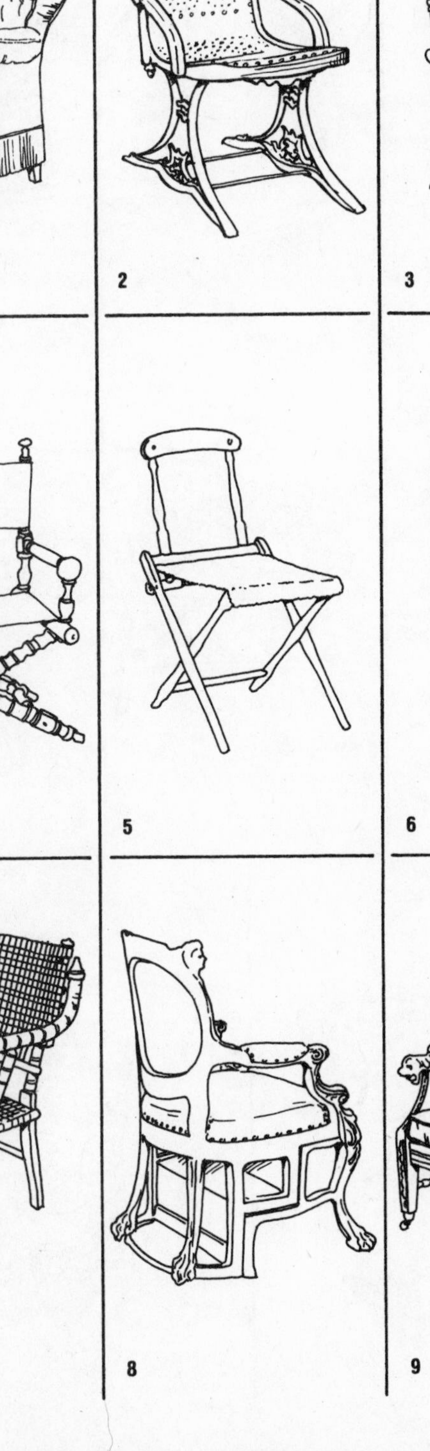

1

2

3

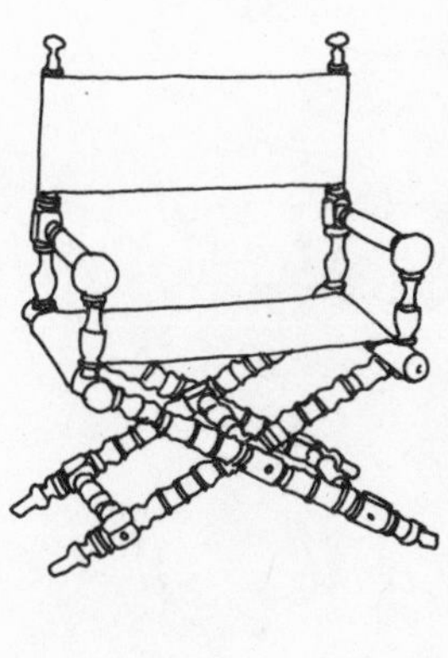

4

5

6

7

8

9

1. Upholstered armchair. America. "Turkish" frame composed of iron rod back and springs covered by fabric. Only legs and connecting elements are of wood. c. 1895.

2. Platform rocking armchair. New York. Had iron spring platform. Maker known for continuous back and seats of pierced plywood. (By Gardner & Co., 1863–1888.) Patented 1872.

3. Platform rocking chair. America. Popular type of chair at turn of 20th century. c. 1900.

4. Folding armchair. Probably Baltimore, Maryland. Similar in design to today's "director's" chair. c. 1860.

5. Folding chair. America. Simple tapestry seat and slat support for back. (By B. J. Harrison, obscure maker.) c. 1866.

6. Folding chair. Closter, New Jersey. Back of seat Late Classical in style. (By Collignon Factory.) Patented 1869.

7. Armchair. New York. Turned members resemble bamboo. Has wire mesh seat. (By George Hunzinger.) Patented 1879.

8. Library armchair. Boston. Can be converted into library steps. (By Augustus Eliaers, active 1849–1865.) Patented 1853.

9. Reclining armchair. Philadelphia. Based on so-called "Morris" chair, invented by William Watt and first made by Morris & Co. in England. (This example by little-known company of Allen & Brothers , 1847–1902.) After 1894.

1. Chair. America. Copied from bentwood furniture imported to America by such Viennese manufacturers as the Thonet Co. and Jacob & Joseph Kohn. c. 1915.

2. Rocking armchair. Possibly New York. So-called "rustic," "bent twig," or "Adirondack" chair. c. 1900.

3. Rocking armchair. Possibly New York. Cane grown in East Indies was imported to New York via Belgium and the Netherlands. c. 1850.

4. Reclining armchair. America. Structural members are bamboo, with seat, back, arms and headrest of cane. c. 1875.

5. Corner chair. America. Wicker furniture can be made of willow or rattan. 1890–1915.

6. Armchair. Boston. Upholstered chair with back, arms, and legs of horn. c. 1880.

1

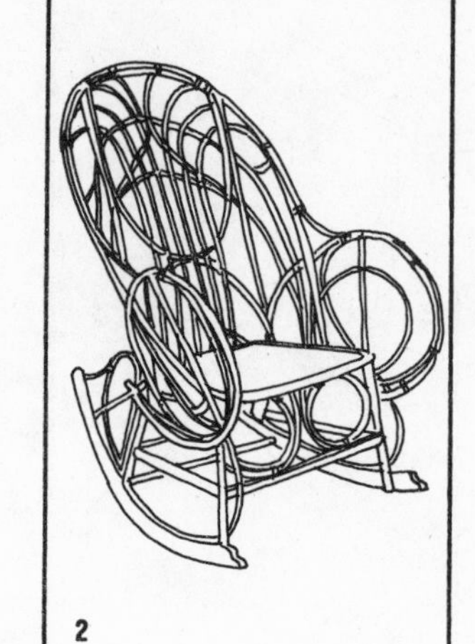

2

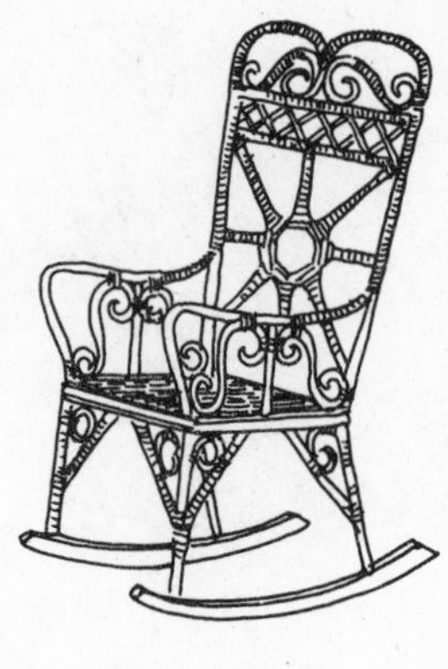

3

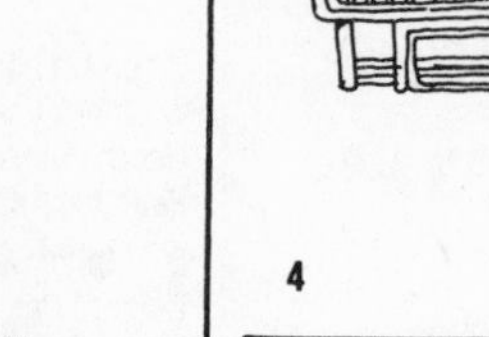

4

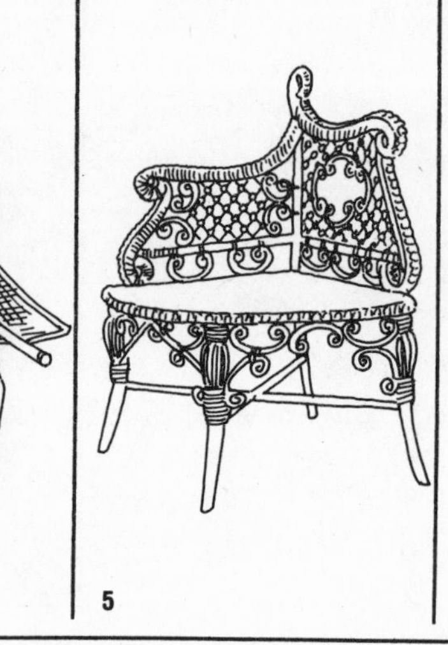

5

6

Exotic and Eclectic

1. Armchair. Possibly New York. So-called "Turkish style" chair, often made *en suite* for Turkish "cozy corners." c. 1885.

2. Armchair. Possibly New York. Such Moorish-style furniture stressed comfort. Both of these chairs were made for the John D. Rockefeller, Sr., house in New York. c. 1885.

1

2

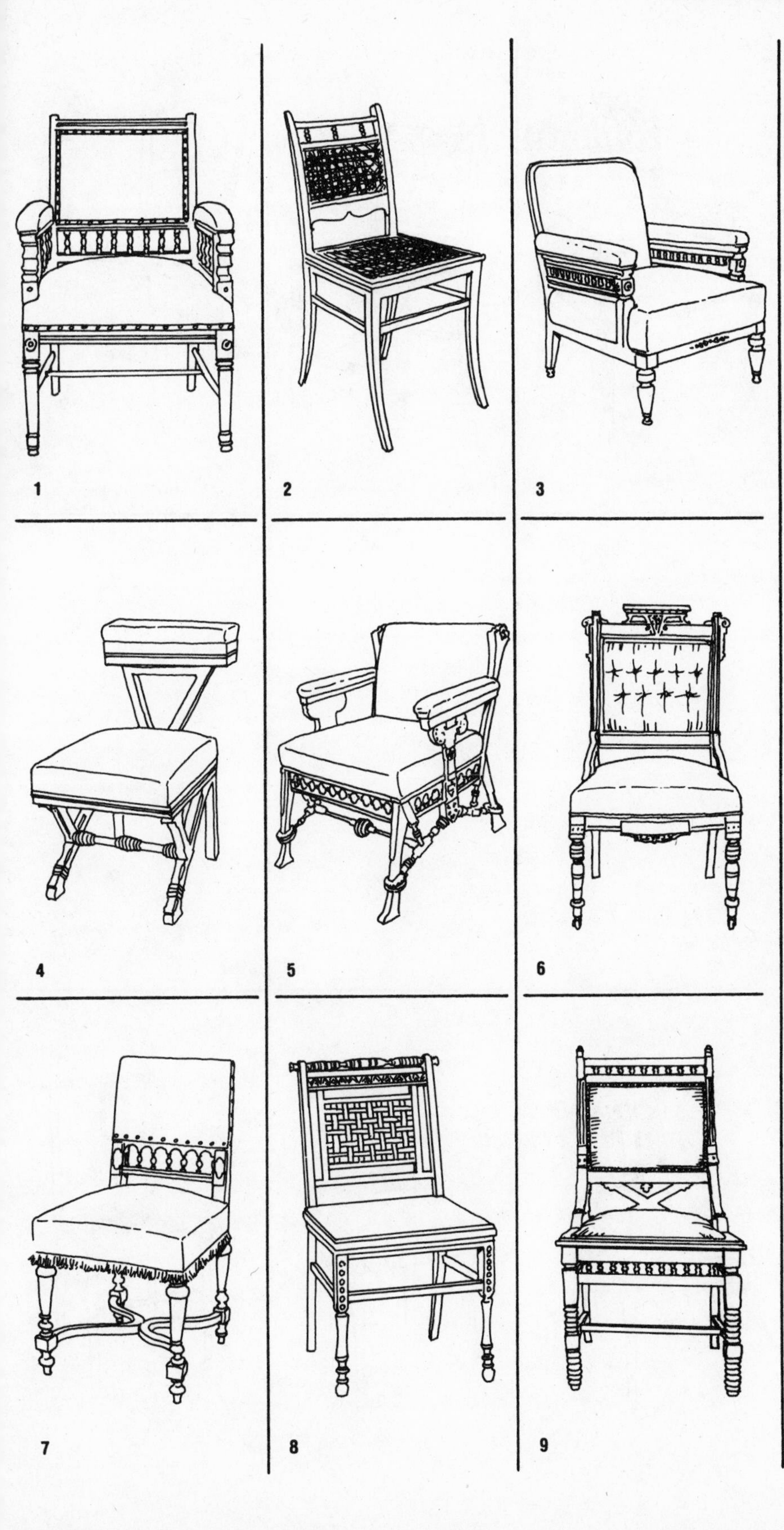

1. Armchair. Probably New York. Spindles above or below back panel were Eastlake-style characteristic. c. 1877–1880.

2. Chair. New York. Caned back and seat. (Possibly by Herter Brothers, a firm noted for creating fine furniture in the Eastlake taste.) c. 1880.

3. Armchair. New York. While Charles Locke Eastlake's (1836–1906) *Hints on Household Taste* (1868) was avidly read by Americans, not all Eastlake-influenced furniture made in the United States followed his tenets. Note, for example, the presence of inlaid details, not favored by Eastlake. c. 1880.

4. Chair. Philadelphia. Geometric in overall design and details. (Designed by architect Frank Furness, 1839–1912 and probably executed by noted furniture maker Daniel Pabst.) 1875.

5. Upholstered armchair. America. Has turned and incised ornamentation of the type seen on other Eastlake-influenced furniture. c. 1875.

6. Chair. America. Incised details on crest rail and skirt characteristic of style. c. 1875.

7. Chair. America. Chair of a similar design pictured in Eastlake's *Hints on Household Taste.* c. 1880.

8. Chair. America. Maker has combined turned and carved ornamentation. Note carved lattice back. 1880–1890.

9. Chair. America. Most Eastlake-style furniture is rectilinear in overall form. 1880–1890.

1. Armchair. America. Use of oak rather than another hardwood suggests this relatively late date. 1880–1890.

2. Chair. America. Common cane-seated chair, incorporating Eastlake-inspired details. 1800–1890.

3. Chair. America. Spindles in back only. Eastlake-style attribute on an otherwise vernacular-style chair. 1880–1890.

1

2

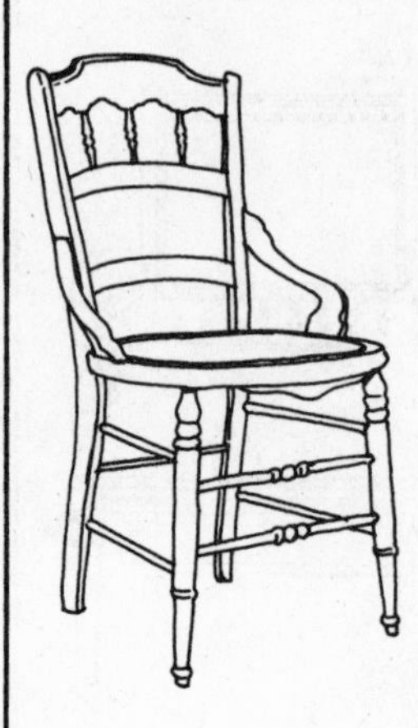

3

Art and Japanese-Inspired Furniture

1. Chair. New York. Ebonized example decorated by means of marquetry. (By Herter Brothers.) c. 1880.

2. Chair. New York. Example of Art Furniture in Anglo-Japanese taste. (By Herter Brothers.) c. 1880.

3. Chair. Probably New York. Part of a *faux* bamboo bedroom set. Made of turned maple. The excitement caused by Japan's exhibit at the Centennial Exposition of 1876 was one reason for the popularity of this style. c. 1880.

1

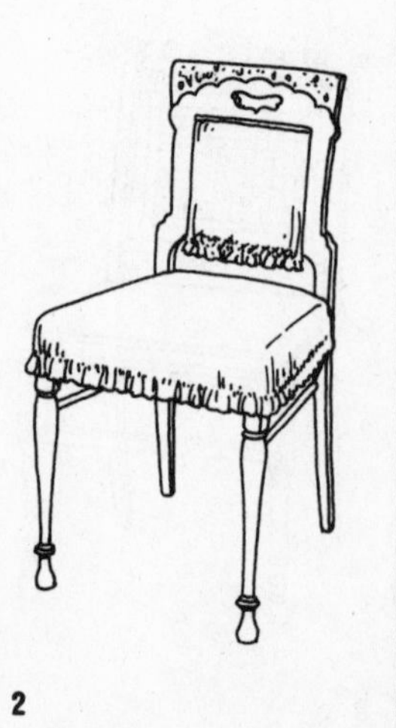

2

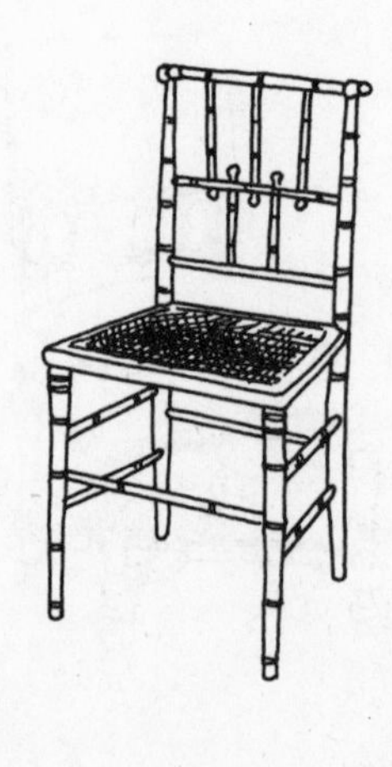

3

1. Chair. Buffalo, New York. Note Art Nouveau influence. (Rare design by Charles Rohlfs, 1853–1936.) c. 1898.

2. Chair. Milwaukee, Wisconsin. Spindle-back designed by Frank Lloyd Wright (1869–1959) and made by George Niedecken. c. 1895.

3. Chair. Chicago. Bold example of style. (Designed by architect George W. Maher, 1864–1929.) 1897.

4. Chair. East Aurora, New York. Made at Elbert Hubbard's (1856–1915) Roycroft Shops. English Arts and Crafts prototypes favored. 1901–1916.

5. Chair. Eastwood (Syracuse), New York. By Gustav Stickley's Craftsman Workshops (1900–1915), the most famous Arts and Crafts furniture producer. c. 1901.

6. Chair. Eastwood (Syracuse), New York. Inlay unusual feature often associated with Harvey Ellis (1852–1904), who designed this chair. Decal of Gustav Stickley's Craftsman Workshops. 1903–1904.

7. Armchair. Eastwood (Syracuse), New York. Flaring arm supports and square through-tenons visible on surface of arms common Mission-style characteristics. Labeled by Gustav Stickley's Craftsman Workshops. 1907–1912.

8. Chair. Media, Pennsylvania. Made at Arts and Crafts community of Rose Valley. Inspired by medieval styles. (Designed by William Price, 1861–1916.) 1901–1909.

9. Armchair. Grand Rapids and Holland, Michigan. Charles P. Limbert Co. made Mission furniture for over ten years beginning in 1902. Some designs not as severely straight as Stickley's. c. 1905.

1. Armchair. Pasadena, California. Influence of Oriental design evident. (Made by Peter Hall and designed by architects Charles and Henry Greene, active c. 1893–c. 1910, for the Gamble House.) c. 1908.

2. Armchair. Eastwood (Syracuse), New York. Spindle-back, one of many variants on basic slat-back chair. (By Gustav Stickley's Craftsman Workshops.) c. 1905–1908.

3. Reclining or "Morris" armchair. Eastwood (Syracuse), New York. Named after William Morris (1834–1896), leader of the Arts and Crafts movement in England. c. 1905.

4. Armchair. Eastwood (Syracuse), New York. Form less popular than that of "Morris" chair. Branded by Gustav Stickley's Craftsman Workshops. c. 1912.

5. Rocking armchair. Fayetteville, New York. Labeled by Gustav Stickley's competitors and brothers, Leopold and J. George Stickley, who made Mission furniture into the 1920s. 1900–1920.

6. Upholstered armchair. Grand Rapids, Michigan. The Stickley Brothers Co., which produced this chair, was headed by brothers of Gustav, Leopold, and J. George. Stickley Brothers and many other less famous factories made Mission-style furniture. c. 1908.

1 2 3

4 5 6

Tables

1. Trestle table. New England. Top and stretcher can be removed to collapse table. Furniture that could be disassembled was important in small 17th-century homes. 1650–1680.

2. Trestle table. Possibly Virginia. Legs and stretcher chamfered. 1700–1750.

3. Draw table. Windsor, Connecticut. Flat leaves pulled from underneath tabletop can double length. 1640–1660.

4. Table with drawer. Southeastern Massachusetts. Wide overhang typical early feature. 1640–1660.

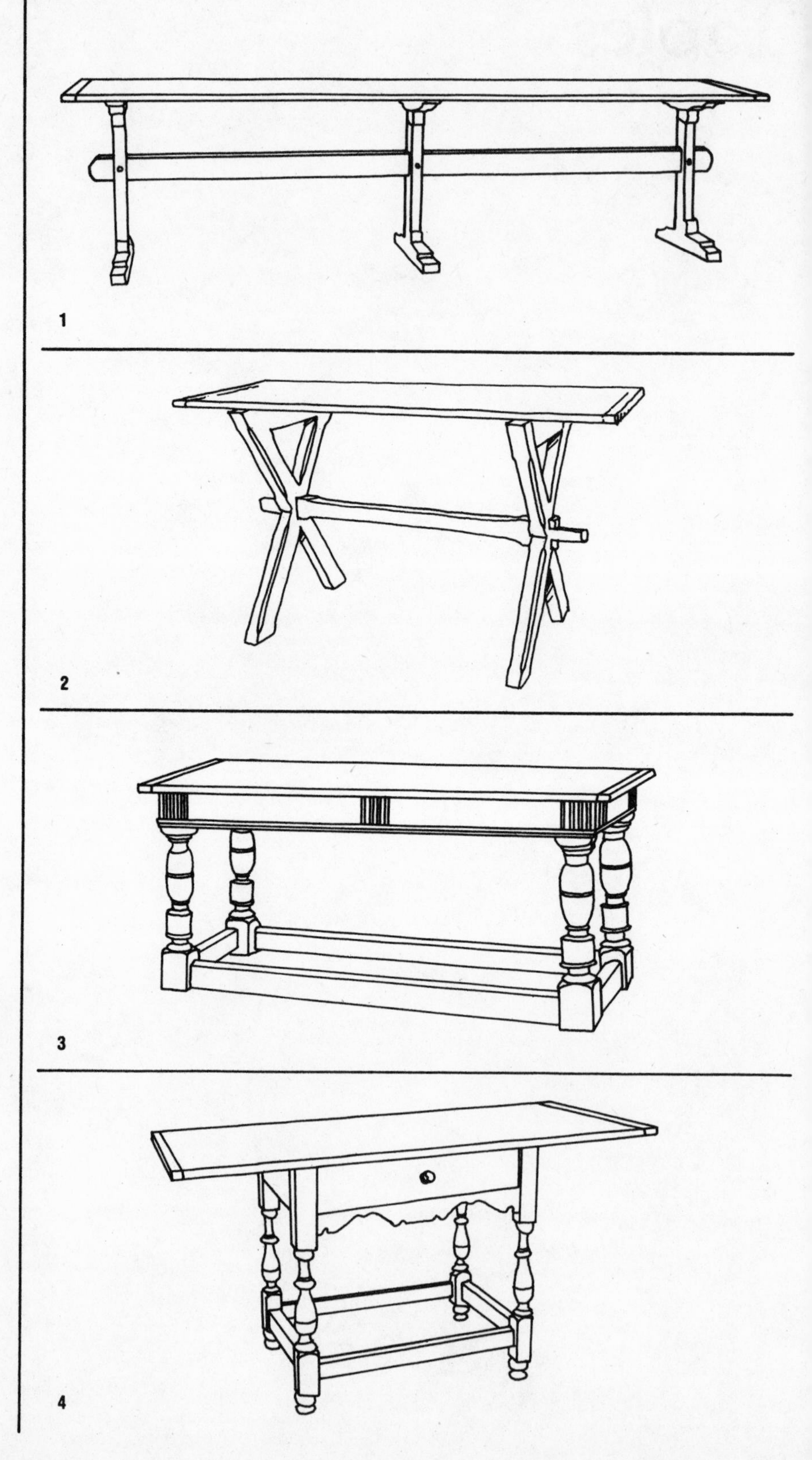

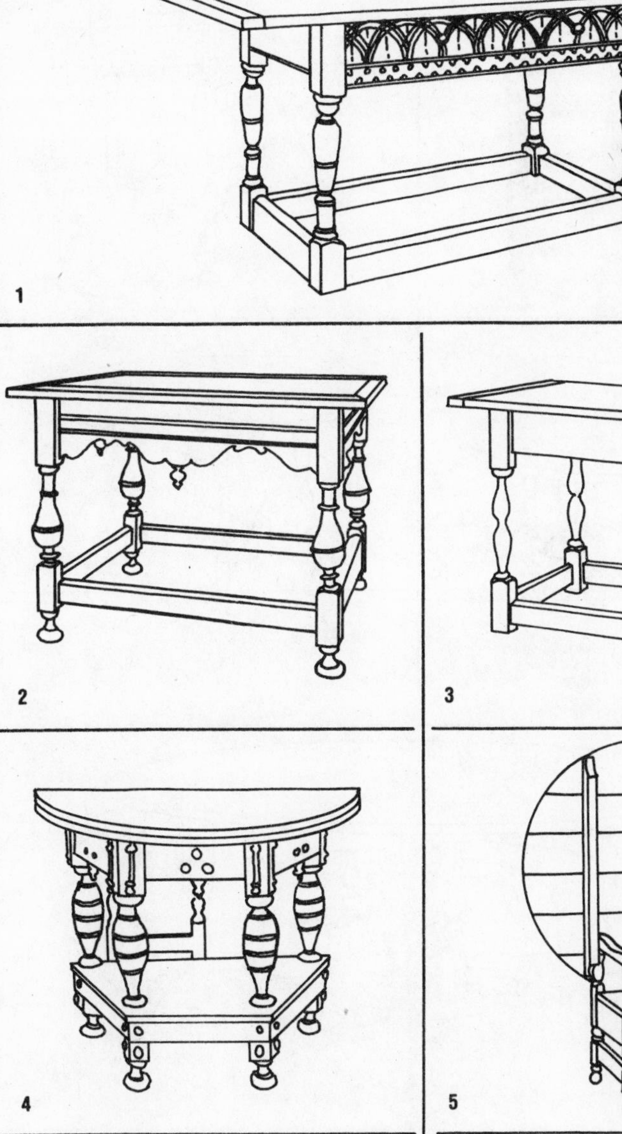

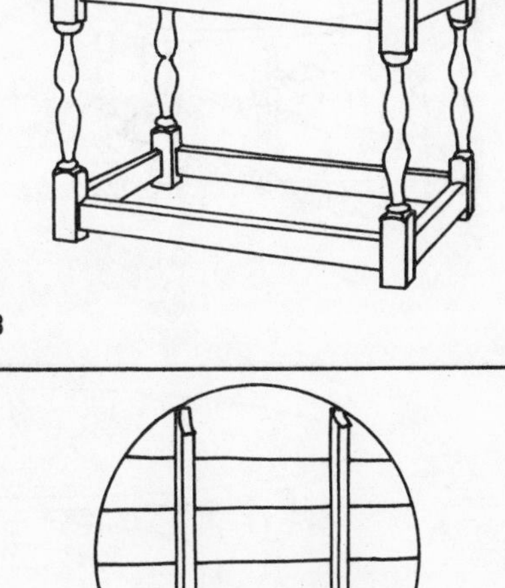

1 2 3 4 5

1. Stretcher table with drawer. Plymouth, Massachusetts. Carving on drawer laid out with draftsman's compass. 1660–1680.

2. Stretcher table. New England. Joiner used molding plane to decorate sides. 1670–1690.

3. Stretcher table. Massachusetts. Once-common form as evidenced by number of extant examples. c. 1700.

4. Folding table. Essex County, Massachusetts. Boldly designed space saver. 1660–1690.

5. Chair-table. Massachusetts. Multifunctional furniture important with space at a premium in the 17th-century home. 1680–1710.

1. Gateleg table. Virginia. Also called "drop-leaf." Distinctive ring and ball turnings borrowed from English work. c. 1690.

2. Gateleg table. Note how two turned swinging legs supported leaves. Rediscovered in Rhode Island. 1700–1735.

3. Gateleg table. New England. Spanish foot, seen here, rarely used on tables. 1700–1730.

4. Gateleg table. New England. Today called "butterfly" table because of distinctively shaped supports. 1700–1730.

5. Gateleg table. New York City. "Baluster and cup" turnings used in New York. 1700–1750.

6. Gateleg table. New York. Note plain swing legs. 1680–1700.

7. Folding table. New England. Easily closed and stored away. 1710–1740.

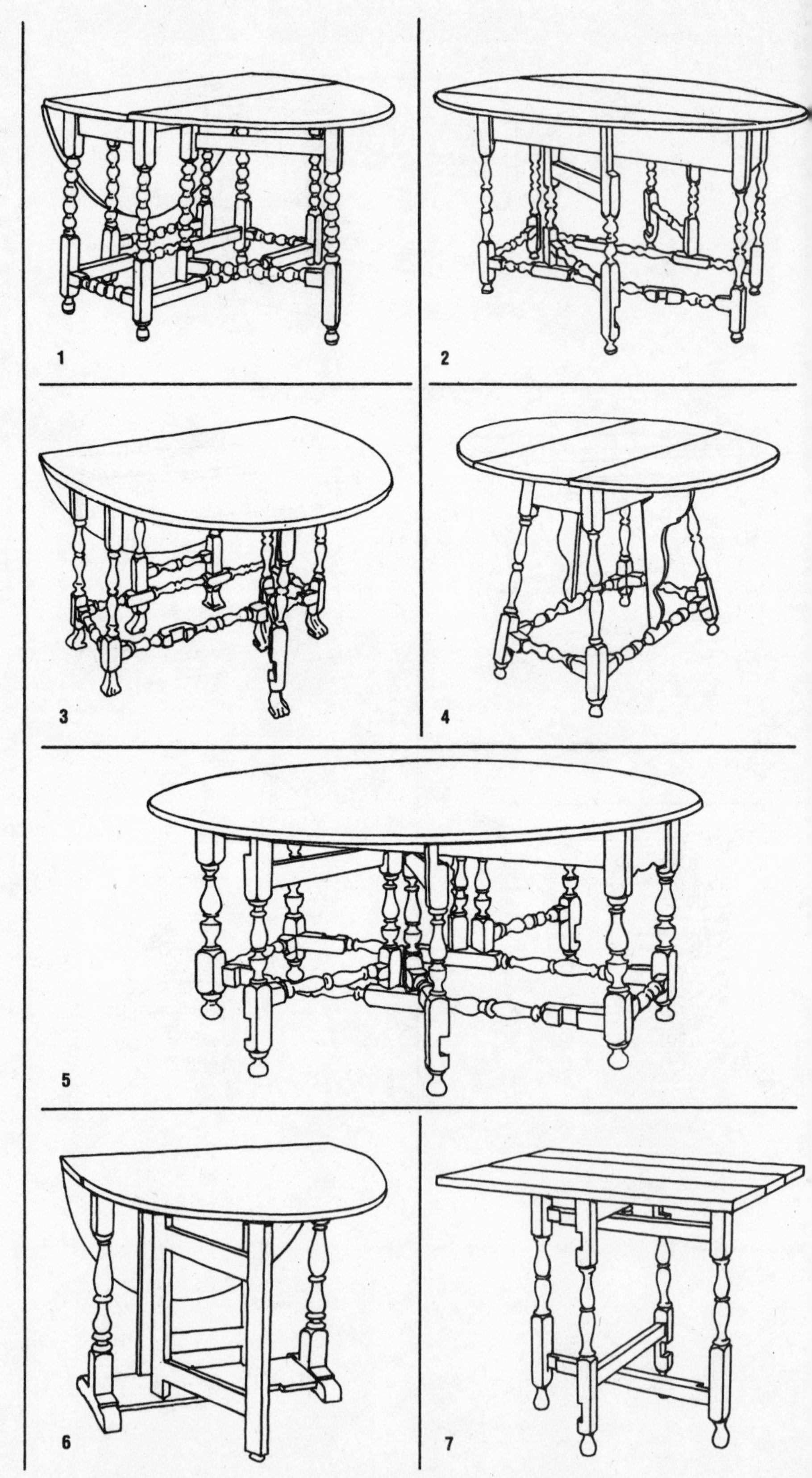

1

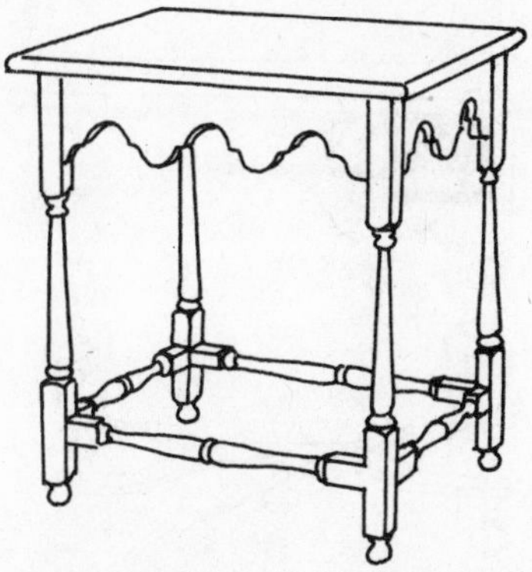

2

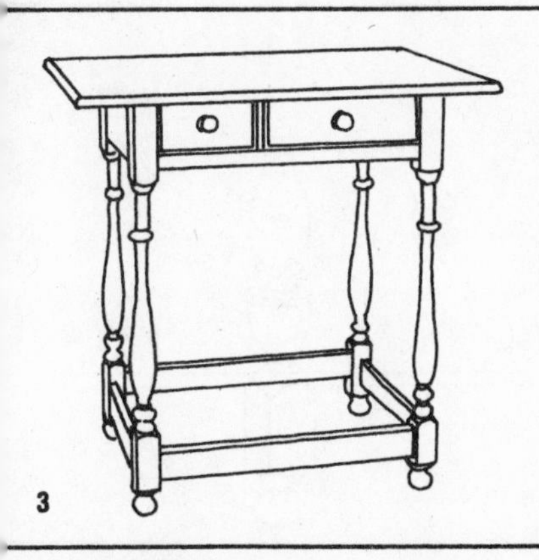

3

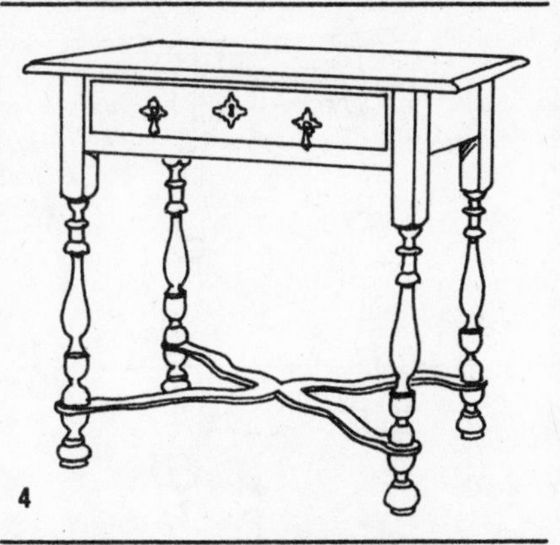

4

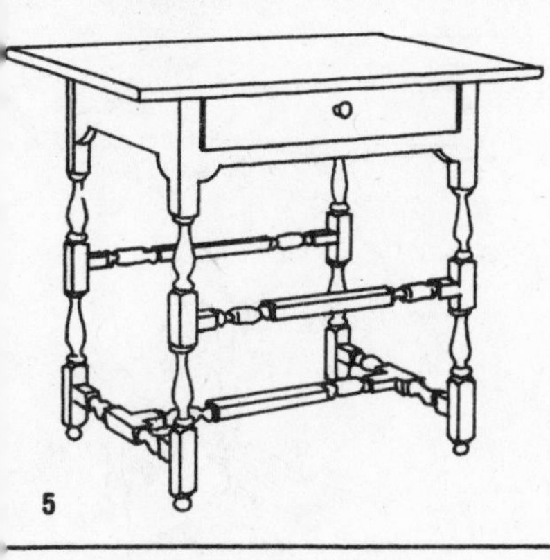

5

6

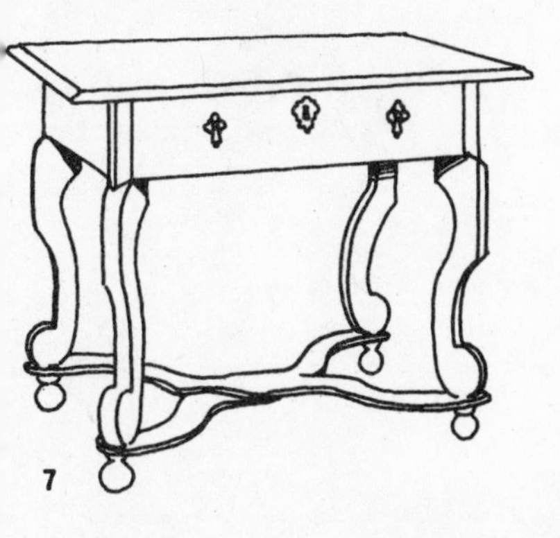

7

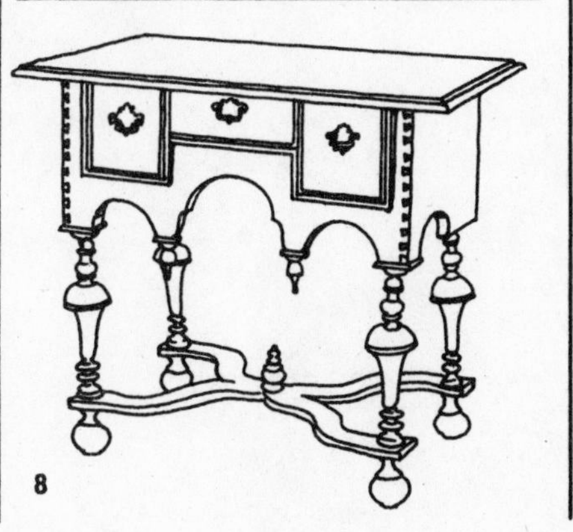

8

1. Stretcher table. New England. Has crisp turnings, Spanish feet, and bold splay of legs. 1700–1740.

2. Tea table. Virginia. Ritual of taking tea prompted development of this form. c. 1710.

3. Stretcher table. Probably Pennsylvania. Tables with one long and one short drawer associated with Pennsylvania and the South. 1720–1780.

4. Table with drawer. Virginia or North Carolina. Note serpentine stretchers, use of period drawer pulls, and escutcheon. 1690–1730.

5. Stretcher table. Possibly South Carolina. Survival rate of Southern furniture low because of unfavorable climate. 1690–1730.

6. Mixing table. New England. Slate top imported from Switzerland. 1700–1720.

7. Dressing table. New York or New Jersey. Outline of sharply scrolled legs reflected in cross stretchers. c. 1700.

8. Dressing table. New England. Deep drawers flanking shallow center drawer was standard arrangement. 1700–1720.

1. Dressing table. Pennsylvania. Canted corners on top unusual. Reel separating cup and trumpet turnings on legs seen in other Pennsylvania tables. Dated 1724.

2. Dressing table. Similar cutouts in skirts seen on English examples. 1700–1720.

3. New England William and Mary turning from table leg. 1700–1730.

4. "Baluster and cup" turning distinctive of New York furniture. 1700–1750.

5. "Butterfly" support from New England gateleg table. 1700–1730.

6. Drop finial from Boston mixing table. Not all tables retain original finials. 1700–1720.

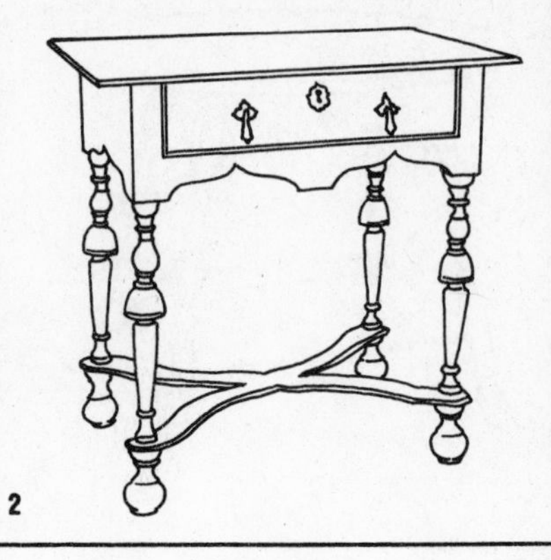

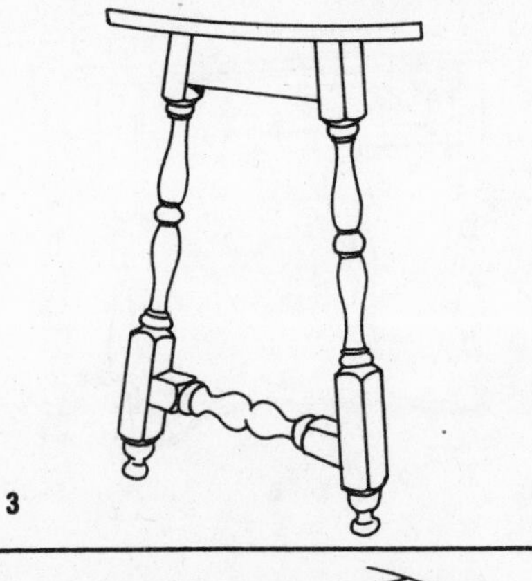

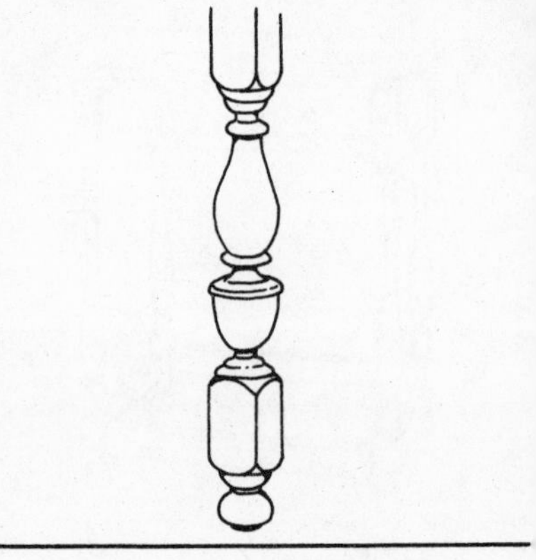

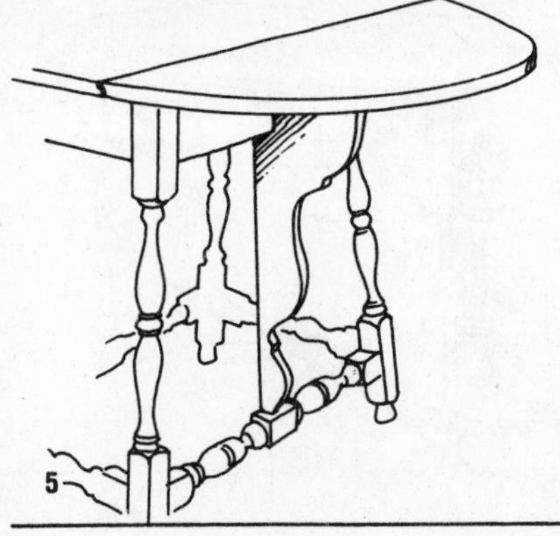

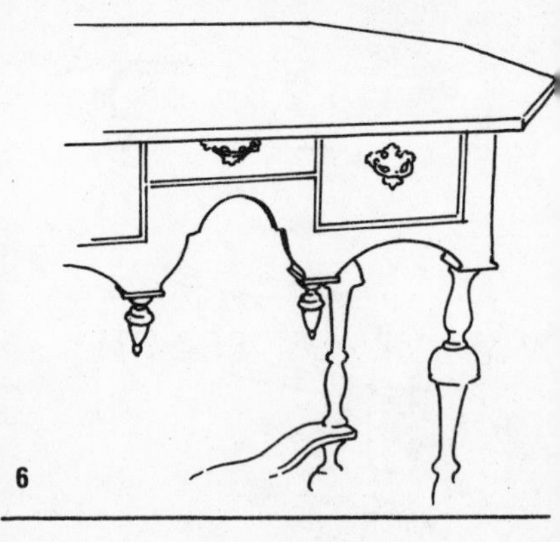

1

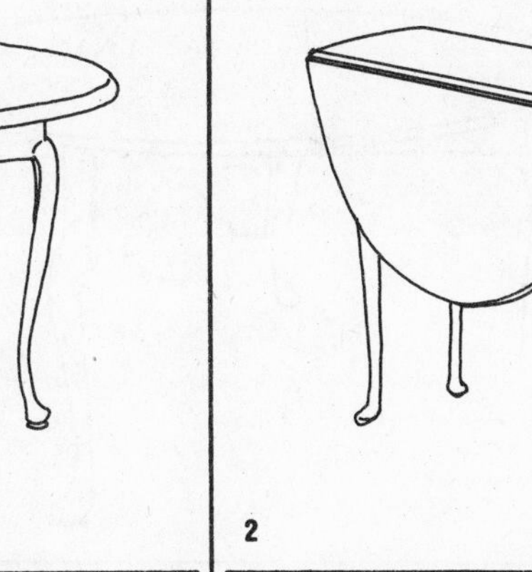

2

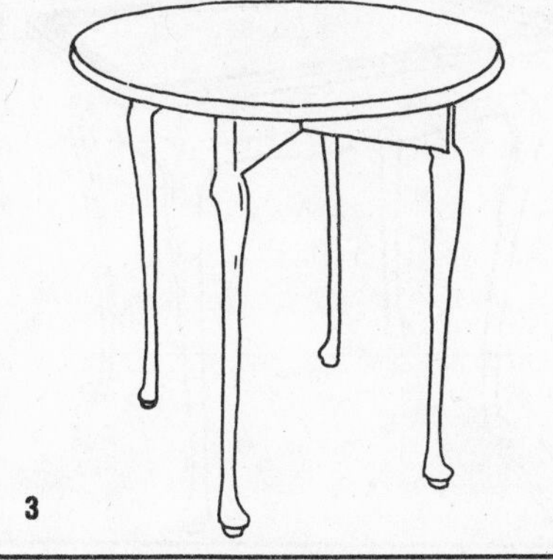

3

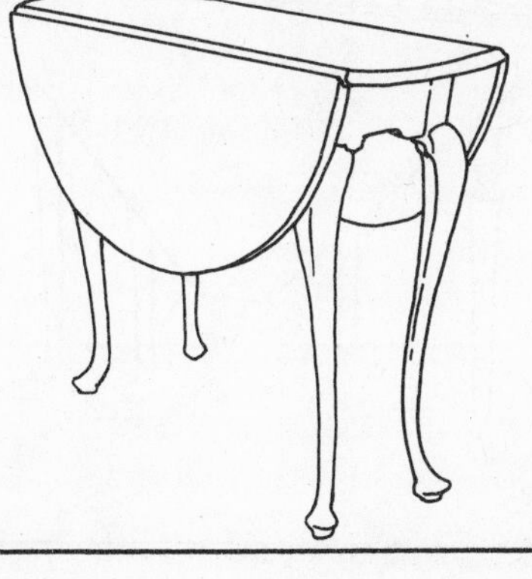

4

5

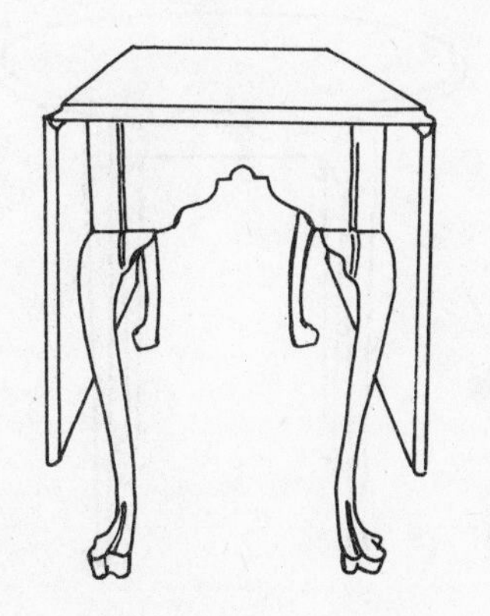

6

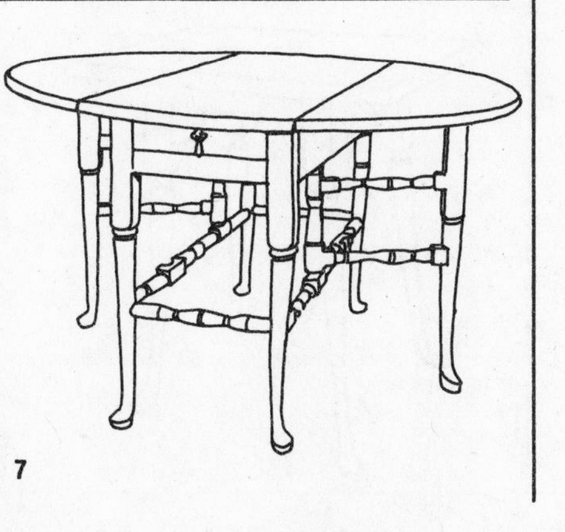

7

1. Drop-leaf table. Massachusetts. Note pad foot resting on flattened ball, a New England characteristic. 1725–1745.

2. Drop-leaf table. Boston. Table has scalloped skirt, squared-off knees, and very thin ankles. 1730–1760.

3. Drop-leaf table. Probably Portsmouth, New Hampshire. Legs swing and top pivots on "tuckaway" table. Minimal storage space required. 1740–1760.

4. Drop-leaf table. Newport, Rhode Island. Note generous, squared-off knee. 1730–1750.

5. Drop-leaf table. New York. Thick "slipper" feet often seen on New York tables. 1730–1750.

6. Drop-leaf table. New Jersey. Presence of trifid feet attests to Philadelphia influence, but deeply scalloped skirt not a high-style Philadelphia characteristic. 1740–1780.

7. Drop-leaf table. Probably Virginia. Conically turned legs stylistically latest feature on this table with stretchers and side hung drawers. 1720–1740.

1. Drop-leaf table. Probably Virginia. Stout leg Southern feature. 1725–1740.

2. Drop-leaf table. Virginia. Easily fit into a corner. Many colonists placed furniture against walls when not in use. 1720–1740.

3. Tea table. Massachusetts. Overall design underlines this form's origin as separate tea tray and frame. 1720–1740.

4. Tea table. Massachusetts. Overall lightness and cut corners on top were period characteristics. 1730–1750.

5. Tea table. Boston area. Note deeply scalloped skirt. 1720–1750.

6. Tea table. New England. Extreme cut in skirt, bold rake to legs, and very thick ankles with ducklike feet suggest this was product of rural or simple city shop. 1720–1750.

7. Tea table. New England. Turner substituted conically turned for cabriole legs. 1740–1750.

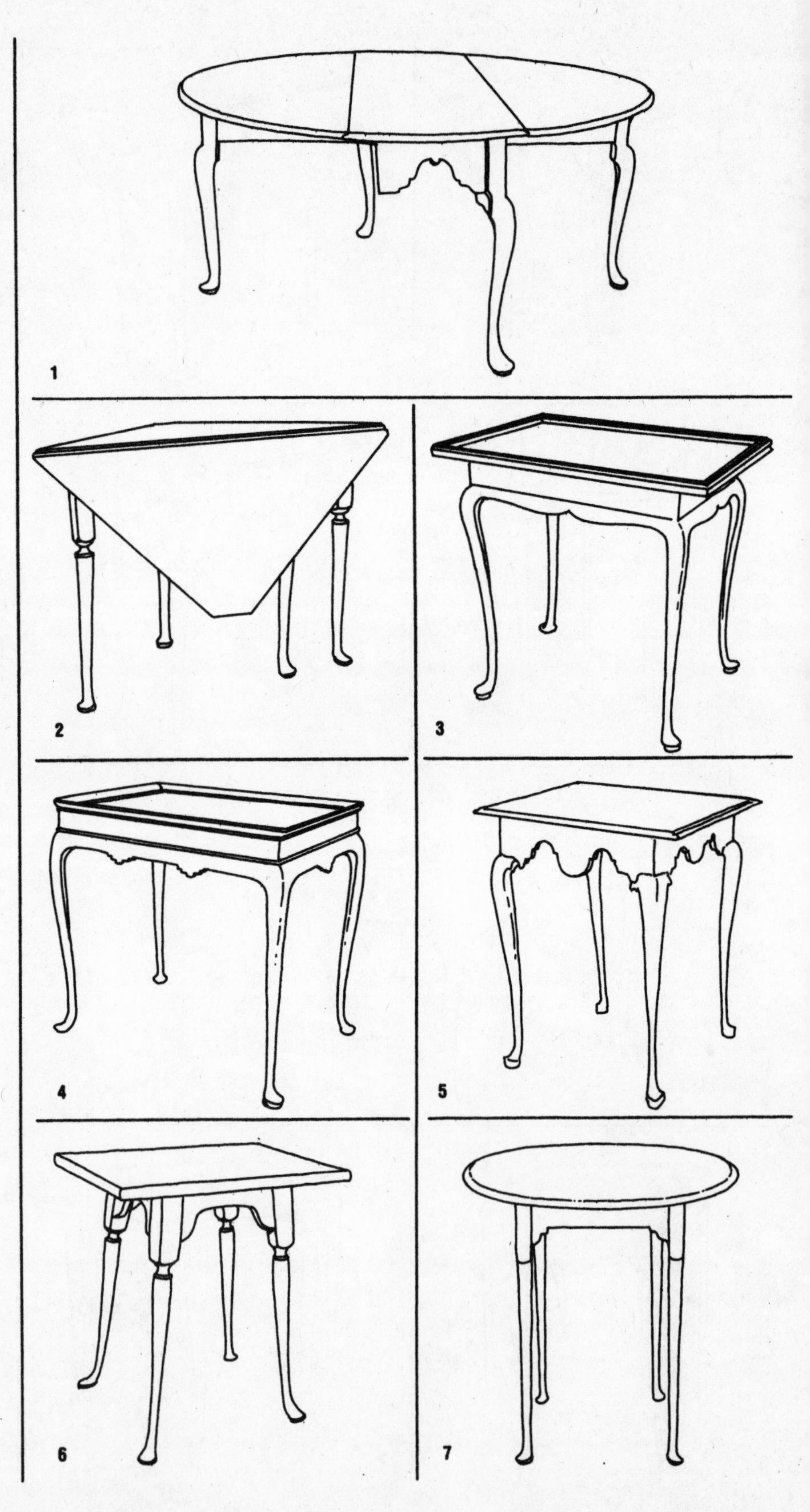

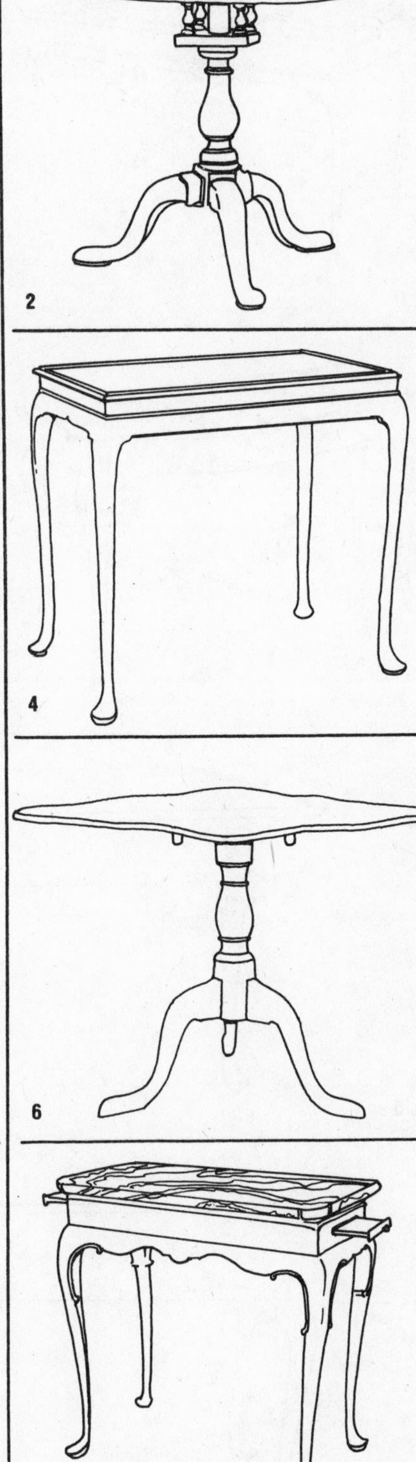

1. Tea table. Connecticut. Rhythmic scalloping of top and skirt seen on many Connecticut tables. 1740–1790.

2. Tea table. New York. Top swings vertically on birdcage device for ease in storing. 1735–1750.

3. Tea table. Probably Long Island. Extremely delicate table. Spade feet relatively common on New York tables. 1740–1790.

4. Tea table. Williamsburg, Virginia. Similarly sturdy legs appeared on other Southern tables. 1730–1740.

5. Tilt-top tea table. Salem, North Carolina. Made in Moravian settlement noted for highly developed crafts. (By little-known maker Jonathan Gavet.) 1784.

6. Tilt-top tea table. America. Some tilt-tops have gently undulating, rectangular tops. 1750–1790.

7. Mixing table. Massachusetts. Protective top of delft tiles original. 1720–1740.

8. Mixing table. New York. Table with grey marble top, used for preparing alcoholic drinks. 1735–1745.

1. Side table with marble top. Massachusetts. Similar to some Massachusetts tea tables in restrained overall design. 1720–1740.

2. Side table with marble top. Massachusetts. Small ankles and large pad feet seen on other Massachusetts tables. 1740–1760.

3. Side table with marble top. Newport, Rhode Island. Of simple but elegant design. 1750–1790.

4. Side table. Rhode Island. Long and straight-sided Rhode Island slipper foot slightly different from those found in Middle Colonies. 1720–1740.

5. Side table. New England. Rather plain painted table, vernacular in style. 1740–1800.

6. Side table. New York. Note volutes on corners of legs and inlaid star pattern. 1740–1755.

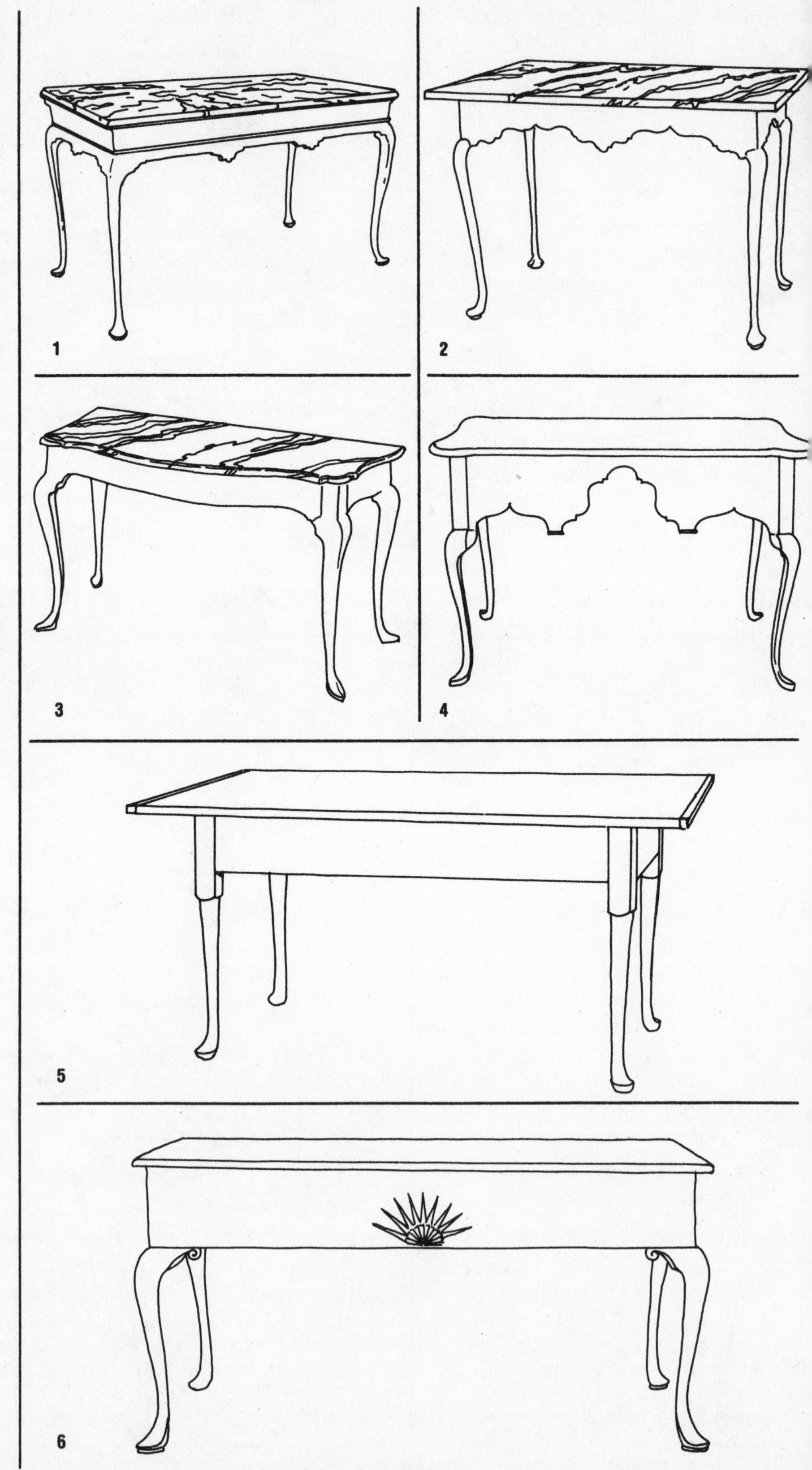

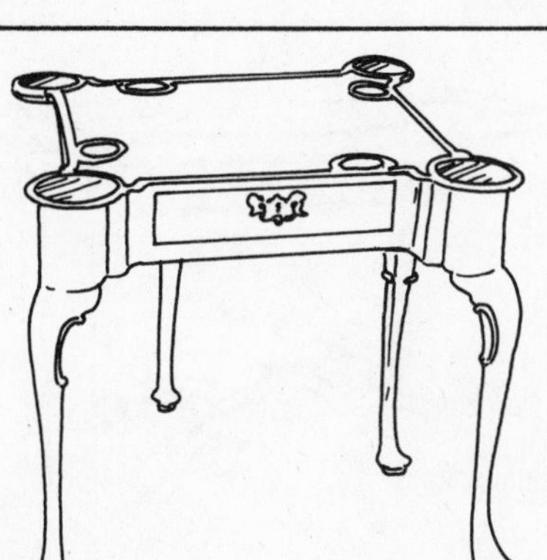

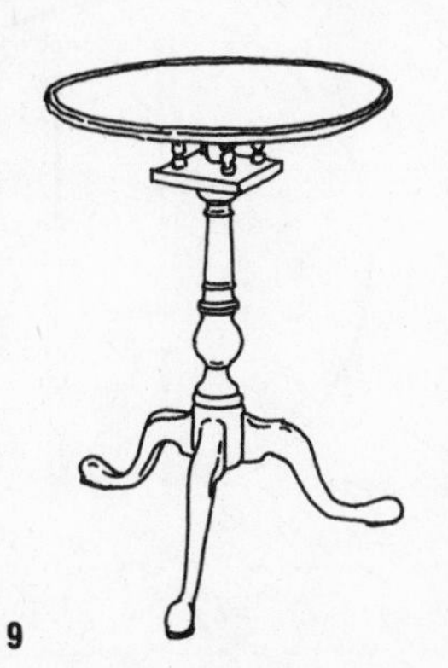

1. Side table with marble top. Newport, Rhode Island. Note boldly serpentine front and sides. Documented by bill dated September 15, 1775. (Made for Captain Anthony Low by John Goddard, 1773–1785.) 1775.

2. Side table. Pennsylvania. Shows Pennsylvania preference for one wide and one narrow drawer. Brasses are Chippendale in style. 1755–1800.

3. Side table. Virginia. Turnings at top of legs often associated with William and Mary period but used on a number of Queen Anne objects. 1730–1750.

4. Card table. Probably Boston. Delicate example with swing leg for supporting top in open position. 1730–1750.

5. Card table. Boston. Note canvaswork playing surface. Circular card table rare in American furniture, but many English examples survive. 1730–1760.

6. Card table. Virginia. Note open top and position of swing leg. Very similar to Irish prototypes. 1745–1785.

7. Stand. New England. Diminutive example with octagonal top and "button" feet. 1725–1750.

8. Candlestand and firescreen. Pennsylvania. Tilt-top multifunctional: protects lit candles from drafts, keeps wax-based make-up from melting when people sit near fire, and stores away easily. 1740–1760.

9. Candlestand. Philadelphia. Has smaller dimensions than most tilt-top tables. 1740–1750.

1. Tea table. Probably Portsmouth, New Hampshire. Note unusual domed, double C-scrolled stretchers and delicately pierced gallery around top. Gallery prevented tea set from falling off table. 1765–1785.

2. Tea table. Boston. Turret top of rhythmic design. Each turret can hold a cup and saucer. 1750–1775.

3. Tea table. Newport, Rhode Island. Letter documents that John Goddard (1723/4–1785) finished this serpentine table on June 30, 1763. Very similar tables also made by John Townsend (1732/3–1809) of Newport.

4. Tea table. New York. Gothic-style pierced gallery. Flat gadrooning seen on other New York tables. 1765–1785.

5. Tea table. Philadelphia. Shape inspired by Chippendale's *Director*, Plate 34. 1770–1785.

6. Tilt-top tea table. Massachusetts. Today this type of foot is sometimes called "rat-claw." 1760–1780.

7. Tilt-top tea table. Connecticut. Stout, pillarlike baluster seen on other Connecticut tables. 1780–1790.

8. Tilt-top tea table. New York. Some New York tilt-top tables have long, lean baluster. 1760–1780.

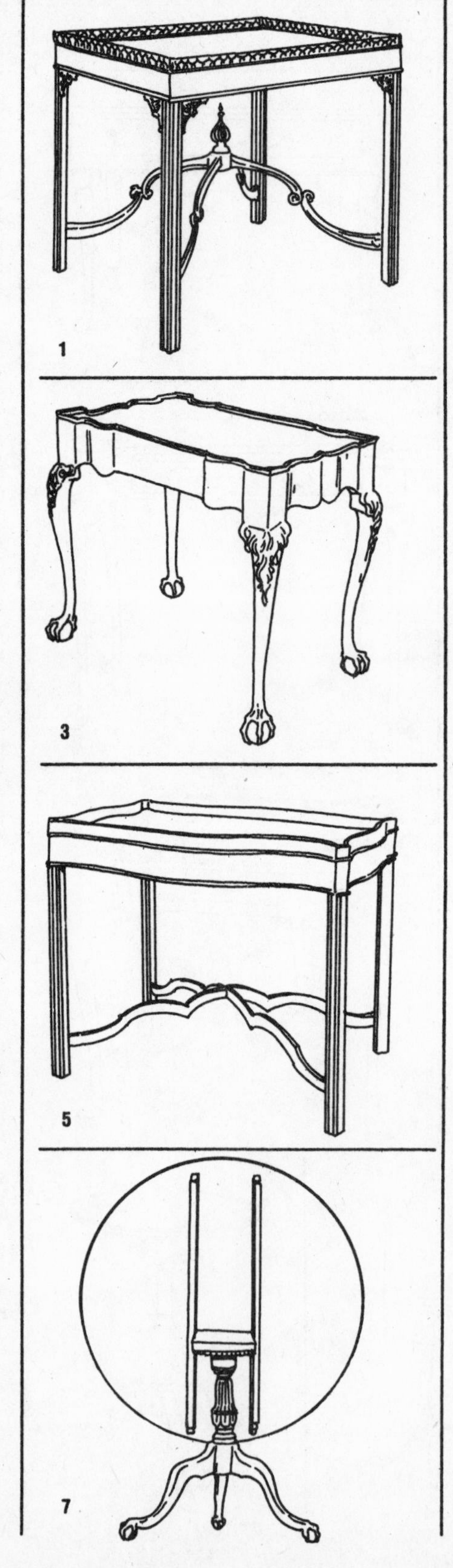

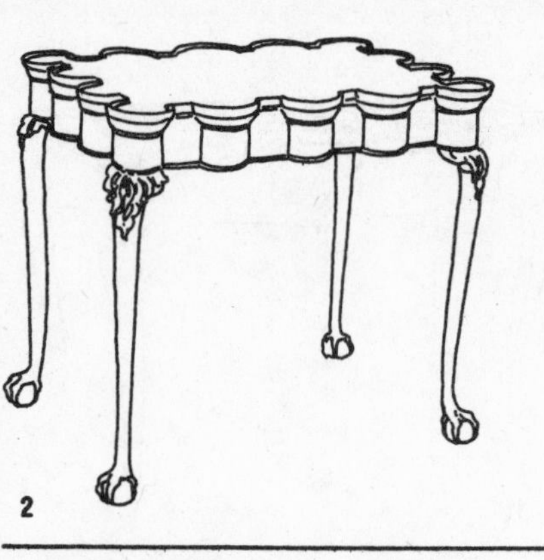

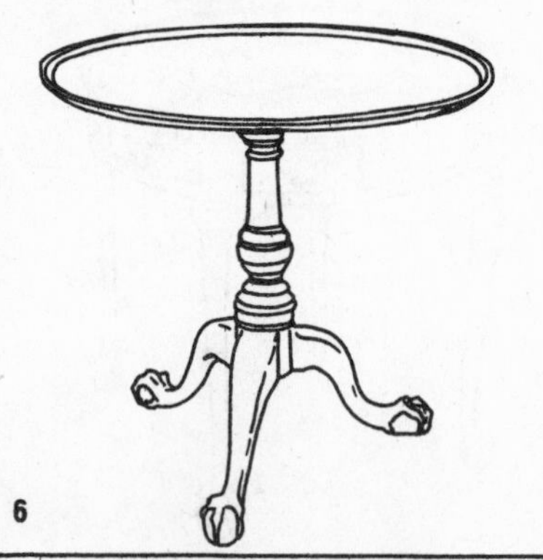

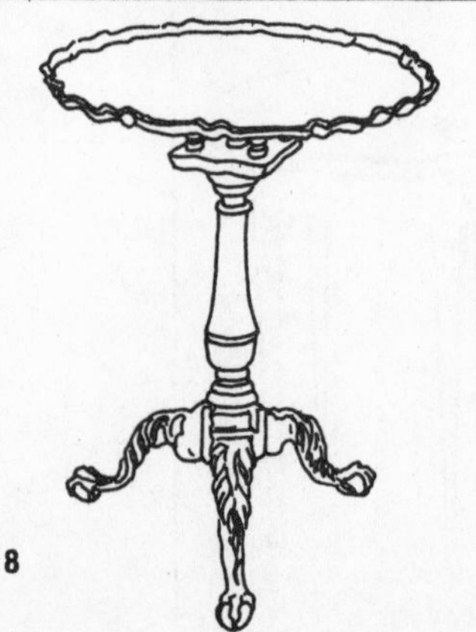

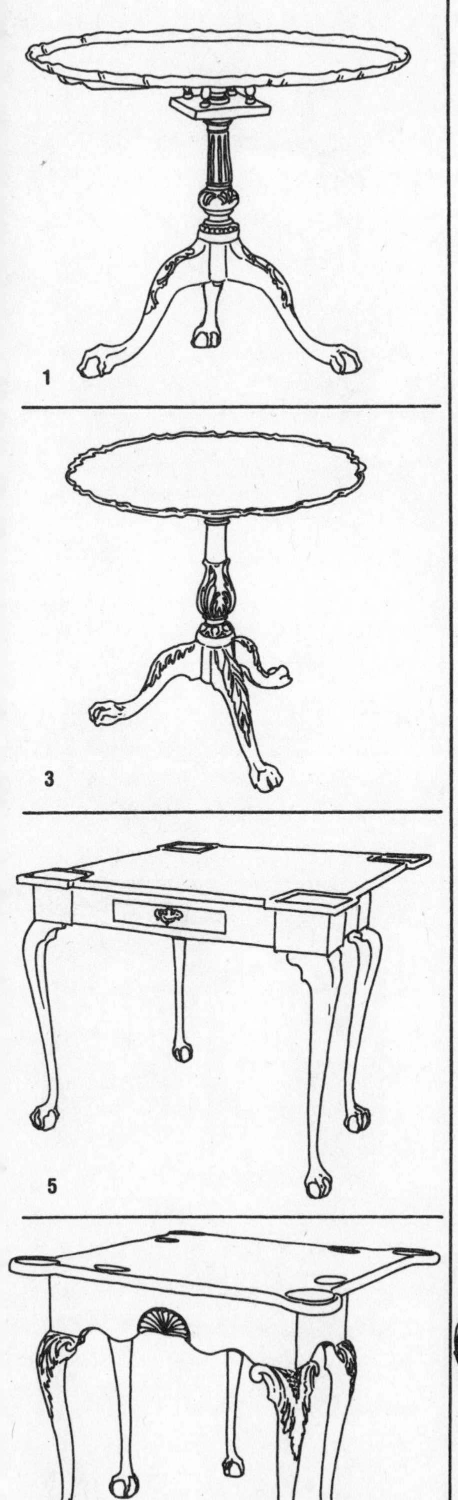

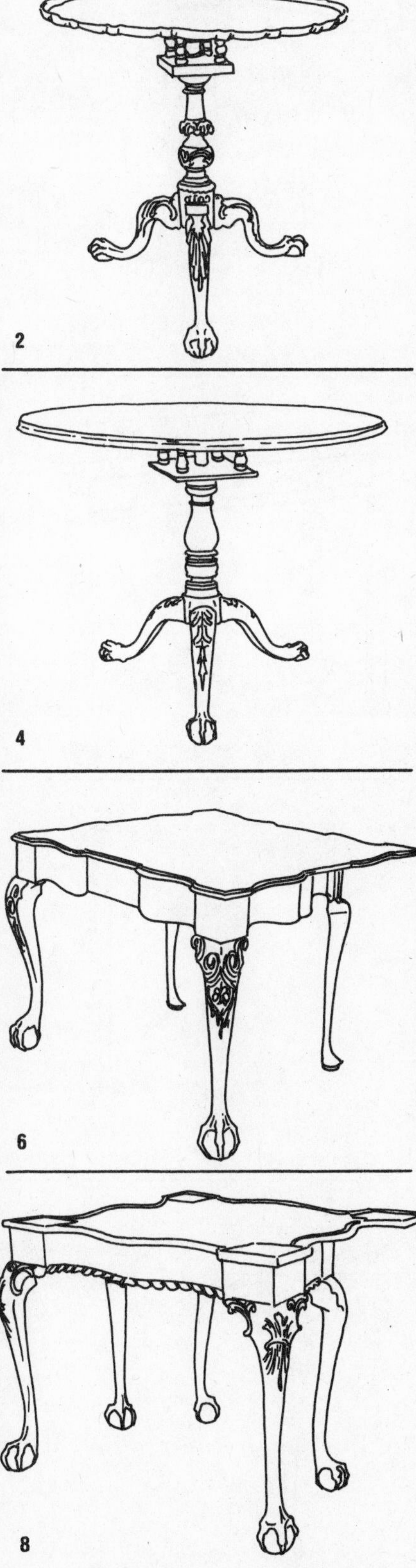

1. Tilt-top tea table. Philadelphia. Popular form in that city. Flattened ball below pillar was common. 1765–1775.

2. Tilt-top tea table. Philadelphia. Pillar and baluster turnings another Philadelphia alternative. 1765–1780.

3. Tilt-top tea table. Charleston, South Carolina. Had acanthus leaf carving on baluster. 1760–1780.

4. Tea table. Lancaster County, Pennsylvania. Heavy molding around top, incised carving on knees. (Possibly by Jacob Bachman.) 1760–1780.

5. Card table. Charlestown, Massachusetts. Lean design and claw-and-ball foot with raked back side talons Massachusetts characteristics. Labeled by famous maker Benjamin Frothingham (1734–1809). 1770–1785.

6. Card table. Newport, Rhode Island. Form also called gaming table. Rear legs ending in pad feet seen on other Newport Chippendale furniture. 1760–1780.

7. Card table. New York. Top has dished-out section for holding counters and candlesticks. Note typical New York foliate and cross-hatched carving on knees. 1740–1755.

8. Card table. New York. Serpentine front common. Fifth swing leg on card tables New York characteristic. 1760–1775.

1. Card table. Philadelphia. Carving on apron similar to that on some Irish tables. 1750–1790.

2. Card table. Philadelphia. Card tables with turreted front corners also seen in Britain. 1750–1790.

3. Card table. Philadelphia. Other Philadelphia card tables have Marlborough legs. These Marlborough legs end in blocked feet. 1760–1790.

4. Card table. Edenton, North Carolina. Note distinctive scalloping of skirt. 1760–1780.

5. Console table. Boston. Rare example of form and of use of mask carving. 1740–1770.

6. Side table with marble top. Massachusetts. Curved skirt and reeded Marlborough legs highlighted by Chinese fretwork. 1760–1775.

7. Side table with marble top. Massachusetts. Gothic fret appears in Plate 196 of Chippendale's *Director.* 1762–1775.

8. Serving table. New York. Wide serpentine molding around top unusual. 1760–1780.

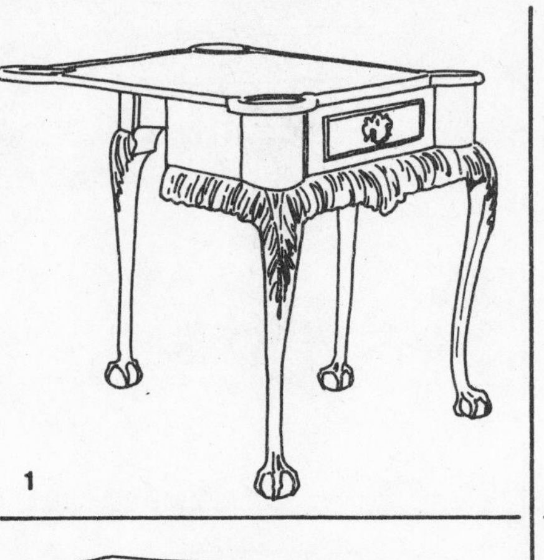
1

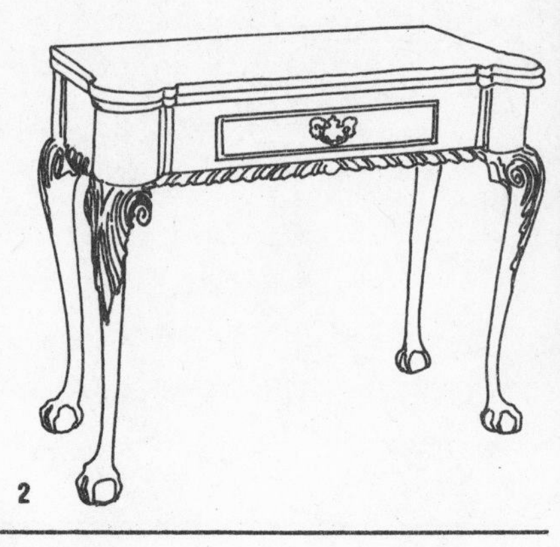
2

3

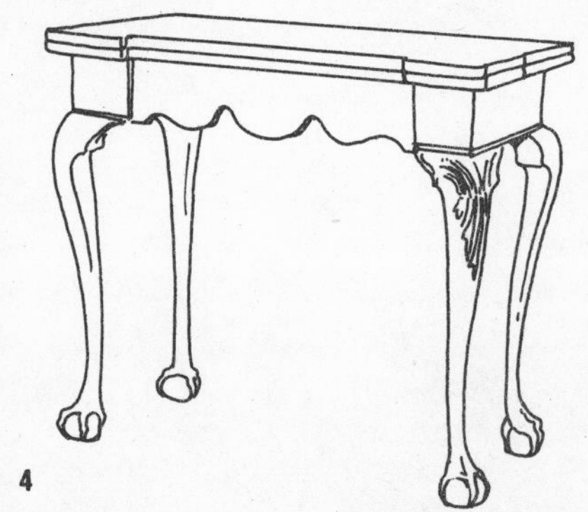
4

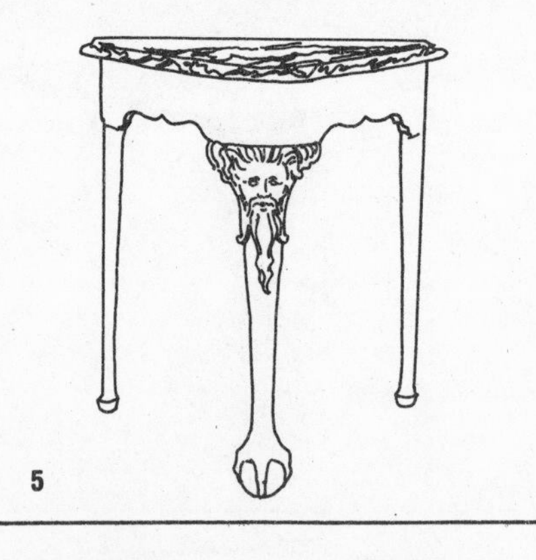
5

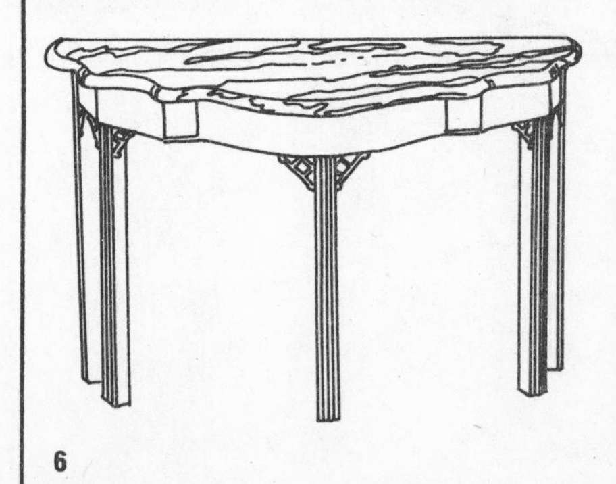
6

7

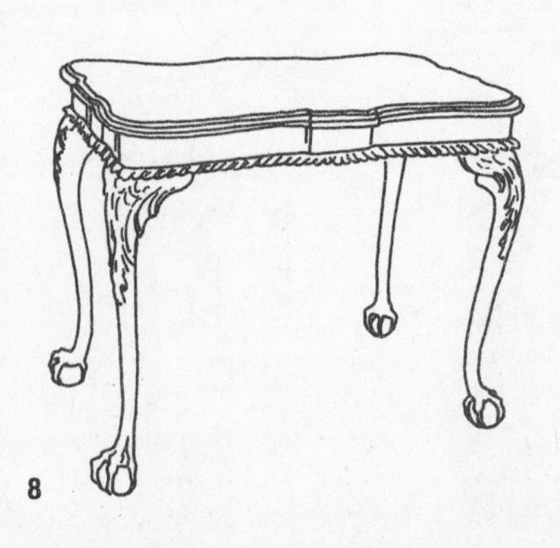
8

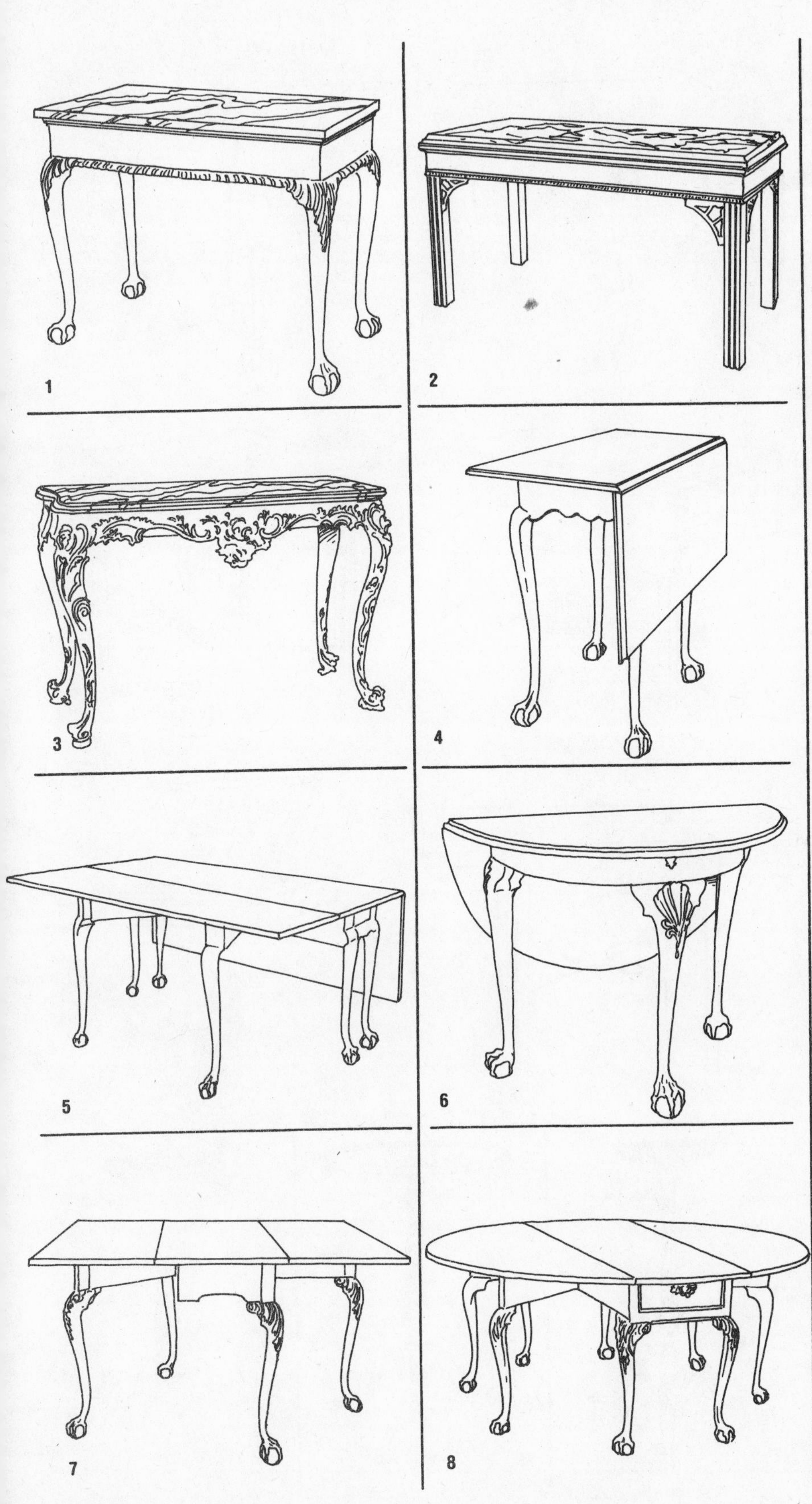

1. Side table with marble top. New York. Of relatively simple design, piece has gadrooned edge and typical New York carving on knees. 1760–1775.

2. Side table with marble top. New York. Similar "sideboard table" in Chinese taste published in *Director.* 1760–1775.

3. Side table with marble top. Philadelphia. Overall form of table, including use of scroll feet and complex carving, underline maker's acquaintance with London styles. (Made by Benjamin Randolph and owned by John Cadwalader.) 1769.

4. Drop-leaf table. Massachusetts. Single drop-leaves not often seen on American tables. 1750–1760.

5. Dining table. Charleston, Massachusetts. Six-legged drop-leaf tables rare. (Labeled by Benjamin Frothingham.) 1755–1790.

6. Drop-leaf table. New York. Top may also be opened to full round or completely pivoted to a vertical position similar to a tilt-top. Carved features suggest New York attribution. 1750–1760.

7. Dining table. New York. Four-legged drop-leaf tables also seen in New England and Philadelphia. 1755–1765.

8. Dining table. New York. Oval top alternative to rectangular one. 1760–1770.

1. Dining table. Philadelphia. Such tables could easily seat eight people. 1758–1780.

2. Drop-leaf table. Philadelphia. Designed to be stored in corner. 1750–1770.

3. Pembroke table. Newport, Rhode Island. "Dot and dash" piercing of stretchers associated with Rhode Island. (Labeled by John Townsend.) 1760–1800.

4. Pembroke table. Philadelphia. Pattern of piercing in stretchers borrowed from Chippendale's *Director,* Plate 53. 1760–1780.

5. Pembroke table. North Carolina. Note use of flat stretchers and blocked feet. 1770–1800.

6. Draftsman's table. New Jersey. Base similar to that on some Philadelphia tilt-tops. Note adjustable drawing surface. 1760–1775.

7. Candlestand. Massachusetts. Typical Massachusetts characteristics include "rat-claw" feet, long fluted column, and urn with spiral carving. 1770–1790.

8. Candlestand. Newport, Rhode Island. Stop-fluting also seen on Newport chair legs. 1760–1780.

9. Kettle stand. Probably Connecticut. Form used at tea parties. Shares characteristics with Newport examples. 1775–1785.

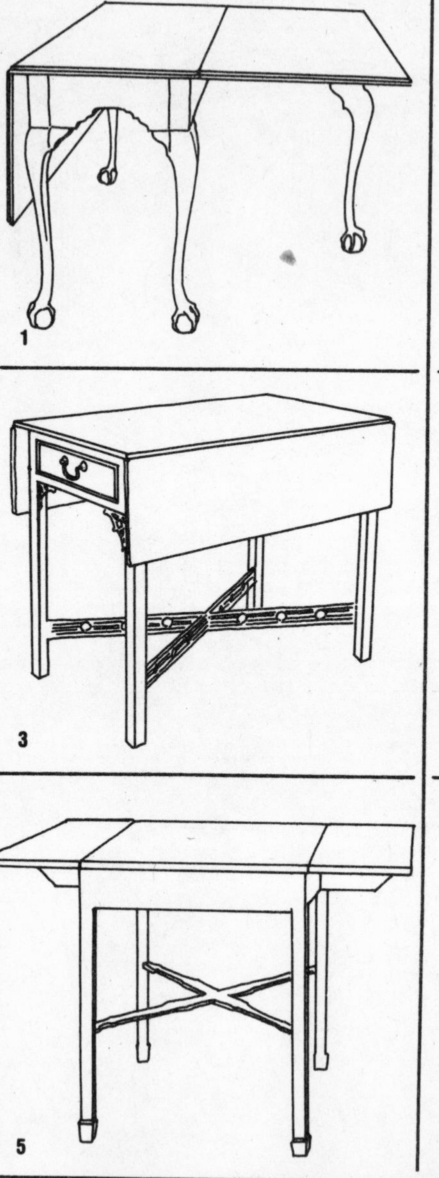

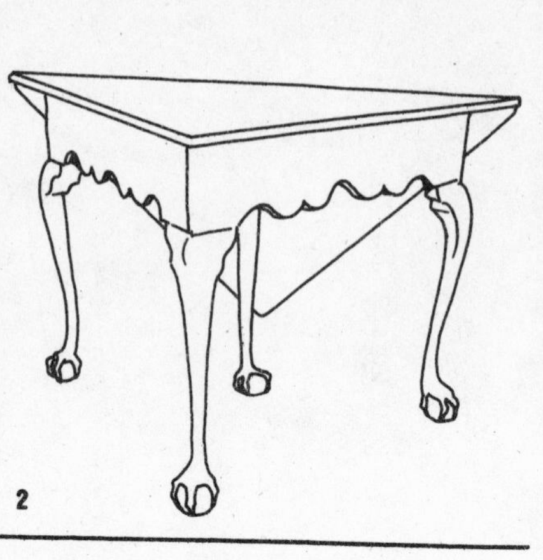

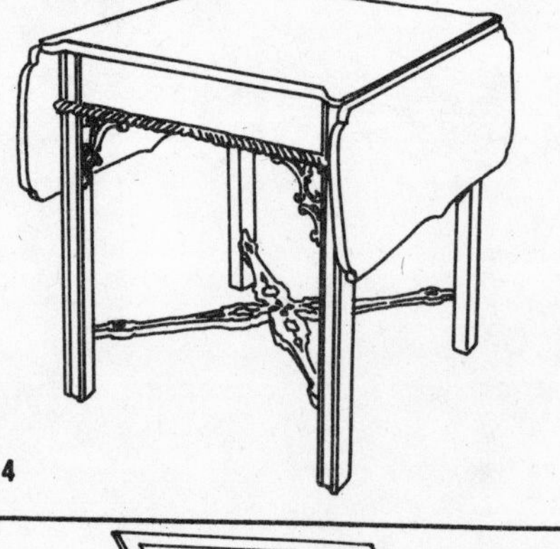

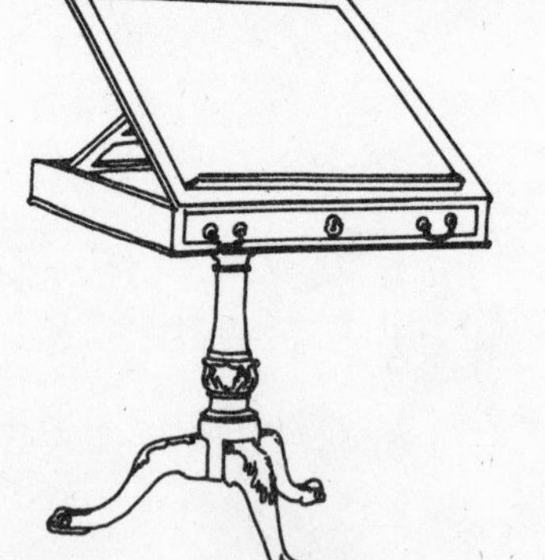

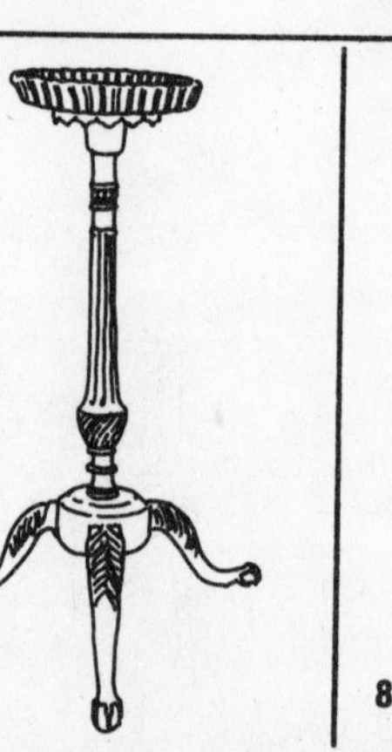

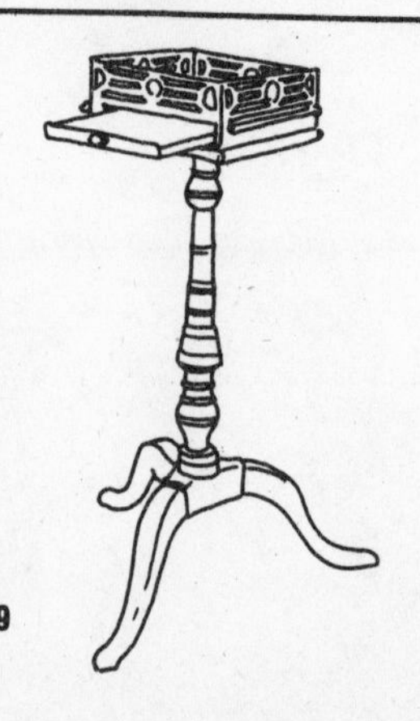

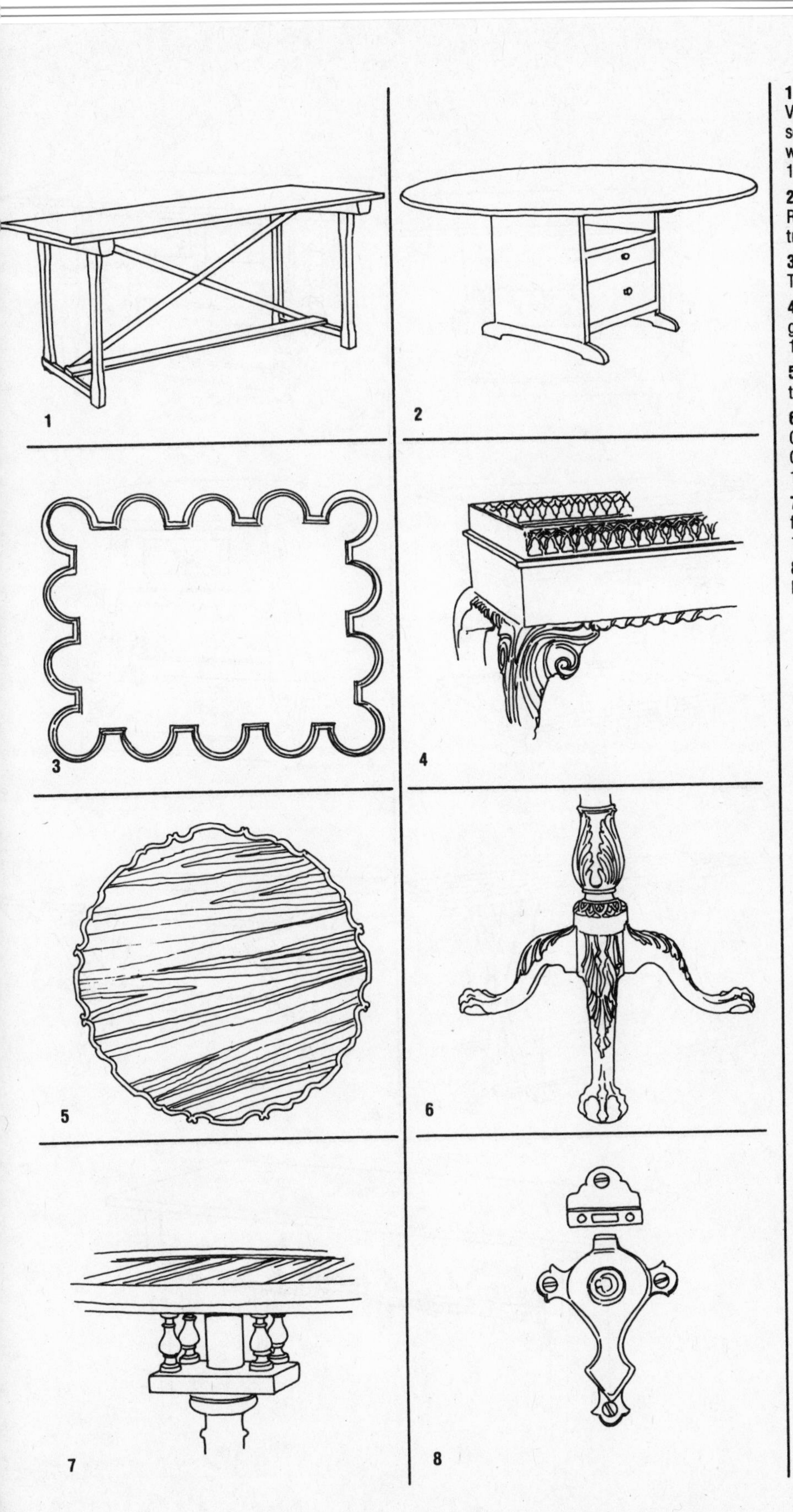

1. Table. Hudson River Valley. X-bracing, seen on some Dutch tables, used widely in this region. 1740–1790.

2. Chair-table. Hudson River Valley. Example with trestle feet. 1750–1800.

3. Turret-top tea table. Top view. 1750–1775.

4. Detail of Gothic-arched gallery on tea table. 1765–1785.

5. Piecrust-shaped top of tilt-top table. 1765–1780.

6. Tripod base of Charleston, South Carolina, tilt-top table. 1760–1780.

7. "Birdcage" device from New York tilt-top. 1740–1770.

8. Tilt-top table catch and lock to secure tabletop.

1. Table with drawer. Pennsylvania. Wide overhang of top and carving of skirt regional characteristics. 1720–1750.

2. Table with two drawers. Pennsylvania. Deeply scalloped and pierced skirt. Drawers of unequal size seen on other Pennsylvania tables. 1720–1770.

3. Table. Ebenezer, Georgia. Made by a member of the Salzburgers, a religious sect that settled here in 1733. Ball-turned legs and stretchers seen on other Germanic tables. 1735–1745.

4. Table. Pennsylvania. Variant of stretcher table with oval top. 1750–1780.

5. Table. Pennsylvania. X-based stretcher table has footrests that help steady table. 1750–1780.

6. Table. Wachovia (now Salem), North Carolina. Art of joining practiced until relatively recently among Germanic furniture makers. Germans often carved the X-bases on these tables. 1750–1780.

7. Table with drawers. Pennsylvania. Fan inlay and dentiling enliven this simple table. 1790–1810.

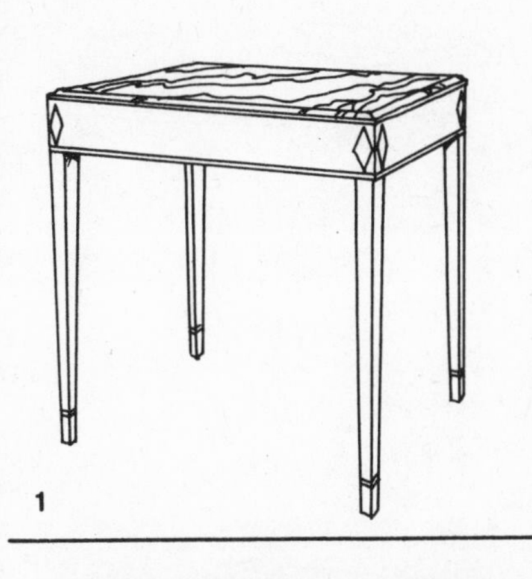

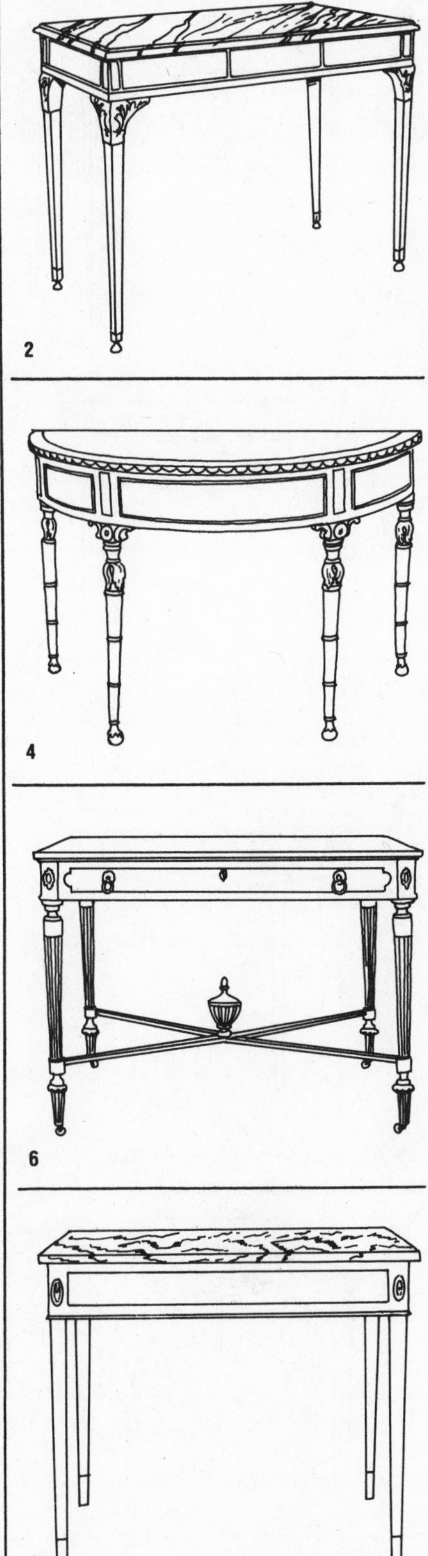

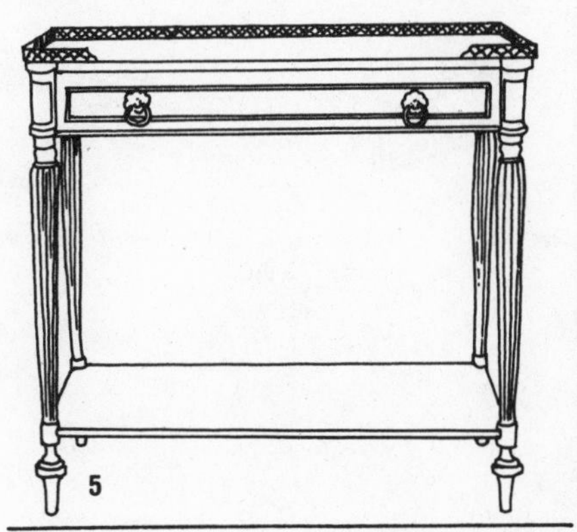

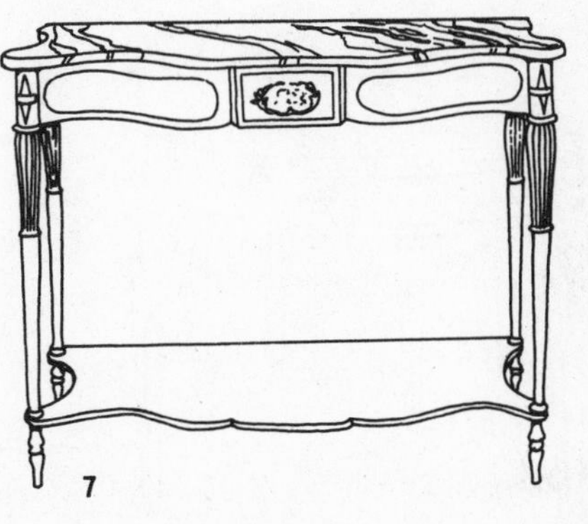

1. Mixing table. Probably northeastern Massachusetts. Delicate table with tapering legs and marble top. 1790–1810.

2. Serving table. Boston. Dark mahogany is combined with light panels of veneered birch around sides of top and legs. Table has marble top. (Probably by John and/or Thomas Seymour.) c. 1800.

3. Serving table. Salem, Massachusetts. Marble top and serpentine shape of table's front and sides cut to follow each other. Note reeded legs. (Labeled by maker William Haskell, active c. 1817–1859.) 1815–1820.

4. Side table. Probably Boston. Unlike most American tables of this period, this one has applied gilt-over-composition details, used widely on French furniture. 1800–1810.

5. Pier table. New York. Stylistically identical to French furniture produced c. 1800, including use of brass galleries and inlay. American woods and stamp of emigré cabinetmaker Charles-Honoré Lannuier identify it as a product of New York. c. 1805.

6. Pier table. New York. Although made by Lannuier, this table is closer stylistically in overall form to New York tables based on English designs. (Stamped and labeled.) 1805–1810.

7. Serving table. Philadelphia or Baltimore. Marble top followed contour of table's front and sides, as did shelf below. *Églomisé* panel is a copy of Plate 2 in Sheraton's *Drawing-Book* (1802). (Possibly by fairly well-known cabinetmaker Joseph B. Barry.) 1802–1810.

8. Serving table. Baltimore. Oval and band inlays ornament this otherwise simple, marble-topped table. c. 1790.

1. Huntboard. Maryland. This form for serving food associated with the South. Always placed against a wall. c. 1790.

2. Corner table. South or possibly Pennsylvania. Strings of inlay lighten surface of this table. Rare form. 1790–1810.

3. Table with one drawer. Eastern Shore, Massachusetts, or Portsmouth, New Hampshire. Panels and bands of inlay and delicate pulls ornament this table with half-serpentine sides. 1790–1810.

4. Table with one drawer. New England. Simple stand with tapering legs decorated with sponge decoration. 1790–1830.

5. Oval table with drawer. New York or Newport, Rhode Island. Elegant and rather unusual form. 1790–1810.

6. Center table. New York. Of the eight drawers, two are shams, four are regular drawers, and two have angled fronts. Heavy urn pedestal and snake feet seen on other New York tables. 1790–1800.

7. Three-part dining table. Newport, Rhode Island. Inlaid motifs seen on other objects by maker John Townsend. Dated 1797.

1. Card table. New England (probably Boston). Radiating motif on front also seen on English work. 1790–1810.

2. Card table. Boston. Table of light and dark woods ornamented by inlay. Ringed corners top delicately reeded legs. (Labeled by makers Samuel Adams and William Todd, active 1798–1800.) 1798–1800.

3. Card table. Boston. Sharp corners interrupt D-shape of table. Inlays used most often associated with this region. Back leg swings to support top in open position. 1795–1810.

4. Card table. Probably Massachusetts. Relatively straight legs appear even thicker due to lack of inlay. Dark banding runs around top and sides, in contrast to light wood veneers. c. 1800.

5. Card table. Probably Boston. Note that top followed line of canted and ovolo corners. c. 1810.

6. Card table. Salem, Massachusetts. Flower-basket carving on front seen on other Salem furniture. c. 1810.

7. Card table. Massachusetts. Typical Massachusetts card table of this period. Note heavy ring turning and reeded legs, as well as presence of castors. 1810–1820.

8. Card table. Connecticut. A host of Classical motifs decorate this painted table, including trophies, urns, festoons, and rosettes. 1795–1810.

1. Card table. Newport, Rhode Island. Fluted frieze or "book" inlay associated with Newport. Patera common Neo-classical ornament in all regions. (Labeled by John Townsend.) 1790–1800.

2. Card table. Newport, Rhode Island. John Townsend, who made this table, primarily remembered for his Chippendale-style furniture. 1790–1800.

3. Card table. Probably Rhode Island. Tables of this design appeared in Hepplewhite's *Guide* and were thus made in Britain in great numbers as well. 1790–1810.

4. Card table. Providence, Rhode Island. Among the most elegant surviving examples of Federal furniture made in Providence. Boasts complex contour of sides and front and subtle yet striking geometric ornamentation. (Labeled by maker Joseph Rawson, active c. 1790–1835.) c. 1800.

5. Card table. New York. Note use of pierced brackets, Chippendale-style holdover. As in the Chippendale period, many New York Federal tables also have fifth swing leg. 1790–1800.

6. Card table. New York. Five-lobed top follows contour of sides and front. Seen on other New York furniture. (Labeled by relatively obscure maker John T. Dolan.) c. 1810.

7. Card table. New York. Distinctive type of New York card table with five-lobed top and carved tripod base. Once thought to have been made only by Duncan Phyfe, a supposition now known to be erroneous. c. 1810.

8. Card table. New York. Note use of canted corners, a lyre base, and four legs. c. 1815.

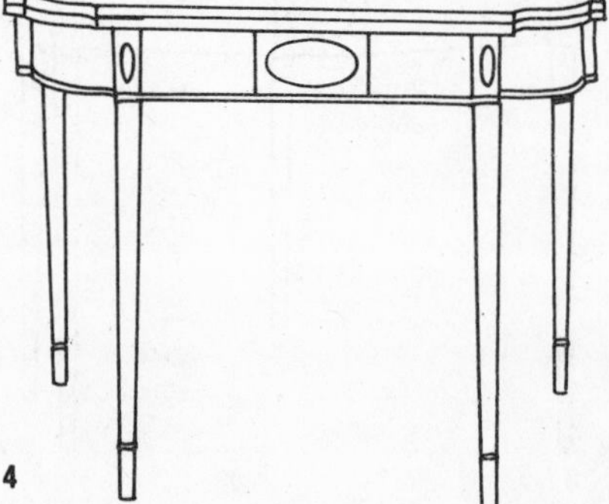

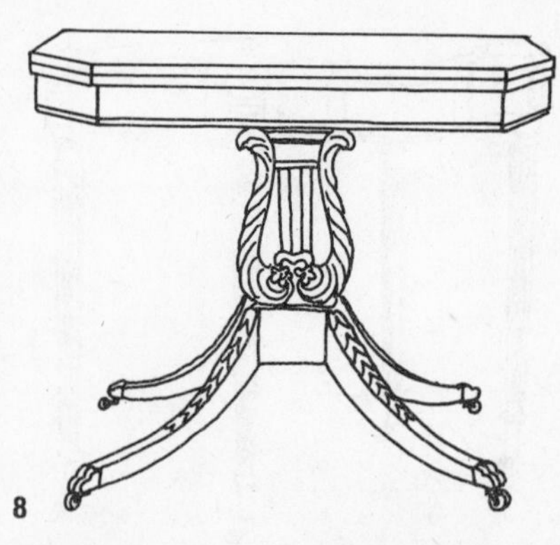

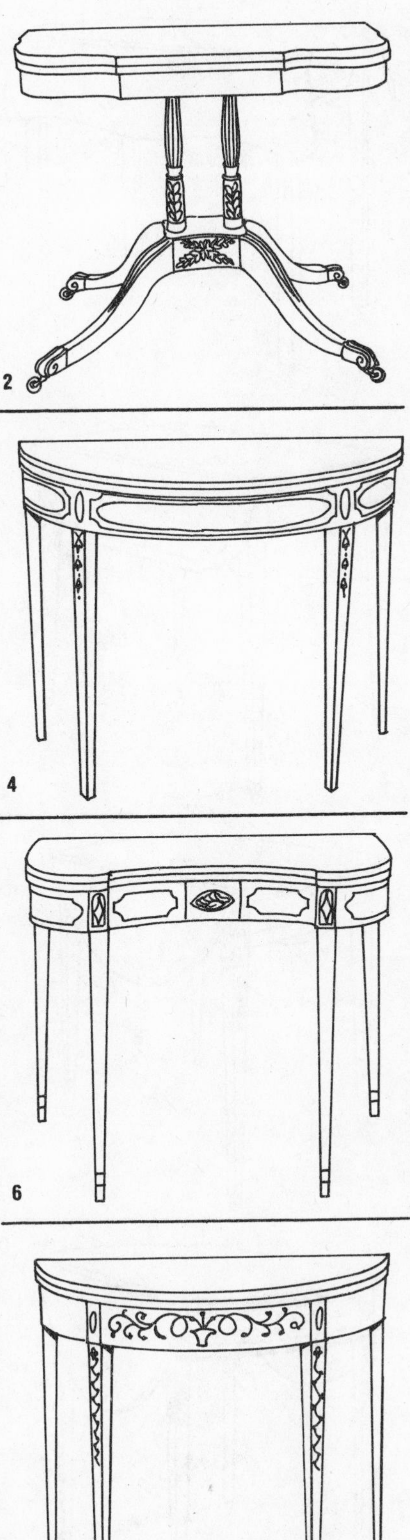

1. Card table. Philadelphia. Presence of brackets and heavy, block feet suggest continuing influence of Chippendale style. (Attributed to noteworthy cabinetmaker Jonathan Gostelowe.) c. 1790.

2. Card table. Philadelphia. Top rests on four carved colonettes. c. 1810.

3. Card table. Baltimore. Urn and floral veneered panels illustrate the artistry of Baltimore cabinetmakers, who were noted for their skillful veneers. 1780–1810.

4. Card table. Baltimore. Wide stretches of veneer associated with the region. c. 1800.

5. Card table. Baltimore. Has typical Baltimore husk inlay with long center petal and inset *églomisé* panels. c. 1800.

6. Card table. Baltimore. Kidney-shaped table has inlaid conch-shell panel, also seen on other Maryland furniture. 1800–1810.

7. Card table. Baltimore. Cuffed foot on this painted table was a Baltimore attribute. 1810–1820.

8. Card table. Charleston, South Carolina. Scrolling, naturalistic inlay covers front and front legs of table. 1800–1815.

1. Pembroke table. Salem, Massachusetts. Form also referred to as breakfast table. This example has many Chippendale-style features. (Labeled by makers Elijah and Jacob Sanderson, active c. 1779–1810.) 1779–1800.

2. Pembroke table. Connecticut. Pierced brackets and scalloped top, Chippendale-style characteristics, blend with overall Hepplewhite design. 1790–1800.

3. Pembroke table. Probably New York. Note use of ovolo corners on drop leaves. 1790–1800.

4. Pembroke table. New York. New York features include leaves without corners, reel turning above delicately reeded legs, and distinctive bulbous foot. (Labeled by maker George Woodruff, active 1808–1816.) 1808–1810.

5. Pembroke table. New Brunswick, New Jersey. Note highly unusual variety of inlays on legs. Cabinetmakers often purchased ready made inlays. (Attributed to Matthew Egerton, Sr. or Jr., active after 1750–1836.) 1795–1815.

6. Drop-leaf table. Georgetown, Maryland. Style of carving and cut corners of top suggest a closer relationship to New York than to Philadelphia counterparts. (By Gustavus Beall.) 1811.

7. Pembroke table. Charleston, South Carolina. Incised husk inlay seen on other Charleston objects. 1800–1815.

8. Pembroke table. Charleston, South Carolina. Note how shape of top is echoed in the panel on side of this table. (By James Main.) 1813–1822.

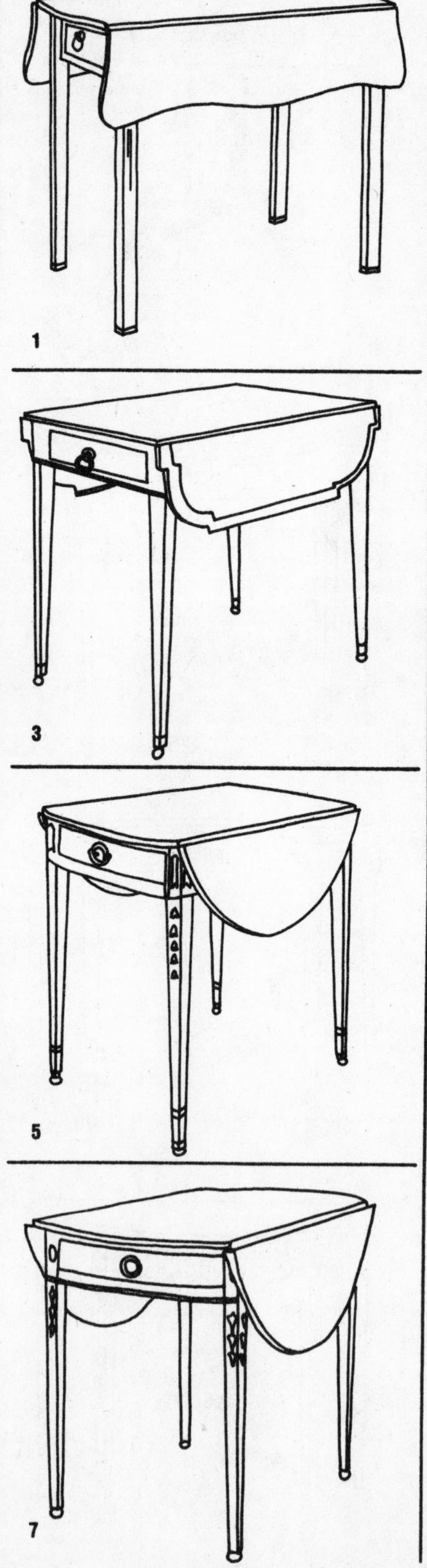

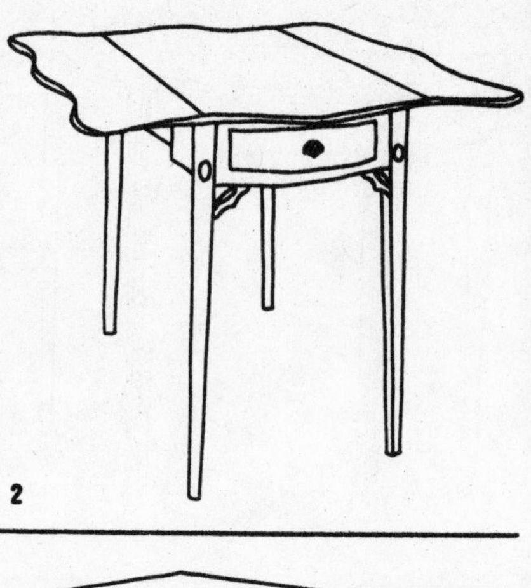

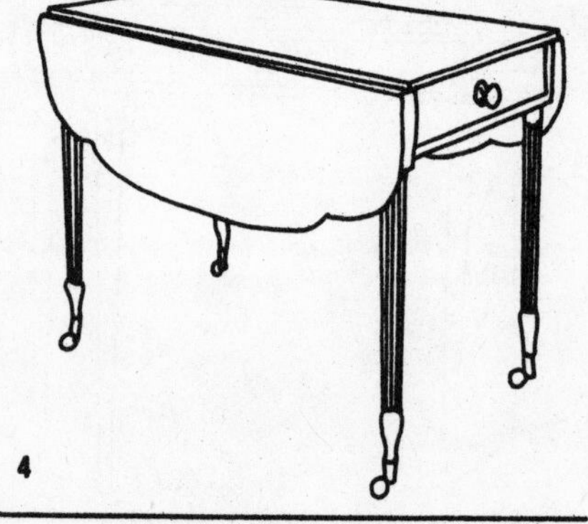

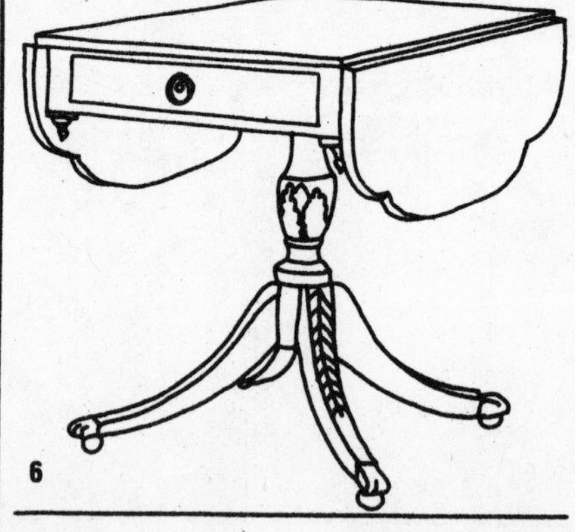

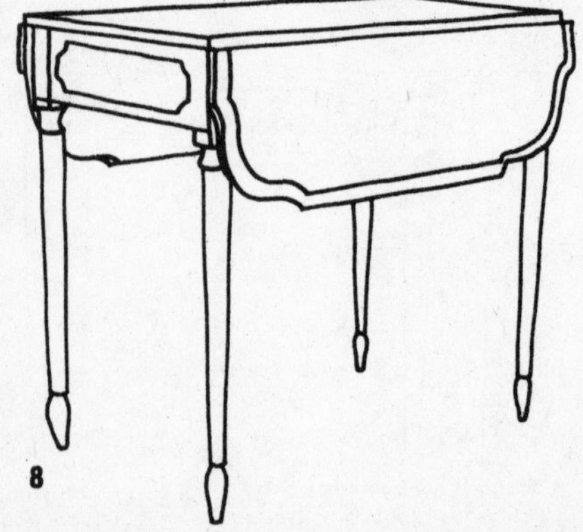

1. Candlestand. Boston or Salem, Massachusetts. Tripod legs end in spade feet. Top of radiating veneer. 1790–1810.

2. Candlestand. Newburyport, Massachusetts. Has tilt-top and petal carving on base. One of a very few labeled candlestands. (By Joseph Short.) c.1800.

3. Candlestand. Boston or Salem, Massachusetts. Noteworthy details include scalloped top, fluting on pedestal, and tear-drop carving on knees. c. 1800.

4. Tilt-top table. New York. Extremely simple compared to carved New York tripod tables. c. 1810.

5. Candlestand. Probably Charleston, South Carolina. Regional attribution based on inlaid eagle. Similar one appears on known Charleston cellaret. c. 1805.

6. Urn or kettle stand. Probably Massachusetts. Relatively rare form. Pull-out support can hold cup and saucer. c. 1800.

7. Urn stand. Charleston, South Carolina. Serpentine-sided stand inspired by plate in Hepplewhite's *Guide*. c. 1790.

8. Oval table. Springfield, Massachusetts. Unusual combination of inlaid hearts, pendants, and dotted band ornaments this otherwise simple table. (Attributed to William Lloyd, active c. 1802–1845.) 1802–1810.

9. Work table. Boston. Form for storing writing and sewing equipment introduced during Federal period. (This example, with canted corners, possibly by John and/or Thomas Seymour, noted Boston cabinetmakers.) c. 1800.

1. Work table. Boston. The lower drawer has no bottom and is used to support bag for storing fabric and tools. On castors for ease in moving. c. 1800.

2. Work table. Salem, Massachusetts. Ring turnings at top of legs and elongated bulbous feet seen in other Massachusetts tables. c. 1805.

3. Work table. Boston. Few objects have both inlaid and painted decoration as this table does. (Signed by Vose and Coates, active 1808–1818.) 1808–1818.

4. Work table. Rhode Island. Unusual inlaid motifs include tassels on legs, obelisks, and light-and-dark diagonal banding around the top. c. 1815.

5. Work table. New York. Stylistically owes much to maker's French origin. (Bears printed label of maker Charles-Honoré Lannuier, active 1803–1819.) 1803–1810.

6. Work table. New York. Form called astragel-end table, referring to rounded sides. Popular in New York and Philadelphia. Note reeded storage area and unusual saber legs. 1805–1815.

7. Work table. Philadelphia. In this example, top ends open to reveal storage space. Unusual turned feet seen on some Philadelphia chests of drawers. (Inscribed "John Sailor maker Phila July 11, 1813." Unfortunately, not much is known about him.)

8. Work table. Philadelphia. Masterfully designed and executed kidney-shaped table with delicately carved details. 1805–1810.

9. Work table. Philadelphia. Astragel-end table has typical Philadelphia reeded leg ending in bulbous foot and some real and some sham drawers. 1805–1810.

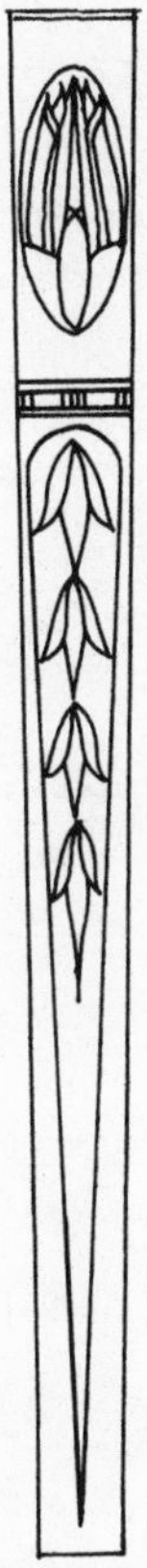

1 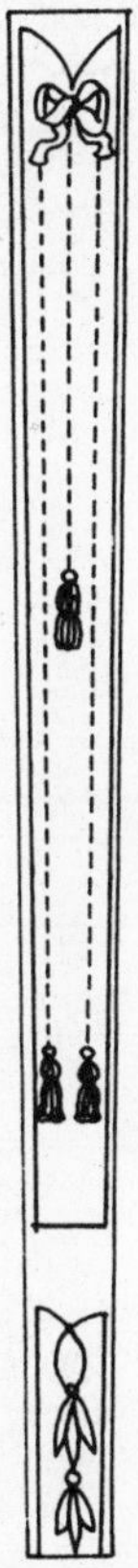 2 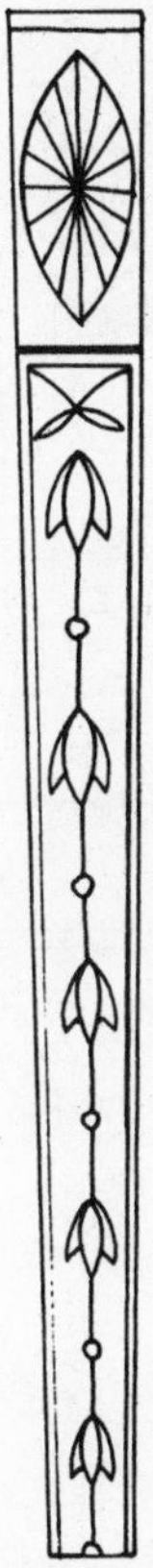 3  4

5

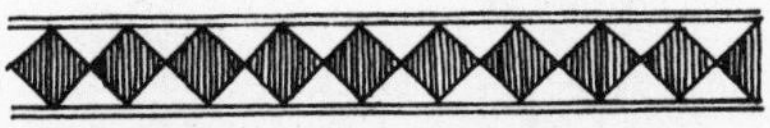

6  7  8  9

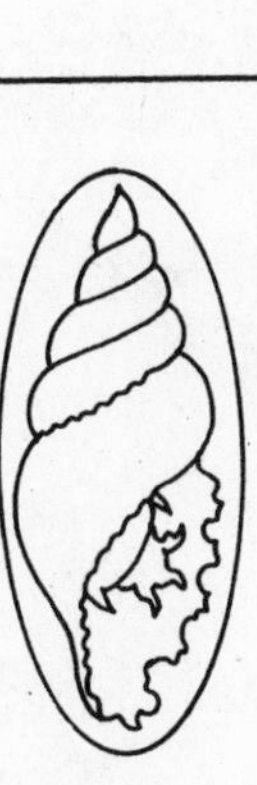

10 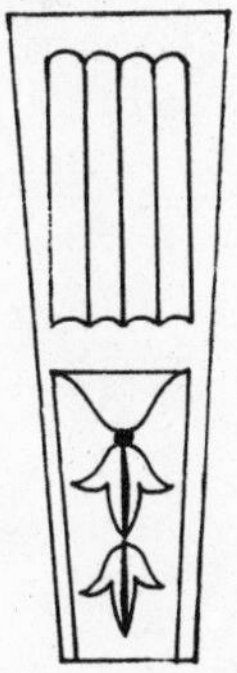 11 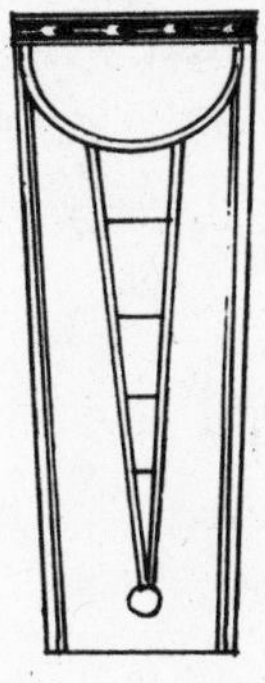 12 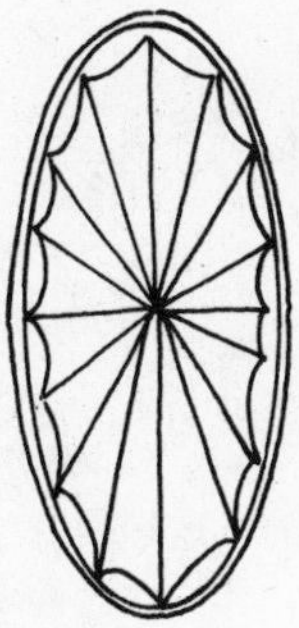 13

1. Ear of corn and bellflower or husk inlay from Baltimore table, c. 1800. Maryland bellflowers typically have long center petal.

2. Delicately inlaid bowknot, tassels, and bellflower from Baltimore side table. 1790–1800.

3. Example of bellflower inlay from table, probably made in Rhode Island. 1795–1815. Motif used in all regions.

4. Floral and bellflower inlay from New York circular card table. c. 1800.

5. Eagle inlay from Massachusetts card table illustrates interest in patriotic motifs during Federal period.

6. Black diamond banding from Newburyport, Massachusetts, card table. c. 1800. Because some banding and stringing were imported, these are not always reliable clues to an object's origin.

7. Distinctive inlay seen on Philadelphia work tables. 1805–1810.

8. Triangle inlay associated with Massachusetts but occasionally seen in other areas.

9. Stringing used on New Jersey Pembroke table, made between 1795–1815.

10. Shell inlay used on corners of Massachusetts card table. c. 1800.

11. Fluted frieze, or book inlay, most often seen on Rhode Island or New York furniture.

12. Distinctive banded pendant, or "icicle" inlay, seen on some Massachusetts, Connecticut, and Rhode Island work.

13. Type of patera often used on New York furniture.

1. Center table. Boston. Three pillars support this simply designed marble-topped table. c. 1820.

2. Center table. New York. Of much heavier proportions than Federal tables. Particular form used in parlors. 1815–1840.

3. Sofa table. New York. Leaf-carved colonettes and eagle support tabletop. This form was often placed in front of sofas. (Attributed to Charles-Honoré Lannuier.) 1815–1820.

4. Drum table. New York. Unusual in that feet are carved of wood rather than cast brass. 1818–1830.

5. Center table. Philadelphia. Masterfully carved table has inset top. (By Antoine-Gabriel Quervelle, 1789–1856.) c. 1830.

6. Sofa table. Philadelphia. Intersecting lyres form the base of the table. Winged animal paw feet common on tables of this period. c. 1820.

7. Card table. New York. Combination of swans' heads and basket of fruit and flowers rare. 1815–1825.

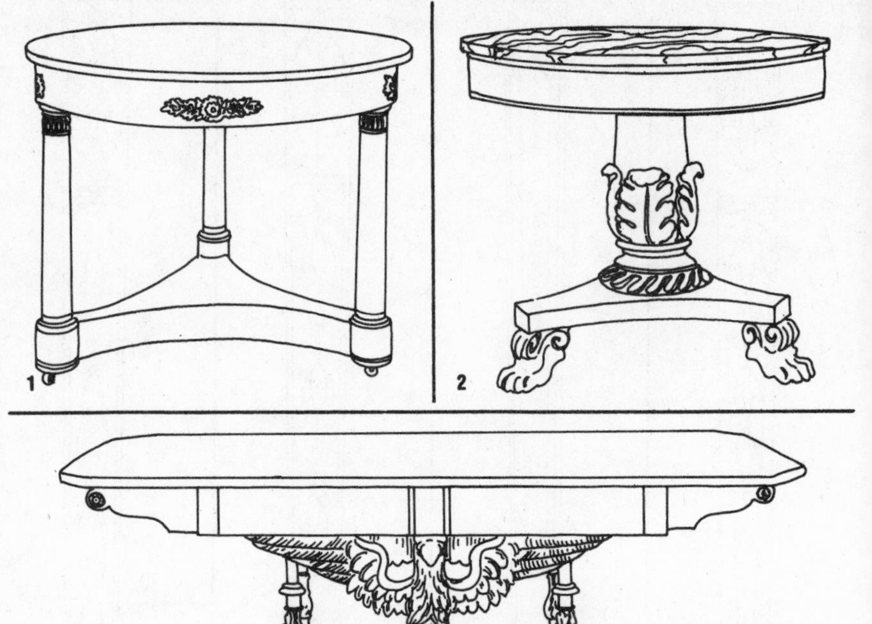

1

2

3

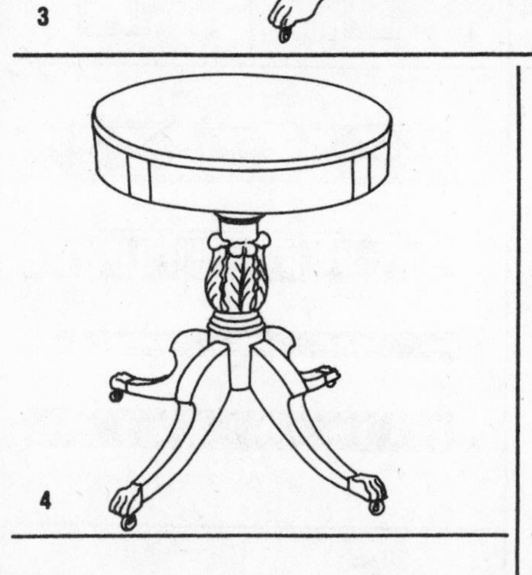

4

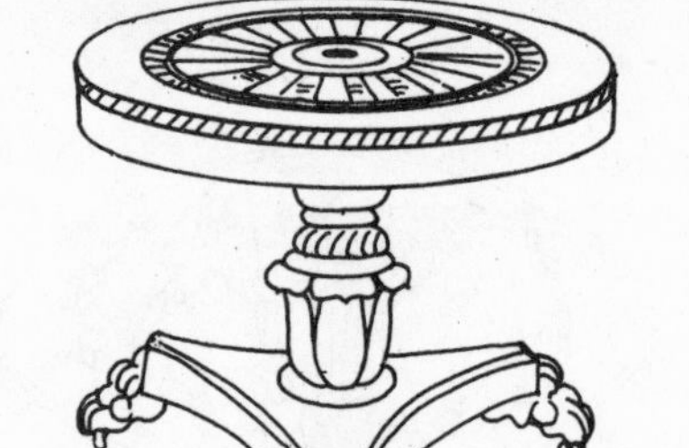

5

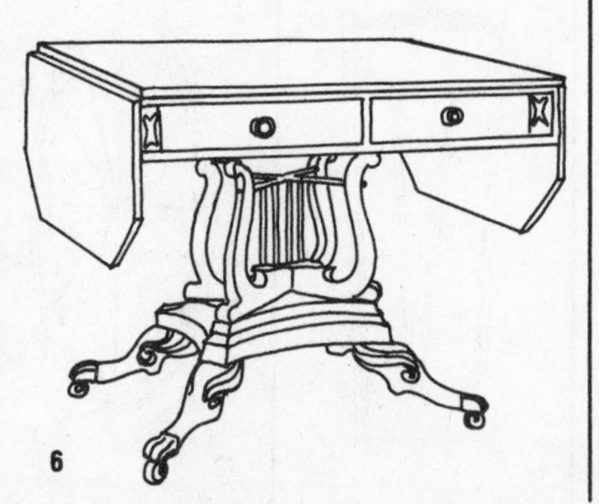

6

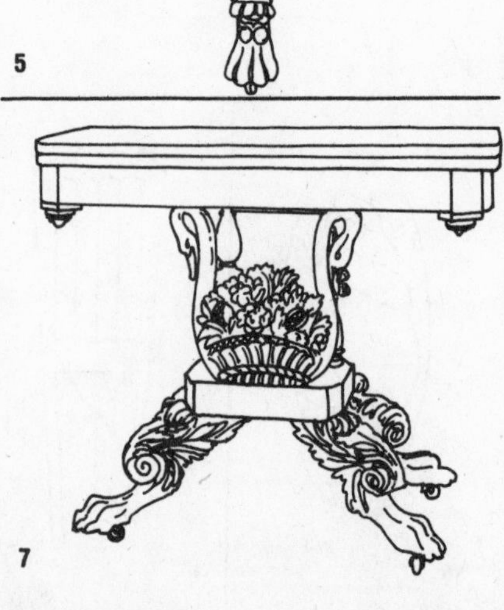

7

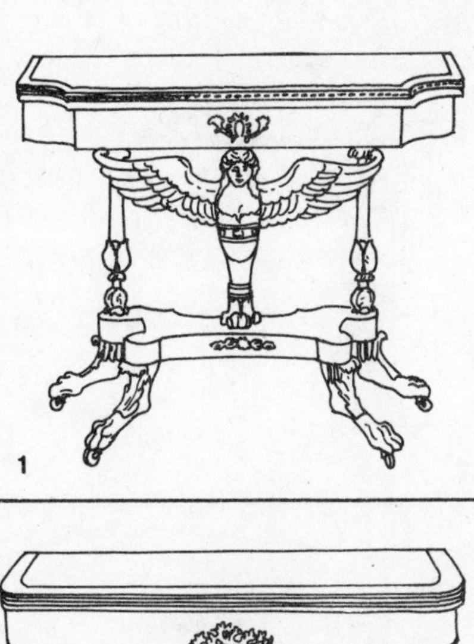

1

2

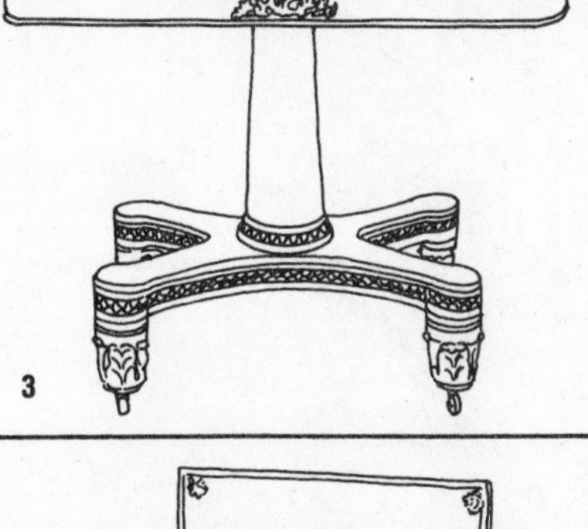

3

4

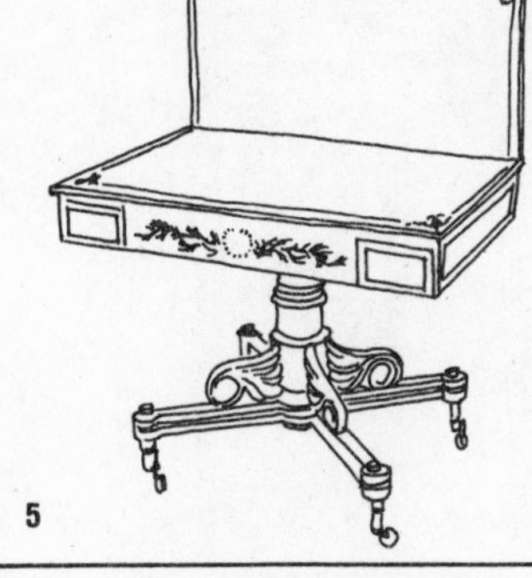

5

6

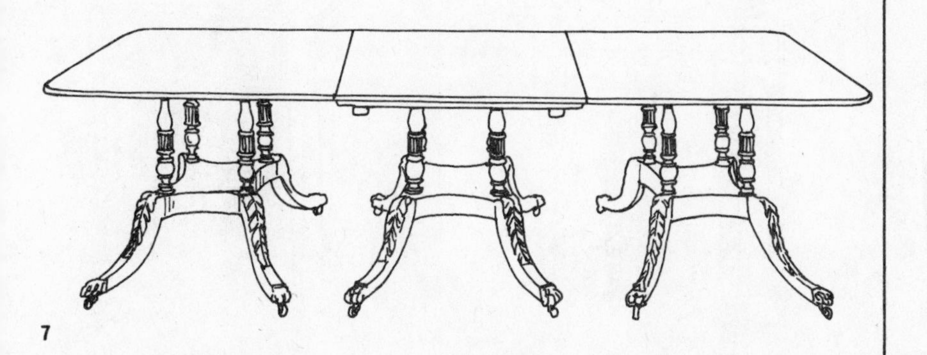

7

1. Card table. New York. Winged caryatid pedestal. (Attributed to Charles-Honoré Lannuier.) c. 1815.

2. Card table. New York. Note gilt and ormolu decoration on this table, made for Stephen Van Rensselaer IV and his wife Harriet Elizabeth Bayard. (Labeled by Charles-Honoré Lannuier.) c. 1817.

3. Card table. New York. Ormolu mounts and trim decorate this pedestal table, based on French Restauration style. 1820–1830.

4. Card table. Philadelphia. Scrolls dominate overall design from feet to pedestal to apron. 1820–1830.

5. Card table. Baltimore, Maryland. Scrolled brackets soften transition between pedestal and X-base. Pine grained to look like rosewood. 1820–1830.

6. Drop-leaf table. Massachusetts. Grained and marbleized decoration on table of relatively heavy proportions. (Signed by Philip H. Saunders.) 1820–1840.

7. Dining table. New York. Sectional dining room table of pedestal type popularized by Thomas Sheraton. 1815–1830.

1. Drop-leaf table. New York. Has leaves with cut corners, as do many earlier New York tables. 1830–1840.

2. Pier table. New York. Table rests on column and caryatid supports and dolphin feet. Similar to designs by Percier and Fontaine. c. 1815.

3. Pier table. New York. Table combines ormolu mounts, marble, and mahogany veneered over pine. Feet are painted and gilded. 1815–1820.

4. Pier table. Philadelphia. Table of powerful design also has marble top and pillars. Pier tables were usually placed between two windows. Their mirrored backs reflected light. c. 1830.

5. Work table. Salem, Massachusetts. Swollen and heavily reeded legs are topped by flaring, leafy cups. c. 1815.

6. Work table. Probably Salem, Massachusetts. Ovolo corners carved with rosettes and leaves, a motif appearing in Sheraton's designs. c. 1815.

7. Work table. Massachusetts. Note ring, reel, and twist turnings on legs. c. 1820.

8. Work table. New York. Note use of lion's-paw castors, lion's-head pulls, and wooden storage compartment. c. 1810.

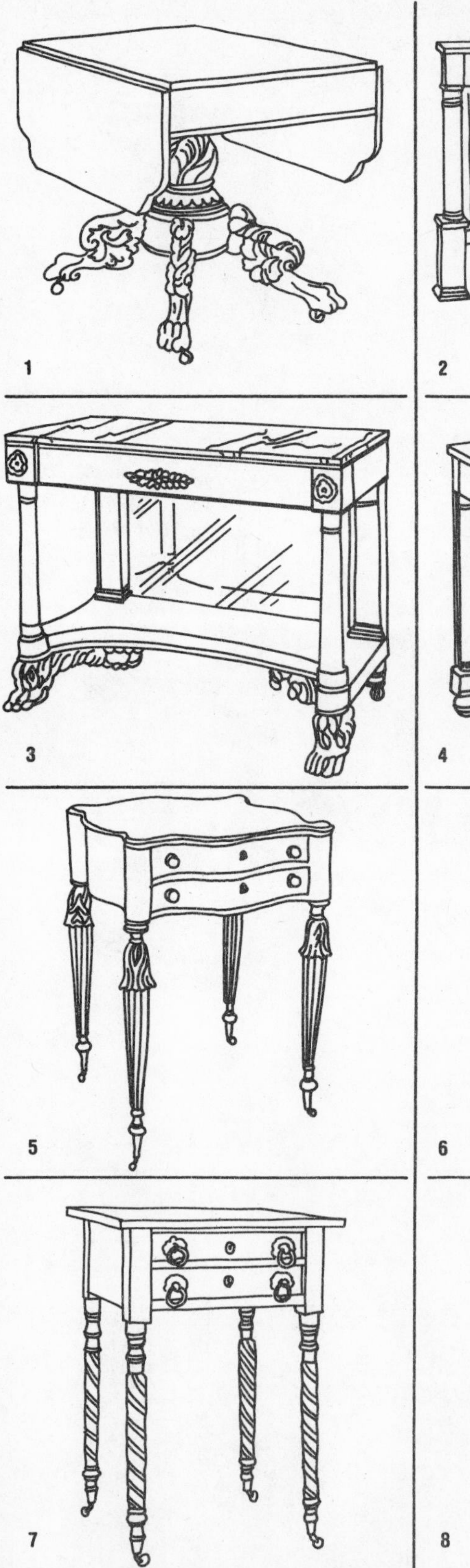

1

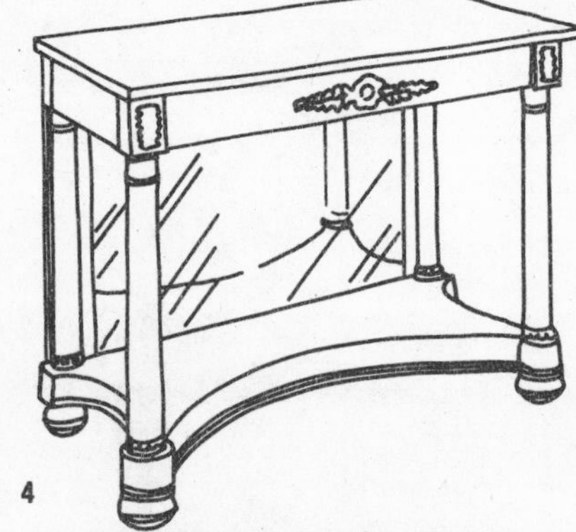

2

3

4

5

6

7

8

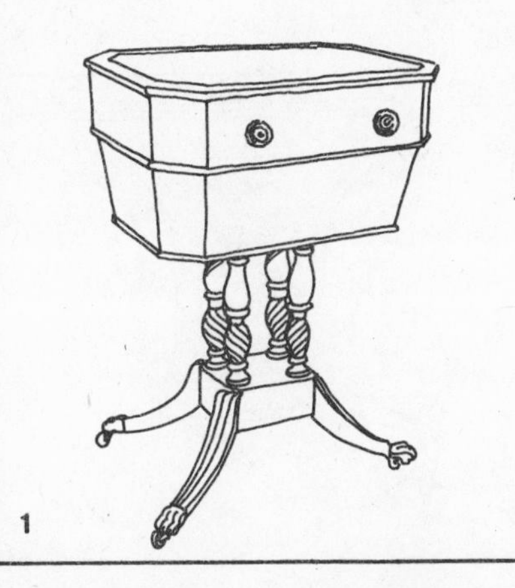

1

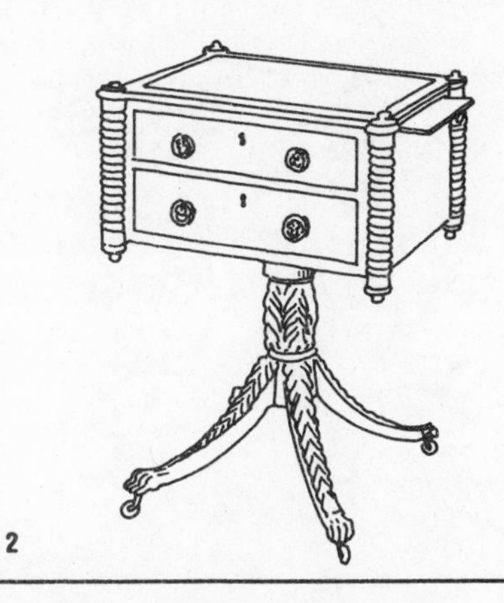

2

3

4

1. Work table. New York. Square with canted corners, this work table bears the label of Duncan Phyfe. c. 1815.

2. Work table. New York. Pedestal-based table with bird's-eye maple veneer on top and fronts of drawers. Note ring-turned ovolo corners and slide for holding candlestick or sewing equipment. c. 1815.

3. Work table. New York. Note lyres ending in swans' necks. (Labeled by maker Michael Allison.) c. 1820.

4. Work table. New York. Much heavier and simpler than earlier American work tables. 1815–1840.

1. Center table. Boston. Typically heavy proportioned table with serpentine sides and scrolled legs. (Signed by obscure maker and/or retailer "S. Beal.") 1830–1850.

2. Card table. Probably New York. Late Classical or "pillar and scroll" furniture tends to be relatively simple in form with little ornamentation other than broad expanses of veneer. c. 1840.

3. Card table. Probably New York. Hexagonal urn pedestal base. c. 1840.

4. Card table. Northeastern America. Pedestal-type table of extremely simple design rests on four flattened-ball feet. 1830–1850.

5. Pier table. Probably New York. Double-scrolled sides support marble top. c. 1840.

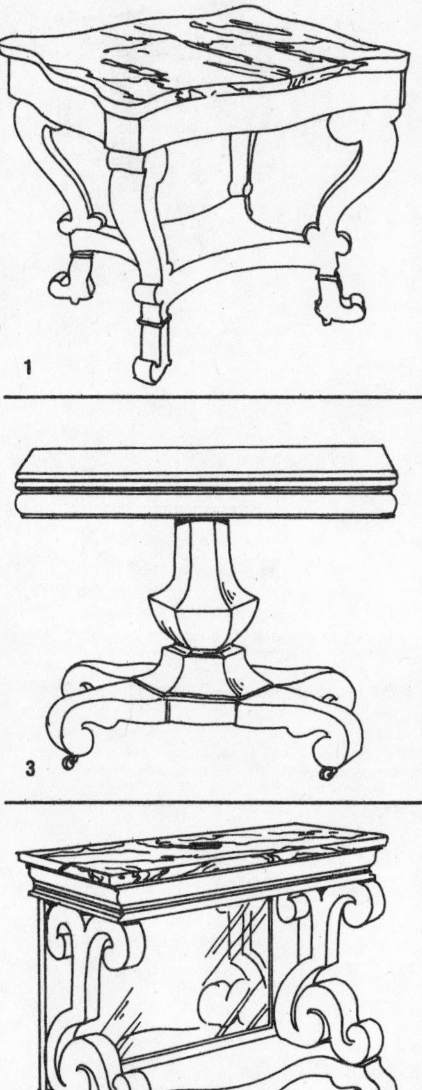

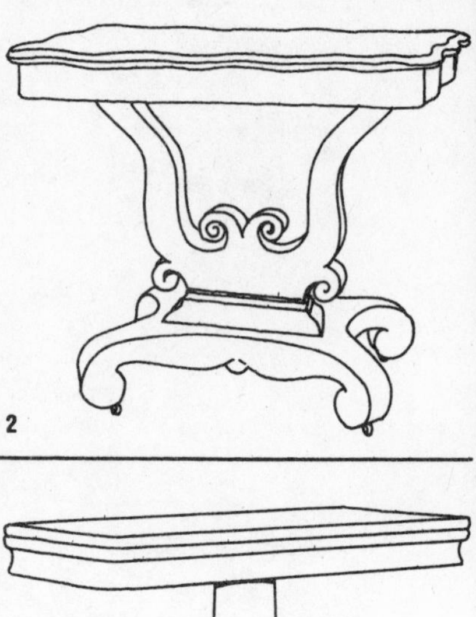

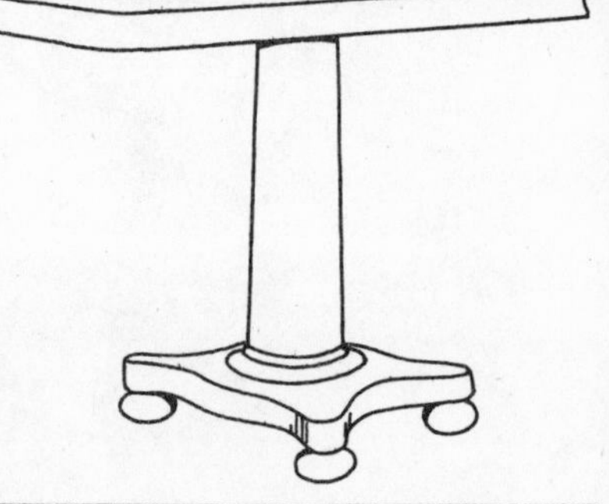

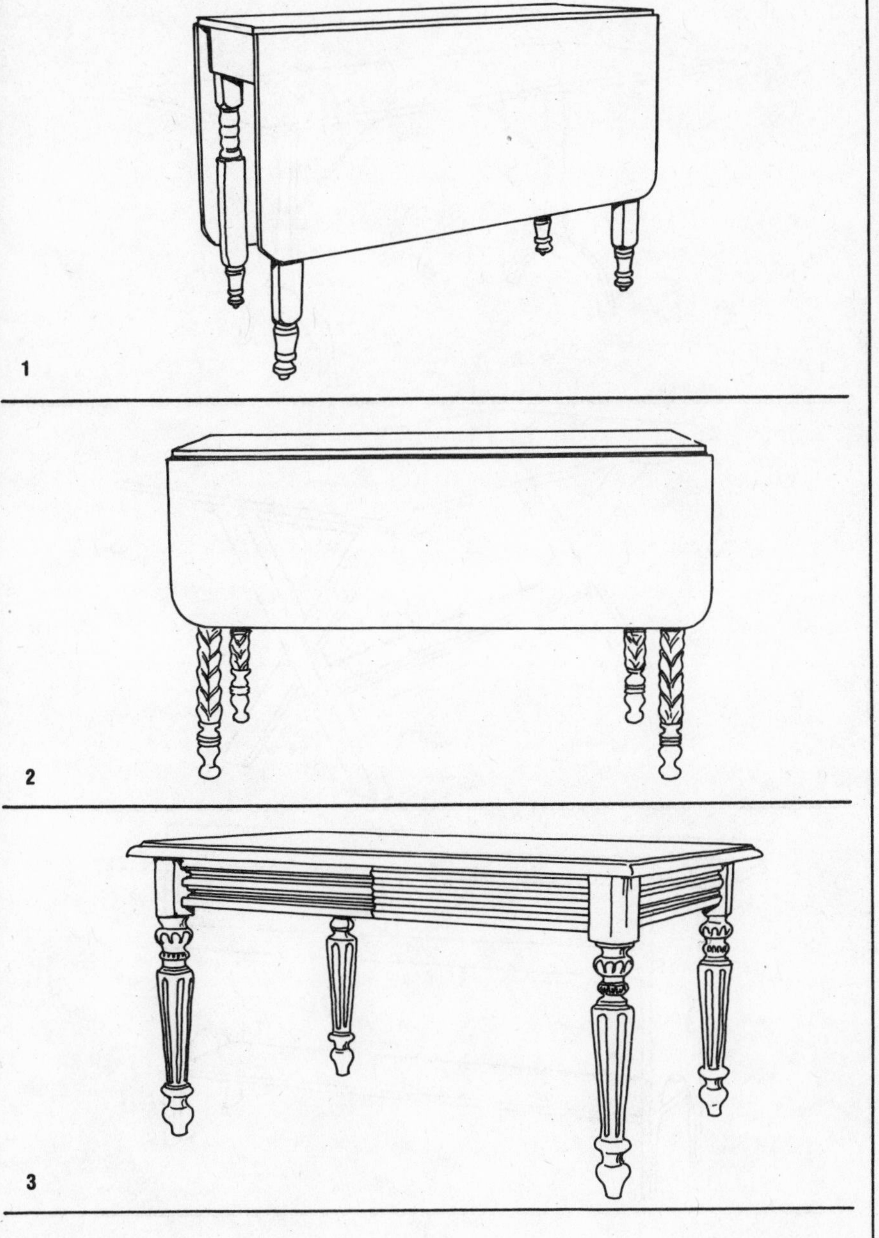

1. Drop-leaf table. America. Vernacular table with vase-turned legs above square section. 1820–1890.

2. Drop-leaf table. America. Has acanthus leaf carving on legs. 1830–1850.

3. Library table. New York. Note use of extremely late version of reeded leg. (Designed by architect Richard Upjohn, 1802–1878.) c. 1842.

1. Dining table. Harvard, Massachusetts. Iron braces support table, leaving plenty of leg room. 1825–1850.

2. Ironing table. Enfield, Connecticut. X-braced work table. 1810–1860.

3. Baking table. Mount Lebanon, New York. Utilitarian form designed for comfort of workers. c. 1820.

4. Drop-leaf table with one drawer. Hancock, Massachusetts. Work table with gracefully turned legs. 1815–1825.

5. Drop-leaf table with two drawers. Hancock, Massachusetts. Innovative Shakers interested in space-saving furniture designs. c. 1820.

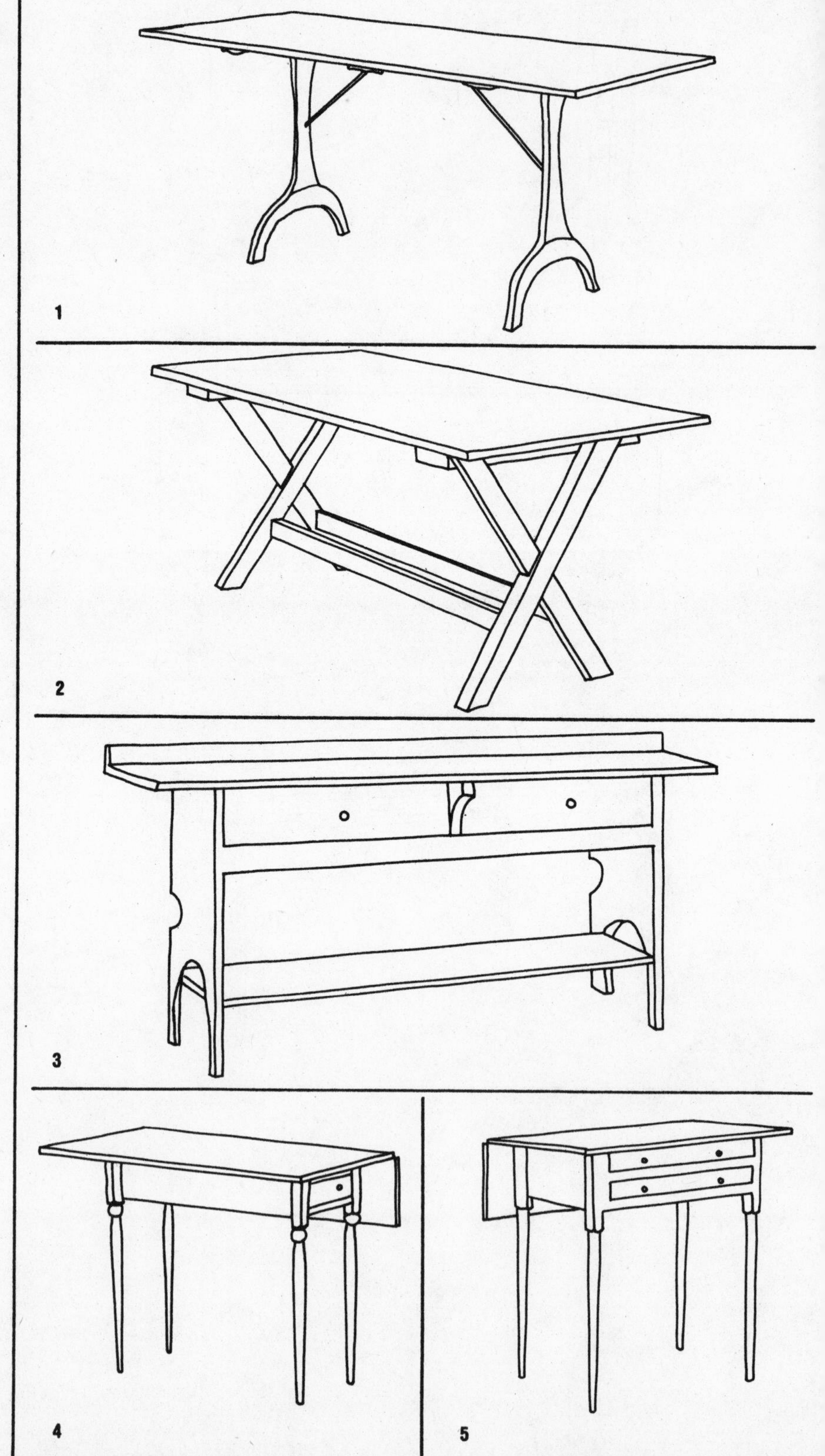

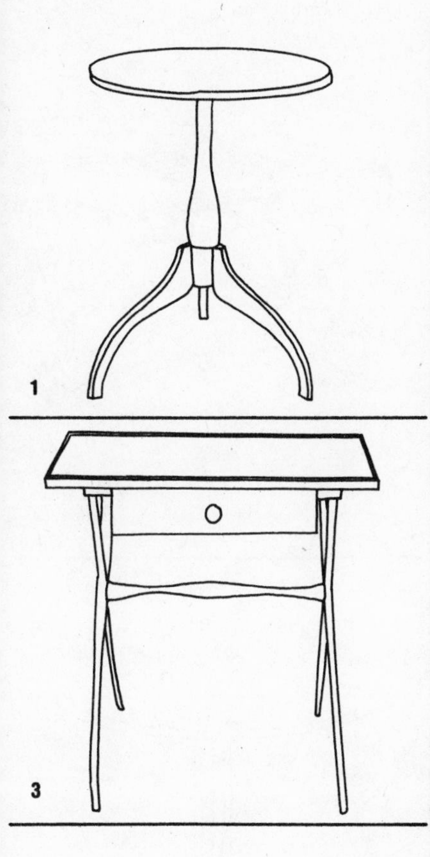

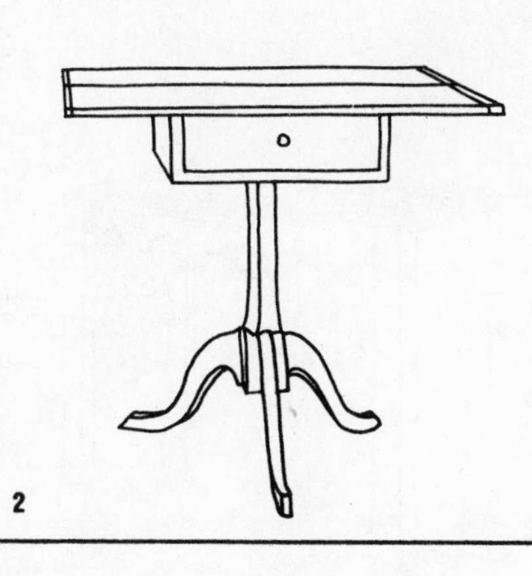

1. Candlestand table. Probably Mount Lebanon, New York. Appearance of tripod candlestand harkens back to late 18th-century "worldly" furniture design. 1820–1830.

2. Sewing stand. Mount Lebanon, New York. Elegant yet highly utilitarian furniture form. 1830–1850.

3. Sewing table. Mount Lebanon, New York. Extremely delicate legs and stretcher substitute for more common tripod base. c. 1850.

1. Serving table. Boston. This presentation piece has pink marble top. Gothic ornamentation used in reserve on sides and front and in brackets. c. 1837.

2. Gaming table. New York. Quatrefoils cut through apron. Basic form of table is Late Classical. 1829–1835.

3. Dining table. New York. Gothic Revival style not often used for dining-room furniture. c. 1840.

4. Table. New York. (Designed by Alexander J. Davis for Lyndhurst and probably executed by Ambrose Wright or Richard Byrne.) c. 1842.

5. Table. America. Scrolling under top, suggesting arches, and turned finials ornament this side table. c. 1850.

6. Sofa table. Baltimore, Maryland. Crocket decoration around base. (Made by John Needles, 1786–1878, for his daughter's marriage in 1857. A number of objects made and labeled by him survive.

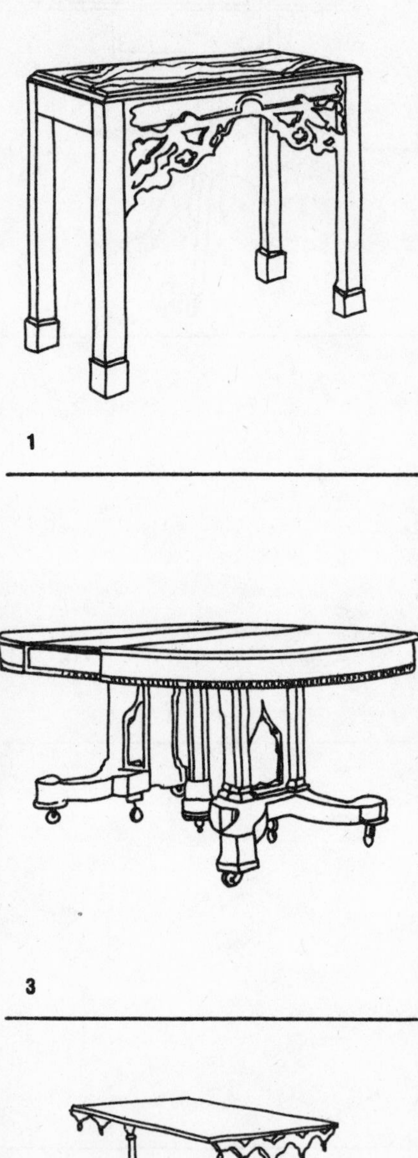

1

2

3

4

5

6

1

2

3

4

1. Card table. New York. Back legs swing to support top. (Bears stenciled name of maker Charles A. Baudouine, 1808–1895.) 1852.

2. Center table. New York. Highly sculptural in overall design. (One of few known objects labeled by John Henry Belter.) 1856–1861.

3. Center table. New York. Marble-topped table made by one of many New York cabinetmakers who worked in this style. 1850–1865.

4. Sewing table. Cincinnati, Ohio. As the 19th century progressed, Midwestern cities rivaled their Eastern counterparts in furniture production. (By Robert Mitchell, 1811–1899, and Frederick Rammelsburg, 1814–1863.) c. 1860.

1

Louis XVI Revival

1. Library table. New York. Inspired by French Classical style. (Attributed to Leon Marcotte.) 1872.

1. Card table. Boston or New York. Carving on front similar to carved crest rails seen on other Renaissance Revival–style furniture. c. 1850.

2. Table. New York. Pedestal of this ornate table decorated with bosses. (Labeled by little-known makers Sumner Kingman and Robert H. G. Murphy.) 1868–1872.

3. Work table. New York. Incised ornamentation made by rotary-powered chisel. (Stamped by relatively unknown maker George Hess, active c. 1864–after 1882.) c. 1876.

4. Library table. New York. Heavy ornamentation lightened by marble mosaic. Made for the William V. Vanderbilt house in New York. (By Herter Brothers.) 1882.

5. Table. Probably Philadelphia. Much Renaissance Revival furniture tended to be made of angular, flat elements, as seen here, in contrast to emphasis on three-dimensionality in Rococo Revival style. 1865–1880.

6. Dining table. Grand Rapids, Michigan. Rectilinear supports ornamented by bosses. (By Berkey & Gay.) 1873.

1

2

3

4

5

6

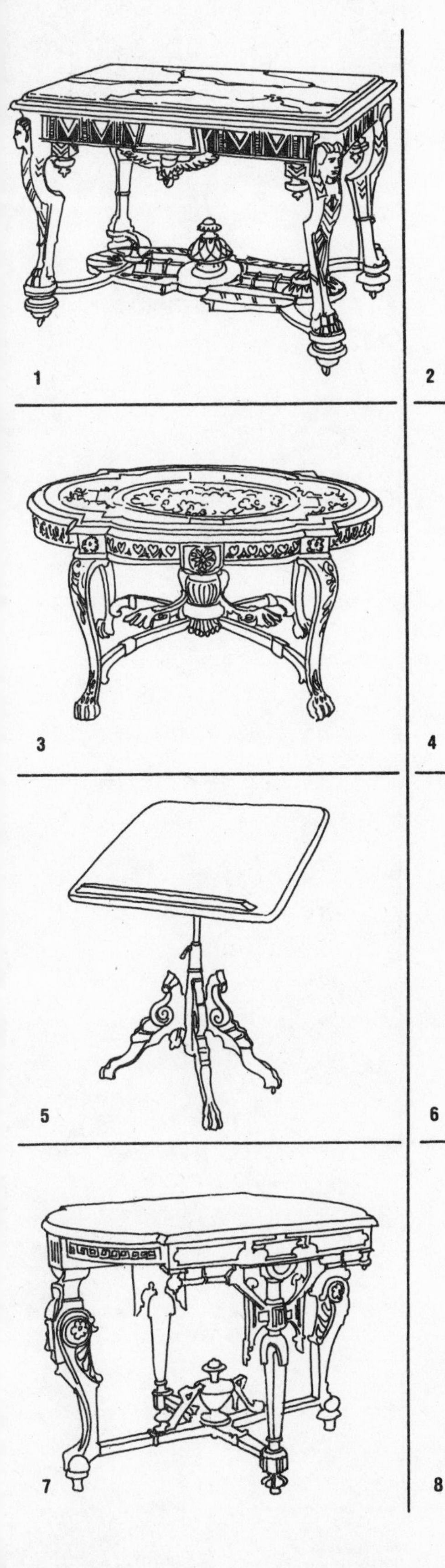

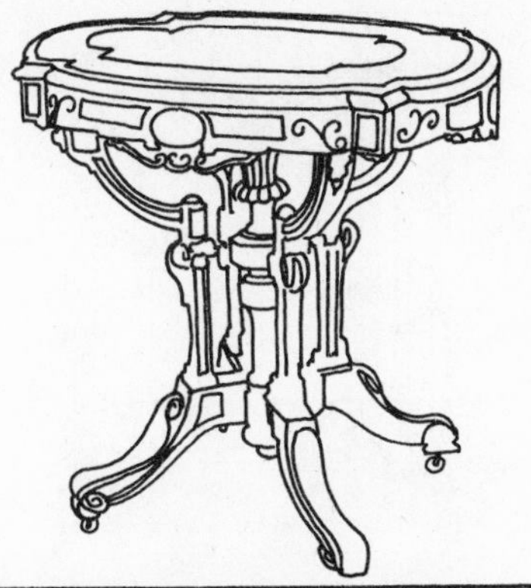

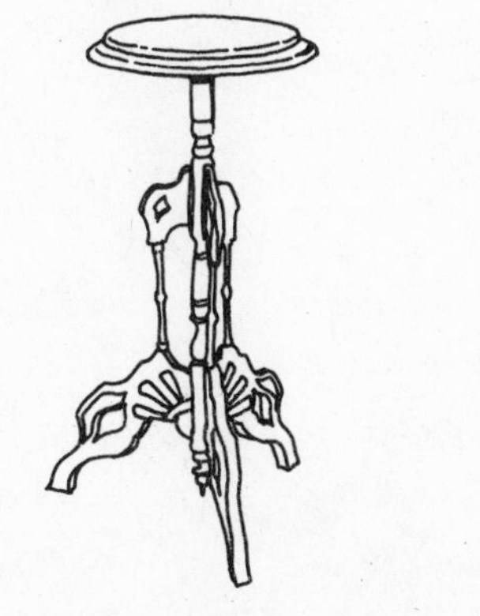

1. Table. Probably New York. Egyptian motifs often appear in this style, with boldly carved and gilded decoration. c. 1870.

2. Table. Probably New York. Use of such bosses and shield also seen on Renaissance Revival furniture. c. 1870.

3. Table. Probably New York. Palmette motif, often found on Neo-Grec furniture, here appears inlaid, incised, and carved. c. 1875.

4. Table. Newark, New Jersey. Pedestal base table with four supports. (Attributed to John Jelliff & Co.) c. 1870.

5. Drafting table. Philadelphia. Animal paw feet seen on some Neo-Grec tables. (By obscure maker G. Gates.) c. 1877.

6. Table. Grand Rapids, Michigan. Table illustrates angular elements and flat decoration favored at this time. (By Berkey & Gay.) 1870–1880.

7. Table. Grand Rapids, Michigan. Has ebonized and gilded decoration. Note use of urn and caryatids. 1870–1885.

8. Table. Grand Rapids, Michigan. Less expensive example in Neo-Grec style. 1870–1880.

1. Table. America. Has painted cast iron base and marble top for outdoor use. 1860–1890.

2. Table. America. Rustic table made of roots and unfinished wood. 1860–1900.

3. Table. Boston. Rather quiet example in rattan. Fragility of material has caused much wicker furniture to be lost. (By Wakefield Rattan Co., 1844–1897.) After 1877.

4. Sewing stand. Litchfield, Connecticut. Most *papiér-mâché* furniture used in America was imported from England. This object was an exception. By Litchfield Manufacturing Co., 1850–1854, a short-lived and little-known American company. 1850–1854.

1

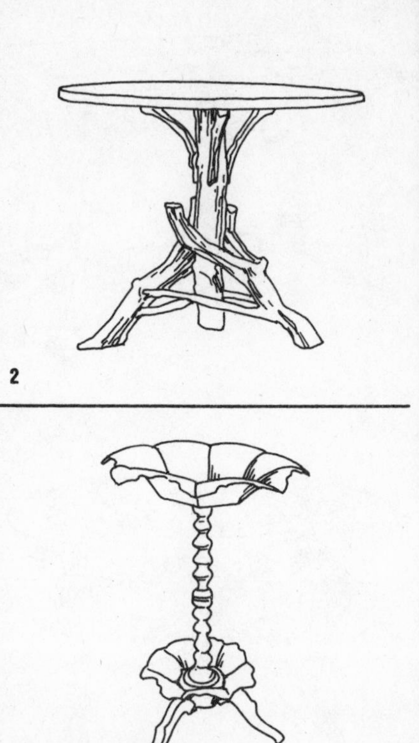

2

3

4

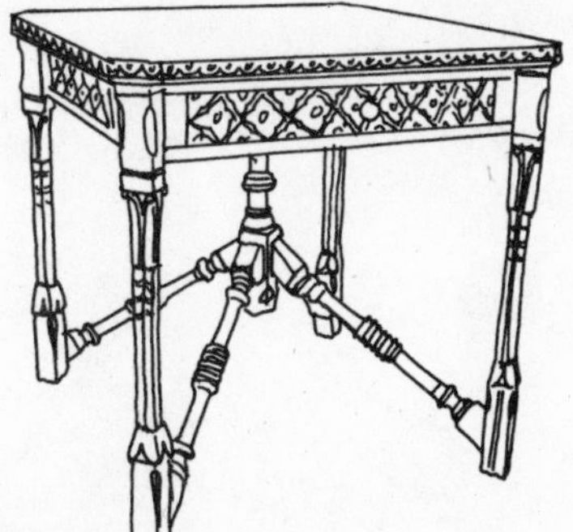

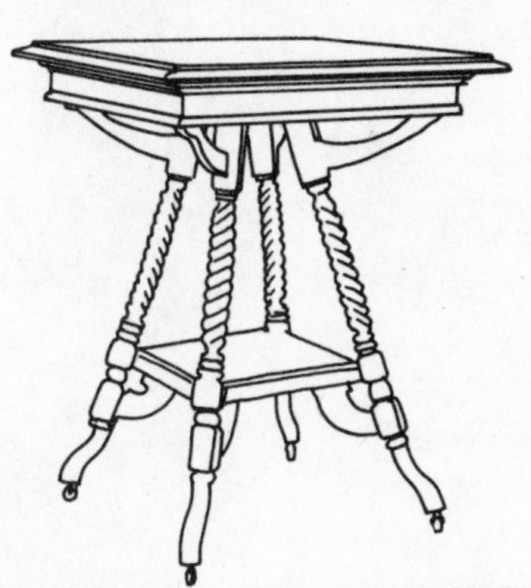

1. Library table. New York. Rectilinearity of members and flat ornamentation characteristic of Eastlake style. 1875–1885.

2. Library table. New York. Eastlake urged simplicity in furniture design. This table reflects his influence. (Labeled by Kimbel & Cabus.) c. 1880.

3. Library table. Probably New York. Some Eastlake-influenced furniture, such as this table, looks Oriental. 1880–1885.

4. Table. Probably New York. Same distinctive ring turning appears on Eastlake-inspired chairs. c. 1880.

5. Table. Chicago. Stylized sunflowers were popular Eastlake-influenced ornament. (By Rudolph E. Pohle, b. 1854, & Co.) c. 1885.

6. Table. Grand Rapids, Michigan. Rope-turned legs and incised floral carving are Eastlake-influenced features on this mass-produced form. 1880–1900.

7. Extension dining table. America. Oddly enough, Eastlake did not approve of this form since he believed such tables should be of a "uniform length." (Made by an unknown American factory.) c. 1877–1880.

1. Table. New York. Saber legs, here tipped in brass, also appear on English Art Furniture. c. 1880.

2. Table. Probably New York. Wooden members turned to produce the illusion of bamboo. c. 1880.

1

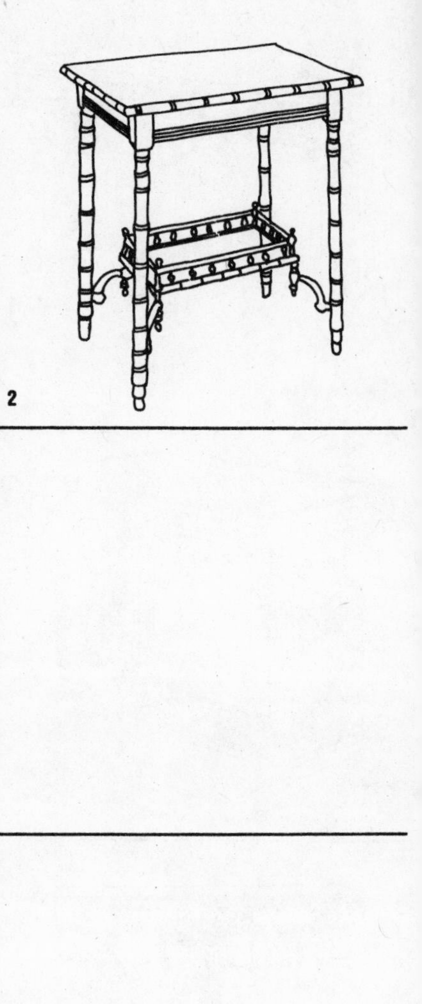

2

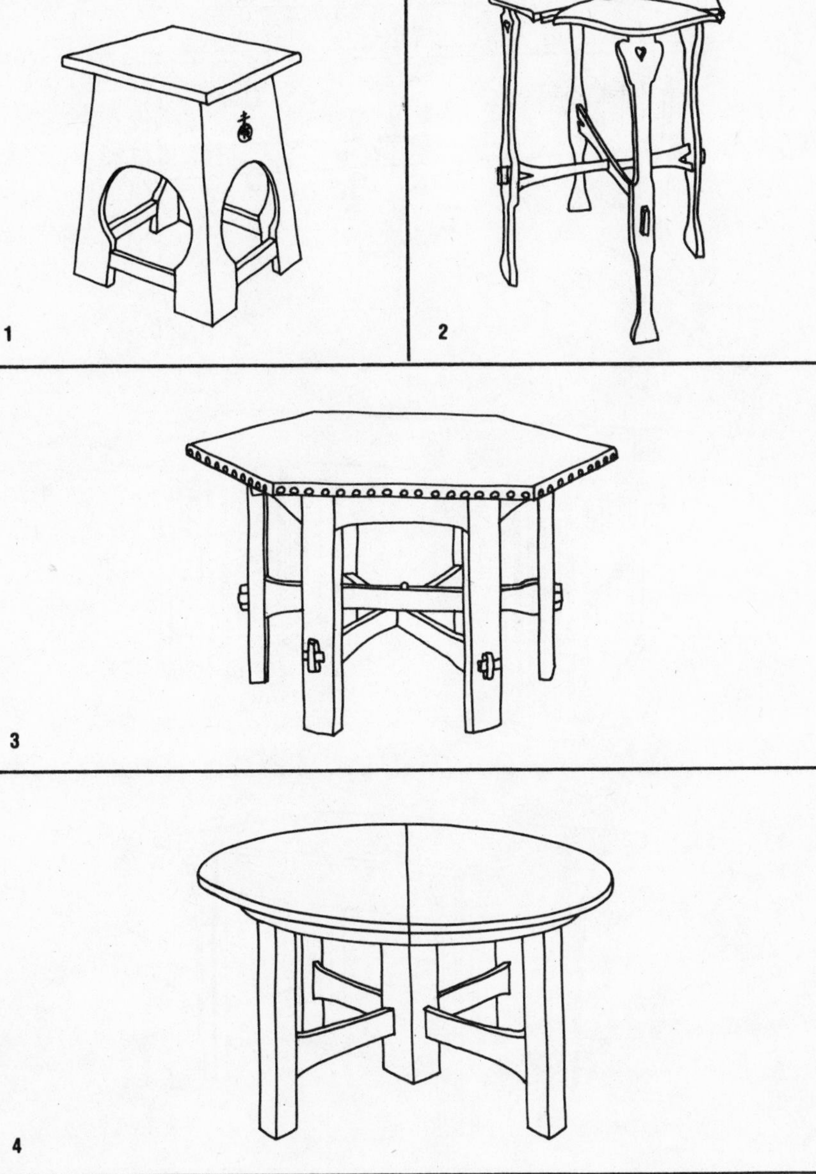

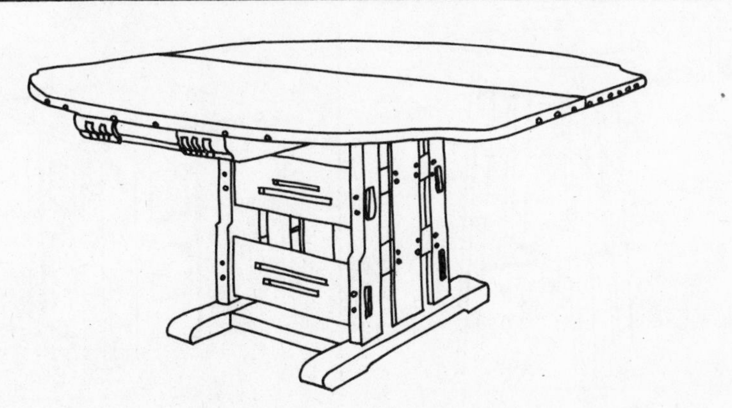

1. Tabouret. East Aurora, New York. Branded "R" within orb and cross, Roycroft symbol. (By Roycroft Shops.) c. 1912.

2. Tea table. Syracuse, New York. Table of organic form by Gustav Stickley Co. Table also appeared in an ad for Tobey Furniture Co. of Chicago, where Stickley had worked. 1900–1901.

3. Library table. Eastwood (Syracuse), New York. Hexagonal top covered in leather. Note use of pinned through-tenons, commonly found on Arts and Crafts furniture. (Bears decal of Gustav Stickley's Craftsman Workshops.) 1902–1903.

4. Dining table. Eastwood (Syracuse), New York. Rather awkward fifth leg gives table more support. (Labeled by Gustav Stickley's Craftsman Workshops.) c. 1906.

5. Dining table. Pasadena, California. Resembles earlier "hutch" table in form. (Designed by architects Charles and Henry Greene and made by Peter Hall.) c. 1908.

1. Library table. Eastwood (Syracuse), New York. Inspired by medieval stretcher tables. (By Gustav Stickley's Craftsman Shops.) 1909–1912.

2. Library table. Chicago. Note "spindle" slats and molded feet. (Designed by Frank Lloyd Wright for a Chicago home.) 1908.

3. Library table. Grand Rapids and Holland, Michigan. Flaring posts seen on other furniture by Charles P. Limbert Co. (Branded inside drawer.) 1912.

4. Table. Fayetteville, New York. Stand with long legs supported by slightly flaring stretchers. (By Leopold & J. George Stickley.) c. 1910.

5. Table. Grand Rapids and Holland, Michigan. Boxlike stand has square cut-outs. (By Charles P. Limbert Co.) 1912.

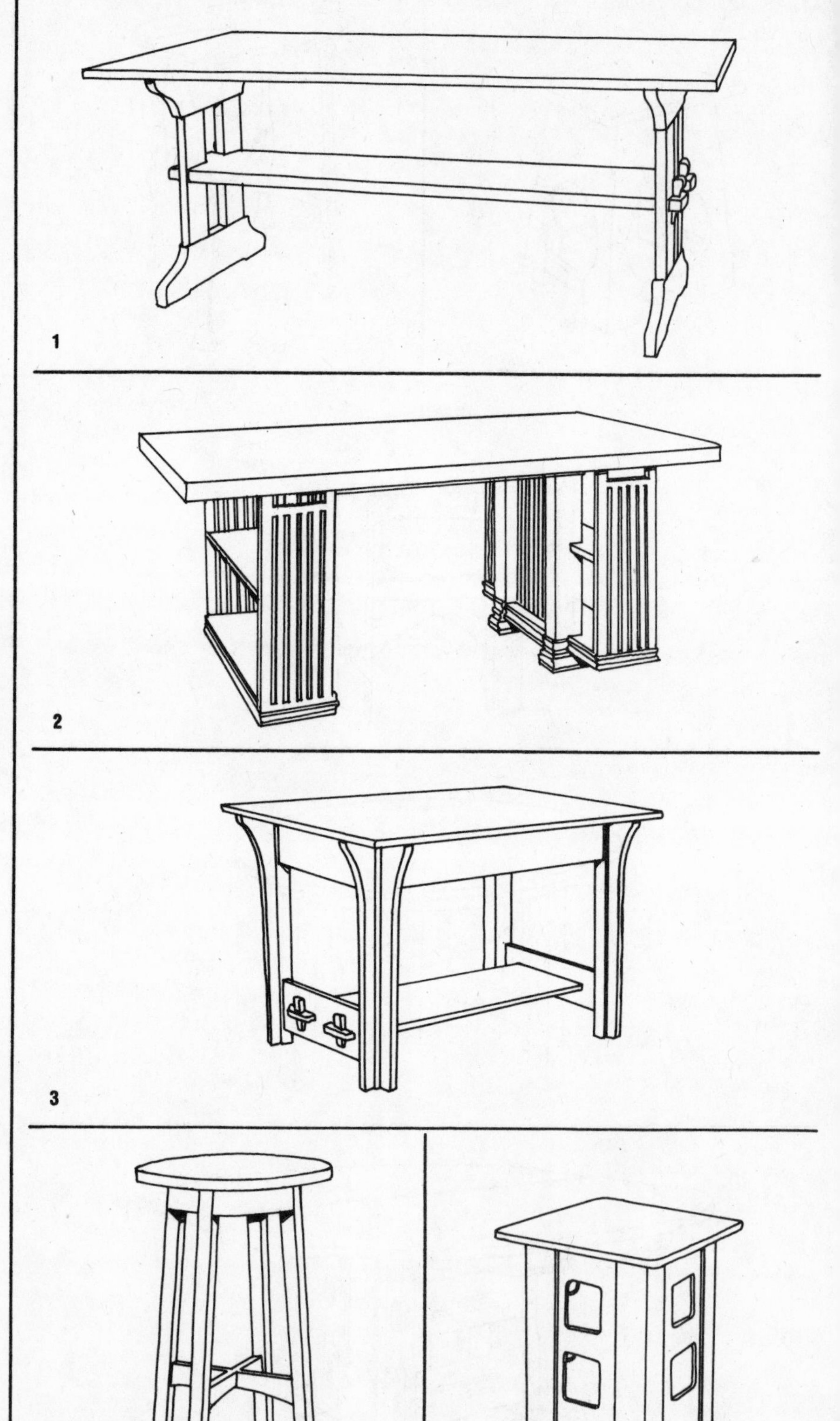

Beds

1. Turned bedstead. Eastern Massachusetts. Stylistically earliest American bedstead known. 1690–1730.

2. Wicker cradle. The Netherlands or possibly Boston. Believed to have held infant Peregrine White aboard *Mayflower.* 1620–1680.

3. Cradle. Plymouth Colony, Massachusetts. Of panel construction. c. 1650.

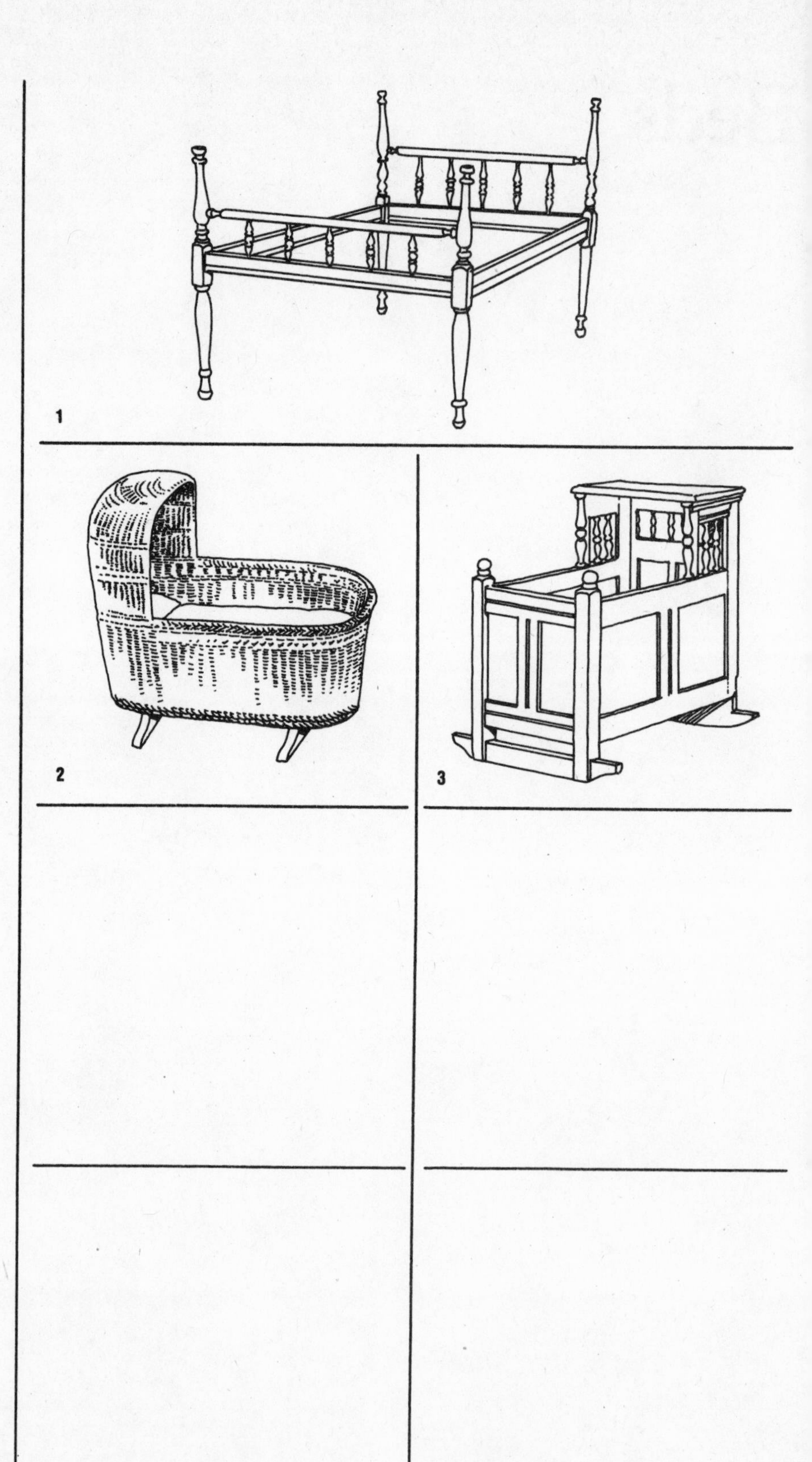

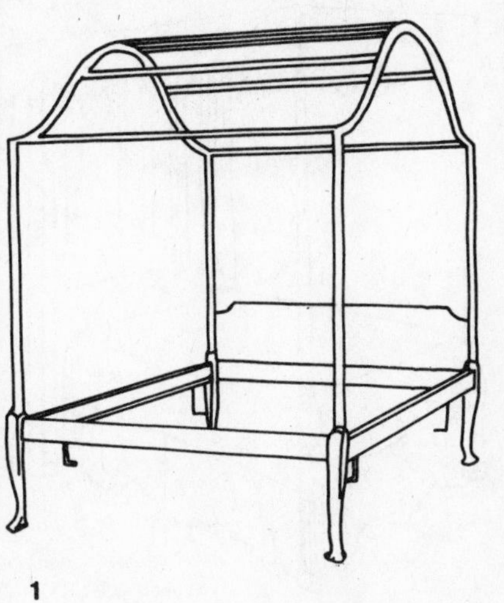

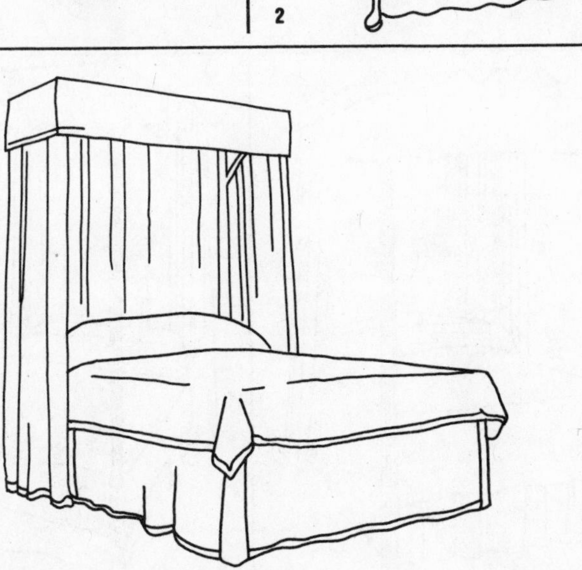

1. Tester bedstead. New England. Also called "field" or "tent" bedstead. 1725–1780.

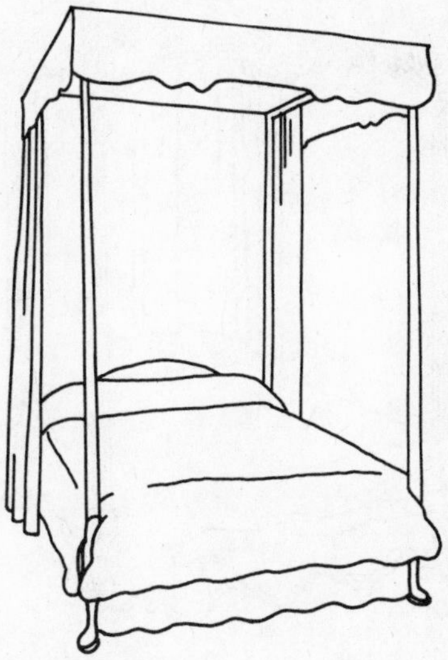

2. High-post bedstead. Rhode Island. Few bedsteads with pad feet survive. 1725–1750.

3. Bedstead. New England. Frame folds up and can be concealed by curtains. 1730–1800.

1. High-post bedstead. Massachusetts. Flat acanthus leaf carving on knees. Brass medallions cover screws used to hold bedstead together. 1760–1775.

2. High-post bedstead. Connecticut. Marlborough legs are fluted and end in blocked feet. 1770–1785.

3. High-post bedstead. New England. Bedposts fluted from top to bottom. 1770–1785.

4. High-post bedstead. New York or Rhode Island. Stop-fluting also seen on Connecticut and Newport examples. 1770–1785.

5. High-post bedstead. New York. Carving on foot posts typical feature on New York furniture. 1760–1775.

6. High-post bedstead. Philadelphia. Bed hangings, then called "bed furniture," extremely costly—at times more expensive than bedstead. 1750–1770.

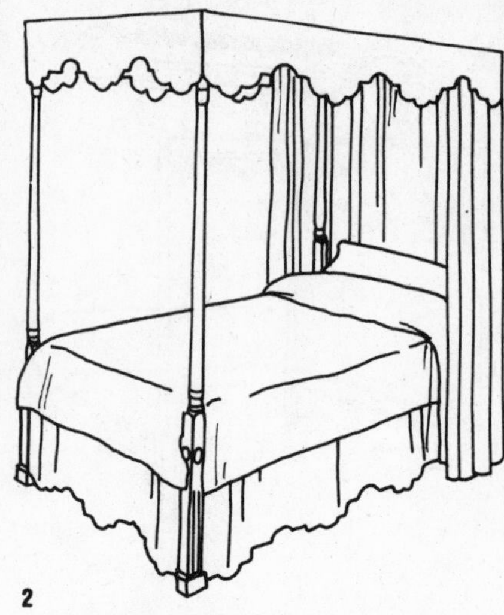

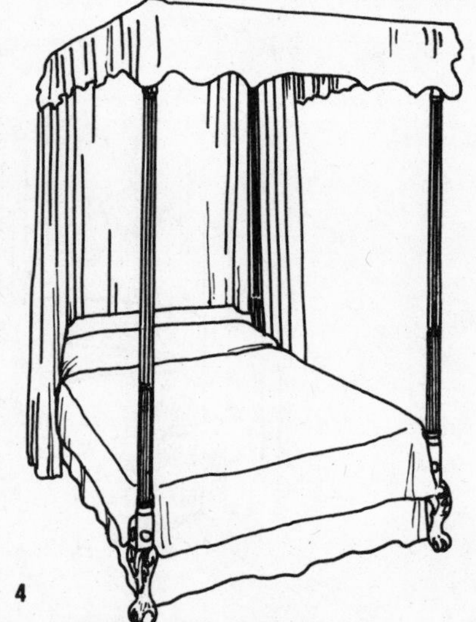

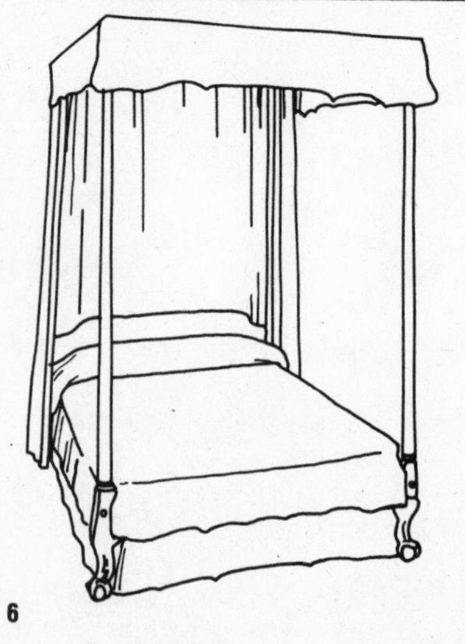

1

2

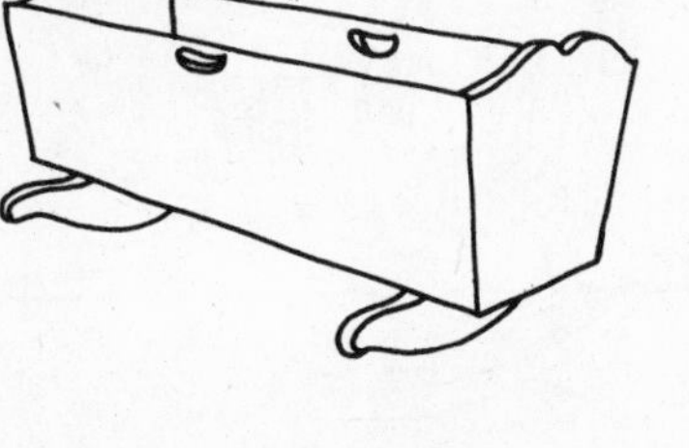

3

4

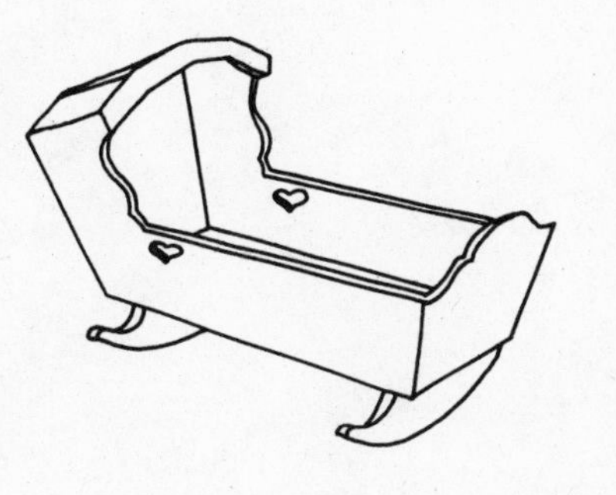

5

1. Bedstead. Philadelphia. High-style low-post bedsteads rare in 18th-century America. 1750–1760.

2. Trundle bedstead. New England. Form usually on wheels because it was rolled under another bedstead during daytime for storage. 1720–1800.

3. Cradle. New England. Has gently scalloped headboard and footboard and cut-out handles on sides. 1770–1800.

4. Deception bed. Philadelphia. Early hideaway bed. Brasses are Federal in style. 1780–1790.

5. Cradle. Probably New York. Similar hooded cradles made all along East Coast. 1775–1820.

1. Cradle. Probably New England. Taller than most Windsor cradles. 1780–1810.

2. Cradle. New England. Has bamboo-turned spindles. 1800–1820.

3. Cradle. Pennsylvania. Turnings on corner posts similar to those on Philadelphia low-back Windsor chair legs. 1780–1810.

4. Cradle. Philadelphia. Hooded cradle with steam-bent hickory spindles. (Branded "I. Letchworth" by maker John Letchworth, b. 1759.) 1790–1810.

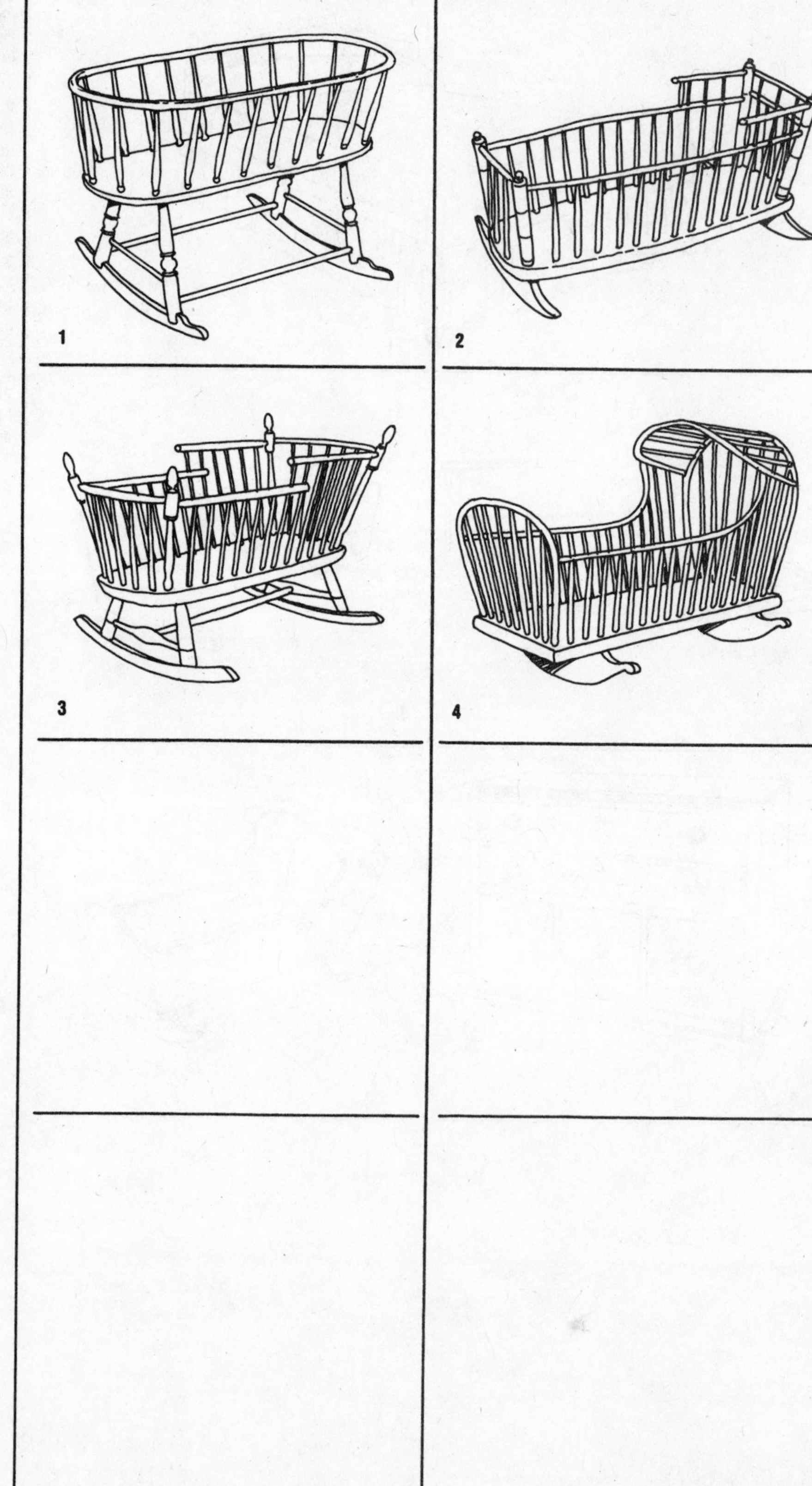

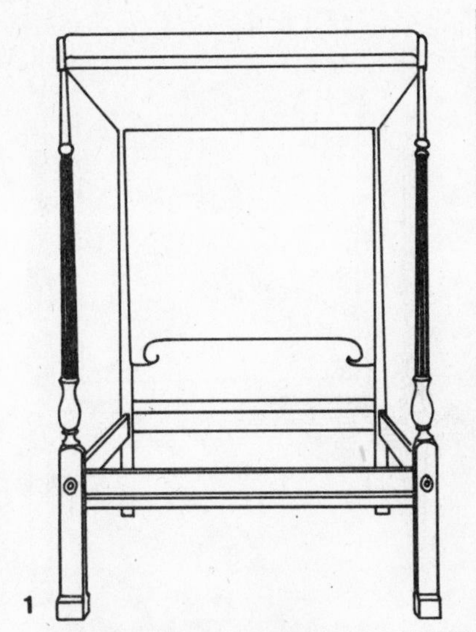

1

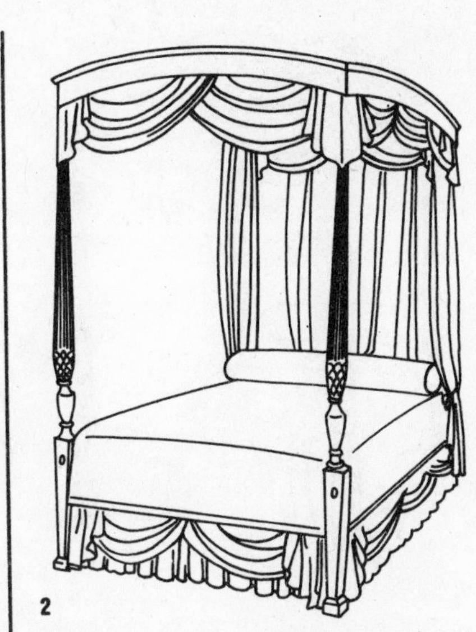

2

3

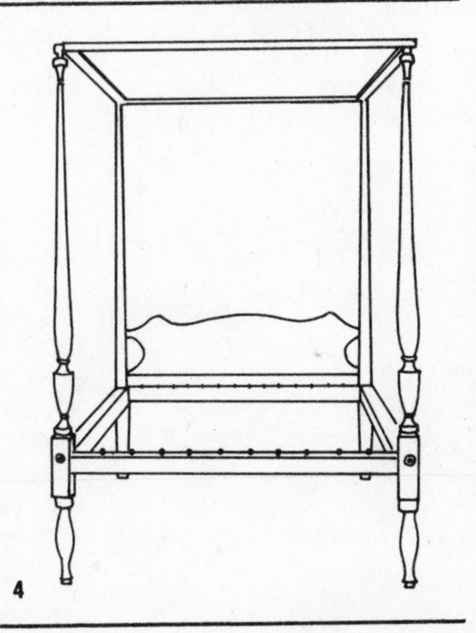

4

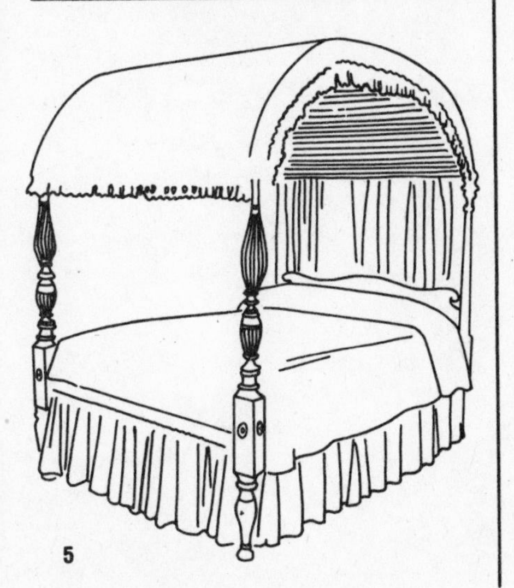

5

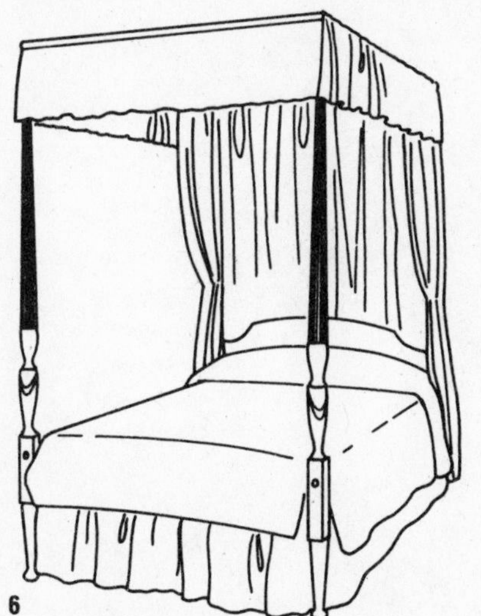

6

1. High-post bedstead. New England. Foot posts have turnings similar to those in Plate 105 of Hepplewhite's *Guide*. 1785–1800.

2. High-post bedstead. Salem, Massachusetts. Design of hangings based on Hepplewhite's *Guide*. c. 1795.

3. High-post bedstead. Northeastern Massachusetts. Extremely high-style bedstead with boldly turned and carved foot posts which boast veneered panels, a painted cornice in the shape of an archer's bow, and two other motifs associated with love—a quiver of arrows and a torch. 1800–1810.

4. High-post bedstead. Middle Atlantic states. Delicately turned foot posts and octagonal head posts. 1790–1815.

5. High-post bedstead. New York. Note swollen turnings on foot posts. 1820–1830.

6. High-post bedstead. Philadelphia. Foot posts are carved with swags and reeding. 1785–1800.

1. High-post bedstead. Philadelphia. Unlike makers in other regions, Philadelphia craftsmen tended to carve both the foot and head posts. 1800–1810.

2. High-post bedstead. Charleston, South Carolina. Carved rice on foot posts regional characteristic. 1790–1810.

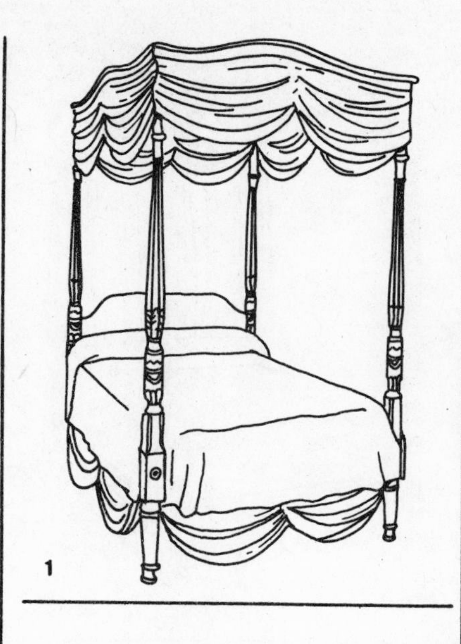

1

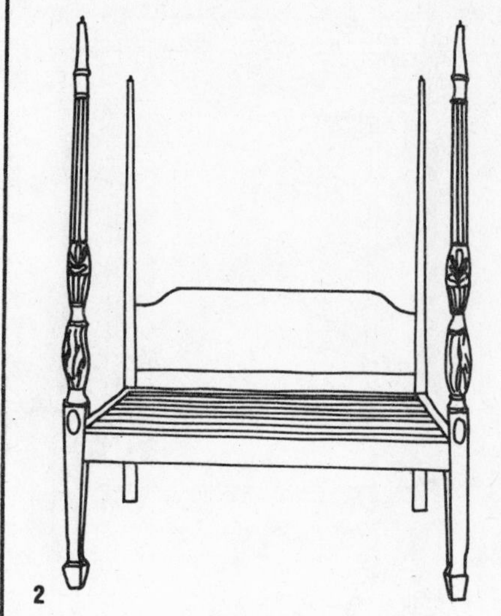

2

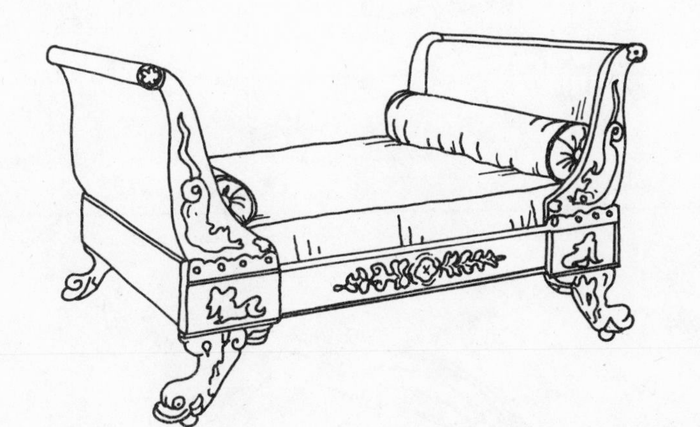

1. High-post bedstead. New York. Louis XVI style. (Attributed to Charles-Honoré Lannuier.) 1805–1819.

2. High-post bedstead. Charleston, South Carolina. Heavily proportioned bedstead with eagle and foliate carving and ring turning. 1810–1820.

3. Sleigh bedstead. New York. Inspired by French style. Van Rensselaer family possession. (Labeled by maker Charles-Honoré Lannuier.) c. 1815.

1. Sleigh bedstead. New York or Newark, New Jersey. "French" bedstead was period term. 1835–1845.

2. Sleigh bedstead. America. Form inspired by French design. c. 1840.

3. High-post bedstead. New Orleans, Louisiana. Note massive proportions of bedstead and heavy cornice. (By Prudent Mallard, 1809–1879.) c. 1850.

1

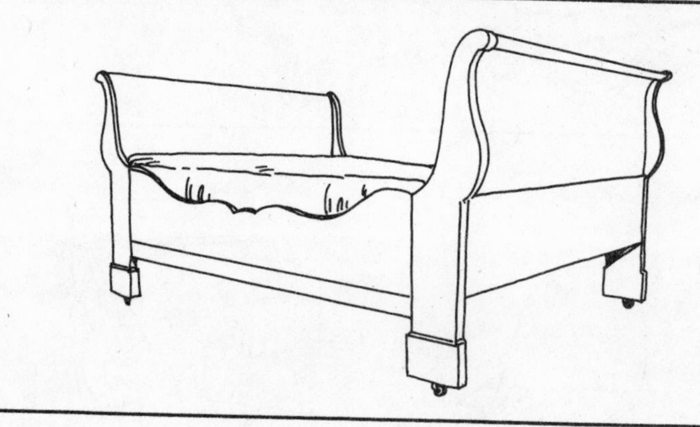

2

3

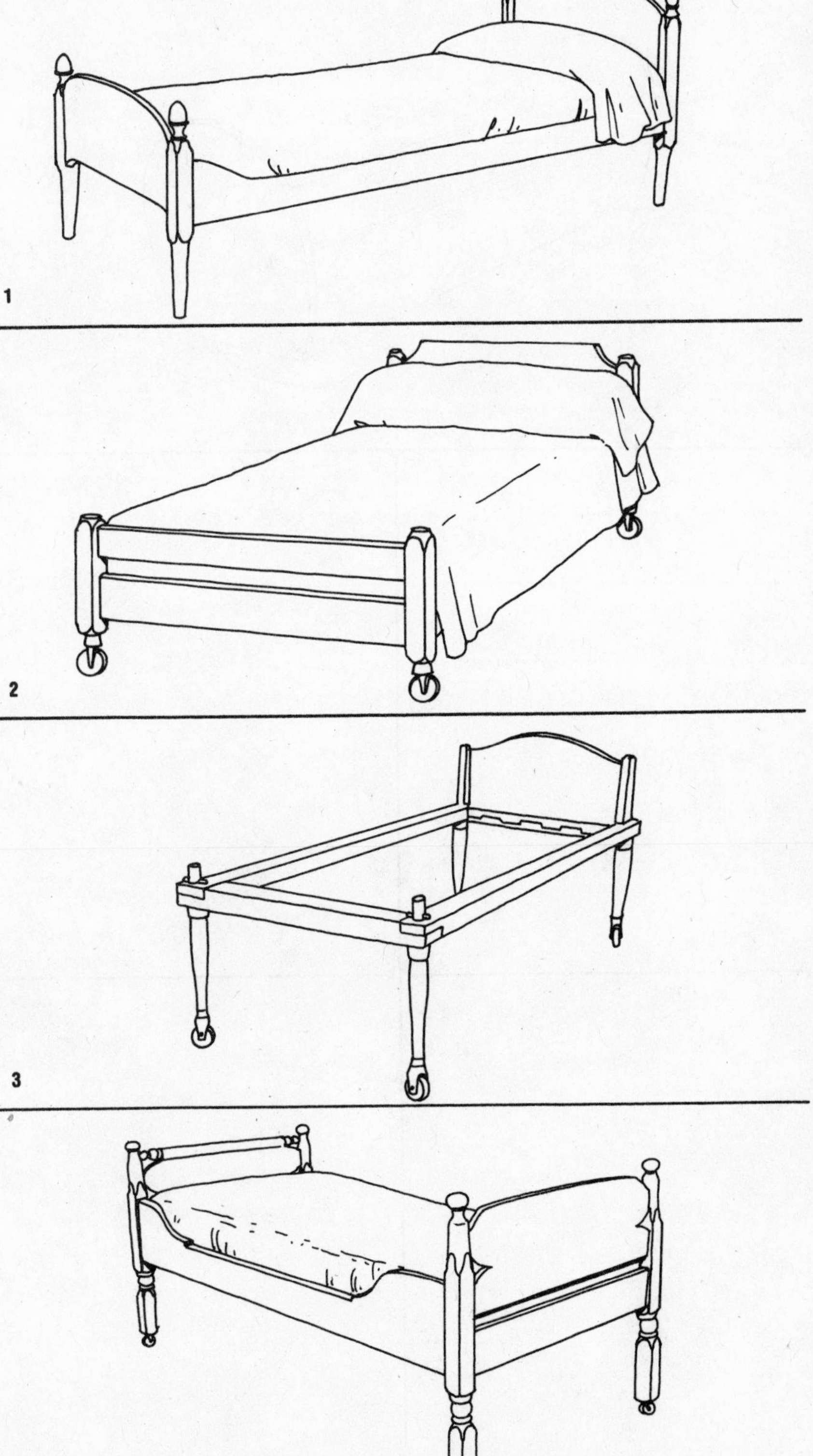

1. Bedstead. Mount Lebanon, New York. Wooden slats connected by tapes support mattress on this simple bed. 1867–1880.

2. Low bedstead. Mount Lebanon, New York. Shaker bedsteads often on wheels so that they could be rolled away from wall for ease in making beds and cleaning floors. 1840–1860.

3. Bedstead. Mount Lebanon, New York. If keys at corners are pulled, bed may be easily dismantled. c. 1880.

4. Bedstead. South Union, Ohio. Acquaintance with "worldly" furniture seen in turned legs and rail topping headboard. c. 1860.

1. Cradle. Pleasant Hill, Kentucky. Used for rocking two children. Shakers also rocked sick and elderly adults in large cradles. 1830–1870.

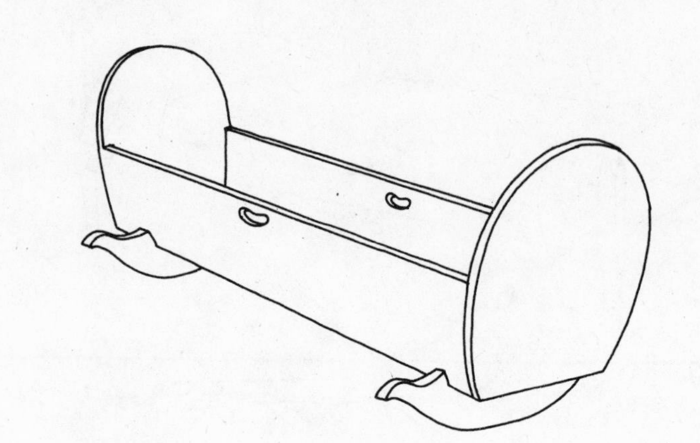

1

1. Bedstead. Probably Philadelphia. Note incorporation of lancet arches and crockets. Joseph Bonaparte gave this bedstead to Nicholas Biddle for use in the Gothic-style cottage at Andalusia. c. 1833.

2. Child's bed or settee. America. Spool turning associated with Elizabethan Revival style. 1840–1860.

1. Bedstead. New York. Outline of bed is one undulating curve. (Die-stamped by maker John Henry Belter.) c. 1853.

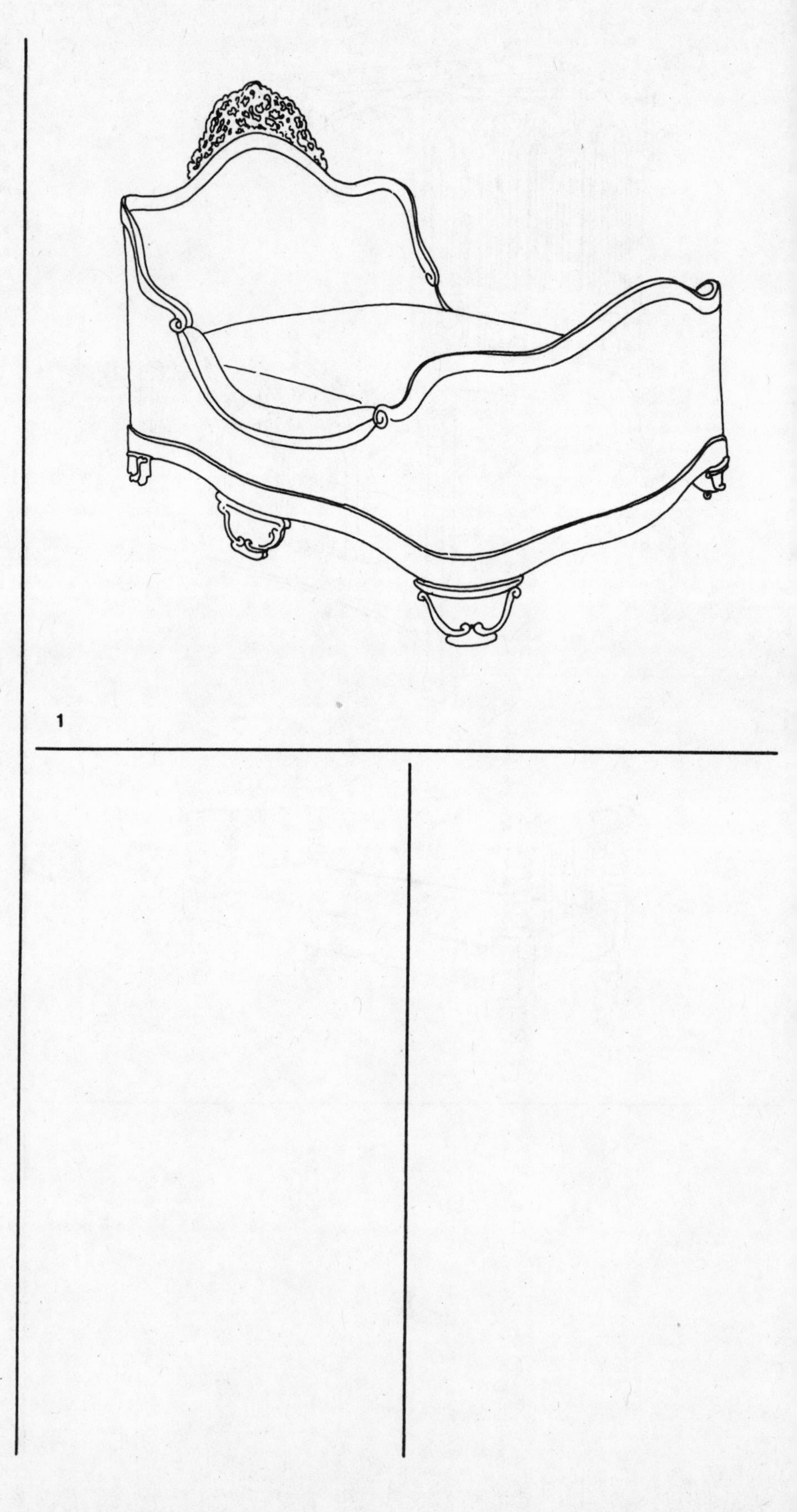

1

1

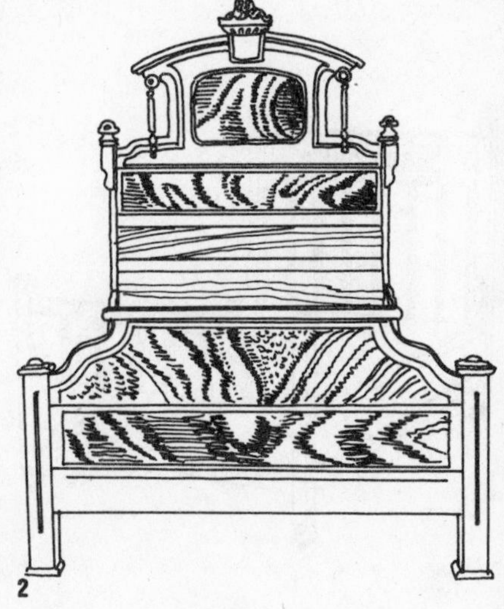
2

4

3

1. Child's bedstead. New York. Sides have particularly Renaissance flavor with pierced work in imitation of strapwork carving and bosses. (Bears stenciled inscription of Alexander Roux.) c. 1855.

2. Bedstead. Probably Northeastern United States. Grained, "cottage" bedstead in Renaissance Revival style. 1875–1890.

3. Bedstead. Grand Rapids, Michigan. Bedsteads with architectural pediments decorated with flat, applied ornamentation were hallmark of this style. 1870–1880.

4. Bedstead. Grand Rapids, Michigan. Part of a bedroom suite exhibited by makers Berkey & Gay at the Centennial Exposition of 1876 in Philadelphia. c. 1876.

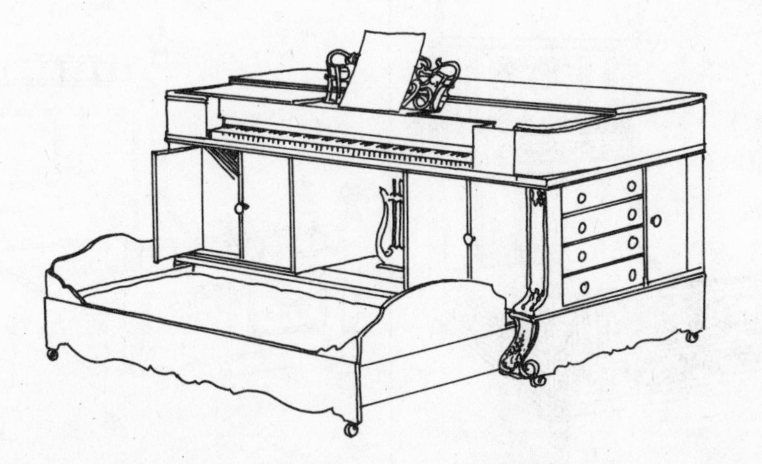
1

Innovative

1. Piano-bed. Cincinnati, Ohio. Indicative of heights reached by the convertible craze. Form was indeed manufactured. (Designed by Charles Hess.) Patented 1866.

1. Bedstead. New York. Top-of-the-line panel bed, popular form in this style. (By Herter Brothers). 1880–1890.

2. Bedstead. Probably Grand Rapids, Michigan. Accent on rectilinearity, as in other Eastlake-inspired furniture. c. 1880.

1

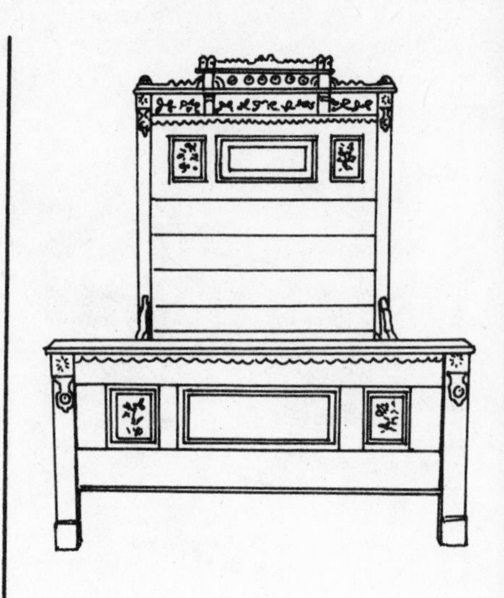

2

Art and Japanese-Inspired

1. Bedstead. New York. Restrained floral marquetry often based on Art Furniture. (By Herter Brothers.) 1880–1885.

2. Bedstead. Probably New York. *Faux* bamboo furniture underlines the great interest in the Orient at the end of the 19th century. c. 1880.

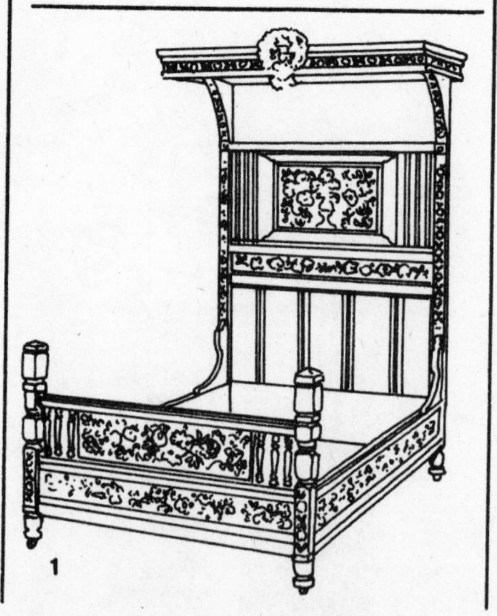

1

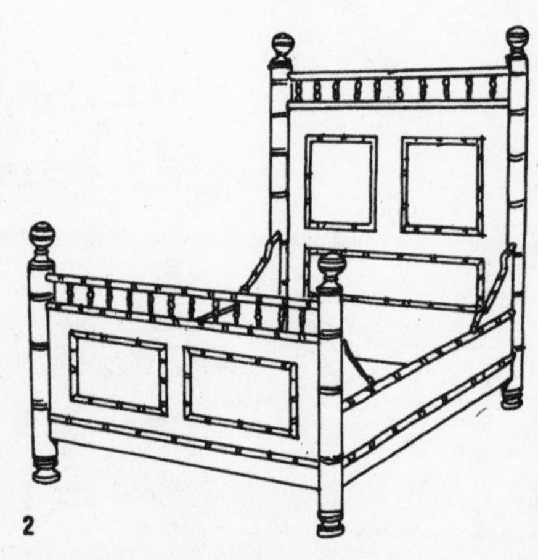

2

1

1. Bedstead. Eastwood (Syracuse), New York. Simple Mission design was translated into bedstead form by many furniture manufacturers. (By Gustav Stickley's Craftsman Workshops.) c. 1910.

Daybeds, Sofas, Benches, Settees

1. Form. Plymouth Colony, Massachusetts. Once-common seating option. 1650–1700.

2. Joint stool. Eastern Massachusetts. Used as seat or as table. 1650–1700.

3. Couch. Boston. Note original turkeywork upholstery. Initially had adjustable wings attached to arms and back for protection from drafts. 1660–1700.

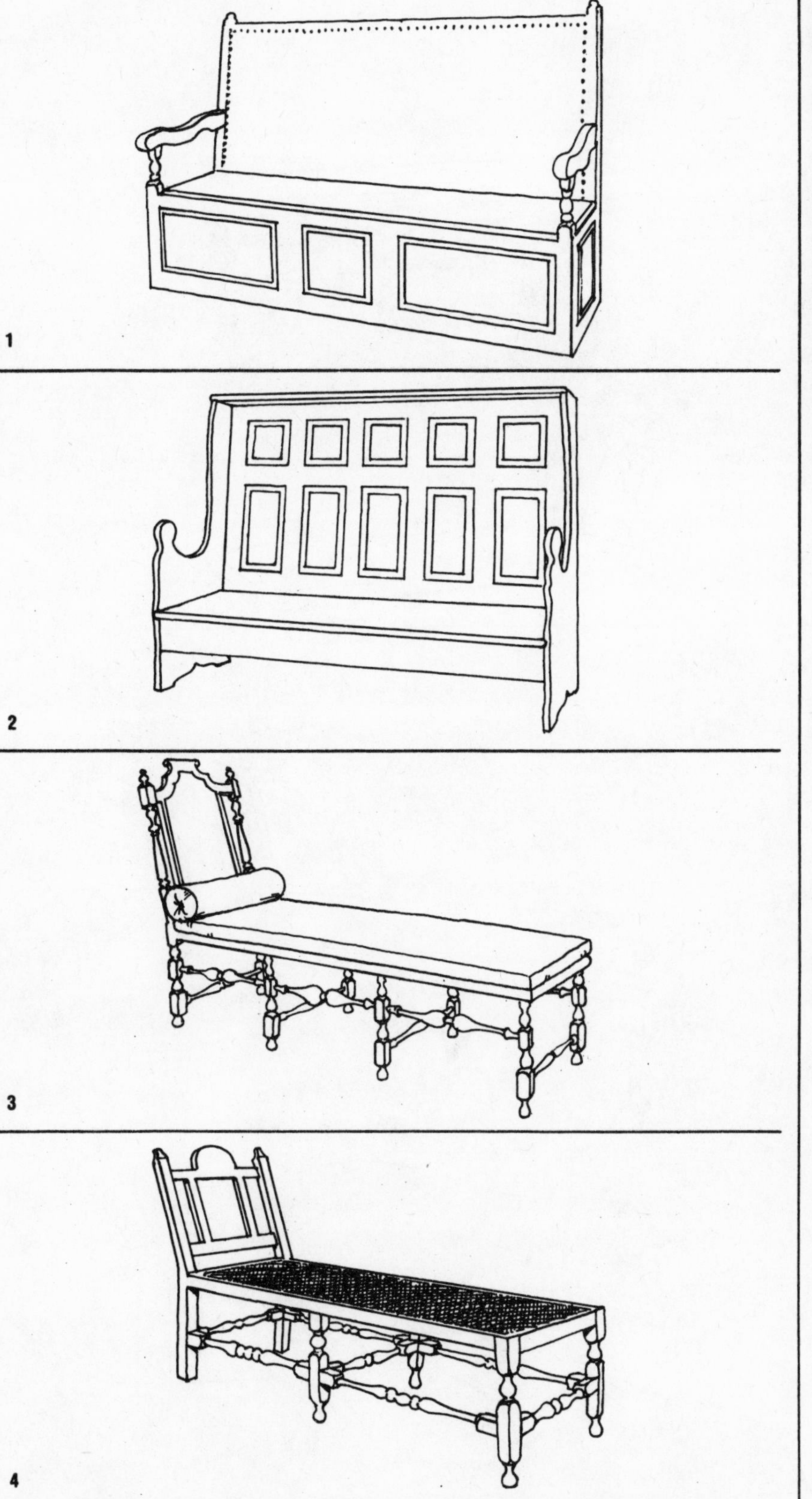

1. Settle. Probably Pennsylvania. Upholstered in leather. Communal seating was important for warmth during cold months. 1700–1750.

2. Settle. Middle Colonies. Such furniture often pulled up to fireplace for warmth. Few survive because of large size. 1700–1750.

3. Couch. Pennsylvania. Also called daybed. Form introduced to America during William and Mary period. Back may be raised or lowered. 1710–1740.

4. Couch. Virginia or North Carolina. Of joined construction. 1710–1730.

1. Daybed or couch. Connecticut. Note boldly turned stretchers and widely flaring Spanish feet. 1710–1725.

2. Daybed or couch. Philadelphia. Example with double splats also has pad feet and stump rear legs. 1730–1750.

3. Daybed or couch. Philadelphia. Has cross-stretchers for support. 1740–1750.

4. Sofa. Philadelphia. Even by this date, still rare form in American furniture. 1730–1770.

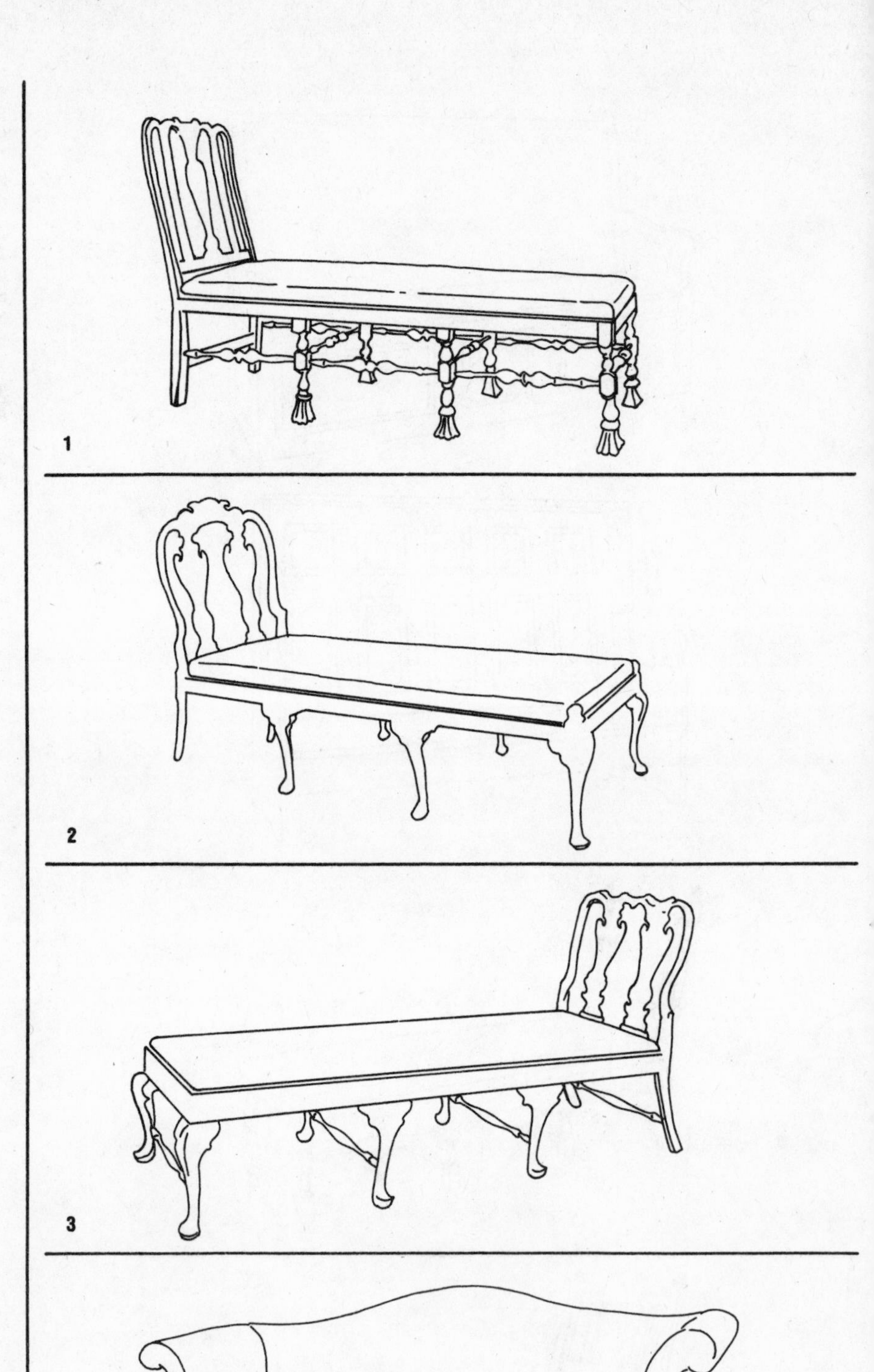

1

2

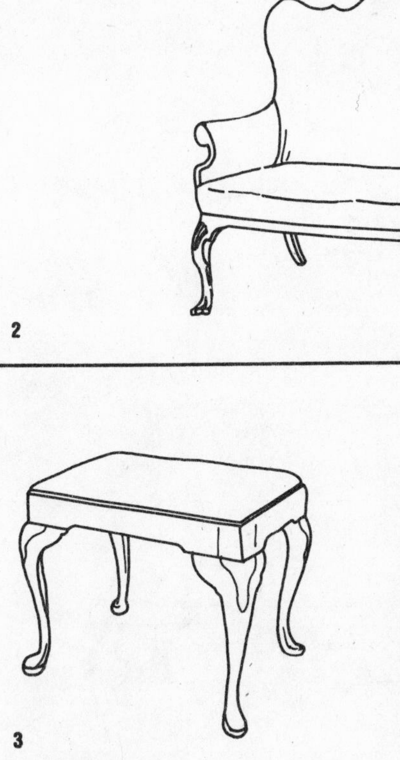

3

4

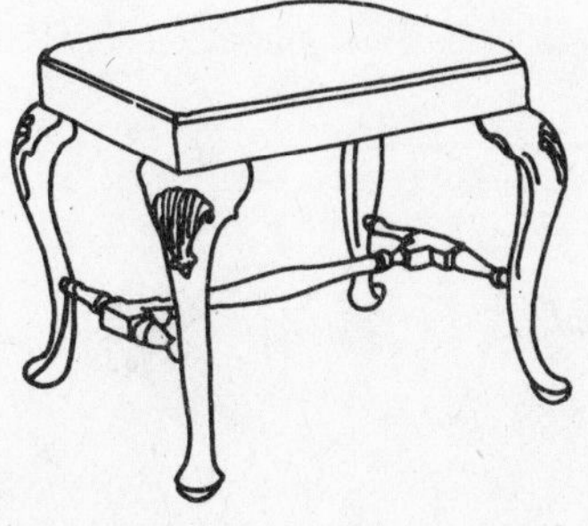

5

6

1. Sofa. Philadelphia. Note carved web feet and scrolled knees. 1740–1750.

2. Settee. Philadelphia. Scrolled legs with shell-carved knees and trifid feet. Unusual form. 1730–1740.

3. Stool. Probably Connecticut. Legs with generous knees end in pad feet. 1730–1770.

4. Stool. Newport, Rhode Island. Squat stool with pad and flattened-ball feet. 1720–1740.

5. Stool. Newport, Rhode Island. Stretchers unusual. Note shell with pendant carving. 1730–1760.

6. Stool. Probably New Jersey. Delicate overall design. 1740–1750.

1. Couch. Probably Middletown, Connecticut. Banister-back consisting of Queen Anne–style splats contained within Chippendale-style back. 1755–1810.

2. Couch. Rhode Island. Adjustable Queen Anne–style back between uprights ending in ears. 1740–1760.

3. Double-chair-back settee. Boston. Form fairly rare in America. 1760–1775.

4. Settee. Boston area. Note Massachusetts claw-and-ball feet with swept-back talons. Vertically rolled arms stylistic holdover from earlier period. 1760–1780.

1

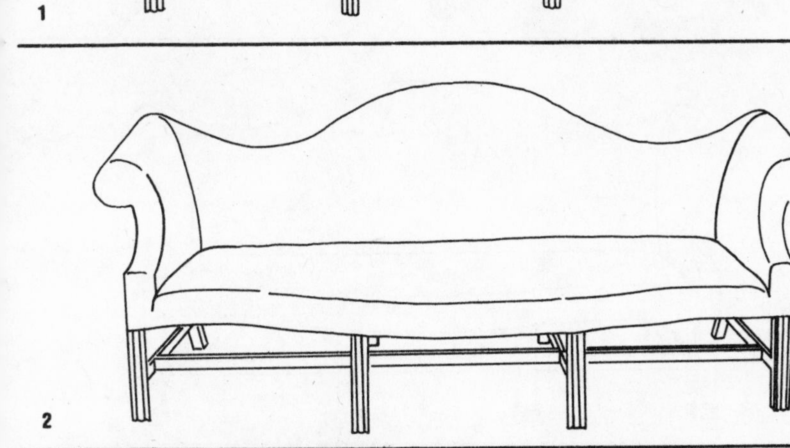

2

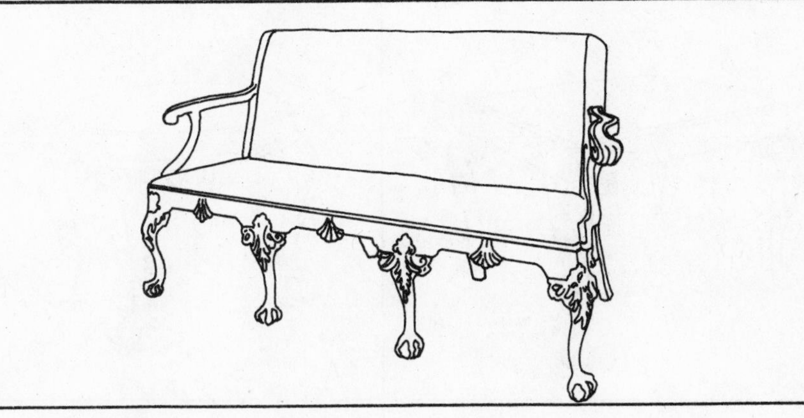

3

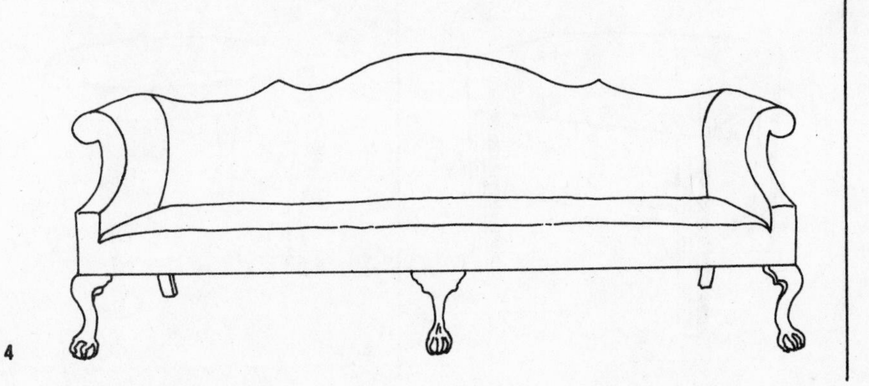

4

1. Sofa. Newport, Rhode Island. Serpentine back combined with Marlborough legs. (Signed and dated by maker: "Made by Adam S. Coe April 1, 1812 for Edw. W. Lawton." Little, if any, other furniture is known to have been made by Coe.)

2. Sofa. Probably New York. Note deep curves of serpentine back and curved front seat rail. 1770–1795.

3. Settee. Philadelphia. Regional characteristics on this unusual form include scallop shells on front rail, C-shaped arm supports, and deeply carved foliage on knees. 1765–1775.

4. Sofa. Philadelphia. Very elegant double-peaked serpentine sofa form associated with Philadelphia. 1765–1780.

1. Sofa. Philadelphia. Relatively rare form during 18th century because of fine mahogany used in the carved cabriole legs, and cost of fabric. 1775–1780.

2. Sofa. Philadelphia. Serpentine sofa with squatter proportions and Marlborough legs. 1770–1780.

3. Stool. New York. Typical New York foliate and cross-hatched carving on knees. 1740–1770.

4. Stool. New York. Legs have bold curve and end in boxy, New York–style claw-and-ball feet. c. 1760.

5. Stool. New York. Stretchers help to support stool's fluted Marlborough legs. 1770–1785.

6. Stool. Philadelphia. Two-part foliate carving, favored in Philadelphia, seen here. 1755–1775.

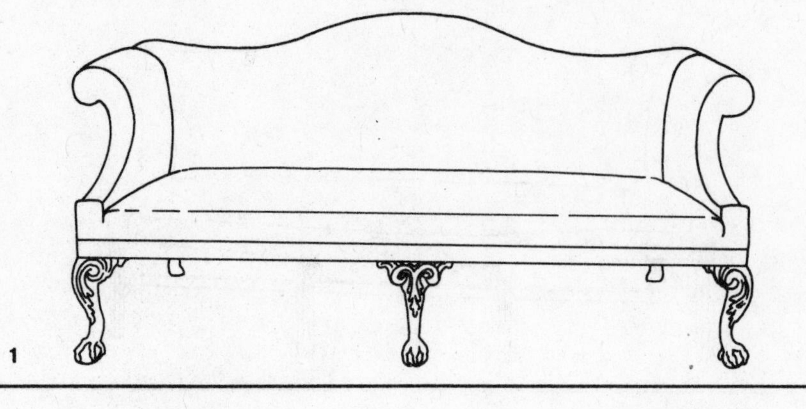

1

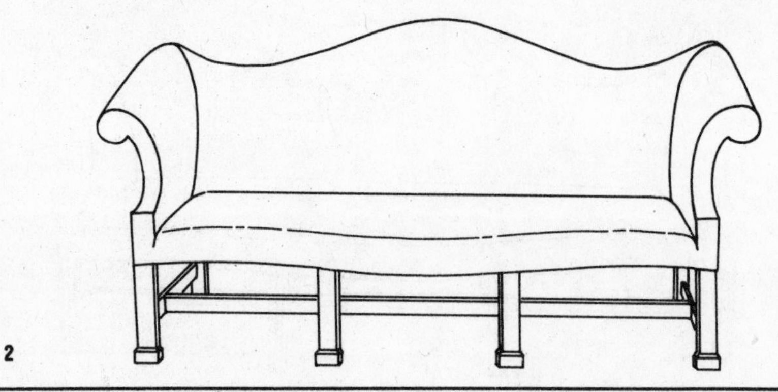

2

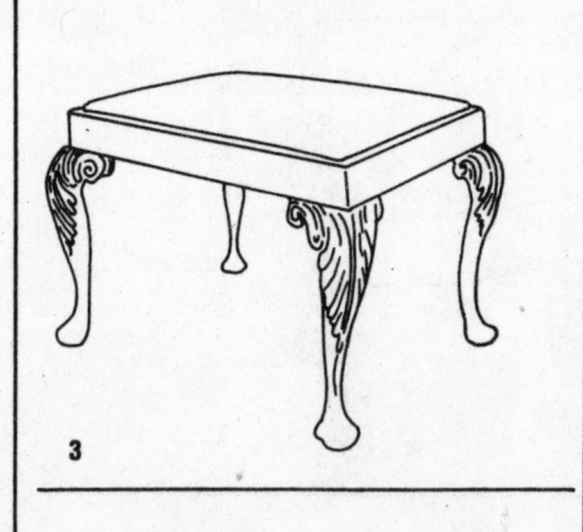

3

4

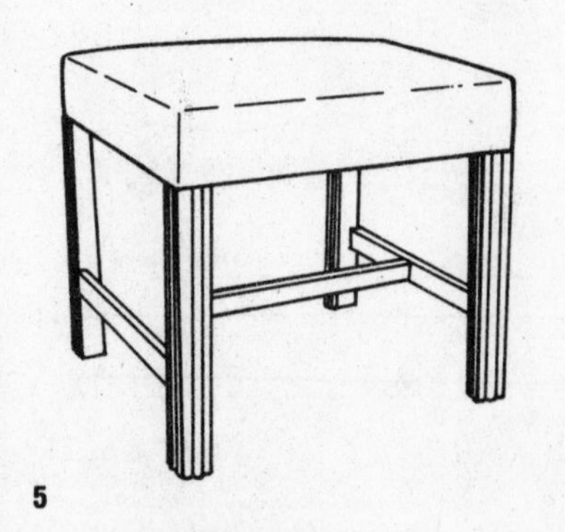

5

6

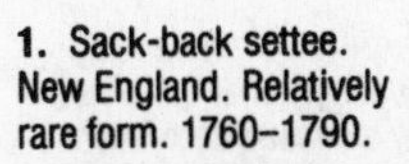

1. Sack-back settee. New England. Relatively rare form. 1760–1790.

2. Rod-back settee. Massachusetts. Resembles Sheraton-style ballroom chairs. Note rush seat. 1805–1820.

3. Rocking settee and cradle. New England. Known as "Mammy's bench," form could be made into a long settee. 1835–1850.

4. Low-backed settee. Philadelphia. Early six-legged example extremely unusual survivor. 1760–1780.

1. Arrow-back settee. Pennsylvania. Enlivened by stenciled decoration. Popular form. 1820–1830.

2. Footstool. America. Common form. 1760–1780.

3. Stool. Philadelphia. Probably used at high accounting desk. 1790–1810.

4. Candlestand. Pennsylvania. Resembles high stool in overall form. Turnings echo those seen on chairs from same area. 1770–1790.

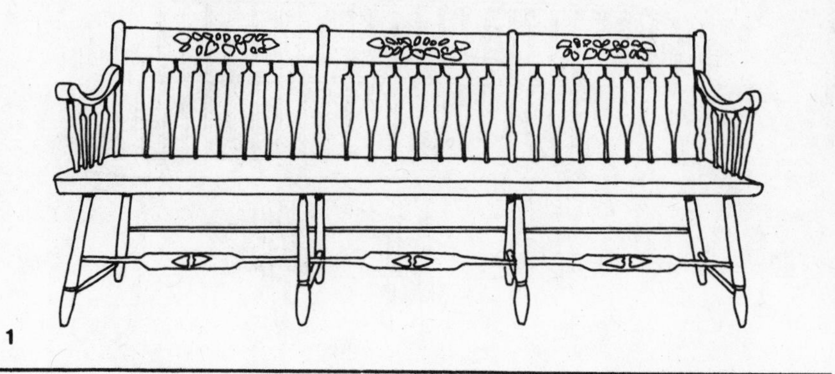

1

2 3 4

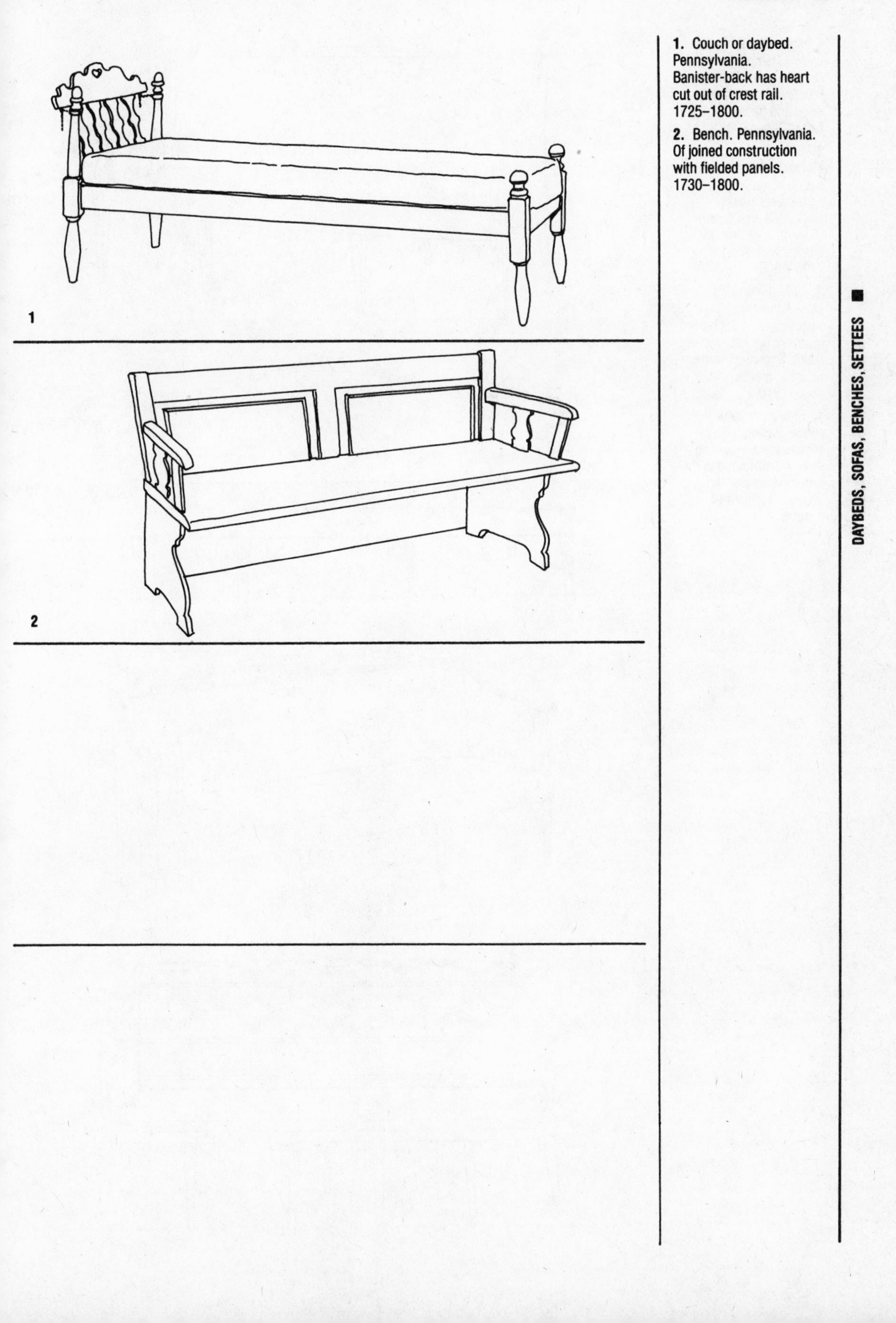

1. Couch or daybed. Pennsylvania. Banister-back has heart cut out of crest rail. 1725–1800.

2. Bench. Pennsylvania. Of joined construction with fielded panels. 1730–1800.

1. Sofa. Massachusetts or New Hampshire. Delicate example with veneered tablet of light wood and pendant inlay in legs. 1790–1800.

2. Sofa. Salem, Massachusetts. Carved basket containing fruit and flowers usually associated with Salem. (Carving attributed to Samuel McIntire.) 1795–1800.

3. Sofa. Salem, Massachusetts. "Snowflake" punch used to stipple background of tablet. Snowflake pattern Salem characteristic. 1800–1810.

4. Five-chair-back settee. Boston. Of complex and appealing design. (Attributed to the shop of John and/or Thomas Seymour.) c. 1805.

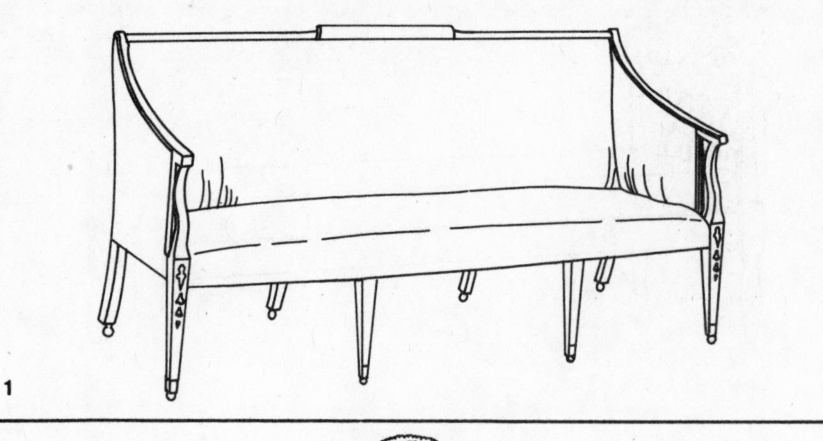

1

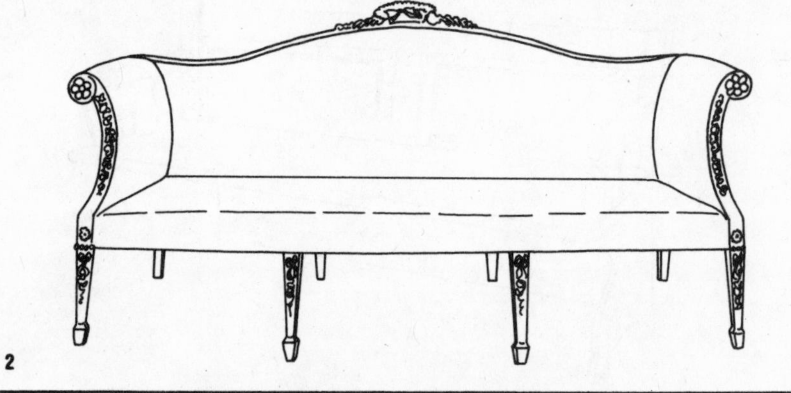

2

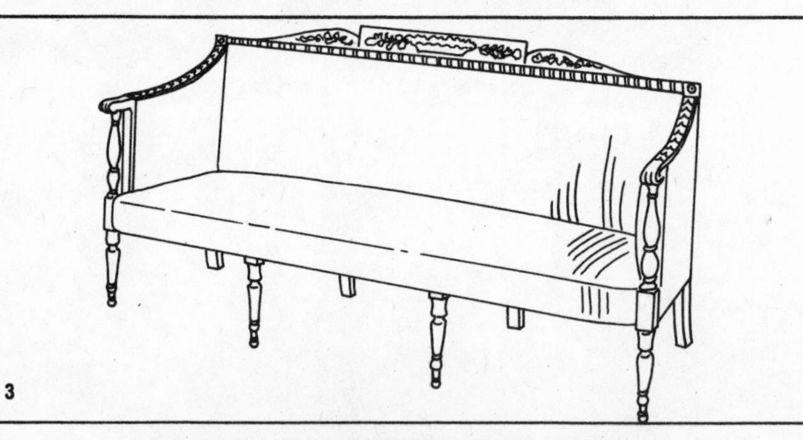

3

4

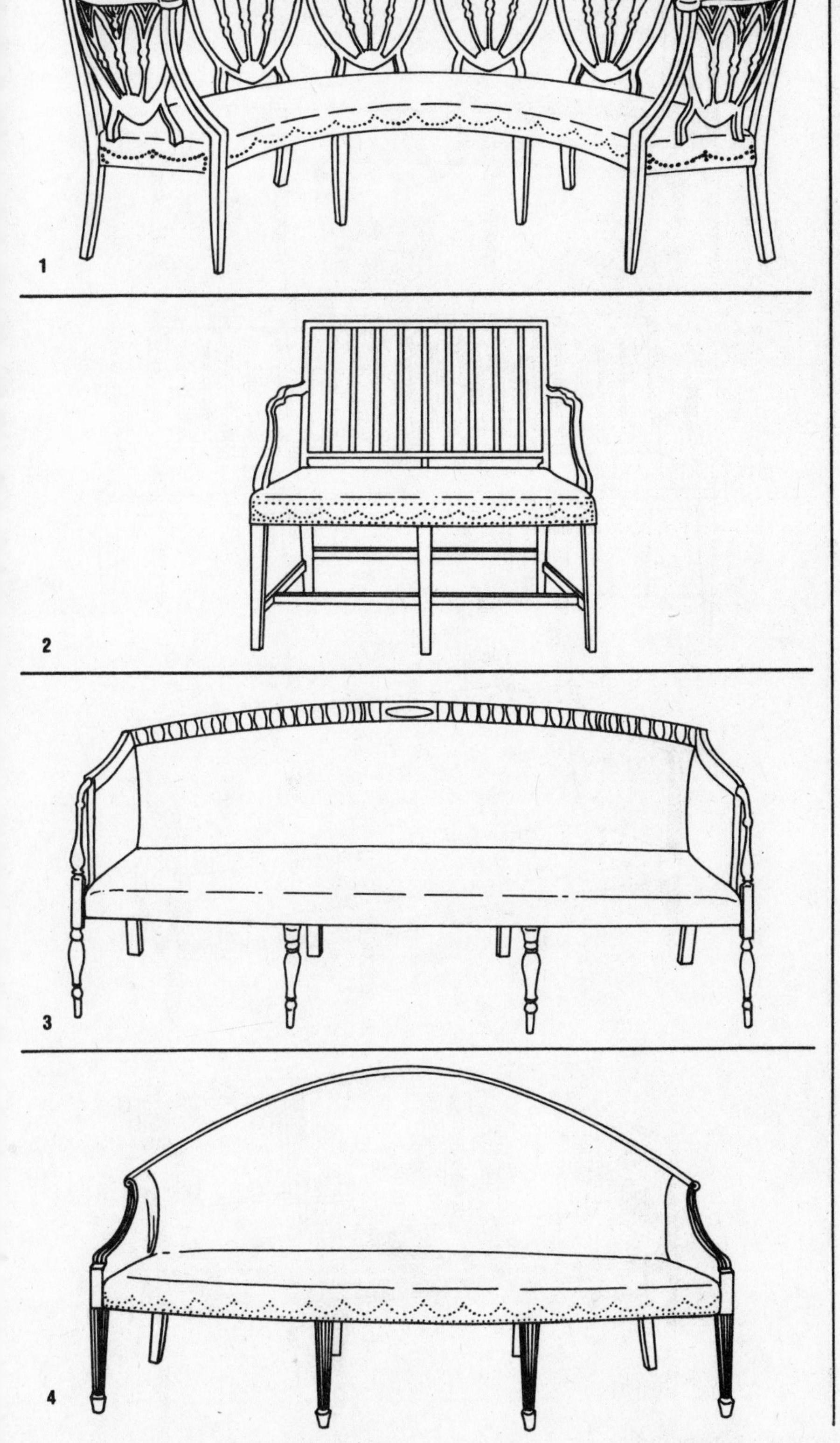

1. Six-chair-back settee. Probably Portsmouth, New Hampshire. Made to fit in curved alcove. Based on Hepplewhite design. c. 1800.

2. Two-chair-back settee. Probably Portsmouth, New Hampshire. Based on a plate in Hepplewhite's *Guide*. Has molded vertical slats. 1800–1815.

3. Sofa. Northeastern Massachusetts or Portsmouth, New Hampshire. Gently curving back ornamented by figured birch veneer. Note reeded arm supports and legs. 1800–1810.

4. Cabriole sofa. New York. "Cabriole" refers to curve of back. Based on designs in Hepplewhite's *Guide*. 1795–1805.

1. Sofa. New York. Square-backed with carved patera within tablet. (Design of tablet associated with the workshop of Slover & Taylor, in partnership 1802–1804.) 1800–1805.

2. Four-chair-back settee. New York or Albany. Overall design extremely unusual in American furniture. Note popularity of square-back chairs in New York during this period. 1800–1810.

3. Sofa. New York. Swags and spikes of wheat joined by a bowknot are motifs associated with Duncan Phyfe. (Possibly by Phyfe.) 1805–1815.

4. Sofa. New York. Note that all elements of this carved sofa are reeded. (Possibly by Duncan Phyfe.) 1805–1815.

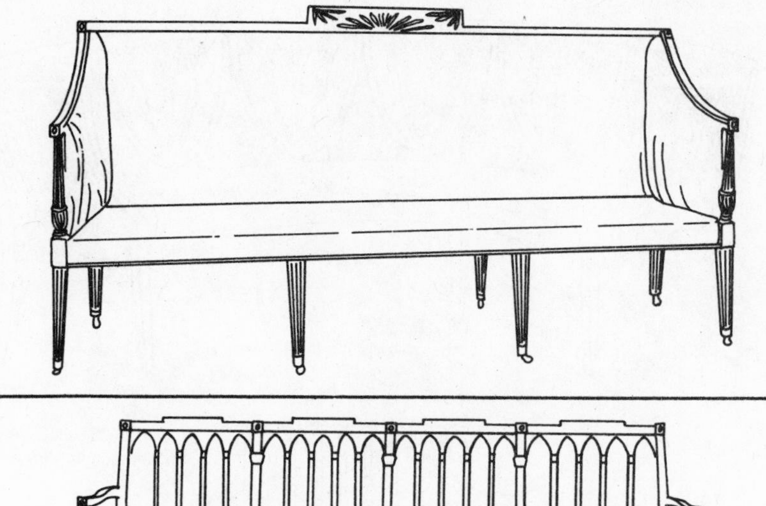

1

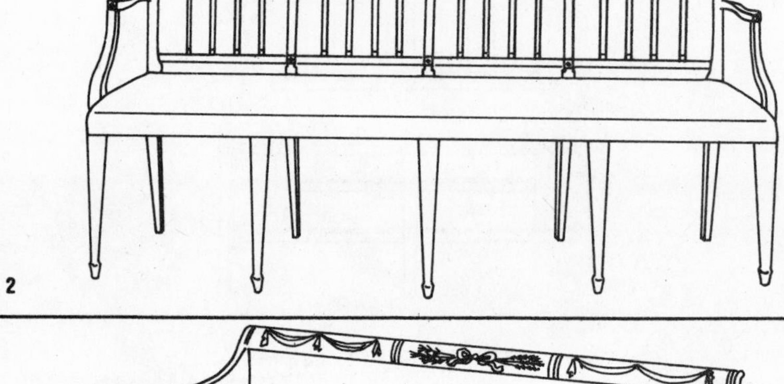

2

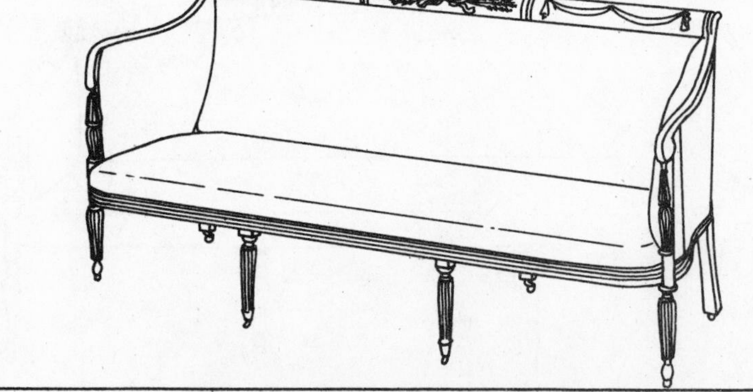

3

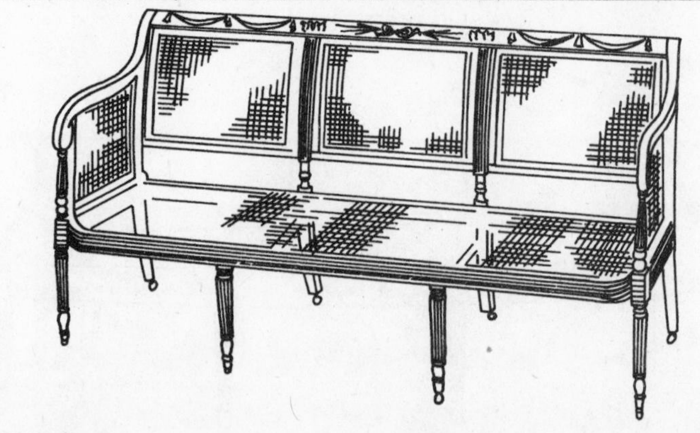

4

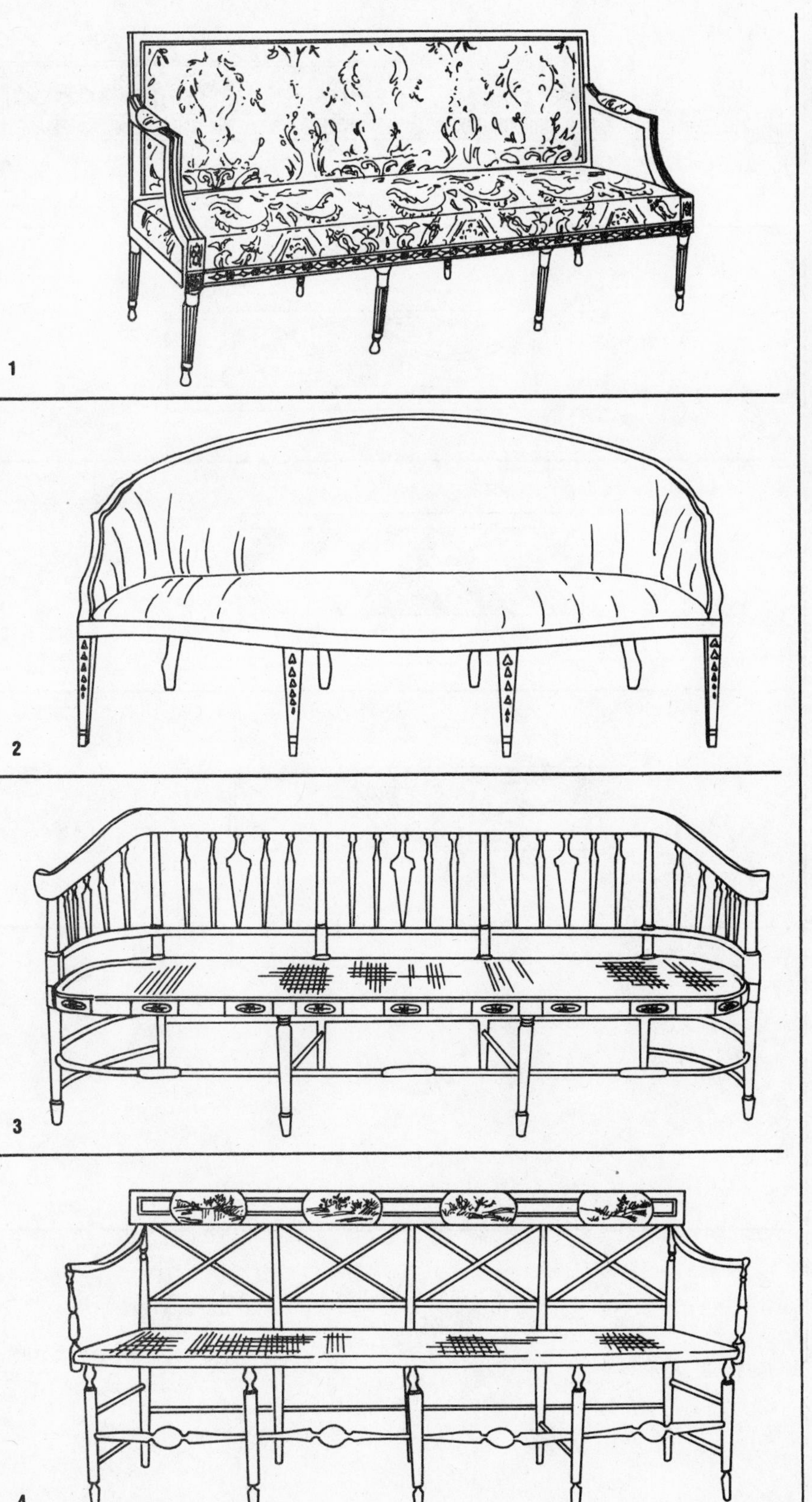

1. Sofa. Philadelphia. Some Americans who had traveled to France at this time developed a taste for Louis XVI–style furniture. Decorated by gilt over white paint. 1790–1810.

2. Cabriole sofa. Baltimore, Maryland. Not only is back of sofa curved, but so too are sides, front, and rear legs. 1790–1800.

3. Settee. Maryland. Note unusual curved stretchers and raked arms. 1800–1810.

4. Four-chair-back settee. Baltimore, Maryland. X-backed settee has painted landscapes in reserves on crest rail. 1805–1810.

1. Fruit-and-flower-basket motif characteristic of Salem, Massachusetts, area. 1800–1815.

2. Swag-curved tablet common New York feature.

3. Banding from curved six-chair-back settee from Portsmouth, New Hampshire. c. 1800.

4. Tablets with carved paterae associated with New York. 1800–1810.

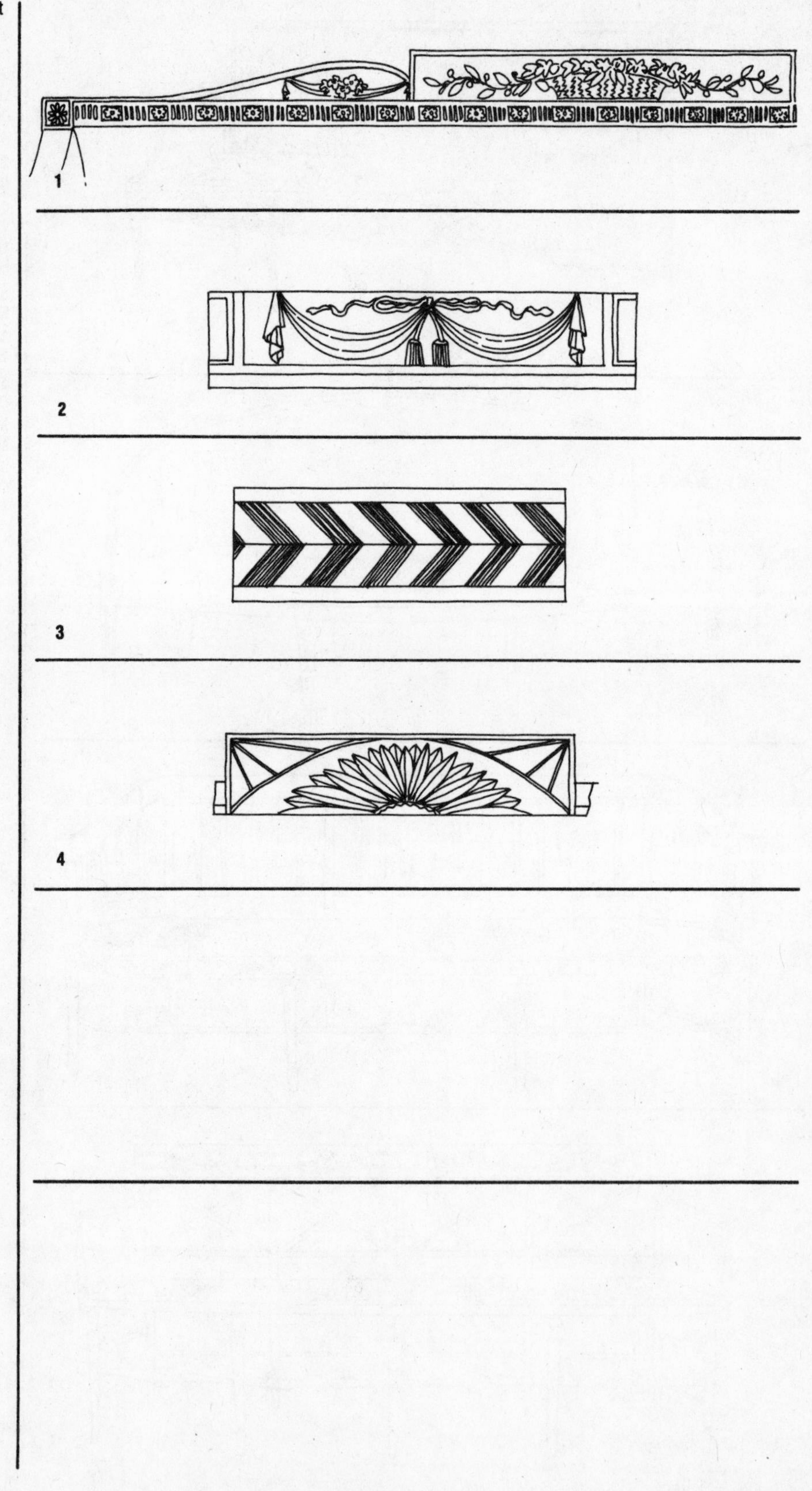

1

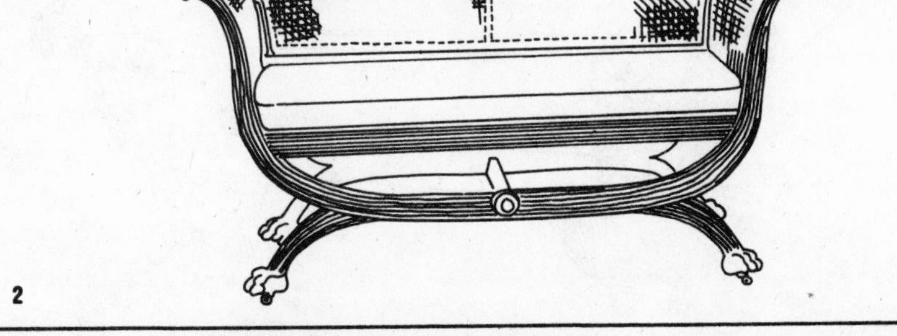

2

3

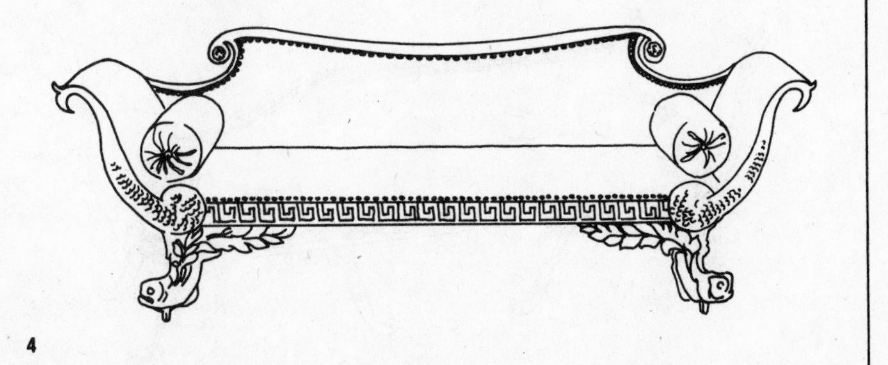

4

1. Sofa. Boston. Copied from plate that appeared in an 1821 issue of Ackerman's *Repository of Arts, Literature, Fashions, etc.*, periodical published in London 1809–1829. 1821–1830.

2. Sofa. New York. Form of curule expanded to sofa-size. (Possibly by Duncan Phyfe.) 1810–1815.

3. Sofa. New York. Scroll-ended sofa has monopodium feet with cornucopia brackets. 1815–1835.

4. Sofa. New York. Incorporates two motifs popular during the archeologically inspired period of Classicism, the dolphin and the Greek key border. 1815–1830.

1. Sofa. Philadelphia. Simpler version of scroll-ended sofa with scroll-shaped legs and ormolu mounts. 1810–1820.

2. Sofa. Philadelphia. Leafy carving decorates the scroll ends and legs of this sofa on castors. c. 1830.

3. Couch. Salem, Massachusetts. Form inspired by ancient Greek and Roman examples. (Labeled by maker Thomas Needham, active c. 1800–after 1830.) c. 1820.

4. Couch. Salem, Massachusetts. Form referred to as "Grecian" couch or sofa in period price and pattern books. Cornucopia and vine carvings on punched "snowflake" background. 1805–1815.

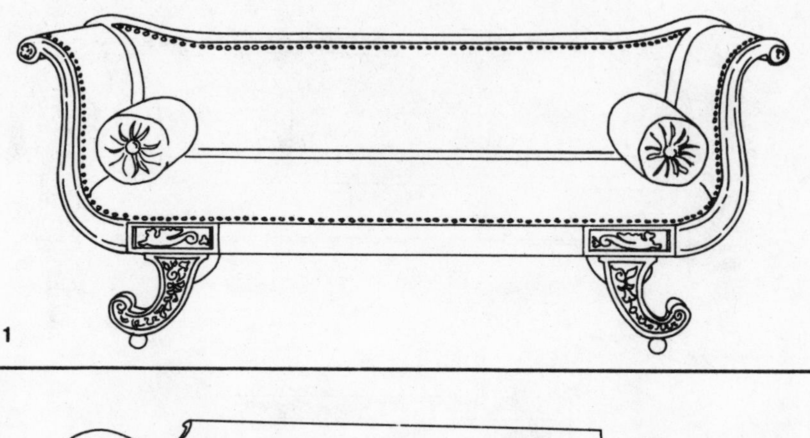

1

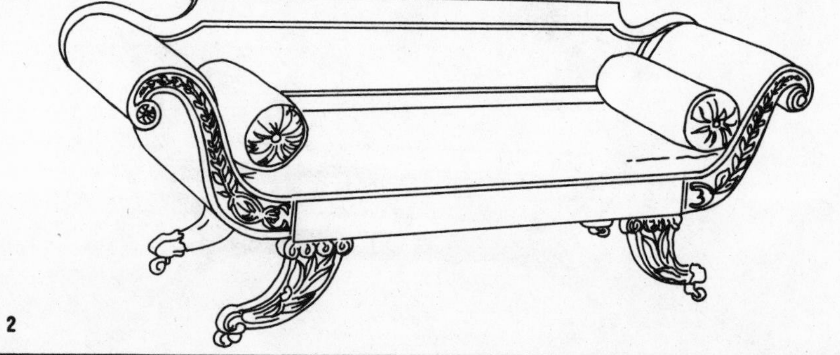

2

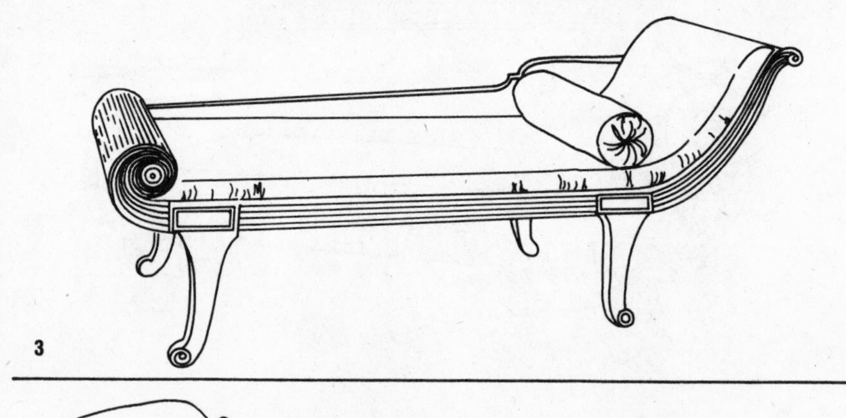

3

4

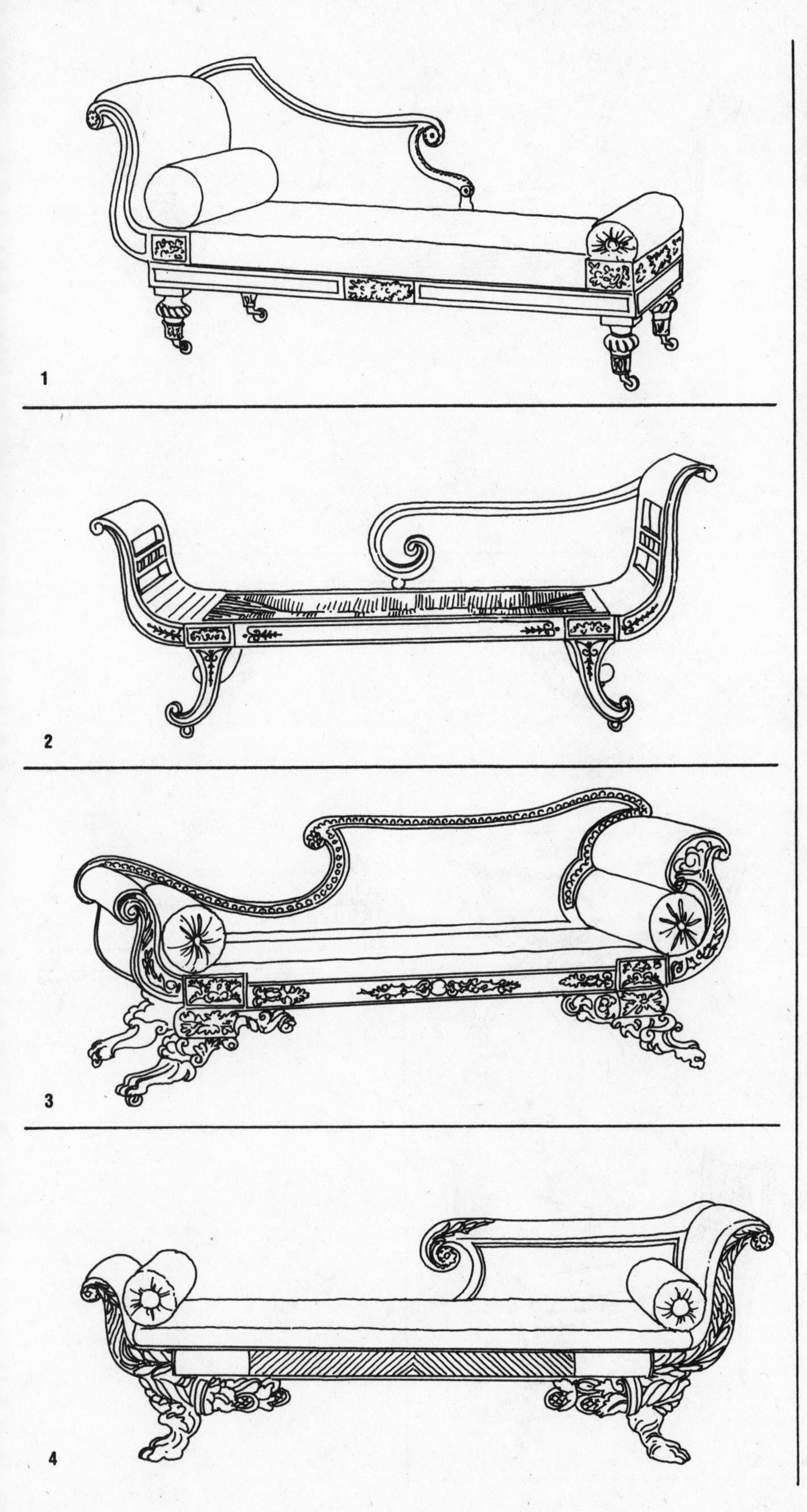

1. Couch. Boston. Note skilled use of inlaid brass. 1818–1830.

2. Couch. New York. Such couches were often used with loose cushions. Note ring turning along front rail. c. 1820.

3. Couch. New York. Robust design with lively carved and gilt decoration. 1820–1830.

4. Couch. Probably New York. Lush, carved ornamentation on couch includes leafy carving ending in rosettes, diagonal reeding, cornucopiae containing fruit and leaves, and monopodia. 1825–1835.

1. Couch. Baltimore, Maryland. Outline of couch accents reeded decoration. 1810–1820.

2. Window bench. Baltimore, Maryland. The fluid, Neoclassical ornamentation on this example is associated with Baltimore. 1820–1830.

3. Stool. Probably Salem, Massachusetts. X-stool highlighted by rosette, leafy, reeded, and animal paw carving. 1810–1815.

4. Window bench or ottoman. With some modifications, form remained popular through much of the 19th century. (Signed by Duncan Phyfe.) c. 1820.

5. Window bench. New York. Unusual form with lyre-backs and animal paw feet. (Possibly by Duncan Phyfe.) 1810–1815.

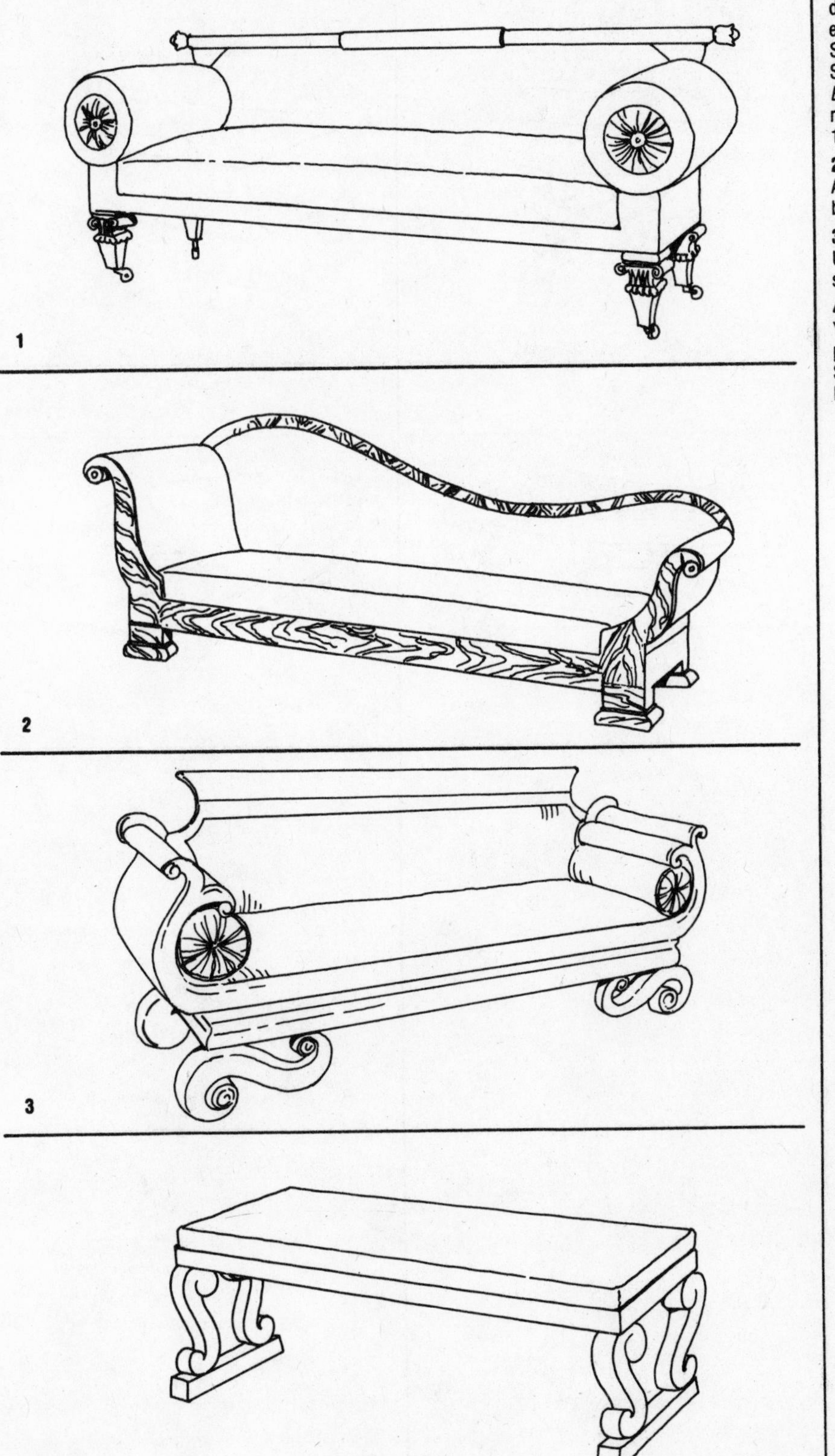

1. Sofa. Boston. A drawer is housed within each of the circular arms. Similar sofas appear in Sheraton's *Cabinet Encyclopedia*. (Labeled by maker William Hancock.) 1826–1828.

2. Sofa. New York. Asymmetrical with broad bands of veneer. 1837.

3. Sofa. Northeastern United States. S-scrolls support sofa. c. 1840.

4. Window bench. New York. Part of a suite of parlor furniture made for Samuel Foot by Duncan Phyfe. 1837.

1. Stool. Probably New York. X-based stool inspired by ancient Roman prototype. 1815–1835.

2. Stool. Albany, New York. Note ogee curve of sides and feet. (Labeled by little-known maker J. W. Netterville, active 1833–1867.) 1840–1850.

3. Stool. America. X-legged stool has caned seat. 1835–1850.

4. Stool. America. Outline of stool follows S-scroll. 1835–1845.

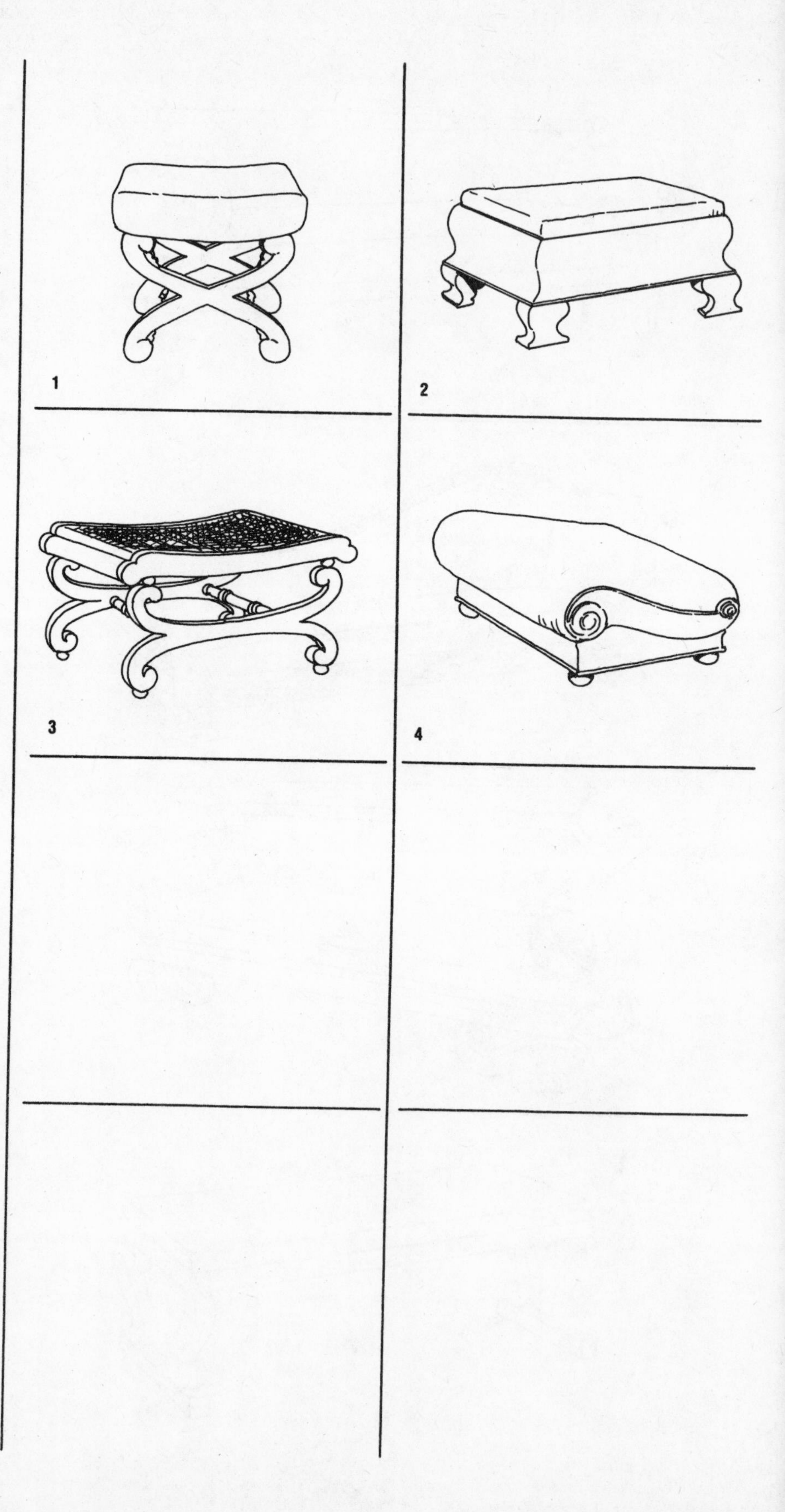

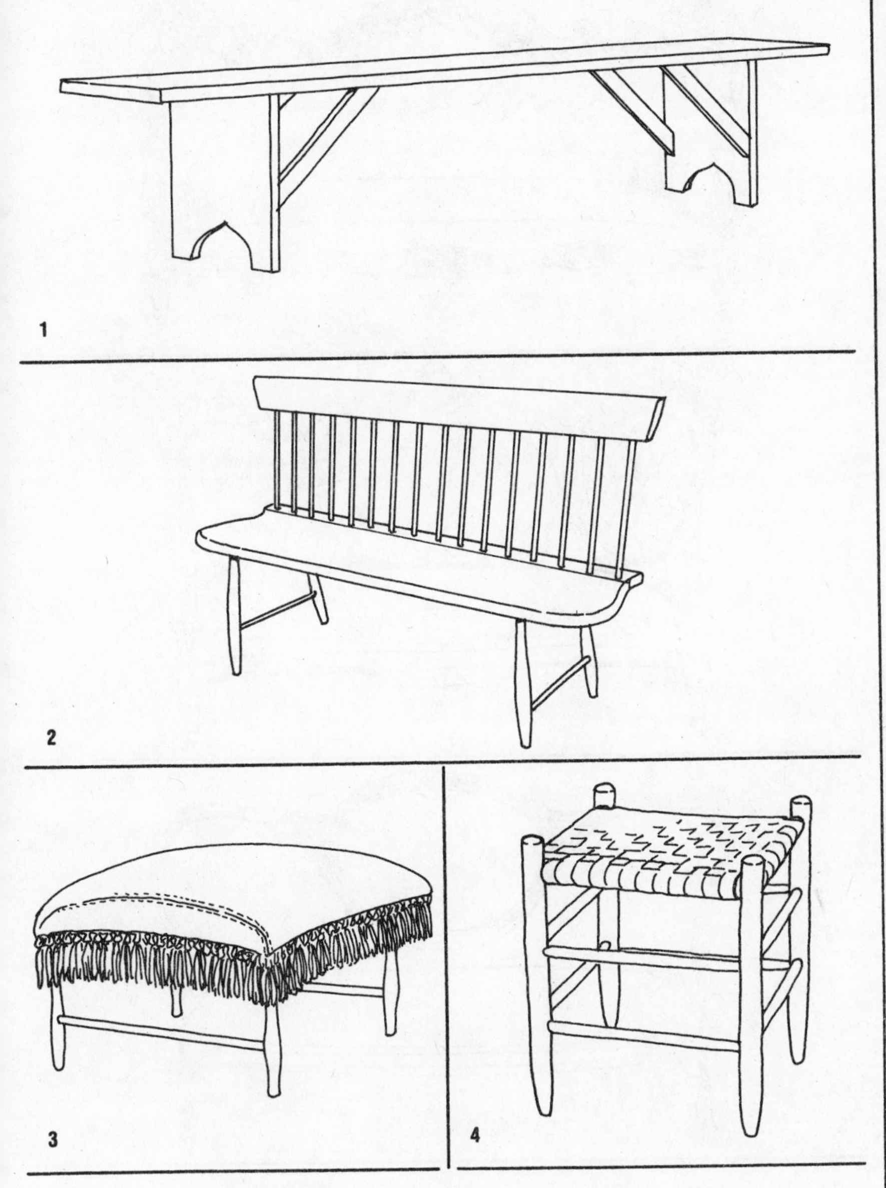

1. Bench. Probably Mount Lebanon, New York. Benches commonly used in meeting houses. 1800–1890.

2. Bench. Enfield or Canterbury, New Hampshire. Specific type associated with Enfield but also found in other communities. 1820–1840.

3. Stool. Mount Lebanon, New York. Upholstered footstool sold commercially. 1875–1900.

4. Stool. Mount Lebanon, New York. Another product of Shakers' commercial line. 1875–1900.

1. Sofa. New York. This type of open carving, here consisting of gnarled vines and flowers, termed "Arabasket" during 1850s. (Attributed to John Henry Belter.) 1850–1860.

2. Sofa. New York. Heads of George Washington, Thomas Jefferson, and Benjamin Franklin appear on this example. (Attributed to John Henry Belter.) c. 1860.

3. Sofa. Simple versions of the Rococo Revival style remained popular for decades. 1860–1890.

4. Tête-à-tête. New York. Invention of lamination allowed for the development of this fluid furniture form. (Attributed to John Henry Belter.) 1850–1860.

1

2

1. Méridienne. New York. Sinuous and rather fragile furniture form used for lounging. c. 1850.

2. Méridienne. Northeastern United States. Sculptural in design, like many other examples of Rococo Revival furniture. c. 1860.

3. Ottoman. Philadelphia. President James Buchanan bought this for the White House from Gottlieb Volmer. 1859.

3

Louis XVI Revival

1. Sofa. New York. Louis XVI style much more subdued in overall design than Rococo Revival. (Attributed to Leon Marcotte.) c. 1860.

1

1. Sofa. New York. Similar in overall design to chairs patented by maker. (By George Hunzinger & Sons.) c. 1870.

2. Sofa. Probably New York. Part of a parlor suite made for the Wilcox house in Meriden, Connecticut. c. 1870.

3. Sofa. Newark, New Jersey. Architectural cresting piece, carved tassels at upper corners, caryatid arm supports and tapering legs were all part of the Renaissance Revival design vocabulary. (By John Jelliff & Co.) 1865–1870.

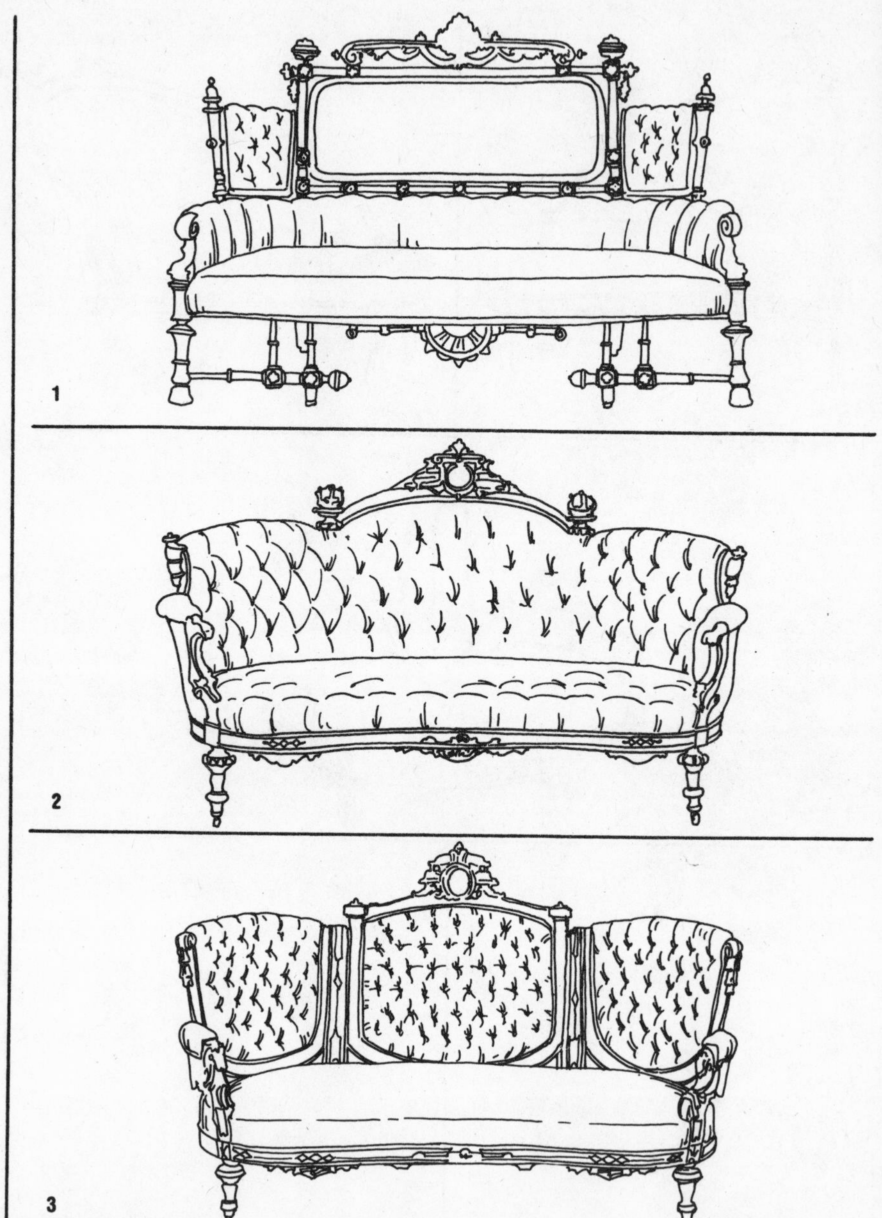

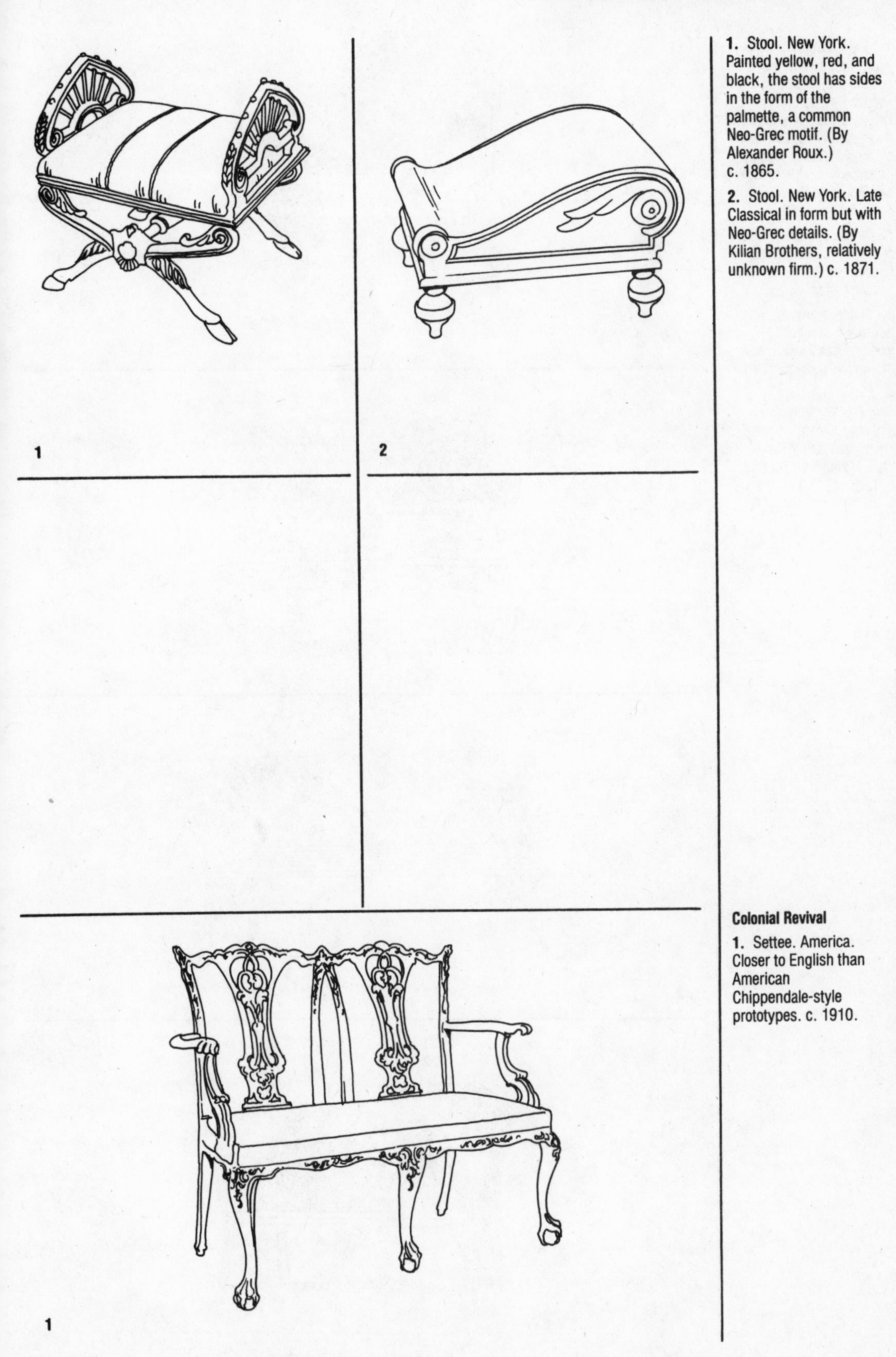

1. Stool. New York. Painted yellow, red, and black, the stool has sides in the form of the palmette, a common Neo-Grec motif. (By Alexander Roux.) c. 1865.

2. Stool. New York. Late Classical in form but with Neo-Grec details. (By Kilian Brothers, relatively unknown firm.) c. 1871.

Colonial Revival

1. Settee. America. Closer to English than American Chippendale-style prototypes. c. 1910.

1. Settee. Brooklyn, New York. Cast iron settee combines elements of the Rococo Revival, Renaissance Revival, and Neo-Grec styles. (Marked by John Timmes, who produced more utilitarian cast iron than he did furniture.) c. 1880.

2. Settee. America. Also of cast iron, this too has Rococo and Renaissance Revival motifs. c. 1870.

3. Settee. America. This fern-back cast iron example has a seat made of wooden slats. c. 1870.

4. Settee. Hartford, Connecticut. Of willow and pine. (Made by the short-lived Colt-Willow Ware Manufacturing Co., c. 1865–1873.) c. 1865.

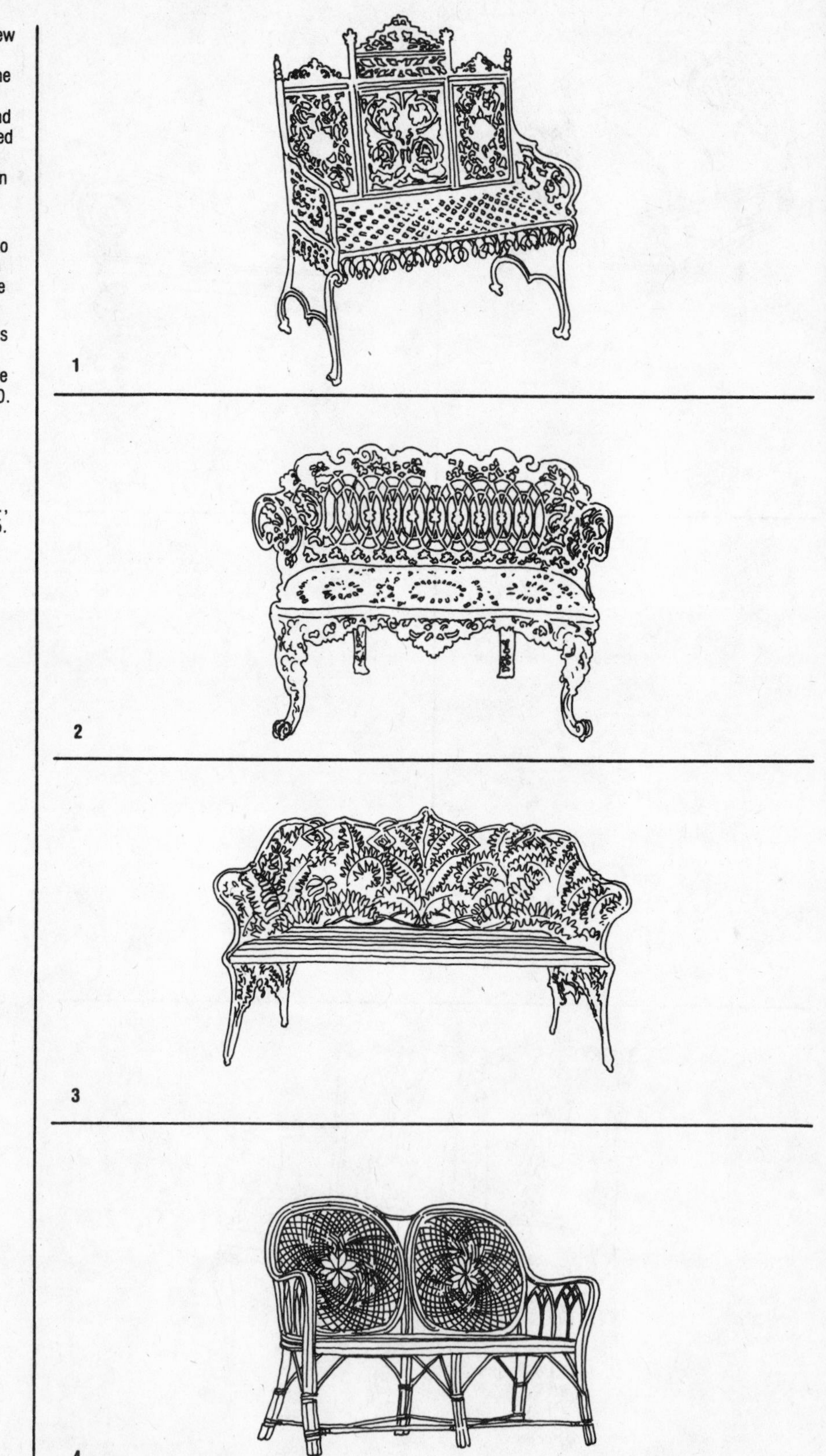

1

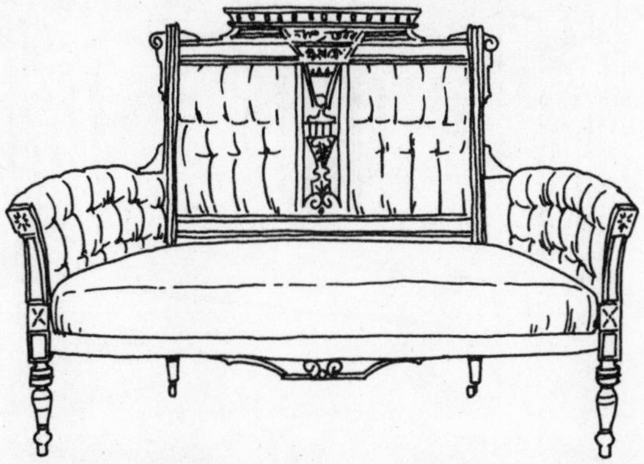

2

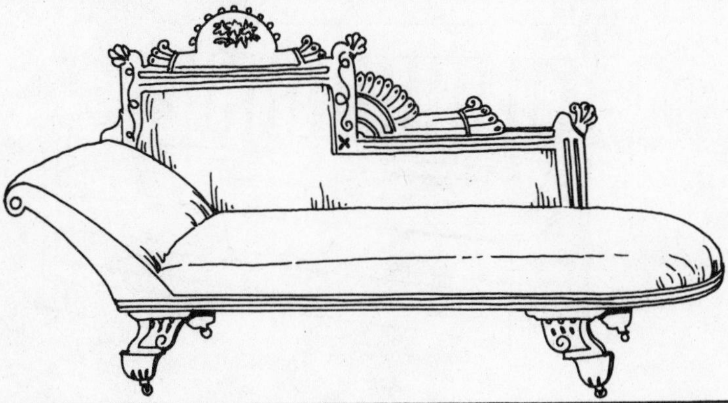

3

1. Tête-à-tête. New York. Style's reliance on rectangular form here aptly illustrated. Note use of tiles. (Attributed to Kimbel & Cabus.) c. 1880.

2. Settee. Probably Grand Rapids, Michigan. Mass-produced example. Note rolled arms, a feature of which Eastlake disapproved. c. 1875.

3. Couch. America. Curving outline of this form does not follow Eastlake's dicta. 1885–1890.

1. Bench. Boston. (Designed by H. H. Richardson, 1806–1886, and has similarities to his Romanesque-style architecture. Attributed to Boston Furniture Co.) 1876–1879.

2. Settee. Fayetteville, New York. Slats used on sides and on back of settee. (Decal of Leopold & J. George Stickley.) c. 1910.

3. Settee. Eastwood (Syracuse), New York. This style simply a lengthwise extension of slat-back chair. (By Gustav Stickley's Craftsman Shops.) c. 1908.

4. Stool. Eastwood (Syracuse), New York. Stool popular Mission form. Upholstered in leather. c. 1910.

5. Stool. Eastwood (Syracuse), New York. Some stools had slip seats; others were upholstered over the rail. 1900–1915.

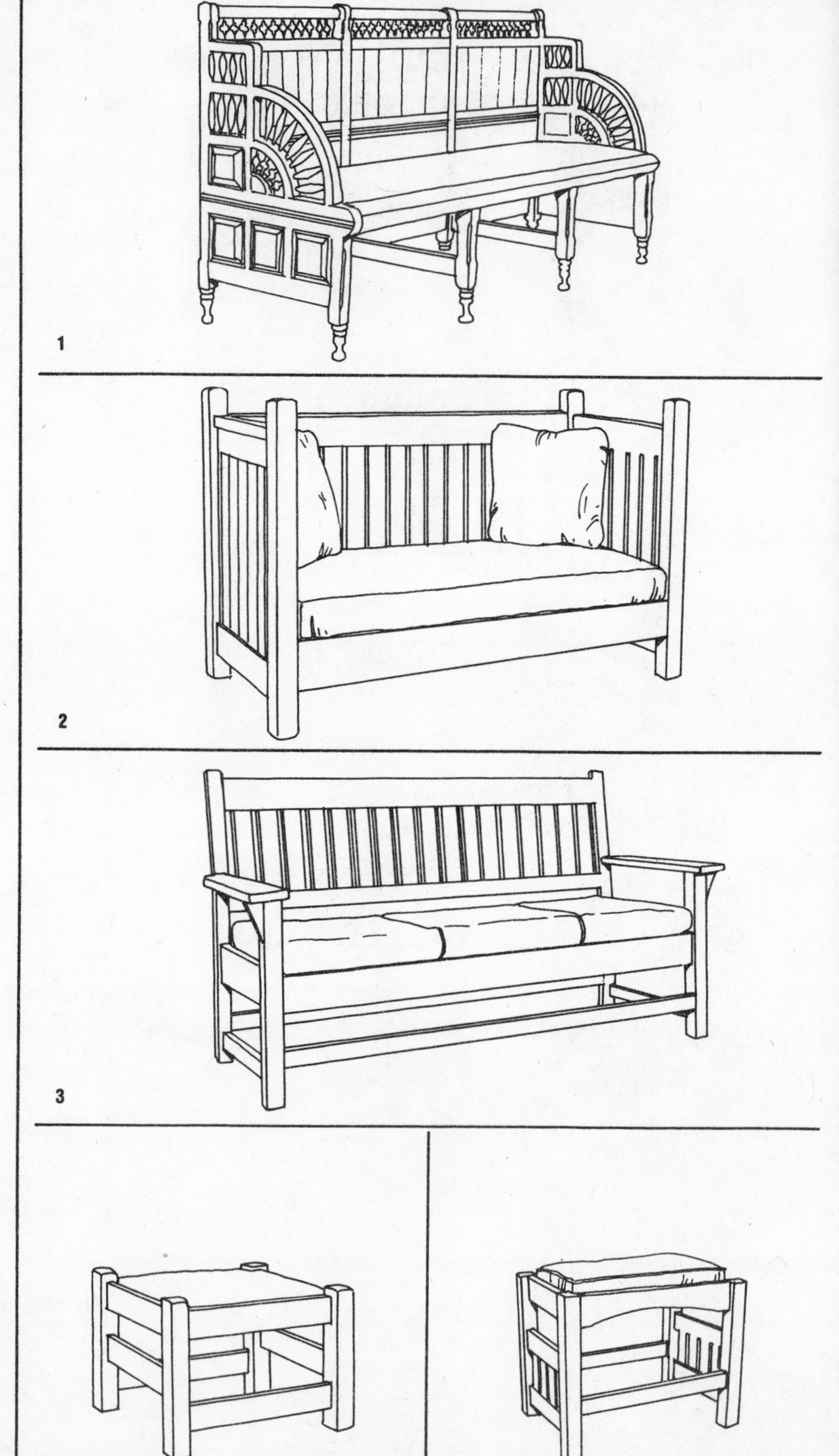

Lift-Top Chests

1. Box. Ipswich, Massachusetts. Carved decoration of leafy S- and reverse S-scrolls. (Possibly by Thomas Dennis, active 1663–1706, or William Searle.) 1670–1700.

2. Box. Probably Connecticut. Shallowly carved in tulip and leaf pattern. 1680–1700.

3. Box. America. International style of carving called "chip" or "Friesland." 1680–1710.

4. Cabinet. Probably Ipswich, Massachusetts. Split spindles, bosses, and panels applied. Note strapwork carving on sides. Dated 1679.

5. Chest. Probably Connecticut. Of six-board construction. Woodworker ran molding plane along front for decoration. 1680–1710.

6. Board chest. New England. With stamped decoration. Dated 1673.

7. Board chest with drawer. Guilford-Milford area, Connecticut. Arrangement of applied elements simulates front of joined chest. 1670–1700.

8. Joined chest. New England. Type of chest made well into 18th century. 1620–1660.

1. Joined chest. Connecticut. Carving very similar to that on English prototypes. 1640–1680.

2. Chest. Ipswich, Massachusetts. Masterfully designed and executed carved chest. (Attributed to Thomas Dennis or William Searle.) 1670–1700.

3. Chest with one drawer. Salem, Massachusetts. Originally had bosses in centers and corners of large panels. 1660–1690.

4. Wethersfield-type chest with drawers. Wethersfield, Connecticut. Note flat sunflower and tulip carving. 1675–1700.

5. Hadley-type chest with drawers. Upper Connecticut River Valley. Carving covers surface of front. Names or initials of female owners often added. c. 1700.

1. Wainscot chest. Virginia or North Carolina. Southern version of joined chest. 1690–1720.

2. Chest with three drawers. Eastern Massachusetts. Top two are false front drawers. Painted to give illusion of chest of drawers. 1700–1720.

3. Chest with drawer. Guilford-Saybrook area, Connecticut. Example of distinctive regional painting, inspired by English precedents. 1700–1720.

4. Chest with drawers. Coastal Connecticut. Delicately painted chest has vertical thrust. Dated 1724.

5. Chest with drawer on frame. Eastern Massachusetts. Movement toward development of high chest of drawers. Painted decoration includes trees. 1700–1720.

6. Chest with drawer. Probably Taunton, Massachusetts. Small and simply constructed. Painting attributed to Robert Crossman. 1730–1740.

1

3

5

1

2

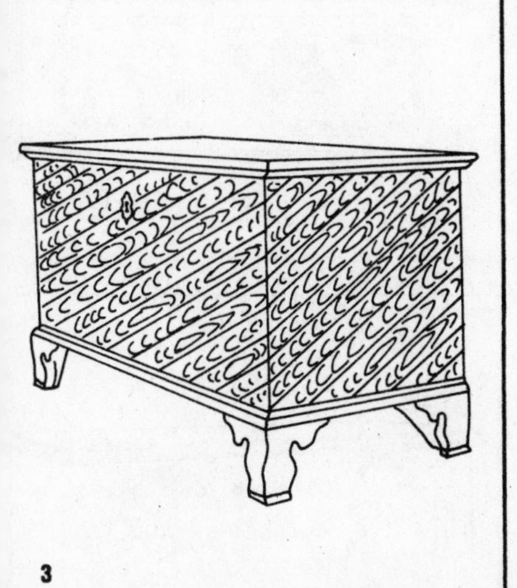

3

4

1. Cabinet. Pennsylvania. Note bold ogee bracket feet. 1750–1770.

2. Cabinet. Chester County, Pennsylvania. Delicate inlay associated with that area. 1750–1770.

3. Chest. Painting in imitation of oyster veneer. 1750–1770.

4. Chest with two drawers. Long Island, New York. This form continued to be made through the 18th century. Updated through use of bracket feet. 1770–1790.

1. Box. Pennsylvania. Abstract floral and geometric painting decorate sides and sliding lid. 1770–1780.

2. Box. Pennsylvania. With rather intricate inlaid decoration. 1790–1820.

3. Chest. Hudson River Valley. Painted in imitation of oyster shell veneer. ("IW 1765" painted on front.)

4. Chest. Lebanon County, Pennsylvania. (Decorated by noted painter Christian Seltzer, 1749–1831. Signed and dated by him.) 1775.

5. Chest with drawers. Berks County, Pennsylvania. Unicorns, men on horseback, and floral designs cover chest. Meaning of symbols probably long-forgotten; now simply part of cultural repertoire of ornamentation. 1780–1800.

6. Chest. Lancaster County, Pennsylvania. Birds and vines contained within arched panels. Bears date 1782.

7. Chest with drawers. Pennsylvania. Name Maria Kutz, date 1783, and naturalistic ornamentation inlaid on front.

8. Chest. Lebanon County, Pennsylvania. Abstract flower and vase designs hallmark of Christian Seltzer's work. (Signed and dated by him.) 1784.

1. Chest. Frederick, Maryland. Bears name Adam Neff, date 1791, and initials I.T. Decorated by means of sgraffito, top layer of color cut away to reveal bottom layer. Technique associated with decoration of ceramics.

2. Chest. Wythe County, Virginia. Some Germanic influence spread to South by Pennsylvania Germans who migrated through Shenandoah Valley. 1800–1820.

1. Chest. Northeastern Massachusetts. Panels of figured birch veneer decorate chest with domed lid. Few such high-style chests were made at this late date. 1790–1800.

1

Shaker

1. Chest. Enfield, Connecticut. Form was holdover from earlier joined chests. Till, a little box with cover attached to the side of the chest, inside. c. 1830.

2. Chest with two drawers. Mount Lebanon, New York. Shakers refined many earlier forms, such as the chest of drawers, in the 19th century. 1820–1850.

3. Chest with one drawer. Canaan, New York. (Branded on back "Made April 1837, Canaan." Because of a dictum against signing and dating objects, relatively little known about early individual Shaker craftspeople.)

1

2

3

Chests of Drawers

1. Cupboard. Eastern Virginia. One of two extant Southern examples of this specific form. 1640–1660.

2. Court cupboard. Salem, Massachusetts. One of the most status-associated furniture forms in 17th-century America. Used to serve food and display plate. Dated 1680.

3. Press cupboard. Essex County, Massachusetts. Used to store household textiles. Unlike most court cupboards, press cupboards have enclosed bottoms. Note applied and carved decoration. 1670–1700.

4. Chest of drawers. Boston. Furniture form prompted development of chest with drawers. 1670–1700.

5. Chest of drawers. Newbury, Massachusetts. Because of variety of applied, carved, and painted ornamentation, nicknamed "vocabulary" chest of drawers during 20th century. Dated 1678.

6. Chamber table. Salem, Massachusetts. 17th-century dressing table. Dated 1690.

7. Side view of side hung drawer. Massachusetts. Slots fit runners inside case. Note lack of dovetails. c. 1680.

8. Press. Eastern Virginia. Architectural in design. Clothes hung on pegs inside. 1680–1700.

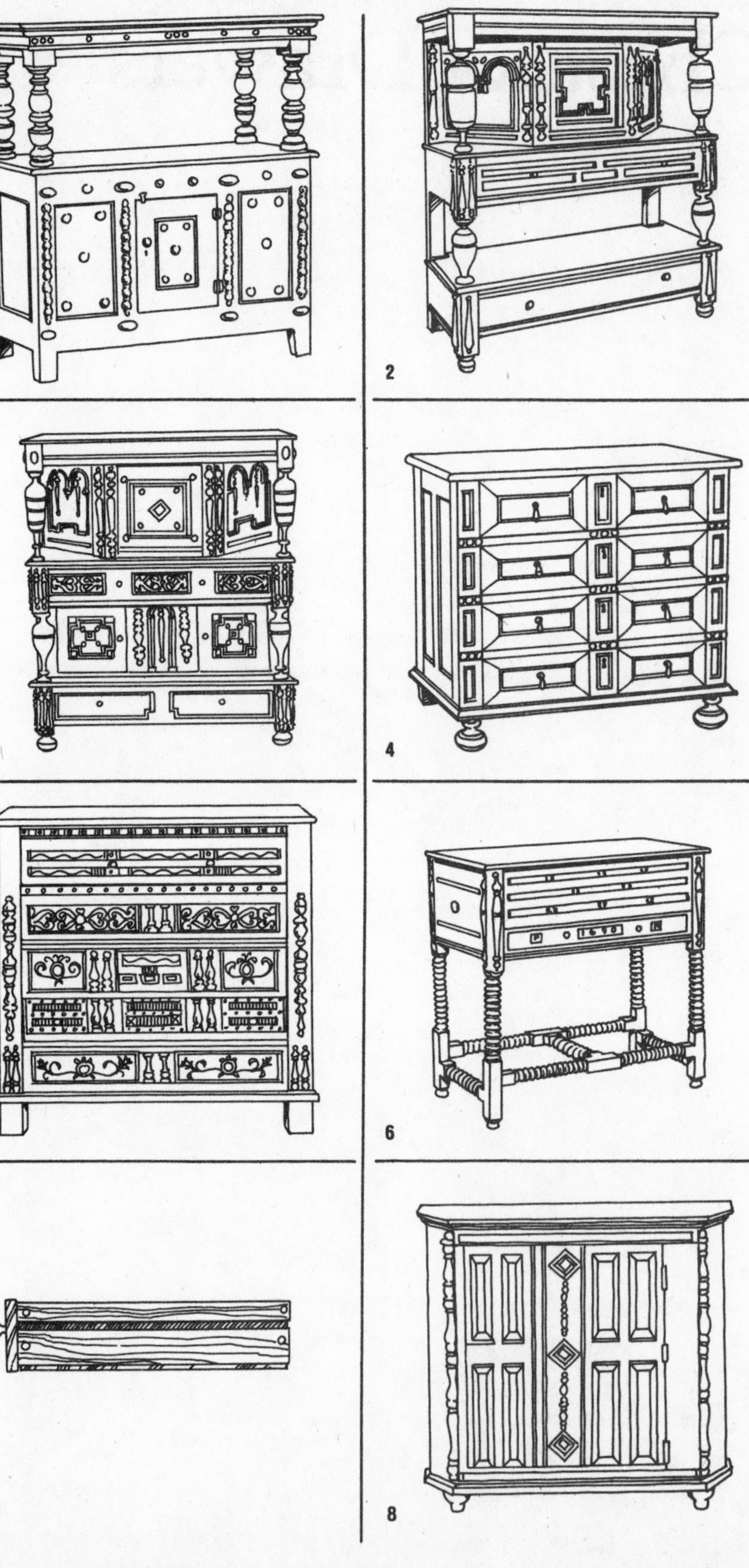

1

3

2

4

5

6

1. Double chest of drawers, or chest-on-chest. Massachusetts. Beveled applied moldings and period hardware decorate front. 1690–1710.

2. Chest of drawers. Boston. Note use of highly figured veneer. Original bracket feet make form unusual in America. 1720–1730.

3. Chest of drawers. Philadelphia. Note that framing of sides is very evident. (Signed and dated "William Beakes 1711" by maker.)

4. Chest of drawers. Chester County, Pennsylvania. Delicate inlay seen on many Chester County objects made through much of 18th century. 1720–1760.

5. High chest of drawers. Probably Boston. Japanned to give illusion of Oriental lacquer. 1700–1730.

6. High chest of drawers. Massachusetts or Connecticut. Note heavy molding around top. 1700–1735.

1. High chest of drawers. Probably Massachusetts. Legs painted to match burled veneer on surface of chest. Triple arched apron an early feature. 1700–1720.

2. High chest of drawers. New York City. First used in colonies during William and Mary period. Note broad proportions and unusual spiral-twist turnings. c. 1700.

3. High chest of drawers. Flushing, New York. (Inscribed "This was made in ye Year 1726 by me Samuel Clement of Flushing June 8.")

4. High chest of drawers. Pennsylvania. Regional features include use of two pulls on each bottom drawer and wide spaces between bottom drawers. 1700–1725.

1

3

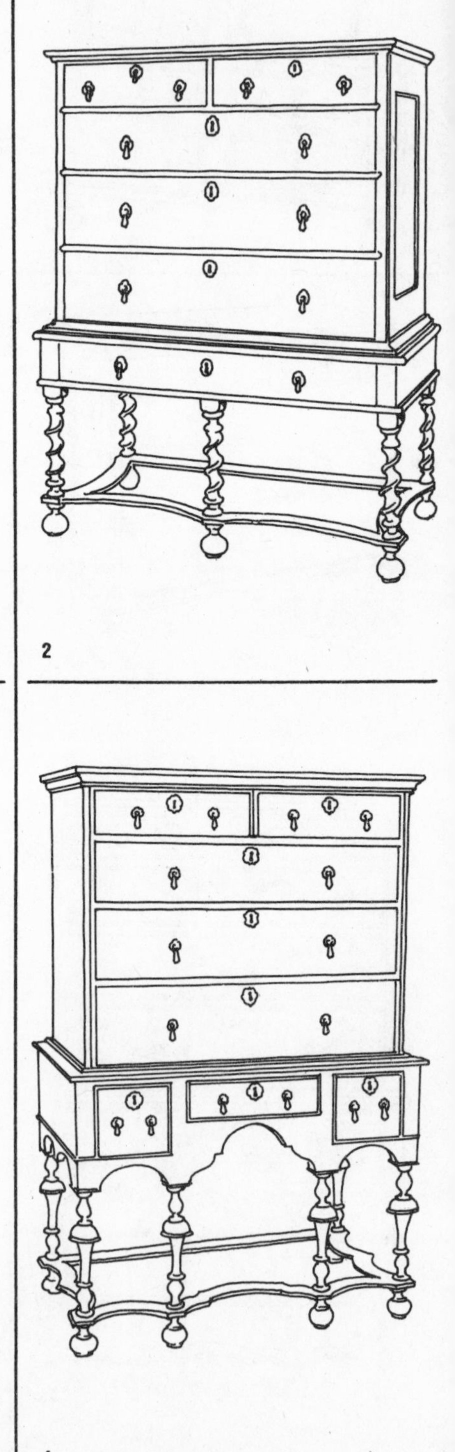

2

4

1

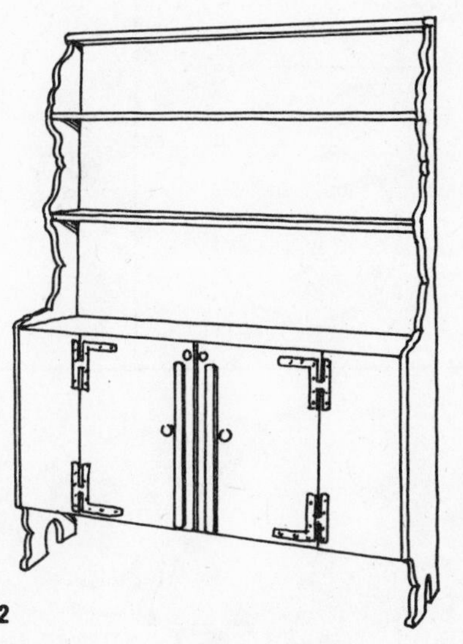

2

3

1. Cupboard. New York. Of simple board construction with shelves inside. Decorated in tones of grey, technique known as *grisaille* painting. 1700–1750.

2. Cupboard. New York. Sometimes called "pudder bank," or pottery cupboard. Found in Brooklyn. 1710–1740.

3. Kast. New York. Preferred storage form in 18th-century New York and New Jersey. 1720–1770.

1. Ball foot used in all regions during William and Mary period. 1690–1730.

2. Diamond-shaped escutcheon. Associated with William and Mary period. 1690–1730.

3. "Teardrop" pull. (Modern terminology.) 1690–1720.

4. Cup-turned leg from Massachusetts high chest of drawers. 1700–1720.

5. Trumpet-turned leg from New England high chest of drawers. 1715–1735.

6. Side view of William and Mary drawer. Note introduction of dovetails. 1700–1730.

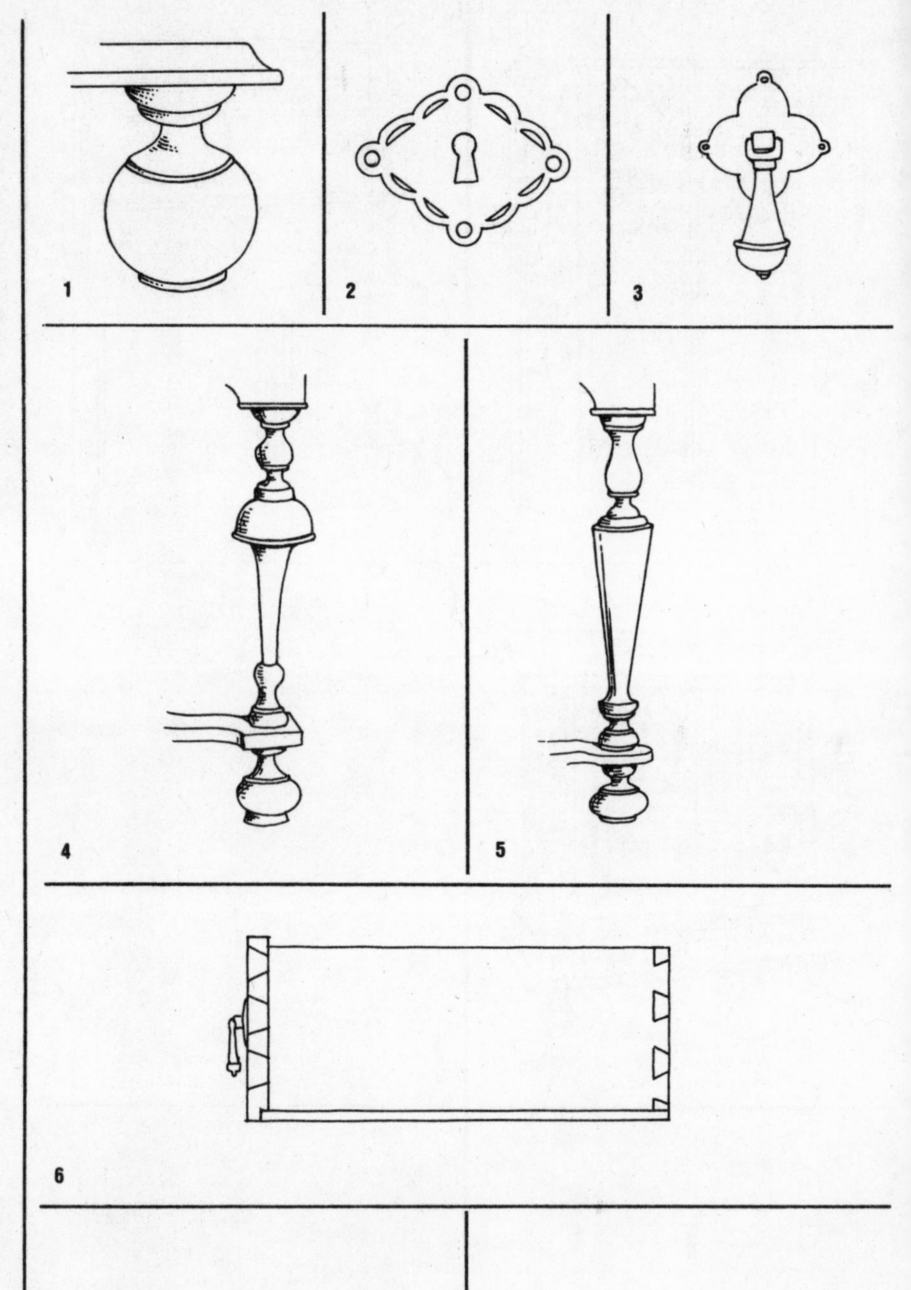

1

2

3

4

1. Chest-on-frame. Massachusetts. Early step in development of high chest of drawers. 1730–1750.

2. Chest-on-frame. North Carolina. Brasses are Federal in style due to late date of object. (Attributed to Jesse Needham, active 1793–1839.) 1795–1815.

3. High chest of drawers. Boston. Japanned in imitation of Oriental lacquer. (Case by John Pimm.) 1740–1750.

4. High chest of drawers. Ipswich, Massachusetts. Low broken-arch pediment Ipswich feature. 1740–1760.

1. High chest of drawers. Salem, Massachusetts. Flat top early feature. 1740–1770.

2. High chest of drawers. Concord, Massachusetts. Blocked front helps make object visually exciting. Chippendale-style brasses used. (Attributed to Joseph Hosmer, 1736–1821.) 1750–1800.

3. High chest of drawers. Massachusetts or Portsmouth, New Hampshire. Bands of inlay outline drawers. 1725–1750.

4. High chest of drawers. Portsmouth, New Hampshire. Deeply scalloped skirt and tall, thin legs give it great vertical thrust. 1730–1750.

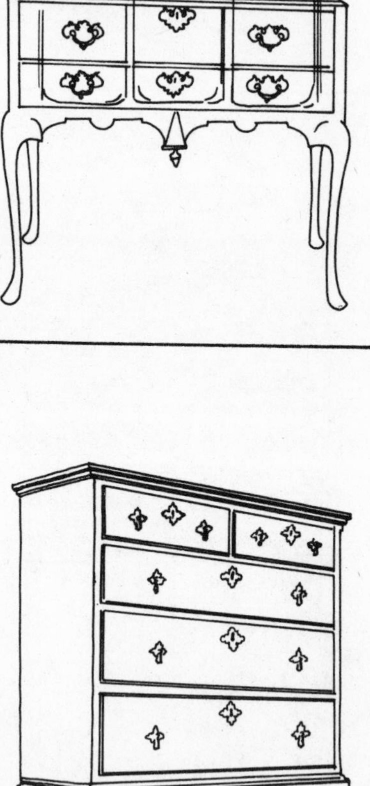

1

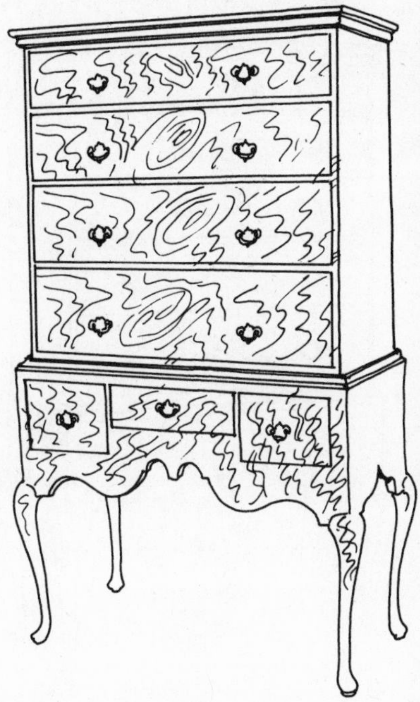

2

3

4

1. High chest of drawers. Windsor area, Connecticut. "Springy" legs and "hockey puck" feet unusual features on this japanned high chest. Date 1736.

2. High chest of drawers. Connecticut. Front grained in imitation of fine veneers found on more expensive furniture. 1740–1760.

3. High chest of drawers with step top. Connecticut. Separate shelving made for display of ceramics. 1748–1760.

4. High chest of drawers. Newport, Rhode Island. Tapering central element and decreasing drawer height toward top are two features that lead eye upward. 1730–1750.

1. High chest of drawers. Newport, Rhode Island. Note delicate slipper feet and original brasses, the latter Chippendale in style. 1730–1760.

2. High chest of drawers. Lawrenceville, New Jersey. Unusual carving on knees echoes pilasters on upper case. c. 1740.

3. Chest-on-chest. Connecticut. Form new during this period. 1750–1800.

4. Queen Anne–style "bat wing" brass with bail handle. 1730–1750.

5. Detail of inlaid star from Boston dressing table. Motif borrowed from England. c. 1730–1750.

6. Spire-shaped finial from Connecticut high chest of drawers. 1740–1800.

7. One of many variant finials seen on Connecticut high chests. 1740–1800.

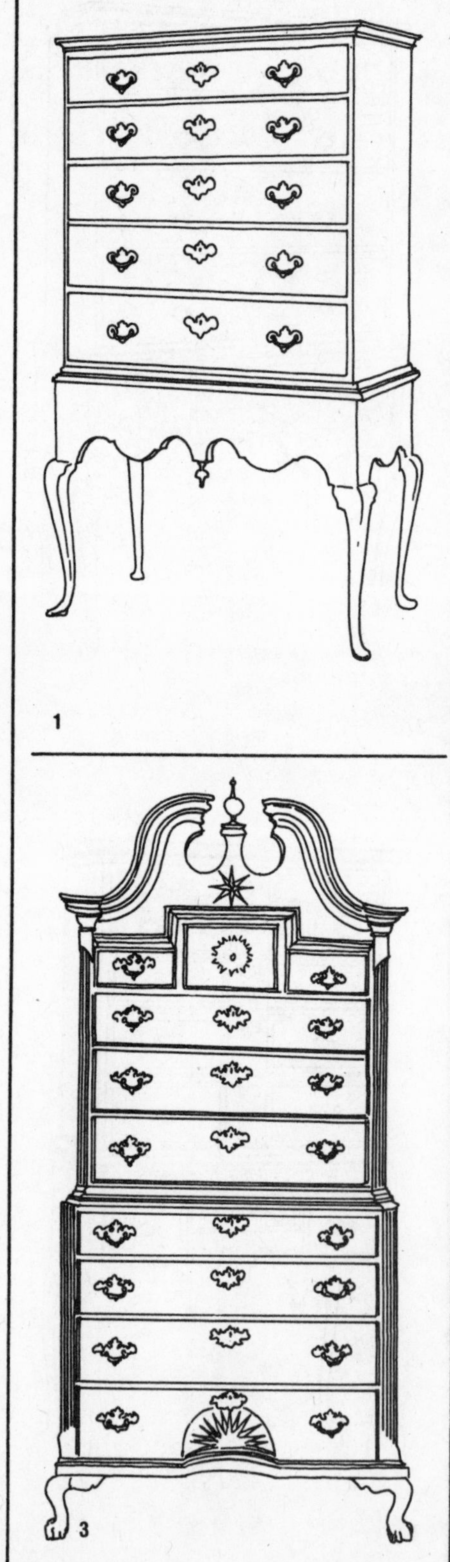

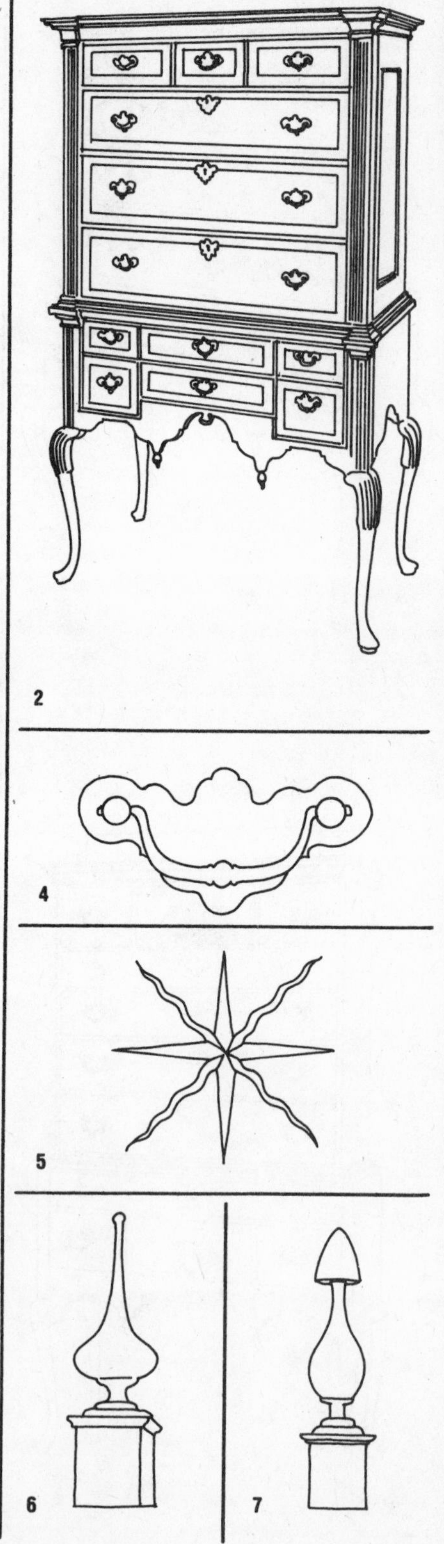

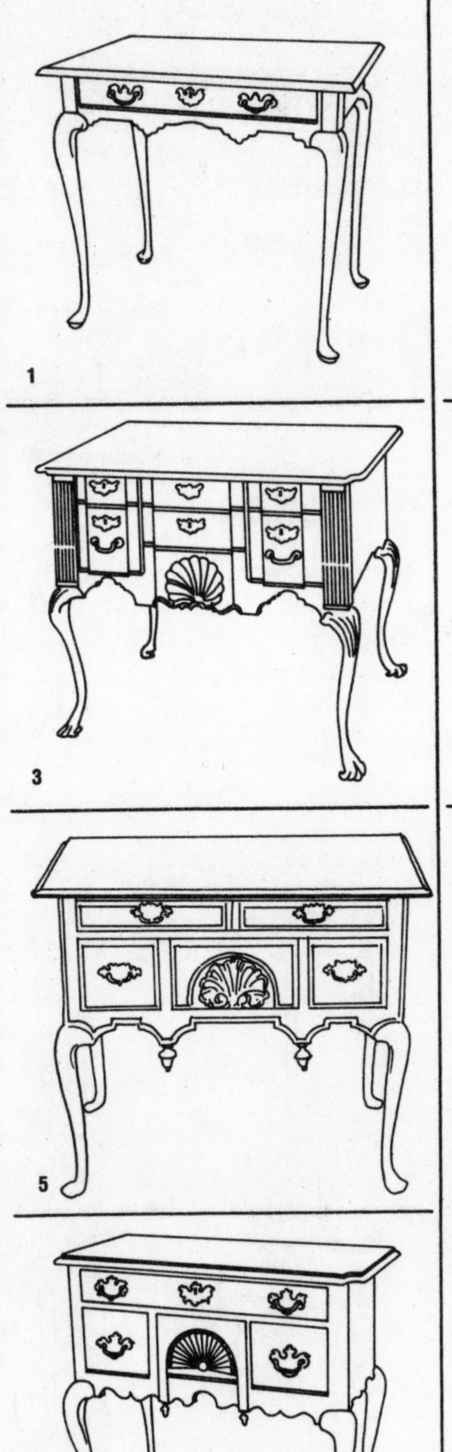

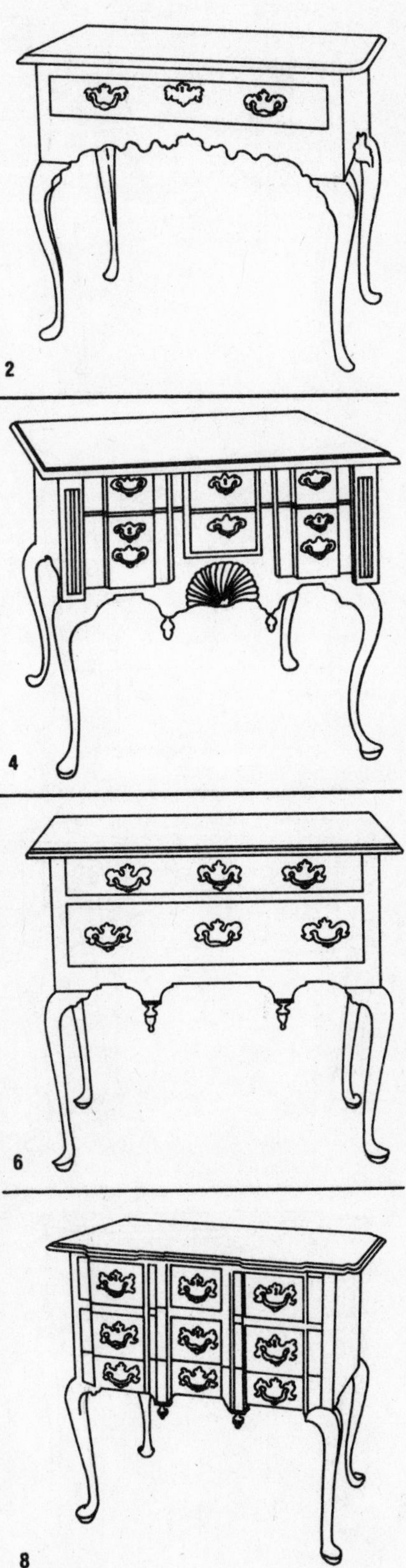

1. Dressing table. Massachusetts. By middle of Queen Anne period, most dressing tables had evolved into case pieces. 1720–1740.

2. Dressing table. Probably Pennsylvania. Similar to English examples. 1740–1770.

3. Dressing table. Boston area, Massachusetts. Early and awkward blockfront. 1720–1740.

4. Dressing table. Boston. Blockfront made by craftsman once apprenticed by Job Coit, first cabinet-maker known to have used blockfront technique in America. (By Joseph Davis, active 1726–1732.) c. 1730.

5. Dressing table. Boston. Note inlaid decoration and carved and gilded shell. 1730–1740.

6. Dressing table. Massachusetts. Plain but well-proportioned, elegant example. 1740–1760.

7. Dressing table. Massachusetts. Note unusual features including cut corners, ribbed fan, and scalloped skirt. 1740–1760.

8. Dressing table. Massachusetts. A well-integrated blockfront. Top molding parallels shape of case's front. 1740–1750.

1. Dressing table. Connecticut. Widely overhanging, deeply scalloped top echoes line of skirt. 1740–1760.

2. Dressing table. Newport, Rhode Island. Has sharp and curvaceous lines. 1740–1770.

3. Dressing table. New Jersey. Note use of "Spanish" or scroll feet, usually associated with William and Mary period. 1720–1735.

4. Dressing table. Philadelphia. Deeply carved skirt unusual. Legs have shell carving on knees and end in trifid feet. 1730–1760.

5. Dressing table. Southeastern Virginia. 1740–1750.

6. Dressing table. Charleston, South Carolina. Abrupt knees relate to English prototypes. 1740–1750.

7. Dressing table. Charleston, South Carolina. Elaborately carved fleurs-de-lis and shells visually connect legs and case. 1740–1760.

8. Dressing table. Southern Colonies. Slightly bowed legs suggest cabriole legs. c. 1750.

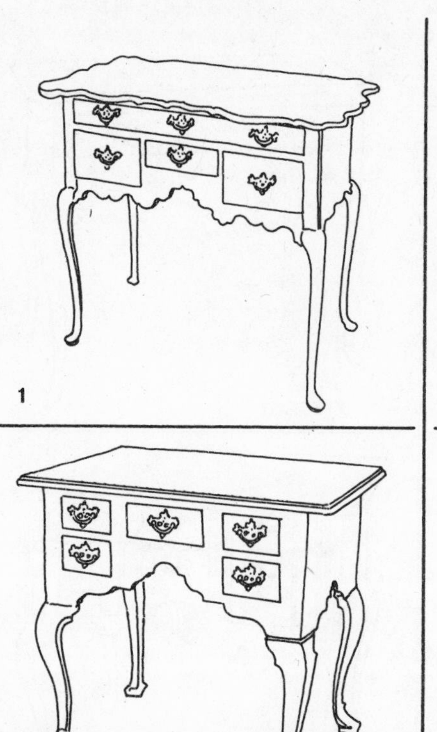

1

2

3

4

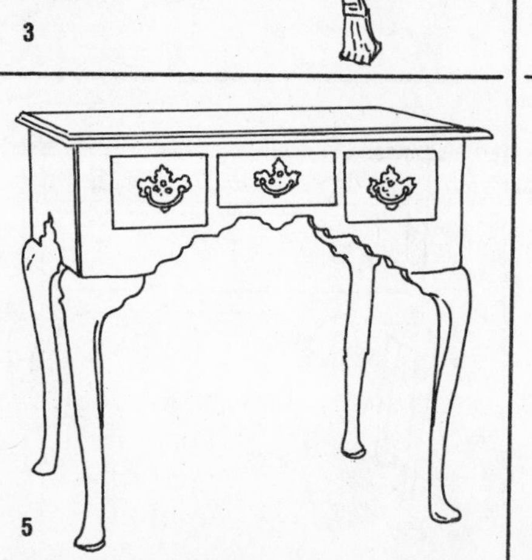

5

6

7

8

1. Blockfront chest of drawers. Massachusetts. Pleasing division of front's surface. 1750–1790.

2. Blockfront chest of drawers. Massachusetts. Claw-and-ball feet alternative to bracket feet. Note how top parallels movement of front. 1760–1780.

3. Chest of drawers. Boston. Note *bombé* sides. 1765–1780.

4. Chest of drawers. Boston. In America, *bombé* case pieces only made in Massachusetts. 1765–1775.

5. Chest of drawers. Probably Connecticut. Similar to simple British prototypes. 1750–1790.

6. Chest of drawers. Connecticut. Influenced by Newport blockfront design. 1770–1790.

7. Chest of drawers. Connecticut. Reverse serpentine front seen more often on British work. 1780–1800.

8. Chest of drawers. Connecticut. Less sophisticated example with reverse serpentine or "oxbow" front. (Inscribed "This buro was made in the year of our Lord 1795 by Bats How," unknown maker.)

1. Chest of drawers. New England. Tall chest of drawers not often seen during this period. 1760–1795.

2. Bureau. Newport, Rhode Island. Blocked drawers flank center compartment. Note bold shell carving associated with Newport. (Attributed to John Townsend.) 1760–1775.

3. Chest of drawers. Philadelphia. Note heavy bracket feet and fluting at corners on this serpentine-front chest. (Made by Jonathan Gostelowe for his wife.) 1789.

4. Chest of drawers. Chester County, Pennsylvania. Distinctive regional inlay decorates surface. 1730–1760.

5. Chest of drawers on frame. Shenandoah Valley, Virginia. Furniture from this area influenced by Pennsylvania and Maryland styles. 1770–1790.

6. Chest of drawers. South Carolina. Quarter-columns vie with full-blown Chippendale brasses for viewer's attention. 1770–1780.

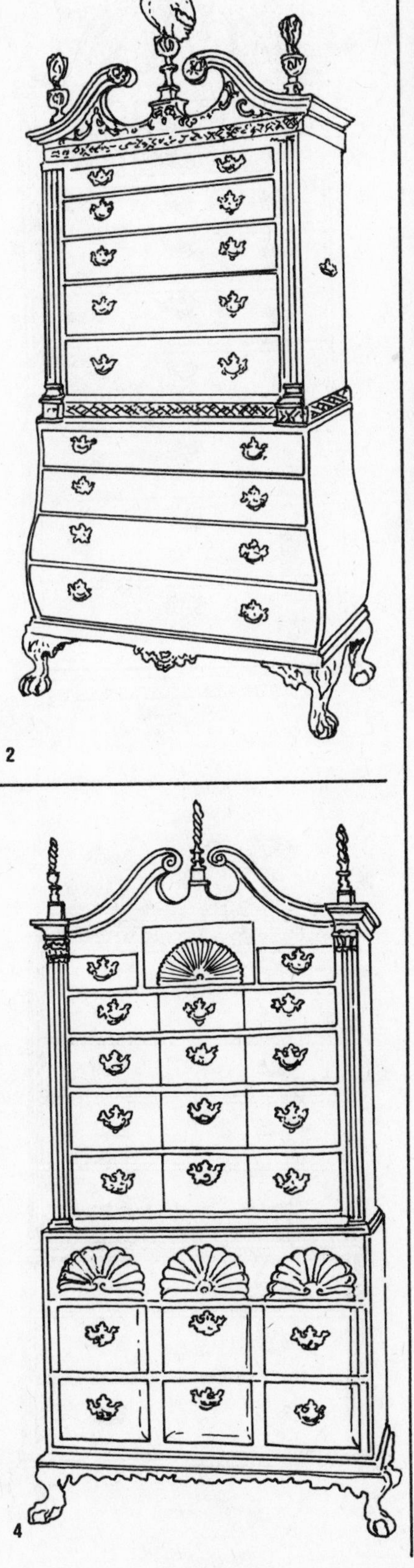

1. Chest-on-chest. Massachusetts. Flat pilasters often favored over rounded quarter columns in Massachusetts. Literally interpreted "fan" carving. 1770–1785.

2. Chest-on-chest. Boston. Note *bombé* bottom. (Signed by maker "John Cogswell, Middle Street, Boston, 1782.")

3. Chest-on-chest. Newport, Rhode Island. Masterfully designed and executed object. Blockfront with nine carved shells. (Attributed to Townsend-Goddard school.) 1765–1780.

4. Chest-on-chest. Norwich area, Connecticut. Inspired by Newport blockfront furniture. Possibly a marriage, since top and bottom differ so in ornamentation. 1755–1810.

1. Chest-on-chest. Kent, Connecticut. Idiosyncratic features include conical finials, carved swirl, and heart-shaped cutouts. (By obscure maker Reuben Beman, Jr.) c. 1800.

2. Chest-on-chest. Pennsylvania, probably Philadelphia. Closely related to English examples. Note dentiling along cornice. 1765–1795.

3. Chest-on-chest. Philadelphia. Bouquet finial, pierced lattice pediment, and fretted frieze seen on other Philadelphia work. 1770–1790.

4. Chest-on-chest. Charleston, South Carolina. Canted corners and particular design of frieze seen on other objects associated with Thomas Elfe (active 1747–1775), so this object is attributed to him. c. 1770.

1

2

3

4

1. Linen press cupboard. New York. Doors hide shelves. Form based on English prototypes. 1785–1795.

2. Linen press cupboard. Virginia. Of massive size. Note pierced gallery around top, flat pilasters, and fielded panel with bowed top and cut corners. 1770–1790.

3. High chest of drawers. New Hampshire. Features seen on other objects by Dunlap family of cabinetmakers include pierced basket-weave cornice with fan carving and small broken pediments, shell carving and S-curves at bottom, and barbs on cabriole legs. (Attributed to Samuel Dunlap II, 1751–1830.) 1775–1800.

4. High chest of drawers. Eastern Connecticut. Nonhigh-style attributes include cone-shaped finial, heavy rosettes on scroll pediment, rope turning, and abstract, ribbed shell at bottom. 1755–1810.

1. High chest of drawers. Newport, Rhode Island. Rhode Island characteristics include squared-off cabriole legs and carved shell incorporated into undulating bottom. 1755–1790.

2. High chest of drawers. New York. Form not often made in New York during Chippendale period. 1750–1770.

3. High chest of drawers. Philadelphia. Simple yet elegant version of Philadelphia high chest. (Labeled by maker William Savery.) 1755–1788.

4. High chest of drawers. Philadelphia. Creator of this monumental object borrowed design of urns from Chippendale's *Director* and scene on bottom drawer from Thomas Johnson's *A New Book of Ornaments* (1762). 1765–1775.

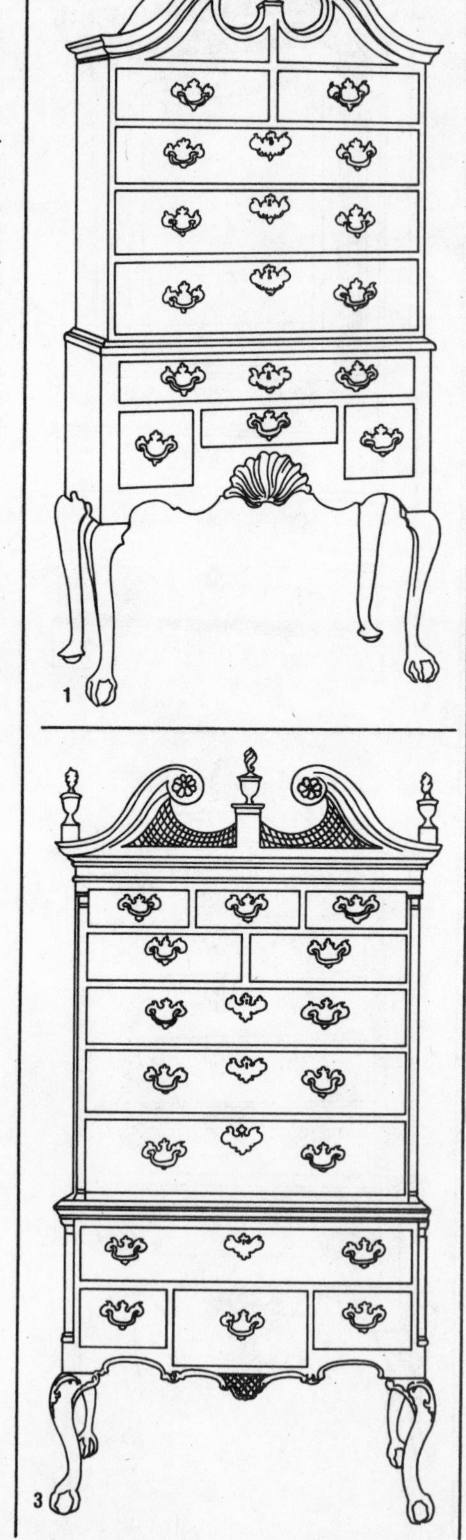

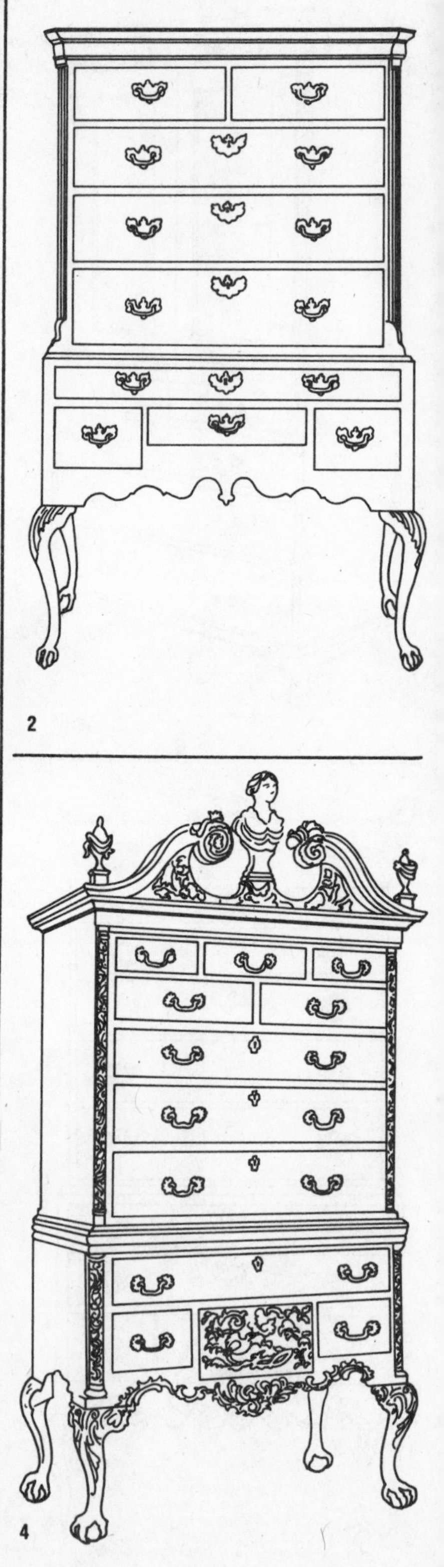

1. High chest of drawers. Philadelphia. Boldly carved example. Scene of fox and grapes from Aesop's fables on lower drawer borrowed from period print. 1765–1775.

2. High chest of drawers. Philadelphia. Note Rococo ornamentation. (Made for wealthy Philadelphians Michael and Miriam Simm Gratz.) 1769.

3. Dressing table. Piedmont area, Virginia. Note thin cabriole legs with corner volutes ending in claw-and-ball feet. 1760–1780.

4. Dressing table. Probably Newport, Rhode Island. Unusual example has scalloped corners on top and legs that appear barely connected to case. 1740–1750.

5. Dressing table. New Jersey or Philadelphia. Flat chamfered corners, boldly arched skirt, and scallop shell on knees suggest Middle Colonies provenance. 1740–1750.

6. Dressing table. Philadelphia. Swan carving probably inspired by Aesop's fables. Note elaborately pierced Chippendale-style brasses. 1760–1780.

1. Dressing table. Philadelphia. Here, Rococo-style carving is restricted to lower drawer, skirt, and legs. 1765–1775.

2. Dressing table. Pennsylvania. Closely related to English examples, 1755–1790.

3. Dressing table. Lancaster County, Pennsylvania. Carving flatter and cruder than that seen on most high-style Philadelphia case pieces. 1755–1810.

4. Dressing table. Probably Maryland. Shares features with other Maryland objects, such as chamfered corners and scalloping of skirt. Piercing of skirt is an unusual feature. 1745–1780.

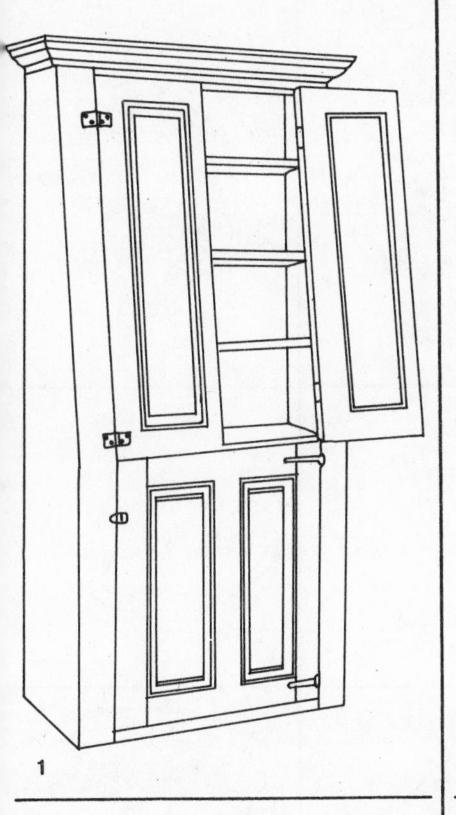
1

2

3

4

1. Cupboard. Massachusetts. Top doors cannot inadvertently swing closed when open because of case's slant. 1740–1780.

2. Corner cupboard. Oakville Center, Connecticut. Very architectural with dentiled cornice, keystone, and boldly molded arch. 1776.

3. Kast. New Brunswick, New Jersey. Some later *kasten* have bracket feet. (Labeled by maker Matthew Egerton, Junior.) 1780–1790.

4. Cupboard. Rowan County, North Carolina. Closely related in style and construction to Pennsylvania examples. (Attributed to James Gheen.) 1780–1795.

1. Asymmetrical finial from high chest of drawers. East Windsor, Connecticut. 1771–1807.

2. Cartouche and cabochon from Philadelphia high chest of drawers. 1765–1780.

3. Vase-and-flowers finial from another Philadelphia high chest.

4. Chippendale-style flattened-urn brass with bail handle used in all regions during period.

5. Intricately pierced brass with bail handle found on some Chippendale-style furniture.

6. Bail handle commonly seen during Chippendale period.

7. Elaborate bail handle with rosette from Massachusetts chest of drawers. 1765–1780.

8. Undercut claw-and ball foot seen on some Newport, Rhode Island, tables and case pieces.

9. Detail of carving from Connecticut corner cupboards. 1776.

10. Fluted, chamfered corner from New York high chest of drawers ending in lamb's-tongue carving. 1750–1770.

11. Fluted quarter-column from Philadelphia high chest of drawers. 1755–1788.

12. Quarter-column from Philadelphia high chest of drawers with Rococo carving rather than fluting. 1765–1775.

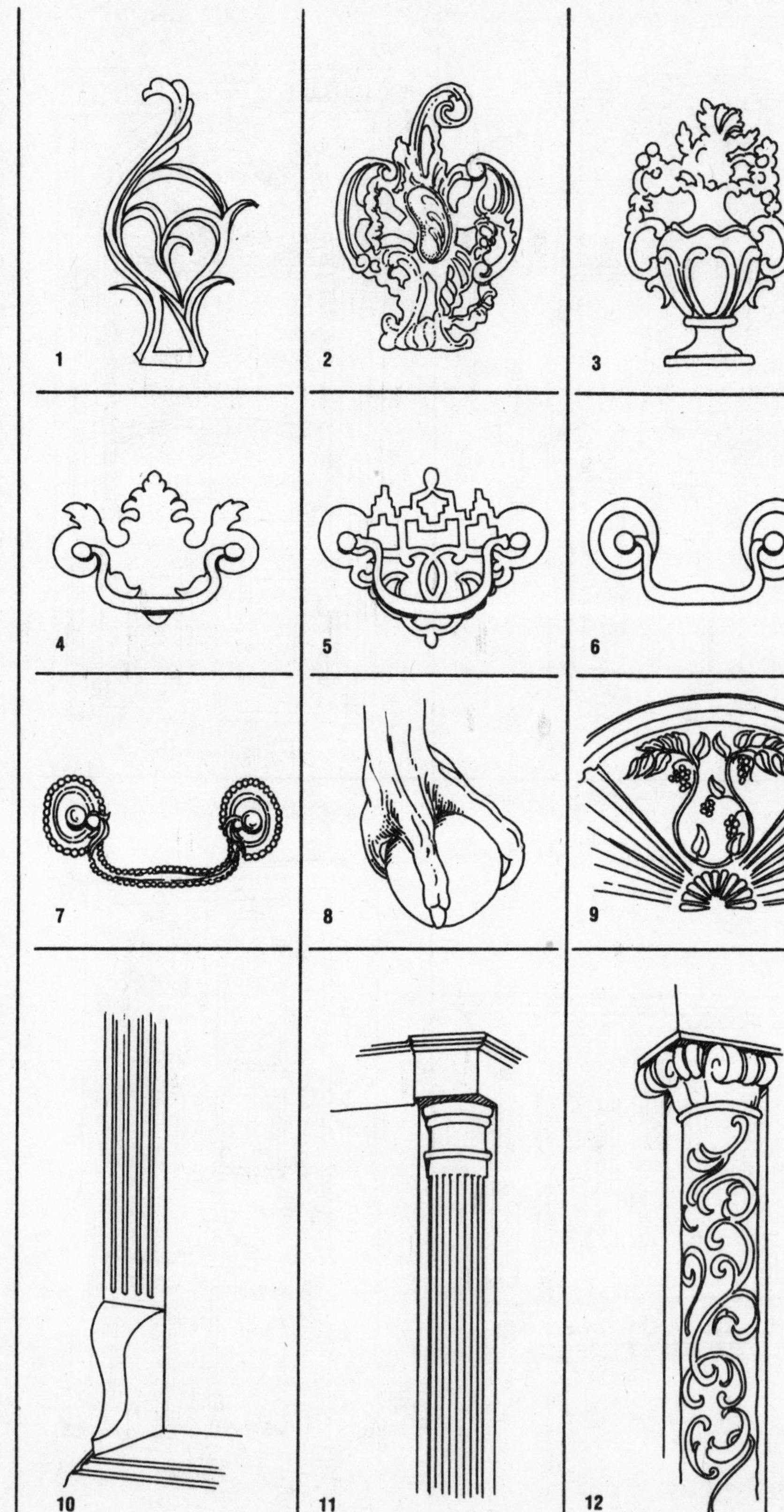

1

2

1. Schrank. Lancaster County, Pennsylvania. (Made for Emanuel Herr and his wife by D. I. Mertz.) Dated February 17, 1768.

2. Schrank. Pennsylvania. Germanic form of kast. ("Georg Huber Anno 1779" written in inlaid wax decoration on doors, referring to schrank's owner.)

1. Schrank. Berks County, Pennsylvania. Rag-painted decoration popular in this county. 1780–1800.

2. Corner cupboard. Pennsylvania. Heart cut-outs and scalloped edge seen on other Pennsylvania furniture. 1780–1800.

3. Corner cupboard. Wachovia (now Salem), North Carolina. (Made by Moravian Brethren's workshops. Sect highly valued fine craftsmanship.) 1750–1770.

1

2

3

1

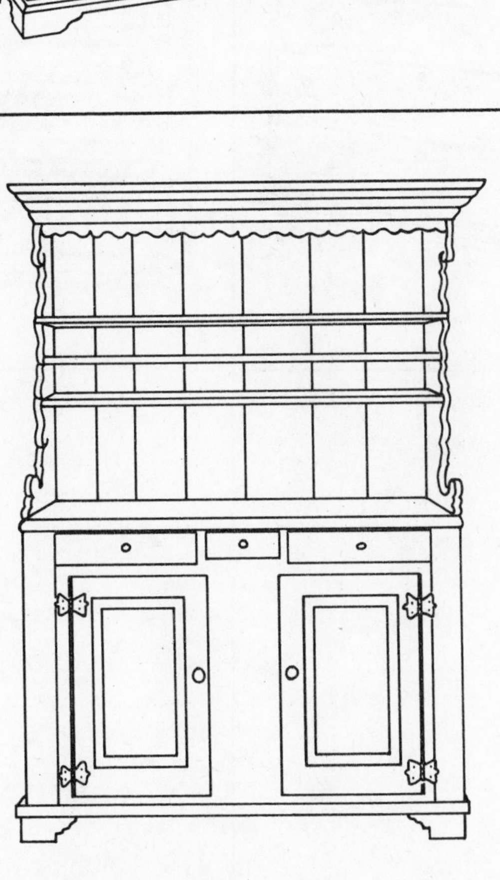

2

1. Cupboard. Pennsylvania. Form combined open and closed shelving and drawers. 1770–1800.

2. Cupboard. Pennsylvania. Note broad proportions and scalloped decoration, seen on other Pennsylvania German objects. 1780–1800.

1. Hanging cupboard. Pennsylvania. Note "HL" hinges and heavy molding around bottom. 1750–1800.

2. Hanging cupboard. Pennsylvania. Has fielded panel in door and flaring cornice at top. Dated 1790.

3. Chest of drawers. Lancaster County, Pennsylvania. Distinctive ogee bracket feet commonly used in Pennsylvania furniture. 1780–1800.

4. Chest of drawers. Mahantango Valley, Pennsylvania. Painted decoration of this sort associated with this region. 1830–1840.

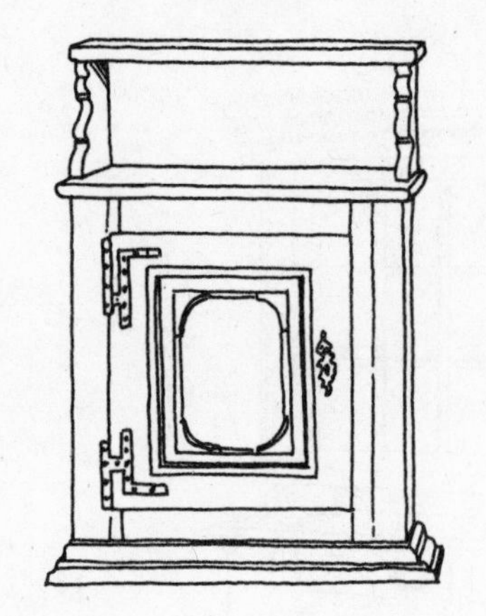

1

2

3

4

1, 2, 3, 4, 5, 6, 7, 8

1. Chest of drawers. Portsmouth, New Hampshire. Bow-front broken up by panels and band of contrasting veneer. 1790–1800.

2. Chest of drawers. Probably eastern Massachusetts. Note use of long French feet on this highly refined, serpentine-front chest of drawers. 1790–1815.

3. Chest of drawers. Northeastern Massachusetts or New Hampshire. Craftsmen in this region favored lavish use of stringing and occasionally employed a "drop tablet" on the bottom front, as seen here. 1790–1810.

4. Child's chest of drawers. Probably Massachusetts. Reverse serpentine front. 1800–1810.

5. Commode. Boston. Exceptional example of Boston Federal-style furniture. (Made for Elizabeth Derby by Thomas Seymour, decorated by noted painter John Ritto Penniman, 1783–1837, and probably carved by Thomas Whitman.) 1809.

6. Chest of drawers. Salem, Massachusetts. Swell- or bow-front chest of drawers has ovolo corners decorated with carved grapevines and punched background above carved, leafy caps. 1810–1815.

7. Chest of drawers. Norwich, Vermont. *Bombé* front chest of drawers has fan inlays at the corners of the drawers and on the front corners of the top. (Inscribed in drawer "Made by G. Stedman Norwich Vermont." Maker is obscure.) 1800–1820.

8. Chest of drawers. Livermore, Maine. Has painting in imitation of stringing. (Inscribed "Made by E. Morse. Livermore. June 7, 1814," by obscure maker.)

1. Chest of drawers and dressing glass. Boston. First introduced as combined form during Federal period. 1810–1820.

2. Chest of drawers and dressing glass. Boston. Swell-front ornamented by figured birch veneer. Note graceful S- and C-curved brackets that support swinging looking-glass. (Labeled by maker Levi Ruggles, active 1813–1855.) 1813–1816.

3. Chest of drawers. Hartford, Connecticut. Cabinetmaker used C-shaped bracket feet to enliven this serpentine-front example. c. 1800.

4. Chest of drawers. Probably Rhode Island. Note quarter fan inlay in corners. 1780–1795.

5. Chest of drawers. Philadelphia or Baltimore. Has the most highly contoured front of any known American Federal-style chest of drawers. 1795–1810.

6. Chest of drawers. Western Maryland or northern Virginia. Note unusual outline of front, inspired by Baltimore furniture. 1790–1800.

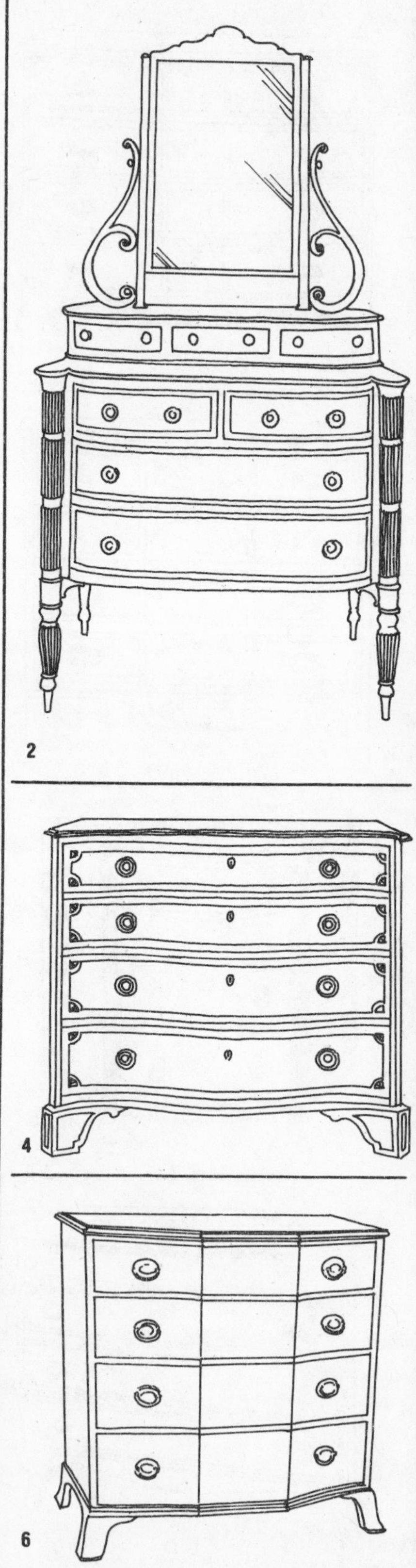

1. Chest of drawers. Norfolk, Virginia. Note flare of French feet and distinctive outline of skirt, characteristics associated with Norfolk furniture. 1790–1800.

2. Chest of drawers. Piedmont area, North Carolina. Related to earlier Chippendale style in overall form. c. 1820.

3. Chest-on-chest. Dorchester Mills, Massachusetts. Monumental object with allegorical figures (carved by John and/or Simeon Skillin) resting on pitch pediment. (Stephen Badlam made this piece for Elias Hasket Derby of Salem.) 1791.

4. Chest-on-chest. Salem, Massachusetts. This serpentine-front chest-on-chest was also made for a member of the Derby family. Overall form closely relates to Chippendale-style predecessors. (Probably carved by Samuel McIntire. Attributed to cabinetmaker William Lemon.) 1796.

1. Wardrobe. New York. Feather and eagle inlays and curved line of skirt are characteristic of objects by Michael Allison. (Attributed to Michael Allison.) 1800–1815.

2. Corner cupboard. Probably Philadelphia. Note fine dentiling and lattice doors on this movable corner cupboard. 1795–1810.

3. Corner cupboard. Davidson County, North Carolina. Note holdover of such details as broken scroll pediment, pilasters, and rope-turned carving at corners. (Attributed to Mordecai Collins.) 1805–1820.

4. Enclosed pier table. Salem, Massachusetts. With half-serpentine sides and storage area behind tambour doors. (Labeled by maker Mark Pitman, 1779–1829.) 1800–1810.

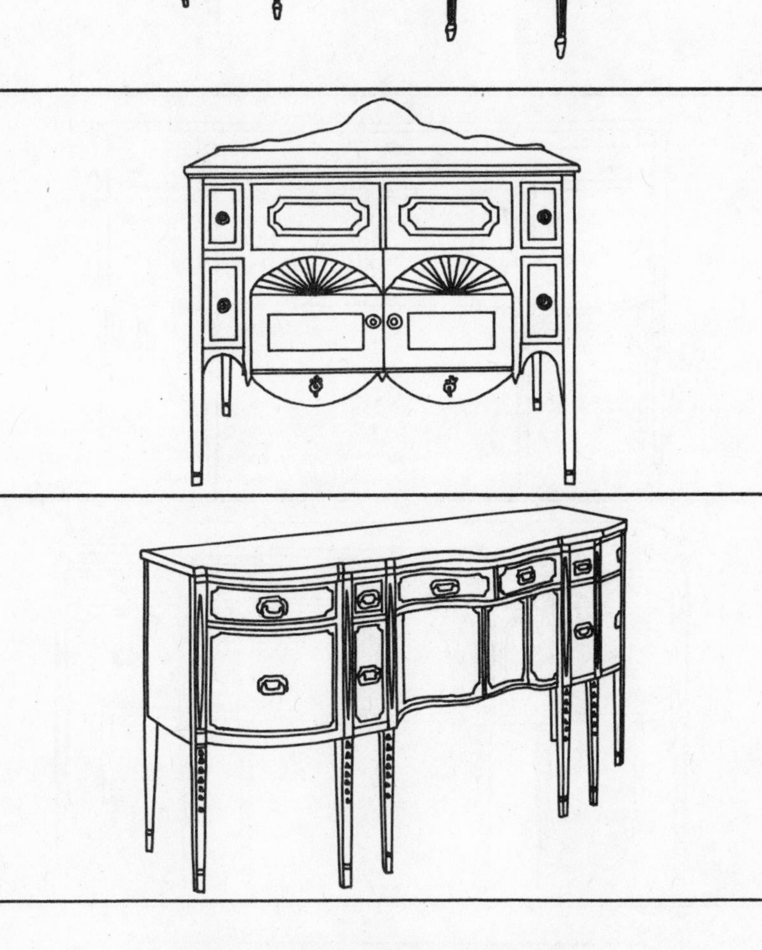

1. Sideboard. Boston. Pendant seen on other sideboards by the Seymours. (Attributed to John and/or Thomas Seymour.) 1800–1810.

2. Sideboard. Newburyport, Massachusetts. Variety of ornamentation not well unified. (Branded by maker Abner Tappan.) c. 1800.

3. Sideboard. Hartford, Connecticut. Serpentine-front sideboard. (Made by Aaron Chapin, as documented by a bill dated November 22, 1804.)

4. Sideboard. Newport, Rhode Island. Serpentine-sided example with highly unusual brasses. 1790–1800.

1. Sideboard. Probably Newport, Rhode Island. Use of oval, circular, and lunette motifs also seen on British sideboards of this general type, 1790–1810.

2. Sideboard. New York. Oval shape of brasses and inlay echoed by rounded corners of sideboard. 1790–1810.

3. Sideboard. New York. The eight legs on this masterfully designed and executed sideboard are just one of its unusual features. 1795–1805.

4. Sideboard. New Brunswick, New Jersey. Similar in overall design to some New York sideboards. (Labeled by maker Matthew Egerton, Jr., active 1785–1837.) 1790–1800.

1

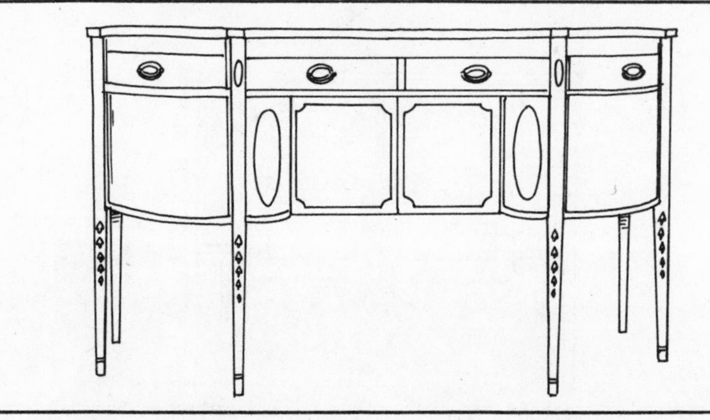

2

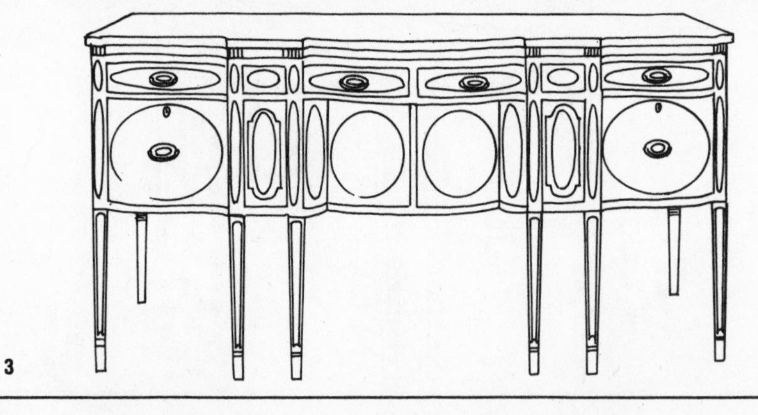

3

4

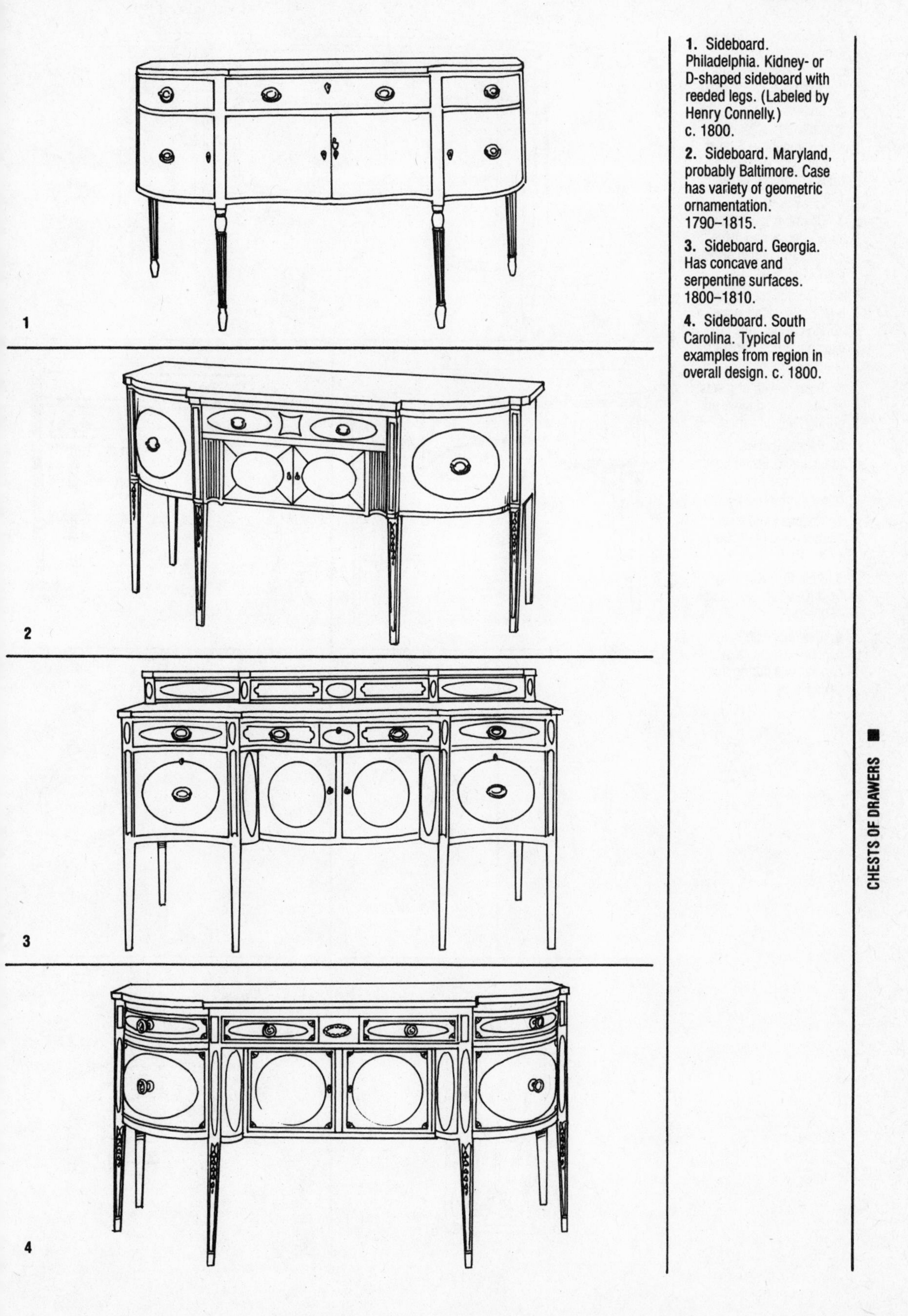

1. Sideboard. Philadelphia. Kidney- or D-shaped sideboard with reeded legs. (Labeled by Henry Connelly.) c. 1800.

2. Sideboard. Maryland, probably Baltimore. Case has variety of geometric ornamentation. 1790–1815.

3. Sideboard. Georgia. Has concave and serpentine surfaces. 1800–1810.

4. Sideboard. South Carolina. Typical of examples from region in overall design. c. 1800.

1. Sideboard. Kentucky. Extremely deep sides have blocked fronts on this example. c. 1810.

2. Chamber table. Probably Portsmouth, New Hampshire. Similar in overall form to some British chamber tables. 1790–1810.

3. Chamber table. New York. Has reeded ovolo corners and period ormolu pulls. 1810–1830.

4. "French" or bracket feet. Form widely used during period. This example from Vermont chest of drawers.

5. Rosette with ring was an alternative drawer pull during Federal period.

6. Federal-period escutcheon. Escutcheons could be made of ivory or brass during this period.

7. Rosette knob from Boston chest of drawers. 1790–1810.

8. Acanthus leaf inlay from New York wardrobe. 1800–1815.

9. Oval pull with bail handle perhaps most popular pull during this period.

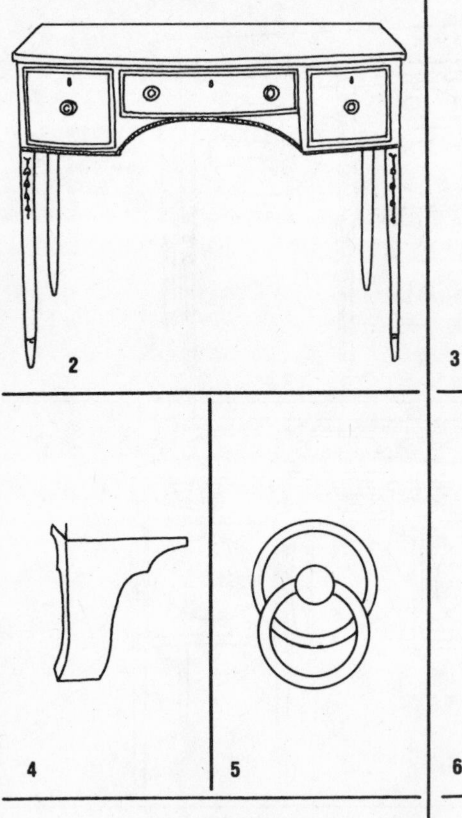

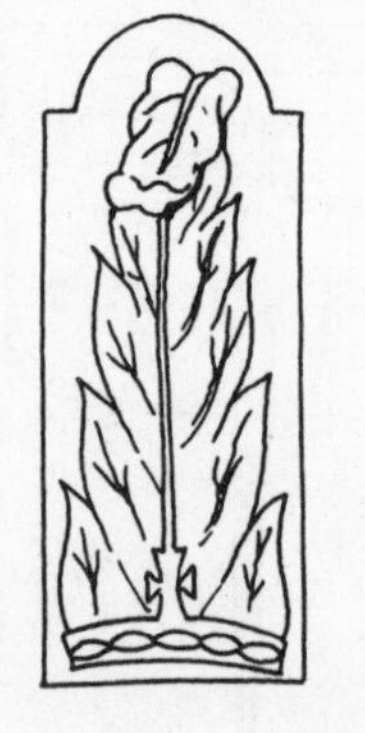

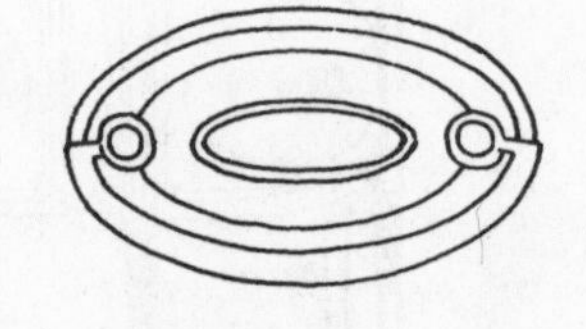

1

2

3

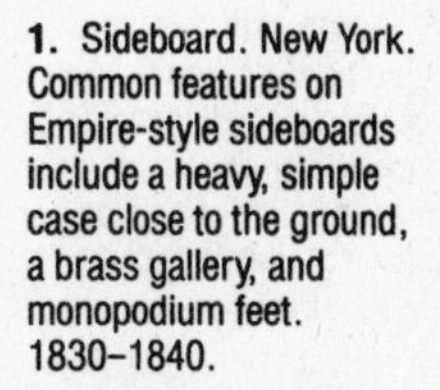

1. Sideboard. New York. Common features on Empire-style sideboards include a heavy, simple case close to the ground, a brass gallery, and monopodium feet. 1830–1840.

2. Sideboard. New York. Example has tambour doors and lion's-head pulls. c. 1820.

3. Sideboard and knife boxes. Ornament includes elaborate brass inlay and carving. (Made for the Gratz family. Possibly by Joseph Barry.) 1820–1830.

1. Sideboard. New York. Four heavy pillars decorated by diagonal and faceted carving. Late manifestation of second phase of Neoclassicism. 1830–1850.

2. Chest of drawers. New York. Note heavy split-spindle carving with acanthus leaf carving. 1830–1850.

3. Chest of drawers. Probably Boston. Follows French Restauration examples closely in simplicity of design and use of ormolu trim. 1820–1825.

4. Wardrobe. New York. Wide panels of figured mahogany and monopodium feet decorate wardrobe. New Yorkers favored this form, perhaps because of its close association to the kast. (Similar example initialed by Lannuier.) 1810–1820.

5. Chest of drawers with attached looking-glass. New York. Drawers are outlined by gilt decoration. 1820–1840.

1

2

3

4

5

1

2

3

4

1. Wardrobe. Probably New York. Plain style referred to as "Grecian" during 19th century. 1830–1850.

2. Wardrobe. Baltimore, Maryland. Taken from a design in John Hall's *The Cabinet Maker's Assistant*, popular source book published in 1840. c. 1840.

3. Server. Probably New England. Late Classical features include rectangular legs with turnings above and below, glass drawer pulls, and scrolled back board. 1825–1855.

4. Sideboard. New England. Such plain and heavy objects were made throughout America during this period. 1830–1850.

1. Chest of drawers with looking-glass. New York. (Appeared in advertising broadside for famous firm of Joseph Meeks & Sons.) 1830–1850.

2. Dressing table with attached looking-glass. America. Legs with turnings above square section quite common. 1830–1850.

3. Wardrobe. Baltimore, Maryland. Also taken from Plate 37 in Hall's pattern book. c. 1840.

4. Such pressed knobs of glass were very popular during the mid-19th century.

5. C-scroll foot seen on many "pillar and scroll" period objects.

1

2

3

4

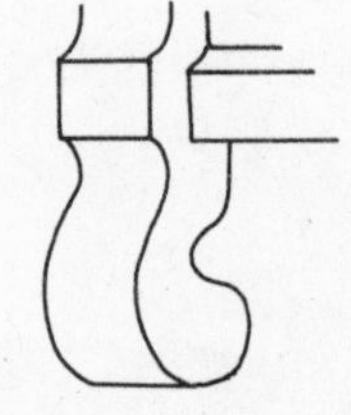

5

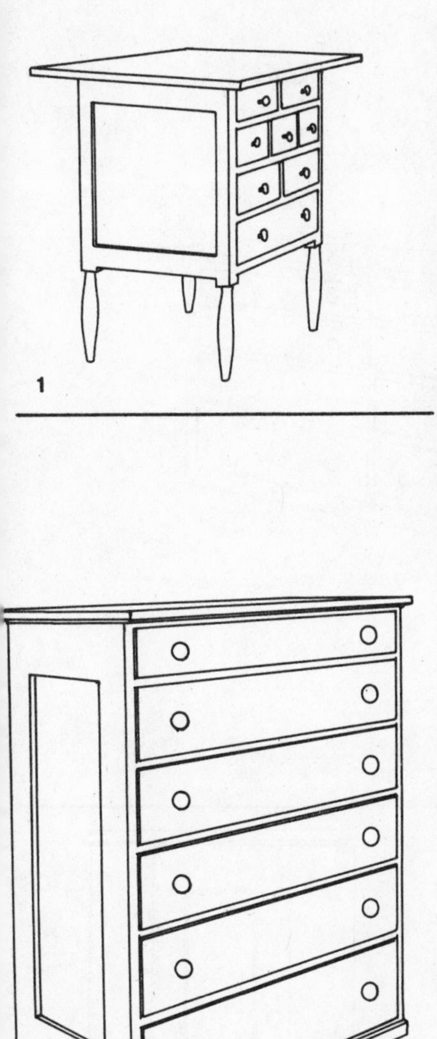

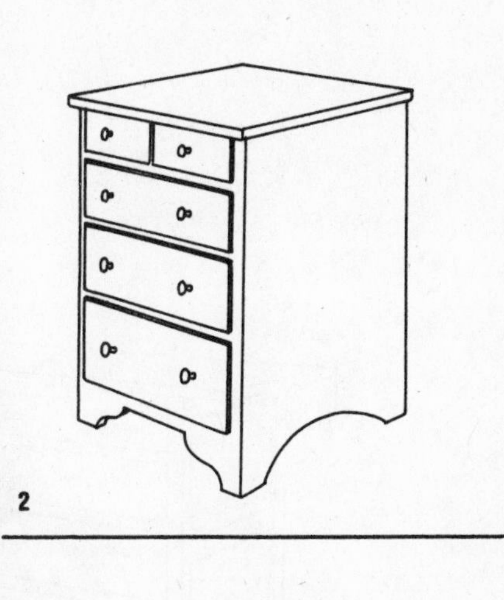

1. Sewing cabinet. Hancock, Massachusetts. Small drawers used for storing sewing equipment and materials. 1830–1850.

2. Chest of drawers. Enfield, Connecticut. (Marked "Enfield, Conn. May 16, 1849 Abner Alley AE age 66." Inscribed furniture unusual among Shakers. By relatively unknown Abner Alley.) 1849.

3. Chest of drawers. North Union, Ohio. Feet were cut down at later date. c. 1880.

4. Cupboard or wardrobe. Pleasant Hill, Kentucky. Objects made in Western communities tended to have Empire-style characteristics. c. 1850.

1. Tailoring counter. Mount Lebanon, New York. This form made in Mount Lebanon and Hancock, Massachusetts, 1825–1850.

2. Tailoring counter. Niskeyuna, New York. Tailoring was an important trade at Shaker communities and counters were standard in their shops. c. 1830.

3. Hanging cupboard. Hancock, Massachusetts. Shakers liked to use walls for storage, as illustrated by such hanging cupboards and rows of pegs. 1800–1870.

1

2

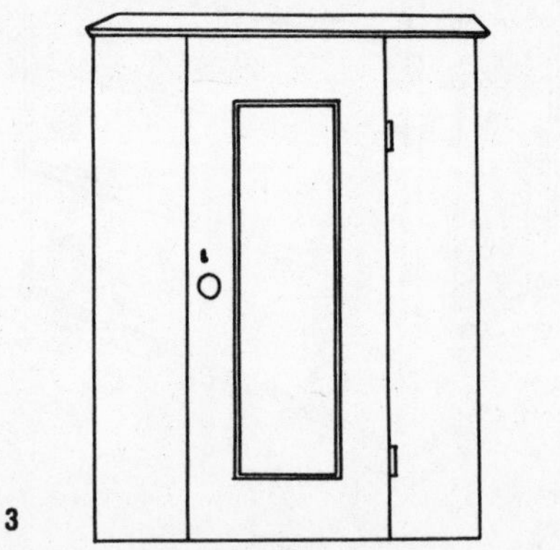

3

1

2

3

1. Built-in cupboards and drawers. Hancock, Massachusetts. With this communal sect's emphasis on orderliness, built-in furniture common. c. 1830.

2. Cupboard-on-chest. Watervliet, New York. Case pieces from Watervliet tend to have slightly more elaborate moldings than those on objects from neighboring communities. c. 1830.

3. Cupboard-on-chest. Pleasant Hill, Kentucky. Curved cornice suggests influence of Empire style. 1820–1855.

1. Double cupboard-on-chest. Watervliet, New York. Cupboards, at times combined with drawers, remained a favored furniture form among Shakers. 1830–1850.

2. Cupboard. Mount Lebanon, New York. Designed to occupy as little space as possible. 1800–1820.

3. Cupboard. Mount Lebanon, New York. Three doors hide shelves. c. 1820.

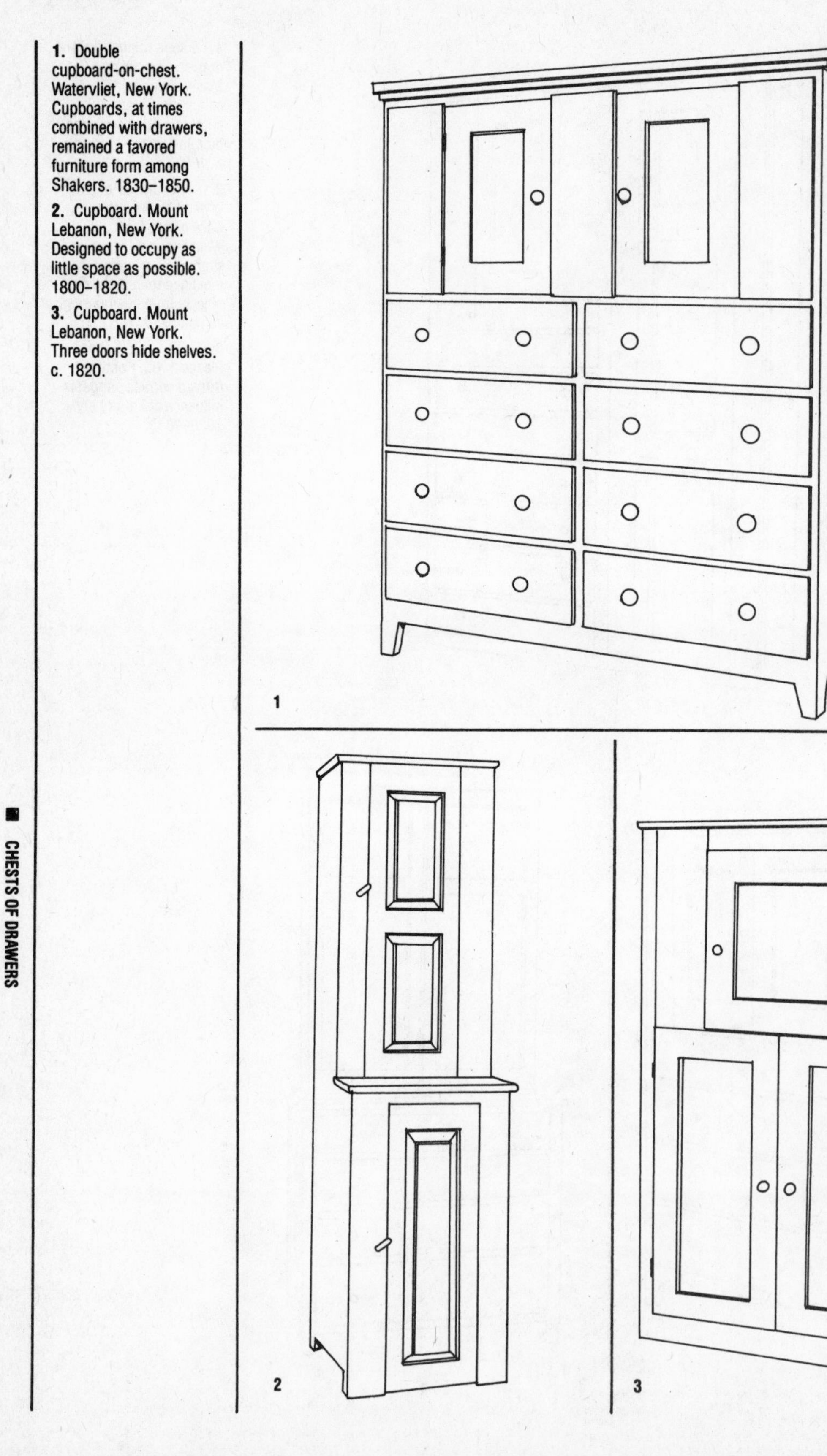

1

2

3

1. Chest of drawers with looking-glass. New York. Extremely architectural in form. (By Richard Byrne.) c. 1850.

2. Etagère. Probably New York. Has open shelves at top for display and enclosed bottom for storage. Panels at bottom are mirrored. c. 1860.

3. Chest of drawers with looking-glass. New York. "Cottage" chest of drawers combines Elizabethan Revival and Rococo Revival elements. The split-spindle turnings are characteristic of the former. c. 1850.

1. Chest of drawers with looking-glass. Such painted "cottage" chests of drawers were often Rococo Revival in style. c. 1850.

2. Chest of drawers with looking-glass. Philadelphia. Has hard enamel finish. By Hart, Ware & Co. 1850–1860.

3. Chest of drawers with looking-glass. New York. Sides and front made of shaped, laminated wood. (Attributed to John Henry Belter on basis of patent drawing.) c. 1860.

4. Chest of drawers. New York. Serpentine front of laminated wood. c. 1860.

1

2

3

4

1

2

3

1. Chest of drawers with attached looking-glass. Baltimore, Maryland. Lightness of looking-glass contrasts with heavy base. (Labeled by John Needles, 1786–1878.) 1840–1853.

2. Dressing table with looking-glass. New Orleans, Louisiana. Has marble top. (By Prudent Mallard.) c. 1860.

3. Sideboard. America. Shell-shaped pulls. c. 1870.

1. Etagère. Troy, New York. C-shaped scrolls support shelves above enclosed bottom. (Attributed to Elijah Galusha, 1804–1871.) c. 1850.

2. Etagère. New York. Fancifully carved and turned elements topped by asymmetrical cartouche. (Attributed to J. and J. W. Meeks on basis of similar labeled examples.) 1850–1860.

1

2

Louis XVI Revival

1. Cabinet. New York. Details picked out in gilt on this Louis XVI object. c. 1860.

1

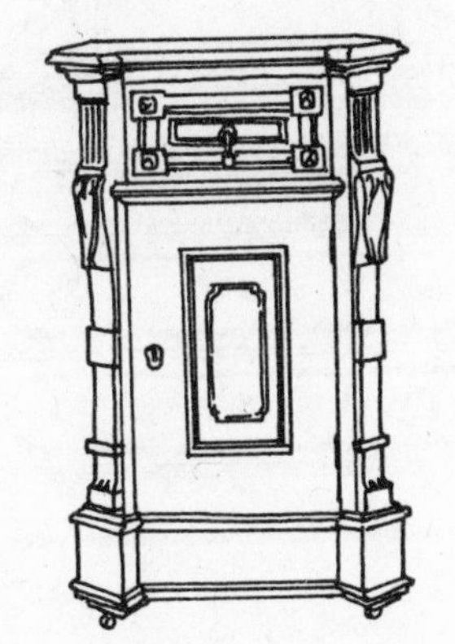

1

2

3

4

1. Bedside cabinet. America. By this time, much furniture was produced and sold *en suite*. 1860–1890.

2. Washstand. America. Here, round knobs rather than pendant pulls have been used. Has marble top. c. 1870.

3 Cabinet. New York. One of a pair made for the William B. Astor house in Barrytown, New York. (By Alexander Roux.) 1850–1857.

4. Cabinet on stand. New York. (Designed by architect Bruce Price, 1843–1903, to hold his wife's jewelry.) 1873.

1. Chest of drawers. Grand Rapids, Michigan. Note use of the side lock seen on other case pieces dating from the mid-to-late 19th century. (Attributed to little-known firm of Nelson, Matter & Co.) c. 1876.

2. Chest of drawers with attached looking-glass. New York. Part of Theodore Roosevelt's bedroom suite. (By Leon Marcotte & Co.) c. 1870.

3. Chest of drawers with attached looking-glass. Cincinnati, Ohio. Mostly Renaissance Revival in style, but has some Rococo Revival details. (By Mitchell & Rammelsburg.) 1865–1870.

4. Chest of drawers with attached looking-glass. Grand Rapids, Michigan. Part of suite made for Centennial Exposition by Berkey & Gay Co. c. 1876.

1

2

1. Sideboard. Philadelphia, Pennsylvania. During mid-19th century, the sideboard became a vehicle for competition among rival furniture manufacturers. (By Daniel Pabst, 1827–1910.) c. 1870.

2. Sideboard. New York. Like previous example, this essentially Renaissance Revival form also includes such characteristics of Louis XIV Revival style as dripping game. (By B. E. Rochefort.) c. 1851.

1. Cabinet. New York. Varieties of veneer play against inlaid, carved, and gilded details. (By Leon Marcotte.) 1865–1875.

2. Cabinet. Probably New York. Such cabinets were designed as showpieces for the display of artwork, not as sideboards. c. 1870.

1

2

1

2

1. China cabinet. America. Form based on Federal-style desk and bookcase. 1890–1910.

2. High chest of drawers. One might expect more carving on face of pediment on an actual 18th-century example. On some reproductions, construction methods, rather than design, reveal age. c. 1890.

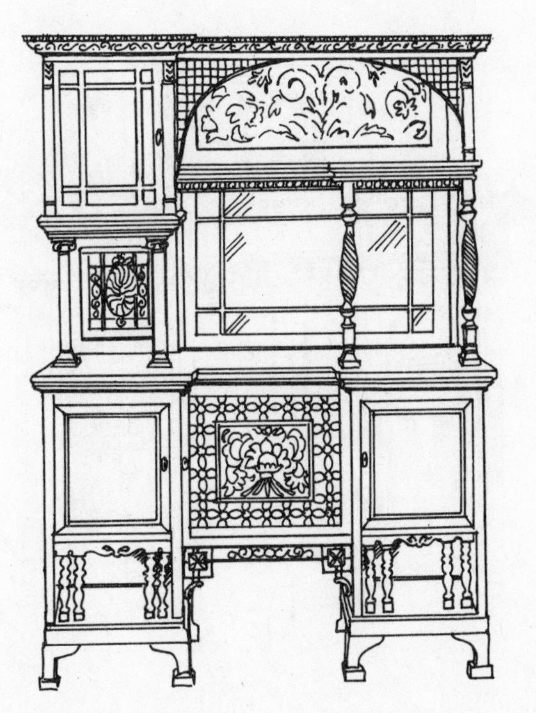

1

Exotic and Eclectic

1. Cabinet. New York. Designed to display exotic curiosities. Note carved and inlaid decoration. (By Charles Tisch, active 1870–1890. No other furniture known by this maker.) c. 1884.

1. Cabinet. New York. Medieval style of this example recalls Eastlake. (Attributed to Kimbel & Cabus.) c. 1876.

2. Chest of drawers with attached looking-glass. Has inset Japanese tiles. (By Herter Brothers.) 1880–1890.

3. Cabinet. America. Spindle gallery and quarter-rounds seen on other Eastlake-influenced furniture. *Églomisé* panels illustrate a variety of revival syles. 1875–1885.

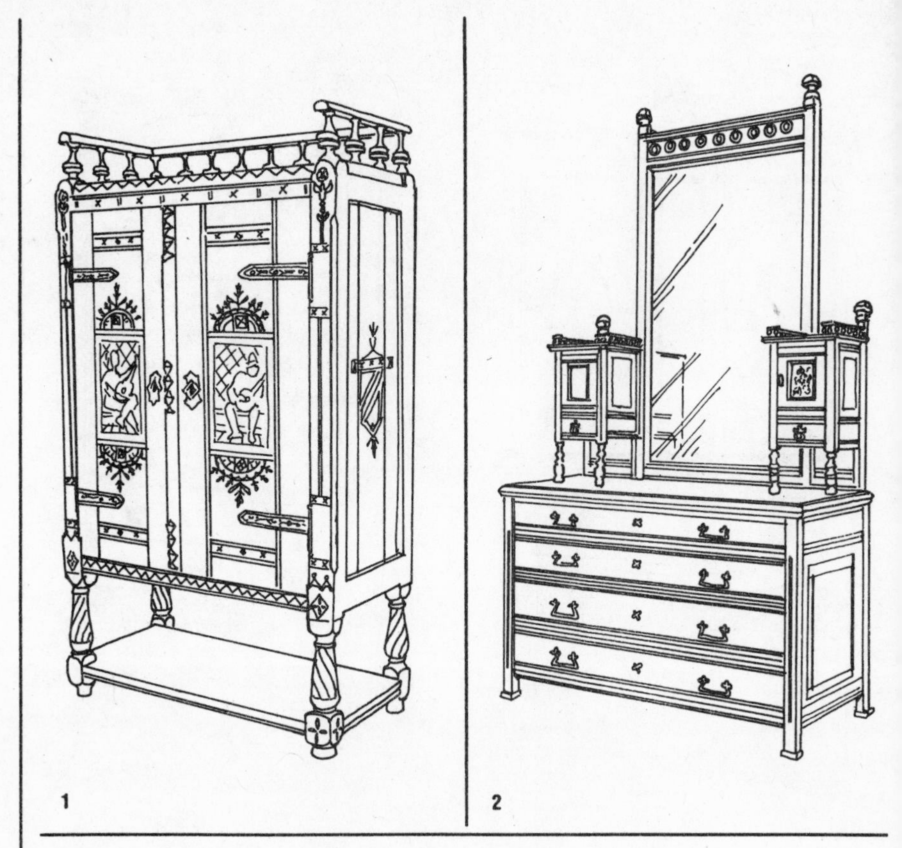

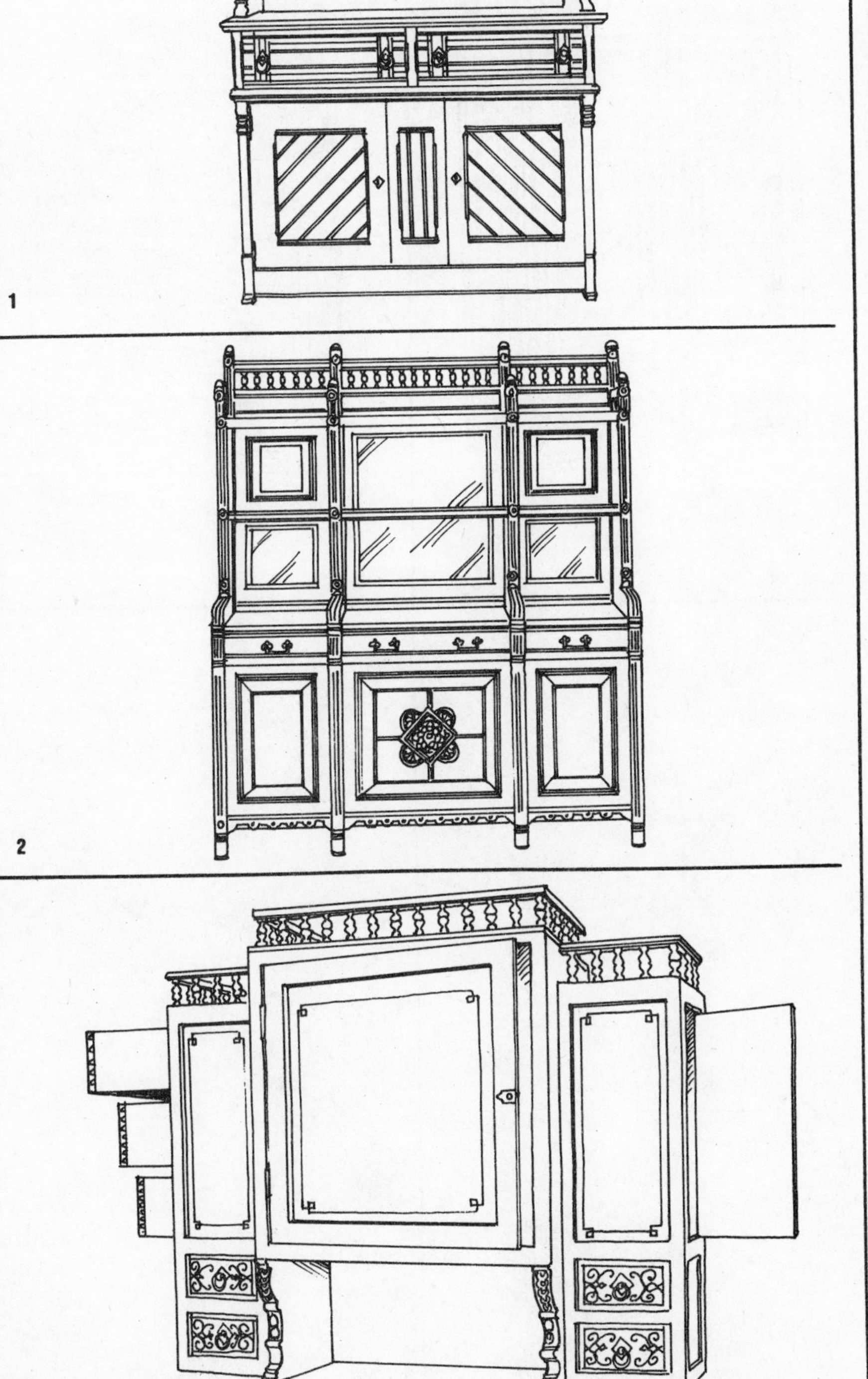

1. Sideboard. Possibly New York. Incised line decorations on drawers commonly found on Eastlake-influenced furniture. 1875–1880.

2. Sideboard. New York. Note minimal ornamentation. Some panels on back are mirrored. c. 1877–1880.

3. Hanging cabinet. America. Ebonized finish. c. 1880.

1. Wardrobe. New York. Ebonized with inlay flowers of yellow. Ordered by the actress Lillian Russell. (By Herter Brothers.) c. 1880.

2. Chest of drawers with looking-glass. Brooklyn, New York. While made of bamboo, not at all Oriental in form. (Labeled by Nimura & Sato Co.) c. 1915.

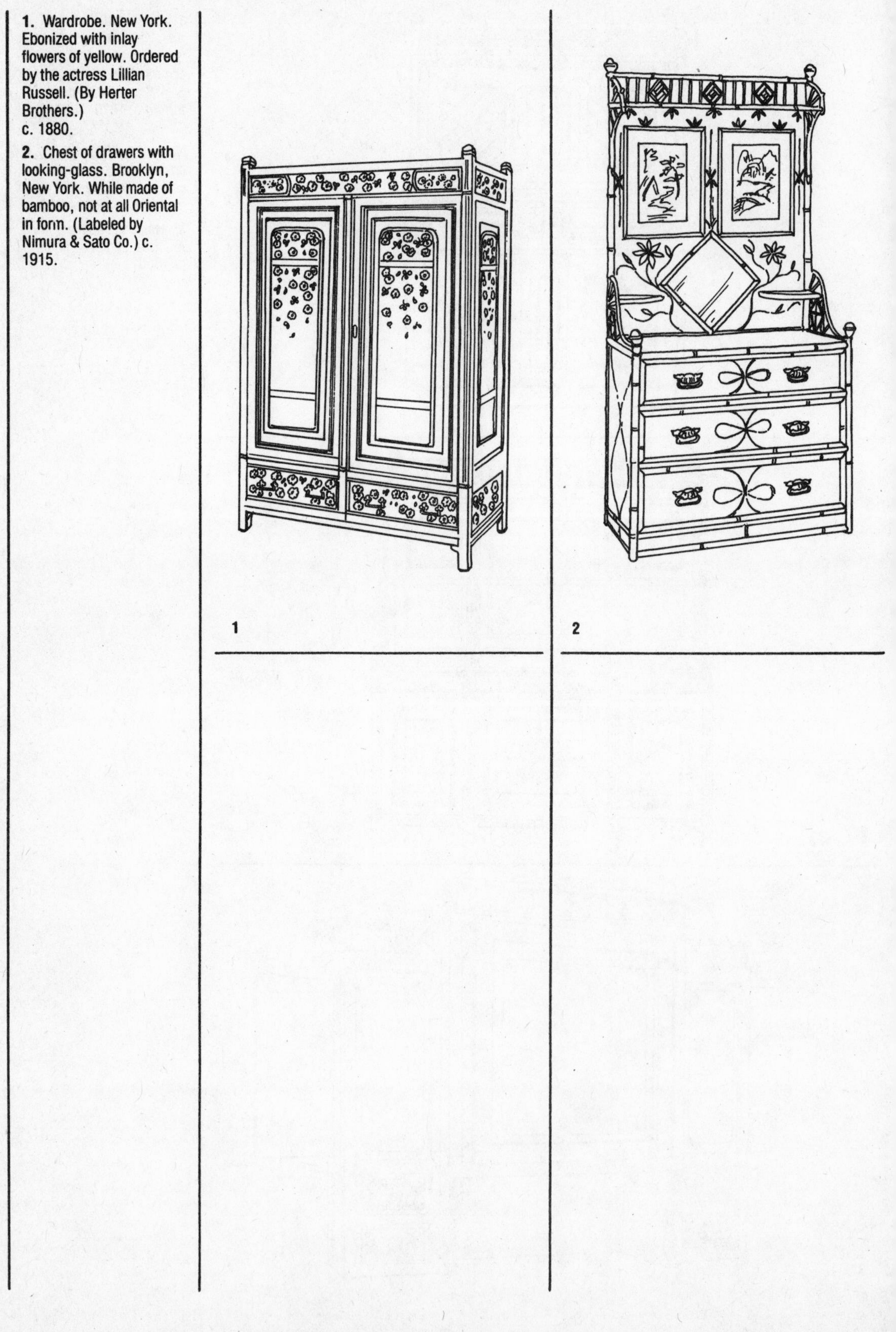

1. Chest of drawers with looking-glass. Eastwood (Syracuse), New York. Of extremely simple design. (By Gustav Stickley's Craftsman Workshops.) c. 1906–1912.

2. Chest of drawers. Eastwood (Syracuse), New York. Metal pulls attached by rectangular mounts decorate object. (Burned-in mark of Gustav Stickley's Craftsman Workshops.) 1907–1911.

3. Server. Eastwood (Syracuse), New York. Smaller alternative to sideboard. (Decal by Gustav Stickley's Craftsman Workshops.) 1907–1911.

4. Sideboard. Eastwood (Syracuse), New York. Warm color of oak and curve of skirt and pulls soften lines of sideboard. (Decal of Gustav Stickley's Craftsman Workshops.) c. 1908.

5. Sideboard. Fayetteville, New York. Massive sideboard has plate rack and strap hardware. (Decal of Leopold and J. George Stickley.) 1912–1915.

1. Cabinet. Providence, Rhode Island. In style of English Arts and Crafts furniture. (By Sydney Burleigh and Charles W. Stetson of the Art Workers Guild.) c. 1894.

2. China closet. Eastwood (Syracuse), New York. Mission dining room furniture was particularly popular. (Labeled by Gustav Stickley's Craftsman Workshops.) 1912–1915.

3. China closet. Grand Rapids and Holland, Michigan. Flaring supports favored by its maker, Charles P. Limbert Co. c. 1910.

1

2

3

Desks and Bookcases

1. Desk-on-frame. New York. Step in evolution of form from portable box with slanted lid for writing to stationary piece of case furniture. 1690–1720.

2. Desk. New York or Pennsylvania. While New England examples exist, this example assigned to Middle Colonies due to presence of tulip poplar, a preferred regional wood. 1690–1710.

3. Bureau-cabinet. Flushing, New York. Note widely overhanging cornice and boldly turned feet. Decorative inlay related to Dutch love of marquetry. 1690–1720.

4. Bureau-cabinet. Philadelphia. Unusual form; few large desks made in America at this early date. (Stamped "Edward Evans 1707," possibly by maker or owner.)

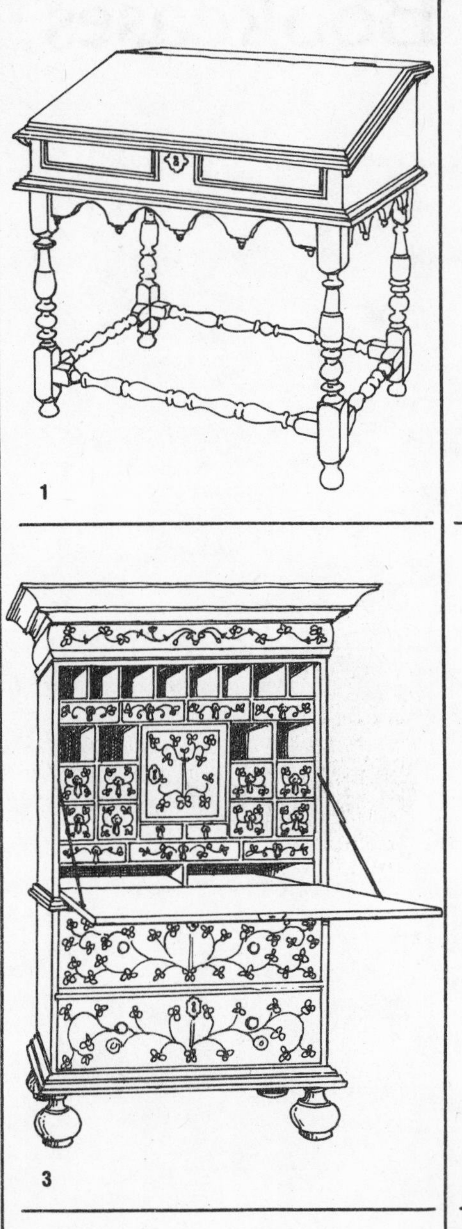

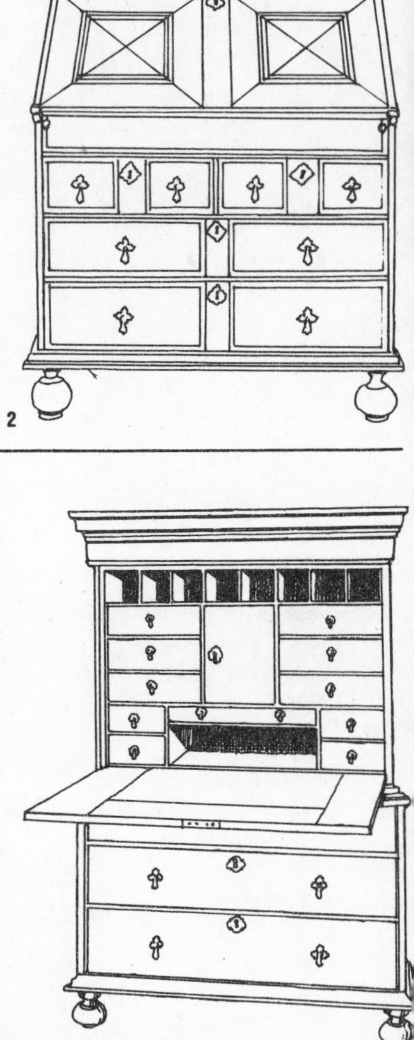

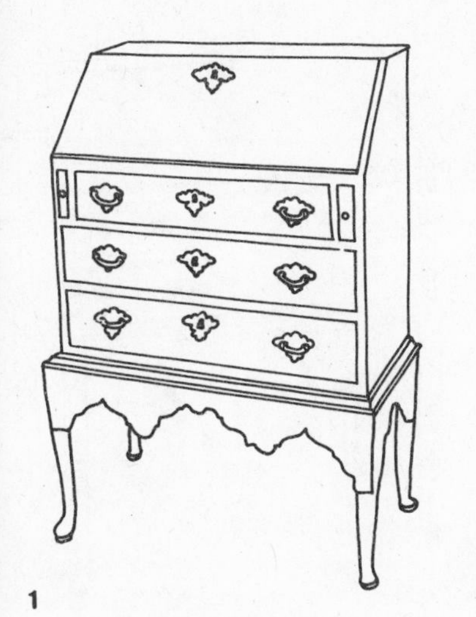

1

2

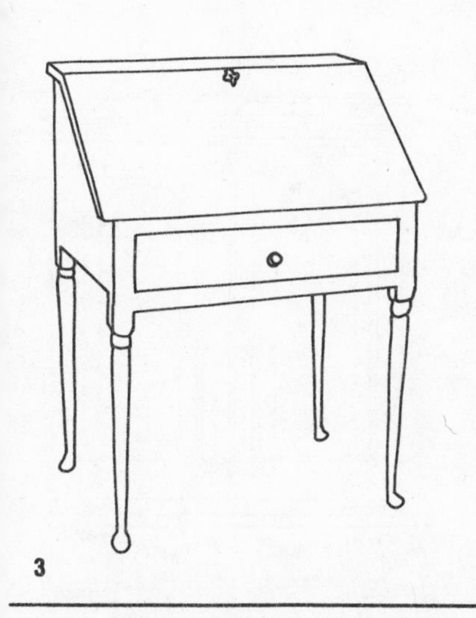

3

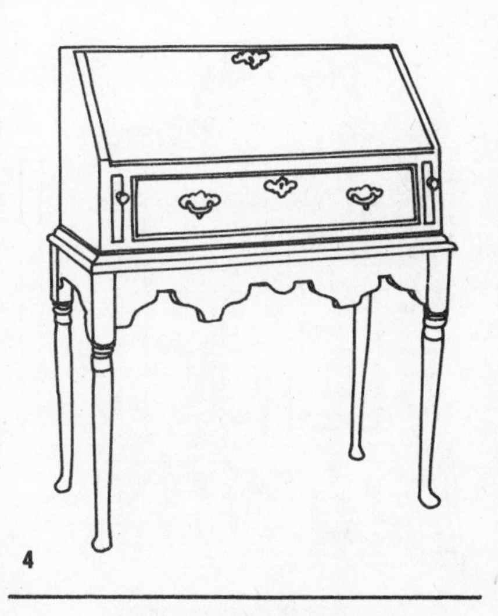

4

5

6

1. Desk-on-frame. New England. Form with drawers introduced during Queen Anne period. 1720–1740.

2. Desk-on-frame. Eastern Massachusetts. High-style example with cabriole legs and delicately scalloped apron. 1730–1750.

3. Desk. New England. Has minimal ornamentation and no pull-outs to support lid when open. 1740–1805.

4. Desk-on-frame. New England. Example closest to William and Mary desk-on-frame in form. 1750–1800.

5. Desk-on-frame. Connecticut. Built lower to the ground and with more drawers, stylistic developments of later Queen Anne desk-on-frame. 1730–1750.

6. Desk-on-frame. Connecticut. Note elaborate treatment of desk's interior and brasses on side of case to make lifting easier. 1740–1760.

1. Desk-on-frame. East Windsor, Connecticut. Design of cut-out on skirt also seen on at least one Connecticut high chest. (Attributed to Eliphalet Chapin, 1741–1807.) 1771–1807.

2. Desk-on-frame. Probably Rhode Island. Flattened-ball and reel turnings visually separate case from straight-turned legs. 1740–1805.

3. Desk and bookcase. Connecticut. Note broken-scroll pediment and arched doors, Queen Anne features. 1740–1760.

4. Desk and bookcase. Albemarle Sound region, North Carolina. Although essentially William and Mary in design, arched panels show Queen Anne influence. 1720–1740.

1

2

3

4

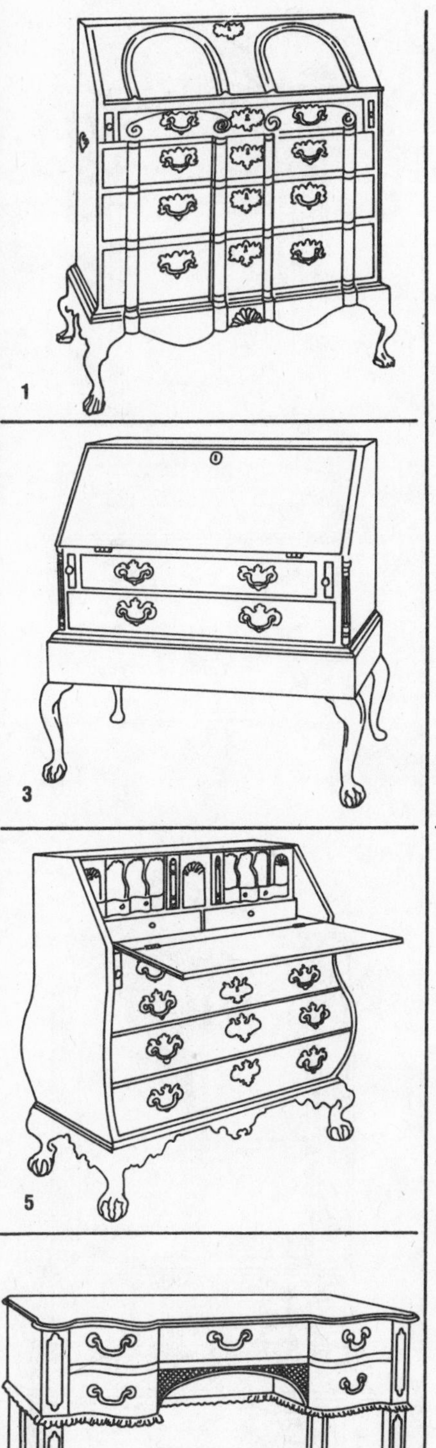
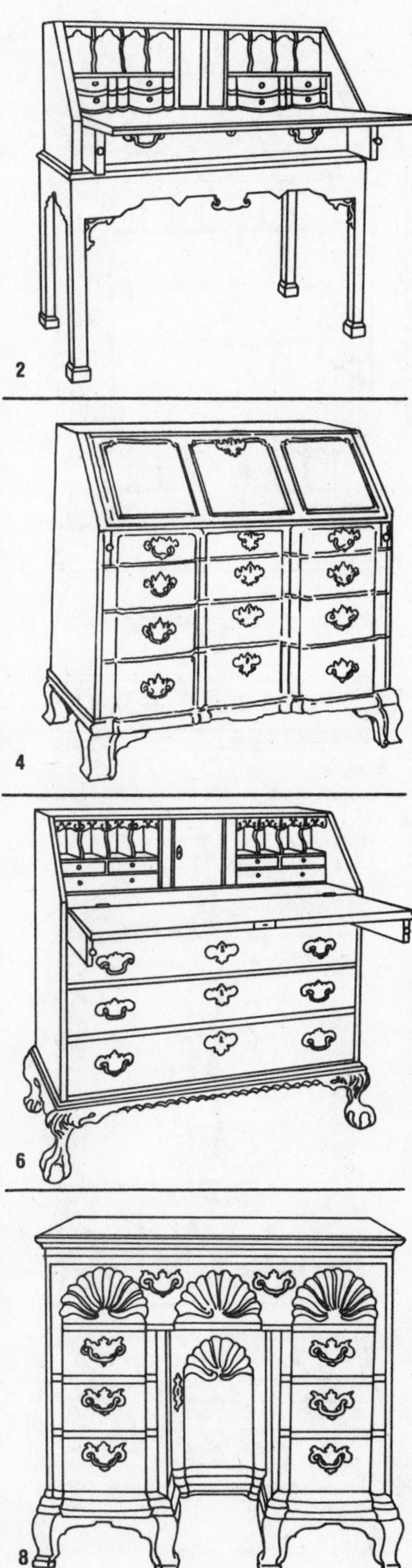

1. Desk-on-frame. Probably Hartford, Connecticut. Idiosyncratic features include Spanish feet, volutes crowning blocking, and arched panels on desk top. 1790–1815.

2. Desk-on-frame. Philadelphia. Note "Chinese Chippendale" style of frame. 1760–1770.

3. Desk-on-frame. Pennsylvania. Of low, broad, and somewhat awkward proportions. 1780–1810.

4. Desk-on-frame. Boston or Charlestown, Massachusetts. Maker famous for blockfront furniture. (Attributed to Benjamin Frothingham.) 1765–1800.

5. Desk. Salem area, Massachusetts. Such case pieces with swelled sides referred to as *bombé* in form. 1760–1790.

6. Desk. New York. Gadrooning on skirt also seen on some New York tables. 1760–1780.

7. Desk. Philadelphia. Inspired by Chippendale's "library table"; never a popular form in America. 1770–1790.

8. Bureau-table. Newport, Rhode Island. Similar form seen in Chippendale's *Director.* (Labeled by maker Edmund Townsend.) 1765–1780.

1. Desk and bookcase. Charlestown, Massachusetts. Steeply arched pediment and *bombé* bottom seen on other Massachusetts case pieces. (Signed by either Benjamin Frothingham, Senior, 1708–1765, or Benjamin Frothingham, Jr., 1734–1809 and dated 1753.)

2. Desk and bookcase. Massachusetts. Porcelain jars have replaced original finials on highly Rococo example of Massachusetts work. 1760–1780.

3. Desk and bookcase. Boston. Rivals some Philadelphia examples in finesse of carved detail. (Attributed to John Cogswell, d. 1818.) 1770–1785.

4. Desk and bookcase. Boston. Unusual quality and quantity of ornamentation for case piece made in Boston. (Purchased in 1778 by Josiah Quincy, 1710–1784.)

1

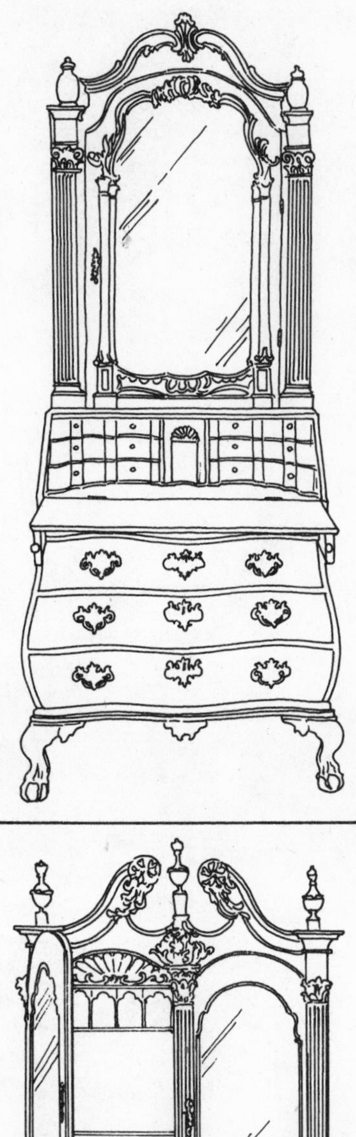

2

3

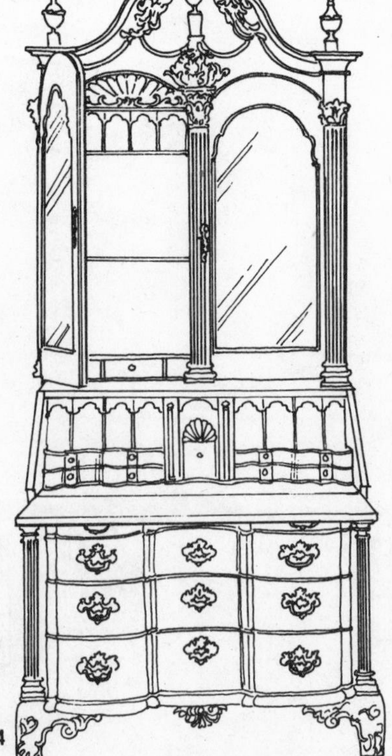

4

1. Desk and bookcase. Connecticut. Of heavier proportions than most desks of period. 1750–1770.

2. Desk and bookcase. East Windsor, Connecticut. Fluted quarter-columns and pierced lattice pediment illustrate maker's strong ties to Philadelphia. (Attributed to Eliphalet or Aaron Chapin.) 1770–1790.

3. Desk and bookcase. Newport, Rhode Island. Convex and concave panels echo blocking of base. 1770–1790.

4. Desk and bookcase. New York. Example with similar pitch pediment, fretwork, and claw-and-ball feet labeled by Samuel Prince (d.1778). 1770–1775.

1. Desk and bookcase. New York. One of the most ornate New York examples. Illustrates New Yorkers' preference for broadly proportioned furniture during Chippendale period. 1760–1780.

2. Desk and bookcase. Philadelphia. Top copied from Plate 78 of the 1754 edition of Chippendale's *Director.* Truly monumental example. 1755–1775.

3. Desk and bookcase. Philadelphia. Unusual features include small drawers serving as writing surface supports and pierced *rocaille* shell. 1765–1780.

4. Desk and bookcase. Charleston, South Carolina. Very architectural. (Attributed to William Axton, Jr.) 1765–1780.

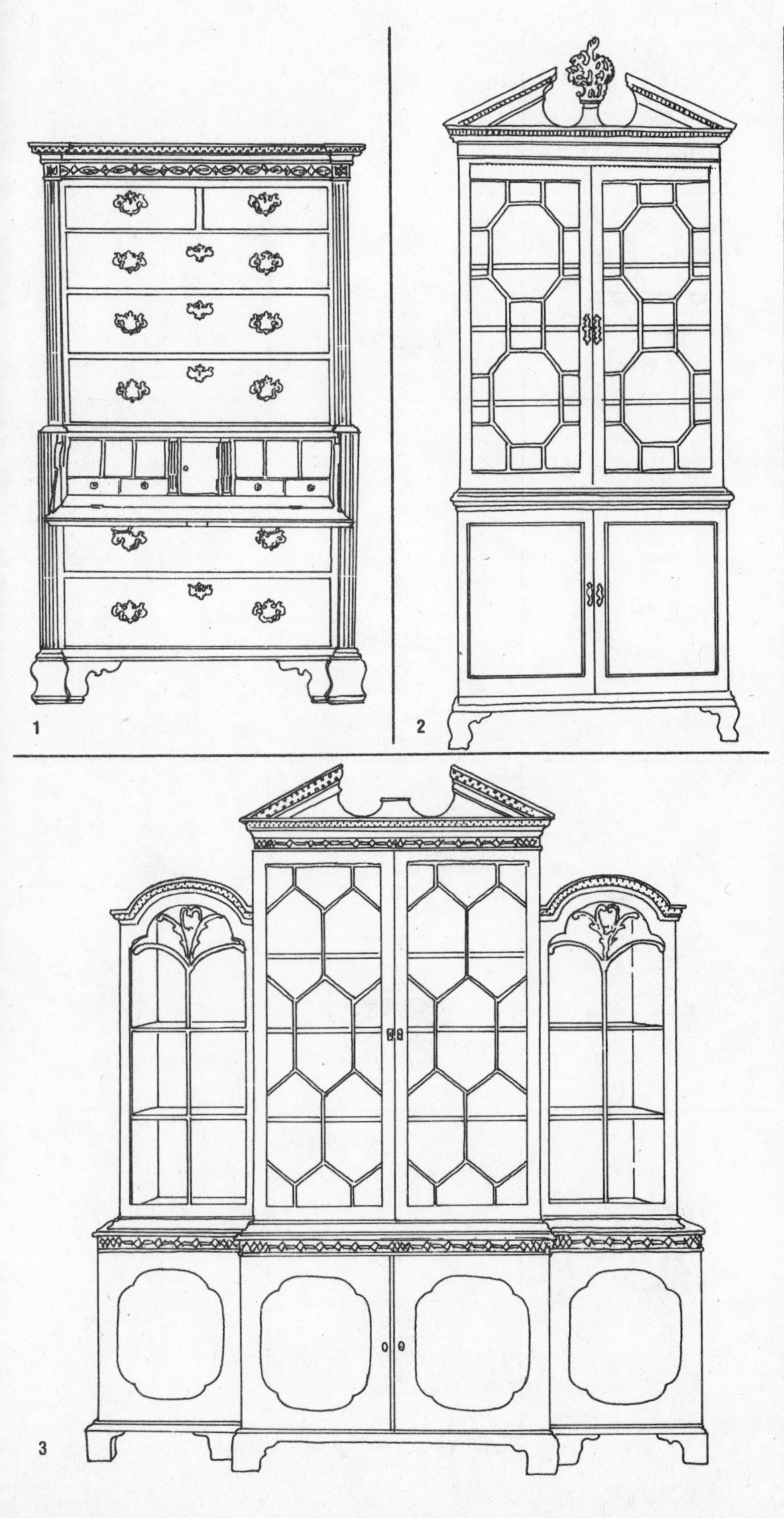

1. Desk and bookcase. Charleston, South Carolina. Note stop-fluting and heavily molded feet. (Attributed to workshop of Thomas Elfe.) c. 1770.

2. Bookcase. Philadelphia. Latticework doors seen on other desks and bookcases. 1760–1775.

3. Library bookcase. Charleston, South Carolina. Closely based on Plate 93 of Chippendale's *Director* (1754). 1755–1775.

1. Spiral finial from Massachusetts desk and bookcase, 1760–1775.

2. Flame-and-urn finial with fluted and foliate carving from Boston desk and bookcase. 1765–1775.

3. Abstract flame on flattened ball from Connecticut desk and bookcase. 1765–1780.

4. Spirelike finial seen on desk and bookcase. East Windsor, Connecticut. (Attributed to Eliphalet or Aaron Chapin.) 1770–1790.

5. Finial from desk and bookcase. Newport, Rhode Island. Dated 1770–1780.

6. Eagle finial from New York desk and bookcase. c. 1770.

7. Urn-shaped central finial from desk and bookcase. (Attributed to New York cabinetmaker Samuel Prince.) 1770–1775.

8. Classical bust topping Philadelphia desk and bookcase, 1755–1775, suggests growing interest in the ancient world.

9. Light and asymmetrical finial from Philadelphia desk and bookcase. 1760–1780.

10. Flame finial on a Philadelphia desk and bookcase. Dated 1775.

11. Idiosyncratic finial from Lancaster County, Pennsylvania desk and bookcase. 1770–1790.

12. Shell finial from desk and bookcase. (Attributed to William Axton, Jr., of Charleston, South Carolina.) 1765–1780.

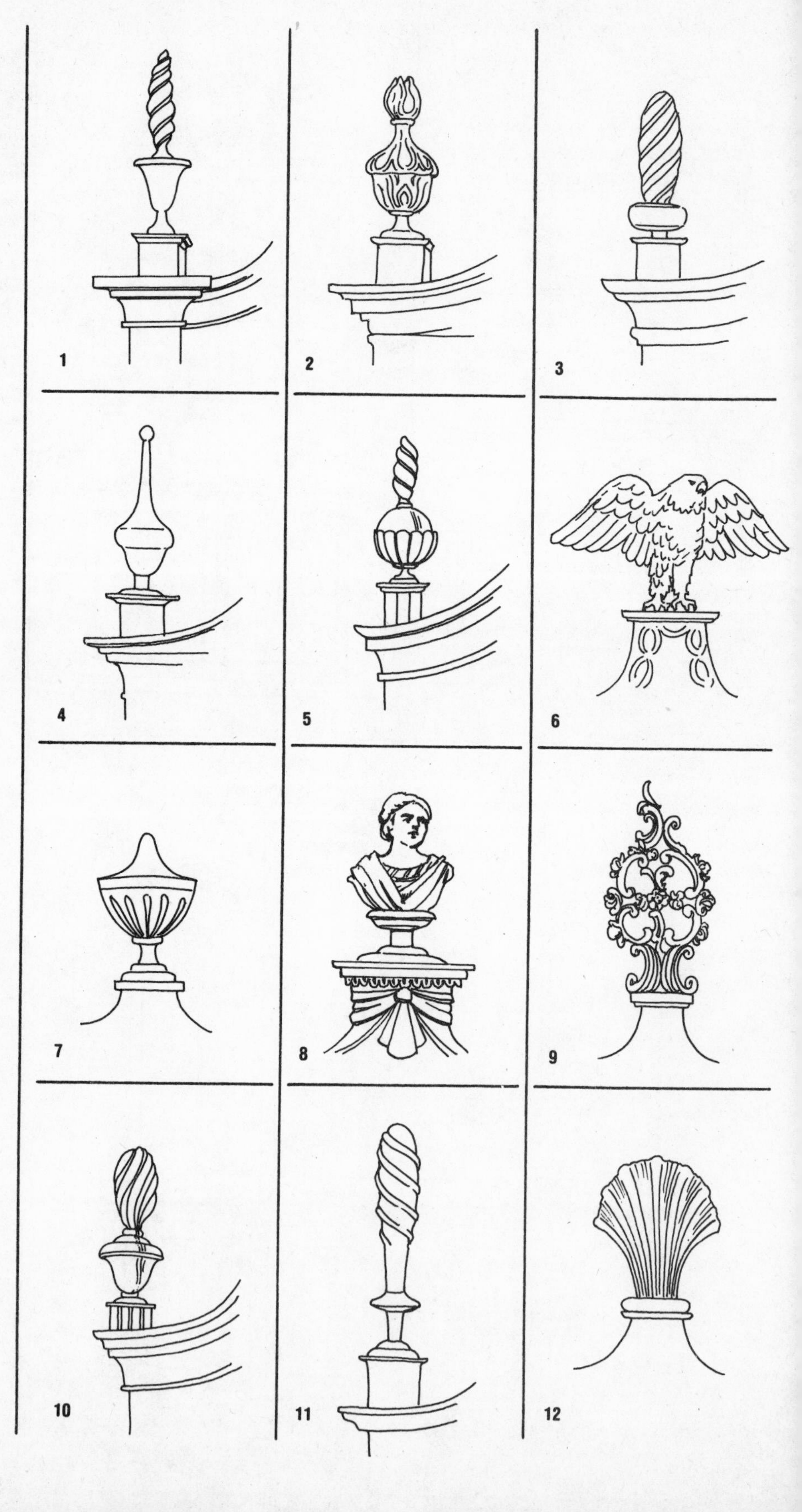

1. Desk. Pennsylvania. Note variety of inlaid decoration including herringbone banding, sunburst, crown, and date 1771.

2. Desk. Mahantango Valley, Pennsylvania. See chest of drawers with similar regional style of painting (shown on page 286). Dated 1834.

3. Desk and bookcase. Lancaster County, Pennsylvania. Has fine foliate carving on pediment. 1780–1810.

4. Desk and bookcase. Piedmont area, North Carolina. Has highly ornamental inlay. Distinctive fall-front supports seen on some Pennsylvania furniture. 1790–1800.

1. Desk and bookcase. Salem, Massachusetts. Secretary drawer innovation during period. (Labeled by maker William Appleton, active c. 1794–1822.) 1795–1804.

2. Lady's desk and bookcase. Massachusetts. Like work table, new form introduced during Federal period. 1800–1810.

3. Lady's desk and bookcase. Salem, Massachusetts. Shows secretary drawer in closed position. (Possibly by Mark Pitman, 1779–1829.) c. 1800.

4. Desk and bookcase. Probably Hartford, Connecticut. Unusual features include latticework, broken-scroll pediment, eagle-and-shield and C-scroll bracket feet. 1790–1810.

1

2

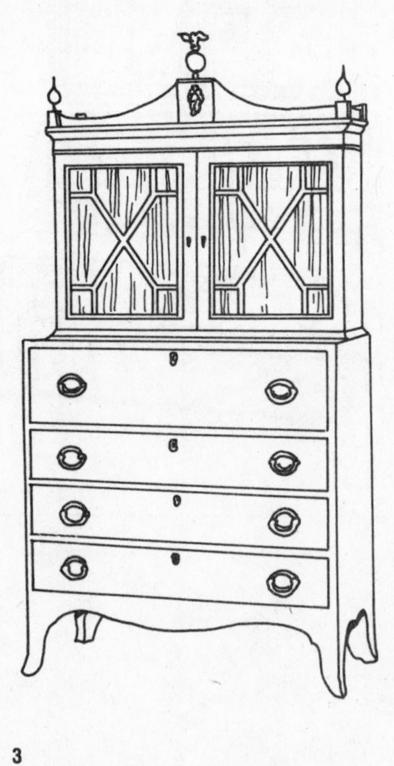

3

4

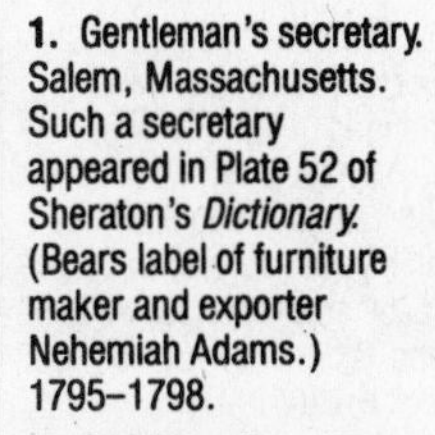

1. Gentleman's secretary. Salem, Massachusetts. Such a secretary appeared in Plate 52 of Sheraton's *Dictionary.* (Bears label of furniture maker and exporter Nehemiah Adams.) 1795–1798.

2. Gentleman's secretary. Salem or Newburyport, Massachusetts. Relatively popular form in Salem area. c. 1800.

1. Tambour desk. Boston. Note how swag designs of light-colored wood have been worked into tambour doors on this highly refined piece. (Labeled by makers John and Thomas Seymour.) 1794–1804.

2. Drawing table. Salem, Massachusetts. Inspired by a plate in Sheraton's *Drawing-Book*. Some drawers are sham. (Labeled by maker Thomas Needham, active 1775–after 1827.) c. 1800.

3. Writing table or desk. Probably Boston. Thought to have been among the furnishings made for the New Hampshire State House, completed in 1819. 1818–1819.

4. Counting desk. Hartford, Connecticut. The ornamentation on this utilitarian form includes paterae and bellflower inlay, cup-shaped drawer pulls, and spade feet. 1790–1800.

5. Lady's desk. New York. This fall front desk follows the French style. 1780–1810.

6. Table-desk. New York. Turnings on legs and feet used on other New York furniture. (Labeled by maker Michael Allison.) c. 1823.

1

2

3

4

5

6

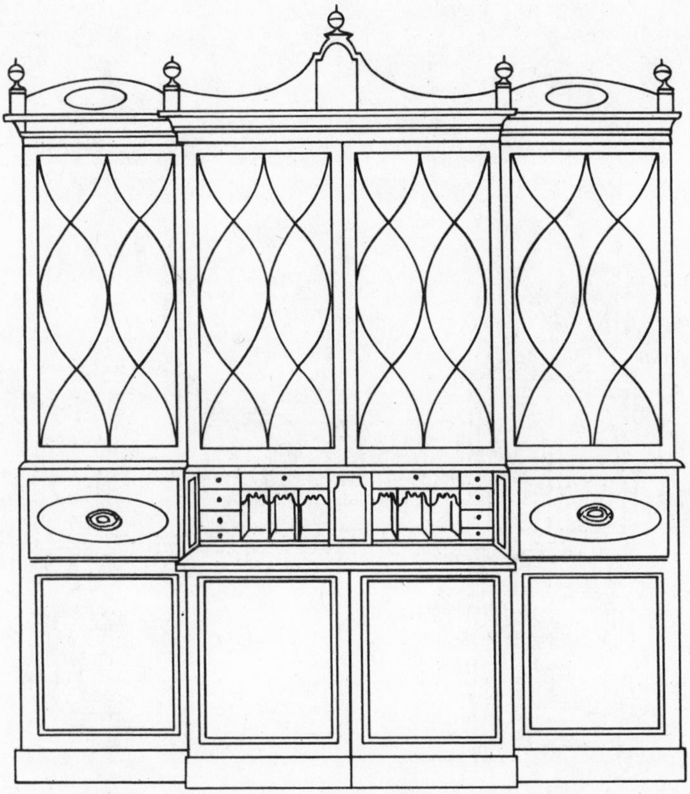

1

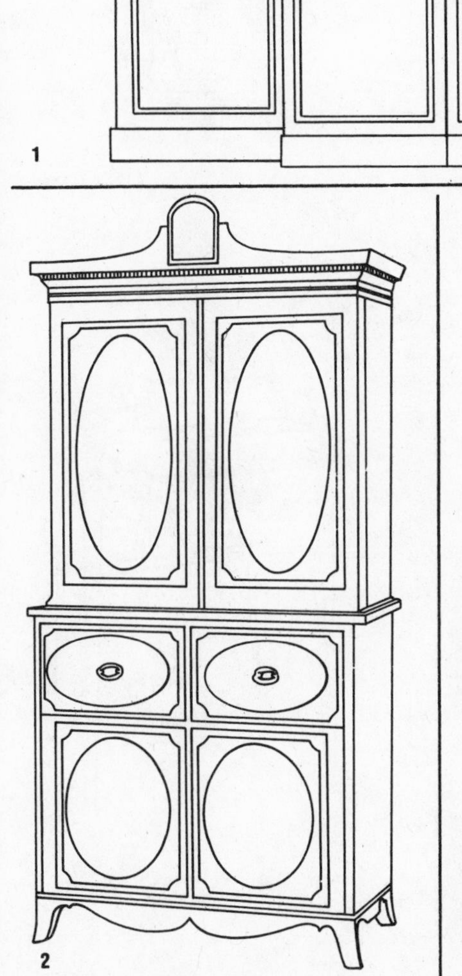

1. Library bookcase. New York. Breakfront form. Note pattern of glazed doors. 1796.

2. Desk and bookcase. Philadelphia. Has mirrored top doors. (Signed by little-known makers John Davey and John Davey, Jr., active 1797–1822.) 1805–1810.

3. Lady's cabinet and writing table. Baltimore, Maryland. Based on Plate 50 of Sheraton's *Drawing-Book*. Has *églomisé* panels on doors and lower sides. Illustrates sophisticated nature of much Federal period furniture made in Baltimore. 1795–1810.

1. Desk and bookcase. Baltimore, Maryland. Inspired by a plate in Sheraton's *Cabinet Dictionary.* Extremely rare form in American furniture. Dated 1811.

2. Desk and bookcase. Lincoln County, North Carolina. Note distinctive inlay on object. Desk is stylistically more akin to Chippendale style rather than Federal period. 1795–1800.

3. Lady's desk. New Bern, North Carolina. Delicate desk has very deep drawers with bail handles. c. 1800.

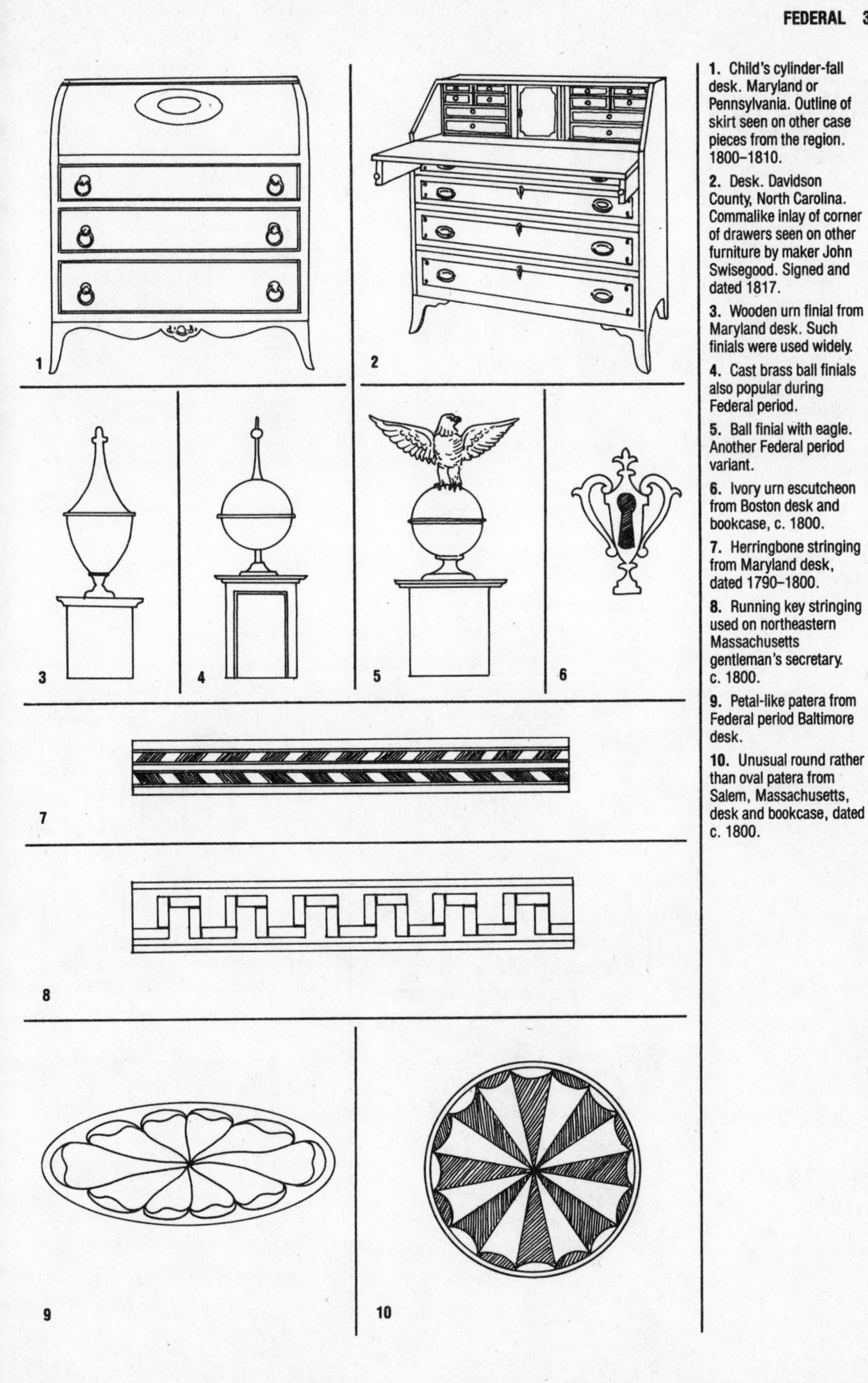

1. Child's cylinder-fall desk. Maryland or Pennsylvania. Outline of skirt seen on other case pieces from the region. 1800–1810.

2. Desk. Davidson County, North Carolina. Commalike inlay of corner of drawers seen on other furniture by maker John Swisegood. Signed and dated 1817.

3. Wooden urn finial from Maryland desk. Such finials were used widely.

4. Cast brass ball finials also popular during Federal period.

5. Ball finial with eagle. Another Federal period variant.

6. Ivory urn escutcheon from Boston desk and bookcase, c. 1800.

7. Herringbone stringing from Maryland desk, dated 1790–1800.

8. Running key stringing used on northeastern Massachusetts gentleman's secretary. c. 1800.

9. Petal-like patera from Federal period Baltimore desk.

10. Unusual round rather than oval patera from Salem, Massachusetts, desk and bookcase, dated c. 1800.

1. Writing table. New York. Has lion's-head pulls, heavy reeded legs, and extendable writing surface. 1800–1825.

2. Writing table. New York. Top lifts to reveal writing surface. Rope or twist turning popular early to mid-19th century. (Labeled by maker John Budd, active 1817–1840.) c. 1817.

3. Desk and bookcase. New York. High-style, painted example with pleated silk curtains and brass tracery in glass doors. (Attributed to Joseph Meeks & Sons.) c. 1825.

4. Desk and bookcase. Philadelphia. Flaring cornice, lunette design formed by panels of veneer; monopodium feet seen on other desks of period. (Labeled by Antoine-Gabriel Quervelle.) c. 1820.

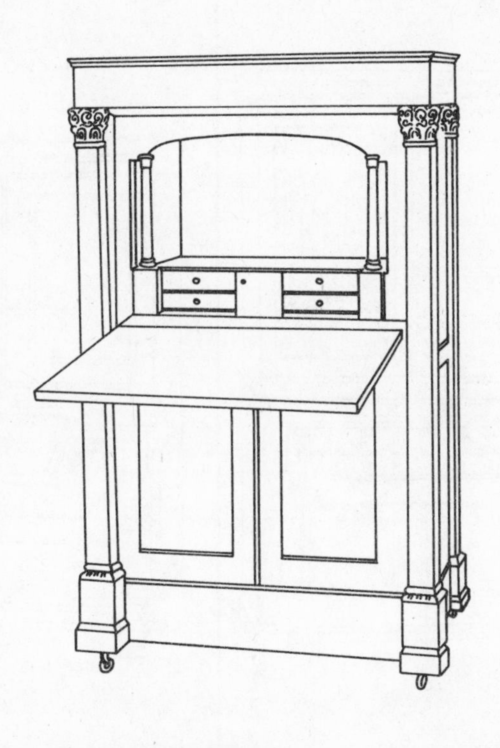

1

2

1. Fall front desk. New York. Ormolu capitals and base on columns. (Belonged to DeWitt Clinton, governor of New York.) c. 1820.

2. Fall front desk. Philadelphia. Closely follows the French Restauration style in overall form and ornamentation. 1815–1820.

1. Desk and bookcase. Baltimore, Maryland. Note unusual design of glazed doors. From Hall's *The Cabinet Maker's Assistant*. c. 1840.

2. Desk and bookcase. Baltimore, Maryland. Writing surface is contained within top drawer. c. 1840.

3. Bookcase. Probably New York. Note broad panels of veneer common on "pillar and scroll" furniture. c. 1850.

1

3

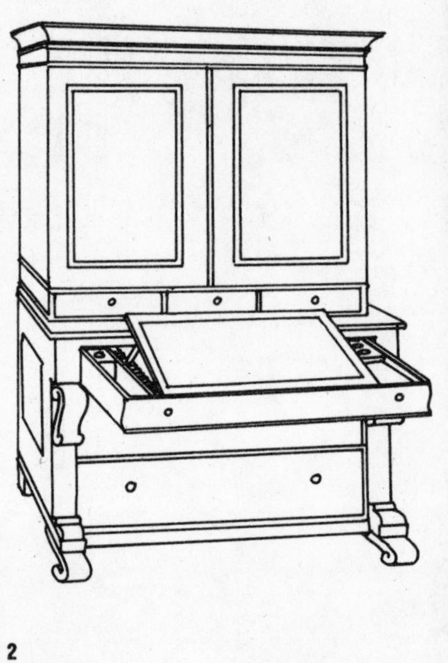

2

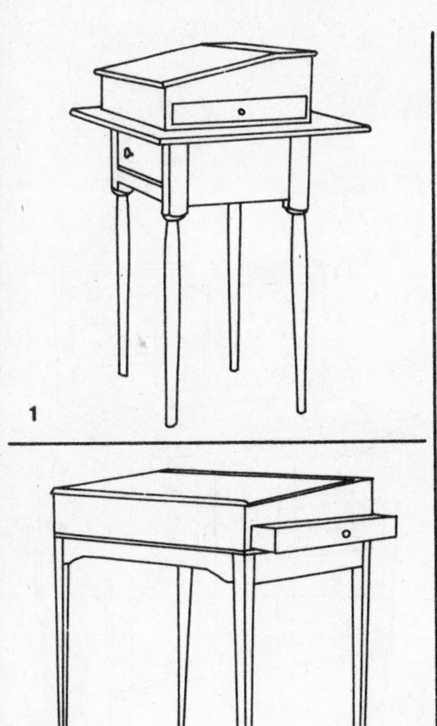

1

3

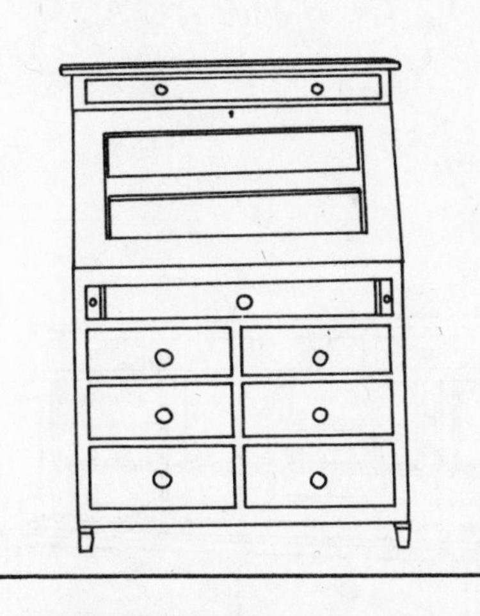

2

4

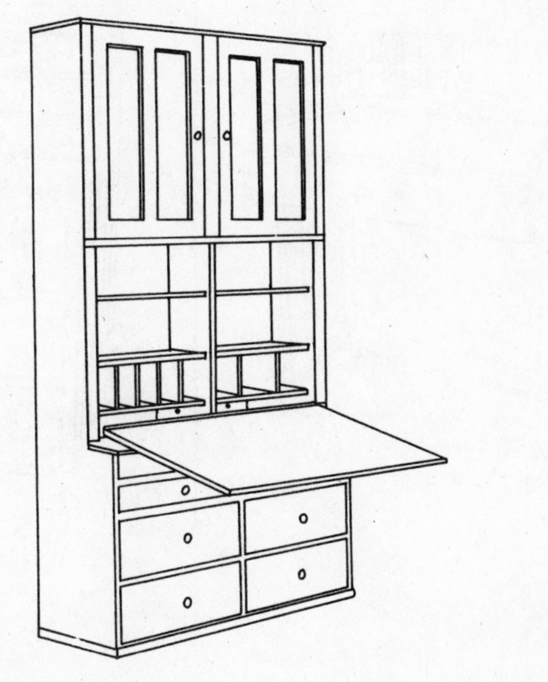

5

1. Lap desk. Canterbury, New Hampshire. Popular form made for domestic use as well as for sale to outside world. Here seen on table. 1810–1860.

2. Desk. Canterbury, New Hampshire. Late example. 1860–1890.

3. Child's desk. Hancock, Massachusetts. Side drawer favored by Shaker craftspeople. 1815–1875.

4. Desk. Hancock, Massachusetts. With tripod base, similar in form to some sewing tables. 1830–1850.

5. Double desk and bookcase. Probably Mount Lebanon, New York. Thought to have been made for deacons of the church. Design suggests communality of sect. Joined desks relatively rare since desks are traditionally a private furniture form. c. 1830.

1. Desk. Mount Lebanon, New York. Variety of storage spaces contained behind doors. 1830–1850.

2. Sewing desk. Canterbury, New Hampshire. Has drawers on two sides and pull-out work top. Late form in Shaker communities. c. 1860.

3. Sewing desk. Union, Ohio. Similar to desks made across America during second half of 19th century. 1870–1890.

4. Sewing desk. Watervliet, New York. Porcelain knobs are original and are seen on other Shaker case pieces of this date. 1880–1900.

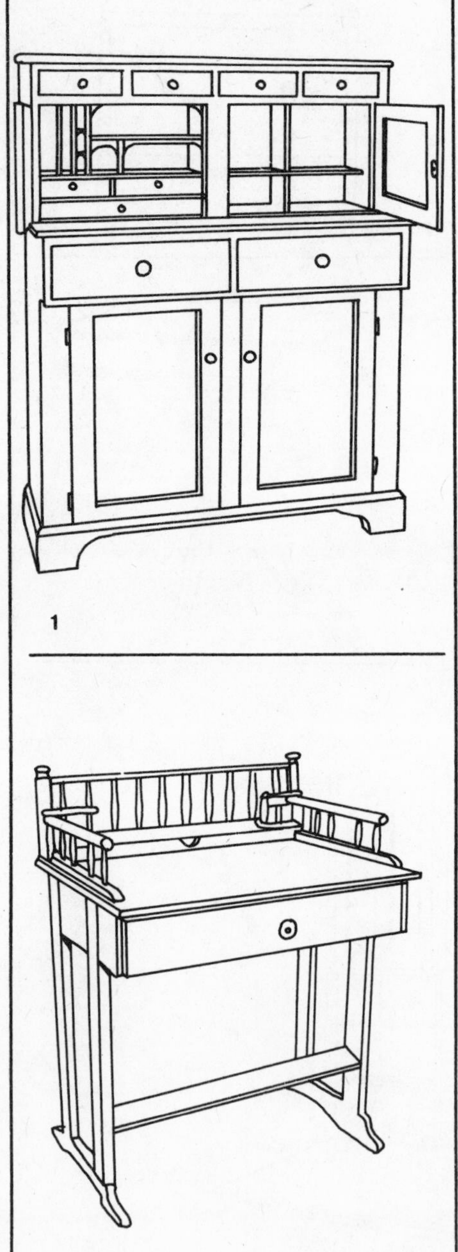

1

2

3

4

1

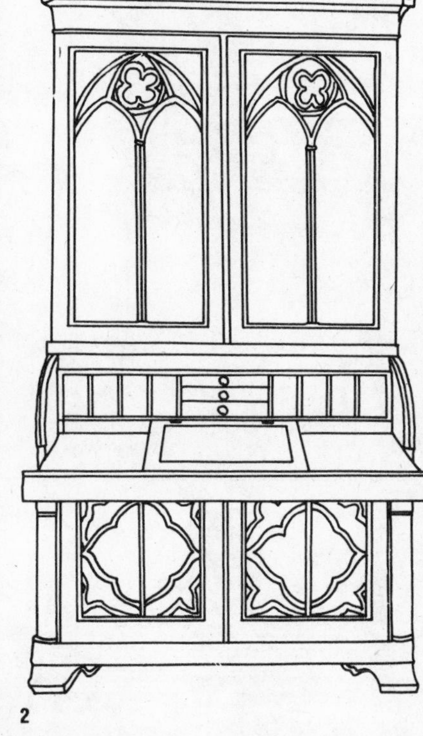
2

3

1. Cabinet and bookcase. New York. Basically Restauration in form with Gothic-style details; common combination. 1830–1840.

2. Desk and bookcase. New York. Quatrefoils are an important design element. (Stenciled by makers J. & J. W. Meeks.) 1836–1850.

3. Bookcase. Probably New York. Has Romanesque as well as Gothic ornamentation. Made for Robert Kelly's New York house, built c. 1842.

1. Lady's desk. New York. So-called "spinet" desk with delicately carved details. 1850–1860.

2. Lady's desk. Newark, New Jersey. Although John Jelliff's sketches of Rococo Revival furniture survive, this is the only extant object he made in this style. 1850–1860.

Renaissance Revival

1. Wooten's Patent Desk. Indianapolis, Indiana. Produced in four "grades" or models for 19th-century businessmen. (Made at factory established by desk's designer William S. Wooten, active 1874–1897.) 1875–1884.

2. View of same desk open. Multitude of compartments advertised as an aid to busy merchants and professional men.

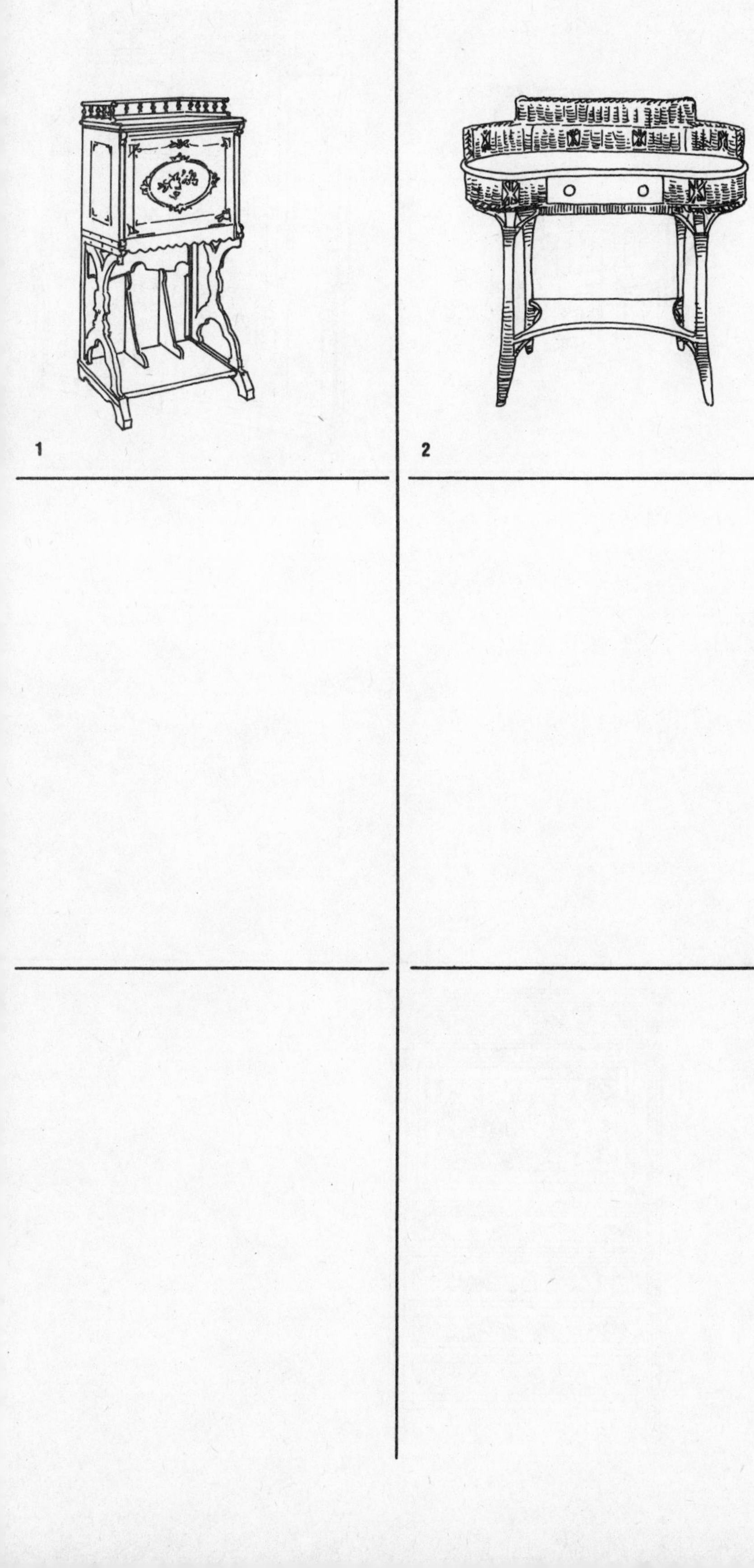

1. Desk/music stand. Moosic, Pennsylvania. Fall front hides pocket compartments for storage of books and papers. (Designed by George W. Hessler.) Patented 1879.

2. Desk. America. Wicker desk with wrapped legs. 1880–1910.

1. Desk. Chicago. (Designed by Isaac E. Scott, 1845–1920, for Mr. and Mrs. John J. Glessner.) c. 1879.

2. Bookcase. Chicago. Here, the decoration, in form of carving and inset ceramic tiles, is medieval in inspiration. (Designed by Isaac E. Scott.) c. 1875.

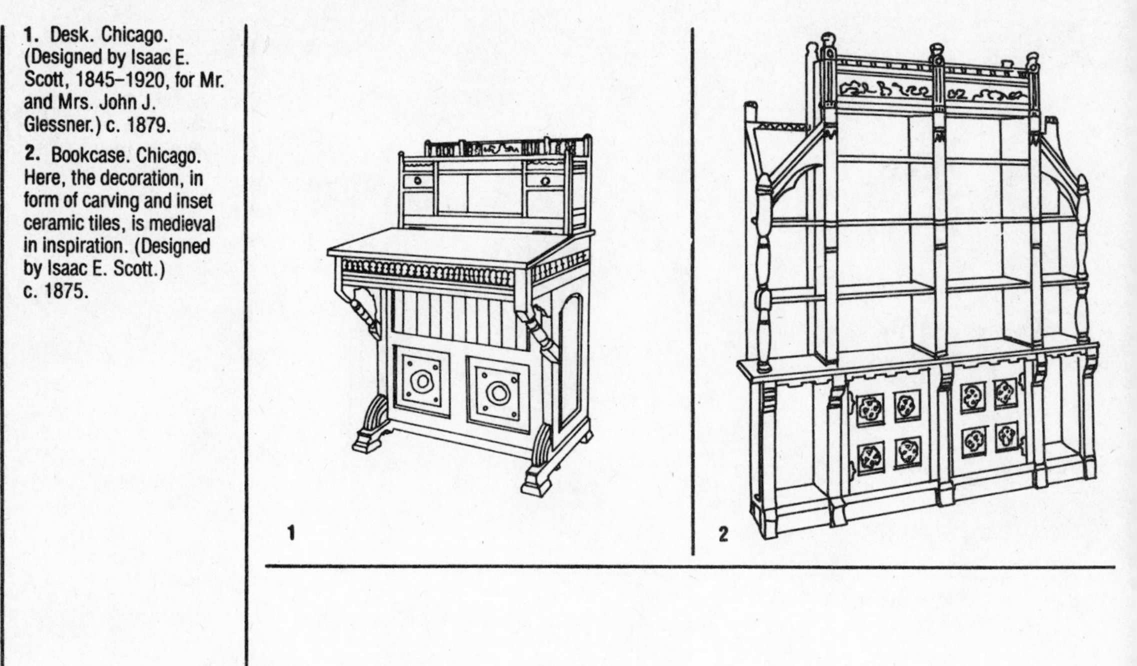

Art and Japanese-Inspired

1. Secretary. New York. With stylized floral decoration. (Belonged to Jay Gould. By Herter Brothers.) c. 1882.

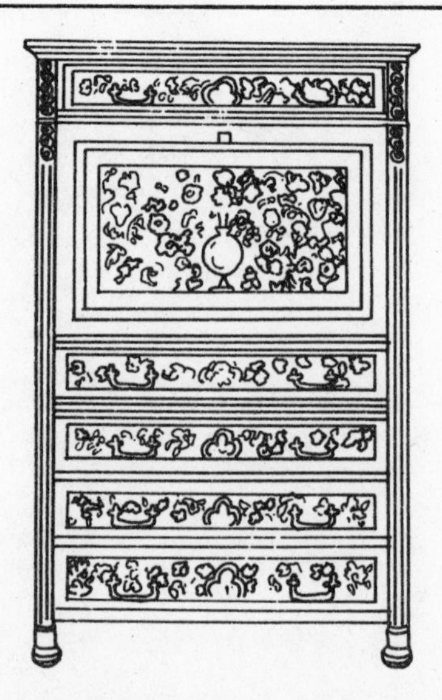

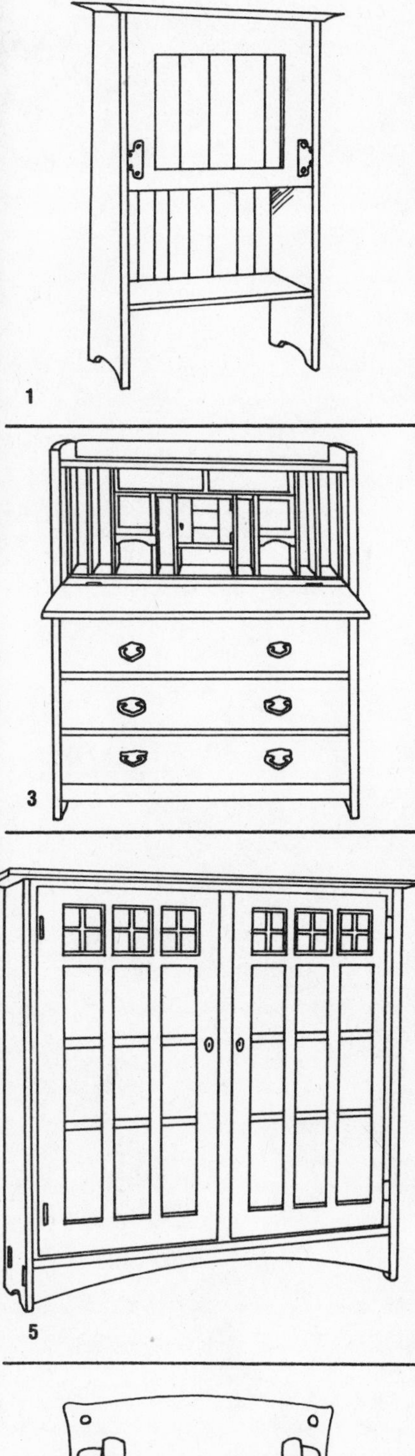

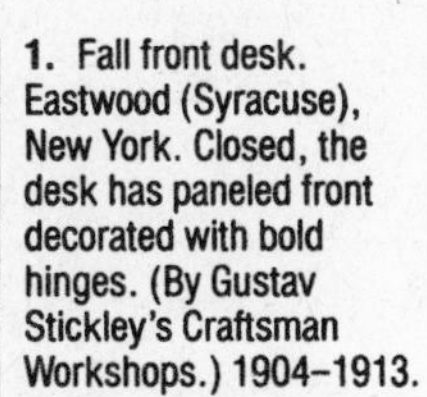

1 2 3 4 5 6 7

1. Fall front desk. Eastwood (Syracuse), New York. Closed, the desk has paneled front decorated with bold hinges. (By Gustav Stickley's Craftsman Workshops.) 1904–1913.

2. Desk. Eastwood (Syracuse), New York. Desk pared down to its essential form. (Decal of Gustav Stickley's Craftsman Workshops.) 1907–1908.

3. Fall front desk. Eastwood (Syracuse), New York. Sides and back extend above top to form gallery to protect ceramics or books on display. (Labeled by Gustav Stickley's Craftsman Workshops.) c. 1908–1911.

4. Magazine stand. Syracuse, New York. Fairly ornate, typical of Stickley's early designs. (By Gustav Stickley Co.) c. 1900.

5. Bookcase. Eastwood (Syracuse), New York. Unlike a china cabinet, has wooden, not glass sides. (Decal of Gustav Stickley's Craftsman Workshops.) 1903–1904.

6. Typical hammered Arts and Crafts–style pull from fall front desk by Gustav Stickley's Craftsman Workshops. c. 1908–1911.

7. Bookcase. Fayetteville, New York. Note appearance of pinned through-tenons. (Marked by Leopold & J. George Stickley and Gustav Stickley.) c. 1918.

Miscellaneous

1. Looking-glass. Rectangular frame imported from England, carved crest added in New England, as shown by woods. 1700–1735.

2. Looking-glass. New England. Very prestigious object due to expense of materials involved. 1700–1740.

1 2

3

4

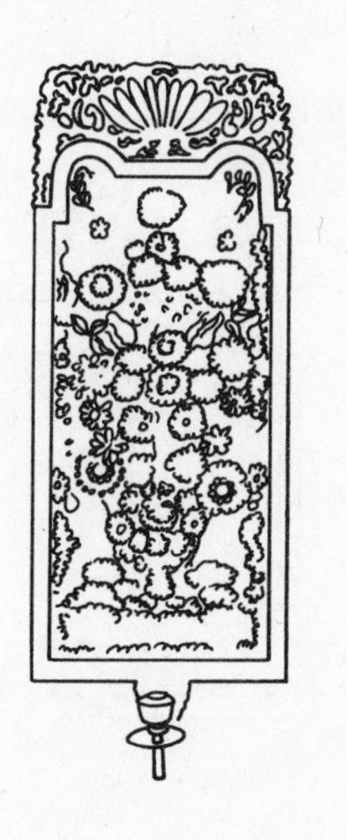

5

1. Looking-glass. New York. Most looking-glasses imported from England at this time. 1725–1735.

2. Looking-glass. New York. Scrolled top reminiscent of that on high chest with broken-scroll pediment. 1725–1735.

3. Looking-glass with sconces. Probably New York. Form designed to hang over fireplace. 1720–1730.

4. Shaving stand with looking-glass. Rhode Island. Note cyma reversa-curved blocking drawers. 1725–1750.

5. Quillwork sconce. America. Contain arrangements of elaborately cut and folded paper, painted and gilded as well as wax figures. 1730–1750.

1. Cellaret. Northeastern North Carolina. Form used to store wine bottles. 1792–1796.

2. Firescreen. Massachusetts. Columnar shaft with swirled cup base. 1765–1780.

3. Firescreen. New York. Bold baluster shaft also seen on New York tables. 1760–1775.

4. Firescreen. Philadelphia. Exquisitely turned and carved base ending in hairy-paw feet. 1765–1780.

5. Looking-glass. New England. Form became more common during Chippendale period. 1750–1780.

6. Looking-glass. Probably Massachusetts. Scrolled pediment seen on other forms of furniture during Chippendale period. Mirror reflected light from candles held by branches. 1760–1770.

1

2

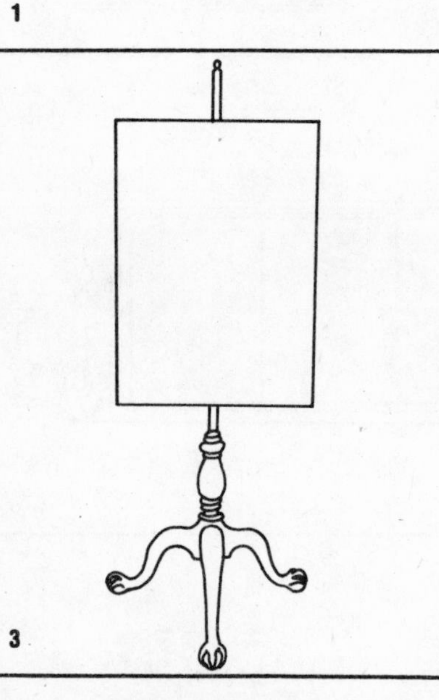
3

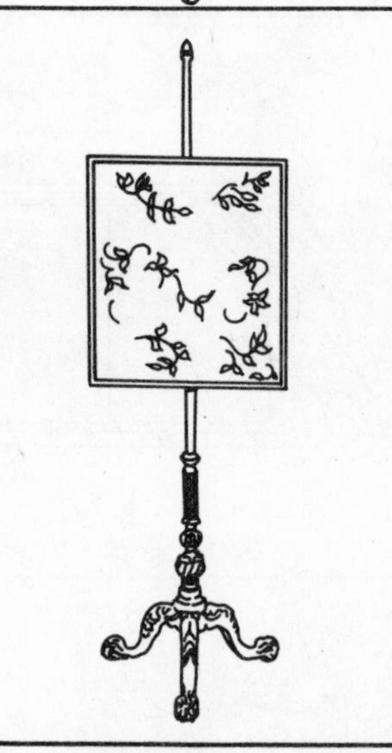
4

5

6

1

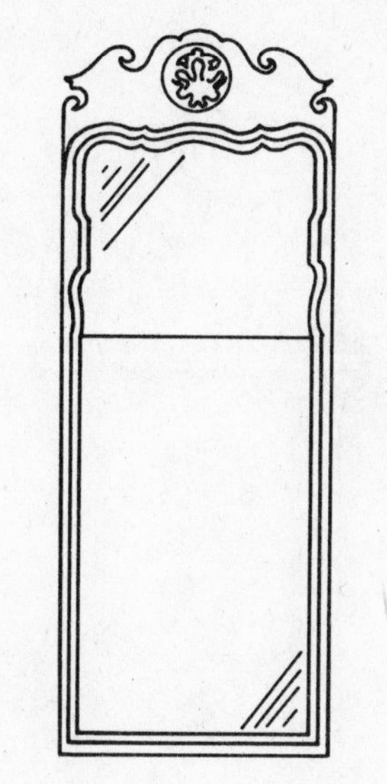

2

3

1. Looking-glass. Probably New York. Similar to at least one other known New York looking-glass. 1780–1790.

2. Looking-glass. Probably Philadelphia. (Labeled by John Elliott, Sr. Elliott imported English looking-glasses, but some that he sold were made in Philadelphia.) 1753–1761.

3. Looking-glass. Philadelphia. Of airy and fragile design. (Attributed to James Reynolds, 1739–1794, on basis of bill to John Cadwalader.) 1770–1771.

1. Looking-glass. Pennsylvania. Incorporates three motifs associated with Germanic work: tulip, heart, and pinwheel. 1800–1820.

2. Watchbox. Pennsylvania. Form used to hold portable timepiece at night. 1740–1780.

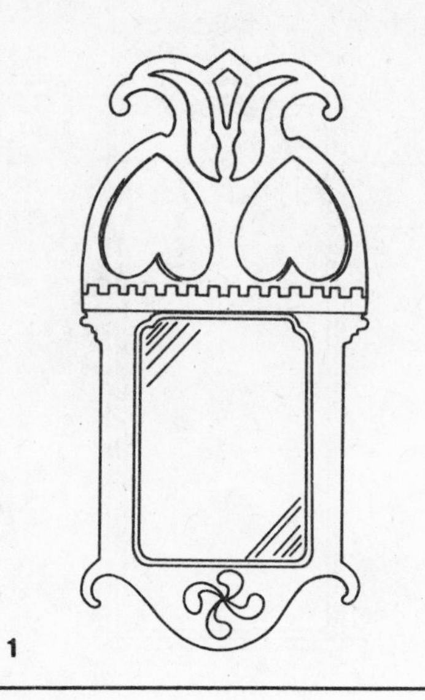

1

2

1

2

3

4

5

6

1. Girandole. Roxbury, Massachusetts. Name comes from the French for "branched candlestick." Sconces were often part of these convex looking-glasses with gilt-covered wooden and gessoed frames. (Attributed to now-famous John Doggett, 1780–1857, on basis of similar labeled example.) 1810–1825.

2. Looking-glass. New England, possibly Boston. Looking-glasses of this overall design with heavy cornices with ball ornament popular during first quarter of 19th century. 1815–1825.

3. Looking-glass. Portland, Maine. Stylistically earlier example than label suggests. Possibly labeled when repaired. (Labeled by James Todd, active 1820–1866.) c. 1825.

4. Looking-glass. New York. Ornamentation includes stringing, inlaid shell, *églomisé* panel, and gessoed and gilded vines and urn with flowers. (Bears stenciled inscription of the Del Vecchio family.) 1780–1805.

5. Looking-glass. New York. Such eagles and urn-shaped vases top many looking-glasses of this period. c. 1800.

6. Looking-glass. Philadelphia. *Églomisé* panel depicts Commodore Perry's victory on Lake Erie. (Labeled by sellers Caleb P. Wayne and Charles Biddle, in partnership 1811–1822.) c. 1815.

1. Cheval glass. New York. Such standing glasses became popular during this period. Note how sconces and storage trays swing forward and back. 1810–1820.

2. Dressing glass. Boston. Shares many details seen on swell-front chest of drawers made in same area. (Labeled by Stephen Badlam, Jr.) 1800–1825.

3. Dressing glass. New Jersey. Attributed to this region by means of inlaid butterflies used on a tall New Jersey case clock. c. 1810.

4. Firescreen. Salem, Massachusetts. Has rare feature of drop-leaf shelf. 1790–1805.

5. Firescreen. America. Shield shape seen on Federal furniture. 1800–1810.

1

2

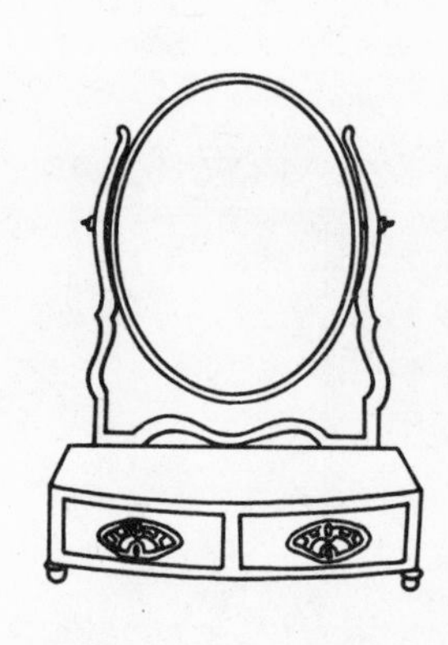

3

4

5

1

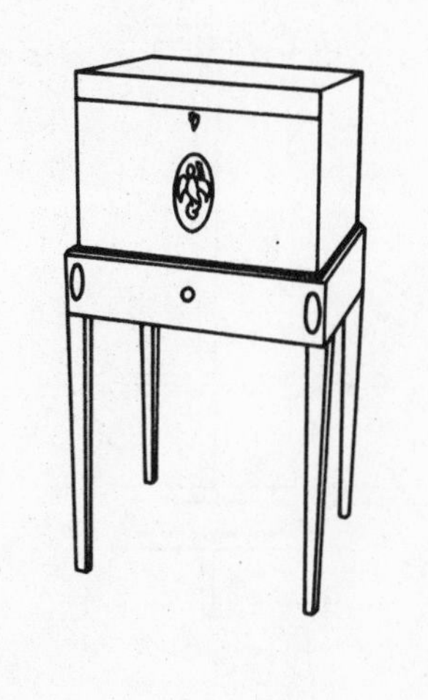

2

3

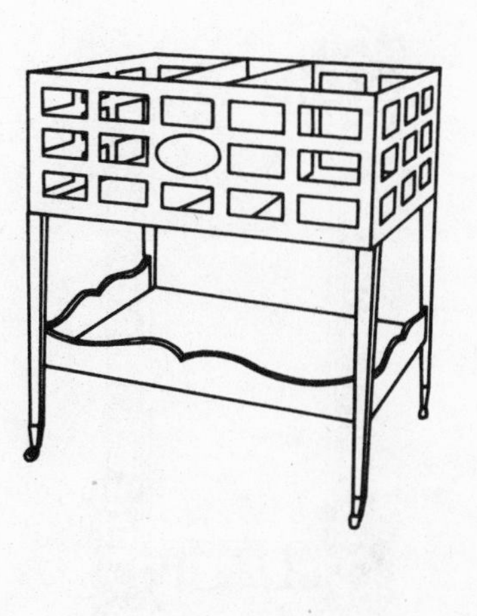

4

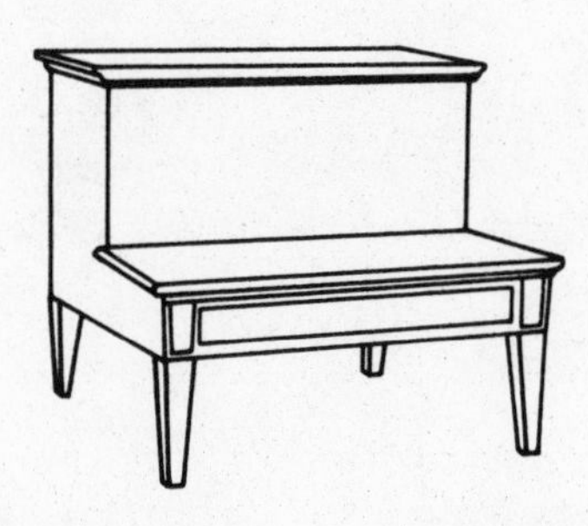

5

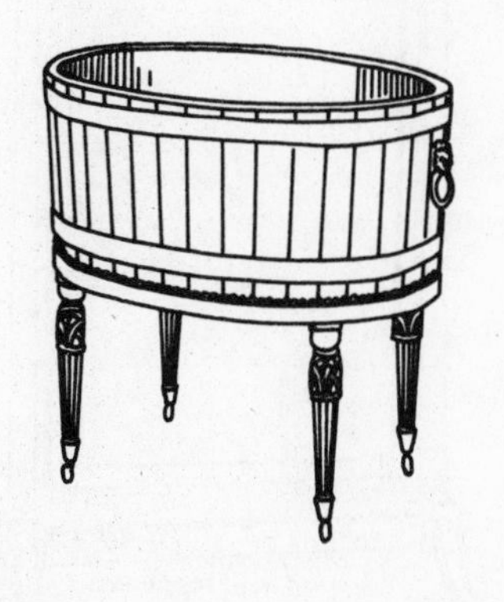

6

1. Basin stand. Baltimore, Maryland. Form fits in corner and holds ewer and basin. c. 1800.

2. Cellaret. Probably Charleston, South Carolina. Attributed to South Carolina due to presence of cypress wood. 1795–1805.

3. Canterbury, New York. Form used to store music and books. Drawer pulls are of pressed glass. 1815–1825.

4. Canterbury. Probably Charleston, South Carolina. This music rack is rather large and has open-backed shelf. 1790–1800.

5. Bedsteps. Possibly Charleston, South Carolina. Top step swings open to reveal space for chamberpot. 1790–1810.

6. Cellaret. Boston. Banded with brass and has lead liner. Used to cool wine bottles. 1805–1810.

1. Easel. New York or Boston. Note swans'-head termini. (Probably belonged to Boston painter Henry Sargent.) 1805–1815.

2. Firescreen. New York. Similar to English Regency examples. c. 1820.

3. Looking-glass. New York. Divided mirror has pilaster surrounds. (Attributed to Isaac Platt, active 1815–1835, on basis of similar labeled example.) 1825–1835.

4. Looking-glass. America. Reverse painting on glass panel depicts woman reclining. 1820–1830.

5. Cheval glass. New York. Inspired directly by French design. (Owned by the Livingston family.) 1815–1825.

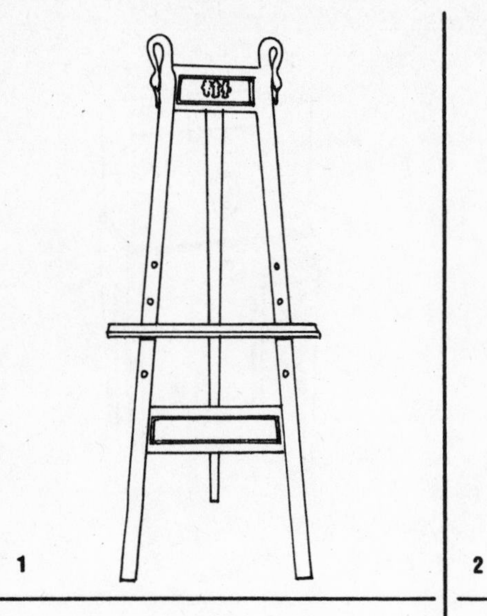

1

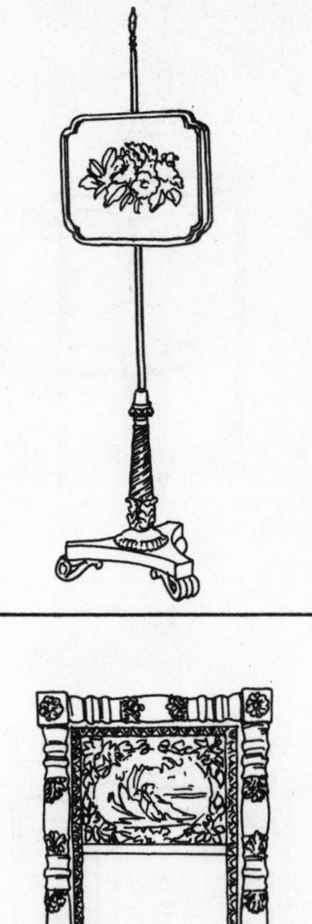

2

3

4

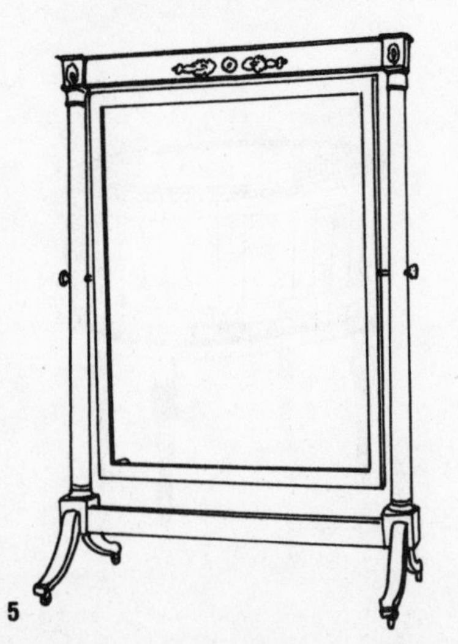

5

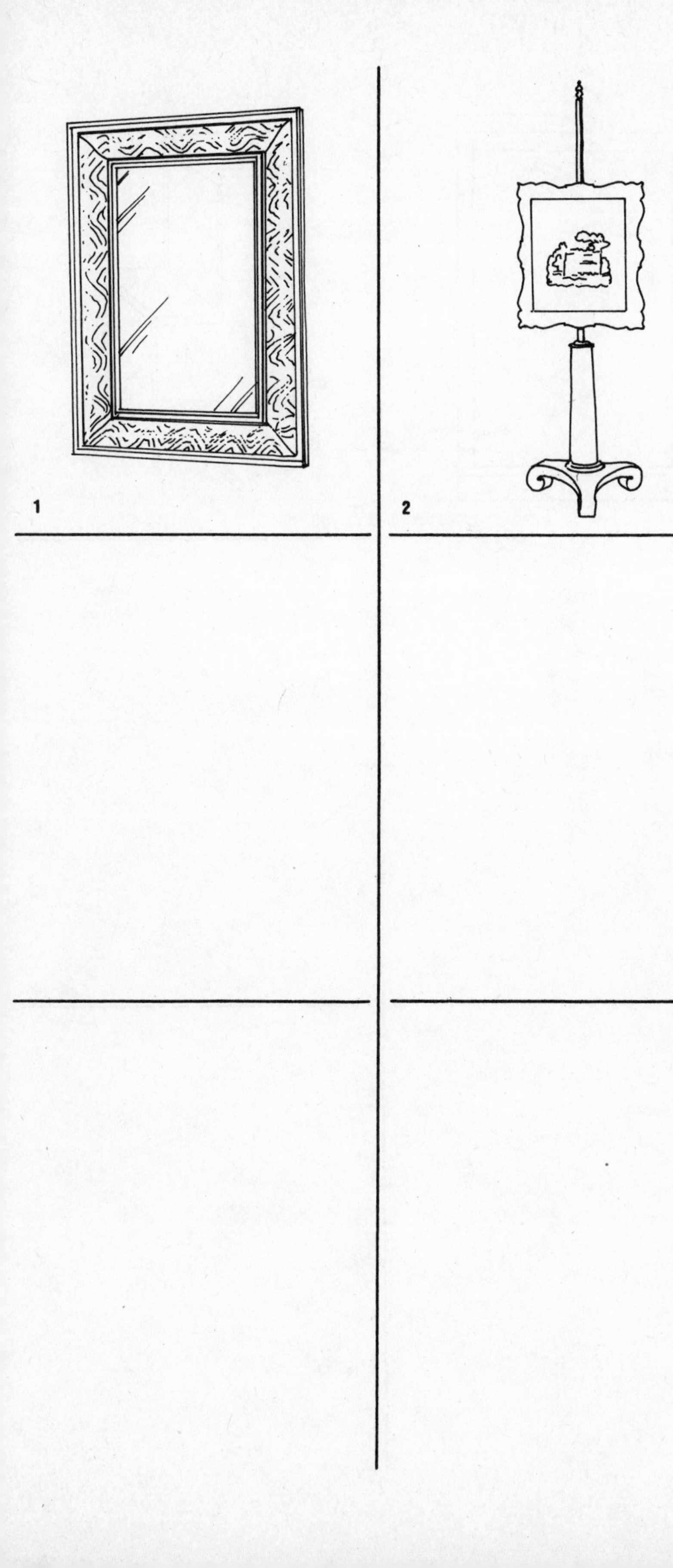

1. Looking-glass. America. Type referred to as ogee-frame because of its contour. 1830–1850.

2. Firescreen. America. Of severe and plain overall form. 1830–1850.

1. Looking-glass. Hancock, Massachusetts. Meant to be hung on a peg. 1830–1880.

2. Step stool. Probably Mount Lebanon, New York. Used to reach high storage areas such as the tops of cupboards. 1800–1890.

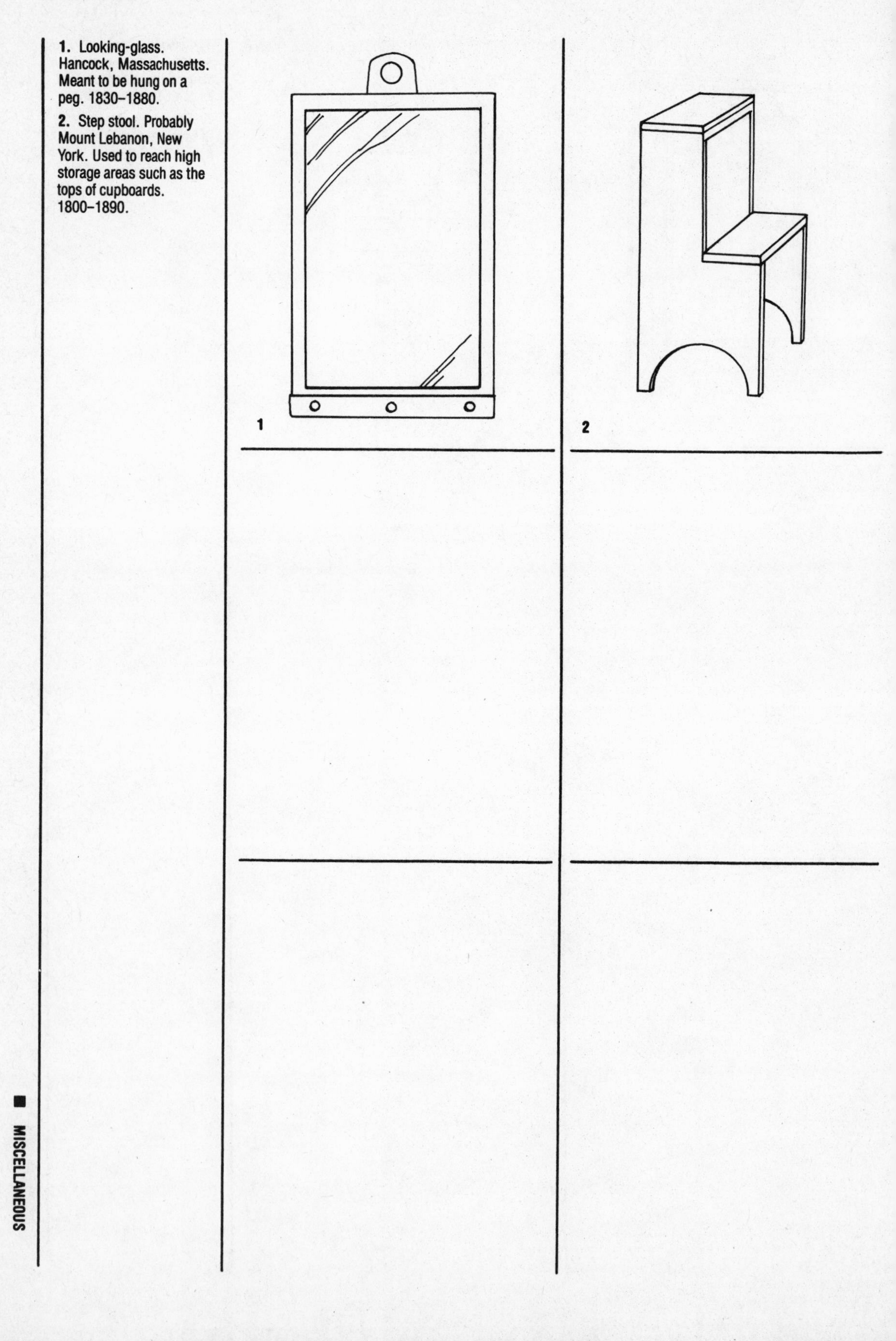

1. Etagère. New York. Tour de force composed of C- and S-scrolls has female bust at center of skirt. (Labeled by Alexander Roux.) 1850–1857.

2. Etagère. Boston. Form used to display curios. (Labeled by George Croome & Co.) 1864.

3. Coat rack. Charleston, South Carolina. Ornamental yet utilitarian hall furniture. c. 1860.

1

2

3

1. Looking-glass. Northeastern Massachusetts. Has pierced crest rail with Rococo ornamentation. 1850–1860.

2. Looking-glass. Boston. Elaborately carved glass ornamentation decorates top and bottom. c. 1860.

Renaissance Revival

1. Etagère. New York. Largely Renaissance Revival in style as evidenced by turned legs and pillars and carved tight scrolls. (Stenciled by maker Julius Dessoir, active 1842–1866.) 1855–1860.

1

2

1. Pedestal. Northeastern United States. This stand for sculpture is covered by Classical ornamentation. c. 1870.

2. Easel. New York. Also used to hold artwork. Note extravagant use of gilded and incised detail on easel's relatively flat members. (By Kilian Brothers.) c. 1871.

1

2

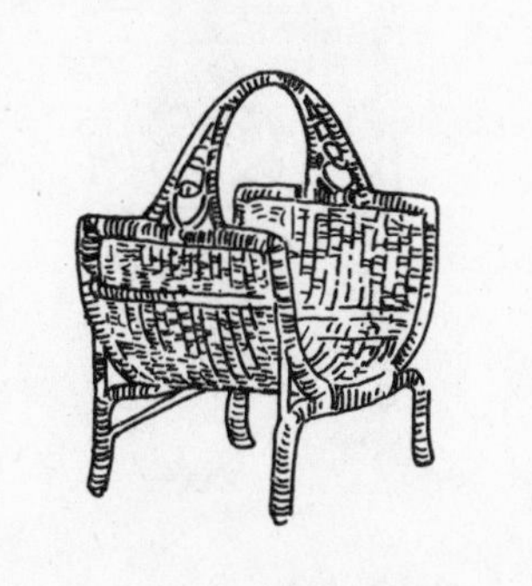

3

Innovative

1. Hat rack and umbrella stand. Multipurpose piece of cast iron hall furniture. c. 1860.

2. Canterbury. New York. Classical in overall style. Note how border imitates "ribbon" molding seen on early European looking-glass frames. (By Gaspar Godone, active 1830–1870.) 1835–1850.

3. Stand. Boston. Wicker was used in a variety of forms. (By Wakefield Rattan Co., 1844–1897.) c. 1880.

1. Pier looking-glass. Probably New York. Note emphasis on two-dimensional ornamentation. c. 1875.

2. Looking-glass. Pennsylvania. Common Eastlake-influenced form. 1870–1880.

3. Easel. Probably New York. Bottom swings open to hold portfolio of prints. 1870–1885.

4. Pedestal. Probably New York. Incised quarter-round popular Eastlake motif. c. 1880.

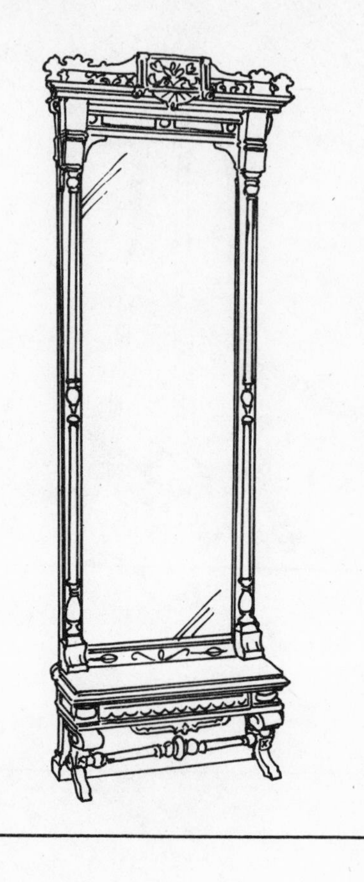

1

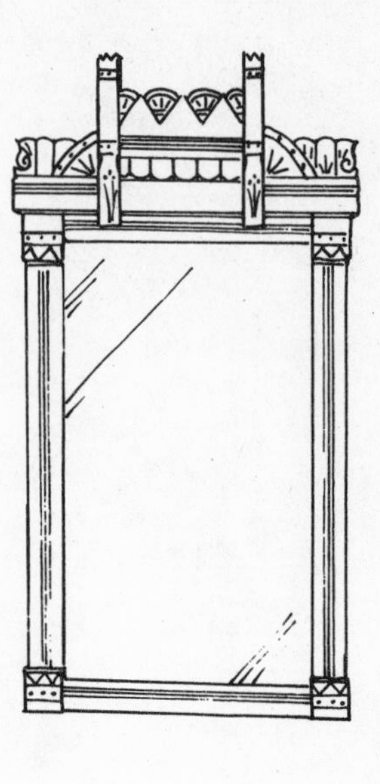

2

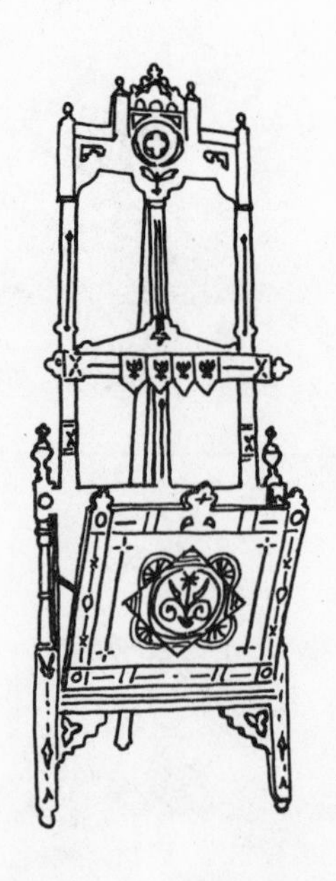

3

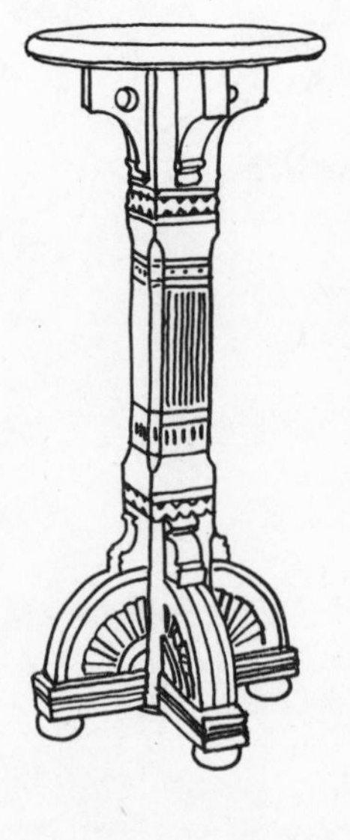

4

1

2

3

4

1. Bookstand. Media, Pennsylvania. Indicative of later Gothic Revival associated with the Arts and Crafts movement, particularly in Britain. (Designed by William L. Price. Made by Rose Valley shops.) 1901–1909.

2. Smoker's stand. Eastwood (Syracuse), New York. Note use of through-tenons. (Labeled by Gustav Stickley's Craftsman Workshops.) c. 1912.

3. Screen. Eastwood (Syracuse), New York. Note how slats are keyed together. (By Gustav Stickley's Craftsman Workshops.) c. 1913–1915.

4. Music cabinet. Eastwood (Syracuse), New York. Similar to English Arts and Crafts prototypes. (Decal of Gustav Stickley.) c. 1904.

Sources of Furniture Illustrated

Every attempt has been made to present generic examples of American antique furniture as a guide to identifying styles. The particular sources for the illustrations used in this work are cited below. This is not to suggest that these pieces are unique or found only in the sources cited. Indeed, much of what is reproduced in this work can be located at antique dealers, auction houses, other private collections, and in homes throughout the country. Sources are listed here by page number, followed by italicized figure number.

AUCTION HOUSES AND ANTIQUE DEALERS 93,7; 105,7; 106,5; 107,2,6,9; 123,1; 124,1,8; 136,1; 144,6; 150,2,3; 151,4,5; 152,3; 158,2; 162,7; 163,6; 165,2,4; 166,6; 168,2,3; 174,3; 176,3; 182,3; 184,7; 186,4; 187,1; 191,4; 197,1; 203,1; 213,2; 215,2,3; 216,2; 227,1; 236,1; 243,3; 245,1a; 255,2; 271,5; 272,2; 273,1,5,7; 274,1; 278,2,3; 281,1,2; 292,1,4; 298,2; 300,3; 305,3; 311,1; 321,2,3,5,6; 329,1; 343,2; 345,1,2; 350,5; 357,1,2.

PRIVATE COLLECTIONS 92,2; 93,3; 95,9; 97,1; 98,2,8; 106,5; 107,3; 111,2,8; 112,5; 117,1,2,8,9; 118,3; 119,1,4; 120,1,4,5,6; 122,4,5; 125,4; 128,6; 132,3; 133,9; 134,8; 136,3; 137,1,2,3; 138,4,5,7,8; 139,1; 140,3,8,9; 141,1,2,3,4; 142,1,3; 143,4; 144,1; 146,4,5,6; 147,1,2,3,4,7,9; 148,6; 151,2,4,6,7; 152,2,4,5; 158,2,4,6; 159,6,8; 161,6; 165,1; 166,7,8; 170,5; 177,6; 178,2,7; 182,4,6,8; 183,1,5,7; 184,3,4; 185,2,4; 186,1,2; 187,2; 188,1,2,3,4,5; 189,1,2; 190,1,2; 194,3; 195,1; 197,2,4; 198,1,4,5; 205,3; 206,3; 210,1,3; 211,2; 212,1; 213,1,2; 214,1; 223,5; 226,4; 228,3; 236,2; 238,5; 241,1; 242,2; 243,1,1a; 248,2,5; 252,8; 255,1,4; 258,1; 263,3,4; 267,4; 270,1; 271,2,4; 272,4; 274,5; 275,4; 277,2; 286,1,2,3; 287,6; 288,3; 293,4; 296,2,3,4; 299,1,2; 300,1,2; 301,1,2; 304,1,3; 307,3; 312,3; 313,3; 315,2,3,4,5; 316,1,2; 326,2; 329,3; 337,2; 339,1,5; 340,1; 342,1a,1b; 345,3,4,5,7; 356,3,4; 358,2; 359,3; 360,2; 362,1.

PERIOD SOURCES 36,1; 84,2; 139,3; 146,2; 148,3,4; 151,9; 152,6; 194,2; 198,3; 215,1a; 217,1; 241,3; 245,2; 246,3; 247,1; 297,2; 298,1,3; 309,2; 315,1,3; 338,1,2; 361,2,3a.

ALBANY INSTITUTE OF HISTORY AND ART, ALBANY, NEW YORK 108,1; 158,5; 181,2; 209,3.

AMERICAN MUSEUM IN BRITAIN, BATH, ENGLAND 268,4.

ART INSTITUTE OF CHICAGO, CHICAGO, ILLINOIS 91,6; 198,2; 254,6; 265,3.

BALTIMORE MUSEUM OF ART, BALTIMORE, MARYLAND 111,9; 174,1; 190,6.

BOWDOIN COLLEGE ART MUSEUM, BRUNSWICK, MAINE 90,2.

BROOKLYN MUSEUM, BROOKLYN, NEW YORK 99,2; 141,5; 143,1,6; 144,4; 148,2; 149,8; 159,7; 164,3; 184,2; 237,3; 238,4; 252,3; 254,5; 303,2; 304,4; 314,2; 362,3.

THE CHARLESTON MUSEUM, CHARLESTON, SOUTH CAROLINA 112,9; 276,4.

CHESTER COUNTY HISTORICAL SOCIETY, WEST CHESTER, PENNSYLVANIA 206,4; 274,4.

CHICAGO SCHOOL OF ARCHITECTURE FOUNDATION, GLESSNER HOUSE, CHICAGO, ILLINOIS 344,1,2.

COOPER UNION, NEW YORK, NEW YORK 146,8.

CHICAGO HISTORICAL SOCIETY, CHICAGO, ILLINOIS 195,5.

THE CONNECTICUT HISTORICAL SOCIETY, HARTFORD, CONNECTICUT 106,7; 156,3; 263,1.

COLONIAL WILLIAMSBURG FOUNDATION, WILLIAMSBURG, VIRGINIA 90,8; 97,8; 109,7; 110,2; 112,2,3; 113,2; 114,3; 118,4; 156,2; 159,5; 163,4; 165,6; 226,2; 272,8; 320,4; 323,4.

DETROIT INSTITUTE OF ARTS, DETROIT, MICHIGAN 252,2.

DIPLOMATIC RECEPTION ROOMS, DEPARTMENT OF STATE, WASHINGTON, D.C. 166,1; 324,1; 326,1.

ESSEX INSTITUTE, SALEM, MASSACHUSETTS 192,1; 220,3.

THE GAMBLE HOUSE, GREENE AND GREENE MUSEUM AND LIBRARY, PASADENA, CALIFORNIA 152,1; 197,5.

GRAND RAPIDS PUBLIC MUSEUM, GRAND RAPIDS, MICHIGAN 143,8; 192,6; 193,6,8; 215,4; 308,4.

HENRY FORD MUSEUM AND GREENFIELD VILLAGE, DEARBORN, MICHIGAN 92,6; 105,3; 113,1; 119,3; 123,4; 124,2; 136,2; 142,6; 143,7,9; 146,3; 148,1; 149,6; 161,4; 165,9; 175,1; 177,8; 183,6; 184,1; 195,3; 206,1,2; 247,2,3; 254,3; 256,2,6; 269,3; 287,1,8; 295,2; 322,3; 349,5.

HENRY FRANCIS DU PONT WINTERTHUR MUSEUM, WINTERTHUR, DELAWARE 90,9; 91,1,3; 92,1,3,5; 94,1; 95,4,6,7,8; 96,9; 97,3,4,9; 98,4,5,6,7; 99,3,4,6; 100,1,2; 106,1; 107,1,7,8; 108,4,5,9; 109,6,8; 110,1,3,4,6,7,9; 111,1,3,4,5,6,7; 113,3,6; 114,1,2,6; 119,6,9; 122,1,2,3; 123,3; 124,4,5; 125,2,3,6,7,8,9; 126,1,2,8; 127,1,2,3,4,5,6,7,8; 128,2,3,4,5,9; 129,1,3,5,6,8,9; 130,2,3,5,6; 131,2,3,5,6; 132,1; 133,5,7,9; 134,1,4,6; 135,3,4,5; 136,6; 138,9; 159,1; 161,1,5,7; 162,1,3,4,5; 163,7,8; 164,1,4,8; 166,3,4,5; 167,1,2,4,5,6,7,8; 168,1,6,7,8; 169,2,4,5,6,7; 170,1,2,3,4,7,8,9; 173,1,2,3,4,5,6,7,8; 174,2,5,6; 175,4,5,6,8; 176,2,4,5,7,8; 177,1,5,7; 178,1,3,4,5; 179,1,2,3,4,5,6,8,9; 180,1,2,3,4,5,6,7,8,9; 181,1,2,3,4,5,6,7,8, 9,10,11,12,13; 184,5,6,8; 185,1; 203,1; 204,1,2,3,5,6; 205,1,4; 207,1,6; 208,1; 209,1; 220,1,3; 221,1; 222,1,3,4; 223,1,4,6; 224,1,4; 225,1,3; 226,1,3,5,6; 229,1; 230,2,4; 231,1,2,3,4; 232,2; 233,2,3; 236,3,4; 237,4; 238,2; 252,4; 254,4; 255,7; 258,1; 262,2,5,6; 267,1,3; 268,1,2; 269,1; 270,3; 271,1,7,8; 272,1,3; 273,2,3,4,6; 274,2; 275,1,3; 276,1; 277,3; 279,2,4,5; 280,1,4; 283,1; 285,2; 287,3,4,7; 288,1,2,4,5; 290,1,2,4; 291,2,4; 292,3; 305,1; 321,1; 323,2,6; 324,2,3,4; 325,1,4; 327,1; 329,2; 330,1,2,4; 331,1,2; 332,1,2,3,4,6; 333,1,3; 334,3; 335,1; 348,1; 349,1,2,3; 350,2,3,4,6; 351,1,2,3; 353,2,3,4,5,6; 354,2,3,4,5; 355,1,2,4.

HERITAGE CENTER OF LANCASTER COUNTY, LANCASTER, PENNSYLVANIA 120,3.

THE HERMITAGE, HO-HO-KUS, NEW JERSEY 313,1.

HISTORIC DEERFIELD, DEERFIELD, MASSACHUSETTS 106,2; 158,3; 175,2; 291,1; 294,4; 325,2.

HOUSTON MUSEUM OF FINE ARTS, BAYOU BEND COLLECTION, HOUSTON, TEXAS 94,2; 221,3; 222,2; 224,3; 276,3.

HUDSON RIVER MUSEUM, YONKERS, NEW YORK 195,2; 312,1.

INDEPENDENCE NATIONAL HISTORICAL PARK, PHILADELPHIA, PENNSYLVANIA 117,4; 119,7,8; 131,4; 228,3.

INDEX OF AMERICAN DESIGN, WASHINGTON, D.C. 256,1,6.

JOHN BROWN HOUSE, RHODE ISLAND HISTORICAL SOCIETY, PROVIDENCE, RHODE ISLAND 107,4; 174,7.

KENTUCKY MUSEUM, WESTERN KENTUCKY UNIVERSITY, BOWLING GREEN, KENTUCKY 340,3.

LITCHFIELD HISTORICAL SOCIETY, LITCHFIELD, CONNECTICUT 194,4.

THE LOS ANGELES COUNTY MUSEUM OF ART, LOS ANGELES, CALIFORNIA 227,2.

LOUISIANA STATE MUSEUM, NEW ORLEANS, LOUISIANA, 305,2.

LYMAN ALLYN MUSEUM, NEW LONDON, CONNECTICUT 239,3; 356,2.

LYNDHURST, NATIONAL TRUST FOR HISTORIC PRESERVATION, TARRYTOWN, NEW YORK 140,3; 149,2,3; 150,2a; 190,4; 216,1; 312,2.

MARGARET WOODBURY STRONG MUSEUM, ROCHESTER, NEW YORK 141,9; 146,5; 149,9; 182,2; 183,3; 191,4; 193,7; 195,6; 244,1; 297,3,4; 307,1; 308,1.

MARK TWAIN MEMORIAL, HARTFORD, CONNECTICUT 150,1.

MASSACHUSETTS HISTORICAL SOCIETY, BOSTON, MASSACHUSETTS 105,9.

METROPOLITAN MUSEUM OF ART, NEW YORK, NEW YORK 85,1,2; 90,6; 96,2; 97,2; 99,5; 108,3; 124,6; 133,1; 136,4,5; 140,5,6; 141,6; 142,1a,2a,3a; 143,2,5; 144,2,3; 145,2; 146,1; 147,5; 149,1; 150,3a; 156,1; 157,4; 164,6; 169,3,8; 182,5; 183,4; 185,3; 190,5; 191,1a,192,4; 193,1,2; 195,7; 196,2; 197,3; 216,1a,2a; 223,2,3; 227,4; 228,4; 235,4; 239,1,2,4; 242,1,4; 244,2; 245,1,2; 256,5; 263,5; 264,2; 278,4; 280,3; 306,1a; 310,2; 311,1a; 313,2; 314,1; 320,1; 323,7; 333,2; 334,1; 336,1; 341,1,2; 344,1a; 354,1; 359,1; 360,1,1a; 361,1,2a; 362,4.

MONMOUTH COUNTY HISTORICAL ASSOCIATION, FREEHOLD, NEW JERSEY 227,3; 281,3.

MUNSON-WILLIAMS-PROCTOR INSTITUTE, UTICA, NEW YORK 141,7,8; 187,3; 190,3; 191,1; 296,1,5; 306,1; 309,1; 341,3; 342,1.

MUSEUM OF ART, RHODE ISLAND SCHOOL OF DESIGN, PROVIDENCE, RHODE ISLAND 118,1,5,8; 156,4; 294,2.

MUSEUM OF THE CITY OF NEW YORK, NEW YORK, NEW YORK 108,2,8; 140,2,7; 148,2a; 176,6; 191,2; 193,3; 196,1; 215,1; 307,4; 320,3; 336,2; 337,1; 356,5.

MUSEUM OF EARLY SOUTHERN DECORATIVE ARTS, WINSTON-SALEM, NORTH CAROLINA 98,9; 112,1,4,6,7,8; 158,1; 159,4; 162,2; 165,3; 167,3; 168,4; 172,3,6; 178,6,8; 179,7; 221,4; 233,4; 254,1; 257,1,2,6,7; 262,1,8; 267,2; 272,5; 274,6; 279,3; 281,4; 288,6; 289,1,2; 290,3; 293,3; 322,1; 326,4; 327,1,3; 329,4; 334,2; 335,2; 350,1.

MUSEUM OF FINE ARTS, BOSTON, MASSACHUSETTS 90,3; 91,4,5; 95,3; 96,6,8; 97,2; 105,6; 113,5; 123,2; 125,1; 126,3; 131,1; 133,1,2,5; 135,2; 140,1; 145,2a; 147,8; 158,7; 161,3; 162,5; 163,5; 164,2; 165,5; 166,2; 168,5; 170,6; 177,3,4; 202,1; 205,2; 221,2; 235,1; 237,1; 248,1; 253,2,3,4,5; 262,3; 268,3; 270,2; 275,2; 279,6; 287,5; 289,4; 323,5,8; 330,3; 349,4; 353,1; 355,6; 356,1; 359,2.

NELSON-ATKINS MUSEUM OF ART, KANSAS CITY, MISSOURI 176,1.

NEW HAMPSHIRE HISTORICAL SOCIETY, CONCORD, NEW HAMPSHIRE 93,6; 96,1.

NEW HAVEN COLONY HISTORICAL SOCIETY, NEW HAVEN, CONNECTICUT 269,2.

NEW-YORK HISTORICAL SOCIETY, NEW YORK, NEW YORK 93,1; 186,3.

NEWARK MUSEUM ASSOCIATION, NEWARK, NEW JERSEY 109,1; 133,3; 143,1; 144,5; 186,5; 192,2,3; 193,4; 244,3; 306,2; 308,4; 310,1; 311,2; 342,2.

OLD SALEM INC., WINSTON-SALEM, NORTH CAROLINA 122,6.

OLD STURBRIDGE VILLAGE, STURBRIDGE, MASSACHUSETTS 124,9; 133,4; 174,4; 224,1; 252,6; 263,6; 267,1.

PARK DISTRICT OF OAK PARK, CHICAGO, ILLINOIS 151,3.

PEABODY MUSEUM, SALEM, MASSACHUSETTS 125,5.

PHILADELPHIA MUSEUM OF ART, PHILADELPHIA, PENNSYLVANIA 110,8; 114,5; 117,5; 134,7; 149,4; 150,1a; 151,8; 160,1; 172,2,4,5,7; 225,4; 229,2; 233,1; 279,1; 283,2; 284,2; 285,1; 286,4; 293,1; 295,3; 304,2; 326,1; 336,4; 352,1,2.

PILGRIM HALL, PLYMOUTH, MASSACHUSETTS 90,4,5; 202,2.

PRESERVATION SOCIETY OF NEWPORT COUNTY, NEWPORT, RHODE ISLAND 96,7.

PRINCETON MUSEUM COLLECTION, PRINCETON, NEW JERSEY 151,1.

MISSISSIPPI SOCIETY DAUGHTERS OF THE AMERICAN REVOLUTION "ROSALIE" NATCHEZ, MISSISSIPPI 338,3.

SAGAMORE HILL NATIONAL HISTORIC SITE, OYSTER BAY, NEW YORK 149,5; 195,4.

SHAKER COMMUNITY INC., PITTSFIELD, MASSACHUSETTS 138,3; 189,3; 339,3,4; 358,1.

SHAKER MUSEUM, OLD CHATHAM, NEW YORK 138,1,2,6; 139,4; 211,1; 241,2,4; 258,1,2; 299,3,4; 301,2; 302,1,3; 339,2; 340,2,4.

SHAKERTOWN AT PLEASANT HILL, PLEASANT HILL, KENTUCKY 301,3.

SHAKERTOWN AT SOUTH UNION, SOUTH UNION, KENTUCKY 211,4.

SHELBURNE MUSEUM, SHELBURNE, VERMONT 164,5; 262,4.

SLEEPY HOLLOW RESTORATIONS, TARRYTOWN, NEW YORK 91,2; 92,7; 93,5; 96,5; 97,6,7; 98,3; 108,6,7; 117,3; 119,2; 126,6; 127,9; 128,1; 133,6; 137,4,5; 142,4,5; 161,2; 163,2; 165,7; 169,1; 171,1,2; 172,1; 175,3,7; 203,3; 205,5; 207,5; 210,2; 225,2; 232,1; 235,3; 240,1,4; 243,2; 255,3; 256,3; 265,1,2; 277,1; 292,2; 294,3; 295,1; 297,1; 303,3; 320,2; 332,5; 336,1; 348,2; 353,4; 355,3; 361,1a.

SMITHSONIAN INSTITUTION, WASHINGTON, D.C. 142,3; 147,6; 149,7; 157,1,3; 243,3; 303,1; 343,1.

THE SOCIETY FOR THE PRESERVATION OF LONG ISLAND ANTIQUITIES, SETAUKET, NEW YORK 118,2.

THE SOCIETY FOR THE PRESERVATION OF NEW ENGLAND ANTIQUITIES, BOSTON, MASSACHUSETTS 130,4; 148,2; 207,2.

J. B. SPEED ART MUSEUM, LOUISVILLE, KENTUCKY 294,1.

THEODORE ROOSEVELT BIRTHPLACE, NEW YORK, NEW YORK 143,3; 308,2.

WACHOVIA HISTORICAL SOCIETY, WINSTON-SALEM, NORTH CAROLINA 284,3.

WADSWORTH ATHENEUM, HARTFORD, CONNECTICUT 156,2; 202,3; 246,4; 291,3.

WALTERS ART GALLERY, BALTIMORE, MARYLAND 182,1.

WARREN COUNTY MUSEUM, LEBANON, OHIO 139,6.

WESTERN RESERVE HISTORICAL SOCIETY, CLEVELAND, OHIO 139,5.

WILLIAM PENN MEMORIAL MUSEUM, HARRISBURG, PENNSYLVANIA 192,5; 193,5; 228,1; 256,4; 284,1.

YALE UNIVERSITY ART GALLERY, MABEL BRADY GARVAN AND RELATED COLLECTIONS, NEW HAVEN, CONNECTICUT 90,1,7; 92,2,4,8,9; 93,4; 95,1,2; 96,3,4; 97,4; 98,1; 99,1; 105,1,2,4,5,8; 106,3,4,8,9; 109,2,3,4,5,9; 110,5; 113,4; 114,4; 117,6,7; 118,6,7,9; 120,2; 124,3,7; 126,4,5,7,9; 128,7,8; 129,2,4,7; 130,1; 133,2,3,6,8; 137,6; 139,2; 141,5; 145,1a,3a; 157,5; 159,3; 160,2; 163,1,3; 204,4; 207,1,4; 208,2; 209,2; 230,1,3; 232,3,4; 235,2; 237,2; 238,1,3; 240,2,3; 252,1,7; 253,1; 254,2; 263,2; 264,4; 268,1; 269,4; 271,2; 273,8; 274,3; 276,2; 277,4; 278,1; 280,1; 287,2; 289,3; 293,2; 322,2; 323,1,3; 325,3; 355,5.

Outstanding Collections of American Antique Furniture

It is invaluable for the interested reader to view original pieces of furniture. Only in this manner is it possible to develop a sense of furniture connoisseurship. The following institutions are strongly recommended.

Albany Institute of History and Art, Albany, New York
Art Institute of Chicago, Illinois
Baltimore Museum of Art, Maryland
Brooklyn Museum, New York
Colonial Williamsburg, Williamsburg, Virginia
Connecticut Historical Society, Hartford, Connecticut
Essex Institute, Salem, Massachusetts
Hancock Shaker Village, Pittsfield, Massachusetts
Henry Ford Museum and Greenfield Village, Dearborn, Michigan
Henry Francis du Pont Winterthur Museum, Winterthur, Delaware
High Museum of Art, Atlanta, Georgia
Historic Deerfield, Deerfield, Massachusetts
Hudson River Museum, Yonkers, New York
Independence National Historical Park, Philadelphia, Pennsylvania
Margaret Woodbury Strong Museum, Rochester, New York
The Metropolitan Museum of Art, The American Wing, New York, New York
Monmouth County Historical Association, Freehold, New Jersey
Munson-Williams-Proctor Institute, Utica, New York
Museum of Early Southern Decorative Arts, Winston-Salem, North Carolina
Museum of Fine Arts, Boston, Massachusetts
Museum of Fine Arts, Houston, Bayou Bend Collection, Texas
Museum of the City of New York, New York
National Museum of American History, Smithsonian Institution, Washington, D.C.
National Trust for Historic Preservation, Lyndhurst, Tarrytown, New York
Newark Museum, Newark, New Jersey
Old Salem, Winston-Salem, North Carolina
Old Sturbridge Village, Sturbridge, Massachusetts
Philadelphia Museum of Art, Pennsylvania
Pilgrim Hall, Plymouth, Massachusetts
Shaker Museum, Old Chatham, New York
Shakertown at South Union, Kentucky
Sleepy Hollow Restorations, Tarrytown, New York
Wadsworth Atheneaum, Hartford, Connecticut
William Penn Memorial Museum, Harrisburg, Pennsylvania
Yale University Art Gallery, Mabel Brady Garvan and Related Collections, New Haven, Connecticut

Selected Bibliography

Andrews, Edward Deming and Faith. *Shaker Furniture: The Craftsmanship of an American Communal Sect.* New Haven: Yale University, 1937.

Bacot, H. Parrott. *Southern Furniture and Silver: The Federal Period, 1788–1830.* Baton Rouge: Louisiana State University Press, 1968.

Baltimore Museum of Art. *Baltimore Furniture: The Work of Baltimore and Annapolis Cabinetmakers from 1760 to 1810.* Baltimore: The Baltimore Museum of Art, 1947.

Butler, Joseph T. *American Antiques, 1800–1900: A Collector's History and Guide.* New York: Odyssey Press, 1965.

———. *American Furniture from the First Colonies to World War I.* London: Triune, 1973.

———. *Sleepy Hollow Restorations: A Cross Section of the Collection.* Tarrytown, New York: Sleepy Hollow Restorations, 1983.

Carpenter, Ralph E., Jr. *The Arts and Crafts of Newport, Rhode Island, 1640–1820.* Newport: Preservation Society of Newport County, 1954.

Cathers, David M. *Furniture of the American Arts and Crafts Movement, Stickley and Roycroft Mission Oak.* New York: New American Library, 1981.

Chippendale, Thomas. *The Gentleman & Cabinet-Maker's Director.* 3rd ed. London: Privately printed, 1762. Reprint. New York: Dover Publications, 1966.

Clark, Robert Judson, ed. *The Arts and Crafts Movement in America, 1876–1916.* Princeton: Princeton University Press, 1972.

Comstock, Helen. *American Furniture, Seventeenth, Eighteenth, and Nineteenth Century Styles.* New York: Viking Press, 1962.

Cooper, Wendy A. *In Praise of America: American Decorative Arts, 1650–1830/Fifty Years of Discovery Since the 1929 Girl Scouts Loan Exhibition.* New York: Alfred A. Knopf, 1980.

Davidson, Marshall B., ed. *Three Centuries of American Antiques.* Vol. I: *The American Heritage History of Colonial Antiques.* Vol. II: *The American Heritage History of American Antiques from the Revolution to the Civil War.* Vol. III: *The American Heritage History of Antiques from the Civil War to World War I.* Reprint (3 vol. in 1). New York: Bonanza Books, 1979.

Denker, Ellen and Bert. *The Rocking Chair Book.* New York: Mayflower Books, 1979.

Downs, Joseph. *American Furniture in the Henry Francis du Pont Winterthur Museum. Queen Anne and Chippendale Periods.* New York: Macmillan, 1952.

Eastlake, Charles L. *Hints on Household Taste in Furniture, Upholstery, and Other Details.* London: Longmans, Green and Co., 1868. Reprint, New York: Dover Publications, 1969.

Elder, William Voss III. *Baltimore Painted Furniture, 1800–1840.* Baltimore: The Baltimore Museum of Art, 1972.

———. *Maryland Queen Anne and Chippendale Furniture of the Eighteenth Century.* Baltimore: The Baltimore Museum of Art, 1968.

Fabian, Monroe H. *The Pennsylvania-German Decorated Chest.* Clinton, New Jersey: Main Street Press, 1978.

Failey, Dean F., and others. *Long Island is My Nation: The Decorative Arts & Craftsmen, 1640–1830.* Setauket, New York: Society for the Preservation of Long Island Antiquities, 1976.

Fairbanks, Jonathan L. and Bates, Elizabeth Bidwell. *American Furniture 1620 to the Present.* New York: Richard Marek, 1981.

Fales, Dean A., Jr. *American Painted Furniture, 1660–1880.* New York: E. P. Dutton, 1972.

Garrett, Wendell D., and others. *The Arts in America: The Nineteenth Century.* New York: Charles Scribner's Sons, 1969.

Giedion, Sigfried. *Mechanization Takes Command: A Contribution to Anonymous History.* New York: Oxford University Press, 1948.

Greenlaw, Barry A. *New England Furniture at Williamsburg.* Williamsburg, Virginia: The Colonial Williamsburg Foundation, 1974.

Hagler, Katharine Bryant. *American Queen Anne Furniture, 1720–1755.* Dearborn: The Edison Institute, 1976.

Hall, John. *The Cabinet Makers' Assistant.* Baltimore: John Murphy, 1840. Reprint. New York: National Superior, Inc., 1944.

Hanks, David A. *Innovative Furniture in America from 1800 to the Present.* New York: Horizon, 1981.

Hepplewhite, George. *The Cabinet-Maker & Uphol-*

sterer's *Guide*. 3rd ed. London: I. & J. Taylor, 1794. Reprint. New York: Dover Publications, 1969.

Hipkiss, Edwin J. *Eighteenth-Century American Arts: The M. and M. Karolik Collection of Paintings, Drawings, Engravings, Furniture, Silver, Needlework & Incidental Objects Gathered to Illustrate the Achievements of American Artists and Craftsmen of the Period from 1720 to 1820*. Boston and Cambridge, Massachusetts: Museum of Fine Arts and Harvard University Press, 1941.

Hope, Thomas. *Household Furniture and Interior Decoration*. London: Longman, Hurst, Rees & Orme, 1807. Reprint: New York: Dover Publications, 1971.

Horton, Frank L. *The Museum of Early Southern Decorative Arts: A Collection of Southern Furniture, Paintings, Ceramics, Textiles, and Metalware*. Winston-Salem: Old Salem, Inc., 1979.

Howe, Katherine S., and Warren, David B. *The Gothic Revival Style in America, 1830–1870*. Houston: The Museum of Fine Arts, 1976.

Kane, Patricia E. *300 Years of American Seating Furniture: Chairs and Beds from the Mabel Brady Garvan and Other Collections at Yale University*. Boston: New York Graphic Society, 1976.

Ketchum, William C., Jr. *Chests, Cupboards, Desks & Other Pieces*. New York: Alfred A. Knopf, 1982.

Kirk, John T. *American Chairs: Queen Anne and Chippendale*. New York: Alfred A. Knopf, 1972.

. *American Furniture of the British Tradition to 1830*. New York: Alfred A. Knopf, 1982.

. *Early American Furniture: How to Recognize, Evaluate, Buy & Care for the Most Beautiful Pieces—High Style, Country, Primitive & Rustic*. New York: Afred A. Knopf, 1970.

Loudon, John C. *An Encyclopaedia of Cottage, Farm and Villa Architecture and Furniture*. London: n. p., 1833.

Madigan, Mary Jean Smith. *Eastlake-Influenced American Furniture, 1870–1890*. Yonkers, New York: The Hudson River Museum, 1973.

Meader, Robert F.W. *An Illustrated Guide to Shaker Furniture*. New York: Dover Publications, 1972.

Miller, Edgar G., Jr. *American Antique Furniture: A Book for Amateurs*. 2 vols. Baltimore: Lord Baltimore Press, 1937.

Miller, V. Isabelle. *Furniture by New York Cabinetmakers, 1650 to 1860*. New York: Museum of the City of New York, 1956.

Montgomery, Charles F. *American Furniture: The Federal Period, in the Henry Francis du Pont Winterthur Museum*. New York: Viking Press, 1966.

Nutting, Wallace. *Furniture of the Pilgrim Century (of American Origin), 1620–1720, with Maple and Pine to 1800, Including Colonial Utensils and Wrought-Iron House Hardware into the 19th Century*. Framingham, Massachusetts: Old America Company, Rev. ed., 1924.

. *Furniture Treasury (Mostly of American Origin), All Periods of American Furniture with Some Foreign Examples in America, also American Hardware and Household Utensils*. 3 vols. Framingham, Massachusetts: Old America Company, 1928–33.

Otto, Celia Jackson. *American Furniture of the Nineteenth Century*. New York: Viking Press, 1965.

Randall, Richard H., Jr. *American Furniture in the Museum of Fine Arts, Boston*. Boston: Museum of Fine Arts, 1965.

Santore, Charles. *The Windsor Style in America, A Pictorial Study of the History and Regional Characteristics of the Most Popular Furniture Form of Eighteenth-Century America*. Philadelphia: Running Press, 1981.

Schwartz, Marvin D. *Chairs, Tables, Sofas & Beds*. New York: Alfred A. Knopf, 1982.

Stanek, Edward J; and True, Douglas K. *The Furniture of John Henry Belter and the Rococo Revival: An Inquiry into Nineteenth-Century Furniture Design Through a Study of the Gloria and Richard Manney Collection*. New York: E. P. Dutton, 1981.

Sheraton, Thomas. *The Cabinet-Maker and Upholsterer's Drawing-Book*. 3rd rev. ed. London: T. Bensley, 1802. Reprint. Charles F. Montgomery and Wilfred P. Cole, eds. New York: Praeger Publishers, 1970.

Tracy, Berry B. and Gerdts, William H. *Classical America, 1815–1845*. Newark, New Jersey: The Newark Museum Association, 1963.

Tracy, Berry B.; Johnson, Marilynn; and others. *19th Century America: Furniture and Other Decorative Arts, An Exhibition in Celebration of the Hundredth Anniversary of The Metropolitan Museum of Art*. New York: The Metropolitan Museum of Art, 1970.

Trent, Robert F. *Hearts and Crowns: Folk Chairs of the Connecticut Coast, 1720–1840, as Viewed in the Light of Henri Focillon's Introduction to Art Populaire*. New Haven: New Haven Colony Historical Society, 1977.

Wilson, Richard Guy; Pilgrim, Dianne H.; and Murray, Richard N. *The American Renaissance, 1876–1917*. New York: The Brooklyn Museum, 1979.

Glossary

Acanthus Decorative ornament resembling the scalloped leaves of the acanthus plant. The leaf has been used as a decorative ornament since classical times, and was especially popular in America during the 18th and 19th centuries.

Acorn-shaped finial Distinctively shaped finial topping the uprights of chairs of many styles.

Aesthetic Movement Primarily an English movement which popularized furniture in the Japanese taste during the mid- to late 19th century. In America, Herter Brothers made a version of Aesthetic style.

Anthemion Flat, carved ornament based on the Greek honeysuckle flower and leaf.

Arcaded panel Panel carved with a series of arches supported by columns.

Arch See Lancet arch; Arcaded panel.

Arrow-back Chair Late Windsor chair with a row of thin flaring splats contained within its back.

Art Nouveau An anti-historical European design reform movement popular between the 1890s and early 1900s which created an elaborate curvilinear style. The "whiplash curve" and organic ornamentation are characteristic of the style. In furniture design, Art Nouveau was never very popular in the United States.

Art furniture Another name for Anglo–Japanese-style furniture fashionable during the 1880s. Edwin W. Goodwin's design book *Art Furniture*, published in London in 1877, popularized the style. One taste within the Aesthetic Movement.

Astragal-end table The protruding front and back break the oval formed by the half-rounded sides of such a table. Some Neoclassical work tables are of this configuration.

Balloon-back chair A chair with a back shaped like a hot-air balloon, swelling at the top and tapering in near the seat.

Ballroom chair Slight and easily transportable type of chair used in ballrooms.

Ball-turning Turning in the form of a series of balls was a common design element in the 19th century. Objects decorated with these turnings were often termed "spool-turned" and are associated with the Elizabethan Revival.

Baluster A turned vertical post or pillar, often having a vase- or column-shaped outline. Also known as a *banister.*

Baluster-and-cup-turning Common pattern of turning on 18th-century chair uprights and banisters in the form of a column with cup or U-shaped element below.

Banding Edging of thinly cut woods laid in a particular pattern, such as a herringbone.

Banister-back chair The chair back is composed of a series of upright turned spindles which are topped by a curving crest rail. Banister-back chairs were made in the early 18th century.

Baroque style Characterized by elaborate, flamboyant decoration and expansive forms, the Baroque style was fully developed by about 1620 in Italy. It was adapted and classicized during the Louis XIV period in France, and it was an indirect influence on the William and Mary and Queen Anne styles in England and America.

Batwing brass Escutcheon or drawer pull popular during the Queen Anne period which resembles the outline of a flying bat. Modern terminology.

Bellflower A hanging motif, consisting of several three- or five-petaled flowers, used during the first phase of Neoclassicism. Generally inlaid, it is sometimes called the *husk* motif.

Bentwood furniture Highly curved furniture of wood bent through the use of steam and pressure. Used by Samuel Gragg of Boston but later popularized by Michael Thonet (1796–1871) in Austria-Hungary. Made in large quantities in America.

Bergère Upholstered chair, based on French prototypes, with a rounded back, closed arms, and a loose seat cushion. Popular during the Classical period in America.

Bird-cage support Section of a tilt-top table, consisting of two blocks separated by columns located between the top and the pedestal, which allows the top of the table to tilt and pivot.

Block Section of wood used for support in furniture. Rounded or triangular corner blocks support slip seats in chairs, and glue blocks are used for support in case pieces with drawers.

Block-and-spindle stretcher Eighteenth-century chair stretcher combining baluster or other turned elements with blocks.

Block-and-vase turning Combination of square and vase-shaped sections. Pattern of turnings associated with the William and Mary period.

Blocked foot Rectangular terminus found on some Marlborough legs.

Blocking; Block front In blocking, the front of a case piece is divided visually into three vertical sections: The center section is concave, and the sections on each side are convex. Seldom found outside of 18th-century New England in America.

Blunt-arrow foot Tapered, cylindrical foot. One version found on Philadelphia Windsor furniture.

Bombé Convex or "blown-out" shape found on the front and sides of 18th-century cabinet furniture. In America, the *bombé* shape was an important innovation of the Chippendale period and was used primarily in Boston.

Book inlay Another name for fluted frieze. So called because it resembles the side view of a stack of books. Most often seen on New York and Newport furniture of the first period of Classicism. *Fluted frieze* a period term.

Boss Applied three-dimensional ornament, usually round or oval, seen on 17th-century-style furniture such as court cupboards and Wethersfield chests.

Boston chair Leather upholstered chair made during the early 18th century. So called because the type was exported from Boston to other American cities in large numbers. Period term.

Boston rocking armchair Painted rocking chair with wide crest rail, splat, or spindles in back, and S-shaped rolled seat. First introduced during the early 19th century. Continues to be a popular form.

Bow-front In case furniture, a front which swells horizontally like a bow.

Bow knot Motif of a ribbon tied in a bow, found inlaid on furniture made during the first phase of Classicism, namely the Federal period.

Bracket Curved element which physically and visually connects the leg with the seat rail or bottom rail of an object.

Bracket foot Simple foot, shaped like a bracket with a mitered corner, used on case pieces. It can be plain, scrolled, or molded. See also French foot.

Brettstuhl Term meaning "board chair," that is, a traditional plank chair. Type of chair by some German immigrant groups during the 18th and 19th centuries.

Broken-arch pediment Triangular or curved pediment in which the two ascending sides do not meet at the top, thus leaving a gap. The curved pediment takes the form of either a broken arch or a scroll. Most often seen on Queen Anne, Chippendale, and Federal-style furniture.

Bulb foot Slightly swollen foot which tapers at end. Commonly used on Neoclassical furniture.

Bun foot A turned foot shaped like a flattened ball. Favored foot for such furniture as the kast and the schrank and often used on 17th-century and William and Mary–style case pieces.

Bureau-table Chest of drawers with recessed area in center with a locked storage area at back. Made during the Chippendale period in America. Often referred to as a *kneehole desk*.

Burled wood Tumorlike growth on a tree which, when sliced, provides a highly figured veneer. Use introduced during the William and Mary period. Burled walnut was the most common type.

Butterfly table Small drop-leaf table with deep leaves supported by butterfly-shaped brackets. The legs and stretchers are generally turned. Modern terminology.

Button feet Modern term for small, flattened ball feet.

Buttress-top table See Turret-top table

Cabochon A smooth, unfaceted oval gem, with convex surface; also, the carved furniture ornament that resembles this particular jewel shape.

Cabriole chair According to George Hepplewhite, a chair with an upholstered back.

Cabriole sofa Neoclassical-style sofa with curved top of back.

Cabriole leg The cabriole leg curves outward at the knee and tapers inward at the ankle in a reverse-S line. Popular during much of the 18th century in America, the cabriole leg most often ended in a pad foot. The cabriole leg follows William Hogarth's "Line of Beauty."

Candle-flame finial Modern term for an elongated finial found on the top of the uprights of some Shaker chairs. Particularly associated with the Enfield, New Hampshire, community. Flame finials are also seen on Philadelphia high chests of drawers.

Candlestand A small stand with a proportionately small top designed to hold a candlestick or lamp.

Caning Woven strips of rattan used for chair, sofa, and couch backs and seats.

Canterbury Movable stand on casters with racks and drawers used to store sheet music, magazines, and books. Form introduced to America c. 1800.

Canvaswork Period term for needlepoint, that is, wool or silk thread worked on a linen background. It was sometimes used as upholstery on chairs.

Capital The uppermost section of a column, often carved, which is separated from the rest of the column by a molding.

Card table Table with a back leg which swings out to support a folding, hinged top. Particularly popular form during the Chippendale and Federal periods. Also called *gaming table*.

Cartouche In furniture, a carved, often asymmetrical device used in American furniture primarily as a finial on Chippendale and Rococo Revival–style case pieces.

Carving Cuts generally deeper and more sculptural than incising. See also Finger-rolled carving.

Caryatid pedestal Support in the form of a female figure borrowed from ancient Greek architecture and used during the Empire; that is, the archeologically inspired phase of Neoclassicism.

Case piece A relatively large, boxlike object having drawers, shelves, or cabinet space which is used for storage.

Cellaret Furniture form used for the storage and, at times, the chilling of wine bottles.

Chamber table Federal-period term for dressing table.

Chamfered Referring to a cut-off, or beveled, edge or corner.

Chest-on-chest Case piece consisting of one chest of drawers placed on top of another and attached. Designed as whole object.

Cheval glass Full-length mirror which pivots vertically on a stand.

Chinoiserie Western imitation, generally inaccurate, of Oriental art and motifs. Particularly popular during the 18th century in America.

Chip carving International style of carving in the form of rather intricate geometric designs. Sometimes called "Friesland" carving. Popular during the 18th century in America.

Claw-and-ball foot Carved foot in the form of a claw grasping a round ball. Often found at the end of a cabriole leg. More expensive feature than a pad foot.

Club foot Thick, slightly pointed foot. In America, seen on some New York Queen Anne–style chairs, but also used in Britain.

Colonette Small column. Term used to describe columns which support tops of some Classical-style tables.

Compass seat Term describing flaring, U-shaped outline of seats used on some Queen Anne and Chippendale chairs.

Continuous arm Refers to chairs and settees where the arms are a continuation of the back, as on some bow-back Windsor chairs.

Coquille Decorative motif carved in the shape of a scallop shell; common Rococo-style ornament.

Cornice In furniture, the horizontal molding which projects from the top of some case pieces.

Cornucopia The "horn of plenty"; a horn-shaped vessel filled to overflowing with flowers and fruit. Common motif on early 19th-century furniture.

Cottage furniture Refers to a type of relatively cheap painted furniture made mid- to late 19th century and popularized by A. J. Downing.

Court cupboard A two-tiered open cupboard used for the display of plates and as a service table. The tiers are supported by turned balusters. Status-oriented form of furniture used in 17th-century New England and Virginia.

Crest rail Exposed horizontal top rail of a chair or sofa. Crest rails are often carved and can be scroll-shaped, arched, and/or pierced.

Crocket In Gothic-style architecture, a pointed device placed along the outer angles of pinnacles and gables. Seen on Gothic Revival–style furniture.

Cromwellian chair Modern term for a chair resembling a stool with a back upholstered in leather. Form used on the Continent and in England and the colonies during the 17th century. Also called a *Farthingale chair.*

Cross stretcher Refers to stretchers which intersect at right angles and connect opposite, rather than adjoining, legs. Used on some Rhode Island Windsor chairs and on some Hudson River Valley tables.

Cuffed foot Tapered foot encircled by a carved band around it several inches above the floor. Associated with Baltimore during the Federal period.

Cupid's bow Motif, composed of a cyma and reverse cyma curve, resembling an archer's bow. Found at the base of the splat on many New York Queen Anne–style chairs. Modern terminology.

Curule chair Chair type used by the "curule," or magistrate, of Rome in classical times. The base of the chair is X-shaped with curved legs. Design popular during the archeologically inspired phase of Classicism.

Cyma curve A double curve which is concave and then convex. Also known as an *ogee.*

Daybed An armless lounge chair, first introduced to America during the William and Mary period. Daybeds are usually upholstered or else have caned or rushed bottoms. Also called *couch.*

Deception bed Bed which folds up into another form of furniture such as a chest of drawers or a sofa.

Dentiling Trim in the form of a series of little rectangles, each separated by a space. Name comes from its resemblance to a row of teeth.

Desk-on-frame Step in evolution of desk form. Slant-top box, with or without drawers below, resting on separate frame.

Diamond-and-scroll splat Splat with interlacing scrolls and diamond motifs favored by New York chair makers during the mid- to late 18th century.

Dolphin Classical decorative motif more recently associated with the Empire style.

Dot-and-dash piercing Pattern of piercing found on some Newport table stretchers dating from the mid- to late 18th century in the form of alternating circles and sets of three horizontal lines.

Dovetail Right-angled joint formed by interlocking, flaring tenons.

Drapery Swaglike draping of cloth used as a carved or inlaid decorative motif on Federal and Empire–style chairs and sofas.

Drawing-room chair Thomas Sheraton used this term to refer to a type of armchair with upholstered back. George Hepplewhite preferred the term *cabriole chair.*

Draw-top table Also known as a *draw table*; a table which can be extended by pulling out leaves located under the tabletop.

Dressing table Table designed to be used by the person completing his or her toilet, usually having drawers to hold toilet articles, and a mirror.

Drop finial Hanging architectural element which was sometimes used on 17th-century furniture such as tables and court cupboards.

Eagle Decorative motif popular during the late 18th and 19th centuries, particularly in America during the Federal period.

Eagle splat See Splat.

Ear of wheat Inlaid or carved ornamental motif in the shape of an ear of wheat used in the Classical style.

Easy chair Padded and upholstered armchair first introduced to America during the William and Mary period. Primarily used by the elderly and infirm during the 18th century. Period term for *wing chair.*

Églomisé Unfired reverse painting or gilding on glass. Found inset in looking-glasses, clocks, desks, and other objects, particularly during Federal period. Favored colors were gold, white, and blue. Also called *verre églomisé*.

En suite Part of a set of furniture. A set of furniture made for a particular room and sold as a whole was an innovation of the 19th century in America.

Entablature Upper part of a classical temple, located above the column and composed of an architrave, a frieze, and a cornice, in that order of ascendance. Also refers to the top of a piece of case furniture.

Escutcheon Key plate, usually of brass, made to protect keyhole on object.

Étagère Shelves, usually freestanding, used to display small objects. Popular during the mid- to late 19th century, the form was also called a *whatnot*.

Fall front Desk or cabinet door designed to open by falling forward. The opened door, supported by struts, doubles as a table.

Fan-back chair Type of Windsor chair with a roughly rectangular crest rail topping a straight-sided, flaring back. Also called a *comb-back*.

Farthingale chair An armless, low-backed upholstered chair with a wide, shallow seat popular during the late 17th century. Also called a *Cromwellian chair.*

Festoon Decorative ornament composed of a U-shaped garland of fruit, flowers, and berries.

Fiddle-back chair Period term for wood turner's version of Queen Anne–style chair. Refers to violin shape of splat. Also called *York chair* in some areas.

Fielded panel Board with chamfered edges which fits into mortise-and-tenon-constructed frame.

Field bedstead Bedstead with arched canopy. Name derives from the story that some of these bedsteads were used by military personnel while at war.

Finger-rolled carving In actuality, distinctive type of molding used on some Rococo Revival–style furniture.

Finial A decorative ornament topping the corners or pediments of furniture. Occasionally finials hang from furniture, and so are referred to as drop finials. Finials were turned or carved in a variety of shapes, including the acorn, urn, candle flame, and corkscrew.

Fluting A series of parallel horizontal channels. Opposite of reeding. Also see Stop fluting.

Foot See Blocked; Blunt-arrow; Bracket; Bulb; Bun; Button; Claw-and-ball; Club; Cuffed; French; Hairy paw; Hoof; Pad; Paintbrush; Rat-claw; Scroll; Snake; Spade; Spanish; Trifid

Form Joined bench. Common type of seating furniture during 17th century.

"French" chair Type of upholstered armchair with Marlborough leg popular during Chippendale period. Term used by Thomas Chippendale.

French foot Tapering, sometimes concavely curved foot used on some case pieces during the Federal period. See also Bracket foot.

Fretwork Openwork pattern of intersecting lines, often cut with a fretsaw. Sometimes used as trim on the top of sides of case pieces. Particularly popular during the Chippendale period.

Gadrooning Curved or swirled fluting and/or reeding, generally applied as an edging.

Gallery "Fence" or balustrade surrounding the edge of a table or other furniture. Designed to keep objects from falling off a surface as well as for decoration.

Gateleg table The turned legs are hinged to central station supports, and can be extended like gates to support the fold-out leaves of the top of the table. Also called *drop-leaf*.

Girandole looking-glass Circular mirror with convex glass and attached sconces popular during the 19th century. *Girandole* comes from the French word for "branched candlestick."

Gothic Refering to medieval style. In Gothic Revival–style furniture, American cabinetmakers incorporated Gothic–style architectural ornament into their furniture designs rather than copying historically-correct furniture forms. Also one of the "tastes" (the other two being *French* and *Chinese*) popularized by Thomas Chippendale in his *Director.*

Grisaille Monochromatic painting in tones of gray. In America, used in New York on a group of kasten and cupboards.

Hadley chest Chest with drawers of joined construction with three panels on the front and carved all over the front with a distinctive abstract design of flowers and leaves. Dating from the early 18th century, such chests were made in the Upper Connecticut River Valley. The name refers to Hadley, Massachusetts, the area where the chests were made.

Hairy paw foot Foot carved to resemble an animal's paw. Seen occasionally on American Chippendale–style furniture, another version of the hairy paw foot was more commonly found on American Empire–style furniture.

Hall chair A chair form used in the hallways of American homes during the mid- to late 19th century. Such chairs were often more sculptural than comfortable and reflect the complicated social ritual of calling practiced during this time.

Hawk Common ancient Egyptian motif found on archeologically inspired furniture.

Heart-and-crown chair Type of turned William and Mary–style chair made along the Connecticut coast during the early to mid-18th century. Name refers to the distinctive outline and piercing of the crest rail.

Heart-shaped back A chair back shaped like a heart. Some Maryland chairs have this variant of the shield-back.

Hieroglyphics Pictorial script used by ancient Egyptians. One of the decorative motifs associated with the Egyptian Revival, popular during the 19th century.

Highboy Modern term for a high chest of drawers.

Hoof foot A chair-leg terminal resembling an animal's hoof.

Horseshoe seat Roughly U-shaped outline of seat found on some Queen Anne–style chairs.

Huntboard Form peculiar to the South, consisting of a tall table, sometimes with drawers, placed along a wall and used for the service of food and drink. When made as a case piece, also called *hunt sideboard.*

Husk inlay Another name for *bellflower* inlay used on Federal furniture.

Icicle inlay Inlay in the form of a tapering pendant seen on some Federal-style objects.

Incising Shallow indentation into surface; not carved deeply.

Inlay A technique similar to that used to form a mosaic. In most cases, differently colored woods are set into a recessed, carved section of an object to form a decorative pattern or motif. Other materials such as ivory and metal are also used.

Jacobean Period The reign (1603–1625) in England of King James I. Inaccurate term when used to describe American furniture.

Japanning The European and American practice of imitating Oriental lacquerwork on a wood base covered with layers of varnish and color. Motifs, animals, and figures on the surface were built up with gesso and then were gilded or silvered.

Joining Technique of constructing mortise-and-tenon joints used widely in the 17th century. The tenon, or tablike projection, is fitted snugly into the mortise, a hole which has been chiseled to size. A peg placed through both pieces holds them together.

Joint Point where two parts of an object meet and are structurally connected.

Joint stool Joined, backless seat with turned legs made during the 17th century.

Kast Distinctive cupboard based on Continental Dutch prototypes produced by settlers from the Lowlands and descendants, primarily in New York and New Jersey and on Long Island. It is a large wardrobe on bun or ball feet, with varying arrangements of fitted drawers and/or shelves inside, and with paneled doors. Kasten were made during much of the 18th and early 19th centuries with little variation in design and ornament.

Kettle base Convex or "blown-out" shape, so called because of its resemblance to a pot-bellied kettle. Also known as *bombé.*

Kettle stand A small table designed to support a teapot or urn, usually having a pull shelf for holding teacup and saucer.

Key plate Also known as an *escutcheon*, the key plate is a protective metal piece which surrounds a keyhole and protects the wood from scratches.

Klismos A chair form designed by the ancient Greeks. Its tapering saber legs slope upward to the curved uprights and crest rail. Extremely popular form during the second and third phases of Classicism.

Knuckled arm Knuckle-shaped carving at the end of an arm. Often used on Queen Anne and Chippendale–style armchairs.

Kylix A term used in Greek pottery to denote a kind of drinking cup. Motif incorporated into backs of some Federal-period chairs, particularly in Newport.

Lamb's-tongue carving A softly-pointed tonguelike pendant which "hangs" from the front corners of some Chippendale–style case pieces.

Lancet arch A narrow and pointed arch favored as a Gothic Revival motif.

Latticework pediment In furniture, a decorative feature found on the tops of case pieces shaped in an openwork fret, or geometrical pattern of intersecting lines.

Leg See Cabriole; Marlborough; Saber; Stump

Library table Relatively large, rectangular-topped table, sometimes with a wide stretcher base. Used for the reading and storage of books. Often has short leaves at the ends of the table rather than at the sides. Also called a *sofa table.*

Linenfold pattern Carved ornament designed to resemble folded linen. It is found in medieval paneling and cupboards.

Lolling chair Upholstered armchair with exposed wooded arms, tall back, and low, deep seat. Name comes from the word loll, meaning "to recline in an indolent manner." *Martha Washington chair* a later term.

Lotus One of the ancient Egyptian decorative motifs, repopularized in part by Napoleon's Egyptian campaigns, and used to ornament furniture, silver, and ceramics.

Louis XVI style Design style popular in France from the mid-1750s to the mid-1780s, approximately, and thus not strictly reflective of the reign of Louis XVI, which began in 1774. The style is simpler and plainer than the Louis XV Rococo style which preceded it. Straight, geometrical lines replaced the curved, elaborate Rococo forms, and Classical ornamentation was adopted at this time. Furniture in this style was also made in America in the 18th and 19th centuries, in the latter century as a revival style.

Lowboy Modern term for 18th-century dressing table.

Lunette A crescent-shaped or semicircular motif.

Lyre Stringed instrument used during ancient times. A favored motif on Classical–style furniture.

Mammy's bench Modern term for a rocking settee with a row of holes across one-half of the front of the seat, into which fits a short "fence" or "gate," thus safely accommodating a sleeping infant while an adult sits rocking the settee.

Marlborough leg A square leg, sometimes fluted and terminating in a blocked foot, first popular in the mid-18th century.

Marquetry Pictorial type of inlay using wood or other materials to decorate furniture. Innovation of the William and Mary period.

Marriage In furniture study, the joining of two or more sections of an object which were not part of the same object originally.

Medallion An ornamental motif of rounded, oval, or spherical shape.

Méridienne Reading or lounging sofa often of asymmetrical form. Classical and Rococo Revival preferred styles.

Milk-bottle turning Gourd-shaped turning preferred by New York woodworkers.

Mixing table Table with a stone top, such as marble or slate, used for preparing drinks.

Molding A strip of wood used for ornamental trim.

Monopodium Animal foot and the extension from it, often in the form of a wing or a cornucopia, found on Empire furniture.

Morris chair Low-seated, high-backed armchair with adjustable slanting back and loose pillows first made by Morris, Marshall, Faulkner & Company in London. Name refers to William Morris, the leader of the English Arts and Crafts Movement. Popular form during the late 19th and early 20th centuries.

Mortise-and-tenon joint The tenon, or tablike projection, is fitted snugly into the mortise, a hole (usually square or rectangular) which has been chiseled to size. A peg holds both pieces together.

Ogee An ornamental molding shaped like the letter S. Another name for *cyma curve*.

Ormolu mount Bronze decorative furniture mounts which are covered in fire gilt. Particularly popular during the Empire period.

Ovolo corner Rounded element or outline which breaks the square corner of a case piece or table. Seen on some Neoclassical furniture.

Oxbow front Another term for *reverse serpentine front*.

Pad foot A softly rounded foot which rests on a small disc, or platform. A popular terminal for the cabriole leg.

Paintbrush foot See Spanish foot

Palmette Decorative motif in the shape of a fan, or palm leaf. Commonly found on Neo-Grec-style furniture.

Patera Round or oval motif, often with segments radiating from the center. Popular element in the Federal style.

Pediment In furniture, the section found on the tops of desk-bookcases and high chests corresponding to the triangular architectural projection above the portico of a classical building. See also Broken pediment; Latticework pediment.

Pembroke table Variant of the drop-leaf table, having two hinged rectangular leaves, four legs, and a single drawer. Popular Federal-period form. Also called a *breakfast table*.

Piecrust top A circular tabletop having scalloped edges that resembles the pressed crust of a pie. Found on tea tables and candlestands.

Piercing Carved openwork, sometimes cut with a fretsaw.

Pier table Type of table originally designed to stand against a wall between two windows. Commonly associated with the Empire period.

Pilaster A flat, rectangular column which is used for ornamental rather than functional purposes. For instance, pilasters decorate the corners of some Chippendale–style high chests, chest-on-chests, and desks and bookcases.

Pillar and scroll Common name for the Late Classical period. Refers to the simple design elements employed to create such furniture.

Pinwheel pattern Radiating decorative motif in the form of a pinwheel.

Plank chair Simple form of a chair with boards forming the back and seat. The legs are composed of sticks stuck into the seat. In America, Germanic-inspired form.

Plinth The section under the base of a column.

Pointed arch A decorative motif in the shape of a

peaked arch. See Lancet arch.

Press cupboard A storage cupboard with shelves, commonly used to hold clothes, linen, and other articles. Similar to a court cupboard except that the press cupboard has an enclosed, rather than open, bottom.

Prie dieu A prayer chair, usually having a high back and a very low seat, for sitting or kneeling upon. The back often has an upholstered shelf at the top, used for an armrest or book stand.

Prince of Wales feathers A carved ornamental motif resembling three ostrich feathers, the symbol of the Prince of Wales.

Quarter-fan inlay Quarter-circle motif, often with lines radiating from what would be the center of the circle. Favorite motif on Federal furniture.

Rat-claw foot Distinctive claw-and-ball foot, found on some Chippendale–style tripod tables, consisting of an elongated ball with flattened bottom topped by a claw. Modern term.

Récamier couch A chaise longue with a single high armrest which can also serve as a back. Name comes from Madame Récamier, who was immortalized reclining on such a couch in a painting by Jacques-Louis David (1748-1825).

Reeding Carved ornamentation in the form of a series of parallel vertical convex lines. The opposite of fluting.

Reel turning Turned element in the form of a spool.

Regency style The English version of the Empire style, which was characterized by the practice of copying furniture from Greek and Roman models. Popular from the late 18th to early 19th centuries. Named for the Prince Regent, later George IV.

Relief Projection of design from flat background.

Reserve An enclosed area.

Restauration The style current in France before and during the reign of Charles X (1824–1830). The furniture is a simplified version of the Classical style: Ormolu mounts disappeared, and light fruitwoods were preffered to mahogany.

Ribbon-back splat Chippendale-style splat with carved "gathers of ribbon" worked into the back of the chair.

Rice carving Decorative motif resembling the ripe grain of the rice plant. Found on some South Carolina furniture.

Riddle-back chair Chair with a back composed of a series of pierced slats.

Ring turning Turning in the form of a ring.

Rococo Eighteenth-century style which originated in France and featured asymmetrical curves and naturalistic motifs such as shells, foliage, and rocks. The style came to America via England.

Rod-back Type of Windsor chair or settee with a rectangular back composed solely or primarily of bamboo-turned vertical spindles. Popular during the early years of the 19th century.

Rope turning Turning resembling the twisted strands of a rope.

Rosette Circular ornament sometimes divided like the petals of a rose.

Roundabout chair Alternate period term for *corner chair.* In such a chair the seat and legs have been rotated forty-five degrees, so that it has one leg in the front, two on the side, and one at the back. The back is generally in the shape of a semicircle.

Ruffle carving Carving in the form of a gathered piece of cloth.

Rush seat A chair seat composed of the twisted stems of marsh grass.

Rustic furniture Furniture of natural materials and organic form generally used as camp and garden furniture during the late 19th and early 20th centuries in America. Also called *bent twig* or *Adirondack furniture.*

Saber leg A chair leg tapered to resemble a cavalry saber. First used on the Greek *klismos* chair.

Sack-back chair Type of Windsor armchair with a rounded back in which the vertical spindles pierce the horizontal arm rail. Made mid- to late 18th century.

Saddle seat Concave, upholstered seat of a chair. Rarely seen in America but used on a set of Chippendale–style chairs made in Philadelphia by Benjamin Randolph.

Saddled Scooped. Used to describe the shaped yokes of some chairs.

Salem rocker A rocking chair in the Windsor style, having a lower back than the Boston rocker.

Sausage turning Modern term for bead-shaped turning used on some 18th-century chairs. Often associated with New York.

Scallop Curved projection.

Schrank Distinctive cupboard or wardrobe form used by Pennsylvania Germans during the late 18th and early 19th centuries.

Scroll Curved element which came in a variety of forms including single, double, S-, and C-scrolls.

Scroll-back chair Another name for the Greek *klismos* chair. Period term.

Scroll foot A chair foot shaped like a rolled-up scroll. Favored by Thomas Chippendale in his *Director,* but rarely used in America. Period term for William and Mary style *Spanish foot.*

Serpentine Curve which is convex in center and concave at each end. Often refers to the curve of a chest of drawers or table front.

Serving table Table with a top of marble or some other stone used for the display and serving of food.

Settee A small sofa.

Settle A wooden bench with high back and arms, used to keep drafts off those seated upon it. Seventeenth- and early 18th-century form. Form also revived at the turn of the 20th century.

Sgraffito From the Italian word meaning "to scratch." Refers to the technique of scratching through a surface coat to reveal a different color below. Primarily a technique used on ceramics, it was occasionally employed on furniture.

Sham Fake; used to refer to false-fronted drawers.

Shell carving Carving resembling seashells, in particular scallop shells. Shell carving on furniture first became popular in America during the early to mid-18th century.

Shield-back chair A chair back shaped like a shield, commonly found on Federal-style furniture based on patterns of the English designer George Hepplewhite.

Sideboard A wide and relatively low case piece placed against the wall in a dining room for the display and serving of food.

Six-board construction The six-board chest is an alternative to the joined chest. *Six-board* refers to its construction. Five boards are nailed together to form a box, and the top is hinged on. A universal construction technique.

Skirt Section of a table found where the legs meet the top, below the under-framing.

Slat-back chair A chair composed of parallel horizontal slats. Also called a *ladder-back*.

Sleigh bedstead Form based on French prototypes and popular during the Classical period. Headboard and footboard are of the same height and are curved, thus resembling the outline of a sleigh.

Sling-seated armchair Upholstered armchair with an X-shaped base and fabric- or leather-covered back and seat of a single piece. Based on Spanish prototypes and popular during the Classical period, particularly in New Orleans and New York. Also called a *Campenchy* or *Spanish armchair*.

Slipper chair Upholstered chair with a high back and low seat. One story has it that such chairs were used to put on shoes, hence the name. Introduced during the Queen Anne period.

Slipper foot Elongated and pointed foot used on some Queen Anne-style furniture such as tables.

Snake foot Softly rounded foot which was used on some New York Federal pedestal tables.

Snowflake punch Stippled background design punched into some Federal furniture made in Salem, Massachusetts. Associated with Samuel McIntire.

Spade foot Terminus of a square, tapering leg somewhat wider than the leg and trowel-like in shape. Seen on chairs and tables based on Hepplewhite design. Common Neoclassical feature.

Spanish foot Another name for the *paintbrush* or *scroll foot*. The vertical scroll curves inward to form the foot's base of support. Modern term.

Spindle-back chair Chair with a back composed of spindles. Particularly popular in Eastlake-influenced furniture. Also refers to Arts and Crafts-style chairs with very thin vertical slats.

Spindle Slender turned rod usually used in a series. See also Split spindle.

Spinet desk Diminutive desk which rests on four legs and has a gallery or shelves at the back of its top.

Sphinx A mythological being, usually composed of the body of a lion and the head of a woman. The sphinx is found in classical Greek and Egyptian art, and was later popular as a decorative motif in furniture design.

Splat The middle section of a chair back, parallel to the uprights on either side of it. Splats could be highly carved, and some of the popular shapes include the scrolled, vase, eagle, and urn.

Splint seat Seat woven of thin strips of wood.

Split spindle Turned length of wood which is flat on one side and is nailed to the surface of a case piece of used in the back of a chair. To create a split spindle the turner glues a soft length of wood, such as pine, between two lengths of harder wood. He turns this block on a lathe, chops out the soft wood, and is left with two "split" spindles.

Spool turning Another name for *ball turning*. Particularly popular during the middle of the 19th century and associated with the Elizabethan Revival style.

Square-back chair Chair with a back in the form of a square or rectangle. Often used to describe Federal chairs with Sheraton-style backs.

Step-down Windsor chair Early to mid-19th-century Windsor chair with a crest rail which is higher in the middle than at the ends. The outline of the crest rail resembles a few stairs going up and then coming down.

Stile Upright or post on a chair.

Stop fluting Fluting in which part of each concave hollow is filled in with reeding.

Strapwork Decorative ornament of interlaced straps, or bands, resembling carved fretwork. Popular on 17th-century-style furniture.

Stretcher Element which connects the legs of an object and stabilizes it.

Stretcher table Table stabilized by stretchers. Early and/or utilitarian form.

Stringing Thin length of decorative inlaid wood, usually lighter than the surrounding wood. Popular technique during the first phase of Classicism.

Stump leg Generally refers to a squarish back leg with chamfered corners. Found on some American Queen Anne and Chippendale-style furniture, but also used in Britain.

Sunburst pattern Design, often inlaid, of a radiating star. Particularly popular in the Queen Anne style.

Sunflower chest See Wethersfield chest with drawers

Swag Inlaid, carved, or painted motif in the form of a gathered length of fabric which hangs lower in the middle. Popular Classical design.

Swan Motif commonly found on Late Classical furniture.

Tambour The gluing of thin strips of wood to a cloth background to create sliding doors or tops on case pieces such as desks. Technique first used during the Federal period in America.

Tea table Form introduced to America c. 1700 as part of the then-novel ritual of the tea party. The earliest style of tea table consisted of a removable tray for the carrying of tea equipment which fit into a separate frame.

Teardrop drawer pull Modern term for the pendant drawer pull used as a component of the William and Mary style.

Tester bed Another term for a high-post bedstead with a frame for holding a canopy.

Tête-à-tête Form of a bench or sofa in which the two seats face in opposite directions. First made in America in the Rococo Revival style.

Through-tenons In some mortise-and-tenon construction the mortise is open-ended and thus reveals the end of the tenon. In America, such through-tenons are found, on Philadelphia and some Connecticut Queen Anne and Chippendale period chairs, as well as some Arts and Crafts period furniture. At times these are pinned for greater strength.

Tilter Metal swivel devices placed on the bottom of each back leg of a chair so that the sitter could lean back. Patented by the Shakers.

Tracery Interlaced lines which form the lacy openwork of a Gothic-style window.

Trapezoidal seat Roughly rectangular seat with flaring sides; corners are pointed, not rounded.

Trefoil A Gothic decorative ornament, shaped like a rosette in three sections, with foil points.

Trestle table Early table form consisting of a board top and legs stabilized by stretchers or cross bracing.

Trifid foot A chair-leg terminal that is divided into three sections resembling toes. Popular on 18th-century Philadelphia chairs.

Trumpet-turning Modern term for flaring conical legs seen on some William and Mary–style tables, dressing tables, and high chests of drawers. Also used on 19th-century Revival–style furniture.

Trundle bedstead Low bedstead on wheels which can be rolled under a regular bedstead for storage during the day.

Turkeywork Canvas-based upholstery of a knotted wool pile which survives on a few 17th-century chairs and couches.

Turning The process or art of shaping wooden objects on a lathe. See also Ball; Baluster; Baluster-and-cup; Block-and-vase; Reel; Rope; Sausage; Spool; Trumpet; Twist.

Turret-top table Table with scalloped outline of top and sides that mirror this curving outline. Tea table form.

Twist turning Length of wood all of which has been carved to resemble a twisted rope. Used on William and Mary–style furniture. Name is actually a misnomer since it is not turned, but carved.

Urn finial Upward projection shaped like curved vase. Classical device.

Veneer Thin layer of exotic or rare wood glued to a cheaper wood base. The technique of veneering was introduced to America during the William and Mary period.

Vernacular furniture Simply constructed furniture, typically less sophisticated than furniture produced in a cabinetmaker's shop. The terms *country* and *primitive* are not accurate synonyms, as such woodworkers operated in urban as well as rural areas, and the furniture they created was often derivative of high-style furniture.

Victorian Renaissance Synonymous with the Neo-Grec style.

Voltaire chair Easy chair, often Late Classical in style, with a tall, often rolled back with exposed wooden trim including the arms. The name refers to the 18th-century French poet, dramatist, satirist, and historian. He is supposedly shown seated in such a chair in a print.

Volute Device in the shape of a scroll or spiral.

Wainscot armchair Seventeenth-century-style joined chair with a paneled back, plank seat, and shaped or turned legs and arms. The fielded panel back is sometimes carved.

Wethersfield chest with drawers Type of joined chest made c. 1700 in the Wethersfield area of Connecticut. Front of chest is typically decorated with applied split spindles, and bosses and panels carved in abstract flower design.

Winged lion paw Common motif used on the feet of archeologically inspired Classical furniture.

Wooton's patent desk Particular type of desk in which the front consists of two three-dimensional doors which are hinged to the sides. When open, the desk reveals seemingly countless storage compartments. Designed for use by businessmen, patented by William S. Wooton, and made in four grades from 1875 to 1884 in the Renaissance style.

Work table Form with one or more drawers, often with a cloth bag hanging below, developed during the Federal period and used for holding women's sewing equipment and materials.

Index